Figured Bass Accompaniment in Europe

Musica Incarnata
Pedagogy, Performance and Market

General Editors
Marcello Mazzetti
Livio Ticli

Volume 2

Publications of the Italian Institute for Applied Musicology

Figured Bass Accompaniment in Europe

Edited by
Livio Ticli

✤

BREPOLS

TURNHOUT

MMXXIII

D/2023/0095/263

ISBN 978-2-503-60851-8

Printed in Italy

Contents

INTRODUCTION
FIGURED BASS IN THE EUROPEAN TRADITION:
CONTINUITIES AND CHANGES OF A PRACTICE

THIS PUBLICATION, alongside its counterpart *Basso Continuo in Italy: Sources, Pedagogy and Performance* edited by Marcello Mazzetti as the first volume of the new 'Musica Incarnata' series, was conceived in the midst of the Covid-19 pandemic. It is important to recall this fact. It was, indeed, at the conference with the same title to the volume that I am introducing, *The Figured Bass Accompaniment in Europe*, which took place virtually from 9 to 11 September 2021, that most of the chapters that make up this book took shape. The amount and quality of research conducted during the congress could not be contained in a single volume, and it was decided, in agreement with the scholarly committee, to separate the chapters dealing with issues of theory, performance practice, pedagogy, and contexts more related to the Italian peninsula from those dealing with the same issues in a wider European context.

Towards the end of his enchanting new chapter featured in this volume, Thomas Christensen asserts objectively that «figured bass always presents novel and intriguing perspectives to each generation, albeit with reluctance to divulge its secrets». This book, therefore, attempts to do justice to the 'fight' (the very idea of 'concerto' as a 'certamen') led by seventeen internationally renowned scholars who ventured to trace figured bass accompaniment in Europe across a wide timespan, from early seventeenth-century Germany to late continuo realisations by Johannes Brahms and Robert Franz. The volume explores various topics, including alternative methods for outlining and extensively documenting instrumental accompaniment, its implementation in practical settings, and instruction on, and the application of, formulas for improvising (and realising) a contrapuntal texture over the bass. For the first time, this study presents a dialogue between counterpoint, basso continuo, and partimento, effectively resolving terminological discrepancies and emphasising the continuity of accompaniment practices spanning over three centuries across France, Germany, England, and Spain.

Detailed case studies illuminate the accompanimental techniques for selected instruments, including the cello and guitar. In this compilation, which scrutinises instruments utilised in accompaniment beyond traditional keyboard instruments, the present volume endeavours to interrogate a number of pivotal issues such as the role of improvisation in nineteenth-century guitar education, and distinctions in harmonic realisation and improvisation by lower string players.

Among the broader research inquiries that this volume aims to address, we find the following:

• The evolution of basso continuo realisation and its impact on counterpoint: how has the evolution of basso continuo realisation influenced the practice of counterpoint, and what are the key developments in this relationship over time?

• Figured bass and its role in the pedagogy of counterpoint: to what extent has figured bass played a role in the pedagogical aspects of counterpoint, and what insights can be drawn from the historical intersection of these two disciplines?

• Basso continuo and partimento in the context of counterpoint practices: how has the utilisation of basso continuo and partimento techniques shaped the practice of counterpoint, and what are the contributions of these approaches to the broader counterpoint landscape?

• National distinctions in contrapuntal techniques and notation: what distinctions can be identified in contrapuntal techniques and their notational conventions across different national traditions, and how have these distinctions contributed to the diversity of counterpoint practices and notation?

• The revival and reinterpretation of thorough bass in contemporary music scholarship: why has thorough bass notation, which was once considered a mechanical shorthand, experienced a resurgence in contemporary music theory and analysis? What are the reasons for the renewed interest in practices like figured bass notation, partimento, and basso continuo in the study of tonal music, and how do they differ from historical notions of thorough bass practices?

Furthermore, this investigation delves into the interrelationships between theory, analysis, composition, and the practical application of basso continuo within the various schools of partimento, offering a comprehensive exploration of this multifaceted subject.

A notable strength inherent within this volume is its adeptness in addressing a noticeable lacuna present within the extant scholarly corpus pertaining to the practice of basso continuo in the European context. Notwithstanding the substantial array of monographic works that have examined various facets encapsulated by the themes expounded within this work, it becomes readily apparent that heretofore, neither a companion compendium devoted to the multifaceted nuances of European basso continuo nor an all-encompassing treatise elucidating the full spectrum of notational, performative, and compositional modalities prevalent across Europe during the temporal expanse from the seventeenth century through the twentieth century has been forthcoming in academic discourse.

***

Introduction

The structure of the book is therefore divided into four main sections covering the following topics: 1. 'Through Alps and Pyrenees to the Sea: Continuity and Discontinuity in Performance Practice' offers a comprehensive exploration of various dimensions of basso continuo in Europe, encompassing diverse historical periods and geographical regions. In the inaugural chapter, David Chung unearths an overlooked manuscript (Bibliothèque nationale de France, Vm^8 1139), with associations to Mr. St. Georges. This manuscript is a repository of 14 preludes meticulously crafted with figured bass accompaniments. Subsequently, the second chapter, by Clotilde Verwaerde, disrupts the established paradigm of French basso continuo realisation. This is achieved by scrutinising the deployment of a more delicate type of three-voice texture, particularly discernible in the latter half of the eighteenth century. Within the third chapter, Marie Demeilliez delves into the labyrinthine realm of articles contained within the *Encyclopédie ou Dictionnaire raisonné des sciences, des arts et des métiers*, a compendium predominantly ascribed to the erudition of Jean-Jacques Rousseau. These entries encompass a myriad of facets pertaining to keyboard instrument accompaniment. Meanwhile, the fourth chapter, authored by Isaac Alonso de Molina, concentrates on a manuscript housed within the Biblioteca Nacional de España in Madrid. This manuscript contains instructive materials pertaining to basso continuo intricacies linked to the Spanish Royal Chapel, thereby unveiling intriguing parallels with the Neapolitan partimento traditions. Finally, the fifth chapter, by Michael Fuerst, embarks on an expedition through the intricate realm of multiple-bass notation in organ music. The author traces the evolutionary trajectory of this musical notation form in the compositions of Hieronymus Praetorius, casting an illuminating beam on the historical context and performance conventions surrounding basso continuo in polychoral compositions within the Hanseatic cities.

2. 'Connected by Strings: Cello Accompaniment Performance Practice' encompassing two additional chapters significantly broadens the investigation of basso continuo practice, offering an expansive and nuanced perspective on its multifaceted nature across Europe. In the sixth chapter, John Lutterman uncovers intriguing connections between unaccompanied cello music and Neapolitan partimento exercises, thereby illuminating the entwined history of written composition and solo improvisation. This chapter also delves into German practices related to thoroughbass realisation, potentially influencing the improvisational techniques employed by cellists. Authored by Hilary Metzger, the seventh chapter delves into the pivotal role of cellists in harmonic realisation within the realm of bass line accompaniment. This chapter builds upon prior research and meticulously explores national distinctions in styles of harmonic performance by cellists, extending the inquiry to encompass later secco recitative repertoire. Furthermore, it offers a comprehensive discussion of the evolving roles of the double bass in European opera orchestras, while also delving into national proclivities concerning arpeggiation, text synchronisation, and voice leading in harmonic realisations by cellists.

3. This section of the book, titled 'From the Page to the Performance through Space and Time', encompasses various facets of basso continuo practice in Europe, providing readers with a comprehensive understanding of the development and adaptation of this practice. The eighth chapter, authored by Valeria Mannoia, delves into the formalisation of figured bass in the German vocal repertoire, emphasising the influence of Italian sacred music and scrutinising its interpretation and adaptation in German settings. In the ninth chapter, penned by Francesca Mignogna, the focus shifts to Pierre-Louis Pollio and his extensive corpus of work. This chapter explores the ontological distinctions between descriptive and prescriptive sources, elucidating their impact on the practice of continuo in his funeral compositions. Chapter ten, authored by Anthony Abouhamad, furnishes insights into basso continuo accompaniment at the organ in eighteenth-century Austria, particularly in Salzburg. This chapter unveils the instructional methods employed by Salzburg organists for realising accompaniments from figured bass, thereby shedding light on their contrapuntal approach to basso continuo. The eleventh chapter, contributed by Martin Ennis, challenges binary perspectives on nineteenth-century basso continuo performance. By examining the practices of Robert Franz and Johannes Brahms, it demonstrates occasional shared artistic practices despite perceived differences in approach, thus highlighting the intricate nature of historical performance practices.

4. This section of the book, titled 'Basso Continuo and Partimento as a Pedagogical Tool Then and Now', delves into several key topics. Chapter twelve, by Thomas Christensen, focusses on the revival of thorough bass, its historical significance, and its role in understanding tonal music, exploring the reasons behind its resurgence and highlighting differences between historical and contemporary notions of thorough bass. The thirteenth chapter, authored by Stephan Lewandowski, centres on Johann Gottfried Vierling and his contributions to music theory, particularly his work on figured bass and the art of preluding in the late eighteenth century, shedding light on the transition in preluding practices and the compositional insights that can be gleaned from his works. Chapter fourteen, penned by Matthew Paul Mazanek, delves into the nineteenth-century transformation of the guitar, its rising popularity among amateur learners, and the shift in music education, particularly focussing on the teaching of improvisation. It explores how guitarists learned to improvise and the pedagogical techniques employed, drawing parallels with the partimento tradition. Justin Ratel, in chapter fifteen, examines the decline of basso continuo in the late eighteenth century and its persistence in French pedagogy at the Paris Conservatoire in the early nineteenth century, emphasising the transformation of this technique into a school subject integrated into harmony studies. The penultimate chapter, written by Thomas Allery, explores the use of figured bass notation as a pedagogical resource in the United Kingdom, particularly its introduction to music students at an early stage of their education. It highlights how figured bass notation can enhance musical education, fostering improvisation skills and a deeper understanding of harmony, ultimately contributing to broader musical proficiency. The

final chapter, authored by Livio Ticli, examines the interrelations between basso continuo and *concertato* practice. Ticli demonstrates their intimate connection and investigates how contrapuntal abilities originating from the ancient *cantores* of musical chapels are adopted and expanded upon in the setting of group improvisation and playing over the bass. Overall, this section investigates the historical and contemporary pedagogical aspects of basso continuo and figured bass, shedding light on their enduring significance and transformative impact on music education and performance.

A multifaceted approach has been employed to investigate various aspects of historical performance practices and pedagogy within the realm of musicology. It encompasses methodologies such as transcription and realisation from original manuscripts, delving into the rich historical sources to uncover the nuances of performance. Aesthetic debates surrounding continuo realisation in eighteenth-century French music are meticulously examined, shedding light on the evolving perceptions of accompaniment texture. Encyclopedic sources, including the *Encyclopédie ou Dictionnaire raisonné des sciences*, provide valuable insights into keyboard accompaniment during the Enlightenment era. A comparative analysis of manuscripts elucidates the evolving practices in diverse geographical regions and historical periods. Historical notation practices, as evidenced in various sources, offer a window into the evolution of musical language and performance. The comparative study of partimento and unaccompanied cello music highlights connections between composition and improvisation. Investigating harmonic realisation by cellists offers a deeper understanding of their role in bassline accompaniment. The historical and comparative analysis of German vocal repertoire brings to light the performance practices in Austria's rich musical tradition. The comparative analysis of descriptive and prescriptive sources distinguishes between the preservation of compositional ideas and practical performance instructions. The study of Salzburg organists' partitura practice uncovers instructional methods for realising a basso continuo. Re-evaluating binary perspectives challenges conventional dichotomies in historical performance debates. Finally, the exploration of the pedagogical role of basso continuo and the utilisation of figured bass notation in music education demonstrates the practical applications of historical practices in modern teaching, fostering a comprehensive understanding of the multifaceted field of historical performance and pedagogy.

Amidst these meticulous operational and methodological declarations to which this volume steadfastly adheres, there is a profound sense of accomplishment in presenting our readers with a work that delineates, within the intricate and expansive landscape of the diverse European milieu, a continuum of performance practices intimately intertwined not only with the linguistic underpinnings of 'playing over the bass' first, encompassing basso continuo and partimento, thereby delving into counterpoint, but also with a fundamental aspect of music — the inseparable aural element that, performance after performance, serves as a poignant reminder of the dynamic and elusive nature of sound when compared to the bare and fragmented representation of notation. This primacy of performance, in a volume that not only acknowledges but embraces the tension between sound and symbol, stands as the most salient and overarching feature of the research underpinning this collection of essays. The focus of our examination, in fact, can only be the language, the lexicon, the reservoir of formulas, and the grammatical and rhetorical components that underpin improvisation and the creative process in the musical milieu of *ancien régime* societies.

One of the principal aims of this volume, as envisaged by its editor and authors, is to provide a valuable resource for academic scholars and practical musicians alike. The book adopts a rigorous language and clear structure, whilst also endeavouring to make the analysis of historical information and various documents more readily understandable.

***

Prior to presenting the literary contents enclosed in this volume to the discerning reader, it is essential for me to express my deep appreciation to the Centro Studi Opera Omnia Luigi Boccherini, epitomised by the distinguished trio of Fulvia Morabito, Roberto Illiano and Massimiliano Sala. Their invaluable aid and committed determination proved instrumental in the systematic arrangement of the conference and the resulting accomplishment of this publication. My sincere gratitude is extended to the diligent scholars whose meticulous research, unwavering dedication, and academic zeal have facilitated the realisation of this intellectual endeavour. My deep appreciation goes to David Force for his unwavering linguistic guidance during the drafting process, which enhanced the readability of the sections that make up this collection of essays. Finally, it is crucial for me to express my profound indebtedness to Marcello Mazzetti, whose contribution surpasses that of a mere co-editor in this series. His insightful analysis, articulate writing style, and intellectual contributions have greatly improved the structural integrity and educational value of each chapter.

Livio Ticli
Mura (Brescia), October 2023

Through Alps and Pyrenees to the Sea: Continuity and Discontinuity in Performance Practice

THE SIGNIFICANCE OF THE PRELUDES WITH FIGURED BASS IN F-PN VM⁸ 1139 FOR KEYBOARD PEDAGOGY IN EARLY EIGHTEENTH-CENTURY FRANCE

David Chung
(HONG KONG BAPTIST UNIVERSITY)

KEYBOARD CONTINUO IN FRANCE

KEYBOARD CONTINUO arrived in France somewhat late, around 1650[1]. Henry Du Mont (1610-1684) was among the earliest musicians to introduce the practice in French music through his *Cantica sacra* (1652). Titon du Tillet reported that «Dumont est le premier de nos Musiciens François, qui ait employé dans ses ouvrages la Basse continue, qui fait un si bel effet dans la composition de la Musique»[2].

The rapid growth of keyboard continuo beginning in the 1670s was largely due to the increasing popularity of operas by Jean-Baptiste Lully (1632-1687), as well as the keyboard continuo's usefulness in Italian chamber music. This growth is evidenced by the publication of numerous treatises from 1689, beginning with D'Anglebert's concise but practical *Principes de l'accompagnement* (included in his *Pieces de clavecin*), along with Nivers's *L'Art d'accompagner sur la basse-continue pour l'orgue et le clavecin*. TABLE 1 lists the major continuo treatises published in Paris between 1689 and 1724. Interestingly, Delair revised and expanded his original 1690 *Traité* and renamed it *Nouveau traité* in 1724[3].

---

[1]. In Italy, basso continuo had flourished since the early 17th century, with a flow of publications by Giulio Caccini (1551-1618), Adriano Banchieri (1568-1634) and other influential writers from 1600; see NUTI 2007, pp. 19-60 for a detailed discussion of the notation and style of basso continuo as evidenced in treatises and other writings published in Italy during the first decades of the 17th century. See also the recent volume MAZZETTI 2023.

[2]. TITON DU TILLET 1727, p. 389.

[3]. For a comprehensive study of French keyboard continuo treatises, see ZAPPULLA 2000.

TABLE 1: MAJOR KEYBOARD CONTINUO TREATISES PUBLISHED IN PARIS BETWEEN 1689 AND 1724

DATE	AUTHOR	TITLE
1689	Jean Henry d'Anglebert	*Principes de l'accompagnement*
1689	Gabriel Guillaume Nivers	*L'Art d'accompagner sur la basse-continue pour l'orgue et le clavecin*
1690	Denis Delair	*Traité d'acompagnement pour le théorbe, et le clavessin*
1700	Jacques Boyvin	*Traité abrégé d'accompagnement pour l'orgue et pour le clavecin* (^{2}1705)
1707	Saint Lambert	*Nouveau traité d'accompagnement du clavecin, de l'orgue, et des autres instruments*
1716	François Campion	*Traité d'accompagnement et de composition selon la regle des octaves de musique*
1719	Jean-François Dandrieu	*Principes de l'accompagnement du clavecin*
1722	Jean-Philippe Rameau	*Principes d'accompagnement*
1724	Denis Delair	*Nouveau traité d'acompagnement pour le théorbe, et le clavessin*

Delair, in his *Traité d'acompagnement pour le théorbe, et le clavessin* (1690), remarked on the popularity of continuo playing: «Accompaniment has never been as widespread as it is today. Almost all who play instruments dabble in accompanying...»[4].

Towards the end of the 17th century, the number of competent continuo players was steadily increasing. For example, Jean-Baptiste de Bousset (1662-1725) drew exceptional praise from Titon du Tillet for his skill in harpsichord accompaniment[5]. Many female musicians, such as Elisabeth Jacquet de La Guerre (1665-1729), Marie-Françoise Certain (1661/2-1711), and Marguerite-Louise Couperin (1675/6-1728), were also distinguished accompanists[6]. In his 1696 biography of Lully, Perrault noted the improved quality of continuo musicians towards the end of the century:

> We admired a master who knew how to accompany [well] on the basso continuo; today, a young girl who plays the harpsichord or the theorbo would find it difficult to hear praises for [having achieved] so little[7].

---

[4]. «[...] l'Acompagnement [*sic*] n'a jamais été si commun qu'il est presque tous ceux qui jouent des Instrumens se meslent d'acompagner...». DELAIR 1991, Preface.

[5]. TITON DU TILLET 1727, p. 604. Bousset, born in Dijon, settled in Paris in the 1690s and developed a thriving career as a composer and organist. See GARDEN 2001.

[6]. Jacquet de La Guerre was a distinguished composer and harpsichordist who made significant contributions to music for accompanied keyboard. See CESSAC 2001. Marie-Françoise Certain, known as 'Mademoiselle Certain', was a close friend (possibly mistress) of Lully. According to La Fontaine, Certain was a brilliant harpsichordist, «dont la rare genie et les brillantes mains surpassent Chambonnières, Hardel, les Couperains». See TITON DU TILLET 1727, p. 637 and GUSTAFSON 2001. Marguerite-Louise Couperin was the daughter of François Couperin 'le Grand'. See FULLER – GUSTAFSON 2001.

[7]. «On admiroit un Maistre qui sçavoit accompagner sur la Basse-Continuë, aujourd'huy une jeune fille qui joüe du Clavecin ou du Theorbe auroit de la peine à s'entendre loüer de si peu de chose». PERRAULT 1696, vol. I, p. 86.

The Significance of the Preludes with Figured Bass in F-Pn Vm⁸ 1139

During the last quarter of the 17ᵗʰ century, the harpsichord was admired for its versatility as both a solo and a continuo instrument. In 1678, the gazette *Mercure* commented on the flexibility of the harpsichord in all kinds of concerts:

> Thus, the harpsichord will accompany all kinds of vocal and instrumental music. It will be ubiquitous for all the concerts you would give, and it is thus the most accomplished of all of the musical instruments[8].

In 1712, the gazette *Mercure galant* reported the building of a harpsichord «tres particulier et tres beau» with four keyboards (two at either end) that would be suitable for all solo and accompaniment contexts: «[...] it is useful for those who give concerts and for those who want to listen to harpsichord pieces played at one end and accompanied at the other»[9].

From the early 18ᵗʰ century, many French composers openly consented to the playing of solo harpsichord music as chamber music, and vice versa. This fluidity between solo and accompanied harpsichord music can be traced back to Gaspard le Roux (d. 1707), who, in his 1705 *Pieces de clavecin*, demonstrates how an instrumental trio comprising two treble instruments and a basso continuo part — itself derived from his own solo harpsichord score — could serve as a blueprint for a two-harpsichord version[10].

In his *L'Apothéose de Lully* (1725), François Couperin emphasised that he often played trio sonatas — scored for two melodic instruments and continuo — as two-harpsichord music with his pupils. In the preface, Couperin explains:

> This trio, as well as the Apothéose de Corelli, and the complete book of trios that I hope to publish next July, may be played on two harpsichords, as well as on all other instruments. I play them this way with my family and with my students, and it works very well, by playing the *premier dessus* and the bass on one harpsichord and the *second dessus* with the same bass in unison on the other one. It is true that this requires two copies of the score instead of one, as well as two harpsichords. But

---

8.   «Ainsi le Clavessin accompagnera toute sorte de Voix et de Musique Instrumentale. Il sera universel pour tous les Concerts qu'on voudra faire, et l'un des plus accomplis de tous les Instrumens de Musique». *Mercure galant* (December 1678), p. 113. The gazette *Mercure galant*, founded in 1672 by the writer Jean Donneau de Visé (1638-1710), informed high society on fashionable events at court, and included anecdotes, news and poems. The published volumes of *Mercure galant* are available from *Gallica* (<gallica.bnf.fr>), the digital library of the Bibliothèque nationale de France.

9.   «[...] il est utile pour ceux qui font des Concerts & pour ceux qui veulent entendre jouer des pieces de clavessin à un bout et les accompagner de l'autre». *Mercure galant*, April 1712, pp. 216-217. English translation mine.

10.   For a discussion of the techniques and stylistic procedures used in converting an instrumental trio into a two-harpsichord version, see McKean 2011, pp. 22-31.

I find that it is often easier to gather these two instruments than four professional musicians[11].

Basso continuo arrived in France during the 1650s and was quickly assimilated into the French keyboard language. The above examples from D'Anglebert to Couperin are indicative of the increasing role of basso continuo in French harpsichord teaching and performance at the time.

F-Pn Vm⁸ 1139

F-Pn Vm⁸ 1139 attests to the importance of basso continuo in early 18th-century French harpsichord pedagogy. The source first attracted modern scholarly attention in 1990 as one of the recently rediscovered manuscripts of original 17th-century French harpsichord music[12]. The manuscript begins with an extensive figured bass treatise (ff. 1r-22v) and a collection of 14 preludes with figured bass (ff. 23r-31r). In 2006, Churchill provided a translation of this treatise and discussed it in the context of other French writings[13].

The author of the figured bass treatise remains unidentified. The inside front cover contains the signature of a certain «Mr. St. Georges», possibly the owner of the manuscript, but attempts to connect this name to a specific musician have been in vain. Two possible candidates are Joseph Boulogne de Saint-Georges (c.1739-1799), known as 'Monsieur de Saint-Georges', and James Francis Edward Stuart (1688-1766), known as 'Chevalier de Saint-Georges'[14].

Both physical evidence (e.g., F4 and C3 clefs) and the repertory suggest an early 18th-century date for the manuscript[15]. Identified harpsichord music includes the 'Fête de Village'

---

[11]. «Ce trio, ainsi que l'Apothéose de Corelli; & le livre complet de trios que j'espere donner au mois de juillet prochain, peuvent s'exécuter à deux clavecins, ainsi que sur tous autres instrumens. Je les exécute dans ma famille; & avec mes éléves, avec une réüssite tres heureuse, sçavoir, en joüant le premier dessus, & la basse sur un des clavecin: & le second, avec la même basse sur un autre à l'unisson: la verité est que cela engage à avoir deux exemplaires, au lieu d'un; & deux clavecins aussi. Mais, je trouve d'ailleurs qu'il est souvent plus aisé de rassembler ces deux instrumens, que quatre personnes, faisant leur profession de la musique». COUPERIN 1725, Preface.

[12]. The manuscript contains original harpsichord pieces by Thomas Bertin de la Doué (no. 16), Louis Couperin (no. 34a), François Couperin (nos. 28, 33), Dandrieu (no. 21) and Jacques Hardel (no. 34). See GUSTAFSON – FULLER 1990, pp. 304-305.

[13]. CHURCHILL 2006, pp. 1-19.

[14]. Gustafson (in GUSTAFSON – FULLER 1990, p. 304) pointed out that if the name is indeed that of Joseph Boulogne de Saint-Georges, the contents of the manuscript would be highly retrospective. As such, James Francis Edward Stuart, proposed by Churchill (in CHURCHILL 2006, p. 13), seems a more suitable match for the name 'Mr. de St Georges'.

[15]. For a discussion of the physical evidence of F-Pn Vm⁸ 1139, see GUSTAFSON – FULLER 1990, p. 304.

(no. 21) by Dandrieu, which was published in 1724, but the version in F-Pn Vm⁸ 1139 is not a copy of the printed score. All other pieces point to an earlier date. 'La Marche des Gris Vetus' (no. 28) and 'Les Vendangeuses' (no. 33) by François Couperin were published in 1713, and pieces by Hardel and Louis Couperin (nos. 34 and 34a), as well as the three arrangements of Lully's music, most likely originated in the 17th century[16].

The figured bass method (ff. 1r-22v), titled 'Règles pour l'Accompagnem[ent]', represents the most substantial handling of the subject in a manuscript. The 21 rules cover all essential points, including intervals, consonance and dissonance, major and minor, the octave, chords, keys and practical information for a variety of situations. Although the treatise is not identical to any other known method, the language and approach are very similar to late 17th-century and early 18th-century treatises, such as those by D'Anglebert (1689), Delair (1690), Saint Lambert (1707) and Dandrieu (1719) (see TABLE 1 above).

PEDAGOGICAL APPROACH

The 'Mr. St. Georges' treatise relies heavily on the so-called rule of the octave but does not actually label it as such. Early in the method, the author expresses the idea that each note of an ascending and descending scale has an implicit chord (f. 3v): «The octave comprises 8 degrees that rise and fall, and each [note] has its own distinct chord»[17].

To explain this principle, the author provides full figures for the C minor scale, first ascending and then descending, and then finishes with a typical cadence (f. 7r). However, the author does not provide any written-out examples. Presumably, the teacher would demonstrate the art of realisation on the keyboard during lessons.

The lessons in the treatise develop from this fundamental exercise, and the rule of the octave is repeated in other keys, including D major and minor (f. 7v), E major and minor (f. 8r), F major and minor (f. 8v), G major and minor (f. 9r), B-flat major and minor (f. 9v), E-flat major and minor (f. 10r), F-sharp major and minor (f. 10v), C-sharp major and minor (f. 11r) and finally G-sharp major and minor (f. 11v)! Curiously, some common keys, such as A major and minor, are omitted. The inclusion of unusual keys such as G-sharp minor suggests that the method is not for beginners, echoing Saint Lambert's observation that those «qui se mettent à l'Accompagnement ne sont pas novices en matiere de Musique»[18].

---

16. Concordances with other French harpsichord manuscripts suggest that the three Lully arrangements in F-Pn Vm⁸ 1139 were very popular teaching pieces. For a list of concordances, see CHUNG 2018.

17. «L'octave est compose de 8 degres qui montent et qui descendent et qui ont chaqun leur accord seur».

18. SAINT LAMBERT 1991, p. 64.

PRELUDES WITH FIGURES

The 14 figured bass preludes accompanying the treatise (f. 23r-31r) apparently fulfil two main purposes: (1) to show how figures are used in the context of compositions and (2) to serve as exercises for both basic and more advanced progressions. They cover all keys beginning on the natural notes of the keyboard, from C major and minor to B major and minor, in alphabetical order and a range of styles and characters.

TABLE 2: PRELUDES IN F-PN VM⁸ 1139

PRELUDE	KEY	TIME	TEMPO/CHARACTER
Prelude 1	C major	[2]	
Prelude 2	C minor	C, 3	Overture
Prelude 3	D major	3	Menuet
Prelude 4	D minor	2	Gavotte
Prelude 5	E major	3	Menuet
Prelude 6	E minor	C	
Prelude 7	F major	2	Vite
Prelude 8	F minor	C	
Prelude 9	G major	2 | 3	Overture
Prelude 10	G minor	3	Sarabande
Prelude 11	A major	3	
Prelude 12	A minor	2	
Prelude 13	B major	C	
Prelude 14	B minor	2	

As the author does not offer any examples to explain how these preludes should be interpreted, I attempt to provide a plausible realisation based on the guidelines laid down in this treatise and information from related French sources.

In terms of notation, each chord is fully figured in the 21 rules preceding the preludes (ff. 12v-22v). For example, a root-positioned chord is represented by 8-5-3, 5-3-8, or 3-8-5, with the number on top indicating the highest note of the right hand (see ILL. 1). In his 1716 *Traité*, Campion became the first theorist to promote the use of full figures, and this practice was fully embraced by Dandrieu in 1719. In the preludes of the St. Georges manuscript, however, the indications of the figures are both full and partial. When figures are full, it makes sense to follow the implied voice-leading with the top number assigned to the highest note of the right hand. In passages with partial figures (e.g. 7-6, 4-3), however, the notes implied by the figures can be assigned to an inner or outer voice. Le Roux's 1705 preludes confirm this flexible approach (see ILL. 2-3).

ILL. 1: Full figures in 'Quatreme Regle pour faire l'Accord de la quinte' (F-Pn Vm⁸ 1139, f. 14r).

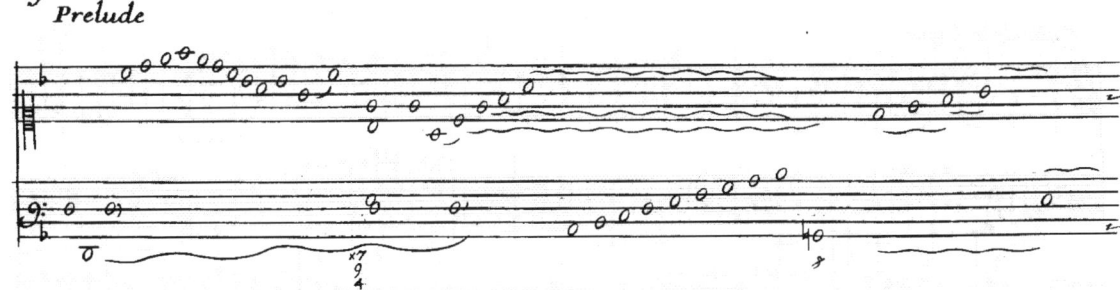

ILL. 2: Gaspard Le Roux, F major Prelude (1705, F-Pn Vm⁷ 1858, p. 32), opening.

ILL. 3: Gaspard Le Roux, D minor Prelude (1705, F-Pn Vm⁷ 1858, p. 1), opening.

In all 14 preludes of the St. Georges manuscript, the author uses diagonal or horizontal straight lines to indicate notes that do not need to be harmonised. Full figures are expected for chromatic and dissonant chords. The trill over a figure is an unusual notational feature found in some preludes. In practice, an expert musician would certainly embellish the texture with additional ornaments.

MY REALISATION OF THE FIGURED BASS

In the musical examples below, the bass lines and figures are original, and they are reproduced without editing except for the tacit adjustment of accidentals to conform to modern practice. In the manuscript, the scribe uses both F4 and C3 clefs; in my examples, only F4 clefs are used. In addition, the octave duplication of accidentals in key signatures, which was common at the time, has been suppressed. All of the continuo figures are original and placed above the bass notes, as in the original version, and my realisation is given in the upper staff. In practice, an experienced player, whether past or present, would vary the realisation each time, playing according to factors such as the instrument(s), the interpretation and the acoustics of the venue, and as such, there is no single ideal version. The written-out realisations in this article serve purely to motivate discussion of how these preludes might contribute to our understanding of continuo practice and keyboard pedagogy in early 18th-century France.

Ex. 1: *Prelude en C sol ut majeur, ton naturel* (F-Pn Vm⁸ 1139, f. 23r).

Prelude 1 demonstrates the rule of the octave in a musical context and discusses how a simple repetition of the dominant an octave lower (bar 6) provides a musically satisfying way to complete the G major scale (see Ex. 1). Bars 12-13 illustrate a descending octave from *c'*. The succession of dissonances and consonances adds flow to the music. In bar 15, for example, the delayed resolution of the dominant seventh chord over the subdominant bass creates a spicy, dissonant effect, enhancing the momentum to the last cadence. The complete figures, such as 3-6-3 and 3-6-5 in bar 5, allow the details of voice-leading to be traced with ease. In the

Ex. 2: *Prelude en C sol ut mineur, ton qui n'est point naturel* (F-Pn Vm^8 1139, f. 23v).

penultimate bar, the trill (*tremblement*) below the figure induces an idiomatic gesture to add variety and interest to the texture.

The author offers additional ways of shaping the bass octave in other preludes. Prelude 2 in C minor, which has the structure of a Lullian overture, is a notable example (see Ex. 2). The opening phrase would be an excellent drill for spicy dissonant and chromatic 7th and 9th chords. Certainly, this is not an exercise for beginners! This prelude shows different ways of approaching cadences and demonstrates how displacing the bass note an octave higher (not lower, as in the above prelude) allows the bass to continue the downward movement (bars 10-11). In the second livelier section in 3rd time, the author demonstrates that not every note of the scale needs to be harmonised, as explained by Saint Lambert in 1707:

Ex. 3: *Prelude en D la ré majeur, ton qui n'est pas naturel* (F-Pn Vm⁸ 1139, f. 24r).

When the bass notes move by consecutive degrees, one is not obligated to accompany them all. One may accompany just the first of each pair of notes [i.e., with one chord for each pair]... You will notice furthermore that one may pass over (without specifically accompanying) just the [bass] notes that occur between two beats in the measure...[19]

Prelude 9 in G major is also in the style of the French overture. Its time signature of 2 suggests a quick opening section with a correspondingly slower harmonic movement. The realisation of this prelude is relatively straightforward.

Preludes 3 and 5, in 3 time, are in the style of the minuet, in which harmonic movement fluctuates between one chord per beat to one chord per bar (see Ex. 3). A flexible texture would be musically desired.

---

[19]. «Quand les notes de Basse vont pas degrez successifs, on n'est pas oblige de les accompagner toutes. On peut n'accompagner que de deux notes l'une alternativement... Vous remarquerez encore qu'on ne passe sans accompagnement particulier que les notes qui se trouvent entre deux temps dans la mesure...». SAINT LAMBERT 1991, pp. 100-101.

Ex. 4: *Prelude en D la ré mineur, ton naturel* (F-Pn Vm⁸ 1139, f. 24v).

Prelude 4 in D minor begins with some warm-ups with the root and first inversion chords (see Ex. 4). The detailed figuring in bars 18-22 contains enough information to work out the challenging chromatic progression that builds up to the climax with an augmented 7th chord in bar 20, after which the music relaxes into the cadence.

Prelude 5 in E major offers an opportunity to practise the 'circle of fifths' in a lively triple time, first with 5th chords and then with 7th chords (bars 14-24). In bars 27-31, the embellished bass line requires only one change of harmony every bar (see Ex. 5). This again echoes Saint Lambert's advice:

Ex. 5: *Prelude en E Si mi majeur, ton qui n'est pas naturel* (F-Pn Vm⁸ 1139, f. 25r).

When the measure is in three beats and the air is played quickly, one can be content with accompanying just the first [bass] note of each measure, provided that the [bass] notes move by consecutive degrees...[20]

---

[20]. «Quand la mesure est a trois temps, & que l'Air se joue vîte, on peut se contenter d'accompagner seulement la premiere note de chaque mesure; pourvû que les notes marchent par degrez successifs...». *Ibidem*, p. 101.

Ex. 6: *Prelude en F ut fa mineur, ton qui n'est pas naturel* (F-Pn Vm⁸ 1139, f. 27r).

Preludes 6 and 7 provide additional exercises for consolidating skills mastered earlier in different musical situations. Prelude 8 in F minor, in contrast, is a step up in difficulty, frequently requiring a change of chord every quaver, with modulations first to A-flat major (bar 6) and then to C major (bar 10) (see Ex. 6). A great deal of chromatic vocabulary is packed into this relatively short prelude (14 bars).

Prelude 10 in G minor is in the style of a sarabande or a light chaconne/passacaille (see Ex. 7). The opening phrase has the character of Lully's 'Les Songes agréables' from the *Atys* (LWV 53/58)[21]. The chromatic bass movement, with an expressive change of

---

[21]. Lully's 'Les Songes agréables' from *Atys* (LWV 53/58) was a favourite piece among 17th-century harpsichordists. D'Anglebert's own arrangement was published in his *Pieces de clavecin* (1689, p. 60), and no fewer than seven other arrangements have survived in manuscripts of both French and non-French provenance. For source information, including incipits of concordant keyboard versions, see CHUNG 2018, 'The Catalogue', <https://digital.lib.hkbu.edu.hk/OTCL/ids/OTC-000218>, accessed October 2023.

Ex. 7: *Prelude en Ge ré sol mineur, ton qui n'est pas naturel* (F-Pn Vm⁸ 1139, f. 28v).

Lully, Les Songes agréables from *Atys* (LWV53/58)

cf. Passacaille d'Armide (LWV 71/61), bars 97-99

harmony on the second beat of bars 34-35, calls to mind Lully's 'Passacaille d'Armide' (LWV 71/61)[22].

22. Lully's Passacaille from *Armide* (LWV 71/61) is another harpsichord piece that was popular during the 17th century. Seven versions have survived in both French and non-French sources. See CHUNG 2018, 'The Catalogue', <https://digital.lib.hkbu.edu.hk/OTCL/ids/OTC-000220>, accessed October 2023.

Ex. 8: *Prelude en B fa si becare mineur, ton naturel* (F-Pn Vm⁸ 1139, f. 31r).

The other preludes (nos. 11-14) challenge the pupil to apply skills acquired previously with the reduced marking of figures, as some are missing (e.g. Prelude in A major, bar 17). At this stage, the learner should have accumulated enough experience to decipher the possible voice-leading between chords without the need for a detailed prescription of the figures. In bars 2-3 of the B major prelude, the author simply writes the number 9 for each 9th chord. In the last prelude, in B minor, the realisation of several '4' chords (bar 29) requires the player to mentally supply accidentals (see Ex. 8).

David Chung

Reflection and Conclusion

The 14 preludes in F-Pn Vm^8 1139 serve a clear didactic function, allowing the pupil to develop fluency in reading figures introduced earlier in the musical context. The treatise preceding the preludes generally provides full figures for all of the bass notes. In the preludes, however, detailed figuring of chords is usually reserved for chromatic and dissonant chords as well as for more advanced progressions. In addition, the straight lines, usually horizontal or diagonal, indicate notes that do not need to be harmonised, such as passing notes and quick notes in livelier tempos. With practice, the learner should gradually develop the competence to realise bass parts that are partially figured.

The mingling of solo and continuo materials is not uncommon in the French keyboard tradition. D'Anglebert's 1689 *Pieces de clavecin* contains a concise continuo treatise titled 'Les Principes de l'Accompagnement', in addition to five organ fugues and nearly 20 transcriptions of Lully's music that are integrated into the composer's original works. Examples of concise figured bass pedagogical materials in French harpsichord manuscripts include US-NH Misc. Ms. 154 (ff. 32v-36r) and F-Pn Rés Vmd Ms. 115[23]. As the most substantial figured bass treatise in French harpsichord manuscripts, F-Pn Vm^8 1139 confirms the view that during the early 18th century, the solo harpsichord style went hand in hand with the accompaniment style. Clearly, developing fluency in keyboard continuo was fundamental to the training of harpsichordists as well as for mastering the art of composition.

In the process of working out possible realisations of these preludes, I have gained insight into how an 18th-century harpsichordist developed skills of accompaniment. The 14 preludes are ideal exercises for practising both basic and advanced harmonic progressions involving diminished and augmented chords, seventh and ninth chords in the overture, menuet, gavotte and other genres characteristic of the French style. Although the method is not as comprehensive as some printed treatises, such as those by Delair (1690), Saint Lambert (1707) and Rameau (1722), the St. Georges method, which is based on the rule of the octave, is very accessible to musicians of average abilities. Significantly, it provides a window into the teaching studio of a Parisian teacher active during the early decades of the 18th century.

---

[23]. US-NH Misc. Ms. 154, compiled around 1710 in France, includes over 40 harpsichord pieces and transcriptions by Chambonnières, Clarke, Corelli, F. Couperin, Keller, Lebègue, Jean-Baptiste Lully, Louis Lully, Marais and Mascitti. The manuscript contains an incomplete introduction to figured bass in pp. 64-71. See Gustafson – Herlin 2017, vol. II, p. 230. F-Pn Rés Vmd Ms. 115, compiled in France in 1686-1689, is a collection of some 100 keyboard (mainly harpsichord) pieces, mostly by 17th-century composers, including Chambonnières, D'Anglebert and Lully. The manuscript opens with rudimentary materials for beginners, such as «nom et valeur des notes» (p. 2), and closes with figured bass exercises (pp. 179-180). See Gustafson 2019, 'Musical Sources'.

The Significance of the Preludes with Figured Bass in F-Pn Vm⁸ 1139

Bibliography

Cessac 2001
Cessac, Catherine. 'Jacquet de La Guerre, Elisabeth', in: *Grove Music Online*, 2001, <https://www.oxfordmusiconline.com/grovemusic/>, accessed October 2023.

Chung 2018
Chung, David. *Online Thematic Keyboard of Lully Keyboard Arrangements*, 2018, <https://digital.lib.hkbu.edu.hk/OTCL/>, accessed October 2023.

Churchill 2006
Churchill, Sara-Anne. 'Monsieur de Saint-Georges' *Règles pour l'accompagnement*: A Translation and Commentary', in: *Performance Practice Review*, XI/1 (2006), pp. 1-19.

Couperin 1725
Couperin, François. *L'Apothéose de Lully*, Paris, [author], 1725.

Delair 1991
Delair, Denis. *Traité d'acompagnement pour le théorbe, et le clavessin*, Paris, [author], 1690; English translation by Charlotte Mattax, *Accompaniment on Theorbo & Harpsichord*, Bloomington & Indianapolis, Indiana University Press, 1991.

Fuller – Gustafson 2001
Fuller, David – Gustafson, Bruce, 'Couperin, Marguerite-Louise', in: *Grove Music Online*, 2001, <https://www.oxfordmusiconline.com/grovemusic/>, accessed October 2023.

Garden 2001
Garden, Greer. 'Bousset, Jean-Baptiste (Drouard) de', in: *Grove Music Online*, 2001, <https://www.oxfordmusiconline.com/grovemusic/>, accessed October 2023.

Gustafson 2001
Gustafson, Bruce. 'Certain, Marie-Françoise', in: *Grove Music Online*, 2001, <https://www.oxfordmusiconline.com/grovemusic/>, accessed October 2023.

Gustafson 2019
Id. *Chambonnières: A Thematic Catalogue*, in: *JSCM Instrumenta 1*, 2019, <https://sscm-jscm.org/instrumenta/instrumenta-volumes/instrumenta-volume-1/>, accessed October 2023.

Gustafson – Fuller 1990
Id. – Fuller, David. *A Catalogue of French Harpsichord Music 1699-1780*, Oxford, Clarendon Press, 1990.

Gustafson – Herlin 2017
Id. – Herlin, Denis. *Jacques Champion de Chambonnières: The Collected Works*, 2 vols., New York, The Broude Trust, 2017.

David Chung

MAZZETTI 2023
Basso Continuo in Italy: Sources, Pedagogy and Performance, edited by Marcello Mazzetti, Turnhout, Brepols, 2023 (Musica Incarnata: Pedagogy, Performance and Market, 1).

MCKEAN 2011
MCKEAN, John. *Gaspard Le Roux's « Pièces de Clavecin » and the Harpsichord Duet: Context and Performance Traditions*, unpublished M.Phil. Thesis, Cambridge, University of Cambridge, 2011.

NUTI 2007
NUTI, Giulia. *The Performance of Italian Basso Continuo: Style in Keyboard Accompaniment in the Seventeenth and Eighteenth Centuries*, Aldershot, Ashgate, 2007.

PERRAULT 1696-1700
PERRAULT, Charles. *Les hommes illustres qui ont paru en France pendant ce siècle, avec leur portrait au naturel.* 2 vols., Paris, Antoine Dezallier, 1696-1700.

SAINT LAMBERT 1991
SAINT LAMBERT, Michel de. *Nouveau traité de l'accompagnement du clavecin, de l'orgue et des autres instruments*, Paris, Ballard, 1707; English translation by John S. Powell, *A New Treatise on Accompaniment*, Bloomington-Indianapolis, Indiana University Press, 1991.

TITON DU TILLET 1727
TITON DU TILLET, Evrard. *Description du Parnasse François*, Paris, J. B. Coignard fils, 1727.

ZAPPULLA 2000
ZAPPULLA, Robert. *Figured Bass Accompaniment in France*, Turnhout, Brepols, 2000 (Speculum Musicae, 6).

The Three-voice Texture in Eighteenth-Century French Continuo

Clotilde Verwaerde
(Université Paris 8 – Musidanse)

I F WE THINK OF A MODEL of eighteenth-century French continuo, the first example that comes to mind is probably a four-part realisation in accordance with Dandrieu's method. Indeed, if we browse the French methods gathered in the six-volume edition by Fuzeau[1], most examples written out on two staves display at least four-note chords and several of them claim a direct connection to Rameau's principles — i.e., a complete chord in the right hand including the doubling of the bass note. On the very first page of the *Maître de clavecin*, Corrette stipulates that «the accompanist always plays three parts, and sometimes four at a time, against the bass»[2], and further specifies that the second way is «the easiest and most common at present»[3]. In this context, Rousseau's opposition to Rameau is obvious regarding chord texture but seems to go against the normal practice. In the entry 'Accompagnement' of his *Dictionnaire*[4], he claims that a note should be removed from most dissonant chords and that intervals of a second — corresponding to Rameau's «joined fingers» (*doigts joints*) — must especially be avoided because of their harshness. This can be linked to the comparison he made between Noblet, the Opera's accompanist, and Felice Bambini in the midst of the famous *Querelle des buffons*:

> Do you recall, Sir, having sometimes heard, in the Intermezzi which have
> been played for us this year, the son of the Italian Impresario, a young boy at most

---

[1]. SAINT-ARROMAN 2006.

[2]. CORRETTE 1753, p. 1: «l'accompagnateur fait toûjours entendre trois parties et quelque fois quatre a la fois contre la Basse». (All excerpts are translated by the author unless otherwise specified.)

[3]. *Ibidem*, p. 38: «Cette manière est la plus aisée et la plus en usage presentement».

[4]. ROUSSEAU 1768, pp. 11-12.

ten years old, sometimes play the accompaniment at the Opera? We were struck from the first day by the effect produced by the accompaniment of the Harpsichord under his little hands; and the whole theatre perceived from his precise and brilliant playing that he was not the usual Accompanist. I immediately sought the reasons for this difference, for I did not doubt that Signor Noblet was a good harmonist nor that he did not accompany very exactly; but what was my surprise, when observing the little gentleman's hands, to see that he almost never filled out the chords, that he omitted many notes and very often employed only two fingers, one of which almost always sounded the octave of the Basse! What! I said to myself, complete harmony produces less of an effect than mutilated harmony, and by filling out all the chords our Accompanists produce only a confused noise, while this one, with fewer notes, makes its accompaniment more perceptible and more pleasant! This was a disturbing problem for me, and I understood its whole importance still better when, after other observations, I saw that the Italians all accompanied in the same manner as the little lad, and that, consequently, this spareness in their accompaniment must depend on the same principle as that which they apply to their scores[5].

Paradoxically, Rousseau considers Bambini's accompaniment bright and precise although hardly ever more than two notes were sounded simultaneously in the right hand. Rousseau could not miss such an opportunity for calling Rameau's principles into question — the latter's *mécanique des doigts* (fingering technique) is based on complete four-note chords in the right hand and the distribution around the joined fingers formed by the seventh and the root placed above it[6]. Those «mutilated» chords — as Rameau calls them in his *Code de musique pratique* (1760) — correspond to a three-part texture (the bass note played by the left hand and a two-note accompaniment provided by the right hand).

In his thorough survey on French continuo practice, Robert Zappulla concludes that «few universal rules can be derived from French accompaniment treatises about even the most fundamental aspects of figured bass realization»[7]. The chord texture usually varies from three to five voices. However, considering the prevalence of the full-chord model in French music, the implementation and the contexts of use of this lighter three-part texture require a more thorough investigation, especially in the second half of the century, following the writings of Rousseau. Instructions from methods and theoretical writings are first gathered and compared. The use of a three-part texture is then studied in relation to the aesthetic debate between French and Italian music. Finally, some collections with written-out accompaniments are surveyed. The purpose is to assess to what extent this model may represent an asset with an eye on the amateur market or a halfway solution in the hitherto declining continuo practice in France.

---

[5]. ROUSSEAU 1753, pp. 51-53, translated in SCOTT 1998, p. 160.
[6]. RAMEAU 1732, pp. 25-31.
[7]. ZAPPULLA 2000, p. 86.

The Three-voice Texture in Eighteenth-Century French Continuo

Three-Part Texture in Theory

From the beginning of the century, Saint-Lambert mentions the possibility of removing a note from the right hand in three cases: when the hands are too close to one another, to avoid a faulty progression, and to balance the sound in relation to the soloist. When the hands are too close to each other, omitting a note from the right hand is an alternative to a parallel movement of the hands. The musical example attached to this instruction contains only triad chords, in which the first omission considered is that of the octave of the bass. Saint-Lambert specifies that this accompaniment of only two notes can be maintained for several successive chords[8]. Faulty progressions such as two successive fifths or octaves can be avoided by 'subtracting a part' — in this case, it is more appropriate to consider two parts in unison rather than an omission, as Saint-Lambert points out[9]. Finally, omissions are part of the license of the accompanist declined under the term 'taste of accompaniment': «For extremely delicate voices, one may as we have said remove a stop or two from the harpsichord, or else omit a note in each chord, reducing the accompaniment to two parts»[10]. The first omission considered by Saint-Lambert is again the octave of the bass.

Doubling the bass note with the right hand is indeed a recurring question in French methods and it may lead to a five-part texture when playing seventh- or ninth-chords. Playing such full chords offers a didactic advantage as the chord position can be kept in the right hand for the root chord and its inversions, thus openly displaying the relation between the various chords. This can however lead to consecutive fifths or octaves which are clearly prohibited by most authors. A four-part realisation of a seventh-chord progression involves the omission of the fifth (replaced by the octave) every two chords so that each seventh is properly prepared and resolved as can be seen in Ex. 1 ('Suite de Septieme à Trois Parties') — this fifth-free seventh-chord is often designated as the *petite septième*[11]. Laporte gives the following instructions:

> Very often, one or two chordal notes are kept in the following chord. The
> hand should be shifted only when the chord gets too low or the bass line rises too
> high. If this concerns one or two notes, one should rather not play the chord instead
> of interrupting the progression (i.e., take the bass note within the chord without

---

[8]. SAINT-LAMBERT 1707, p. 34.

[9]. *Ibidem*, p. 42. Although Arnold's survey is not restricted to French continuo, it is worth mentioning here that he noted from the second half of the seventeenth century «a great tendency to drop at the slightest provocation, from four-part into three-part harmony». ARNOLD 1965, vol. I, p. 331.

[10]. *Ibidem*, p. 61: «Pour les voix extrêmement delicates, on peut comme nous avons dit ôter un jeu ou deux du Clavecin, ou bien retrancher une note dans chaque accord, reduisant l'Accompagnement à deux Parties».

[11]. CORRETTE 1753, pp. 40-41, LAPORTE 1753, p. 36.

displacing it). Not only can the octave be omitted, but another note can be removed when it is deemed appropriate[12].

The conditions described here are the same as those previously mentioned. Although Laporte does not explain more precisely where those omissions *a discretion* should be applied, he gives musical examples «à deux parties» (see Ex. 1) — the second-chord progression even displays imitations between left and right hands and parallel thirds in the right hand, a feature found later on in written-out accompaniments (see Exs. 5 and 6). Compared with Saint-Lambert's musical example there is a significant evolution here; a three-part texture is strictly maintained throughout the progression «à deux parties» (with the exception of the first and last chords). However, this choice still belongs to the accompanist's license. What if the composer were to specify the chord texture intended?

Ex. 1: Laporte, *Traité théorique et pratique de l'accompagnement du clavecin* (1753), excerpts from the chord progressions, pp. 36-41.

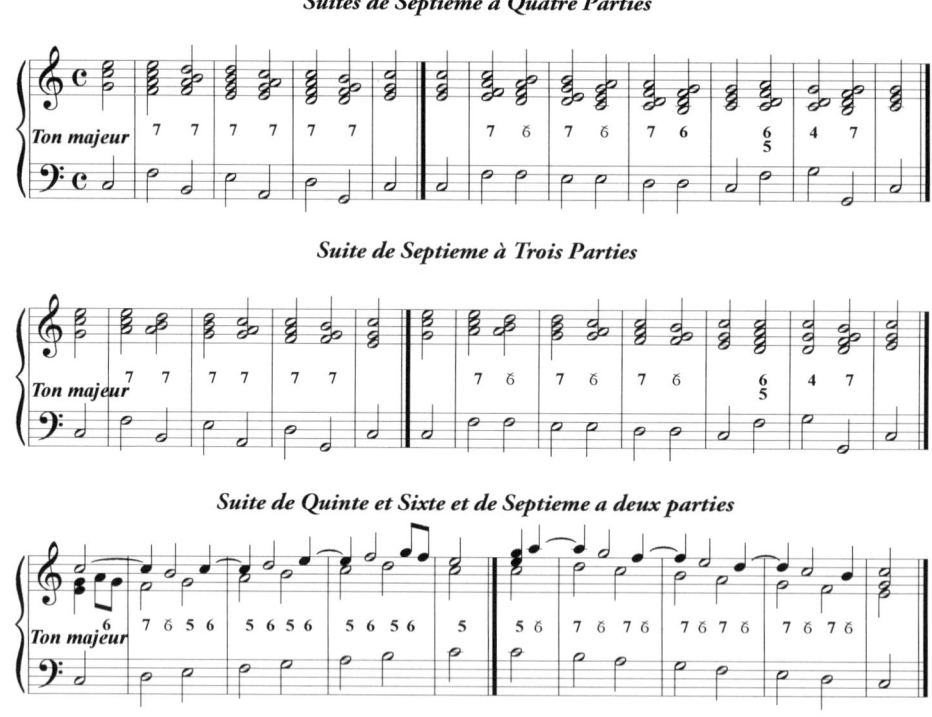

Suites de Septieme à Quatre Parties

Suite de Septieme à Trois Parties

Suite de Quinte et Sixte et de Septieme a deux parties

---

12. LAPORTE 1753, p. 36: «Très souvent une Note ou deux de l'Accord que l'on tient sert a former celui qui suit. Il ne faut point deranger la main, que lorsque l'Accord descend trop bas, ou que la Basse monte trop haut, encore, s'il ne s'agit que d'une note ou deux, il vaut mieux supprimer l'Accord que d'en interrompre la succession, c'est-à-dire, prendre la Note de Basse, dans l'Accord meme sans le deranger. Non seulement l'on peut supprimer l'Octave de la Basse dans les Acords Mais l'on peut supprimer encore une Note avec elle, quand on le juge a propos».

Suite de Seconde a deux parties

In the entry 'Accompagnement' of the *Encyclopédie méthodique*[13], Framery starts with Rousseau's *Dictionnaire* and comments on the latter's observations. As regards the chord texture, he asserts that the accompanist does not need to know how many notes a chord can comprise, but only the very notes the composer has in mind: the accompanist has to perform according to the composer's ideas. This notion is already developed by Jean-Baptiste Mercadier de Belesta, author of a new theoretical and practical system of music in 1776. His reflections on figures led to new symbols in which the exact composition of the chord can be indicated. The root of the chord is designated by its letter in the alphabetical notation. Calligraphic differences are made to specify the types of chord; for instance, an upright capital letter is used for a perfect triad whereas an italic capital letter calls for a seventh-chord. A dot placed after the letter indicates that all intervals are required; a barred letter means that the root must be removed; a barred letter followed by a dot means that the chord is complete but for its root; for other omissions, the composition of the chord is clearly indicated by the corresponding numbers placed above the root-letter[14] (see Ex. 4).

So far, three-part texture has been seen as a way of firstly avoiding faulty or clumsy motions, and secondly of providing variety and lightness. Another argument is showcased by Catel in the last chapter of his treatise devoted to the way of figuring a bass — a chapter he claims as essential to those who want to accompany on a harpsichord[15]. He states that one should accompany with three parts only by adding the most essential interval to the figures. This type of accompaniment can never lead to mistakes because he claims this three-part harmony as the purest. When a simple figure is placed above the bass note, only one accompaniment note needs to be added, none when the figure is double. The risk of adding a faulty interval is indeed limited, since there is hardly ever more than one possibility indicated to complete a harmony designated by a simple figure. For instance, the third is the sole interval one should consider adding to a chord figured 5, 6, 7, 8, or 9. Musical examples displaying this three-part texture are included not only in this chapter, but also in the previous ones. This principle was taken over by Jean-Baptiste Rey a few years later[16].

13.   Framery – Ginguené 1791, p. 17.
14.   Mercadier de Belesta 1776, pp. 156-157.
15.   Catel 1802, p. 68.
16.   Rey 1807, p. 196.

Mercadier de Belesta's new symbols have not been used (figured basses were already scarce in the 1770s) but a connection can be established between Catel's «pure harmony» and the way the figured bass should be realised in the *Principes élémentaires* and *Solfèges* of the Conservatoire[17]. In the first pages of the second book of the *Principes élémentaires*, a new symbol called «zero» appears in the figured bass. Short explanations are provided in footnotes: used alone, the zero calls for no chord above the bass note; placed above other numbers, it informs the accompanist that no other interval should be added to the chord. For instance, 0 above a barred 5 indicates a diminished fifth without adding a sixth (see Ex. 2).

Ex. 2: excerpts from the *Principes élémentaires du Conservatoire* (1799), Livre second pp. 3 and 38; (*) The zero above the 5 indicates that the chord must be played without sixth.

5. ANDANTE
AUTRE HARMONIE

(*) Le zéro au-dessus du cinq indique qu'il ne faut pas de Sixte dans l'accord.

58. GOSSEC
LARGHETTO

17. Agus *et al.* 1799 and Agus *et al.* 1802.

Ex. 3: Antoine Bemetzrieder, *New Lessons for the Harpsichord* (1782), p. 72; «The same example, the harmonies positioned according to the observations of the note».

This zero is not to be found in any treatise or method published in France before 1800, but it is used in a similar way by Antoine Bemetzrieder in his *New Lessons for the Harpsichord* published in London in 1782 with instructions both in English and French:

> Total and complete combinations are marked by their abridged signs.
> Incomplete combinations are marked by their figures with a *zero* over them, which points out an omission.
> [...]
> To play this and following examples on the harpsichord, it must be observed, 1st, that the bass and any simple accord may be doubled; but in the signs with a *zero* above them, the accords must be placed as they are written, i.e., the upper above, and the lower below[18].

According to these explanations and as confirmed by the various bass lines presented in the third part of the treatise, 'The science and the practice of accords', the «zero» is primarily meant to better control the chord rendition by giving an exact translation in figures of the

---

18.   BEMETZRIEDER 1782, Introduction, p. xxii.

right-hand part, i.e., the number of pitches and their order from lowest to highest. This level of precision prevents any abbreviated notation. Nonetheless, this symbol is most convenient for indicating which interval should be redoubled in the «sixte doublée» or in a fifth-free perfect triad, in which case four figures are stacked on top of each other (see Ex. 3). Incomplete combinations can be requested above written-out octaves in the bass staff, the possibility of doubling the bass being clearly stated in the instructions. Bemetzrieder's approach differs from Catel's notion of «pure harmony» since his written-out example and his figures show a texture varying from two to five voices — even six if the octave of the bass is added in the left hand — but the use of three-part texture clearly stands out and is extended to complete phrases. Some of the subsequent basses comprise three-note chords almost exclusively.

Browsing the two volumes of the Conservatoire's *Principes élémentaires* and *Solfèges*, one also finds vocal exercises in which elements of realisation are written-out on the bass staff (see Example 2, no. 58): the variety of chord texture may be compared to the one observed in Bemetzrieder's examples with again a marked preference for two-note chords in the right hand.

CHORD TEXTURE CONSIDERED WITHIN THE AESTHETIC DEBATE

Mercadier de Belesta's idea of taking the texture into account in the chord symbols clearly derives from Rousseau whose *Dictionnaire de musique* and *Lettre sur la musique Françoise* he explicitly cites to justify his position: «What would come out of all this filling? The vocal part would be muffled, harmony would go with monotony and often result in a confused noise. That is why some sounds are often omitted from the chords one plays, depending on the context and thus giving the ear the pleasure of recreating them»[19]. Michel Corrette comes to the same conclusion and specifically mentions Italian arias. In this repertoire, reducing the number of voices per chord is indeed presented as a means of lightening the texture, along with switching the right hand to the upper keyboard[20]. In a later edition of his *Prototypes*, he adds a whole new part devoted to the Italian way of accompanying the voice. He asserts that most Italian female singers play the harpsichord themselves while singing in a concert and apply only three fingers in soft passages. The octave of the bass is then omitted and Corrette reminds his reader that

---

[19]. MERCADIER DE BELESTA 1776, pp. 149-150: «que résulteroit-il de tout ce remplissage? Le chant seroit étouffé, la monotonie seroit presqu'inséparable de l'harmonie, & celle-ci ne produisoit bien des fois qu'un bruit confus. Aussi retranche-t-on souvent quelques sons des accords dont on fait usage, selon que les occasions l'exigent, & on donne à l'oreille le plaisir de les sous-entendre». Rousseau's criticisms are also echoed in Geminiani's *L'Art de bien accompagner du clavecin* (1754); among the differences between the French and English versions of his work, we note in particular the attacks on accompanists whose struck chords «degenerate into noise and clatter» and offer only «massive harmony» (see VERWAERDE 2015, pp. 239-243).

[20]. CORRETTE 1754, p. 15.

such practice is contrary to the principles developed by Rameau in his theory of fundamental bass[21]. However, this three-finger accompaniment differs from the texture discussed here. It results in four-note chords when both hands are taken into account as the arias with written-out keyboard part illustrate in the following pages of this augmented edition.

Mercadier de Belesta was not the first to attempt to express textural differences in thoroughbass figures. François-André Philidor composed in 1755 a Cantatille titled *L'Été*. Although no relation to Italian aesthetics can be guessed from the front page, the composer gives precise instructions as to the way it should be performed, but first and foremost he specifies the type of accompaniment he intended:

> As Mr Philidor requests that his *Cantatilles* be accompanied with the same delicacy with which the Italians accompany their music, he urges the amateurs to abide by the rules prescribed here below.
>
> Symphonies and recits can never be too full of harmony, but the airs must be accompanied with much discretion because one should hardly ever sound more than two notes as an accompaniment when a voice is singing in order to avoid confusion.
>
> The Ariettes
>
> I. No fifth in the seventh-chord unless it is a dominant chord, in which case it can be played without sounding displeasing to the ear.
>
> II. No fourth in the major sixth chord (commonly called *petite sixte*) major sixth without fourth (♯6 or ˣ6), major sixth with the fourth (♯6̸ or ˣ6̸)
>
> III. No sixth with the diminished fifth unless the chord is figured 6/5̸
>
> IV. No second with the augmented fourth unless the chord is figured ♯4/2
>
> V. No sixth in the second-chord unless explicitly called for[22].

These instructions are illustrated in Ex. 4: chords numbered II to IV are inversions of the dominant seventh chord in which he removes the root; the last chord considered is the third inversion of a seventh chord other than a dominant in which this time the fifth of the root position is removed. Philidor's choices are in accordance with the instructions of both Rousseau and later Mercadier de Belesta. Looking at the whole score of this cantatille, one might even

---

[21]. Corrette 1775, pp. 46-47.

[22]. Philidor 1755, Avertissement: «Mr Philidor desirant que ses Cantatilles soient accompagnées avec la même délicatesse que les Italiens accompagnent leurs Musiques il prie les Amateurs de se conformer aux régles prescrites cy dessous. Les Symphonies et les Recitatifs ne peuvent jamais être trop chargées d'harmonie, mais les Airs doivent être accompagnés avec beaucoup de discretion car il ne faut presque jamais toucher plus de deux nottes d'accompagnement lors qu'une voix chante afin d'eviter la confusion. Les Ariettes I. Il ne faut point mettre de 5ᵗᵉ dans l'accord de 7ᵉ a moins que ce ne soit sur une Dominante, alors cette 5ᵗᵉ peut-être frappée sans choquer l'oreille. II. Point de 4ᵗᵉ dans l'accord de 6ᵗᵉ majeure (appellée communément petite 6ᵗᵉ) Sixte Majeure sans 4ᵗᵉ (♯6 ou ˣ6) Sixte majeure avec la 4ᵗᵉ ♯6̸ ou ˣ6̸. III. Point de 6ᵗᵉ dans l'accord de Fausse quinte qu'elle ne soit marquée 6/5̸. IV. Point de 2ᵈᵉ dans l'accord de Triton qu'elle ne soit marquée ♯4/2. V. Point de 6ᵗᵉ dans l'accord de 2ᵈᵉ qu'elle ne soit marquée».

Ex. 4: Illustration of Philidor's instructions (accordingly numbered I to V) with Philidor's figures above the bass staff and their correspondence with Mercadier de Belesta's new symbols below the staff.

wonder why he makes such specific distinctions among the figures since he never uses the ones intended for complete chords in the ariettes. If we respect the composer's intentions as we are urged to in the *Encyclopédie méthodique*, this should result in a constant three-part texture in the sung passages of the ariettes[23]. Commenting on this mid-century Italian influence, David Tunley notes that «the wheel has, indeed, turned full circle!»[24].

Philidor's very detailed and performance-oriented foreword could certainly apply to works by other Italianate composers. All aspects of Antoine Bailleux's musical activities for instance suggest artistic choices from both composer and performer in accordance with the Italian aesthetics. As an editor, Bailleux actively promoted Italian composers such as Antonio Lolli, Luigi Boccherini or Felice Giardini[25]. In 1770, he wrote a method containing a hundred vocal exercises in the «new taste» for one or two voices, advice for a healthy training, instructions regarding the usual vocal embellishments, and a glossary of Italian musical terms with their translation in French. A substantially augmented edition was released in 1783 with the addition of a second part containing *solfeggi* by Leo, Durante, Piccini and Sacchini among others[26]. In 1779, Bailleux launched his *Journal d'ariettes italiennes*. This periodical was dedicated to the Queen, proposed each month two ariettes by Italian composers, and was regularly published until 1795. Prior to these publications, he composed a series of cantatilles explicitly labelled

---

[23]. A parallel can be drawn between Philidor's attempt at controlling the chord texture and the indications given by Veracini in his *Sonate Accademiche* (1744) with letters indicating single notes or *tasto solo*: «This is an example of a most controlled use of continuo, where the presence of more or fewer notes in the chords is marked by the composer directly on the score». NUTI 2007, p. 129.

[24]. TUNLEY 1997, p. 181; Tunley especially points out «the trend towards a staid, plodding bass» (p. 179) in works corresponding to the last stage of the cantatille as a genre and the assimilation of a new style by most composers of this last generation, marked by the aesthetic quarrel.

[25]. For instance: Luigi Boccherini, *Six Trios dialogués pour deux violons et un violoncelle, Œuvre XXVIII, mis au jour par Mr Bailleux*, Paris, Bailleux, 1779; Felice Giardini, *Sei Duetti per due Violini, Opera X, mis au jour par Mr Bailleux*, Paris, Bailleux, 1768.

[26]. A first selection of Italian *solfeggi* was published by Pierre Levesque and Jean-Louis Bêche as early as 1772. Bailleux's selection differs from this edition and several exercises of his own are inserted in this second «Italian» part to ensure a better gradation of difficulty.

in the Italian taste: *Le Bouquet de l'amitié* (1758), *Borée et Orithie* (1760), *Le Prix de la beauté* (1760), *La Vengeance de l'amour* (1761), *L'Hymne à Bacchus* (1766) and *Pigmalion* (1770)[27]. The *Journal de musique* praised the latter as being a «successful blend of our [French] music's majesty and the lightness of the Italian taste»[28]. There are no performance instructions but a thorough examination of the figures in *La Vengeance de l'amour* reveals a possible hint at the chord texture. Bailleux resorts several times to pedal notes with second- and dominant-chords above the tonic resulting in the following succession of figures: 8 – 2 – [8 –] 7× – 8. In the recitative «De ses transports l'amour ne fit que rire» (p. 6), all intervals (6/4/2) are indicated for the second-chord. A complete chord rendition seems an exception within the whole score but, according to Philidor, it is befitting here as it occurs within a recitative.

The Italian manner is most certainly required when works by Italian composers are considered. Trained in the famous Neapolitan school, Egidio Giuseppe Antonio Albanese came to Paris in 1747 and entered the service of the King. Acclaimed for his performances of Pergolesi's *Stabat mater* at the Concert spirituel, he is listed among the teachers of Italian taste (*maîtres de goût italien*) in the *Almanach musical* from 1770. His published works span four decades from the 1760s and are in the fashionable vocal genres of songs, romances and ariettes, with varied instrumental settings: strings, guitar, harp, harpsichord, the latter with a continuo or *obbligato* part. Within some of his collections, continuo figures and a written-out part for the right hand are combined, thus clearly displaying his choice of texture. This unusual layout is explained in the foreword of *La Soirée du Palais Royal*: «The bass of my airs is figured for the convenience for those who will not be able to play the written-out right-hand part; I only urge them to keep in the harmony they use the accompaniment turn that I have applied to each piece in particular. It is essential to strictly abide by the soft and loud nuances that are marked»[29]. The fact that dynamic markings are not directly correlated to the chord texture could be ascribed to his explicit preference for the pianoforte. Three-part texture seems predominant, and first and second inversions of dominant chords are often realised in accordance with Philidor's instructions (omission of the fundamental note). However, «joined fingers» are not avoided,

---

[27].   Years of publication are derived from the announcements (see Devriès-Lesure 2005, p. 24), all works are preserved except *L'Hymne à Bacchus*. It should be noted that these works are gathered under the heading 'Cantatilles dans le gout italien' in Bailleux's catalogues, thus insisting on the Italian brand: the seventh work listed in this category, *Le Retour de Printems*, is probably by Antoine Légat de Furcy (see Tunley 1997, p. 258), another composer for whose works it might be worth considering this type of accompaniment.

[28].   *Journal de musique*, March 1770, p. 38: «l'heureux assemblage de la majesté de notre Musique, & de la légèreté du goût italien».

[29].   Albanèse 1775, Avertissement: «La Basse de mes Airs est chiffrée pour la commodité des personnes qui ne pourront pas s'assujettir à exécuter de la main droite les traits qui sont écrits; je les prie seulement de conserver dans l'Harmonie qu'ils employeront, la tournure d'accompagnement que j'ai voulu rendre propre à chaque morceau en particulier. Il est essentiel d'observer exactement les doux et les forts qui sont marqués».

Ex. 5: Antoine Albanèse, *La Soirée du Palais Royal* (1775), pp. 4-5.

especially in 6/5 chords in which he prefers to omit the third. Discrepancies between figures and realisation may be noticed, often resulting from melodic motions when the accompaniment doubles the vocal part with parallel thirds or sixths. In such passages, the added accompaniment resembles a second vocal part as can be seen in Ex. 5 (for instance bars 1-4 or 8-10). It also calls to mind the parallel motions observed in Laporte's *Suite de Seconde à deux parties* (Ex. 1).

Whether the connection to thoroughbass is explicitly maintained or not (by way of a figured bass), written-out keyboard accompaniments constitute a relevant source of information in relation to chord texture.

THE 'ITALIAN TRIO' IN WRITTEN-OUT ACCOMPANIMENTS

Already in the first edition of his *Prototypes*, Corrette hints at other features of the Italian manner: «In Italian ariettes, chords can be arpeggiated on long notes and the right hand may double the vocal part from time to time. This sometimes sounds better than a struck accompaniment which, by its too great conformity, becomes tedious, tasteless, flat, confused and stifles the delicacy of the voice. But one must be a great musician to accompany in such a way»[30]. The 1775 edition contains three arias by Pergolesi, Galuppi and Rinaldo. In the first two, the right-hand part and the vocal part share the same staff with chords written-out when the voice is *tacet*; in sung passages, the keyboardist is instructed to play «the right hand like the voice». Here this feature is not applied 'from time to time' only, but systematically, with no second voice added as an accompaniment. Such passages with the right hand merely doubling the vocal part also occur in Albanese's works — this is limited to one or two beats in Ex. 5, but it may be used throughout several bars with the right hand even an octave higher.

The possible resemblance between an inner part added as an accompaniment in the right hand and a second vocal part has been mentioned previously. This idea of doubling the two upper (vocal) parts with the right hand can be found in another work by Albanèse, *Les Soirées du Bois de Boulogne*. This collection no longer contains a figured bass, but the fortepiano is designated as the accompanying instrument for the arias, songs and duets, with the exception of an arietta for a which a string ensemble is required. The Idille 'La Récompense de Mr Leonard' is written for a single voice, but it is specified in the margin of the first system that «the small notes mark a second vocal part if one wishes» (Ex. 6a.); the right-hand part takes up these two parts with a tessitura inversion in the second statement (mm. 3-4) to ensure a minimum of variety in the keyboard part. A few pages further, another Duo is notated on three staves, two vocal parts with text and a bass part. The vocal configuration is similar to the previous example, with an exchange of parts in the second statement of the initial motive in the third bar. The mention «Accompaniment with song» seems to call for an accompaniment comparable to that of the Idille, the keyboardist having this time to reconstitute his right-hand part from the two vocal parts (Ex. 6b.).

---

[30]. CORRETTE 1754, p. 16: «Dans les Ariettes Italiennes on peut harpeger les accords sur les notes longues et jouer de tems en tems de la main droite la partie chantante cela fait quelque fois mieux qu'un accompagnement plaqué qui par sa trop grande conformité devient ennuyeux, insipide, plat, confus et étouffe la delicatesse de la voix, mais pour accompagner de cette façon il faut être grand Musicien».

Ex. 6: ALBANÈSE, Égide-Joseph-Ignace-Antoine. *Les Soirées du Bois de Boulogne, nouveau recueil d'airs, de chansons et de duo pour le forte-piano avec une ariette à grand orchestre et une pièce en pantomime, œuvre XII*, Paris, Bureau d'abonnement musical, 1779, excerpts from pp. 4 and 22.

At any rate, playing the vocal part with the right hand is the simplest way of sustaining the singer and every single pitch is effectively doubled without the need for harmonic abilities. This is even recommended by Despreaux for the accompanists who have not yet acquired the habit of instantly finding the right chords[31]. Such performance modalities should not be disregarded as the continuo practice gradually lost ground in France during the second half of the eighteenth century. Thoroughbass skills were no longer required to perform chamber music thanks to a whole new repertoire of accompanied keyboard sonatas. «There is a fury today», Albanese complains, «to perform dazzling pieces only and to neglect what really leads to a solid talent, which is Accompaniment»[32]. However, doubling the voice can also provide the primary layout for a halfway solution between continuo realisation and written-out accompaniment. It leads to the «Italian trio» as described in the *Encyclopédie méthodique*:

> The Italians despise figures when they play from the score, because figures are
> and should only be the representative signs of the accompanying notes, used by the
> composer in his score. Besides, they are not in the habit of striking chords, except in

---

[31].   DESPREAUX 1783, p. 2.

[32].   ALBANÈSE 1775, foreword: «On a la fureur aujourd'huy de ne jouer que des pièces, dont l'exécution éblouit; et on néglige ce qui mène véritablement à un talent solide, qui est l'Accompagnement».

the recitative. They prefer to play the vocal line or the most prominent orchestral parts with the right hand. It is thus not true that they do not need the score, but they can sometimes do without it. They then accompany from the bass placed below the vocal part. Playing the former with the left hand and the latter with the right hand, they only have to add one note of accompaniment to complete the harmony for they seldom sound more than the trio. [...] The interval formed by the bass note and the vocal part being known, the third note is readily identified, either through the rank of the bass note within the tonality, the rule of the three movements or that of the cadences[33].

Reference is evidently made here to the rule of the octave which is presented later in the same entry and deemed sufficient by the author, provided that the accompanist has properly identified the tonality or the modulation. Albanese's three-part accompaniment corresponds to this description but it is also striking for its melodic qualities as parallel motions are frequently observed.

Collections of vocal music with written-out accompaniment for harpsichord, fortepiano or harp directly relate to this 'Italian trio' model, a light texture being a recurrent feature in them. Two-note right-hand chords often alternate with harmonic figurations in which usually one note is sounded at a time. Fuller chords may be applied to penultimate and/or final notes, tensed harmonies or heavily affect-loaded passages. Instructions sometimes enlighten us as to the way the accompaniment was devised. For instance, Charles Gabriel Foignet's approach may be related to the description provided by the *Encyclopédie méthodique*. From the first volume of his collection of airs and songs *Les Plaisirs de la Société*, he addresses amateurs whose harmonic training is insufficient as shown by the following comment on the front page:

Those who are not accomplished pianists will find here the means to accompany themselves with great ease. Instead of three staves, there are only two, one for the vocal part and one for the bass, but, in the upper staff, I have placed below the normal size notes of the vocal line those of the accompaniment with

---

33. Framery – Ginguené 1791, p. 17: «Les italiens méprisent les chiffres quand ils ont la partition sous les yeux, parce que les chiffres ne sont & ne doivent être que le signe représentatif des notes d'*accompagnement, employées par le compositeur* dans sa partition. D'ailleurs, ils sont peu dans l'habitude de *plaquer* les accords, si ce n'est dans le récitatif: ils préfèrent d'exécuter de la main droite ou le chant, ou les parties d'orchestre les plus saillantes. Il n'est donc pas vrai que la partition leur soit peu nécessaire: cependant ils peuvent quelquefois s'en passer. Ils accompagnent alors sur la basse jointe au chant; & l'on voit qu'exécutant l'une de la main gauche & l'autre de la main droite, ils n'ont plus qu'une note d'*accompagnement* à deviner pour completter l'harmonie; car ils font rarement entendre plus que le *trio*. [...] Or, cet intervalle formé par la note de la basse & par celle du chant étant donné, la troisième note leur est facilement connue, soit par le rang que la note de basse tient dans le ton, soit par la règle des trois mouvemens, soit par celle des cadences».

smaller noteheads; this accompaniment may be performed or dispensed with since the bass line is developed enough to replace any other accompaniment[34].

Another collection of vocal music illustrates the transition from thoroughbass to written-out accompaniment. *Les Délassemens de Polymnie*, a periodical launched by Porro in January 1786 proposes a selection of opera transcriptions and genuine society songs, and claims to be useful for both teachers and amateurs. It initially comprises three parts: the upper one intended for the voice and the first violin (thus doubling the vocal part), the middle one for another violin providing an accompaniment, and the lower one for the bass (labelled for cello or harpsichord). The middle part often resembles a keyboard right-hand part alternating harmonic figurations, short melodic patterns and chords, and it is conveniently placed above the bass part, but no performance alternative is explicitly suggested. Figured bass was maintained throughout the first year of publication — this being one of the very last occurrences of figured bass in musical works or periodicals published in France — but disappeared at the beginning of 1787, although the bass part was still intended for 'harpsichord or bass'. In the seventh issue, the layout clearly calls for the accompaniment part (middle staff) to be performed on the keyboard. This part features the elements discussed earlier: the vocal part is doubled by the violin and partly by the harpsichord, parallel thirds are occasionally added to complete the harmony, and the overall keyboard texture remains thin, often displaying three parts.

In the course of the eighteenth century, which was rich in didactic works, theoretical debates and aesthetic reflections, the three-voice texture in the French basso continuo was considered from different angles. Inscribed in the prerogatives of the performer, it constitutes first of all a technical solution. On the scale of the keyboard realisation, it contributes to keeping the chords in the medium register, limits the useless movements of the right hand, and prevents certain faulty progressions; it is then applied in a very punctual way to a few successive chords at the most. On the scale of the whole ensemble, it allows for a rebalancing of the sound forces present so that the solo part is not stifled; it can be applied to larger passages, or even to an entire movement. The question of texture becomes a stylistic argument when the composer favours an Italianate style. This preference is not satisfied with the sole renunciation of the doubling of the bass in the right-hand chord, and it is necessary to make targeted omissions in the seventh chords and their inversions. The identification of these omissions consequently becomes an issue in the designation of chords, as shown by Philidor's adaptation of the figures in his

---

34. FOIGNET 1781: «Les personnes qui ne sont pas fortes sur le Piano y trouveront une grande facilité pour s'accompagner: au lieu de trois lignes, il n'y en a que deux, celle du Chant et celle de la Basse, mais, dans la première ligne, j'ai mis sous les Nottes du chant qui sont grosses celles de l'accompagnement qui sont petites et que l'on n'exécutera qu'à volonté la basse étant assez travaillée pour suppléer à tout autre accompagnement».

cantatille. This parameter is also integrated into the design of the symbols that Mercadier de Belesta proposed with his new harmonic system in 1776. In both cases, the approach expresses a desire to take control of this aspect of the realisation usually left to the free appreciation of the continuo player.

The question needs to be considered in a different light as thoroughbass practice gradually declined in France in the last decades of the century. It is no longer so much one of knowing how to adapt the realisation of chords stylistically, but rather of having the necessary skills to correctly interpret the figures and play the corresponding chords. In later theoretical works such as those by Catel and Rey, three-part harmony is presented as the purest. This assertion is not based on aesthetic arguments, but on the possibility of avoiding harmonic pitfalls through omissions. The term 'omission' itself becomes inappropriate, since the process does not consist in removing sounds from a complete chord, but in completing the elements available on the score. In this respect, Catel's pure harmony can be compared to the solution described in the *Encyclopédie méthodique*. By taking as a basis on one side the bass and a figure, and on the other the bass and the upper (vocal) part, only one interval remains to be added, the common interest being to facilitate the accompaniment. Amateurs were the main target audience of the numerous periodicals that flourished in the second half of the century. They constituted a public with more fragile harmonic skills to whom it was advisable to offer ever easier learning methods and adapted performance solutions. The development of written-out accompaniments coincides with the growth of accompanied keyboard repertoire. This characterises a period of transition in the years 1770-1780, during which different formats were considered or experimented with, in terms of the number of staves, the doubling of the vocal part, and the way in which the necessary accompaniments were indicated (figures or small notes directly on the staff). As the last journal to include a figured bass part, *Les Délassemens de Polymnie* illustrates the different stages of transition and the implementation of this light texture at the keyboard. Whether or not the ease of performance is related to aesthetic choices, the resulting three-voice texture, with or without vocal doubling, can indeed be observed in many written-out accompaniments of the second half of the century. It deservedly takes its place among the possibilities of thoroughbass realisation in the French vocal music repertoire of the second half of the eighteenth century. This repertoire combines works initially conceived for a small chamber ensemble with transcriptions of opera arias, with figured bass or written-out accompaniment for keyboard — it was on the accompaniment of a stage work that Rousseau established his comparison between Noblet and Bambini. Playing lighter chords and doubling the solo part should also be considered as an expression of the influence of orchestral accompaniments in opera.

Bibliography

Agus *et Al.* 1799
Agus, Henri *et al. Principes élémentaires de Musique arrêtés par les Membres du Conservatoire pour servir à l'étude de cet établissement; suivis des Solfèges par M. M. Agus, Catel, Cherubini, Gossec, Langlé, Lesueur, Méhul et Riegel Première Partie*, Paris, Imprimerie du Conservatoire, 1799.

Agus *et Al.* 1802
Agus, Henri *et al. Solfèges pour servir à l'étude dans le Conservatoire de musique: seconde partie*, Paris, Imprimerie du Conservatoire, 1802.

Albanèse 1775
Albanèse, Égide-Joseph-Ignace-Antoine. *La Soirée du Palais Royal, nouveau recueil d'airs à une, deux et trois voix de dessus et de basse-taille avec accompagnement de forte-piano ou de harpe, la basse chiffrée, œuvre IX*, Paris, l'auteur-Cousineau, 1775.

Arnold 1965
Arnold, Franck Thomas. *The Art of Accompaniment from a Thorough-Bass*, unabridged and unaltered republication, 2 vols., Mineola (NY), Dover, 1965.

Bemetzrieder 1782
Bemetzrieder, Antoine. *Nouvelles leçons de clavecin – New Lessons for the Harpsichord*, London, the author, 1782.

Catel 1802
Catel, Charles-Simon. *Traité d'harmonie*, Paris, Imprimerie du Conservatoire, 1802.

Corrette 1753
Corrette, Michel. *Le Maître de clavecin pour l'accompagnement, méthode théorique et pratique*, Paris, l'auteur, 1753.

Corrette 1754
Id. *Prototipes contenant des leçons d'Accompagnemt par demandes et par reponses; Pour Servir d'Addition au Livre intitulé Le Maitre de Clavecin pour l'Accompagnement. Avec des Sonates pour le Violon, la Flûte, le Pardessus de Viole, où les accords sont notés sur la Basse pour guider les Commençans; ce qui dévoile les prétenduës difficultées de l'Accompagnement en moins de six mois*, Paris, l'auteur et aux adresses ordinaires, 1754.

Corrette 1775
Id. *Prototype pour servir d'addition au Maître de Clavecin. Méthode pour l'Accompagnement [...] Nouvelle Edition augmentée d'Ariettes Italiennes, et la maniere de les accompagner*, Paris-Lyon-Rouen-Dunkerque, Adresses ordinaires, [1775].

Despréaux 1783
Despréaux, Louis-Félix. *Cours d'éducation de clavecin ou piano-forte. Première partie contenant les premiers principes de la musique, suivis de cinquante leçons, avec la basse chiffrée*, Paris, Le Duc, [1783].

The Three-voice Texture in Eighteenth-Century French Continuo

Devriès-Lesure 2005
Devriès-Lesure, Anik. *L'Édition musicale dans la presse parisienne au XVIIIᵉ siècle: catalogue des annonces*, Paris, CNRS éditions, 2005.

Foignet 1781
Foignet, Charles Gabriel. *Les Plaisirs de la société. Recueil d'ariettes choisies des meilleurs opéra, opéra comiques et autres, arrangées pour le forte piano ou le clavecin, avec un accompagnement de violon ad libitum*, Paris, Boyer-Le Menu, 1781.

Framery – Ginguené 1791
Framery, Nicolas-Étienne – Ginguené, Pierre-Louis. *Encyclopédie méthodique, ou par ordre de matières: par une société de gens de lettres, de savants et d'artistes. La Musique, tome I*, Paris, Panckoucke, 1791.

Laporte 1753
Laporte, Claude de. *Traité théorique et pratique de l'accompagnement du clavecin, avec l'art de transposer dans tous les tons et sur tous les instrumens*, Paris, Bayard-Vernadé, 1753.

Mercadier de Belesta 1776
Mercadier de Belesta, Jean-Baptiste. *Nouveau système de musique théorique et pratique*, Paris, Valade, 1776.

Nuti 2007
Nuti, Giulia. *The Performance of Italian Basso Continuo: Style in Keyboard Accompaniment in the Seventeenth and Eighteenth Centuries*, Aldershot, Ashgate, 2007.

Philidor 1755
Philidor, François André Danican. *L'Eté Cantatille a Voix Seule avec Simphonie deux Violons un Alto et Basse*, Paris, L'Auteur-Le Clerc-Bayard-Castagneri, 1755.

Rameau 1732
Rameau, Jean-Philippe. *Dissertation sur les différentes méthodes d'accompagnement pour le clavecin ou pour l'orgue avec le plan d'une nouvelle méthode établie sur une méchanique des doigts*, Paris, Boivin, 1732.

Rey 1807
Rey, Jean-Baptiste. *Exposition élémentaire de l'harmonie, théorie générale des accords d'après la basse fondamentale vue selon les différens genres de musique: ouvrage classique servant à l'intelligence de tous les traités, systèmes d'harmonie et méthodes d'accompagnement, pouvant servir aussi d'introduction à la composition*, Paris, l'auteur, [1807].

Rousseau 1753
Rousseau, Jean-Jacques. *Lettre sur la musique française*, Paris, Le Sueur, 1753.

Rousseau 1768
Id. *Dictionnaire de musique*, Paris, Duchesne, 1768.

SAINT-ARROMAN 2006
Méthodes & Traités. Basse continue. France 1600-1800, 6 vols., edited by Jean Saint-Arroman, Courlay, Fuzeau, 2006.

SAINT-LAMBERT, 1707
SAINT-LAMBERT. *Nouveau traité de l'accompagnement du clavecin, de l'orgue et des autres instruments*, Paris, Ballard, 1707.

SCOTT 1998
ROUSSEAU, Jean-Jacques. *Essay on the Origin of Languages and Writings Related to Music*, edited and translated by John T. Scott, Hanover (NH), University Press of New England, 1998.

TUNLEY 1997
TUNLEY, David. *The Eighteenth-Century French Cantata*, Oxford, Clarendon Press, ²1997.

VERWAERDE 2015
VERWAERDE, Clotilde. *La pratique de l'accompagnement en France (1750-1800): de la basse continue improvisée à l'écriture pour clavier dans la sonate avec violon*, Ph.D. Diss., Paris, Paris-Sorbonne, 2015, <https://theses.hal.science/tel-04267902>, accessed December 2023.

ZAPPULLA 2000
ZAPPULLA, Robert. *Figured Bass Accompaniment in France*, Turnhout, Brepols, 2000 (Speculum Musicae, 6).

The *Encyclopédie ou Dictionnaire raisonné des sciences, des arts et des métiers* (1751-1772): A Source for Basso Continuo Accompaniment in Eighteenth-Century France

Marie Demeilliez
(Université Grenoble Alpes)

IN THE 28 VOLUMES of the *Encyclopédie ou Dictionnaire raisonné des sciences, des arts et des métiers* published between 1751 and 1772 under the direction of Diderot, D'Alembert, and Jaucourt, several articles deal with basso continuo accompaniment. Like numerous articles on musical subjects, most of them were written by Jean-Jacques Rousseau, as a first draft of his *Dictionnaire de musique*. These texts address different aspects of accompaniment by keyboard instruments. The article 'Accompagnement' (vol. I) defines the principles of its teaching and practice. 'Règle de l'octave' (vol. XIV) teaches which chords are to be played on an unfigured bass. 'Chiffrer' (vol. III) deals with the chord notation system. 'Doigter' (vol. V) and 'Face' (vol. VI) deal with the position of the hand and fingers, and their movement in the chord sequence. 'Accompagnateur' (vol. I) lists the qualities one is expected to have in order to play the accompaniment. 'Arpeggio' (vol. I) and 'Harpègement' (vol. VIII) describe the ways of arpeggiating the chords, on the harpsichord and on the cello. This last article also examines the particular case of the accompaniment of recitatives.

These texts have given rise to numerous comments since the 18th century: since its publication in 1751, Rousseau's article 'Accompagnement' has been at the root of a long controversy between Rameau and Rousseau. Indeed, these articles are part of a dual quarrel: on the one hand regarding Rameau's theories, on the other hand between the supporters of Italian music and the defenders of the French aesthetic. Beyond these controversies, these texts also provide valuable information on performance of basso continuo in France in the mid-18th century[1].

---

1. This chapter is based on my work as a critical editor of these articles within the ENCCRE project (collaborative and critique digital edition of the *Encyclopédie*): <http://enccre.academie-sciences.fr/encyclopedie/>, accessed October 2023.

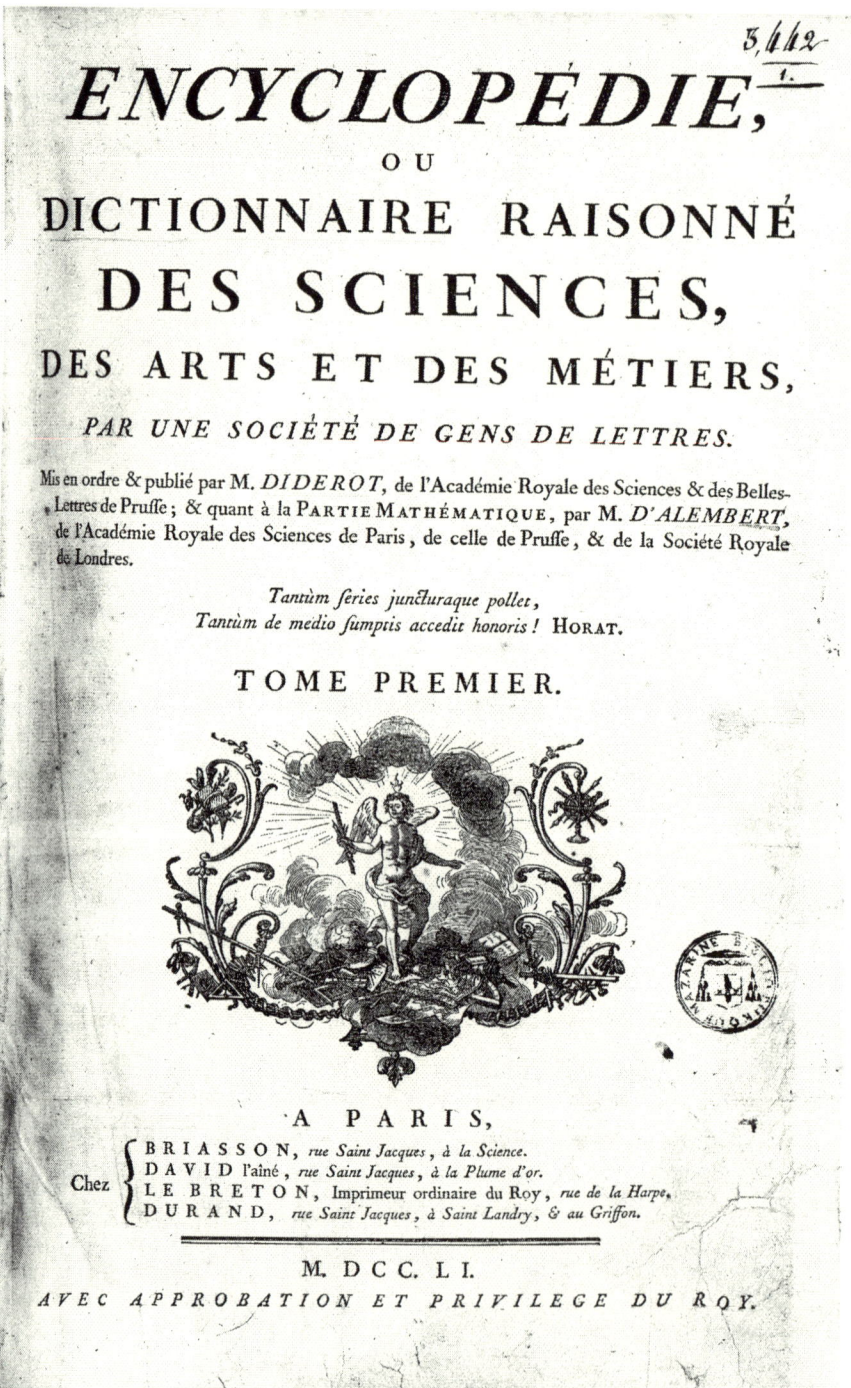

ILL. 1: Title-page of *Encyclopédie ou Dictionnaire raisonné des sciences, des arts et des métiers*, vol. I, edited by Denis Diderot and Jean Le Rond d'Alembert, Paris, Briasson-David l'aîné-Le Breton-Durand, 1751.

The Corpus

Rousseau signed seven of the eight articles in the *Encyclopédie* dealing with accompaniment ('Accompagnateur', 'Accompagnement', 'Arpeggio', 'Chiffrer', 'Doigter', 'Face', 'Règle de l'octave'). They were published between 1751 and 1765. The fact that these articles for the *Encyclopédie* were republished, sometimes expanded or modified, in his *Dictionnaire de musique* in 1768 has meant that these texts are mostly commented on from their recast version, the content of which is sometimes quite different. Yet, these articles for the *Encyclopédie* are of considerable interest: they are written at a turning point in Rousseau's thinking, before the shattering statements linked to the *Querelle des Bouffons*. Indeed, Rousseau's entire contribution to the *Encyclopédie* was written and delivered in 1749[2]. One article remains anonymous: 'Harpegement', published in 1765, but we can assume that it may have been written by D'Alembert[3].

These texts on accompaniment are linked to all the articles devoted to harmonic theory. The article 'Accompagnement' is in fact what we could refer to as a 'crossroads article' (*article-carrefour*)[4] in the *Encyclopédie*, in the sense that it is the centre of a constellation of more detailed articles organised by networks of cross-references. The composition of chords, the rules for consonances and dissonances, which are sometimes displayed in accompaniment methods, are to be found in several articles of the *Encyclopédie* such as 'Harmonie' (vol. VIII), 'Basse fondamentale' (vol. II), 'Consonnance' (vol. IV), 'Dissonnance' (vol. IV), 'Composition' (vol. III), 'Supposition' (vol. XV), 'Suspension' (vol. XV), 'Ton' (vol. XVI), 'Cadence' (vol. II), 'Modulation' (vol. X), 'Renversement' (vol. XIV) written by Rousseau, 'Accords fondamentaux' (vol. VII) and 'Basse fondamentale' (vol. VII) written by D'Alembert.

A Main Source: Rameau's Writings

Rousseau bases his articles on harmony and accompaniment on the writings of Jean-Philippe Rameau[5]. For the trilogy *Accompagnement*, *Doigter* and *Chiffrer*, which aims to expose in a simple way the main issues of keyboard accompaniment, the main source is the *Dissertation*

---

[2]. Cernuschi 2000, p. 111.

[3]. The article 'Harpegement' appears to be an indirect response to Rameau's criticisms of the *Encyclopédie* and particularly to Rousseau's 'Accompagnement', which was vigorously attacked in the *Erreurs sur la musique dans l'Encyclopédie* (1755). It is therefore likely that D'Alembert, who was responsible for editing Rousseau's contributions, wrote this article 'Harpegement', which duplicates Rousseau's article 'Arpeggio' published in vol. I (Demeilliez 2020-2022). In vol. VII, D'Alembert had already done so, signing a new article *Basse fondamentale* to complete a homonymous article co-signed with Rousseau five years earlier for vol. II (O'Dea 2003).

[4]. Cernuschi 2000, p. 113.

[5]. Even though he mentions the names of Delair and Campion in Rousseau 1751 (p. 75) and Rousseau 1765, he seems to know their texts through reading Rameau. There are other sources that complement Rameau's writings for the more than 400 articles on music that Rousseau wrote for the *Encyclopédie*: for example Chambers'

sur les différentes méthodes d'accompagnement published in 1732. The whole of the first part of 'Accompagnement' (§ 1-27), like the bulk of the 'Doigter' article (§ 4-16), borrows large passages from Rameau's *Dissertation*, sometimes word for word, sometimes reformulating or summarising Rameau's ideas. Even if the borrowings are less literal, the material and logic of 'Chiffrer' also come from the same *Dissertation*.

The choice to base his articles mainly on this *Dissertation* rather than on the *Principes d'accompagnement* included in Rameau's *Traité de l'harmonie* (1722), reveals a concern close to Rousseau's heart: the wish to simplify musical notation, which he considered too complex[6]. A text such as Rameau's *Dissertation* [...] *with the help of which, one can become a learned composer, and a skilled accompanist, even without knowing how to read music*[7] was therefore ideal in its teaching ambitions. The aim of Rameau's *Dissertation* was to propose a new method of teaching the accompaniment that would enable beginners without any theoretical background to acquire harmonic reflexes quickly on the harpsichord. The idea was to have the fingers memorise a limited number of typical sequences in a mechanical way, which the accompanist would be able to replace according to the musical context. Intended for novice harpsichordists, the chords should be played with the right hand, moving the fingers as little as possible. To limit the number of chords to be played, Rameau uses the fundamental bass: the chords are played not according to the continuo bass line notated by the composer, but according to the fundamental bass line. This considerably reduces the number of chords to be learned, since all the inversions of a chord are played as if they were in their root-position. With this method, accompaniment becomes a mechanical process of finger movement, a «méchanique des doigts». Rameau combined this innovative pedagogy with the invention of a new system of notation: he proposed to replace the traditional figured bass, characterised by a large number of chords and several dozen different figures, with a system composed of seven characters that made it possible to accompany without even knowing how to read the music[8]. This system of notation was not followed up[9], Rameau

---

Cyclopaedia, Brossard's *Dictionnaire de musique*, French *Dictionnaires universels* (Furetière and Trévoux), Blainville's *Harmonie théorico-pratique*. See CERNUSCHI 2000, MARTIN 2012, DEMEILLIEZ 2020-2022.

[6]. Rousseau's article 'Notes, en musique' (*Encyclopédie*, vol. XI) betrays the same concern.

[7]. Its complete title is: *Dissertation sur les différentes métodes d'accompagnement pour le clavecin, ou pour l'orgue; avec le plan d'une nouvelle métode, établie sur une méchanique des doigts, que fournit la succession fondamentale de l'harmonie: et à l'aide de laquelle on peut devenir sçavant compositeur, & habile accompagnateur, même sans sçavoir lire la musique.* In English: Dissertation on the different methods of accompaniment for the harpsichord, or for the organ, with the plan of a new method, established on a mechanics of the fingers, which the fundamental succession of harmony provides, and with the help of which one can become a learned composer, and a skilled accompanist, even without knowing how to read music. All translations of French quotations into English are by the present author, unless otherwise specified.

[8]. For an overview of this method, see HAYES 1974, CHRISTENSEN 1993, pp. 58-61.

[9]. Although some theorists (Nicolas-Louis Le Dran, Pierre-Joseph Roussier for example) tried to develop systems of figured bass notation close to that of Rameau, these were not adopted by music publishers and copyists.

himself did not use it in his music[10], and thirty years later, he admitted his inadequacy[11]. A few years before writing his articles for the *Encyclopédie*, Rousseau himself had developed a new system of notation, in which the pitches of notes are expressed by numbers and dots. He had presented this *Projet concernant de nouveaux signes pour la musique* unsuccessfully to the Académie des Sciences in 1742 and developed it in his *Dissertation sur la musique moderne* (1743). For the accompaniment, he planned a system of notation whose principle was quite close to that of Rameau, announcing a work in which he would propose:

> [...] a novel means of figuring the accompaniment of the Organ or Harpsichord entirely different from all those of this sort that have appeared until now, and such in way that with four signs alone I figure all sorts of Thoroughbasses in a way that always makes the modulation and the Fundamental Bass perfectly known to the Accompanist, it being otherwise possible for him to be mistaken about it. Following this method, one can, without seeing the Figured Bass, accompany quite correctly by the numerals alone, which, instead of being related to that Figured Bass, are related directly to the Fundamental[12].

This work was never written to the best of our knowledge. In the *Encyclopédie*, underlining the complexity of the figures of the accompaniment and calling for a renewal of the notation and the teaching of it proved to be a way for Rousseau to militate for the simplification of the music notation system.

The ideas of Rameau's *Dissertation* synthesised by Rousseau in this trilogy *Accompagnement-Chiffrer-Doigter* are distributed as follows: in the article 'Accompagnement', paragraphs 1-5 define the nature of accompaniment in music, note and try to explain the difficulties of learning how to accompany (mainly the abundance of figures); then paragraphs 6-11 describe the methods used for teaching accompaniment and the inadequacies thereof. Finally, paragraphs 12-27 set out the principles of the method invented by Jean-Philippe Rameau. Paragraphs 4-16 of 'Doigter' continue the discussion of Rameau's teaching method, describing the movements of the fingers needed to play chords according to the movements of the fundamental bass. Finally, the article 'Chiffrer' describes the system of notation for the

---

See VERNET 2016, VERWAERDE 2015, pp. 157-159.

[10]. CHRISTENSEN 1993, p. 60.

[11]. RAMEAU 1760, p. 74.

[12]. ROUSSEAU 1743, pp. xv-xvi: «J'y traiterai d'une nouvelle manière de chiffrer l'accompagnement de l'Orgue et du Clavecin entièrement différente de tout ce qui a paru jusqu'ici dans ce genre, & telle qu'avec quatre signes seulement je chiffre toute sorte de Basses continues, de manière à rendre la modulation & la Basse-fondamentale toujours parfaitement connues de l'Accompagnateur, sans qu'il lui soit possible de s'y tromper. Suivant cette méthode, on peut, sans voir la Basse-figurée, accompagner très-juste par les chiffres seuls, qui au lieu d'avoir rapport à cette Basse-figurée, l'ont directement à la fondamentale». English translation: SCOTT 1998, p. 33.

figured bass invented by Rameau. After explaining how it works, Rousseau notes its main flaw: the signs are so dependent on each other that if the musician gets lost mistaking one finger for another, it is no longer possible to recover until the next perfect triad.

Nevertheless, Rousseau's articles are not only a summary of Rameau's *Dissertation*. The failure of its new method of notating and teaching accompaniment, and more generally the encyclopaedic project of proposing an inventory of the art of music, led Rousseau to expose other aspects of accompaniment. The article 'Chiffrer' thus offers the most comprehensive table of figures of its time, for Rousseau aims to list all the figures in use in different countries (mainly France and Italy) and by the various composers (ILL. 2). The article 'Règle de l'octave' (Rule of the octave) describes precisely this pedagogical tool used by 18th-century French musicians to teach accompaniment and composition: a standardised method of harmonising ascending and descending major and minor scales. However, although the musical example reproduced in the volume VII of the *Recueil de planches* of the *Encyclopédie* corresponds to the version usually reproduced in French methods in the middle of the 18th century (ILL. 3)[13], Rousseau is not satisfied with it and devotes paragraphs 4-8 of his article to re-examining the chord placed on the sixth ascending degree. The rule prescribes playing a first-inversion triad, which, for Rousseau,

ILL. 2: Table of figures for accompaniment (from ROUSSEAU 1753A).

---

13.   DIDEROT 1769, pl. VI.

Chiffres.	Noms des Accords.
3 ♮	Accord parfait, tierce naturelle.
♮ 3	Idem.
* ♮	Idem.
5 / ♮	Idem.
6 / 3	Accord de sixte-tierce.
* 6	Idem.
	Les differentes sixtes se marquent dans cet accord, comme les tierces dans l'accord parfait.
* 6 / 4	Accord de sixte-quarte.
6	Idem.
7 / 5 / 3	Accord de septieme.
7 / 5	Idem.
7 / 5	Idem.
* 7	Idem.
* ※	Septieme avec tierce majeure.
* 7 / ♭	Idem avec tierce mineure.
* 7	Idem avec tierce naturelle.
7 ♭	Accord de septieme mineure.
* ♭ 7	Idem.
7 ※	Accord de septieme majeure.
* ※ 7	Idem.
※ 7 ♮	De septieme naturelle.
* ♮ 7	Idem.
7 / ※	Septieme avec une fausse quinte.
7 / ♭ 5	Idem.
7 / 5 ♭	Idem.
* 7	Accord de septieme diminuée.
7 ♭	Idem.
♭ 7	Idem.
7 ♭ / ※	Idem.
7 ♭ / 5 ♭	Idem.
♭ 7 / ※	Idem.
♭ 7 / ♭ 5	Idem.
7 ♭ / 5 ♭ / 3	Idem, &c.
* ※ 7	Septieme superflue.
7 ※	Idem.
7	Idem.
※ 7 / 5 / 4 / 2	Idem.
※ 7 / 6 / 4 / 2	Idem.
7 / 2	Idem.
7 ※ / 4 / 2	Idem, &c.
7 ※ / 6 ♭	Accord de septieme superflue avec sixte mineure.
× 7 / ♭ 6	Idem.
× 7 / ♭ 6 / 2	Idem.
× 7 / ♭ 6 / 4	Idem, &c.
7 / 6	Accord de septieme & seconde.
* 6 / 5	Accord de grande sixte.
6 / 5	Idem.
* 5̸	De fausse quinte.
5 ♭	Idem.
♭ 5	Idem.
6 / ♭ 5	Idem.
6 / 5	Idem, &c.
6 / 5̸	Accord de fausse quinte avec sixte majeure.
× 6 / ♭ 5	Idem.
6 ※ / 5 ♭	Idem.
4 / 3	Accord de petite sixte.
6 / 4 / 3	Idem.
* 6̸ / 6	Idem.
× 6̸	Idem, majeure.
× 6 / 4 / 3	Idem, &c.
* × 6̸	Petite sixte superflue.
× 6 / 4 / 3	Idem.
※ 6 / 6 ※	Idem.
6 / 4 / 3	Petite sixte, quand la quarte est superflue.
6 / × 4 / 3	Idem.
6 / × 4	Idem.

ILL. 2: Table of figures for accompaniment (from ROUSSEAU 1753A), cont.

47

Chiffres.	Noms des Accords.
× 4 / 3	Idem.
✻ 2	Accord de seconde.
4 / 2	Idem.
6 / 2	Idem.
✻ 5 / 2	Accord de seconde & quinte.
6 / 4	De triton.
6 / 4 ×	Idem.
6 / × 4	Idem.
6 / 4	Idem.
6 / 4 / 2	Idem.
4 / 2	Idem.
4 × / 2	Idem.
× 4 / 2	Idem.
4 × / 2	Idem.
✻ × 4 / 4	Idem.
4 × / 3 b	Triton avec tierce mineure.
4 / b	Idem.
6 / 4 / 3 b	Idem.
✻ × 4 / b	Idem, &c.
✻ × 2	Seconde superflue.
× 4 / × 2	Idem.
4 / 2	Idem.
6 / 4 / × 2	Idem.
✻ 9	Accord de neuvieme.
9 / 5	Idem.
9 / 3	Idem.
✻ 9 / 7	Neuvieme avec la septieme.
7 / 5	Idem.
4	Quarte ou onzieme.
5 / 4	Idem.

Chiffres.	Noms des Accords.
4 / 9	Quarte avec la neuvieme.
9 / 4	Idem.
4 / 7	Quarte & septieme.
× 5 / 5 ✻	Accord de quinte superflue. Idem.
× 5 / 9	Idem.
× 5 / 9 / 7	Idem.
9 / 7 / × 5	Idem.
× 5 / b 4	Quinte superflue avec la quarte.
5 × / 4 b	Idem, &c.
7 / 6	Septieme & sixte.
9 / 6	Neuvieme & sixte.

Quelques auteurs avoient introduit l'usage de couvrir d'un trait toutes les notes de basse qui passoient sous un même accord : c'est ainsi que les charmantes cantates de M. de Clerambault sont *chiffrées* ; mais cette invention étoit trop commode pour durer ; elle montroit aussi trop clairement à l'œil toutes les syncopes d'harmonie.

Aujourd'hui, quand on soûtient le même accord sur quatre différentes notes de basse, ce sont quatre chiffres différens qu'on leur fait porter ; desorte que l'accompagnateur induit en erreur, se hâte de chercher l'accord même qu'il a déjà sous sa main. Mais c'est la mode en France de charger les basses d'une confusion de chiffres inutiles. On *chiffre* tout, jusqu'aux accords les plus évidens ; & celui qui met le plus de chiffres croit être le plus savant. Une basse ainsi hérissée de chiffres triviaux rebute l'accompagnateur de les regarder, & fait souvent négliger les chiffres nécessaires. L'auteur doit supposer que l'accompagnateur sait les élémens de l'accompagnement ; il ne doit pas *chiffrer* une sixte sur une médiante, une fausse quinte sur une note sensible, une septieme sur une dominante, ni d'autres accords de cette évidence, à moins qu'il ne soit question d'annoncer un changement de ton. Les chiffres ne sont faits que pour déterminer le choix de l'harmonie dans les cas douteux. Du reste, c'est très-bien fait d'avoir des basses *chiffrées* exprès pour les écoliers. Il faut que les chiffres montrent à ceux-ci l'application des regles ; pour les maîtres, il suffit d'indiquer les exceptions.

M. Rameau dans sa *dissertation sur les différentes méthodes d'accompagnement*, a trouvé un grand nombre de défauts dans les chiffres établis. Il a fait voir qu'ils sont trop nombreux, & pourtant insuffisans, obscurs, équivoques, qu'ils multiplient inutilement le nombre des accords, & qu'ils n'en montrent en aucune maniere la liaison.

Tous ces défauts viennent d'avoir voulu rapporter les chiffres aux notes arbitraires de la basse-continue, au lieu de les avoir appliqués immédiatement à l'harmonie fondamentale. La basse-continue fait sans doute une partie de l'harmonie ; mais cette harmonie est indépendante des notes de cette basse, &
elle

ILL. 2: Table of figures for accompaniment (from ROUSSEAU 1753A), cont.

constitutes a «fault» against the «elementary rules of harmony»[14]. Rousseau therefore tries to find another solution by exploring several options in succession, before concluding that the best chord on this sixth degree is the root-position seventh chord. In this case, Rousseau considers this chord not as a seventh chord in its root position, but as the inversion of a *sixte ajoutée* on the first degree. This allows him to consider that the fundamental bass progresses by descending fifths (which is permitted by the rules of harmony)[15]. This solution was not to be followed: the treatises of accompaniment published in the second half of the 18th century continued to adhere to the commonly accepted version with a first-inversion triad.

ILL. 3: 'Règle de l'octave', in: *Encyclopédie ou Dictionnaire raisonné des sciences, des arts et des métiers, Recueil de planches*, t. VII, pl. VI Musique, 1769.

Apart from this discussion of the harmonisation of the sixth degree, Rousseau's understanding and exposition of the *règle de l'octave* is largely inspired by Rameau's writings. The definition of the rule and its (erroneous) attribution to Denis Delair come from the *Dissertation*[16]. But above all, Rousseau drew from the *Traité de l'harmonie* the understanding of the *règle de l'octave* through Rameau's theory of the fundamental bass. Indeed, the latter is

---

[14]. ROUSSEAU 1765, p. 22: «J'ai cependant peine à pardonner qu'une formule destinée à la pratique des *regles* élémentaires de l'harmonie contienne une faute contre ces mêmes *regles*». The sequence root-position triad on the dominant followed by a first-inversion triad on the sixth degree corresponds to a fundamental bass progression of a second. However, in Jean-Philippe Rameau's theory, which influenced Rousseau, the fundamental bass must progress by intervals of fifths (or its inversion the fourth) or thirds (or its inversion the sixth). Progression by intervals of a second (as in this case) is considered a license.

[15]. It is notable that Rousseau does not mention Jean-Philippe Rameau's explanation of this problematic sequence in the *Traité de l'harmonie* (RAMEAU 1722, p. 382). If Rameau admits the progression of root-position triad on the dominant (G) to a first-inversion triad on the sixth degree (A), it is because he considers this not as the inversion of a root-position triad on the fourth degree (F), but as the inversion of a seventh chord of the second degree (D). In this case the fundamental bass progresses by fourths.

[16]. Rousseau traces the history of the Rule of the Octave to a work by Étienne Denis Delair dated 1700, although Delair did not publish anything in 1700. This comes from Rameau who mentions in his *Dissertation* «[Delair's] Treatise on Accompaniment engraved in 1700 [which] determines the succession of the Chords on

systematically integrated into the explanations and musical examples of the *règle de l'octave* in the Rameau's treatise[17].

Other elements also come from Rameau's writings, even if the composer is not always cited: some technical details such as the avoidance of the right-hand thumb[18], the basic texture of the accompaniment (bass in the left hand, chords in the right)[19], and the right-hand fingerings in playing chords. Like Rameau in the *Traité de l'Harmonie*, Rousseau stresses the importance of adapting the accompaniment to the musical context. One must proportion the realisation to the character of the music and to that of the instruments or the voices one accompanies:

> [...] thus, in a chorus one strikes full chords in the right hand, and one doubles the octave or the fifth, and sometimes the whole chord, in the left hand. On the contrary, in a slow and soft solo, when there is only a flute or a weak voice to accompany, one omits notes, one softly arpeggiates, one takes the upper manual[20].

This observation is in line with what Rameau, like other authors of accompaniment methods[21], called for:

> The accompaniment must conform to the character of the voices, and to that of the airs, entering into the spirit of the words or of the sole expression of the

---

that of the Bass» (RAMEAU 1732, p. 5). The first publication of the Rule of octave in France was in fact by François Campion, author of a *Traité d'accompagnement et de composition, selon la régle des octaves de musique* (Paris, 1716).

17. RAMEAU 1722, pp. 212 and 382-383.
18. *Ibidem*, p. 371; RAMEAU 1732, pp. 58-60.
19. RAMEAU 1732, p. 17.
20. ROUSSEAU 1751, p. 76: «Il faut toûjours proportionner le bruit au caractere de la Musique, & à celui des instrumens ou des voix qu'on a à accompagner: ainsi dans un chœur on frappe les accords pleins de la main droite, & l'on redouble l'octave ou la quinte de la main gauche, & quelquefois tout l'accord. Au contraire dans un récit lent & doux, quand on n'a qu'une flûte ou une voix foible à accompagner, on retranche des sons, on les arpege doucement, on prend le petit clavier».
21. For example, GERVAIS 1733, p. 27: «On doit même un peu harpeger les Accords, c'est-à-dire, en toucher les Notes l'une prés l'autre, avec un mouvement égal, en commençant par celle qui est la plus prés de la Basse. Cette façon d'accompagner se pratique dans les Recitatifs, les Airs tendres & gracieux. Lorsque l'on accompagne des morceaux d'un mouvement vif, ou de grandes Symphonies, comme les Concerto; il est mieux de frapper ses Accords tout d'un coup, & même d'en doubler quelques-uns, de la main gauche, autant que l'on le peut faire; l'accompagnement ne pouvant être trop rempli dans ces occasions-là». (One must even arpeggiate the chords a little, that is to say, play the notes one after the other, with an equal movement, beginning with the one closest to the bass. This way of accompanying is practised in recitatives, tender & graceful airs. When accompanying lively pieces, or large symphonies, such as concerto's, it is better to strike the chords all at once, and even to double some of them, with the left hand, as much as one can do: the accompaniment cannot be too full on such occasions).

air, if there are no words. This accompaniment must be equally proportioned to the strength of the voices, or of the instruments, so that they are not covered up by too much noise, or not supported enough by the opposite, being able to double with the left hand the chords that are touched with the right hand, excepting the dissonances from this rule, or being able to remove from the chords the octaves, or even certain dissonances, as appropriate[22].

The recommendation, in a context of long notes in the bass, to restrike the chords on the first beats of the measures or on the strong beats (Rousseau's third observation) is also taken from Rameau[23], as is the distinction between the ways of accompanying from the organ and from the harpsichord (sixth observation):

> Although *accompaniment* by the organ might be the same as that by the harpsichord, the style is different. Since the sounds of the organ are sustained, their progression should be sweeter and less uneven. One must lift the entire hand as little as possible, glide the fingers from one key to another without removing those which, in the place where they are, can be used in the chord into which one is passing. Nothing is so disagreeable as hearing that type of dry and detached *accompaniment* that one is forced to practise on the harpsichord[24].

---

[22]. Rameau 1722, p. 426: «Il faut conformer son accompagnement au caractere des voix, & à celui des Airs; entrant dans l'esprit des Paroles ou de la seule expression de l'Air, s'il n'y a point de paroles: Il faut proportionner également cet accompagnement à la force des Voix, ou des Instruments; de sorte qu'on ne les étouffe point par un trop grand bruit, ou qu'on ne les soûtienne pas assez par le contraire; pouvant doubler de la main gauche les Accords que l'on touche de la main droite, en exceptant les Dissonances de cette regle, ou pouvant retrancher des Accords les Octaves, ou même certaines Dissonances, selon le cas».

[23]. Rousseau 1751, p. 77: «Quand on a à refrapper les mêmes touches dans une note longue ou une tenue, que ce soit plûtôt au commencement de la mesure ou du tems fort, que dans un autre moment: en un mot, il faut ne rebattre qu'en bien marquant la mesure». See Rameau 1722, p. 427: «Quand le Son du Clavecin ou du Theorbe se perd; l'on peut repeter un même Accord, faisant en sorte que ce soit plûtôt sur le premier temps de la Mesure, que sur aucun autre, & avec la derniere syllabe d'un mot; car cette repetition faite au milieu d'un mot, ou même au milieu d'une phrase, pourroit empescher souvent d'en entendre le sens».

[24]. Rousseau 1751, p. 77: «Quoique l'accompagnement de l'orgue soit le même que celui du clavecin, le goût en est différent. Comme les sons y sont soûtenus, leur marche doit être plus douce & moins sautillante. Il faut lever la main entiere le moins qu'on peut, faire glisser les doigts d'une touche à l'autre sans lever ceux qui, dans la place où ils sont, peuvent servir à l'accord où l'on passe; rien n'est si désagréable que d'entendre sur l'orgue cette espece d'accompagnement sec & détaché, qu'on est forcé de pratiquer sur le clavecin». English translation Scott 1998, p. 203. See Rameau 1722, p. 372: «Cette Position de la main, qui regarde principalement le Clavecin, ne souffre d'exception pour l'Orgue, qu'en ce que les Nottes de chaque Accord doivent y être touchées ensemble; qu'il ne faut jamais quitter une Touche, qui après avoir servi à un Accord, peut encore servir à celui qui suit, & que les Sons doivent y être liez, autant que cela se peut».

Marie Demeilliez

Rousseau's Quarrel with Rameau

Rousseau bases his articles on the art of accompaniment on Rameau's *Dissertation*, but he does not hesitate to add to it and above all to underline its fragilities. At the end of 'Accompagnement', he explicitly criticises a characteristic of the system of accompaniment set out in the *Dissertation*: the idea that all the tones of the chords must be played systematically, which is what the application of Rameau's method leads to. Firstly, Rousseau denounces the sound effect produced («unbearable with all this filling out»), and secondly, the non-respect of the compositional rules forbidding parallel fifths and octaves[25]: the fact that the chords played with the right hand do not differ from the root-position to the various inversions induces repetition and parallels usually avoided between the right hand and the bass line. These recommendations regarding realisation (avoid parallel fifths and octaves, do not double the leading note, do not play all the notes of certain dissonant chords) can be found in most 18th-century methods of accompaniment, including the *Principes d'Accompagnement* of Rameau's *Traité de l'harmonie*[26]. In the *Dissertation*, however, Rameau defends a greater tolerance of the rules of composition, considering that the accompanist already has much to do without having to worry about avoiding parallel fifths and octaves, which only an informed listener is able to perceive[27]. This sudden indulgence can be explained by the fact that the method presented by Rameau is a teaching method intended for novices, who should be able to accompany correctly within a few months' learning.

The articles on accompaniment illustrate the ambivalent relationship between Rousseau and Rameau. Rousseau recognised in Rameau's theory an invaluable contribution to the understanding of music and the *Encyclop*édie was an effective vehicle for the dissemination of Ramist theory, especially with regard to composition and accompaniment. However, although Rousseau's musical training owed much to his reading of Rameau's writings, particularly the *Traité de l'Harmonie*, the composer's public disdain for him became an effective spur to his

---

[25]. Rousseau 1751, p. 76: «Quoi que suivant les principes de M. Rameau il faille toucher tous les sons de chaque accord, il ne faut pas toûjours prendre cette regle à la lettre. Il y a des accords qui seroient insupportables avec tout ce remplissage. Dans la plûpart des accords dissonans, surtout dans les accords par supposition, il y a quelque son à retrancher pour en diminuer la dureté; ce son est souvent la septieme, quelquefois la quinte, quelquefois l'une & l'autre. On retranche encore assez souvent la quinte ou l'octave de la basse dans les accords dissonans, pour éviter des octaves ou des quintes de suite, qui font souvent un fort mauvais effet, surtout dans le haut; & par la même raison, quand la note sensible est dans la basse, on ne la met pas dans l'accompagnement; au lieu de cela, on double la tierce ou la sixte de la main droite. En général on doit penser en accompagnant, que quand M. Rameau veut qu'on remplisse tous les accords, il a bien plus d'égard à la facilité du doigter & à son système particulier d'accompagnement, qu'à la pureté de l'harmonie».

[26]. Rameau 1722, p. 410.

[27]. Rameau 1732, pp. 60-61.

willingness to challenge the universal claims of Rameau's theoretical system[28]. Rousseau's criticism of Rameau's method and theory goes hand-in-hand with his conviction of the superiority of Italian music. At the end of the article, Rousseau distinguishes an Italian way of accompanying on harpsichord, simple and beautiful, in contrast to the «noisy» French accompaniments, characterised by full harmony and numerous ornaments.

Rameau's reaction to these few criticisms was strong. The article 'Accompagnement', published in the first volume of the *Encyclopédie*, and one of its most developed musical articles, inaugurated a polemic that would place Rousseau and Rameau in opposition for two decades. In the *Erreurs sur la musique dans l'Encyclopédie* published in 1755, he vigorously and extensively criticised the article 'Accompagnement'[29]. The main elements contested are the deviations and criticisms of his theory, as well as the references to the superiority of the Italians in music. Rousseau responded to Rameau's criticisms in a text entitled *Examen de deux principes avancés par M. Rameau dans sa brochure intitulée: Erreurs sur la musique dans l'Encyclopédie*, unpublished, and then in the republication of the article 'Accompagnement' which he reworked a few years later for his *Dictionnaire de musique*, emphasising his opposition to Rameau[30]. At the same time, the praise of the simplicity of Italian-style accompaniments, as opposed to the rich, overly complex harmonies of French accompaniments, was to become a recurrent theme in Rousseau's discourse. In the *Lettre sur la musique française*, published in 1753 in the context of the *Querelle des Bouffons* (and also criticised in RAMEAU 1755), Rousseau deepens his criticism of French accompaniments, which he considers noisy and inexpressive. He illustrates his point with the description of a very young Italian musician heard at the Opéra (Felice Bambini), who exemplifies the superiority of the Italians in harpsichord accompaniment:

> Do you recall, Sir, having sometimes heard, in the Intermezzi, which have been played for us this year, the son of the Italian Impresario, a young boy at most ten years old, sometimes play the accompaniment at the Opera? We were struck from the first day by the effect produced by the accompaniment of the Harpsichord under his little hands; [...] but what was my surprise, when observing the little gentleman's hands, to see that he almost never filled out the chords, that he omitted many notes and very often employed only two fingers, one of which almost always sounded the octave of the Bass! What! I said to myself, complete harmony produces less of an effect than mutilated harmony, and by fulling out all the chords our

---

[28]. O'DEA 1994.

[29]. RAMEAU 1755, pp. 3-72.

[30]. In this dispute over the article 'Accompagnement', we can also mention D'Alembert's articles 'Accords fondamentaux' and 'Basse fondamentale' (*Encyclopédie*, vol. VII), LE DRAN 1765 («dedicated to the *Encyclopédie*») and the continuations and other editions of the *Encyclopédie* (Lucques, Livourne, Pellet, Yverdon, Lausanne and Berne, the *Supplément*, the *Encyclopédie méthodique*) which publish either the 1751 version of the article, or that of the *Dictionnaire de musique*, sometimes with additional commentary.

Accompanists produce only a confused noise, while this one, with fewer notes, makes its accompaniment more perceptible and more pleasant[31]!

However exaggerated this praise of the accompaniment played by an Italian child with two fingers, whose simplicity is placed above that of the accompanists of the *Académie royale de musique*, it reveals that the question of accompaniment had its place in the quarrel between Italian and French music in the middle of the 18th century[32].

Italian and French Style in Keyboard Accompaniment

In the articles of the *Encyclopédie*, the criticism of Rameau and of French aesthetics bears witness to the existence of another way of accompanying, in an Italian style, in use in France in the middle of the 18th century. The fifth observation at the end of *Accompagnement* contrasts two ways of playing accompaniment, depending on the repertoire:

> One should not accompany Italian music as one does for French music. In the latter, one must sustain the sounds, arpeggiating them gracefully and continually from low to high, stick to filling out the harmony as much as possible, play the bass *proprement*[33] — for French composers today give it all the small ornaments and grace notes of the treble. On the contrary, when accompanying the Italian, one must strike the notes from the bass simply, produce neither trills nor embroidery, reserve for it the grave and steady progression which suits it; the accompaniment should be dry, and without arpeggios. One may suppress notes without scruple, but those notes, which are to be heard, must be well chosen. The Italians attach little importance to noise; a third, a well-adapted sixth, even a simple unison when good taste demands it, is more pleasing to them than all our din of parts and of accompaniment; in a word, they want nothing to be heard in the accompaniment

---

[31].   Rousseau 1753b, pp. 51-53: «Vous ressouvenez-vous, Monsieur, d'avoir entendu quelquefois dans les Intermédes qu'on nous a donnés cette année le fils de l'Entrepreneur Italien, jeune enfant de dix ans au plus, accompagner quelques fois à l'Opéra. Nous fumes frappés dès le premier jour, de l'effet que produisoit sous ses petits doigts, l'accompagnement du Clavecin; [...] quelle fut ma surprise en observant les mains du petit bon homme, de voir qu'il ne remplissoit presque jamais les accords, qu'il supprimoit beaucoup de sons, & n'employoit très-souvent que deux doigts, dont l'un sonnoit presque toujours l'octave de la Basse! Quoi! disois-je en moi-même, l'harmonie complete fait moins d'effet que l'harmonie mutilée, & nos Accompagnateurs en rendant tous les accords pleins, ne font qu'un bruit confus, tandis que celui-ci avec moins de sons fait plus d'harmonie, ou du moins, rend son accompagnement plus sensible & plus agréable!». English translation: Scott 1998, p. 160.

[32].   In addition to Rameau's criticism of these pages (Rameau 1755), we can cite that of Louis Travenol, a violinist at the *Académie royale de musique* (Travenol 1754, pp. 37-42).

[33].   NB: in the 18th century, *jouer proprement* means playing with care and grace.

or in the bass that might distract the ear from the principal subject, and they are of the opinion that attention vanishes for having been divided[34].

Rousseau's description of French accompaniment is consistent with other theoretical sources from the early 18th century onwards: full harmony, arpeggiated chords, ornamentation. Theoretical and musical sources of the 18th century indicate that French musicians clearly expected the continuo player to regularly add ornaments to the realisation and sometimes to the written bass line as well[35]. Thus, the small ornaments and *tours de chant* that the harpsichordist adds to the bass to play it *proprement* were theorised in Saint-Lambert's treatise (1707): «When the Basses are not very full of notes, & when they dawdle too much for the Accompanist's liking, he may add other notes»[36]. The choice and placement of *agréments* in the bass part are still specified in Michel Corrette's *Prototipes* in 1754, a few years after Rousseau had written the article 'Accompagnement': «*Cadences* are very appropriate on the 4th note of the scale when ascending and on the leading tone; [...] with regard to the *pincé*, it may be played on all long notes; however one must avoid it on those, where one plays the diminished 7th and the augmented 2nd [...]»[37]. Rousseau's testimony makes this propensity to ornament the basses a marker of French style. As for arpeggiated chords, the various methods of accompaniment for keyboard players published in France give examples of them since the 17th century[38]. Rousseau prefers the Italian way of accompanying, which he describes as characterised by greater sobriety: a bass line played simply without embellishment, chords played struck, not arpeggiated, and not very full, so as not to cover the soloist. It is interesting to note that the comparison between Italian

---

34. ROUSSEAU 1751, p. 77: «On ne doit pas accompagner la Musique Italienne comme la Françoise. Dans celle-ci il faut soûtenir les sons, les arpéger gracieusement du bas en haut; s'attacher à remplir l'harmonie, à joüer proprement la basse: car les Compositeurs François lui donnent aujourd'hui tous les petits ornemens & les tours de chant des dessus. Au contraire, en accompagnant de l'Italien, il faut frapper simplement les notes de la basse, n'y faire ni cadence, ni broderie, lui conserver la marche grave & posée qui lui convient: l'accompagnement doit être sec & sans arpéger. On y peut retrancher des sons sans scrupule; mais il faut bien choisir ceux qu'on fait entendre. Les Italiens font peu de cas du bruit; une tierce, une sixte bien adaptée, même un simple unisson, quand le bon goût le demande, leur plaisent plus que tout notre fracas de parties & d'accompagnement: en un mot, ils ne veulent pas qu'on entende rien dans l'accompagnement, ni dans la basse, qui puisse distraire l'oreille du sujet principal, & ils sont dans l'opinion que l'attention s'évanoüit en se partageant».

35. ZAPPULLA 2000, pp. 100-118.

36. SAINT-LAMBERT 1707, p. 57: «Quand les Basses sont peu chargées de notes, & qu'elles traînent trop au gré de l'Accompagnateur, il peut y ajoûter d'autres notes pour figurer d'avantage». See also p. 63, about adding ornaments.

37. CORRETTE 1754, p. 11: «Les cadences font fort bien sur la 4me note du ton en montant et sur la note sensible [...] à l'égard du pincé il se peut faire sur toutes les notes longues il faut cependant l'eviter sur celles, ou l'on fait la 7e diminuée et sur la 2d superfluë [...]».

38. ZAPPULLA 2000, pp. 93-100.

and French accompaniment has been reversed since the beginning of the 18th century: in 1715, Bourdelot and Bonnet's *Histoire de la musique* denounced Italian accompanists of their time, who, by ornamenting and doubling the basses, arpeggiating the chords, and emphasising their virtuosity, caused an extraordinary cacophony and drowned out the voices they accompany[39].

However, in 1749, Rousseau's words shed light on the *Avertissement* published by the Italian-trained violinist Louis-Gabriel Guillemain at the beginning of his *Six sonates en quatuors, ou, Conversations galantes et amusantes pour flûte, violon, basse de viole et basse continue* (1743): «if one wishes to play the Harpsichord, one must accompany only on the upper manual and play the chords in the Italian style»[40]. A few years later, François André Danican Philidor gives similar advice in his *cantatille L'Eté* (1755) to be accompanied «with the same delicacy as the Italians accompany their music»: «Airs must be accompanied with great discretion, for one should almost never play more than two notes of accompaniment when a voice is singing in order to avoid confusion»[41]. Philidor then recommends, for the accompaniment of airs, the suppression of a few notes in the realisation of the chords: the fifth in the seventh chord (except on the dominant), the sixth in the *fausse quinte* and *accord de seconde*, the fourth in the *petite sixte* and the second in the *triton*[42]. This idea that it is good not to constantly play all the notes of dissonant chords is defended by Rousseau in 'Accompagnement', in opposition to Rameau's method: «In the majority of dissonant chords, above all in chords by supposition, some notes have to be omitted in order to diminish their harshness. This note is often the seventh, sometimes the fifth, sometimes both. The fifth or the octave of the bass is also fairly often omitted in dissonant chords»[43].

The three-voice texture intended by Philidor (and Rousseau) for the accompaniment is rarely described in early 18th-century French sources, where mainly four or five-part realisations

[39]. Bourdelot – Bonnet 1715, pp. 434-436: «une basse continue toujours doublée, qui souvent est une espece de batterie, d'accords, et un harpegnement, qui jette de la poudre aux yeux [...], ne sont bons qu'à faire briller la vitesse de la main de ceux qui accompagnent. [...] la voix en est étouffée [...] ce qui cause une cacophonie extraordinaire».

[40]. Guillemain 1743: «si l'on veut se servir du Clavecin, il faut n'accompagner que sur le petit Clavier et plaquer les accords à l'Italienne».

[41]. Philidor 1755: «Mr. Philidor desirant que ses Cantatilles soient accompagnées avec la même délicatesse que les Italiens accompagnent leurs Musiques, il prie les amateurs de se conformer aux règles prescrites cy dessous. Les Symphonies et les Recitatifs ne peuvent jamais être trop chargées [*sic*] d'harmonie, mais les Airs doivent être accompagnés avec beaucoup de discretion car il ne faut presque jamais toucher plus de deux nottes d'accompagnement lors qu'une voix chante afin d'eviter la confusion». Present author's translation.

[42]. See example 4 in the chapter by Clotilde Verwaerde in this volume.

[43]. Rousseau 1751, p. 76: «Dans la plûpart des accords dissonans, surtout dans les accords par supposition, il y a quelque son à retrancher pour en diminuer la dureté; ce son est souvent la septieme, quelquefois la quinte, quelquefois l'une & l'autre. On retranche encore assez souvent la quinte ou l'octave de la basse dans les accords dissonans». Present author's translation.

(including the bass) are taught. However, several examples are found in Laporte's treatise[44], and this trio texture, associated with the influence of Italian music, will become more frequent in the accompaniments of the second half of the century[45]. In a paragraph that was to disappear from the *Dictionnaire de musique* (probably so as not to belittle Italian music), Rousseau also mentions an Italian practice of doubling the vocal part with the right hand instead of playing chords: «The Italians sometimes play the whole song instead of the accompaniment, and this is done well enough in their genre of music. But whatever they may say about it, there is often more ignorance than taste in this manner of accompanying»[46]. This practice is rarely mentioned in France in the middle of the 18th century, although it is briefly described by Corrette in his *Prototipes*:

> In Italian ariettes, chords can be arpeggiated on long notes and the right hand may double the vocal part from time to time. This sometimes sounds better than a struck accompaniment which, by its too great conformity, becomes tedious, tasteless, flat, confused and stifles the delicacy of the voice[47].

The 1775 reprint[48] of the *Prototipes* includes a section entitled 'Pour accompagner les voix à la manière italienne' (To accompany the voices in the Italian manner), which describes this usage at greater length with musical examples.

Written a few years after Rousseau's texts, the article 'Harpegement' is also rich in information. It should be noted that neither Rousseau's article 'Arpeggio' (vol. I, 1751) nor the article 'Harpegement' (vol. VIII, 1765) distinguish between the terms *harpègement* (with or without H) and *arpeggio*, which are clearly differentiated in the musical sources of the 18th century. *Harpègement* (or *arpègement*, or *harpégé*) is an ornament widely used in French music since the 17th century, particularly by harpsichordists and lutenists. It can be simple or

---

[44]. LAPORTE 1753, pp. 36, 40-41.

[45]. See the chapter by Clotilde Verwaerde in this volume.

[46]. ROUSSEAU 1751, p. 77: «Les Italiens jouent quelquefois tout le chant au lieu d'accompagnement; & cela fait assez bien dans leur genre de musique. Mais quoi qu'ils en puissent dire, il y a souvent plus d'ignorance que de goût dans cette maniere d'accompagner». English translation: SCOTT 1998, p. 203. In the version of this article in the *Dictionnaire de musique*, Rousseau writes instead: «When one accompanies vocal Music, one should, by means of the Accompaniment, sustain the Voice, guide it, give it the Pitch on all its re-entrances, and put it back onto it when it is off pitch: the Accompanist, always having the Song before his eyes and the Harmony present to his mind, is particularly charged with preventing the Voice from going astray». *Ibidem*, p. 552.

[47]. CORRETTE 1754, p. 16: «Dans les Ariettes Italiennes on peut harpeger les accords sur les notes longues et joüer de tems en tems de la main droite la partie chantante cela fait quelque fois mieux qu'un accompagnement plaqué qui par sa trop grande conformité devient ennuyeux, insipide, plat, confus et étouffe la delicatesse de la voix». C. Verwaerde's translation.

[48]. CORRETTE 1775.

figuré (i.e. in which non-harmonic tones are included). *Arpeggio*, however, is a mode of playing of Italian origin, found in France with increasing frequency in the 18th century, especially in the repertoires of the violin, the cello, or occasionally the harpsichord. Since the 17th century, treatises published in France have considered arpeggiation of chords as an important component of accompaniment, and they sometimes offer beautiful examples to imitate[49]. However, following on from the article 'Accompagnement', the author of 'Harpegement' (probably D'Alembert) recommends avoiding *harpegements* in accompaniments and, more generally, not filling in the chords, at the risk of masking the voice and damaging its expression:

> One almost never arpeggiates in accompaniments: taste and wisdom proscribe anything that might distract from the song and its expression; and the secret of not masking the voice consists not so much in the art of playing softly, as in that of eliminating that note from the chord which, by being heard, would harm the accents and the effect of the song. [...] This wisdom, which forbids the filling of chords in accompaniments, is all the more opposed to *harpegement*[50].

This way of performing accompaniment seems to correspond to what François-André Danican Philidor specified for his *cantatille L'Eté*, as mentioned previously. The rest of the article is interesting because it distinguishes the particular case of recitative. Even in Italian style, the avoidance of arpeggiation does not concern the accompaniment of recitatives, in which the arpeggiated chords structure the piece, while guiding the singer and determining his or her intonation. Philidor gives similar advice:

> A Recitative is begun by striking the chord with a double *Arpegio*. The singer's part then begins, and when it is on the last note of its phrase, the bass note must be struck at the same time with its chord without *arpegio*, and without the slightest interval, the following note must be struck with an *arpegio* to provide the tone to the singer's part. If one encounters a perfect cadences, or other cadences, one must strike the chords without *arpegio*[51].

---

49. Zappulla 2000, pp. 93-100.
50. Anonymus 1765: «On n'*harpege* presque jamais dans les accompagnemens: le goût & la sagesse proscrivent tout ce qui pourroit distraire du chant & de son expression; & le secret de ne point couvrir la voix consiste moins dans l'art de joüer doux, que dans celui de supprimer cette note de l'accord, qui en se faisant entendre, nuiroit aux accens & à l'effet du chant. [...] Cette sagesse qui défend de remplir les accords dans les accompagnemens, s'opppose à plus forte raison à l'*harpegement*».
51. Philidor 1755: «On commence un Récitatif en frappant par un double Arpegio l'accord qui est marqué. La partie chantante pour lors commence et lors qu'elle se trouve sur la derniere notte de sa phrase il faut frapper dans le même tems la notte de la Basse avec son accord sans arpegio et sans le moindre intervalle frapper par Arpegio la notte qui suit pour donner le Ton a la partie chantante. Si l'on rencontre des Cadences parfaites, ou autres, on doit frapper les Accords sans Arpegio».

The article 'Harpegement' does not distinguish between the beginnings and ends of phrases, but it provides valuable additional information on the instrumentation of basso continuo in recitatives. Indeed, it is one of the earliest French testimonies of a long-lasting practice: the realisation of chords by the cello in recitatives:

> To accompany the recitative, the composer writes only the bass note; but the one who accompanies on the harpsichord strikes the chord full and dry as often as this note changes; and the one who accompanies on the cello, plays the same chord by arpeggiation, to help and support the singer in the tone. Then the composer must figure his bass, at least in the difficult places[52].

Harmonic realisation of basso continuo on the cello seems to have been customary in the Italian sonata repertoire since the 17th century[53]. This practice developed in the 18th century for the accompaniment of recitatives, both in Italy and in France. Several cello methods published in French towards the end of the century evince this practice, devoting several pages to the recitative, which cellists learn to accompany with chords[54]. The article 'Harpegement' in the *Encyclopédie* reveals that in 1765, this practice was already in use in France. Moreover, although the cello sometimes provides the harmonic accompaniment to a recitative (this was to be frequent in the 19th century), the division of roles described here, with chords struck on the harpsichord and arpeggiated on the cello, is interesting because it is quite unique in the sources of this period.

***

The small treatise constituted by the articles in the *Encyclopédie* devoted to accompaniment is therefore a precious source for anyone interested in a historically informed performance of basso continuo. It testifies to Rousseau's role in the dissemination of Rameau's theories, despite the quarrels that opposed them for several decades. Rousseau's predilection for Italian music also reveals that the aesthetic opposition between French and Italian music also affected accompaniment: the *Encyclopédie* can therefore be considered a rich source of information on how to accompany Italian or Italian-inspired repertoire performed in France in the mid-18th century.

---

52. ANONYMUS 1765: «Pour accompagner le récitatif, le compositeur n'écrit que la note de la basse; mais celui qui accompagne du clavecin frappe l'accord en plein & à sec aussi souvent que cette note change; & celui qui accompagne du violoncelle, donne le même accord par *harpegement*, pour aider & soûtenir le chanteur dans le ton. Alors le compositeur doit chiffrer sa basse, du-moins dans les endroits difficiles».
53. WATKIN 1996, WHITTAKER 2012.
54. BAUMGÄRTNER 1774, pp. 18-25; RAOUL 1797, pp. 41-42; BAILLOT *ET AL.* 1804, pp. 137-139.

Bibliography

Anonymus 1765
Anonymus [d'Alembert?]. 'Harpegement (*Musique*)', in: *Encyclopédie ou Dictionnaire raisonné des sciences, des arts et des métiers. 8*, edited by Denis Diderot and Jean Le Rond d'Alembert, Neuchâtel, Samuel Faulche et compagnie, 1765, p. 58.

Baillot *et Al.* 1804
Baillot, Pierre – Baudiot, Charles-Nicolas – Catel, Charles-Simon – Levasseur, Jean-Henri. *Méthode de Violoncelle et de Basse d'accompagnement [...] Adoptée par le Conservatoire impérial de musique pour servir à l'étude dans cet établissement*, Paris, Imprimerie du conservatoire, 1804.

Baumgärtner 1774
Baumgärtner, Johann B. *Instructions de musique, théorique et pratique, à l'usage du violoncello [...]*, Den Haag, Daniel Monnier, [1774].

Bourdelot – Bonnet 1715
Bourdelot, Pierre-Michon – Bonnet-Bourdelot, Pierre – Bonnet, Jacques. *Histoire de la musique, et de ses effets, depuis son origine, jusqu'à present*, Paris, Jean Cochart, Étienne Ganeau, Jacques Quillau, 1715.

Cernuschi 2000
Cernuschi, Alain. *Penser la musique dans l'«Encyclopédie». Etude sur les enjeux de la musicographie des Lumières et sur ses liens avec l'encyclopédisme*, Paris, Champion, 2000.

Christensen 1993
Christensen, Thomas. *Rameau and Musical Thought in the Enlightenment*, Cambridge, Cambridge University Press, 1993.

Corrette 1754
Corrette, Michel. *Prototipes contenant des leçons d'Accompagnemt par demandes et par reponses; Pour Servir d'Addition au Livre intitulé le Maitre de Clavecin pour l'Accompagnement. Avec des Sonates pour le Violon, la Flûte, le Pardessus de Viole, où les accords sont notés sur la Basse pour guider les Commençans; ce qui dévoile les prétenduës difficultées de l'Accompagnement en moins de six mois*, Paris, l'Auteur et aux adresses ordinaires, 1754.

Corrette 1775
Id. *Prototype Pour servir d'addition au Maître de Clavecin. Méthode pour l'Accompagnement [...] Nouvelle Edition augmentée d'Ariettes Italiennes, et la maniere de les accompagner*, Paris-Lyon-Rouen-Dunkerque, Adresses ordinaires, [1775].

Demeilliez 2020-2022
Demeilliez, Marie. 'Critical edition of *Accompagnateur, en Musique* (*Encyclopédie*, t. i, pp. 74b-75a), *Accompagnement* (t. i, pp. 75a-77b), *Arpeggio, Arpège ou Arpégement, en Musique* (t. i, pp. 701b-702a), *Chiffrer, en Musique*, (t. iii, pp. 334b-337b), *Doigter, en Musique* (t. v, pp. 16b-17b), *Face, en Musique* (t. vi, p. 357b),

Harpegement (t. VIII, p. 58a-b), *Règle de l'octave, en Musique* (t. XIV, p. 22b), *Renversement, en Musique* (t. XIV, pp. 122b-123a)', in: *Édition numérique collaborative et critique de l'«Encyclopédie» (1751-1772)*, 2020-2022, <http://enccre.academie-sciences.fr/encyclopedie/>, accessed October 2023.

DIDEROT 1769
Recueil de planches, sur les sciences, les arts libéraux et les arts méchaniques, avec leurs explications. 7, edited by Denis Diderot, Paris, Briasson and Le Breton, 1769.

GERVAIS 1733
GERVAIS, Laurent. *Méthode pour l'Accompagnement du clavecin*, Paris, veuve Boivin, 1733.

GUILLEMAIN 1743
GUILLEMAIN, Louis-Gabriel. *Six sonates en quatuors, ou, Conversations galantes et amusantes pour flûte, violon, basse de viole et basse continue*, Paris, Boivin-Le Clerc, 1743.

HAYES 1974
HAYES, Deborah. 'Rameau's *Nouvelle Méthode*', in: *Journal of the American Musicological Society*, XXVII/1 (1974), pp. 61-74.

LAPORTE 1753
LAPORTE, Claude de. *Traité théorique et pratique de l'accompagnement du clavecin*, Paris, l'Auteur-Boivin-Le Clerc, 1753.

LE DRAN 1765
LE DRAN, Nicolas-Louis. *Sur les signes, Do, Di, Ca, pour l'indication des accords en musique. Dédié à l'Encyclopédie*, Paris, Le Prieur, 1765.

MARTIN 2012
MARTIN, Nathan John. 'Rameau's Changing Views on Supposition and Suspension', in: *Journal of Music Theory*, LVI/2 (2012), pp. 121-167.

O'DEA 1994
O'DEA, Michael. 'Rousseau contre Rameau: musique et nature dans les articles pour l'*Encyclopédie* et au-delà', in: *Recherches sur Diderot et sur l'Encyclopédie*, XVII/1 (1994), pp. 133-148.

O'DEA 2003
ID. 'Consonances et dissonances: Rousseau et D'Alembert face à l'œuvre théorique de Jean-Philippe Rameau', in: *Recherches sur Diderot et sur l'Encyclopédie*, XXXV (2003), pp. 105-130.

PHILIDOR 1755
PHILIDOR, François André Danican. *L'Eté Cantatille a Voix Seule avec Simphonie deux Violons un Alto et Basse*, Paris, L'Auteur-Le Clerc-Bayard-Castagneri, 1755.

Rameau 1722
Rameau, Jean-Philippe. *Traité de l'harmonie réduite à ses principes naturels* [...], Paris, Jean-Baptiste-Christophe Ballard, 1722.

Rameau 1732
Id. *Dissertation sur les différentes métodes d'accompagnement pour le clavecin, ou pour l'orgue, avec le plan d'une nouvelle métode, établie sur une méchanique des doigts, que fournit la succession fondamentale de l'harmonie: et à l'aide de laquelle on peut devenir sçavant compositeur, & habile accompagnateur, même sans sçavoir lire la musique*, Paris, Boivin-Le Clair, 1732.

Rameau 1755
Id. *Erreurs sur la musique dans l'Encyclopédie*, Paris, Sebastien Jorry, 1755.

Rameau 1760
Id. *Code de musique pratique, ou méthode pour apprendre la musique, même à des aveugles, pour former la voix & l'oreille, pour la position de la main avec une méchanique des doigts sur le clavecin & l'orgue, pour l'accompagnement sur tous les instruments qui en sont susceptibles, & pour le prélude: avec de nouvelles réflexions sur le principe sonore*, Paris, Imprimerie royale, 1760.

Raoul 1797
Raoul, Jean-Marie. *Méthode de violoncelle. Contenant une nouvelle exposition des principes de cet instrument* [...], Paris, Pleyel, c.1797.

Rousseau 1743
Rousseau, Jean-Jacques. *Dissertation sur la musique moderne*, Paris, G. F. Quillau, 1743.

Rousseau 1751
Id. 'Accompagnateur' and 'Accompagnement', in: *Encyclopédie ou Dictionnaire raisonné des sciences, des arts et des métiers. 1*, edited by Denis Diderot and Jean Le Rond d'Alembert, Paris, Briasson-David l'aîné-Le Breton-Durand, 1751, pp. 74-77.

Rousseau 1753a
Id. 'Chiffrer, en Musique', in: *Encyclopédie ou Dictionnaire raisonné des sciences, des arts et des métiers. 3*, edited by Denis Diderot and Jean Le Rond d'Alembert, Paris-Briasson-David l'aîné-Le Breton-Durand, 1753, pp. 334-337.

Rousseau 1753b
Id. *Lettre sur la musique française*, Paris, s.n., 1753.

Rousseau 1765
Id. 'Regle de l'octave, en Musique', in: *Encyclopédie ou Dictionnaire raisonné des sciences, des arts et des métiers. 14*, edited by Denis Diderot and Jean Le Rond d'Alembert, Neuchâtel, Samuel Faulche et compagnie, 1765, p. 22.

SAINT-LAMBERT 1707
SAINT-LAMBERT, M. de. *Nouveau traité de l'accompagnement du clavecin, de l'orgue, et des autres instruments*, Paris, Christophe Ballard, 1707.

SCOTT 1998
ROUSSEAU, Jean-Jacques. *Essay on the Origin of Languages and Writings Related to Music*, edited and translated by John T. Scott, Hanover (NH), University Press of New England, 1998.

TRAVENOL 1754
TRAVENOL, Louis. *La Galerie de l'Académie Royale de Musique contenant les Portraits, en Vers, des principaux sujets, qui la composent en la présente année 1754. Dédiée à Jean Jacques Rousseau [...] par un zélé partisan de son système sur la Musique Françoise*, Paris, s.n., 1754.

VERNET 2016
VERNET, Thomas. 'Nicolas-Louis Le Dran (1687-1774), «amateur de l'harmonie» et lecteur de Rameau', in: *Rameau, entre art et science*, edited by Sylvie Bouissou, Graham Sadler and Solveig Serre, Paris, École des Chartes, 2016, pp. 143-153.

VERWAERDE 2015
VERWAERDE, Clotilde. *La pratique de l'accompagnement en France (1750-1800): de la basse continue improvisée à l'écriture pour clavier dans la sonate avec violon*, Ph.D. Diss., Paris, Paris-Sorbonne, 2015, <https://theses.hal.science/tel-04267902>, accessed December 2023.

WATKIN 1996
WATKIN, David. 'Corelli's Op. 5 Sonatas: «Violino e violone o cimbalo»?', in: *Early Music*, XXIV/4 (1996), pp. 645-664.

WHITTAKER 2012
WHITTAKER, Nathan H. *Chordal Cello Accompaniment: The Proof and Practice of Figured Bass Realization on the Violoncello from 1660-1850*, DMA Diss., Seattle (WA), University of Washington, 2012.

ZAPPULLA 2000
ZAPPULLA, Robert. *Figured Bass Accompaniment in France*, Turnhout, Brepols, 2000 (Speculum Musicae, 6).

«Acompañamientos con las llamadas del Baxo y lo que se puede tocar sobre cada uno de ellos»: Partimenti Diminuiti in Manuscript M/1188 of the Biblioteca Nacional de España (Madrid)

Isaac Alonso de Molina
(Royal Conservatoire of The Hague)

Introduction: Partimento, Thorough Bass, Counterpoint

The relatively recent rediscovery of partimento has been nothing short of a revolution. From the seminal studies in the 1990s to the proliferation, approximately in the last two decades, of dozens of scholarly articles, monographs, practical manuals, etc., partimento has quickly become an extremely influential topic, reshaping the dominant views on 18th-century music history while also having a tremendous impact in the fields of music theory, analysis, and pedagogy[1]. With regard to the latter, it is without doubt a most welcome revolution, especially to the extent that it has contributed to a fuller understanding of the significance of thorough bass in its widest sense, that is, encompassing all of its many functions: as shorthand notation for accompaniment, as the lowest-sounding part extracted from a polyphonic texture, and as the basis for teaching counterpoint, harmony, improvisation, and composition[2]. Modern practical usage tends to differentiate these functions, applying historical terms to them as if they were unambiguous (basso continuo, basso seguente, partimento), although actual use of these terms in sources is rarely so straightforward.

---

[1]. To avoid an unreasonably long list of relevant works, I will limit myself to citing Cafiero 2020. In particular, the introduction (pp. vii-xii) provides a brief and fairly recent overview of the *status quaestionis*, with exhaustive bibliographical references.

[2]. Felix Diergarten has already pointed to this wider sense of the idea of thorough bass: see Diergarten 2017, especially its second section (pp. 6-9).

Partimento, because of its close relationship to counterpoint, has greatly enriched our understanding of thorough bass beyond its harmonic implications. This does not amount to a rejection of those implications: harmony, as a specific musical discipline in its own right, is built on the former existence of thorough bass structures, but the key for its inception is a process of systematic analysis applied to those structures[3]. In this process, dozens of vertical intervallic combinations and their horizontal connections are abstracted into a handful of possible chords (built by superimposing thirds), practicable variants (root positions and inversions), and standard progressions (identified by degrees or by functions). However, the advent of thorough bass itself around 1600 (let the symbolic date suffice for our purposes here, even if it is an oversimplification) did not go quite so far: it was, primarily, a reorganisation of long-standing contrapuntal techniques. Its main technical advantage lay in the simplification of polyphonic processes, whether these were written or improvised, by consistently taking the lowest voice as the reference point for the whole texture (as opposed to the tenor, for example). The complexity of the multidimensional tables traditionally needed to teach counterpoint in many parts could thus be avoided[4].

The relevance of such a shift cannot be overstated: the expression *sonare sopra il basso*[5] is perhaps best understood when compared to *sopra il canto fermo*. However, these are not mutually exclusive, given that it is perfectly possible to put the plainchant in the lowest voice; such is the case of the famous six recercadas by Diego Ortiz on the plainchant known as La Spagna, «el qual se ha de poner en el Cymbalo por donde esta apuntado por contrabaxo, acompañandole con consonancias y algun contrapunto»[6]. This is as precise a description of accompaniment from a basso continuo part as it gets: the continuities between both practices might thus have outweighed the differences[7]. Amongst such continuities, the furthest-reaching one might be that of contrapuntal collocation[8]: in my opinion, the obvious similarity between the clauses *si cantus ascendit duas voces* found in organum/discantus treatises[9] and *quando il basso sale di grado* found in partimento sources is not a superficial issue, which is to say that the *Klangschritt*

---

[3]. For a detailed comparison of both paradigms, see HOLTMEIER 2007.

[4]. Such tables (presented sometimes with examples, sometimes as actual tables, and sometimes as lengthy textual descriptions) can be found in printed *musica practica* treatises such as ARON 1516 (chapter XVII, f. 43r), ORNITHOPARCUS 1517 (book four, chapter VI), VANNEO 1533 (book three, chapters XIII-XXIX), DENTICE 1533 (second dialogue, p. 7), ARON 1539 (chapter XXI), or BERMUDO 1555 (book five, chapter XXVIII). For a slightly earlier example by Juan de Urrede, surviving in a manuscript leaf, see KNIGHTON 2011.

[5]. As found, for example, in the titles of AGAZZARI 1607 or BIANCIARDI 1607.

[6]. ORTIZ 1553, p. 30.

[7]. For more on these continuities, especially on placing the cantus firmus in the bass for extemporisation of several parts of counterpoint, see MAZZETTI – TICLI 2017.

[8]. See GJERDINGEN 2020, chapter 10.

[9]. On this specific phase of organum (starting ca. 1100), see EGGEBRECHT – ZAMINER 1970, SACHS 1971, FULLER 1981 (especially sections 2-4), SWEENEY 1989, and FULLER 2011 (pp. 53 and following).

doctrine of ca. 1100 already contains, *in nuce*, the fundamental element of collocation, still standing in partimento.

A sizeable part of the scholarly reasearch regarding partimento has been dedicated to its dissemination and reception out of Naples[10], but also to the identification of comparable or parallel traditions, with a variable degree of connection to or independence from the Neapolitan model[11]. It is almost as if partimento-like traditions are surfacing everywhere, now that partimento has been rediscovered and understood[12]. This article belongs to such a strand of research: its focus is the presence of partimento in 18th-century Spain, as an 'imported' pedagogical tool of Neapolitan origin in the wider context of the influence of Italian music.

CONTEXT: THE ITALIAN CONNECTION

The strong political ties existing between Spain and Italy during the whole Early Modern Period date back to the medieval campaigns of Mediterranean expansion of the kings of Aragon, culminating in the conquest of Naples in 1442, preceded by Sicily in 1282 and Sardinia in 1325. The Italian Wars of the Renaissance (1494-1559), with the reincorporation of the Kingdom of Naples into the senior Aragonese branch (1504), plus the annexation of the Duchy of Milan (1559), now under the Habsburg monarch of a unified Spain, brought Italian politics to a *status quo* that remained fairly stable until 1700. In November of that year, the death of a childless Charles II of Spain marked the end of the Habsburg dynasty and its replacement by the Bourbons, and the War of Succession that ensued (1701-1715) reshaped the balance of power in all of Europe, diminishing the Spanish influence in Italy in favour of Austria. Nevertheless,

---

[10]. The case of the Conservatoire of Paris is, perhaps, the most relevant one. Neapolitan methodologies played a central role in curriculum design at the Parisian institution, and the particular transformation of these methodologies during the 19th century had a tremendous influence across all of Europe, due to the role model that Paris represented, in turn, for the subsequent generation of conservatoires founded elsewhere. See CAFIERO 2007, GJERDINGEN 2020.

[11]. Here the cases of Rome and Bologna are amongst the most representative; see SANGUINETTI 2012 (especially chapter 3), MARTINI 2020, MATTEI 2021. Of historical significance is the seminal reference to Banchieri in TAGLIAVINI 1978.

[12]. These 'other partimenti' were not called 'partimenti'. Furthermore, the relevant terms — such as *basso per accompagnamento*, *bassetto*, *partitura*, *Generalbass*, *Bassetgen*, *acompañamiento*, etc. — overlap to various extents with the several meanings of thorough bass mentioned above. Terminological subtleties such as these might have been much less relevant then, as the earliest mention of partimento shows: TRABACI 1605, cited by BORGIR 1987 (p. 12) and SANGUINETTI 2012 (p. 12), is a collection of masses and motets «cum partimento pro organista». The specific organ part has not survived but it was very probably a thorough bass for accompaniment of the *basso seguente* type, as confirmed by the extant part from the second edition of 1616. For more examples of the term 'partimento' used in this sense, see VAN TOUR 2015, p. 214.

part of that influence was regained by the second third of the century: the political ties between Spain and Italy were to be effectively cut only in the 19th century, with the Napoleonic wars and the process of unification and national construction of Italy.

The 18th century has been traditionally identified as a phase of 'italianisation' of Spanish music, starting with the first Bourbon king, Philip V (1683-1746)[13]. The briefly summarised historical overview above suggests, nonetheless, plenty of opportunity for artistic and cultural exchange through the late Middle Ages, the Renaissance, and the 17th century. A detailed analysis of such exchanges is obviously out of the scope of this article, but a quick glance at recent scholarly works documenting the presence of Neapolitan music and musicians in the court of Charles II[14] suffices to suggest that Habsburg Spain was by no means alien to Italian music, and that the role played by the figures that represented the aforementioned political ties, like the viceroy of Naples, was fundamental for such musical exchanges.

At any rate, it is true that during the 18th century the presence of Italian musicians at the Spanish court grew both in size and in its relative importance in institutional terms. In that sense, two specific actions of Philip's musical patronage can be highlighted: the first one is the establishment of an intermittent, secondary royal chapel in the 1720s, intended to serve during his periods of retirement at La Granja de San Ildefonso (the 'little Spanish Versailles'), in which a group of Italians coming from Rome and possibly selected by Francesco Gasparini made up for half the roster[15]; the second one is the appointment of an Italian, Francesco Corselli (1705-1778), to the highest musical position, that of *maestro de capilla*, in 1738. The influence of Philip's second wife, Elisabetta Farnese, or Isabel de Farnesio, is clearly visible in this appointment, as in many other matters[16]: Corselli was the son of the French dancing master Charles Courcelle, who served a young Isabel in Parma and Piacenza, before her wedding to the Spanish king.

The increased presence of Italian musicians in the Royal Chapel, as opposed to being recruited as chamber musicians, is highly significant, due to its public dimension and

---

[13]. For the evolution of this historiographic trend in the last four decades, see MARTÍN MORENO 1985, BOYD – CARRERAS 2006, LEZA 2014.

[14]. See FRUTOS 2009, DOMÍNGUEZ 2009, GONZÁLEZ LUDEÑA 2020. The Neapolitan castrato Matteo Sassano ('Mateucho'), in particular, seems to have made quite a career in the twilight of the Habsburg court, to the point of becoming personal confidant of the queen: a clear precedent to the similar role that Carlo Broschi 'Farinelli' would play some decades later for the Bourbons.

[15]. MORALES 2007, pp. 95-101.

[16]. Isabel never limited herself to the secondary role of queen consort, becoming instead a very active political figure after her marriage to Philip in 1714 till her death in 1766. She greatly contributed to the shift of Spanish politics towards Italy (and away from France, at least in as much as that was possible with a Bourbon on the throne) with her own inheritance: she was heiress apparent to the Duke of Parma and Piacenza (her grandfather) and she had a claim to the Grand Duchy of Tuscany.

institutional implications, and has a deeper and longer-lasting effect in the musical landscape of the court, especially in the aspect that interests us here: Corselli, in his role of chapel master, was also in charge of the Real Colegio de Niños Cantores. Founded in 1590 by Philip II, the Royal College functioned as a boarding school for (on average) ten boys, who were trained as musicians with the goal of staffing the Royal Chapel. The College had several teachers in their staff, to provide for the education of the choirboys in grammar, Christian doctrine, and of course, music. Upon Corselli's appointment as chapel master in 1738, the traditional position of music teacher was split into two: a «maestro de rudimentos» and a «maestro de estilo italiano o moderno», a structure that would survive into the 19th century. The task of the first one was considered complete when a student was able to sing all kinds of solfeggi «con perfección», and «medianamente bien» with a text, at which point the student was accepted into the second, more advanced class, where he was taught the skill of singing «con buen gusto» while also learning accompaniment at the keyboard[17].

The first «maestro de estilo» was the Italian Antonio Corvi Moroti (1709-1771). We have little information about him, and only a handful of surviving pieces: five substitution arias for José de Nebra's zarzuela *Viento es la dicha de Amor*[18], a Salve Regina, and references to two oratorios dedicated to the patron saint of the Royal College, Saint Barbara[19], whose feast on 4th December was elaborately celebrated every year by the school. The fact that Corvi Moroti was a native from Piacenza[20] and that he was entrusted with an important teaching position newly created at the College by Corselli suggests that they were already colleagues back in Italy. At the very least, he followed the same career path: from the Italian dominions of the Farnese to the Spanish court.

Corselli's appointment as chapel master and his reform of the Royal College attest to the full incorporation of the galant style — the pan-European, but Italianate, musical style that was predominant during most of the 18th century[21] — into the Spanish institutions. In particular, the characteristics of the new position of «maestro de estilo» and the inventories of music books of the Royal College, where solfeggi, canons, arias, and duos by Leonardo Leo, Domenico

---

[17]. Although not in the official curriculum, some of the boys also learned organ (probably to be understood as soloistic keyboard playing, especially improvisation for liturgical contexts), other instruments (with external teachers) and, if they were advanced enough, composition. For more information on the Royal College, see Morales 2005.

[18]. See Leza 1997. The substitution arias are edited in Nebra 2009.

[19]. Composed in 1744 and 1750 respectively. Only the libretti are extant, they can be consulted at <http://bdh.bne.es/bnesearch/detalle/bdh0000142715> and <http://bdh.bne.es/bnesearch/detalle/bdh0000142594>, accessed October 2023.

[20]. Birth and death certificates for Antonio Corvi Moroti are cited in Morales 2007, p. 44.

[21]. As initially defined in Ratner 1980 and further developed in Heartz 2003 and Gjerdingen 2007.

Scarlatti or Francesco Durante coexist with choir books and part books of polyphony in the older style[22], point to the expansion of the traditional model of musical instruction at the College, very close to the choir schools of Spanish cathedrals, with the imported *conservatorio* methodology. Furthermore, a manuscript that can be linked to the Royal Chapel attests to the presence of partimento in 18th-century Spain.

THE SOURCE

The manuscript M/1188 of the Spanish National Library in Madrid[23] (hereafter, Madrid 1188) is an oblong volume measuring 22x31 cm and consisting of 73 folios, systematically ruled with 10 staves per page. It is a fair copy, made by two professional scribes (the first one copied ff. 1-21, 37-73, the second one wrote ff. 22r-36v) who must have collaborated, as there is no discontinuity in contents between the parts copied by each of them. Once owned by the composer and musicologist Francisco Asenjo Barbieri (1823-1894), whose collection passed in successive phases to the National Library, the source has been tentatively dated ca. 1790[24], and it incorporates, into a single volume, diverse materials configuring a complete manual for instruction in thorough bass (see TABLE 1).

TABLE 1: CONTENTS OF MANUSCRIPT MADRID 1188

SECTION	FOLIATION	HEADING
1	1r-17r	*Reglas Generales o Escuela de Acompañar [...] De Dⁿ Felix Maximo Lopez [...]*
2	17v-22r	*Sigue la Colección de Baxos por todos Tonos [...]*
3	22v-36r	*Sigue una Coleccion de Bajetes de Dⁿ Josef Lidon, los quales llevan encima la Glosa que les corresponde [...]*
4	36r-44r	*Siguen veinte y quatro Bajetes por los 24 terminos [...] del mismo Autor*
5	44r-61r	*Acompañamientos, con las Llamadas del Baxo, y lo q̃ se puede tocar sobre cada uno de ellos*
6	61v-73r	*Varios Acompañamᵗᵒˢ de Cantadas, de diferentes Autores Ytalianos [...]*

The first section, 'Reglas de acompañar', is a thorough bass treatise by Félix Máximo López (1742-1821), organist of the Royal Chapel. It contains the usual catalogue of rules

---

[22]. For a transcription of the inventories, see MORALES 2005, p. 158.

[23]. Catalogue record and digital reproduction can be found at <http://bdh.bne.es/bnesearch/detalle/bdh0000111600>, accessed October 2023.

[24]. As per the catalogue record. In any case, the first section is ascribed to Félix Máximo López, described as «organista de la Real Capilla», a position that he held since 1775 and until his death in 1821.

for accompaniment (intervals, chords, cadences, rule of the octave, prepared dissonances, bass motions, etc.) found in similar sources elsewhere, roughly corresponding to the classes defined by Sanguinetti[25]. It is followed by a series of 23 figured bass lines, to be realised «according to the preceding rules». No author is expressly mentioned for this second section, but it might also be the work of López. Sections 3-4, due to their ascription to José Lidón (1748-1827), have already received some specific attention[26]. They are two series of partimenti: those of section 3 are presented on two staves, the lower staff containing a reduction («fundamental») of the upper («glosa»)[27], while those in section 4 cover all 24 tonalities. Section 5 is the series of partimenti diminuiti that will be discussed in more detail in the last part of the present article.

Section 6 deserves some special attention. It is an interesting collection of bass lines extracted from cantatas, «de diferentes Autores Ytalianos»: only the bass lines are provided, without the solo part, and with no hint of which cantatas they are extracted from. Of the 17 bass lines that constitute the last section of the manuscript, I have been able to identify 14 as works of Nicola Porpora, as can be seen in TABLE 2. Porpora was undoubtedly one of the most influential Neapolitan musicians of his generation (roughly contemporary with Francesco Durante and Leonardo Leo). Dozens of copies of his set of 12 cantatas published in London in 1735 are scattered all over Europe[28]. The original collection consists of 6 cantatas for soprano and 6 for alto. In Madrid 1188, those bass lines that have been extracted from alto cantatas (nos. 1-8) appear systematically transposed a fourth higher: these could have been transposed as part of the process of extraction, but it seems much more likely that the transposed bass lines were extracted from a specific copy of the collection in which all 12 cantatas were arranged for soprano. It is not far-fetched to suggest that such an arrangement would be especially suitable for an institution, like the Royal College, dedicated to the instruction of choirboys.

---

[25]. SANGUINETTI 2012, chapter 9: 'The Rules'.

[26]. LÓPEZ RUIZ 2017, especially chapter 5. The career of José Lidón is intimately connected to the royal institutions: he was educated as a choirboy in the Royal College (1758-1768); as such, he received specific training in the Italian style by Antonio Corvi Moroti. He entered the Royal Chapel shortly thereafter (eventually becoming chapel master in 1805) and succeeded Corvi Moroti as «maestro de estilo» in 1771.

[27]. This partimento typology has a Neapolitan precedent: the partimenti by Rocco Greco contained in the first 10 folios of I-Nc 32-2-3. For a brief description, see SANGUINETTI 2012, p. 63.

[28]. PORPORA 1735. RISM lists 37 extant copies, under codes P 5116 and PP 5116 of series A/I. See <https://opac.rism.info/search?id=990052520>, accessed October 2023. As for Spain, besides the extracted basses in Madrid 1188, they also found their way into the *Libro de Música de D. Geronimo de Ribas* (E-Bbc M 1321), which is a manuscript compilation of 26 Italian and Spanish cantatas, together with a few canons by Antonio Caldara.

TABLE 2: ARIAS IN SECTION 6 OF MANUSCRIPT MADRID 1188

ARIA	FOLIO	KEY	TEMPO AND TIME SIGNATURE	COMPOSER	CANTATA	SECTION
1	61v	B-flat Major	Adagio, ¢	Porpora	VII. Veggo la selva e il monte	2. Le direi mormorando tra sassi
2	62r	C minor	Lento, 6/8	Porpora	VIII. Or che una nube ingrata	2. Senza il misero piacer
3	62v	G Major	Allegro, 3/8	Porpora	IX. Destatevi o pastori	4. Silvio amante disperato
4	63v	C Major	Afectuoso, 3/4	Porpora	X. O se fosse il mio core in libertà	2. Se lusinga il labro e 'l ciglio
5	64r	G minor	Lento, 6/8	Porpora	XI. O Dio che non è vero	2. Quella ferita ch'io porto in seno
6	64v	C Major	Allegro, 3/8	Porpora	XI. O Dio che non è vero	4. Se mi prestasse i vanni
7	65r	C minor	Andante moderato, 3/8	Porpora	XII. Dal povero mio cor	2. Mesogniera dici spera
8	65v	B-flat Major	Allegro, 3/8	Porpora	XII. Dal povero mio cor	4. A' scogli e rie procelle
9	66v	E Major	Spiritoso, ¢		?	
10	67v	E Major	Spiritoso, ¢		?	
11	68v	A Major	Allegro ma non presto, 3/8		?	
12	70r	A Major	Andante, 3/8	Porpora	II. Nel mio sonno almen talora	3. Parti con l'ombra è ver
13	70v	A minor	Afectuoso, ¢	Porpora	III. Tirsi chiamare a nome	2. Se in amor che sia vicino
14	71r	G Major	Allegro, ¢	Porpora	III. Tirsi chiamare a nome	4. So ben che la speranza
15	71v	G minor	Allegro, 3/8	Porpora	V. Scrivo in te l'amato nome	3. Per te d'amico Aprile
16	72v	A Major	Adagio, ¢	Porpora	VI. Già la notte s'avvicina	1. Già la notte s'avvicina
17	72v	A Major	Allegretto, 3/8	Porpora	VI. Già la notte s'avvicina	3. Non più fra' sassi algosi

When extracted from their original context, the continuo parts of these arias become partimenti, not by their inception as such, but by the way they are used, thus blurring the distinction between thorough bass as a shorthand notation for accompaniment or for self-standing improvisation in a pedagogical context, as was suggested in the introduction. The reason for this case of repurposing pre-existing music as partimenti might simply have been necessity: maybe there were not enough partimento collections available at the time in Spain, or at least not of the musical substance required to serve as the final stage for this particular compilation. There are other cases of connections between pre-existing repertory and partimento pedagogy, featuring specific teaching strategies, such as the references to Corelli sonatas in Padre Martini's *Libro per Accompagnare*[29], or the partimento-fugues of Leonardo

---

29.   This aspect is discussed in Peter van Tour's preface to MARTINI 2020.

Leo and Nicola Sala that correspond to fugal sections from liturgical compositions, recast into partimento notation[30] and representing a link between the basso seguente tradition and partimento proper.

The diverse materials compiled into Madrid 1188 seem to respond in practice to a quite comprehensive and well-organised syllabus for instruction in thorough bass, starting from the most basic rules and proceeding through different series of partimenti, each more challenging than the previous, up to and including bass parts extracted from 'real' compositions. The term *zibaldone*, used also by Sanguinetti for a certain typology of manuscript compilation featuring partimenti and related materials[31], has been applied to this source[32]. However, there is a certain abuse of the term here: if applied indistinctly to all such compilations, the implications suggested by *zibaldone*[33] (mixture of heterogeneous elements, lack of unity or coherence, haphazard process of compilation, etc.) are lost, especially when referring to sources like Madrid 1188 (carefully selected and organised material in a clean, professional copy), or else the specific source is misrepresented.

Partimenti diminuiti in Madrid 1188

As can be seen in Table 3, section 5 of the manuscript contains 37 *acompañamientos*. These are unevenly figured bass lines supplemented with hints for realisation in an idiomatic keyboard texture («lo que se puede tocar sobre cada uno de ellos», i.e. what can be played on each of those), responding to the typology of partimenti diminuiti[34].

Table 3: Acompañamientos in Section 5 of Manuscript Madrid 1188

No.	Folio	Key	Time signature	Reference value	Maniere
Semitono ascendente, in ogni valore					
1	44r	G minor	¢	Minim	9
2	44v	C Major	¢	Crotchet	10
3	45v	E minor	¢	Quaver	6
4	45v	G minor	¢	Minim (alla breve)	5
5	46v	G Major	3/8	Dotted crotchet	14
6	47v	B minor	3/8	Crotchet (off-beat)	4
7	48r	E major	3/8	Quaver	5

---

[30]. On this topic, see Van Tour 2017, chapter 7.

[31]. Sanguinetti 2012, p. 54.

[32]. López Ruiz 2017, p. 244.

[33]. For a definition, see <https://www.treccani.it/vocabolario/zibaldone/>, accessed October 2023.

[34]. The specific typology is briefly described in Sanguinetti 2012, p. 70.

Moto ascendente per grado					
8	48v	C Major	¢	Minim	10
9	49r	D Major	¢	Crotchet	8
10	49v	F Major	¢	Quaver	3
11	50r	E-flat Major	¢	Semibreve (alla breve)	9
12	51r	D Major	3/8	Dotted crotchet	4
13	51v	E minor	3/8	Crotchet	-
14	52r	G Major	3/8	Quaver	3
15	52v	B-flat minor	12/8	Dotted minim	3
16	53r	B-flat minor	12/8	Dotted minim	2
17	53v	E-flat minor	12/8	Dotted crotchet	-
Moto ascendente per terza					
18	54r	A minor	¢	Minim	6
19	54v	D minor	¢	Crotchet	-
20	55r	C Major	¢	Quaver	-
21	55v	D minor	12/8	?	-
22	55v	A Major	12/8	?	1
23	56v	F Major	12/8	?	-
24	56v	G minor	¢	Semibreve (alla breve)	-
25	57r	A minor	3/8	Dotted crotchet	-
26	57v	B minor	3/8	Quaver	-
27	57v	C minor	3/8	Quaver	-
28	58r	C minor	12/8	Dotted minim	-
29	58v	F minor	12/8	Dotted crotchet	-
30	59r	E-flat Major	12/8	Crotchet	-
Moto ascendente per quarta					
31	59v	C Major	¢	Minim	-
32	59v	D minor	¢	Crotchet	-
33	60r	E-flat Major	¢	Quaver	-
34	60r	D Major	¢	Minim (alla breve)	-
35	60v	A Major	3/8	Dotted crotchet	-
36	60v	C Major	3/8	Crotchet	-
37	61r	D minor	3/8	Quaver	-

The series is organised according to two criteria. The first, most obvious one, is the specific bass motion on which each piece is focused, dividing the series into four groups: ascending semitones, ascending steps, ascending thirds, ascending fourths; each group is preceded by a header indicating the bass motion[35]. Inside each group, there is a second, metre-related criterion for organisation: the note value of reference, i.e., what are the note values used in the bass when the specific motion appears (for the sake of clarity regarding this organisation, repeated

---

[35]. Bass motions (*moti* or *movimenti del basso*) were one of the fundamental aspects of partimento pedagogy; for a description see *ibidem*, chapter 9, especially the section 'Class IV: Bass Motions' (p. 135). They were also used to teach counterpoint: see Van Tour 2015, pp. 121-169.

notes have been accumulated into larger values in the table). The metrical aspect is particularly important in the context of partimenti diminuiti, not only because the possible figurations to be played on a bass motion are necessarily different if the rhythm of the bass varies, but also because certain bass motions are reinterpreted as diminutions over other motions when they appear in quicker figurations (e.g., apparent ascending steps in quavers actually outlining an ascending fifth at the level of minims).

The *acompañamientos* in Madrid 1188 closely follow the model of Francesco Durante's partimenti diminuiti. Not only is the typology the same (featuring examples of idiomatic realisation, variously called *diminuzioni*, *maniere*, *modi* or *pensieri* in the sources of Durante), but also the general plan of the series (organised in groups by bass motion) and the internal order of each group (by note value) are analogous to those in Durante's *Studi per cembalo*, his «advanced course», as described by Peter van Tour[36]. Moreover, the connection between these *acompañamientos* and Durante's partimenti is not limited to the formal aspect: some of them are also remarkably similar in musical content. This could seem obvious, given that the goal of such a series is to provide a student with practice pieces focusing on each of the musical commonplaces represented by the bass motions, but the fact is that, for some of the *acompañamientos*, there is a clear precedent in Durante's diminuiti. The extent of the similarities linking an *acompañamiento* to its hypothetical model varies: while some are generally related in terms of comparable musical material, some feature almost the same material in different tonalities and through a different tonal plan.

In order to better appreciate these similarities, Ex. 1 presents the initial bars of the first three *acompañamientos*, all three belonging to the first group in the series (on the ascending semitone). Each of them features the same bass motion in different metres: minims for no. 1, crotchets for no. 2, quavers for no. 3. For comparison, the beginnings of three partimenti diminuiti by Durante (Gj 3, Gj 5, Gj 39[37]) focusing on the same bass motions and note values appear in Ex. 2. Some of the superficial differences can be attributed to division of values into repeated notes: such is the case in no. 1, where four repeated quavers correspond to Durante's minims, and in no. 2, where crotchets correspond to Durante's repeated quavers. Normalising those rhythmic variants would result in virtually identical beginnings for no. 2 and Durante's Gj 5. Furthermore, if we select some of the *maniere* (the suggestions for idiomatic realisation)

---

[36]. Van Tour showed that the customary division of Durante's partimento output into four groups (*regole*, *numerati*, *diminuiti* and *fughe*) does not respond to the original plan: his partimenti seem to have been reorganised into those four categories during the 1790s in the context of the academic restoration process of the Neapolitan schools, blurring the original division into two courses (a basic and an advanced one) that is apparent from a detailed analysis of 18th-century sources, and their comparison to 19th-century ones. See Van Tour 2017.

[37]. Gj numbers were introduced by Robert O. Gjerdingen to identify partimenti in his website *Monuments of Partimenti*: <https://partimenti.org>, accessed October 2023. They are also used by Peter van Tour in *The Uppsala Partimento Database*: <https://www2.musik.uu.se/UUPart/UUPart>, accessed October 2023.

featured by the *acompañamientos* and put them side by side with the relevant ones from Durante, as in Ex. 3, the similarities and analogies are even more apparent. Although it is not possible to talk about these three pieces as mere copies, transpositions, or arrangements, each of them is clearly related to a partimento by Durante, suggesting a process of recomposition based on the same building blocks.

Ex. 1: *Acompañamientos* 1-3 from Madrid 1188.

Ex. 2: Three partimenti by Francesco Durante.

Ex. 3: Comparison of *maniere* for *acompañamientos* 1-3.

Amongst the 37 *acompañamientos* found in Madrid 1188, no. 10 is arguably the one which is closer to its hypothetical model. This is an interesting example because we happen to have not just one, but two very similar partimenti diminuiti by Durante: Gj 7 and Gj 8. All three pieces, presented in full in Ex. 4, feature the same musical material (which, admittedly, is a very typical commonplace) with minor variants and differ mostly in regards to the tonal plan and cadences. The *maniere* are essentially identical (see Ex. 5). It might be relevant to note that Gj 7 and 8 occupy a relatively asymmetrical place in the corpus of Durante's partimenti: while the first one appears in more than twenty sources, the second is only present in five[38], of which at least three are later, 19th-century sources[39]. My suggestion would be that Gj 8 might be related to Gj 7 in the same way that *acompañamiento* no. 10 in Madrid 1188 is related to either or both of them.

---

[38]. Information taken from *The Uppsala Partimento Database*: <https://www2.musik.uu.se/UUPart/UUPart.php>, accessed October 2023.

[39]. See Van Tour 2017, especially note no. 7.

Ex. 4: *Acompañamiento* 10 from Madrid 1188, Partimenti Gj 7 and Gj 8 by Durante.

Durante: Partimento Gj 8

The general impression given by the *acompañamientos* in Madrid 1188 is as if someone educated in the school of Durante intended to reconstruct the master's method with a newly composed series of partimenti. Why would someone do this? Several reasons can be proposed, all of them of course hypothetical. One would consist in undertaking the composition of a series of partimenti in emulation of the master, as a final stage of the process of training. Another could be a wish for expansion: additional partimenti to cover further possibilities, in terms of metres or tonalities (many of the *acompañamientos* are in compound metre, quite some in remote keys, such as B-flat minor or even E-flat minor), to offer more *maniere*, or to bring them closer to an updated musical fashion: although admittedly small, there is a slight stylistic difference between these partimenti and Durante's. A third one would be simple necessity: how to teach young

Ex. 5: Comparison of *maniere* for *acompañamiento* 10.

musicians in Spain with partimenti diminuiti, without having a compilation of Durante's series readily available.

Once the close relationship between the *acompañamientos* of Madrid 1188 and Durante's partimenti diminuiti has been established, it might be interesting to point to some differences. One is in the number of *maniere*: while the majority of Durante's diminuiti offer a couple of *maniere*, the first few ones in Madrid 1188 (those in the first group, focusing on the semitone)

Ex. 6: *Acompañamientos* 21-23 from Madrid 1188.

are presented with many more: from a minimum of 4 to no less than 14 (for partimento no. 5). Then, there is a progression towards fewer and fewer: all except two of the second group have *maniere*, while only two partimenti have them in the third group, and none in the fourth and last group present hints for realisation. This feature conforms to a pedagogic plan in which hypothetical students need more ideas and guidance at the beginning of the process, while becoming increasingly independent as they progress through the series. Another difference consists in the fact that only four bass motions are represented in this series. There is no way to

Ex. 7: *Maniera* for *acompañamiento* 22.

Acompañamiento no. 22

tell whether they belong to a complete series of which only a part survived, or if the author did not actually proceed beyond the section on ascending fourths for some reason. A hypothetical complete series, providing a similar number of partimenti for those bass motions that are not represented (ascending fifths and sixths, plus all the descending motions) would have contained around a hundred items.

Finally, I would like to point to a particular irregularity in the series of partimenti diminuiti from Madrid 1188: the third group of the series contains three partimenti which do not seem to belong there. Nos. 21-23 appear to be designed around the bass motion of ascending semitones, as opposed to ascending thirds (see Ex. 6). Given that partimenti rarely feature a single bass motion, but several of them, it is not always completely obvious which motion represents the main focus of each partimento. Nevertheless, the presence of *maniere* can be used as a confirmation, given that they present idiomatic realisations of the relevant bass motion. Although two of the 'suspicious' partimenti (nos. 21 and 23) feature no *maniere*, the single one accompanying no. 22 seems to confirm the hypothesis that they actually belong to the ascending semitone group (see Ex. 7). Moreover, as a secondary effect, if these three partimenti were to be moved to the first group (after no. 7), the progression of metres and note value of references would be virtually identical to the other groups, and the relative number of items in each group would also be more homogeneous: from 7/10/13/7 to 10/10/10/7 (see TABLE 3).

CONCLUSION

At least until the eventual discovery of similar sources, the presence of partimento in Spain is attested to by manuscript Madrid 1188, a well-organised and comprehensive compilation of pedagogic materials for instruction in thorough bass from the late 18th century. Specifically, the 37 *acompañamientos* of section 5 are modelled on the partimenti diminuiti of Francesco Durante, to the point that some of them have a clear precedent in Durante.

Some or all of the materials of the manuscript might have been used to teach the choirboys of the Royal College: sections 1, 3, 4 (and possibly also 2) are the work of two musicians of the Royal Chapel: José Lidón and Félix Máximo López. Furthermore, Lidón was «maestro de estilo italiano o moderno» at the College since 1771.

The position of «maestro de estilo», created by Francesco Corselli upon his appointment as royal chapel master in 1738, officially incorporates Italian methodology in the curriculum of the Royal College, in the context of a general 'italianisation' of musical life at the court. The first «maestro de estilo» Antonio Corvi Moroti, who taught between 1738 and 1771, and with whom Lidón studied for ten years, might have been directly responsible for the introduction of partimenti in that context.

Bibliography

Agazzari 1607
Agazzari, Agostino. *Del sonare sopra 'l basso con tutti li stromenti e dell'uso loro nel conserto*, Siena, Falcini, 1607.

Aron 1516
Aron, Pietro. *Libri tres de institutione musica*, Bologna, Hectoris, 1516.

Aron 1539
Id. *Il Toscanello in musica*, Venice, Sessa, 1539.

Bermudo 1555
Bermudo, Juan. *Declaración de instrumentos musicales*, Osuna, León, 1555.

Bianciardi 1607
Bianciardi, Francesco. *Breve regola per imparar' a sonare sopra il basso con ogni sorte d'instrumento*, Siena, Falcini, 1607.

Borgir 1987
Borgir, Tharald. *The Performance of the Basso Continuo in Italian Baroque Music*, Ann Arbor (MI), UMI Research Press, 1987.

Boyd – Carreras 2006
Music in Spain during the Eighteenth Century, edited by Malcolm Boyd and Juan José Carreras, Cambridge University Press, 2006.

Cafiero 2007
Cafiero, Rosa. 'The Early Reception of Neapolitan Partimento Theory in France: A Survey', in: *Journal of Music Theory*, li/2 (1986), pp. 137-159.

Cafiero 2020
Ead. *La didattica del partimento. Studi di storia delle teorie musicali*, Lucca, LIM, 2020.

Dentice 1553
Dentice, Luigi. *Duo dialoghi della musica*, Rome, Lucrino, 1553.

DIERGARTEN 2017
DIERGARTEN, Felix. 'Editorial', in: *Eighteenth-Century Music*, XIV/1 (2017), pp. 5-11.

DOMÍNGUEZ 2009
DOMÍNGUEZ, José María. 'Comedias armónicas a la usanza de Italia: Alessandro Scarlatti's Music and the Spanish Nobility c.1700', in: *Early Music*, XXXVII/2 (2009), pp. 201-215.

EGGEBRECHT – ZAMINER 1970
EGGEBRECHT, Hans Heinrich – ZAMINER, Frieder. *Ad organum faciendum. Lehrschriften der Mehrstimmigkeit in nachguidonischer Zeit*, Mainz, Schott, 1970.

FRUTOS 2009
FRUTOS, Leticia. 'Virtuosos of the Neapolitan Opera in Madrid: Alessandro Scarlatti, Matteo Sassano, Petruccio and Filippo Schor', in: *Early Music*, XXXVII/2 (2009), pp. 187-200.

FULLER 1981
FULLER, Sarah. 'Theoretical Foundations of Early Organum Theory', in: *Acta Musicologica*, LIII/1 (1981), pp. 52-84.

FULLER 2011
EAD. 'Early Polyphony to circa 1200', in: *The Cambridge Companion to Medieval Music*, edited by Mark Everist, Cambridge, Cambridge University Press, 2011 (Cambridge Companions to Music), pp. 46-66.

GJERDINGEN 2007
GJERDINGEN, Robert O. *Music in the Galant Style*, Oxford, Oxford University Press, 2007.

GJERDINGEN 2020
ID. *Child Composers in the Old Conservatories*, Oxford, Oxford University Press, 2020.

GONZÁLEZ LUDEÑA 2020
GONZÁLEZ LUDEÑA, Carlos. 'Para que cante Mateucho y todos los demás: música en la Real Cámara en el ocaso de vida de Carlos II', in: *Revista de Musicología*, XLII/1 (2020), pp. 131-154.

HEARTZ 2003
HEARTZ, Daniel. *Music in European Capitals: The Galant Style, 1720-1780*, New York, Norton, 2003.

HOLTMEIER 2007
HOLTMEIER, Ludwig. 'Heinichen, Rameau, and the Italian Thoroughbass Tradition: Concepts of Tonality and Chord in the Rule of the Octave', in: *Journal of Music Theory*, LI/1 (2007), pp. 5-49.

KNIGHTON 2011
KNIGHTON, Tess. 'Gaffurius, Urrede and Studying Music at Salamanca University around 1500', in: *Revista de Musicología*, XXXIV/1 (2011), pp. 11-36.

Leza 1997
Leza Cruz, José Máximo. 'La zarzuela *Viento es la dicha de amor*. Producciones en los teatros públicos madrileños en el siglo XVIII', in: *Música y Literatura en la Península Ibérica: 1600-1750. Actas del Congreso Internacional Valladolid, 20-21 y 22 de febrero, 1995*, edited by María Antonia Virgili Blanquet, Germán Vega García-Luengos and Carmelo Caballero Fernández-Rufete, Valladolid, Sociedad V Centenario del Tratado de Tordesillas, 1997, pp. 393-405.

Leza 2014
Historia de la música en España e Hispanoamérica. 4: La música en el siglo XVIII, edited by José Máximo Leza Cruz, Fondo de Cultura Económica de España, 2014.

López Ruiz 2017
López Ruiz, Luis. *El compositor José Lidón (1747-1827): obra teórica y análisis de su música litúrgica*, Ph.D. Diss., Madrid, Universidad Complutense de Madrid, 2017.

Martín Moreno 1985
Martín Moreno, Antonio. *Historia de la música española. 4: Siglo XVIII*, Madrid, Alianza Música, 1985.

Martini 2020
Martini, Giambattista. *Libro per Accompagnare (1737-38)*, edited by Peter van Tour, Visby, Wessmans Musikförlag, 2020.

Mattei 2021
Mattei, Stanislao. *Scales and Versets in all Major and Minor Keys; Three Partimento Realizations from the Ricasoli Collection*, edited by Peter van Tour, Visby, Wessmans Musikförlag, 2021.

Mazzetti – Ticli 2017
Mazzetti, Marcello – Ticli, Livio. 'Quando de quintis terzisque calabat in unam octavam: Per una storia della prassi esecutiva della musica sacra a Brescia nel tardo Cinquecento', in: *Annali di Storia Bresciana*, V (2017), pp. 223-293.

Morales 2005
Morales, Nicolás. *Las voces de Palacio. El Real Colegio de Niños Cantores de Madrid*, Madrid, Ayuntamiento de Madrid-Área de Gobierno de las Artes, 2005.

Morales 2007
Id. *L'artiste de cour dans l'Espagne du XVIIIᵉ siècle. Étude de la communauté des musiciens au service de Philippe V (1700-1746)*, Madrid, Casa de Velázquez, 2007.

Nebra 2009
Nebra, José. *Viento es la dicha de amor. Zarzuela en dos jornadas*, edited by José Máximo Leza, Madrid, Instituto Complutense de Ciencias Musicales, 2009.

Ornithoparcus 1517
Ornithoparcus, Andreas. *Musice active micrologus*, Leipzig, Schumann, 1517.

Ortiz 1553
Ortiz, Diego. *Trattado de glosas sobre clausulas y otros generos de puntos en la musica de violones*, Rome, Dorico, 1553.

Porpora 1735
Porpora, Nicola. *All'Alteza Reale di Frederico Prencipe Reale di Vallia e Prencipe Elettorale di Hanover* [...] *nuovamente composte opre di musica vocale*, London, s.n., 1735.

Ratner 1980
Ratner, Leonard G. *Classic Music: Expression, Form, and Style*, New York, Schirmer, 1980.

Sachs 1971
Sachs, Klaus-Jürgen. 'Zur Tradition der Klangschritt-Lehre. Die Texte mit der Formel «Si cantus ascendit...» und ihre Verwandten', in: *Archiv für Musikwissenschaft*, xxviii/4 (1971), pp. 233-270.

Sanguinetti 2012
Sanguinetti, Giorgio. *The Art of Partimento: History, Theory and Practice*, Oxford, Oxford University Press, 2012.

Sweeney 1989
Sweeney, Cecily. 'The Regulae Organi Guidonis Abbatis and 12th Century Organum/Discant Treatises', in: *Musica Disciplina*, xliii (1989), pp. 7-31.

Tagliavini 1978
Tagliavini, Luigi Ferdinando. 'Anfänge des Generalbaßsatzes. Die *Cento Concerti Ecclesiastici* (1602) von Lodovico Viadana', in: *Rivista Italiana di Musicologia*, xiii/1 (1978), pp. 174-185.

Trabaci 1605
Trabaci, Giovanni Maria. *Missarum et motectorum quatuor vocum cum partimento pro organista*, Naples, Vitale, 1605.

Van Tour 2015
Van Tour, Peter. *Counterpoint and Partimento: Methods of Teaching Composition in Late Eighteenth-Century Naples*, Uppsala, Acta Universitatis Upsaliensis, 2015 (Studia musicologica Upsaliansia. Nova Series, 25).

Van Tour 2017
Id. 'Partimento Teaching According to Francesco Durante, Investigated through the Earliest Manuscript Sources', in: *Studies in Historical Improvisation: From Cantare super Librum to Partimenti*, edited by Massimiliano Guido, Abingdon-New York, Routledge, 2017, pp. 131-148.

Vanneo 1533
Vanneo, Stephano. *Recanetum de musica aurea*, Rome, Dorico, 1533.

Hieronymus Praetorius, Multiple-Bass Notation in Organ Parts and Continuo Performance Practices of Polychoral Music in the Hanseatic Cities of Northern Europe

Michael Fuerst
(Hochschule für Künste, Bremen)

Any group of continuo players, and foremost among them the organist, requires certain information to accompany polychoral works successfully, the most basic of which is the musical text[1]. The various sources of keyboard parts from the final years of the sixteenth century on into the seventeenth show that several forms of notation were available to composers, publishers, arrangers, and organists, ranging from scores, tablatures, short scores, and single-line organ basses to the multiple-bass notation used in 1594 for the very first printed organ partbook and by Hieronymus Praetorius (1560-1629) for his first *bassus continuus* partbook[2], printed in 1618. The decision to employ multiple-bass notation creates an organ part that allows for a variety of flexible performance practices.

Within the last year, scholarly work has been published reflecting upon the art of accompaniment from organ tablatures[3]. The first visual impression of some of these tablatures, the so-called block tablatures[4], is not unlike that of the notation considered here in that there is instant clarity in discerning which choir is singing at what time. Multiple-bass notation in its essence is simply a reduced portrayal of a polychoral work that presents a *basso seguente* for each

---

[1]. I am greatly indebted to Arndt Schnoor, Marcin Szelest, Kerala J. Snyder, Jeffery Kite-Powell, Esther Criscuola de Laix, and Frederick K. Gable for their guidance and generosity.

[2]. I will use the terms 'organ book' and '*bassus continuus* partbook' interchangeably while respectfully acknowledging the various usages of these books, as will be discussed below.

[3]. Kite-Powell 2021 and Szelest 2021

[4]. See Kite-Powell 2021, pp. 56ff.

individual choir in a score of as many lines as there are choirs (for examples of this notation, see ILLS. 1 and 2 for quadruple-choir pieces and ILL. 7 for a double-choir piece). When one of the choirs is not singing, the measures are filled with rests, just as a block tablature indicates graphically how the choirs are divided and when they perform together by showing rests or blank space when one of the choirs is not active[5]. Its development in Italy has been at the forefront of much musicological discussion, first by Otto Kinkeldey in 1910[6], and recently in Richard Charteris's foreword to his 2014 edition of Giovanni Croce's first book of 8-part motets[7]. In 2004, Irmtraut Freiberg mentioned the notation under the heading *spartitura/partitura*[8], the first printed example of multiple-bass notation having been titled *Spartidura*[9]. I will refer to these parts using the descriptive term multiple-bass[10]. The most detailed examination of the topic was undertaken by Imogene Horsley in 1977[11], who found that while multiple-bass notation was initially developed by the Venetians, they soon all but abandoned it in favour of the single-line *basso pro organo*, and it was primarily in Milan and Bologna that parts with more than one bassline continued to be published[12]. After 1620, two-bass scores for polychoral works appeared only infrequently in Italy, but it was north of the Alps that publishers still brought out organ parts that gave more than a single-line[13]. In this article, I will use the printed *bassus continuus* parts of the Hamburg organist Hieronymus Praetorius as a point of departure to examine the context and usage of multiple-bass organ parts in German-speaking lands, particularly in Hanseatic cities.

Hieronymus Praetorius published his vocal works in Hamburg between 1599 and 1625, which in their final form made up his *Opus musicum*[14], consisting of five volumes[15]. While the

---

[5]. *Ibidem*, p. 56.

[6]. KINKELDEY 1910, pp. 187-215.

[7]. CHARTERIS 2014.

[8]. FREIBERG 2004, pp. 23ff.

[9]. RISM A/I C4429.

[10]. The term *spartitura* can indicate the use of bar lines and is not unambiguous in its meaning. For Banchieri's use of the term, see BELOTTI 2018. For use of the term as meaning the division of parts into measures using bar lines, see CHARTERIS 2014, pp. x-xi.

[11]. HORSLEY 1977.

[12]. Even so, the last example for a multiple-bass score that Horsley gives in the appendix was published in Venice in 1628. See *ibidem*, p. 499.

[13]. *Ibidem*, pp. 496-497. Horsley cites prints by Johann Stadlmayr from 1610 and 1614. Presumably, the 1614 print citation refers to RISM A/I S4286.

[14]. Unless otherwise clarified, the referenced edition is the final Hamburg print.

[15]. The RISM A/I numbers of the final Hamburg editions of each volume are P5338 (OM-1), P5334 (OM-2), P5330 (OM-3), P5341 (OM-4), and P5343 (OM-5). The 1622 edition of OM-3 consists only of the *bassus continuus* part, whereby the final edition of the vocal parts was printed in 1616. OM-4 was only printed in 1618. See CRISCUOLA DE LAIX 2009, p. 128, Table 2-1 for a complete overview of all *Opus musicum* prints with RISM

first three collections in their various editions had initially been released without an organ partbook, in 1618 the composer issued such a part in print for the first time for the fourth part of the *Opus musicum*, titled *Cantiones variae* (hereafter OM-4)[16]. This partbook makes use of multiple-bass notation for the final 14 out of 27 pieces, scored for 8 to 20 voices divided into 2 to 4 choirs[17]. Four years later, in 1622, Praetorius issued a newly conceived *bassus continuus* for the three previously released volumes, *Cantiones sacrae*, *Magnificat octo vocum*, and *Liber Missarum* (hereafter OM-1, OM-2 and OM-3). In these new parts, as will be discussed below, he abandoned multiple-bass notation for the polychoral works in favour of the single-line *basso pro organo*, conforming to what had come to be prevalent in Venetian prints. Every one of his *bassus continuus* partbooks was printed in folio as opposed to the quarto format of the eight vocal partbooks. With the new organ book and newly corrected and revised editions, the composer himself considered the four volumes to be a set and made a collector's edition with a combined title page of his complete works as they stood in 1622[18]. In this same year he presented a copy to St. Peter's church in Lübeck as a gift[19]; this copy is still preserved, although incomplete, in the city's library[20]. As in many other libraries throughout Europe, the four volumes of the *Opus musicum* are combined, bound together in each partbook according to its voice[21]. The Lübeck copy of the *bassus continuus* book is of particular interest as it contains contemporary, handwritten markings, and is the only organ book among the editions once held in Lübeck to have survived[22].

A/I numbers. For modern editions of Hieronymus Praetorius' works, see GABLE 2008 (OM-2) and GABLE 2014 (OM-3); OM-1, OM-4, and OM-5 forthcoming. The Frankfurt reprints are not considered in this article. See fn 39.

[16]. RISM A/I P5341.

[17]. Numbers XXII to XXXIX. Some of the pieces have multiple parts that are given their own number in the collection.

[18]. The 5th volume (OM-5), *Cantiones novae officiosae* (1625), shown by Esther Criscuola de Laix to have been something of an afterthought 3 years later, is not part of the Lübeck copy. See CRISCUOLA DE LAIX 2009, pp. 164-169. On the collector's edition of 1622 see *ibidem*, pp. 169-178. Within each partbook in Lübeck, the volumes of OM-1-4 are bound together; the combined title page is in the tenor partbook, D-LÜh A205b. Other copies with the combined title page include those held in D-Hs, GB-Lbl and D-BGk. The exemplars of the organ partbooks in B-Br and D-SAh both contain OM-1-5, bound together. In PL-Kj, the volumes OM-1-5 are bound together in the vocal partbooks, but the volumes of the organ book are each bound separately, creating 5 partbooks. See APPENDIX 2.

[19]. For two different transcriptions of Praetorius's presentation letter, see STAHL 1931, p. 169, and STAHL 1952, p. 192.

[20]. D-LÜh A205. Cantus: A205a, Tenor: A205b, Septima vox: A205c, Bassus: A205d, Bassus Continuus; A205e. A second complete set of 8 vocal partbooks each containing OM-1-4, A205f-n is not considered here, as there are no handwritten markings in the partbooks, and the organ part is not extant.

[21]. See fn 18. The date of the binding for most exemplars is not clear. While the Lübeck binding is contemporary with the gifting in 1622, bearing a stamp «St. Peters Kirchen», there are indications that some editions were combined much later after coming into the collections of libraries or collectors. See fn 33 for D-LEm II. 2. 11a.

[22]. The copy of OM-1-4 from the choir library of St. Mary's, now held in A-Wg, is missing the organ book which was, however, counted by Martin Lincke in his inventory, albeit with the 9 partbooks recorded as being in 4°,

In 1614, four years before Hieronymus Praetorius released his first printed *bassus continuus*, Adam Gumpelzhaimer of Augsburg published a collection with a multiple-bass partbook[23]. The title page of this so-called *Partitio* reads «...cum duplici Basso in Organorum usum» i.e., «with doubled bass for the use of the organs»[24], suggesting that he conceived these parts for performance on two different instruments by two different people[25]. Such an idea was not novel. Aurelius Ribrochus, in his forward to his 1598 *bassus continuus* settings for works by Josephus Gallus[26], which makes use both of open score and multiple-bass notation, writes:

> First, if you are willing to play and sing this sacred musical work of ours, you ought to have two books of the score itself, so that from the one or the other, that is to say in either "chorus" you will play everything easier, sweeter, and with more polish[27].

The point here is that multiple copies of such printed scores could be obtained for players, making the manuscript production of several copies unnecessary and making sure that both performing organists had a clear picture of the entire piece. This would be a convenient alternative to the practice suggested by Michael Praetorius that a single-line thoroughbass be copied many times, underlining the segments in red where the musicians of a specific choir were meant to play[28]. Heinrich Schütz issued a *basso pro organo* with his 1619 *Psalmen Davids* without any

---

thus disregarding the fact that the *bassus continuus* book is in folio. Presumably, the organ book, not least because of its different size, was kept at the large organ and was overlooked when the St. Mary's choir library was sent to Vienna, only to be destroyed in the bombing of 1942 or lost at some time before that. See SNYDER 2015, p. 1 and p. 5. I am indebted to Kerala J. Snyder for drawing this to my attention.

[23]. RISM A/I: G5143. Gumpelzhaimer declares in his preface that any organist not served by his *Partio* should feel free to prepare a part according to their own methods: «Welchem aber sein weis besser gefelt / oder hiemit ungedient ist: dem stehet es jederzeit frei / nach seiner gelegenheit / gar zu partiern». He emphasises the sentiment by adding a 6-voice canon, labeled *Fuga*, with a chronistichon implying an earlier composition date (1606) than that of the 1614 publication: «*EineM jeDen gefäLLt sein VVeIs.*» i.e., «each person likes his own way [of doing things]» with the Roman numeral MDLLVI integrated into the text.

[24]. Gumpelzhaimer uses the plural again in the parts, adding to the upper left corner of each page the heading *Bassus ad organa*, i.e., «bass for the organs». RISM A/I S4286 also refers to the multiple-bass part in the title: «...cum duplice basso organicorum usui accommodato».

[25]. The idea that *organa* should be translated as organ in the sense of a single instrument seems highly unlikely considering the context. If, however, Gumpelzhaimer is referring to a double organ in the English sense of having two divisions, he would seem to be a proponent of performance as recommended by Matthäus Hertel. See below.

[26]. RISM A/I: G270.

[27]. «Primum. Si hoc nostrum sacrum opus musicum pulsare, concinereq; haud gravabimini, Partiturae ipsius Libri duo sunt vobis habendi, ut hinc & inde, hoc est, in utroq; Choro omnia facilius, suavius, & expolitius modulemini». English translation taken from CHISHOLM 2015, p. 103.

[28]. PRAETORIUS 1619, pp. 144, 124-145, 125. English translation in KITE-POWELL 2004, p. 134.

indication regarding which choir was being accompanied, while stating in the preface that new parts would have to be made based on the vocal parts if multiple organs were to be used[29]. So clearly a culture of creating handwritten parts based on performance needs was prevalent. That said, the book-fair catalogues of Frankfurt and Leipzig do have examples of individual organ books for sale[30], albeit not those printed with multiple-bass notation. It is evident that access to multiple copies of a printed organ book would be convenient for performances of polychoral works, particularly if that organ book were set up in a fashion that makes the division of the choirs clear, and thus useful to organists and directors alike.

Surprisingly, the Leipzig[31] and the Berlin[32] exemplars of the OM-4 *bassus continuus* book may give evidence for the practice of distributing multiple copies of the same print among the musicians involved in a performance. They prove that additional books were produced after the first printing, showing not only continued interest in the collection, but also that more organ books were required. Both exemplars stand alone, not part of a collection of vocal partbooks[33]. In fact, each of these copies is a hybrid edition[34], undocumented as such before now. They mostly use gatherings from the 1618 edition while inserting newly printed, variant gatherings of signatures D, only found in Berlin, and E, found in both Berlin and Leipzig (see ILLS. 1 and 2 for a comparison of the first page of the E gatherings, folio E1r). In both copies, gatherings A, B, C and F are from the original 1618 printing. That the variant gatherings are newer is simple to ascertain since they use a different size of print type than the rest of the part. While the print type in the original 1618 organ book is smaller[35], the variant gatherings use the same larger

---

[29]. RISM A/I S2275. «...(wofern mehr als eine Orgel gebraucht werden soll) durch die Psalmen die Bässe herauß zu ziehen wissen» («...know to extract the basses from the Psalms (if more than one organ is to be used)»). Incidentally, the copy of the organ part held by B-Br shows underlining as suggested by Michael Praetorius, albeit not using red ink.

[30]. For Michaelmas 1618, the organ book to the first part of the *Florilegium portense*, RISM B/I 1618[1], is listed separately, directly under the collection. For Michaelmas 1624, RISM A/I L1033, Caspar Vincentius' organ part to the works of Orlando di Lasso are offered. <http://www.olmsonline.de/purl?PPN525616772>, accessed October 2023.

[31]. D-LEm II. 2. 11a.

[32]. D-B Mus.ant.pract. P 1185a.

[33]. The Leipzig copy of OM-4 is bound together with the 1622 organ books of OM-2 and OM-3. It is worth noting that the pages of OM-2 and OM-3 are cleanly cut, whereas those of OM-4 are raw. Presumably, these editions were separate and only bound together at some later date. The volume stems from the collection of Carl Ferdinand Becker, who may well have had the copies bound together in the nineteenth century. D-LEm II. 2. 11b stems from his collection as well and has a similar binding. It is a copy of the *bassus continuus* from OM-2 with the pages cut to a much smaller size. See APPENDIX 2.

[34]. See BOGHARDT 1993, p. 307.

[35]. For more on the print type used by Hieronymus Praetorius and his printers see CRISCUOLA DE LAIX 2009, pp. 137-139 and p. 162. The smaller print type used in OM-4 appears to be identical with that used by

ILL. 1: Fol. E1r from the *Bassus Continuus* of OM-4 held in D-LÜh. Stadtbibliothek Lübeck, shelfmark A 205e. Used with permission.

type found in all the vocal partbooks and in the *bassus continuus* books published in and after 1622. Hieronymus Praetorius worked with several different printers between 1599 and 1625, and in his works, this smaller print type is exclusively found in the first organ book, printed by Heinrich Carstens for OM-4 in 1618. The unified appearance of the original partbook is compromised by the larger print type, so that it follows that the printing of the variant gatherings must have been undertaken after the composer stopped working with Carstens. For his volumes published in 1622 and 1625, Praetorius worked with the printers Paul Lange and

---

Caspar Vincentius in the organ partbook of *Promptuarium*. See below.

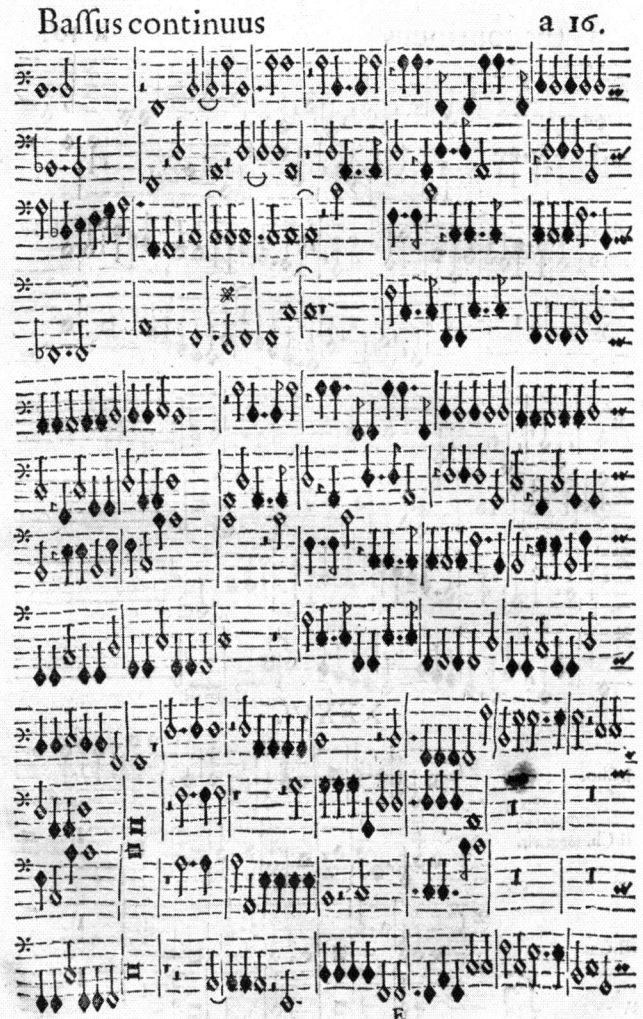

ILL. 2: Fol. E1r from the *Bassus Continuus* of OM-4 held in D-LEm. Leipziger Städtische Bibliotheken-Musikbibliothek, shelfmark II. 2. 11a. Used with permission.

Michael Hering respectively[36]. Assuming the hybrid editions come from one of their shops, these men either did not have access to the smaller print type or they rejected it. A comparison with the reprint of the *bassus continuus* book brought out in 1623 in Frankfurt by Egenolff Emmel[37] reveals that the hybrid edition was an independent undertaking. The resulting version contains some corrections, suggesting the involvement of Hieronymus Praetorius himself,

---

36. The *bassus continuus* books in PL-Kj and B-Br are both complete editions of the entire *Opus musicum*, OM-1-5. Neither version of OM-4 is the hybrid edition. This could be an indication that the hybrid edition was made in or after 1625, presumably by Michael Hering. See APPENDIX 2.

37. RISM A/I P5342.

but unfortunately introduces new errors in other places, bringing about an edition with more misprints than the original. The amount of music printed on each page, even on each line, is mostly identical, but there is some variation. Clearly, more copies of the OM-4 organ partbook were needed, and gatherings no longer available, particularly gathering E, were reprinted and combined with remaining gatherings to create complete copies.

A hybrid edition by its very definition does not intend to be a new edition. Hieronymus Praetorius was keen to bring out new editions, which he advertised as being corrected and augmented as part of their promotion[38], so it is notable that this is not the case for OM-4, which was only issued once in Hamburg[39]. The fact that the title page, folio A1r, is identical in the hybrid and original editions emphasises the point that there was no intention to create a second edition, only increase the number of copies of the first. It was usual to print an overrun of gatherings to make sure that enough copies of each gathering were available for the desired number of books without having to reset the type for another print run in case unusable gatherings were discovered[40]. This would mean any gatherings left over from the initial process could be used, augmented by the reprinting of any missing gatherings, to increase the number of complete books at some later date[41].

It is not impossible that the requirement to reprint these specific gatherings was due to more than just the chance survival of the other parts of the book, considering the contents of gatherings D and E. TABLE 1 lists the pieces included in these gatherings, all in multiple-bass notation; they include the collection's final double-choir work, the two triple-choir works, and, except for the final two lines, the sixteen-voice quadruple-choir works, including *Herr Gott dich loben wir*, Praetorius' setting of the German *Te Deum*[42], (nos. XXXVI-XXXVIII). Gathering F, preserved in the original 1618 printing in all extant copies, contains the conclusion of no. XXXVIII and the final piece of the collection, a twenty-voice, quadruple-choir motet, as well as the index.

---

[38]. CRISCULOA DE LAIX 2009, pp. 159, 175 and 178.

[39]. RISM A/I P5342, the Frankfurt reprint of 1623, was apparently not authorised and is therefore not considered as part of this discussion. See CRISCULOA DE LAIX 2009, pp. 177-178, and ROSE 2019.

[40]. BOGHARDT 1993, pp. 309-310.

[41]. The question as to whether the number of vocal partbooks was similarly increased in this manner could not be researched at this time. Since, however, each of the two surviving hybrid editions of the *bassus continuus* book is individually preserved without being part of a set of vocal partbooks, it seems likely that this phenomenon is limited to the organ book of OM-4. See APPENDIX 2.

[42]. The piece is divided into a *prima pars* (XXXVI) *Herr Gott wir danken dir*, *secunda pars* (XXXVII) *Du König der Ehren*, and *tertia pars* (XXXVIII) *Behüt uns heut, O treuer Gott*. It is followed by the final piece of the collection, number XXXIX with 20 voices in four choirs. See GABLE 1987 and the forward to GABLE 1998 especially pp. xix-xx and xxiii.

TABLE 1

Pieces on Folios of Gatherings D, E, and F in the *Bassus Continuus* Partbook of OM-4

FOLIO	D	E	F
1	XXXII *In convertendo Dominus* à 10 in 2 choirs	Continuation of XXXV XXXVI *Herr Gott dich loben* wir à 16 in 4 choirs Opening (8 breves)	Closing of XXXVIII (15,5 breves) XXXIX *Decantabat populus* à 20 in 4 choirs
2	XXXIII *Angelus ad pastores ait* à 12 in 3 choirs		
3	XXXIV *Tota pulchra es* à 12 in 3 choirs	XXXVII *Du König der Ehren Jesu Christ* à 16 in 4 choirs (Part 2)	
4			Index
5	XXXV *Exultate justi in Domino* à 16 in 4 choirs		
6		XXXVIII *Behüt uns heut O trewer Gott* à 16 in 4 choirs (Part 3)	

Herr Gott dich loben wir was initially printed without an organ part in pamphlet form in 1612[43] and is presumably the same setting of the liturgical text described as having been composed and performed by Hieronymus Praetorius for the dedication of St. Gertrude's chapel in 1607[44]. The piece must have enjoyed several performances over the years considering the many manuscript additions in the Lübeck copies preserved both in D-LÜh and A-Wg[45]. Is it possible that the necessity to create the hybrid edition arose as an unintended result of taking gathering E, which contains the bulk of the work, out of the context of the complete book and distributing multiple copies among the chordal bass players and directors for performances of the *Te Deum*, whereby the final two lines which appear on gathering F could have been copied out by hand? The idea of such use could also apply to the triple-choir works, collected in gathering D[46]. There is no hard evidence of such a practice, but while conjecture, it would follow the recommendation made by Ribrochus to allow more than one person to have maximal information about the piece being performed, thanks to the multiple-bass notation.

Interestingly, the Lübeck copy of OM-4's organ book is missing gatherings E and F except for the first leaf of gathering E, which has been carefully connected to gathering D. This folio

---

43. RISM A/I PP 5344a. See CRISCULOA DE LAIX 2009, pp. 351-354 and 379.

44. GABLE 1998, p. xxiii.

45. See fn. 22. The eight vocal partbooks of OM-1-4, once part of St. Mary's choir library, are held in A-Wg. See SNYDER 2015.

46. It is not unlikely that the double-choir works were accompanied by a single organist. See below.

primarily contains the conclusion of XXXV *Exultate justi* and the opening line of XXXVI *Herr Gott dich loben wir*. Each of these pieces has clearly written text underlay in the *bassus continuus* partbook and many manuscript additions in the vocal partbooks. All this unequivocally points to use of the scores in performances of these works. If it were not for the careful preservation of the first folio of gathering E, resulting in XXXV being complete, one would presume the losses to be a simple matter due to the ravages of time. Considering the actual state of preservation described above, however, the possibility might be entertained that gatherings E and F were intentionally removed from the Lübeck copy of St. Peter's church while carefully leaving the previous motet intact in the organ book. If this is indeed the case, it would indicate that the printed multiple-bass score was needed elsewhere, perhaps by the director, while at the same time, the rest of the book was needed in its usual place, presumably at the organ[47].

In Lübeck, the church of St. Mary's held a position of privilege in the city's musical organisation, where the cantor of St. Catherine's school led the figural music and was able to employ the best municipal musicians on all the primary feast days of the church year. At the beginning of the seventeenth century, *Figuralmusik*, led by the cantor and accompanied by instrumentalists of the finest musical organisation of the city, the *Ratsmusik*, was only heard in St. Peter's four times a year on a Sunday that followed one of the main liturgical feast days of Christmas, Easter, Pentecost, and Michaelmas[48]. This was also true for all the other main churches of Lübeck. In 1620, only two years before Hieronymus Praetorius gifted his printed works, the wealthy parish of St. Peter's was able to secure the employment of the musicians of the *Brüderschaft*, a less prestigious organisation of instrumentalists, so that figural music could be heard on the major feast days as well[49]. These musicians were to be directed not by the cantor but by the choral conductor of St. Peter's, Hermann Bielefeldt, and paid for by special collections taken from the parish. There were also contractual arrangements made in the 1630s to employ musicians from the *Ratsmusik*, augmented by the *Brüderschaft* to play on two additional Sundays each year so that music could be heard from both organs and the choir loft on the rood screen, enabling polychoral works of 3 or 4 choirs to be undertaken[50].

---

[47]. If true, this would imply that the first line of the German *Te Deum* would have been copied out in manuscript to complete the score in the removed gatherings.

[48]. See STAHL 1952, pp. 54-55.

[49]. See *ibidem*, pp. 56-57.

[50]. *Ibidem*, p. 56. Stahl quotes the contract, dated 10 August 1630, as follows: «mit ihren besten Instrumenten als Cornetten, Zinken, Posaunen, Dulcianen, Lauten, Pandoren, Pfeifen, Geigen und andern darzu dienenden Instrumenten auf dem Chor und beiden Orgeln erscheinen und nach ihrem bestenn vermugen den Figural gesang nebenst St. Peters Kirchen Cantore und Organisten bestellen, [...] dazu aus der Brüderschaft soviel tüchtige Personen, als vonnöten sein werden [...], daß ein Musica von 3 oder 4 Chören könne gemacht werden» («appear together with the choir of St. Peter's Church and its organists with their best instruments including cornettos, trombones, dulcians, lutes, pandoras, flutes, violins and other instruments in the chancel [i.e. on the rood screen]

This is the context in which St. Peter's church would have witnessed performances of the large-scale motets in OM-4, confirmed by the manuscript additions in the scores, particularly the Christmas motets for 2 and 3 choirs.

Sadly, the *bassus continuus* book once held by St. Mary's has not survived[51], but the eight vocal partbooks that do survive from the parish's 1622 *Opus musicum* collection, identical to the St. Peter's set, show usage of the German *Te Deum* as well[52]. While there is currently no evidence to suggest that organ partbooks were shared between the churches, considering the musical organisation of the city as described above, it is conceivable that the larger church of St. Mary's might have borrowed from the collection of St. Peter's for the performance of such large-scale works. If the performance was to include multiple continuo players, easily manageable as a *Regalist* was among the instrumentalists employed with the *Ratsmusiker*[53], several handwritten parts would have been copied out. It cannot be denied, however, that more than one person involved with such a large-scale performance would have found the multiple-bass score useful, especially but not only the cantor and the main organist. If the polychoral pieces were performed with maximal spatial separation as suggested in the documents for St. Peter's cited above, multiple-bass notation would have been very useful indeed. Perhaps St. Mary's found a use within its own walls for Hieronymus Praetorius's gift to St. Peter's. In the absence of any proof of such an arrangement, this will have to remain conjecture.

Gumpelzhaimer's indication of the use of multiple organs in his *Partitio* points to another important issue: these parts were primarily conceived for organists, leading to the question of how to interpret any text written into multiple-bass parts or tablatures[54]. Several sources of Hieronymus Praetorius' multiple-bass scores have handwritten additions of text underlay which has caused some to question if they were used by organists at all. Among others, Michael Praetorius recommends supplying the *bassus generalis* to the capellmeister or other directors, and, accordingly, the most prevalent interpretation of handwritten text underlay has been that it is a strong indication of use as a directing score, if not an unequivocal one[55]. This argument

---

and with both organs and bring about figural music, according to their best ability [...] They shall bring along as many competent persons as necessary from the *Brüderschaft* [...] so that a musical performance of 3 or 4 choirs can be achieved»). The organist of St. Peter's from 1619 to 1641was Johannes Ratke. See STAHL 1952, p. 71. If the music sounded from both organs and the rood screen, there was considerable spatial separation between the choirs. See fn. 75 for Michael Praetorius on placement of choirs in churches. See also fn. 74.

[51]. See fn. 22.

[52]. SNYDER 2015, *The Database Catalogue*.

[53]. STAHL 1952, p. 56. Consider also the plucked instruments noted in fn. 50 above.

[54]. For a discussion of direction from *basso continuo* scores see KITE-POWELL 2021, pp. 30-36.

[55]. PRAETORIUS 1619, pp. 144, 124-145, 125. «Es ist auch meines einfältigen erachtens diß der vornembste und beste Nutz des Generalbasses / daß er / sonderlich einem Capellmeister und andern Musicorum Chororum Directoribus zu gut / ein fein Compendium ist / [...] / Damit er nicht allein des Tacts halben / wenn sich derselbe in Tripeln und sonsten verendert / sondern auch einen unnd dem andern Chor einzuhelffen / den gantzen Gesang

has long been in existence; even Kinkeldey makes a point of relativising Emil Bohn's theory that a number of organ tablatures in Wrocław served as directing scores for the capellmeister, pointing out that many are transposed[56]. Transposition is very common in organ scores made for the accompaniment of vocal works, both in the tablatures and in manuscripts using mensural notation as well. One important aspect that would lead to transposition is inherent in the instrument itself, or, more specifically, in its tuning system. In his preface to his 1611 organ part which uses multiple-bass notation, Caspar Vincentius states that he has left all the pieces in the same keys as the vocal parts and then gives the following explanation for transposition: Since d-sharps were not available on the organs in his region, the organ pipe in question being tuned to e-flat, the organists were required to transpose for performances of pieces that otherwise would have used this pitch[57]. Vincentius implies in his discussion that he expected organists to be able to transpose from the printed score without copying out the part. In manuscript scores that are transposed, however, the use of text underlay is actually very common, and these, being transposed, are obviously for organ[58], whether tablatures, multiple-bass parts or even single-line organ basses. Pieces in the Munich copy[59] of OM-4 (see figure 3) even have handwritten note letters to aid in transposition while still using extensive text underlay in the same piece[60]. The Tenor partbook of the same set has an early modern, handwritten addition so that it reads «*deudschen BASSUM CONTINUUM pro Organo*», i.e., «German Basso Continuo for

---

vor sich haben möge» («It is my humble opinion that the best and most effective use of the thoroughbass is as an artful compendium of the parts; such a thoroughbass is ... especially beneficial to the music director and other conductors. [...] This will enable him to be aware not only of a change in the beat to triple meter or something else, but also to assist in cueing in the various choirs»). Translation from KITE-POWELL 2004, p. 134. PRAETORIUS 1619, p. 170 «Alß denn mus der Capellenmeister / oder ein ander der des Tacts gewis / den General-Bass vor sich haben / und den Tact also führen / daß ihn der Chorus Musicorum in der Kirchen auff der einen und die Trommeter auff der andern seiten / sonderlich aber der der die Quint, oder wie sie es meistentheils nennen / den Principal führet / sehen und sich darnach richten können». («With the help of the thoroughbass part, the choirmaster, or whoever is responsible for keeping the beat, must lead the group of musicians in the choir and the trumpeters in the nave, especially the person paying the *Quint* or, as it is usually called, the *Principal*. All members must be able to see him [the person keeping the beat] and follow his lead»). Translation from KITE-POWELL 2004, p. 173.

56. KINKELDEY 1910, p. 191.

57. RISM B/I 1611[1]. «Præterea, quia in his regionibus organorum atque instrumentorum Calculi sive Claves ita confisiuntur, ne in ♮ duro tertium majorem habeamus Organista facile sibi imaginabitur, [C4], esse [F4 with B-flat] & habebit Quintam inferiorem» («Besides, since in these regions the *calculi*, or keys, of instruments are finished (tuned) in such a way that there is no major third with b natural (i.e., d-sharp), the organist will quickly notice that the C4 clef means F4 with a b-flat and use the fifth below»). English translation mine. Thanks to Manfred Cordes for help with the original Latin.

58. As argued by Kinkeldey, transposition would have been of no value to a conductor. KINKELDEY 1910, p. 191.

59. D-Mbs 4 Mus. pr. 64723. This exemplar has old stamps from D-Hs. See NEUBACHER 1997. Especially pp. 21-22. See APPENDIX 2.

60. D-Mbs 4 Mus. pr. 64723. *Bassus continuus*, numbers XXX and VIII.

Ill. 3: Fol. C5r from the *Bassus Continuus* of OM-4 held in D-Mbs. München, Bayerische Staatsbibliothek, shelfmark 4 Mus.pr. 64723. Used with permission.

Organ»[61], which would seem to imply what the original users of this copy of the print thought about its use.

---

[61]. Handwritten additions bold: «Cui in gratiam Musicae peritorum additum habes **deudschen** BASSUM CONTINUUM **pro Organo** («from whom you have in thanks of music an added expert **German** *Bassus Continuus* **for organ**»). The particular 'German-ness' of this organ part needs to be considered. Perhaps the writer meant to distinguish it from parts with figures as produced by disciples of Viadana or even in contrast to single-line organ basses, both of which, being more modern, may have been thought of as Italian. For Michael Praetorius' use of *pro organo* see Kite-Powell 2022, especially p. 15.

There are also examples of handwritten multiple-bass parts[62] and some of these are written in tablature notation[63]. A manuscript basso continuo book[64] written in mensural notation in Fulda around 1615 and now held in Kassel shows two attempts to make an organ part for Hieronymus Praetorius' eight-voice *Angelus ad pastores ait* from an edition of OM-1which predates the printed organ partbook of 1622[65]. The first attempt, a single line *basso pro organo*, is crossed out and then, following another work, the piece appears again written in multiple-bass notation on two lines. Handwritten examples, particularly if transposed, suggest their use took place at the organ, but it is worth considering that the director and organist may have been following the practice described by Lodovico Viadana in 1612, who wrote that «the director must stand in front of this five-part choir, always keeping an eye on the basso continuo of the organist and giving the entries for the choir»[66]. It is equally worth considering that the same book may have enjoyed various kinds of use by different people in different roles for different performances. While it is certainly possible, and in some cases even likely, that a printed organ partbook was used as a conducting score[67], its primary function was to serve organists, and text underlay cannot be considered as conclusive evidence that a book was not used at the keyboard, whether in a printed score or manuscript.

Whereas printed parts support the idea that the use of several copies of the same part for multiple players was the primary reason for multiple-bass notation, handwritten parts of

---

[62]. D-Mbs 4° Mus. Pr. 23/4 is one example. The manuscript is bound together with the Munich copy of RISM A/I G270 and other works. It is dated 1600-1610 and came from the monastery on Tegernsee. See Münster 1968.

[63]. PL-Wn 326 Cim. I am indebted to Marcin Szelest for drawing my attention to this source. See Wojnowska 2016.

[64]. D-Kl 2° Ms. Mus. 62i. See Kahlfuss – Gottwald 1997, pp. 206-207.

[65]. This *bassus continuus* will have been created from the vocal parts from one of the earlier editions, RISM A/I P5336 (OM-1) or RISM A/I P5337 (OM-1), printed in 1599 and 1607 respectively. The 1622 edition that includes the organ part, RISM A/I P5338 (OM-1) uses a single-line *basso pro organo*, not multiple-bass, as stated above. The *Secunda pars* in the manuscript is incomplete, where the final page appears to have been lost.

[66]. RISM A/I V1400. «Il Maestro di Capella, starà nell'istesso Choro a Cinque, guardando sempre su 'l Basso Continuo dell'Organista». Translation from Wielakker 1998, pp. 2-3. Also missing in the German translation in Winter 1964, p. 43, «of the organist» was added by me.

[67]. See discussion of manuscript text underlay in D-LÜh below. In the copy of RISM A/I P5334 (OM-2) in D-LEm ii. 2. 11a, for example, there is a note following a piece that refers to a tablature that can be consulted for clarification regarding the rests in the second choir suggesting that a conductor may have used the *bassus continuus* book. At the same time, the piece in question has thoroughbass figures added suggesting use at the organ. It is possible that one organist played from the printed book while another played from the tablature, whereby the conductor followed the printed copy. The note found on the recto side of the folio with gathering stamp C2 reads: «Allhier soll beÿm 2. Chor zu innerung / gethan werden eines orts wegen <u>der pausen</u> / wie auch anders orts wegen deß Tacts, / welches aus der Tabulatur in Libr A. / sub No: 191. Zu ersehen» (*«Here the second choir should be reminded in one instance because of the rests as well as elsewhere because of the beat which can be seen in the tablature in Libr. A / sub No: 191»*).

the same kind, like those cited above, suggest that this notation may not have this purpose exclusively. In fact, there is plenty of evidence that polychoral music was accompanied by a single organist, and in Northern Europe, particularly in Hanseatic cities, a large organ with several manuals was likely to be available that could provide a colourful and convincing performance. Even in Italy, it appears to have been common for large, fixed single-manual organs, the *grossi da muro*, to accompany polychoral music throughout, unifying the performance and centralising aural orientation, whereby additional, optional positive organs could be added to support individual choirs that were placed further away from the main organ[68]. Viadana's part for the main organ from the 1612 *Salmi* cited above, called *Basso generale per l'organo*, indicates that this instrument is to play continuously through each piece, whereas the organ parts for choirs positioned away from the large organ give rests when the choir to be accompanied is not singing. This is an alternative notation to Michael Praetorius's idea of writing out the entire thoroughbass and underlining the parts to be played in red, although the desired results of both would be identical. Considering the rests, the Viadana parts for the third and fourth choirs can hardly be considered a true *basso continuo*, since they are not continuous for the entire piece. In 1643, Thomas Selle, the cantor of the *Johanneum* in Hamburg, had a name for a bass part that was not written out for an entire piece, calling it a *bassus continuus corruptus*[69]. The 'corruption' of the part is to be understood as decomposition, i.e., the part is a piece of a composite, in contrast to a thorough, or complete bass. According to this line of thinking, a multiple-bass part must be thought of as a *bassus continuus integer*, whereby each individual line of the same multiple-bass part, if taken out of context, would be a *bassus continuus corruptus*.

A large instrument north of the Alps could use different sounds on different manuals, spatially separated in different divisions, to imitate multiple continuo players[70]. The Pelplin tablatures contain examples of double-choir pieces where lowest sounding notes not in the bottom line of tablature are underlined in red[71]. This clarification in red ink would aid the

---

[68]. One clear example of this practice is Viadana's *Salmi*, cited above as RISM A/1 V1400, which includes three separate organ parts: the second two accompany choirs three and four exclusively, while the first organ plays throughout. There is no indication in the first organ part as to which choir sings when, but there is information regarding the number of voices in general at any given time. See also MORELLI 1994.

[69]. D-Hs Skrin 251. The Passion of St. John was copied in manuscript in 1643. Thomas Selle uses the term *bassus continuus corruptus* for the plucked instrument parts that only play at certain times when accompanying certain characters in the passion. The *bassus continuus integer* gives the basso continuo for the entire piece. I have never seen the term *bassus continuus corruptus* applied to polychoral music. See PÖCHE 2018 for more on Selle's Passions.

[70]. See also KITE-POWELL 2021 pp. 53-55 and p. 56.

[71]. PL-PE Ms 305 (SUTOWSKI – OSOSTOWICZ-SUTKOWSKA 1965: Number 241). Thanks to Marcin Szelest for first pointing this information regarding the colouration out to me. The introduction to the facsimile edition also refers to the red colouration on p. viii. Red colouration of the same kind is also found in PL-PE Ms 307 (see p. viii of facsimile edition for a list). See JOHNSON 1989 for an overview of organ tablatures.

organist by ensuring that the realisation be based upon the correct bass note in tutti sections, but it could also be an indication for playing a line in the pedal with a 16' stop, whereby different choirs could be accompanied on different manuals. This precise practice was recommended by Matthäus Hertel in his treatise on the organ and its use from 1666[72].

> Here it is most important to observe that one [plays] an 8-voiced motet that is set with high and low choirs such that the high choir is always [accompanied] on a single manual, be it the *oberwerk* or the *rückpositiv*, and it is the same for the low choir, that it be played on the other manual, so that each choir, where possible, has its own manual [for accompaniment]. And when one manual is more strongly registered than the other, the louder manual with pedal is used when both choirs sing together, in my opinion the *oberwerk* is best suited for this[73].

Although there were surely smaller instruments available in places like Hamburg[74] such as those whose use is recommended for the accompaniment of individual choirs by Michael Praetorius and Viadana, and while these were surely used for polychoral music, particularly in schools and at banquets, the integration of the main organ into church performances must not be dismissed, and multiple-bass notation would have only been beneficial for such use, with the largest instrument giving orientation to the entire group[75]. Looking at the organ parts Hieronymus Praetorius prepared and printed in 1622 and 1625, he attempts to impart the same information a multiple-bass part would give while using a single line. The organ part of the 1622 edition of *Cantiones sacrae* (OM-1) has a short preface[76] in which Hieronymus explains

---

[72]. HERTEL 1666, p. 21. Tablatures such as those by Johann Woltz and from Braunsberg and Oliva also support this playing style. See SZELEST 2021, p 53. See also KITE-POWELL 2022, pp. 2-3 for use of the pedal in the context of Michael Praetorius' music.

[73]. HERTEL 1666, p. 21. Translation mine. «Hierbey ist aber nun vornehmlich zu mercken, das eine Motet von 8, so hoch= und tieff gesetzet, man allezeit das hohe Chor auff einem Clavier alleine, als im Oberwercke oder Rückpositiff: gilt gleiche: spiele, das tieffe aber allezeit auff dem andern Claviere, das also zu jedem Chor, wo man es haben kann, ein sonderlich Clavier nehme, doch das ein Clavier umb ein Stimmwerck stärcker als das ander gezogen werde, wan aber beide Chor zusammen fallen, man alsdann das starcke Clavier nebst dem Pedal gebrauche, hierzu ist aber meines erachtens am bequemsten das Oberwerck».

[74]. Before the 1640s, regals were common instruments for use in the chancel, on choir lofts called *Sängeremporen* that took the place of rood screens in Hanseatic cities. See KJERSGAARD – WÖLFEL 2005, and DAVIDSON 1991, p. 23.

[75]. Michael Praetorius also writes about the various places in churches where one could place choirs, mentioning specifically that suitable places for the separation of choirs can be found in old churches, and that the Italians place one group above the other as in King David's time. PRAETORIUS 1619, pp. 135, 115 and KITE-POWELL 2004, p. 125.

[76]. The OM-1 foreword can be found in APPENDIX 1. This and the short statements referring to it in OM-2, OM-3 and OM-5 can be found in GABLE 2008 (OM-2), pp. xxii-xxiii and GABLE 2014 (OM-3), pp. xxiv-xxv with an English translation.

his use of the numbers 1 to 3 to denote which choir is singing, and his use of *P* (*plenum*) to denote the places where all the choirs sing at the same time. He sometimes uses the *P* quite literally, for example if the choirs overlap for the space of a single note. At other times the *P* seems to be more interpretive, as if showing at what point to start using a louder sound by changing manuals or adding stops. At times, the part has a rather cluttered look that begs to be deciphered. In contrast to other composers who were primarily concerned with an appropriate accompaniment depending on the number of musicians performing at a given time, it appears to have been of great importance to Praetorius to clarify which choir was being accompanied at any given time. Considering this, multiple-bass notation may well have been preferred by the composer, whereby the single-line organ parts he produced later would have been a compromise, albeit more modern and efficient in terms of the number of pages required for a part. The hybrid editions of OM-4, not having been updated into single-line parts but reproduced using their original, multiple-bass notation only supports the presumption that Hieronymus Praetorius saw value in parts of this sort.

The manuscript additions in the Lübeck copy of the OM-4 organ book all follow the observations and interpretations made above and provide insight into the use of multiple-bass parts in a wealthy Hanseatic city. In this exemplar, five works with multiple-bass notation have handwritten entries in the form of text underlay and other signs. No thoroughbass figures were written into the score. The triple-choir motet, XXXIII *Angelus ad pastores ait* shows cleanly written text underlay for all the choirs[77], while XXXV *Exultate justi* for four choirs gives equally clean text underlay for the fourth choir only. This careful writing, unlike that of the text underlay to be discussed below for the double-choir pieces, may well be a sign that for the works for more than two choirs, the *bassus continuus* book was used by the director, Hermann Bielefeldt. It could also be an indication that the organist of St. Peter's, Johannes Ratke, had a particularly important role in *Exultate justi* if the texting of a single choir means that this motet was performed analogously to the description of the German *Te Deum* for the 1607 dedication service of St. Gertrude's in Hamburg where the parts of the entire fourth choir were played by the organ[78], presumably with one of the vocal parts sung so that the entire liturgical text could be heard in full[79]. The other choirs for that performance were all scored for maximal colour, whereby only the first choir, positioned in the front of the church, was sung in all four voices and choirs two and three were performed mostly by instruments. More than half a century later, a member of the next generation of Hamburg organists, Heinrich Scheidemann,

---

77. The fragment of the German *Te Deum*, No. XXXVI *Herr Gott dich loben wir*, consisting only of the first line, has text underlay for all four choirs.

78. GABLE 1998, p. viii. «Dat veerde up de Orgel» quoted from Lucas van Cöllen's sermon of 1609. The piece described here is presumably identical with the setting first published in pamphlet form in 1612 and then in 1618 in OM-4. See also GABLE 1987.

79. GABLE 1998, p. xx.

performed Andreas Hammerschmidt's 12-part motet, *Alleluja, Lobet den Herrn*, published in 1646, «partly from the choir and partly from the organ by the choir, solo singers, and also by an ensemble of five voices and five instruments. Specific stops were pulled on the organ and string and wind instrument sounds (such as violins, flutes, cornettos, trombones, and cymbals) were heard which the text itself requires»[80]. These are two documented examples from the 17th century where the skills of an organist-virtuoso from Hamburg were showcased in performing either an entire choir or significant parts of a large ensemble work as part of an augmented accompaniment in a polychoral motet.

As suggested above, the particular care in the writing of the text observed in the triple-choir and quadruple-choir pieces may be a sign, although not a conclusive one, that the book may have been used by the director for those motets. Other written indications in the scores of the double-choir motets, however, suggest strongly that the organist played from this copy of the *bassus continuus*. The pieces XXVII *Ecce Maria genuit* and XXIX *Ein Kindelein so löbelich* show precisely the kind of additions one might expect a single organist to write into the part (see ILLS. 4 and 5). The carelessly written text underlay[81] appears to indicate the line of music upon which to base the accompaniment. There are also indications showing where to switch lines in *Ecce Maria genuit*. In *Ein Kindelein so löbelich*, similar abbreviations to those used by the composer in and after 1622 are written into the score. The indication *Ple* for *plenum* is written in twice when both choirs are singing more or less homophonically. In one case, the number *2* is written to show that the second choir is singing, which is obvious from the multiple bass score. These additions may indicate registration or manual changes, giving clearer instructions as to how to realise the part and augmenting the more conceptual information of the multiple-bass notation. They may also show that the organist was more comfortable playing from the single-line organ parts in the other volumes and used the abbreviations found there as described above. In another instance, while perhaps redundant due to the change in clef (C3), the indication *T1* is given, emphasising that the printed line doubles the tenor voice from the first choir. In some cases, when both choirs are singing simultaneously, the text is not written under the lowest sounding bass part which shows that the user was not always systematic, at least not in a way readily understood 400 years later. Indications for musical commas may occur in the form of little vertical lines. Beyond clarifying the phrasing, the handwritten additions are anything but

---

80. DIRKSEN 2007, pp. 202-204. «Auf dieselbe ist theils auf dem Chor / theils auf der Orgel / die XXXIIX. Motet aus dem Hammerschmidt / mit zwölf Stimmen / Chor- und concerts-weise / auch der capella von Fünff Stimmen / dazu fünff Instrumenten der gestalt gemachet und figuriret worden / daß die jenigen Stimmen in der Orgel angezogen / und die Instrumenta mit Seyten und Pfeiffen (als Geigen / Flöten / Cornötten / Posaunen und Cymbeln) gebrauchet worden / welche der Text selbst erfodert». English translation in *ibidem* by Frederick Gable. See also SNYDER 2007, pp. 128-129. The motet was taken from RISM A/I H 1931.

81. The writer even uses German *Kurrent* script within Latin words in at least one instance. There are also instances of incorrect texts written into the score.

ILL. 4: Fol. C2r from the *Bassus Continuus* of OM-4 held in D-LÜh. XXVII *Ecce Maria genuit.* Orientation line in the last bar of the third system. Stadtbibliothek Lübeck, shelfmark A 205e. Used with permission.

unequivocal in terms of what they mean specifically for performance, but in each instance, they do augment or reinforce information about the piece itself that the organist would find useful to develop a better accompaniment, much in the same way the red notation in the Pelplin tablatures highlights information that is already there[82]. If the multiple-bass scores can be thought of as a reduction of a block tablature using single-line *basso seguente* notation for each

---

82. See above.

ILL 5: Fol. C4r from the *Bassus Continuus* of OM-4 held in D-LÜh. XXIX *Ein Kindelein so löbelich*. 'T1' in third to last bar of first system. 'Ple' before second to last bar of fourth system. '2' on lowest line of staff four bars before the end of the fourth system. Vertical phrasing mark in last bar of second system. Stadtbibliothek Lübeck, shelfmark A 205e. Used with permission.

choir, then the visual effect of the printed entries could lead a single player to any number of flexible, intuitive solutions in terms of the registration, manual changes, and whether the vocal parts should be doubled or freely embellished[83]. It is the flexibility afforded by this notation through its efficient means of relaying maximal information that is its greatest benefit.

Presuming that Hieronymus Praetorius had very quick access to the newest prints of musical volumes, it is not outside the realm of possibility that he could have seen actual examples of printed organ parts for his own works in anthologies that pre-date his own. His 8-part *Puer qui natus est* (OM-1) was among the multiple-bass parts prepared by Caspar Vincentius (Gaspar Vincent) for the third volume of the *Promptuarium musicum*[84] printed in 1613; the same work was issued in 1621 in the second part of the *Florilegium musicum portense*[85] with a single-line organ part[86]. Both examples use thoroughbass figures. Whether the composer knew either of these collections or not, they are datable examples of the kind of organ parts familiar to him and they or parts like them would have surely influenced his choices in his own publications[87].

In his 1622 preface explaining the indications in the organ book, Praetorius also writes that he does not disapprove of the use of thoroughbass figures, but dismisses the practice, saying that a skilled organist can discern the intervals more easily by hearing them as opposed to seeing them, especially when rests and notes of short values do not allow time to look ahead[88]. Certain ambiguities in the figuring as found in both anthologies could certainly confound a performer and create confusion where otherwise there would be none. In the *Promptuarium*, thoroughbass figures are fairly consistent in terms of the placement of sharps and flats on a line or space corresponding to the note, irrespective of the appropriate octave, that is to be raised or lowered. The *Florilegium* simply places these figures above the staff. That would not necessarily be a problem if accidentals referring to the bass notes were not placed above the staff as well. In one of the most confounding examples from this anthology (see Ill. 6), the figures of three

---

[83]. Kite-Powell 2021, pp. 56-69 as cited above for explanations of 'stacked' and 'block' tablatures. The single-line *basso pro organo*, according to this analogy, would be comparable to a stacked tablature.

[84]. RISM B/I 1613². Hereafter *Promptuarium*.

[85]. RISM B/I 1621². Hereafter *Florilegium*.

[86]. Holger Eichhorn speculated that the *Florilegium* organ part may have been prepared by Vincentius as well. I would argue that whoever made it used the *Promptuarium* as a template but was probably not the same individual. See Eichhorn 1995, especially p. 65.

[87]. There is no indication of either of these compilations having been in Hamburg at the time in question. The *Promptuarium* was in the library of St. Mary's in Lübeck, but it had been purchased by Martin Lincke and thus became part of the library after Hieronymus' death. See Snyder 2015, *The Database Catalogue*.

[88]. This part of Hieronymus Praetorius' foreword was already translated into German by Johann Mattheson in Mattheson 1735, pp. 43ff. who then seeks to prove that figures were indeed necessary by showing harmonically ambiguous examples for the bassline of one of Praetorius' own pieces. Mattheson's translation is quoted in Abraham 1961, pp. 25-26 and again in Freiberg 2004, p. 236. The OM-1 foreword can be found in Appendix 2. See fn. 76.

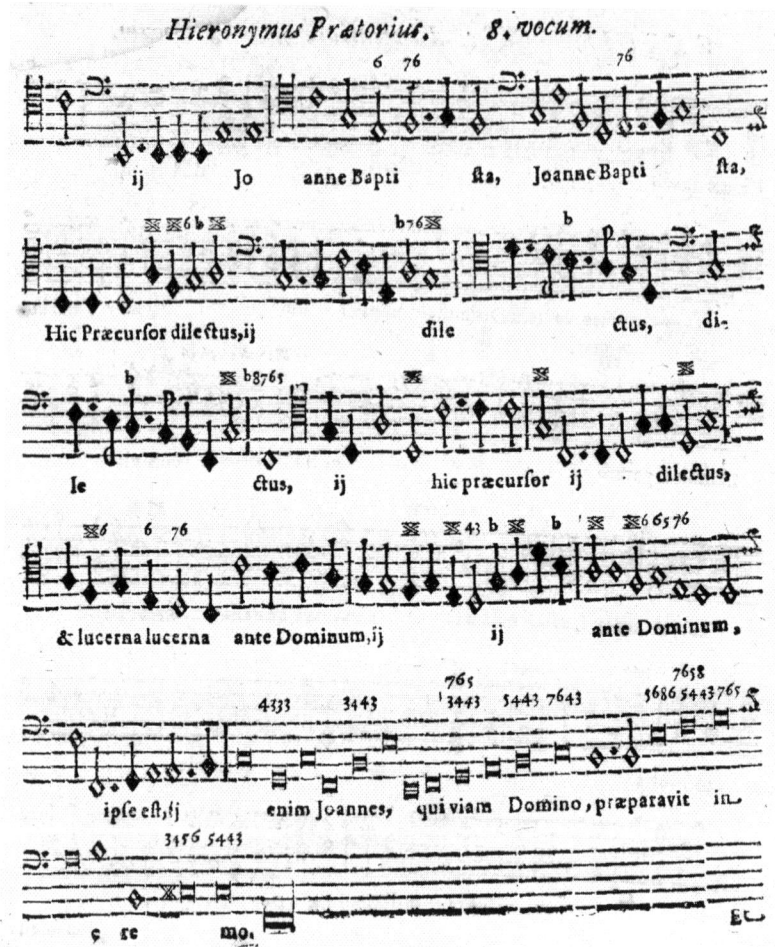

ILL. 6: No. CXXVI *Puer qui natus est* by Hieronymus Praetorius from the *Florilegium Portense II* (RISM B/I 1621²). See the thorough bass figures at the beginning of the second line. SLUB Dresden, <https://digital.slub-dresden.de/werkansicht/dlf/197099/1853#>. (Public domain.)

consecutive notes, all printed above the staff, each mean different things. The first sharp refers to the third above the bass, the second to the bass note itself. The 6b that straddles the g does not indicate an e-flat, as the 6 belongs to the previous bass note, f-sharp, indicated by the accidental above the staff that precedes the 6, while the b refers to the third above the bass note g. Beyond this, considering the inconsistency in Praetorius's own prints of placing accidentals referring to the bass note either before the note or above the note, his concerns about figuring can be imagined. This lack of consistency would seem to be the reason for errors in both anthologies where accidentals referring to the thirds above the bass were incorrectly placed in front of the bass note.

ILL. 7: No. XIX *Puer qui natus est* by Hieronymus Praetorius from the *Promptuarium III* (RISM B/I 1613²). The bass of choir 1 above the second breve (d) in choir 2 of the final system is translated into thorough bass figures in the *Florilegium*. See penultimate note on penultimate line of ILL. 6. Munich, Bayerische Staatsbibliothek shelfmark 4 Mus.pr. 450-1/4. Used with permission.

Unlike Gumpelzhaimer, Vincentius seems to have had a single organ in mind for the part he prepared for the *Promptuarium*. At times, he composes a new organ bass that functions as such for the first choir, but the passages of this kind found in the final systems of *Puer qui natus est* would be very unusual to use as a point of departure for a continuo realisation if they were intended to be played by an additional organist serving the first choir. In fact, the *Florilegium* reduces Vincentius's bassline of the first choir to figures placed over the single-line organ bass, supporting the point that at the very least, some contemporaries thought that this organ part was intended to be interpreted by one person (see ILLS. 7 and 6).

Considering the 1607 dedication service of St. Gertrude's chapel once again, Praetorius himself was the organist, and it is notable that in the original documents it is emphasised that he dedicated the new organ[89] at the same service. He was also paid one *Thaler* more than the cantor, placing even a monetary emphasis on the central role of the main instrument and its player[90]. If sounding continuously during the polychoral works, the 2-manual organ would have surely held each composition together, using different manuals and registrations depending on which choir was sounding at a given time, with the tutti sections using the strongest registration with the pedals. Such a performance structure, although presumably using sub-directors to help keep spatially separated choirs together, would be in line with the contemporaneous English cathedral practice of directing choirs via organ accompaniment rather than by conducting[91]. At the time of the dedication of St. Gertrude's, the printed *bassus continuus* part of 1618 did not yet exist, and it is easy to imagine that this performance and others like it may have influenced Hieronymus Praetorius in his thinking about what information to convey in an organ part and how to convey it, perhaps leading to his decision to use multiple-bass notation.

Multiple-bass notation is flexible. As an abbreviated form of a block tablature or full score in terms of the information it gives, these scores allow for a wide variety of performance options for polychoral accompaniment as they may have taken place in Hanseatic cities. These can be categorised as follows:

1. The basses are divided up among different instruments and players allotted to specific choirs, as recommended by Ribrochus and prepared for by Gumpelzhaimer whereby each organist plays from the same score;

2. The large organ plays everything using multiple manuals and pedal as described by Hertel;

3. The large organ plays everything, while other, smaller instruments placed directly among individual choirs play only with these choirs, as recommended by Viadana and Michael Praetorius;

4. The large organ may perform one of the choirs or parts of a choir by itself as reported for the performances by Hieronymus Praetorius and possibly implied by the Lübeck copy of OM-4 for No. XXXV, or may even add soloistic elements as described for Heinrich Scheidemann's performance in Otterndorf;

[89]. The Scherer organ that was installed under the recommendation of Hieronymus Praetorius is long gone. Johann Kortkamp instigated a rebuild from 1699-1700 by Arp Schnitger, whereby the structure of the instrument, as well as 6 stops, were preserved. It had 2 manuals: Werk, Brustwerk, and Pedal. In 1842 it was destroyed by the great fire of Hamburg. See FOCK 1974, p. 69, and GABLE 1998, pp. xxvi-xxvii.

[90]. KRÜGER 1933, pp. 195-196. See also the descriptions of the organ dedication in Otterndorf in DIRKSEN 2007, pp. 201-204, and SNYDER 2007, pp. 128-129.

[91]. HOLMAN 2020, pp. 43-57, especially p. 44, where Holman writes: «The norm was for the organist to lead the choir just by accompanying it [...]». For more on conducting see KITE-POWELL 2021.

5. Any combination of the above, depending on the place of performance and instruments available for use, and of course a multiple-bass part would be useful for the director of the ensemble, who, if not the organist himself, could follow the organist's part or hold his own copy if multiple copies were available, whether manuscript or printed.

Multiple-bass notation provides the musician or musicians using it with an efficient reduction of the full score making possible various intelligent, multi-faceted accompaniments. By presenting a picture of the entire piece, this notation also serves the purposes of the director of the ensemble, whether the capellmeister, the organist, or both, whether working in tandem from the same score or multiple copies of the same score in different roles. If the performance took place in the back of a large Hanseatic church with a large organ of several manuals and pedals ordering and leading the music throughout, this instrument would be worthy of Athanasius Kircher's analogy of the organ, a *Welt-Orgel*, to the world and of the organist to the creator Himself[92].

Appendix 1

Hieronymus Praetorius' Foreword to the *Bassus Continuus* Book of OM-1, Hamburg, 1622

Lector Benevole, ut Compendium et tibi & mihi Bassi nostri Continui facerem, in ijs, quæ plurium videlicet octo, decem vel duodecim vocum sunt, choros numeris & litera P. distinximus, 1. ergo primum, 2. secundum, 3. tertium, P plenum chorum notat. Solent & alij in hoc Bassi genere numeros notulis subjungere varios pro cantus diversitate indicaturi intervalla, quos ego non improbo, conatum laudo, attamen præter rem eos facere duco; quia enim Bassi hujus Continui solius nec in instrumentali nec in vocali Musica usus est sine reliquarum vocum connexu planè nullus, credo ego Muscæ peritum & organistam commodius & facilius ex auditu discernere intervalla posse quam visu illa assequi, inprimis cum suspiria celerrima visus moram nun patiantur, ut alia taceam impedimenta. Id scire te volui, tu quod ex re tua erit his utere, & nobis bene precare, Vale[93].

Kind Reader, so that I might provide instructions for our basso continuo, both for you and me, in those many-voiced pieces of eight, ten, or twelve parts, I have distinguished the choirs with numbers and with the letter P: 1. is for the first choir, 2. for the second, 3. for the third, P notates the entire chorus. Others are accustomed in this type of bass part to place various numbers as little marks underneath the bass line to indicate the intervals according to the flow of the cantus. I don't disapprove of this, and I praise the attempt. Nevertheless, I follow a different practice in this matter. Because this *bassus continuus* is clearly worthless by itself unless joined with the remaining voices, whether instrumental or vocal, I believe that a skilled musician and organist can discern those intervals more easily and conveniently by hearing them than by seeing them, especially when fast notes and short rests do not allow time to look ahead, not to mention other difficulties. I wanted you to know this. Use this as you will, and pray well for us, farewell[94].

---

[92]. Kircher 1662, p. 253.

[93]. RISM A/I P5338 (OM-1), fol. A1v.

[94]. English translation with help from Hans von Busch. Compare with Gable 2014 (OM-3), pp. xxiv-xxv and Mattheson 1735.

APPENDIX 2

The Sources for the *Bassus Continuus* book of OM-4

B-Br Fétis 1.963 C 4 (RP)

The Brussels copy is part of a complete set of 9 partbooks of OM-1-5, where the volumes are bound together in each partbook. It was originally held by D-B as shown by the stamp «VEND. EX BIBL. REG. BEROL.» The entire source is available online.

D-B Mus. ant. pract. P 1185a

Only the *bassus continuus* partbook of OM-4 is held in Berlin. This copy is a hybrid edition where gatherings D and E are variant[95].

D-BDk K: M 2044

Originally from the St. Katharinenkirche in Brandenburg, this source has manuscript additions including dates of performances. It is bound together with the volumes of OM-1-3 in the 1622 collector's edition, and part of a complete set of 9 partbooks of OM-1-4[96].

D-Hs Scrin. A/617 (4)

The complete set of 9 partbooks of OM-1-4, of which this *bassus continuus* book is part, was presented to the city library of Hamburg by Hieronymus Praetorius in 1623 and is the first book of music to have been obtained by that institution. The 4 volumes of each partbook are elaborately bound together in this clean collector's edition of 1622[97].

D-LEm II. 2. 11a

The city library of Leipzig holds a copy of the *bassus continuus* partbook of OM-4, bound together with those of OM-2 and OM-3; no vocal partbooks are in the collection. OM-4 is a hybrid edition where gathering E is variant. The pages of OM-4 are raw, whereas those of OM-2 and OM-3 are cleanly cut. Manuscript additions are written throughout the source which is available online. A second copy of the *bassus continuus* of OM-2 is held as II. 2. 11b. Both books were once in the collection of Carl Ferdinand Becker[98].

D-LÜh A205e

The Lübeck source of the 1622 collector's edition of OM-1-4 has the four volumes bound into individual partbooks. Hieronymus Praetorius presented the set, which is now incomplete, to St. Peter's church of Lübeck as a gift in 1622. It preserves S, T, B and 7 (A205a-d) together with the *bassus continuus* (A205e) for which the title page of OM-4 and gatherings E and F are missing excepting the first folio of E; pages are also missing from OM-2 and the title page of OM-1 is incomplete. Manuscript additions are found in several pieces throughout all the partbooks. The cover of the *bassus continuus* partbook is stamped «B.C. / S PETERS KIRCHEN / 1622». A

---

[95]. Many thanks to Roland Schmidt-Hensel of the SBB for his assistance.
[96]. Many thanks to Uwe Czubatynski of the Domstiftarchiv in Brandenburg for this information.
[97]. Many thanks to Jürgen Neubacher of the Staats- und Universitätsbibliothek, Hamburg for his assistance.
[98]. Many thanks to Brigitte Geyer of the Stadtbibliothek, Leipzig for her assistance.

second set of 8 vocal partbooks, also with the volumes from OM-1-4 bound together, is held by the library as well; it has no markings and unclear provenance, although it is sometimes referred to as being from the church of St. Giles (A205f-n)[99].

D-Mbs 4 Mus. pr. 64723
This complete set of 9 partbooks of OM-4 is available online. The source has many manuscript additions. It was originally held in Hamburg as seen by the stamp «BIBL: HAMBURG PUBLICA DUPLUM VENDITUM».

D-SAh Y 24 h
The Saalfeld source is part of an incomplete set of OM-1-5 where the volumes are bound together in partbooks. Y 24 a-g are the shelf marks for C, A, 5, 6, 7, 8, and B, whereby T is missing. The *bassus continuus* is currently displayed in a case in the museum[100].

GB-Lbl Music Collections C.78.(4.)
The British Library holds a copy of the OM-4 *bassus continuus* that is bound with those from OM-1, OM-2 and OM-3 as part of a complete set of the 9 partbooks of OM-1-4 in the 1622 collector's edition. According to the catalogue, the combined title page is in the *Bassus* partbook[101].

PL-Kj BJ Mus. ant. pract. P 1185 [4]
Part of complete set of 9 partbooks of OM-1-5, the 5 *bassus continuus* partbooks of OM-1-5 are bound separately into distinct volumes whereas the 8 vocal partbooks of OM-1-5 have the volumes bound together. The *bassus continuus* has manuscript additions of text underlay in red ink. This source was once held in Berlin as shown by the stamp «Ex Biblioth. Regia Berolinensi»[102].

Bibliography

Abraham 1961
Abraham, Lars Ulrich. *Der Generalbass im Schaffen des Michael Praetorius und seine harmonischen Voraussetzungen*, Berlin, Merseburger, 1961.

Belotti 2018
Belotti, Edoardo. 'Adriano Banchieri and the Theory and Practice of Counterpoint and Basso Continuo in the Seventeenth Century', in: *The Organ Yearbook*, xlvii (2018), pp. 49-78.

Boghardt 1993
Boghardt, Martin. 'Partial Duplicate Setting: Means of Rationalization or Complicating Factor in Textual Transmission?', in: *The Library*, xv/4 (1993), pp. 306-331.

---

[99]. Many thanks to Arndt Schnoor of the Stadtbibliothek, Lübeck for his assistance and allowing me to publish my photographs of the Lübeck copy.

[100]. Many thanks to Dirk Henning of the Stadtmuseum Saalfeld im Franziskanerkloster for this information.

[101]. Many thanks to Elias Mazzucco of the British Library for this information.

[102]. Many thanks to Maria Porębska of the Biblioteka Jagiellońska in Kraków for this information.

CHARTERIS 2014
CROCE, Giovanni. *First Book of Motets for Eight Voices and Organ*, edited by Richard Charteris with the assistance of Michael Procter, Hillsdale-New York, Pendragon Press, 2014.

CHISHOLM 2015
CHISHOLM, Leon. *Keyboard Playing and the Mechanization of Polyphony in Italian Music, Circa 1600*, Ph.D. Diss., Berkeley (CA), University of California, 2015.

CRISCUOLA DE LAIX 2009
CRISCUOLA DE LAIX, Esther. *Cultures of Music Print in Hamburg, ca. 1550-1630*, Ph.D. Diss., Berkeley (CA), University of California, 2009.

DAVIDSON 1991
DAVIDSON, Hans. *Matthias Weckmann: The Interpretation of His Organ Music. 1*, Stockholm, Gehrmans Musikförlag, 1991 (Skrifter från Musikvetenskapliga Institutionen 22).

DIRKSEN 2007
DIRKSEN, Pieter. *Heinrich Scheidemann's Keyboard Music*, Aldershot, Ashgate, 2007.

EICHHORN 1995
EICHHORN, Holger. 'Ein Sammeldruck vom Beginn des Dreißigjähring Krieges: Das Florilegium Portense', in: *Musik zwischen Leipzig und Dresden*, edited by Michael Heinemann and Peter Wollny, Oschersleben, Dr. Ziethen Verlag, 1995, pp. 60-84.

FOCK 1974
FOCK, Gustav. *Arp Schnitger und seine Schule*, Kassel, Bärenreiter, 1974.

FREIBERG 2004
FREIBERG, Irmtraut. *Der frühe italienische Generalbass dargestellt anhand der Quellen von 1595-1655. 1*, Hildesheim, Georg Olms Verlag, 2004.

GABLE 1987
GABLE, Frederick K. 'St. Gertrude's Chapel, Hamburg, and the Performance of Polychoral Music', in: *Early Music*, XV/2 (1987), pp. 229-241.

GABLE 1998
Dedication for St. Gertrude's Chapel, Hamburg 1607, edited by Frederick K. Gable, Madison, A-R Editions, 1998.

GABLE 2008 (OM-2)
Hieronymus Praetorius. Collected Vocal Works 2. Opus musicum II: Magnificats and Five Motets, edited by Frederick K. Gable, Middleton (WI), American Institute of Musicology, 2008 (CMM, 110).

GABLE 2014 (OM-3)
Hieronymus Praetorius. Collected Vocal Works 3. Opus musicum III: Six Masses, edited by Frederick K. Gable, Middleton (WI), American Institute of Musicology, 2014 (CMM, 110).

HERTEL 1666
HERTEL, Matthäus. *Orgelschlüssel, Ausgewählte Schriften, Überarbeiteter Neudruck nach Georg Schünemann und Manuskriptauszügen*, edited by Wolf Bergelt and Wolfgang J. Brylla, Berlin, Freimut & Selbst, 2018.

HOLMAN 2020
HOLMAN, Peter. *Before the Baton*, Woolbridge, Boydell & Brewer, 2020.

HORSLEY 1977
HORSLEY, Imogene. 'Full and Short Scores in the Accompaniment of Italian Church Music in the Early Baroque', in: *Journal of the American Musicological Society*, XXX/3 (1977), pp. 466-499.

JOHNSON 1989
JOHNSON, Cleveland. *Vocal Compositions in German Organ Tablatures, 1550-1650: A Catalogue and Commentar*, New York, Garland, 1989.

KAHLFUSS – GOTTWALD 1997
KAHLFUSS, Hans-Jürgen – GOTTWALD, Clytus. *Manuscripta Musica*, Wiesbaden, Harrassowitz, 1997.

KINKELDEY 1910
KINKELDEY, Otto. *Orgel und Klavier in der Musik des 16. Jahrhunderts*, Leipzig, Breitkopf & Härtel, 1910.

KIRCHER 1662
KIRCHER, Athanasius. *Musurgia universalis*, (1662), translated by Andreas Hirsch, edited by Melanie Wald, Kassel, Bärenreiter, 2006.

KITE-POWELL 2004
PRAETORIUS, Michael. *Syntagma musicum. 3*, (1619), translated and edited by Jeffery Kite-Powell, Oxford-New York, Oxford University Press, 2004.

KITE-POWELL 2021
KITE-POWELL, Jeffery. 'Notating-Accompanying-Conducting: Intabulation Usage in the Levoča Manuscripts', in: *Journal of Seventeenth-Century Music*, XXVII/1 (2021), <https://sscm-jscm.org/jscm-issues/volume-27-no-1/notating-accompanying-conducting/>, accessed October 2023.

KITE-POWELL 2022
ID. 'Michael Praetorius's Organ Works: The Notation Conundrum Revisited', <https://www.academia.edu/73964206/Michael_Praetoriuss_Organ_Works_The_Notation_Conundrum_Revisited?auto=download>, accessed October 2023. An abbreviated version may be found in the 2022 issue of the *Schütz-Jahrbuch*.

KJERSGAARD – WÖLFEL 2005
KJERSGAARD, Mads – WÖLFEL, Dietrich. *Zwei Positive des Orgelbauers Jochim Richborn von 1667 und 1673*, Lübeck, Schmidt-Römhild, 2005.

KRÜGER 1933
KRÜGER, Liselotte. 'Johann Kortkamps Organistenchronik, eine Quelle zur hamburgischen Musikgeschichte des 17. Jahrhunderts', in: *Zeitschrift des Vereins für Hamburgische Geschichte*, XXIII (1933), pp. 188-213.

MATTHESON 1735
MATTHESON, Johann. *Kleine Generalbaßschule*, Hamburg, J. C. Kissner, 1735.

MORELLI 1994
MORELLI, Arnaldo. 'Basso continuo on the Organ in Seventeenth-Century Italian Music', in: *Basler Jahrbuch für historische Musikpraxis*, XVIII (1994), pp. 31-45.

MÜNSTER 1968
MÜNSTER, Robert. 'Fragmente zu einer Musikgeschichte der Benediktinerabtei Tegernsee', in: *Studien und Mitteilungen zur Geschichte des Benediktiner-Ordens und seiner Zweige. Her. Von der Bayerischen Benediktinerakademie.* LXXIX/1.4 (1968), pp. 66-91.

NEUBACHER 1997
NEUBACHER, Jürgen. *Die Musikbibliothek des Hamburger Kantors und Musikdirektors Thomas Selle (1599-1663)*, Neuhausen, Hänssler, 1997 (American Institute of Musicology. Musicological Studies and Documents, 52).

PÖCHE 2018
PÖCHE, Juliane. *Thomas Selles Musik für Hamburg. Komponieren in einer frühneuzeitlichen Metropole*, Bern, Peter Lang, 2019.

PRAETORIUS 1619
PRAETORIUS, Michael. *Syntagma musicum. 3*, (1619), facsimile edited by Arno Forchert, Kassel, Bärenreiter, 2001.

RISM A/I C4429
CROCE, Giovanni. *SPARTIDURA | DELLI MOTETTI | A OTTO VOCI. | DI GIOVANNI CROCE | CHIOZZOTTO. | NOVAMENTE POSTA IN LICE. | IN VENETIA, Appresso Giacomo Vincenti. | M.D.XCIV.* Venice, 1594, modern edition cited above as CHARTERIS 2014.

RISM A/I G270
GALLUS, Josephus. *Totius Libri primi | SACRI OPERIS | MVSICI ALTERNIS | MODVLIS CONCINENDI | PARTITIO. | Seu quam praestantiss. Musici PARTITVRAM vocant, | AUTORE M. R. D. IOSEPHO GALLO | Mediolanensi, Religionis Somaschae: | Studio tamen & labore R. D. Aurilij Ribrochi Nobilis Dertho- | nensis in gratiam Organistarum in lucem edita. | MEDIOLANI, | Apud haeredes Francisci, & Simonis Tini. | M.D.XCVIII.* Edited by Aurelius Ribrochus, Milan, Tini, 1598.

RISM A/I G5143
GUMPELZHAIMER, Adam. *PARTITIO | SACRORVM CONCENTVVM | OCTONIS VOCIBVS MODVLANDORVM, | cum duplici Basso in Organorum usum, | AVTORE, | ADAMO GVMPELZHAIMERO. T. E. | CIVE AVGVSTANO. | LIBER SECVNDVS.* Augsburg, 1614.

RISM A/I H1931

HAMMERSCHMIDT, Andreas, *Vierter Theil* | *Musicalischer Andachten Geistlicher* | *Moteten undt Con=* | *certen* | *Mit 5, 6, 7, 8, 9, 10, 12 vnd mehr* | *Stimmen Nebenst einem gedoppelten* | *General-Baß componirt* | *von* | *Andrea Hammerschmieden* | *Erste Stimme* | *Freyberg in Meißen* | *Gedruckt vnd vorlegt* | *druch Georg Beuthern* | *Im Jahr* | *M.DC.XLVI.* Freiberg, 1646.

RISM A/I P5330 (OM-3)

PRAETORIUS, Hieronymus. *BASSUS CON-* | *TINUUS* | *MISSARUM SACRARUM V. VI. IIX.* | *VOCUM.* | *Quae sunt* | *OPERUM MVSICORUM* | *Tomus Tertius.* | *DIVINAE MAIESTATIS HONORI* | *REIPUBLICAE CHRISTIANAE ET MUSICAE* | *BONO* | *OMNIBUS MUSICAE PERITIS* | *Concinnatus &* | *dedicatus* | *ab* | *HIERONYMO PRAETORIO SEN.* | *Organ. ad D. Jacob.* | *HAMBURGI,* | *Ex officina Typographica PAULI LANGI.* | *ANNO M. DC. XXII.* Hamburg, 1622. Modern edition cited above as GABLE 2014 (OM-3).

RISM A/I P5334 (OM-2)

ID. *BASSUS CON-* | *TINUUS* | *CANTICI B. M. VIRGINIS* | *SEU* | *MAGNIFICAT* | *Super Octo Tonos Consuetos octo Vocibus decantati* | *Cum additis Motectis aliquot VIII. X.* | *XII. VOCUM.* | *Quae sunt* | *OPERUM MVSICORUM* | *Tomus Secundus* | *Denuo ab autore revisus correctus & auctus.* | *DIVINAE MAIESTATIS HONORI* | *REIPUBLICAE CHRISTIANAE ET MUSICAE* | *BONO* | *OMNIBUS MUSICAE PERITIS* | *Concinnatus & dedicatus* | *ab* | *HIERONYMO PRAETORIO SEN.* | *Organ. ad D. Jacob* | *HAMBURGI,* | *Ex Officina Typographica PAVLI LANGI.* | *ANNO M. DC. XXII.* Hamburg, 1622. Modern edition cited above as GABLE 2008 (OM-2).

RISM A/I P5336 (OM-1)

ID. *CANTIONES* | *SACRAE DE PRAE-* | *CIPVIS FESTIS TO-* | *tius Anni 5. 6. 7. &* | *8. Vocum.* | *AVTHORE* | *HIERONYMO PRAETORIO* | *Organista in aede S. Iacobi* | *Hamburgensi.* | *HAMBVRGI* | *Excudebat Philippus de Ohr* | *Anno CIƆ IƆ IC.* Hamburg, 1599.

RISM A/I P5337 (OM-1)

ID. *CANTIONES* | *SACRAE, DE FESTIS* | *PRAECIPUIS TOTIUS* | *Anni, 5. 6. 7. 8. 10.* | *& 12. Vocum:* | *Compositae à* | *HIERONYMO PRAETORIO,* | *ORGANISTA IN AEDE S. JA-* | *COBI HAMBURGENSI.* | *Operum Musicorum Auctoris* | *TOMUS PRIMUS.* | *Editio altera* | *Ab ipsomet auctore correcta, & aliquot Motectis* | *aucta.* | *Cum Privilegio S. Caes. Majest. speciali.* | *HAMBURGI,* | *Typis PHILIPPI de OHR,* | *Ex Bibliopolio FROBENIANO, Anno* | *CIƆ. IƆ C. VII.* Hamburg, 1607.

RISM A/I P5338 (OM-1)

ID. *BASSUS CON-* | *TINUUS* | *Cantionum Sacrarum de Festis prae-* | *cipuis totius anni* | *V. VI. VII. IIX. X. XII.* | *VOCUM* | *Quae sunt* | *OPERUM MVSICORUM* | *Tomus Primus* | *Denuo ab autore revisus correctus & auctus.* | *DIVINAE MAIESTATIS HONORI* | *REIPUBLICAE CHRISTIANAE ET MUSICAE* | *BONO* | *OMNIBUS MUSICAE PERITIS* | *Concinnatus & dedicatus* | *ab* | *HIERONYMO PRAETORIO SEN.* | *Organ. ad D. Jacob* | *HAMBURGI,* | *Ex Officina Typographica PAVLI LANGI.* | *ANNO M. DC. XXII.* Hamburg, 1622.

RISM A/I P5341 (OM-4)

ID. *BASSUS CON-* | *TINVVS* | *Cantionum variarum* | *V. VI. VII. IIX. X. XII. XVI. XX.* | *VOCUM* | *Quae sunt* | *OPERVM MVSICORVM* | *Tomus Quartus* | *DIVINAE MAIESTATIS HONORI* | *REIPUBLICAE CHRISTIANAE ET MUSICAE* | *BONO* | *OMNIBUS MUSICAE PERITIS* | *Concinnatus & dedicatus* | *ab* |

117

HIERONYMO PRAETORIO SEN. | *Organ. ad D. Jacob.* | *M DC XVIII.* | *HAMBURGI* | *Excusus ab HENRICO CARSTENS.* | *sumptibus auctoris.* Hamburg, 1618.

RISM A/ɪ P5342 (OM-4)

Iᴅ. *BASSVS CON-* | *TINVVS* | *Cantionum variarum* | *V. VI. VII. IIX. X. XII. XVI. XX.* | *vocum.* | *Quae sunt* | *OPERUM MUSICORUM* | *Tomus Ultimus:* | *DIVINAE MAJESTATIS HONORE* | *REIPUBLICAE CHRISTIANAE ET MUSICAE* | *bono* | *OMNIBVS MVSICAE PERITIS* | *Concinnatus &* *dedicatus* | *ab* | *HIERONYMO PRAETORIO SEN.* | *Oranista ad D. Jacobi.* | *FRANCOFURTI,* | *Ex Officina Typographica Egenolphi Emmelii.* | *Anno M. DC. XXIII.* Frankfurt, 1623.

RISM A/ɪ P5343 (OM-5)

Iᴅ. *CANTIONES NOVAE* | *OFFICIOSAE* | *V, VI, VII, VIII, X ET* | *XV VOC.* | *QUAE SUNT* | *OPERUM MUSI-* | *CORUM* | *Tomus Quintus* | *Cui in gratiam Musicae peritorum additum habes* | *Bassum Continuum* | *Divinae Majestatis honori* | *Reipublicae Christianae & Musicae BONO* | *Concinnatus & dedicatus* | *Ab* | *HIERONYMO PRAETORIO SENIORE* | *ORGANISTA AD D. JACOBI* | *CUM GRATIA ET PRIVILEGIO ELECT. SAXON.* Hamburg, 1625.

RISM A/ɪ PP5344a

Iᴅ. *Das* | *TE DEVM LAVDA-* | *MVS Deutsch:* | *Zu sonderlichen Ehren vnd günstigen wolgefallen:* | *Dem Ehrnvesten* | *Wolachtbaren* | *vnd Hochweisen* | *Herrn Hieronymo Vöglern* | *Der löblichen Stadt Hamburg* | *Bürgermeistern.* | *Seinem insondern Großgünstigen Verrn* [sic] | *Schwagern vnnd mechtigen* | *Befürderern.* | *Mit 16. Stimmen componirt vnd gesetzt* | *Durch* | *HIERONYMUM PRAETORIUM* | *Organisten daselbst vnterdienstlich.* | *Hamburg* | *Durch Heinrich Karstens* | *Im Jahr* | *M. DC. XII.* Hamburg, 1612.

RISM A/ɪ S2275

Sᴄʜüᴛᴢ, Heinrich. *BASSO CONTINOVO* | *Vor die Orgel* | *Lauten* | *Chitaron, Etc.* | *Der* | *Psalmen Davids* | *Sampt* | *Etlichen Moteten und Concerten* | *mit acht vnd mehr Stimmen* | *Nebenst andern zweyen Capellen* | *daß dero etliche* | *auff drey vnd vier Chor nach beliebung gebraucht* | *werden können.* | *Wie auch* | *Mit beygefügten Basso Continovo vor die Orgel* | *Lauten* | *Chitaron* | *etc.* | *Gestellet durch* | *Henrich Schützen* | *Chur. S. Capellmeistern.* | *ANNO M. DC. XIX.* | *In vorlegung des Authoris.* | *Dreßden* | *In Churf. S. Officin durch Simel Bergen.* Dresden, 1619.

RISM A/ɪ S4286

Sᴛᴀᴅʟᴍᴀʏᴇʀ, Johann. *Magnificat. Symphoniae variae secundum varios modos musicos, aliae octonis, una duodenis vocibus compositae & nunc primum in lucem editae cum duplice basso organicorum usui accommodato.* Innsbruck, 1614.

RISM A/ɪ V1400

Vɪᴀᴅᴀɴᴀ, Lodovico. *Salmi a Quattro chori per cantare, e concertare nelle gran Solennità di tutto l'Anno, con il Basso continuo per sonar nell'Organo di Lodovico Viadana Maestro di Capella nel Domo di Fano. Opera XXVII Nouamente composta, & data in luce. Con Privilegio. In Venetia. Appreso Giacomo Vincenti. 1612.* Venice, 1612. Modern edition cited below as Wɪᴇʟᴀᴋᴋᴇʀ 1998.

RISM B/ɪ 1611[1]

PROMPTUARII MUSICI, | *SACRAS HAR-* | *MONIAS SIVE MOTETAS* | *V. VI. VII. & VIII.* | *VOCUM,* | *E DIVERSIS, IISQUE CLARIS-* | *simis hujus & superioris aetatis autoribus, antehac nun-* | *quam in Germania editis, collectas exhibentis, | PARS PRIMA: | QUAE | CONCENTUS SELECTISSIMOS QUI TEMPORE | hyemali S.S. Ecclesiae usui esse possunt, | comprehendit. | COLLECTORE ABRAHAMO SCHADAEO SENFF- | tebergensi, Scholae Spirensium Senatoriae Rectore. | Cui | BASIN VULGO GENERALEM DICTAM, | & ad ORGANA, musicaq. Instrumenta accommo- | datam, Singulari industriâ addidit | CASPAR VINCENTIUS EJUS- | dem civitatis Musicus Organicus. | ARGENTINAE. | Typis Caroli Kiefferi, Sumptibus | Pauli Ledertz. Anno 1611.* Speyer, 1611.

RISM B/I 1613[2]
PROMPTUARII MUSICI, | SACRAS HAR- | MONIAS SIVE MOTETAS | V. VI. VII. & VIII. | VOCUM, | E DIVERSIS, IISQUE CLARIS | simis hujus & Superioris aetatis authori- | bus collectas comprehendentis, | PARS TERTIA: | Quae exhibet | Concentus varios selectioresque, | QUI SOLENNIORIBUS sc. S.S. TRINITATIS, S. JOH | Baptistae, B. Virginis Mariae, S.S. Apostolorum, Martyrum, Confeßorum, | & Virginum Festis per totius anni curriculum inserviunt: cum Corollario | textius ex Canticis canticorum depromente. | COLLECTORE ABRAHAMO SCHADAEO | Senfftebergensi. | Ad quam | BASIN GENERALEM ACCOMMODAVIT | CASPAR VINCENTIVS SPIRENSIVM | Organaedus. | ARGENTINAE. | Typis Caroli Kieffer, Sumptibus Pauli Ledertz. | Anno M. DC. XIII. Speyer, 1613.

RISM B/I 1621[2]
FLORILEGII | MUSICI PORTENSIS, | Sacras Harmonias sive Motetas | V. VI. VII. VIII. X. Vocum. | E Diversis, ijsq praestantißimis aetatis nostrae autoribus | collectus comprehendentis | PARS ALTERA. | Quae exhibet concentus selectissimas. | CL. | Qui partim diebus Dominicis in communi: partim verò in spe- | cie Festis solennioribus, per totius anni curriculum inserviunt, | cum adjecta Basi Generali ad Organa Musicaq] instrumen- | ta accommodata | COLLECTORE ET EDITORE | M. ERHARDO BODENSCHATZIO, | Lichtenbergense, Illustris Gymnasij Portensis olim Can- | tore, nunc verò temporis Ecclesiae Osterhusanae | Pastore. | Cum Gratia & Privilegio Electoris Saxoniæ. | LIPSIAE, | Typis Abrahami Lambergi, & Sumtibus | Gottfridi Grossij Bibliopolae. | ANNO CHRISTI M. DC. XXI. Leipzig, 1621.

Rose 2019
Rose, Steven. *Musical Authorship from Schütz to Bach*, Cambridge, Cambridge University Press, 2019.

Snyder 2007
Snyder, Kerala. *Dieterich Buxtehude: Leben, Werk, Aufführungspraxis*, German translation of revised edition by Hans-Joachim Schulze, Kassel, Bärenreiter, 2007.

Snyder 2015
Ead. 'A Brief History of the St. Mary's Choir Library', in: *The Choir Library of St. Mary's in Lübeck 1546-1674. A Database Catalogue*, 2015, <https://orgeldatabas.gu.se/webgoart/goart/Snyder.php>, accessed October 2023.

Stahl 1931
Stahl, Wilhelm. *Geschichte der Kirchenmusik in Lübeck*, Kassel, Bärenreiter, 1931.

Stahl 1952
Id. *Musikgeschichte Lübecks. 2: Geistliche Musik*, Kassel, Bärenreiter, 1952.

SUTOWSKI – OSOSTOWICZ-SUTKOWSKA 1965
The Pelplin Tablature, a Thematic Catalogue, edited by Adam Sutowski and Alina Osostowicz-Sutkowska, Warsaw, Warsaw Univ. Pr., 1965.

SZELEST 2021
Tabulaturae Brunsbergenis-Olivenses, edited by Marcin Szelest, Warsaw, Wydawnictwo Naukowe Sub Lupa, 2021.

WIELAKKER 1998
VIADANA, Lodovico. *Salmi a Quattro chori*, edited by Gerhard Wielakker, Madison, A-R Editions, 1998.

WINTER 1964
WINTER, Paul. *Der mehrchörige Stil*, Frankfurt, Peters, 1964.

WOJNOWSKA 2016
WOJNOWSKA, Elżbieta. *Thematic Catalogue of 17th-Century Organ Tablatures from the Liegnitz Bibliotheca Rudolphina*, edited by Tomasz Jeż, Warsaw, Biblioteka Narodowa, 2016.

MANUSCRIPT SOURCES

D-Hs Skrin 251
SELLE, Thomas. *Passio secundum Johaneum cum Intermediis*, <https://digitalisate.sub.uni-hamburg.de/detail/?tx_dlf%5Bid%5D=44001&tx_dlf%5Bpage%5D=1&cHash=a1e18b78a0684f747f8bc4e738b1b2d1>, accessed October 2023.

D-Kl 2° Ms. Mus. 62i
Bassus continuus missarum, <https://orka.bibliothek.uni-kassel.de/viewer/!metadata/1558962947000/128/LOG_0026/>, accessed October 2023.

D-Mbs 4° Mus. Pr. 23/4
Motetten, Messen, Magnificatsätze etc., <https://stimmbuecher.digitale-sammlungen.de/view?id=bsb00094037>, accessed October 2023.

PL-PE Ms 305
The Pelplin Tablature, edited by Adam Sutkowski and Alina Osostowicz-Sutkowska, Warsaw, Warsaw Univ. Pr., 1965 (Antiquitates Musicae in Polonia, 3).

PL-PE Ms 307
The Pelplin Tablature, edited by Adam Sutkowski and Alina Osostowicz-Sutkowska, Warsaw, Warsaw Univ. Pr.,1965 (Antiquitates Musicae in Polonia, 5).

PL-Wn 326 Cim.
Tabulatura organowa niemiecka, <https://polona.pl/item/tabulatura-organowa,MjcxNzA3MjE/3/#info:metadata>, accessed October 2023.

Connected by Strings:
Cello Accompaniment Performance Practice

Partimento, German Thoroughbass Practice, and Improvised Solo Performance on the Cello

John Lutterman
(University of Alaska, Anchorage)

As the burgeoning recent scholarship focused on Italian partimento pegagogy attests, continuo realization served as a foundation of both written composition and improvised solo performance well into the nineteenth century. Partimento pedagogy may also have influenced (or reflected) similar German practices, which are given detailed and explicit verbal treatment in the thoroughbass treatises of Niedt, Kellner, Heinichen, Mattheson, C. Ph. E. Bach, Adlung and Wiedeburg. Robert Levin, John Mortensen, and Alma Deutscher, among many others, have demonstrated that the study of such pedagogical practices is a valuable resource for performers concerned with re-creating historical improvisatory practices. While these sources are aimed primarily at keyboard players, there is reason to believe that well-trained musicians would have employed similar techniques when learning to improvise on the cello.

Until recently, little attention has been given to the striking similarities between early examples of unaccompanied cello music and Neapolitan partimento exercises. The fact that many partimento exercises were created by or attributed to celebrated cellists suggests a close relationship between the skills required for partimento realization and solo improvisation. One of the most striking characteristics of the earliest cello treatises is that so many of them give instruction in chordal thoroughbass realization, and some are organized in a manner that appears to reflect the influence of partimento practices (or similar German thoroughbass methods), offering examples of the *Regola dell'Ottava*, simple, double and compound cadences, and sequential patterns like the 'monte' and 'fonte', and suspensions, such as the '7-6 fauxbordoun'. Traces of these practices may also be discerned in many examples of seventeenth- and eighteenth-century compositions for solo viol and cello, traces which offer valuable clues to the idiomatic nature of improvised solo practices on these instruments.

The process of historical analysis is inevitably shaped by subjective biases, both our own and those of the sources we have chosen to examine. While this is an inescapable condition of all forms of cultural research, Pierre Bourdieu's concept of «objectifying the subjective» suggests a way to ameliorate such biases: by specifying our cultural positions and those of our sources as best we can, we may temper the influence of our subjectivity and enable our readers to assess the degree to which our analyses may have been skewed. In the spirit of documenting my own subjectivities, I would like to offer a bit of personal background as a kind of genealogical sketch of my experience with some of the problems that I would like to address in this essay.

My first scholarly foray into thoroughbass studies came during the early 1980s, as a graduate student in musicology at SUNY Stony Brook, where I had the good fortune to take seminars on the history of music theory and performance practice with Leo Treitler, Eric Chafe, Eva Linfeld, Sarah Fuller, Richard Kramer, Thomas Christensen, and Arthur Haas. In 1982, my classmate David Schulenburg, who at the time was finishing his dissertation, published the first of a pair of excellent articles that first made me aware of Friedrich Niedt's *Handleitung*, and of the relationship between thoroughbass practices and composition in the seventeenth and eighteenth centuries[1]. In 1984, a seminar with Richard Kramer on C. P. E. Bach's treatment of *Fantasieren* introduced me to Hans-Joachim Schulze, Hellmut Federhofer, and Karl Fellerer's early writings about partimento practices[2].

In 1985, a graduate seminar with Eva Linfeld on seventeenth-century music theory gave me an excuse to dig into the history of early compositions for the cello and viol, and I quickly became convinced that many of the early compositions for my instruments were intended as didactic illustrations of improvisatory practices. By this time I had decided to pursue a performance degree, and I ended up writing one of my DMA essays on the relationship between G. B. Vitali's Partite for Violone and the examples of ground bass variations appended to treatises on improvisation by Ortiz and Simpson.

In 1989, having completed my DMA at Stony Brook, I spent four years living in Europe, during which time I was able to study performance practice, Baroque cello and Viol with Nicolas Harnoncourt, Christophe Coin and Jaap ter Linden at the Mozarteum, the Schola Cantorum, and the Royal Conservatory in the Hague. I had assumed that learning to improvise in period style would be an essential facet of historically-informed performance at these institutions, but I was surprised to discover that, at that time, there was little attention given to historical improvisatory practices. While harpsichordists studied the rudiments of thoroughbass realization, and soloists would occasionally venture a brief ornamental elaboration of a melody (usually worked out in advance), most performers felt obliged to restrict themselves to offering no more than a tasteful, but literal interpretation of a musical text, more or less as notated.

---

[1]. Schulenberg 1982, Schulenberg 1984.
[2]. Fellerer 1930, Fellerer 1940, Federhofer 1958, Federhofer 1968, Schulze 1978.

Training in improvisatory skills has maintained an unbroken, if somewhat tenuous foothold in the conservatory curriculum for players of keyboard instruments, especially organists, but the importance of such training has been largely overlooked by string players of both the 'modern' and 'early music' varieties. Viol players would occasionally give concert performances of pieces from Simpson's *The Division-Viol* and Ortiz's *Tratado da Glosas*, but I was surprised to find that virtually no one appeared to be interested in cultivating the improvisatory skills that such treatises were intended to teach.

Upon returning to the USA, I decided to embark on a Ph.D. in musicology, this time at UC Davis. In seminars with Anna Maria Busse Berger, David Nutter, and Christopher Reynolds, I began to focus on historical improvisatory practices, across a very broad range of time periods and styles. By this time, Pamela Poulin's translation of Niedt's *Handleitung* had appeared[3], and David Schulenburg had published an article titled 'Composition and Improvisation in the School of J. S. Bach'[4], which I found fascinating, and which has continued to inspire much of my own work.

Also around this time, I became aware of Lydia Goehr's influential *The Imaginary Museum of Musical Works*[5], which served to bolster my own hypotheses about the various functions that notation would have served in the Bach circle. By 1998, I had decided to write a dissertation questioning the ontological status of the Bach Cello suites as musical works, arguing that they could fruitfully be understood as artifacts of historical improvisatory practices[6].

While exploring the relationship between Friedrich Niedt's *Handleitung* and improvisatory practices on the cello, I began to wonder about Niedt's relationship to partimento practices. At the time, so few musicians knew anything about these practices that I frequently used the word partimento as a username or password for my internet accounts, confident that I would be safe from even the savviest hackers. I could scarcely have imagined how quickly that situation would change. In the time since I completed my dissertation in 2006, there has been an astonishing amount of first-rate scholarship focused on partimento practices. Robert Gjerdingen, Giorgio Sanguinetti and Peter van Tour[7] have published ground-breaking monographs, which have firmly established partimento as an important topic for music theorists and musicologists, and the career of the astonishing child prodigy, Alma Deutscher (whose improvisatory skill is a direct result of her training in partimento methods) has brought a much broader public awareness of the practice. Today, there are even Facebook groups and podcasts devoted to partimento. Suffice it to say I no longer feel safe using the term as a password.

---

3. POULIN 1989.
4. SCHULENBERG 1995.
5. GOEHR 1992.
6. LUTTERMAN 2006.
7. GJERDINGEN 2007, SANGUINETTI 2012, VAN TOUR 2015.

In the course of my dissertation work, I began to cross-reference what I little I could find in the available partimento sources with my earlier research on seventeenth-century Italian cello repertoire, and I soon noticed Rocco Greco's name popping up on both lists. I also noticed that many of the Neapolitan partimento exercises bore striking resemblances to passages from the early unaccompanied cello compositions I had been examining by Vitali, Colombi, Gabrielli, Degli'Antoni and Supriani.

In 2004, I presented a paper outlining my arguments at the 11th Biennial Conference on Baroque Music in Manchester, and I was very happy with the positive response my ideas received from an intimidating audience that included Christoph Wolff, Robin Leaver, David Ledbetter, Michael Maul, and several other illustrious Bach scholars. However, my suggestion that the correlations I had found might point to the existence of partimento practices among seventeenth-century cellists was greeted with skepticism, particularly from Gregory Barnett, who had done important work on the Bononcinis, whose sonatas sometimes include simple «composed realizations» for cello in the basso part.

Guido Olivieri, who was initially also somewhat skeptical, was more sympathetic to the idea, and when I met him again at another conference two years later, shortly after completing my dissertation, I was delighted to learn that he had discovered a manuscript at the Abbey of Montecassino, attributed to Rocco Greco, which appears to confirm the existence of such a practice. Since then, Olivieri[8] has published an excellent article on partimento cello practices in Naples, and Giovanna Barbati and Catherine Bahn, among others, have been doing impressive work with the sources that he has discovered.

Turning now to my primary agenda, I would like to sketch some of the connections that I am attempting to flesh out between Italian partimento practices, German thoroughbass methods, and improvisatory solo practices on the viol and cello. In a pair of articles that were developed from papers that I presented at conferences in La Spezia and Lucca[9], I have illustrated many of the relationships I have found between solo improvisatory practices and the skills required for chordal realization of a figured bass on the cello and viol, and I presented some of the methods that I have employed in my attempts to apply these skills in the course of my own improvisations. I will refrain from repeating those arguments here. One of my goals for this essay is to call your attention to evidence of some of the other correspondences I have noticed and am currently pursuing. My hope is that my readers may be in a position to provide evidence (or to find evidence in the future) which could serve to either support or refute the hypotheses that I am in the process of developing.

Recent scholarship has clearly established that Italian partimento practices were influential throughout Europe, in part because of the many Italian musicians who held prominent

---

[8]. Olivieri 2021.
[9]. Lutterman 2011, Lutterman 2019.

positions in cities and courts North of the Alps, but also because of the many important German musicians who had spent part of their careers studying and working in Italy. In my earlier work, I often referred to Friedrich Niedt's *Handleitung* as a treatise on partimento practice, since his strategy of using a bass line to structure the improvisation and composition of particular genres has much in common with partimento pedagogical practices. For convenience, I shall continue refer to Niedt's method, as a type of partimento practice, but it is important to bear in mind that there are significant differences in the way that these practices were documented. We now have a much richer and deeper understanding of the distinctive nature of partimento and solfeggio improvisatory practices, and of the important differences between Italian partimento and German thoroughbass pedagogical strategies.

While Niedt's *Handleitung* was the first of many published German treatises to employ thoroughbass as a framework for improvisation and composition, and while it quite possibly reflects his teacher's adaptation of partimento practices encountered during a journeyman year in Italy, the manner of presentation that Niedt employs reflects a distinctly German approach to pedagogy. The Italian partimento sources are artefacts of a primarily orally-transmitted method for training professional musicians, and their skeletal, enigmatic structures may have been a means of protecting jealously guarded trade secrets. The earliest sources often originated as students' notebooks, reflecting a particular teacher's methods, and they circulated almost exclusively in manuscript copies of bass lines, some figured, but many not, with very little verbal explanation. On the other hand, the fact that Niedt's treatise was published suggests that it was intended to be used by a much broader range of musicians, including *Kenner und Liebhaber* interested in understanding the practices of professional musicians. Niedt provides a substantial theoretical rational for his method, along with thorough verbal instructions for practicing his thoroughbass exercises, which he then illustrates with composed-out realizations.

Thomas Christensen has argued convincingly that the pedagogical organization of many of the early German thoroughbass treatises, including Niedt's, was influenced by a long-standing German tradition of teaching organ improvisation, dating back to the *fundamenta* of Conrad Paumann and Hans Buchner, among others, a method that German scholars have termed *Klangschrittlehre*[10]. In fact, I would suggest an even stronger connection of this *fundamenta* tradition to J. S. Bach than Christensen has proposed, since Bach owned a copy of Elias Ammerbach's *Orgel oder Instrument Tablatur* of 1571, which contained works by Buchner and Hofhaimer. Since many of the early *Klangschrittlehre* thoroughbass methods were published in Augsburg, I cannot help but wonder if they reflect a local practice that could have influenced the cellist Johan Baumgartner, who was born in Augsburg in 1722, and whose treatise of 1774 was the first to provide specific verbal instruction in the art of chordal continuo realization on

---

[10]. CHRISTENSEN 2008.

the cello[11]. Baumgartner's treatise does appear to reflect his familiarity with partimento (or a similar German practice), since he offers examples of several *regole*, some with realizations, as well as an attempt at a Fugue for unaccompanied cello, which makes extensive use of sequential patterns of partimento-like schemata (Ill. 1).

Ill. 1: Johann Baumgartner: Fugue for unaccompanied cello, using partimento schemata (1774).

Of course, the most famous example of a fugue for unaccompanied cello is the Prelude of J. S. Bach's Suite in C Minor, BWV 1011. In my dissertation, I argued that Bach's unaccompanied works may fruitfully be understood as encyclopedic examples of the improvisatory practices of his day[12]. I have felt justified in casting a fairly broad net in my search for evidence that may help us decipher the practices that Bach has documented, but the city of Jena has been a particularly important nexus for many of the sources I have examined in the course of my exploration of correspondences between partimento, thoroughbass, and the improvised practices demonstrated in J. S. Bach's cello suites.

---

11. Baumgartner 1774.
12. Lutterman 2006.

In 1694, Friedrich Niedt entered the University of Jena where he apparently became a student of Johann Nicolaus Bach (1769-1753), the eldest cousin of J. S. Bach. Nicolaus Bach appears to have founded his teaching on partimento-style thoroughbass realization, and as Thomas Christensen has argued, he appears to have fostered interest in a particularly German theory of harmony among musicians in Jena[13]. The organist and theorist Jakob Adlung, lutenist Gottlieb Baron, viol player Ludwig Christian Hesse, and cellist Johann Georg Schetky all studied at the University of Jena, and there were several strong connections between the music faculty at the University and J. S. Bach's family.

It is likely that Niedt's semi-autobiographical description of Tacitus's apprenticeship in the preface to his treatise reflects Niedt's own experience as a student of Nicolaus Bach, and it seems safe to assume that Niedt's treatise was intended to transmit the precepts of a Bach family tradition. Niedt's treatise is of interest for many reasons, not the least of which is his demonstration, in volume II, of a method for manipulating a figured bass line to create a suite of movements by employing partimento methods of elaboration. For a cellist, the fact that the movements Niedt chose for his illustration are exactly those of the first two of Bach cello suites is of particular importance (prelude – allemande, courante, sarabande, minuets and gigue).

I suspect that the older German *fundamenta* tradition and the more modern Italian partimento practices reflect different pedagogical strategies for teaching what may have been similar improvisatory skills, but I also wonder how much Nicolas Bach's teaching may have been directly influenced by Italian practices. We know that Nicolas Bach spent time as a journeyman in Italy, and that he became fluent enough in Italian to teach the language when he returned to Jena, but we have no further information about where he traveled or how long his sojourn lasted. I spent a week during the summer of 2018 in Jena, searching the University archives for further evidence, but to no avail. We know that Nicolas Bach started off on his Italian journey with one of his classmates from the University, Georg Bertouch, who at some point during their travels abandoned his friend for a position with a Danish general and eventually settled in Norway, where he had an influential career as a composer. I have often wondered whether more evidence of their Italian journey might be found in a Scandinavian archive. It is also worth noting that Bertouch lived for a while in Copenhagen, at the same time as Friedrich Niedt, who moved there from Jena in 1700.

One of the most important of the eighteenth-century musicians to discuss improvisation was Jakob Adlung. His *Anleitung zu der musikalischen Gelahrtheit* (1758) is an encyclopedic work that not only gives detailed information on a vast number of musical subjects, but which also provides a critical survey of the most important writings of earlier theorists and historians of music. Like Bach, Adlung (1699-1762) spent his entire career in a small region of central Germany. Born in Erfurt, Adlung's earliest musical training came from his father, an organist.

---

[13]. Christensen 1996.

In 1723, he matriculated at the University of Jena and began organ studies with Johann Nicolaus Bach. He also befriended Johann Gottfried Walther, who proved to be a strong influence in his study of music theory. While still in Jena, Adlung wrote three treatises on music, *Anweisung zum Generalbaße, Anweisung zur italienischen Tablatur, and Anweisung zur Fantasie und zu den Fugen.* All of these were apparently lost when Adlung's home burned down in 1736. Adlung relied on his memory to incorporate some of the material from these treatises in his *Anleitung zu der musikalischen Gelahrtheit,* where these topics receive substantial treatment, though he claimed to have neither time nor energy to reconstruct them completely. However, thanks to the work of Michael Maul, a late eighteenth-century manuscript copy of the *Anweisung zur Fantasie* has recently been discovered, and is now available in an English translation by Derek Remeš[14].

There is little surviving evidence of the compositional activity of Ludwig Christian Hesse (1716-1772), widely regarded as the greatest viol player of his generation, on a par with Karl Friedrich Abel. However, Hesse did leave an abundant collection of chamber music arrangements of popular operas, almost all of which feature the viol as a solo instrument. His father was evidently his only viol teacher, but Ludwig Christian also studied law at the University in Jena, where, like Friedrich Niedt, and Johann Georg Schetky, he would likely have encountered an approach to music strongly influenced by members the Bach circle. In 1741 Hesse took a position in the Hofkapelle of Frederick the Great, where he was listed in payroll records as both viol player and cellist, and where one of his colleagues was Carl Philipp Emanuel Bach.

In 1766, Hesse moved to the court of Friedrich Wilhelm, Prince of Prussia, as viol teacher and court musician. During his tenure at the Prussian court, Hesse was responsible for transcribing and arranging popular operas as duos for viol or cello, often from scores of French operas sent to Friedrich Wilhelm by Jean-Baptiste Forqueray. Many are for solo viol with an *ad libitum* bass, in which case the pitches of the basso are often included as double or triple stops in the solo part. Several of his arrangements feature an unusual kind of shorthand, which indicates double stop passages by means of figures, including ♯s and ♭s, similar to those used in thoroughbass practice, but in Hesse's arrangements they are applied to the solo part and may refer to intervals either above or below the line. Hesse uses figures to indicate intervals ranging from seconds to sevenths, but the most common figures are for passages of consecutive thirds and sixths (Ill. 2).

Cellist Johann Georg Schetky (1737-1824) came from a family of musicians in Darmstadt, and he surely would have known the Hesse family of viol players. Ludwig Christian Hesse had moved to the Berlin court by the time Schetky turned four, but Hesse's father, Ernst Christian, who at the time was much more famous, was active in Darmstadt

14. Remeš – Maul 2021.

ILL. 2: Ludwig Christian Hesse: Opera arrangement for viola da gamba and basso continuo, with shorthand figures indicating intervals both above and below the solo part (c.1760).

until his death in 1762, and it seems likely that Schetky would have studied viol with one of the family.

As a young man, Schetky studied Law at Jena University, as had Ludwig Christian Hesse, and it seems reasonable to assume that the musical practices that these two musicians experienced in Jena would have reflected a Bach family tradition. At some point during the Seven Years War, Schetky abandoned his law studies in Jena and spent time in the military, after which he pursued further studies, this time devoting himself entirely to music. Gerber reports that Schetky moved to Hamburg, and according to Sandys and Forster, «being passionately fond of music, he followed the bent of his inclination, and studied both theoretically and practically under Emanuel Bach»[15]. It may be that Schetky's introduction to Emanuel Bach was facilitated by Ludwig Christian Hesse, who was at that time Emanuel Bach's colleague in the Berlin Hofkapelle. Schetky had further experience of the Bach family tradition when he moved to London in 1770, where he studied viol with Carl Friedrich Abel. Furthermore, Van der Straeten reports that while in London, Schetky also «made the acquaintance, and obtained the patronage of Johann Christian Bach», a report confirmed by Gerber[16].

What could the result of Schetky's encounter with practices of the Bach circle have been?

In 1799, the *Allgemeine musikalische Zeitung* (Leipzig) printed an anonymous description of Schetky accompanying a recitative, playing the cello with an underhand, «viol» bow grip.

> It was in the accompaniment to recitative that this bow-hold was shown to full advantage. The obligation of the violoncellist in the accompaniment of recitatives is to give the main note of the voice above, but at the same time to play so that the chord is heard, along with the bass note. These duties are a legacy bequeathed to the violoncello by the defunct gamba. The violoncellist who strokes only the bass notes in the recitative does not understand the duty of his instrument, or is at most a fiddler to whom thoroughbass is terra incognito[17].

Schetky eventually settled in Edinburgh, where he appears to have had a strong influence on Scottish musicians, particularly John Gunn, whose treatise of 1802 provides an exceptionally detailed and thorough explanation of thoroughbass realization on the cello[18]. In 1811, Schetky published his *Practical and Progressive Lessons for the Violoncello*, which includes instruction on the art of accompanying recitative. Possible further evidence of Schetky's thoroughbass practice may found in his earlier Six Quartettos for two Violins, a Tenor, & Violoncello, Op. VI

---

[15]. Sandys – Forster 1864, p. 184.

[16]. Van Der Straeten 1915, p. 190, Gerber 1790-1792.

[17]. «Im Accompagnement zum Recitativ war diese Bogenhaltung in ihre vollen Kraft. Die Pflicht des Violoncellisten ist im Accompagnement des Recitatives die Hauptnote in der Höhe anzugeben, aber den Akkord mit dem Grundton zugleich hören zu lassen. Mit diesem Amte hat die verstorbene Gambe dem Violoncello ein Legat vermacht. Der Violoncellist, welcher im Recitativ nur die Bassnoten herunter-streicht, versteht die Pflicht seines Instrumentes nicht, oder ist höchstens ein Fiedler, dem der Generalbaß terra incognita ist». Anonymous 1799, pp. 34-38.

[18]. Gunn 1802.

ILL. 3: Johann Georg Schetky: Six Quartettos, Op. VI, cello part of a string quartet with thoroughbass symbols (1777).

published in 1777. Although neither the title page, which is given only in the cello part, nor the cello part itself offer any verbal clue that another continuo instrument is called for, the cello part is extensively figured, and contains *tasto* or *tasto solo* indications under most of the long sustained or repeated notes (see figure 8.33). This suggests that Schetky would have intended these figures to be realized on the cello (ILL. 3).

JOHN LUTTERMAN

One of the most striking characteristics of the published cello treatises that began to appear over the course of the eighteenth century is that so many of them give instruction in thoroughbass realization, especially the later conservatory methods aimed at a more professional market. In most of these sources, continuo realization is discussed in connection with accompanying recitatives, a practice which Baumgartner described as the epitome of the cellist's art. Even the methods that do not explicitly mention thoroughbass realization attach great importance to the skills that would be required for a chordal realization, particularly the study of double-stops and three- or four-voice arpeggiated passages. These skills receive much more attention than they are given in modern string pedagogy, and they are arranged in formulaic patterns of scales, sequences and cadential progressions, with fingerings designed to facilitate the proper approach and resolution of dissonance.

A few of the treatises advise cellists to play only what is written when performing a figured bass line, but there were a variety of reasons for these admonishments, and they should be interpreted with a degree of caution. It is possible that when authors of the treatises proscribed improvising a realization that they simply intended this advice for the amateurs for whom many of these treatises were written. In any case, it is clear that professional attitudes and practices were often quite different. In many cases, the authors were attempting to curb abuses of the practice, and several of the writers who counseled restraint went on to acknowledge that there were certain situations in which an improvised realization was called for. Authors of some treatises probably did intend to proscribe any kind of departure from the notated pitches, but the very fact that they found it necessary admonish performers who took liberties with the scores is evidence that some cellists were in the habit of improvising elaborations.

All of this points to a greater emphasis on harmonic thinking than one would expect for an instrument that is usually considered melodic. While all of the published treatises that deal explicitly with figured bass realization and other harmonic practices on the cello date from after Bach's death, we should bear in mind that there are virtually no treatises of any kind for the cello before the mid-eighteenth century, and that the earliest published treatises were aimed primarily at amateur musicians — they offer only indirect evidence of professional practices. Although we can never be certain of the degree to which later treatises are relevant to Bach's music, the practices that they describe reflect the same kind of harmonic thinking and improvisatory traditions that had clearly been important to viol players for the previous two centuries. Thanks to the work of Olivieri, we now have clear evidence of Italian partimento practices on the cello, and I would argue that Bach's monumental collection of suites, when considered in light of the pedagogical strategies of the German thoroughbass tradition, argue strongly for the existence of similar improvisatory practices North of the Alps.

Bibliography

Anonymous 1799
Anonymous. 'Einige Tonkünstler älterer Zeiten', in: *Algemeine musikalische Zeitung*, no. 3 (1799), pp. 34-38.

Baumgartner 1774
Baumgartner, Johann Baptiste. *Instructions de musique theorique et pratique: a l'usage du violoncello*, La Haye, Monnier, 1774.

Christensen 1996
Christensen, Thomas. 'Johann Nikolaus Bach als Musiktheoretiker', in: *Bach-Jarbuch*, no. 82 (1996), pp. 93-100.

Christensen 2008
Id. '*Fundamenta partiturae*: Thoroughbass and Foundations of Eighteenth-Century Composition Pedagogy', in: *The Century of Bach and Mozart: Perspectives on Historiography, Composition, Theory and Performance in Honor of Christoph Wolff*, Cambridge (MA), Harvard University Press, 2008, pp. 17-33.

Federhofer 1958
Federhofer, Hellmut. 'Zur handschriftlichen Überlieferung der Musiktheorie in Österreich in der zweiten Hälfte des 17. Jahrhunderts', in: *Die Musikforschung*, XI (1958), pp. 264-279.

Federhofer 1965
Id. 'Musiktheoretische Schriften aus Johannes Matthias Spergers Besitz', in: *Sbornik Praci Filosoficke Fakulty Brneske University*, XIV/F9 (1965), pp. 71-77.

Fellerer 1930
Fellerer, Karl Gustav. 'Das Partimentospiel, eine Aufgabe des Organisten im 18. Jahrhundert', in: *Premier congrès. Société International de Musicologie: compte rendu*, edited by Peter Wagner and Wilhelm Merian, Guilford, Billing, 1930, pp. 109-112.

Fellerer 1940
Id. *Der Partimento-Spieler: Übungen in Generalbass-Spiel und in gebundener Improvisation*, Leipzig, Breitkopf & Härtel, 1940.

Gerber 1790-1792
Gerber, Ernst Ludwig. 'Schetky, Christoph', in: *Historisch-biographisches Lexikon der Tonkünstler*, Leipzig, Breitkopf, 1790-1792.

Gjerdingen 2007
Gjerdingen, Robert O. *Music in the Galant Style*, Oxford, Oxford University Press, 2007.

Goehr 1992

Goehr, Lydia. *The Imaginary Museum of Musical Works: An Essay in the Philosophy of Music*, Oxford, Clarendon Press, 1992.

Gunn 1802

Gunn, John. *An Essay Theoretical and Practical, with Copious and Easy Examples on the Application of the Principles of Harmony, Through Bass, and Modulation to the Violoncello*, London, Preston for the Author, 1802.

Lutterman 2006

Lutterman, John. *Works in Progress: J. S. Bach's Suites for Solo Cello as Artifacts of Improvisatory Practices*, Ph.D. Diss., Ann Arbor (MI), UMI Research Press, 2006.

Lutterman 2011

Id. '«Cet art est la perfection du talent». Chordal Thoroughbass Realization and Improvised Solo Performance on the Viol and Cello in the Eighteenth Century', in: *Beyond Notes: Improvisation in Western Music of the Eighteenth and Nineteenth Centuries*, edited by Rudolf Rasch, Brepols, Turnhout, 2011 (Speculum Musicae, 16), pp. 111-128.

Lutterman 2019

Id. 'Re-Creating Historical Improvisatory Solo Practices on the Cello: C. Simpson, F. Niedt, and J. S. Bach on the Pedagogy of *Contrapunctis Extemporalis*', in: *Musical Improvisation in the Baroque Era*, edited by Fulvia Morabito, Brepols, Turnhout, 2019 (Speculum Musicae, 33), pp. 241-260.

Olivieri 2021

Olivieri, Guido. 'The Early History of the Cello in Naples: Giovanni Bononcini, Rocco Greco and Gaetano Francone in a Forgotten Manuscript Collection', in: *Eighteenth-Century Music*, xviii (2021), pp. 65-97.

Poulin 1989

Niedt, Friedrich Erhardt. *The Musical Guide*, edited and translated by Pamela Lee Poulin and Irmgard C. Taylor, introduction and explanatory notes by Pamela Lee Poulin, Oxford, Clarendon Press, 1989 (Early Music Series, 8).

Remeš – Maul 2021

Remeš, Derek – Maul, Michael. 'Jakob Adlung's «Anweisung zum Fantasiren» (c.1725-7): Edition, Translation, and Commentary', in: *Early Music*, lix/3 (2021), pp. 429-439.

Sandys – Forster 1864

Sandys, William – Forster, Simon Andrew. *The History of the Violin and other Instruments Played on with the Bow, from the Remotest Times to the Present*, London, William Reeves, 1864.

Sanguinetti 2012

Sanguinetti, Giorgio. *The Art of Partimento: History, Theory, and Practice*, Oxford-New York, Oxford University Press, 2012.

Schulenberg 1982
Schulenberg, David. 'Composition as Variation: Inquiries into the Compositional Procedures of the Bach Circle of Composers', in: *Current Musicology*, no. 33 (1982), pp. 57-87.

Schulenberg 1984
Id. 'Composition before Rameau: Harmony, Figured Bass, and Style in the Baroque', in: *College Music Symposium*, XXIV/2 (1984), pp. 130-148.

Schulenberg 1995
Id. 'Composition and Improvisation in the School of J. S. Bach', in: *Bach Perspectives 1*, edited by Russell Stinson, (1995), pp. 1-42.

Schulze 1978
Schulze, Hans-Joachim. '«Das Stück in Goldpapier»: Ermittlungen zu einigen Bach-Abschriften des frühen 18. Jahrhunderts', in: *Bach Jahrbuch*, XXXII (1978), pp. 19-42.

Van der Straeten 1915
Straeten, Edmund S. J. van der. *History of the Violoncello, the Viola da Gamba, their Precursors and Collateral Instruments, with Biographies of all the Most Eminent Players of Every Country, the Result of Thirty Years Research*, London, W. Reeves, 1915.

Van Tour 2015
Van Tour, Peter. *Counterpoint and Partimento: Methods of Teaching Composition in Late Eighteenth-Century Naples*, Uppsala, Acta Universitatis Upsaliensis, 2015 (Studia musicologica Upsaliensia. Nova Series, 25).

National Styles in Lower String Accompaniment of Secco Recitatives in the Late Eighteenth and Early Nineteenth Centuries

Hilary Metzger
(Pôle Aliènor, Centre d'études supérieur
de musique à Poitiers)

Over the past twenty-five years, many musicologists and cellists have studied the cello's role in realising harmonies while executing basslines from earlier times. After David Watkin's ground-breaking article on cello accompaniment in Corelli[1], and Valerie Walden's seminal book on cello playing from 1740 to 1840[2], there came a multitude of works on this subject, including writings by Claudio Bacciagaluppi (concerning 19th-century opera in Italy)[3], John Lutterman (in Bach)[4], Nathan Whittaker (in repertoire from 1660-1850)[5], Marc Vanscheeuwijck (as related to different lower string instrument sizes and playing positions)[6], and Christopher Suckling (in Handel)[7]. Recently, much attention has been focused on newly discovered manuscripts from 17th-century Naples documenting the partimento writing and teaching traditions coming from that city, a musical exercise that influenced cellists throughout Italy for two centuries[8].

Many of these investigations have dwelt on the cello's accompaniment role in secco recitatives, the recitatives where only one bass note, with or without figures, is written in

---

1. Watkin 1996.
2. Walden 1998.
3. Bacciagaluppi 2006.
4. Lutterman 2011.
5. Whittaker 2012.
6. Vanscheeuwijck, 2016; Vanscheeuwijck 2020.
7. Suckling 2015.
8. Barbati 2019; Bahn 2021; Olivieri 2021. See also Lutterman's chapter in the present volume and Bahn – Barbati 2023.

support of the vocal line. Here, written instructions, testimonies and examples of harmonic realisations by cellists are particularly well documented throughout Europe, especially from the mid-18th century.

In order to build on these recent analyses, this chapter focuses on national differences in the lower string accompaniments of later secco recitative repertoire, that is, from the late 18th to the mid-19th century. Firstly, it will address the presence and the role of the double bass in these settings; then it will examine differences in harmonic execution on the cello, including choices of voice leading and chordal inversions, text relevance and synchronicity, types of arpeggiation, and styles of preluding.

The Double Bass in Late 18th- and 19th-Century Secco Recitative Accompaniment

Nowadays, in most productions of the operas of Mozart, Rossini, Donizetti etc., the secco recitatives are usually accompanied either by a keyboard instrument alone, or by a keyboard instrument in conjunction with a cello[9]. This practice stands in stark contrast with late 18th- and early 19th-century practice throughout Europe, when the double bass was often considered an essential part of the continuo group in recitative accompaniment. This cello-bass duo formed a team, with the former playing the harmonies and the latter providing the written note in the bass line. Sometimes they played along with a keyboard instrument, but frequently a keyboard instrument either was not present or was relegated to a more marginal position within the continuo group. This situation arose even before the mid-19th century when keyboard instruments were less common in opera orchestras[10].

In London, starting in the late 18th century and continuing for nearly 50 years, Robert Lindley, the cellist, and Domenico Dragonetti, the double bassist, formed a secco recitative accompaniment duo that was celebrated throughout Europe. Although Lindley also performed widely as a soloist and chamber musician and was, for many years after his death, the reference against which all foreign virtuoso cellists performing in Great Britain were compared[11], his obituary in the *Musical Times* singled out only his recitative playing[12]. When, in 1837, a piano

---

[9].   An in-depth examination of current cello recitative accompaniment worldwide will be published soon by the same author in *Performance Practice Review*.

[10].   The presence and role of keyboard instruments in recitative accompaniment is not the focus of this article, and it varied significantly between countries, but by the mid-19th century, most European opera seating plans no longer show a keyboard instrument in the pit.

[11].   Te Haar 2019, pp. 45-47.

[12].   Musical Times 1855, p. 61. Even though Dragonetti and Lindley accompanied the 'sung speech' of others so remarkably in recitatives, they both had difficulty making their own speech understood: Dragonetti constantly

exceptionally replaced this duo to accompany the recitatives during an opera performance, a critic from the *Musical World* pointedly «regretted» that the cello and double bass were absent in this role[13]. Recitative accompaniment by just cello and double bass is documented late into the 19th century in England, with at least one source from that time incorrectly hinting that this combination was a national peculiarity[14].

Franz Joseph Fröhlich, the opera director and pedagogue from Würzburg, published a cello method (and a double bass method) in c.1810, with a lengthy section on secco recitative playing, claiming that this music should be accompanied only by the cello playing chords and the double bass playing the written bass note[15]. In Karlsruhe, the violinist, composer and conductor, Ferdinand Gassner, wrote in 1844 that a cello and a double bass duo (i.e. without a keyboard instrument) was one of the most common recitative accompaniment combinations of his day. None of the four possible recitative accompaniment solutions he cited as most common included the keyboard-cello duo so prevalent today[16].

In Italy, where keyboard instruments are well-documented in recitative accompaniment in the first part of 19th century[17], the concept of a cello-bass 'continuo team' was nonetheless demonstrated by their titles, *violoncello al cembalo* and *contrabbasso al cembalo*: initially the two instruments sat on either side of the harpsichord and all three players read off the same score. These titles continued to define their matched positions during the early 20th century, long after keyboard instruments had disappeared from the opera pit. In non-operatic works from the 19th century, the principal cellist and the principal bass player remained a physically close 'team', as they often still shared a stand[18].

In Vienna and Prague, finally, the double bass was not only known as a virtuoso instrument, but it was also considered important in recitative accompaniment. The operetta composer, Ferdinand Kauer, in his very concise, twelve-page, cello method from 1788, felt it necessary to include a musical example of cello-bass recitative accompaniment[19]. In his 1807 double bass method, the double bass virtuoso Wenze Hause wrote of recitative accompaniment with only the double bass and keyboard[20]. In the section on recitative accompaniment from his c.1829 cello method, Bernard Stiasny, principal cellist at the Prague opera, briefly mentioned the presence of

mixed the vocabulary and syntax of the five languages he spoke to the great confusion of most of his listeners, and Lindley was a stutterer.

13. *MUSICAL WORLD* 1837, p. 126.
14. FISCHER 1891, p. 100.
15. FRÖHLICH 1810, p. 89.
16. GASSNER 1844, p. 118.
17. GALEAZZI 1817; SCARAMELLI 1811.
18. QUARENGHI 1877, Part III/1; BILLE 1922, Part I/4, p. 54.
19. KAUER 1788, p. 12.
20. HAUSE 1807, p. 48.

a harpsichord, but then provided no fewer than 30 pages of recitative accompaniment examples specifying the notes for only the double bass and cello (see ILL. 1). It is clear from his choice of voicings that the double bass was considered indispensable; frequently, only the double bass, sounding an octave lower than printed, supplied the printed bass note of the chord[21].

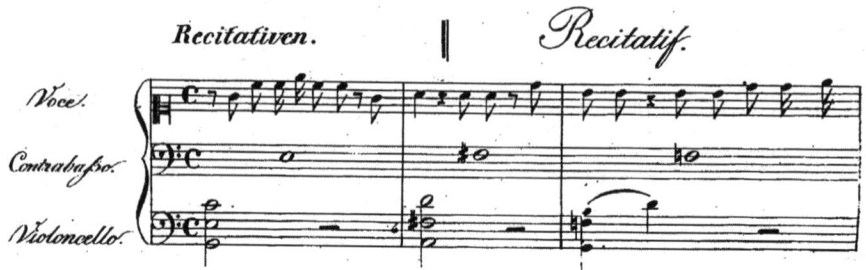

ILL. 1: STIASNY, Bernard. *Violoncell-Schule*, Mainz, Schott, c.1829, p. 21.

In France, on the other hand, the involvement of the double bass in secco recitative accompaniment was less openly acknowledged, though double basses certainly did join cellists in this task in some instances. The list of musicians at the Théâtre Italien in 1818, for example, refers to both a *premier violoncelle d'accompagnement* and a *première contrebasse d'accompagnement*[22]. Giacomo Meyerbeer in *Les Huguenots*, writes out the notes to be played by the first cellist and first double bassist in his recitatives, and like Stiasny, referenced above, he treats the two instruments as a team, using the presence of the bass to allow the cello to play different inversions of the harmonies[23].

Otherwise, sources from France that discuss chordal realisation for cellists in recitative accompaniment from the late 18th and early 19th centuries avoid mentioning the double bass. This includes the 'harpegement' entry written by Rousseau in Diderot's *Encyclopédie* (1765)[24], the reference to recitative accompaniment in Jean Raoul's *Méthode de Violoncelle* (1797)[25], as well as the treatment of cello harmonic realisation found in the Paris Conservatory Cello Method (1804)[26] and in Charles Baudiot's *Méthode de Violoncelle* (1826)[27]. As the latter three sources also do not mention any keyboard instrument, perhaps the authors just assumed the

21. STIASNY 1829, p 21.
22. Archives Nationales, AJ 13, 130, III and V; and AJ 13 131/II. My thanks to Janet Johnson for her help in finding these sources.
23. MEYERBEER 1836, p. 99. Though much of his professional career was spent in France, Meyerbeer was educated in Germany and lived as a young composer for many years in Italy.
24. ROUSSEAU 1765.
25. RAOUL 1797, p. 41.
26. BAILLOT *ET AL.* 1804.
27. BAUDIOT 1826.

presence of both instruments along with the cello in such settings. Nevertheless, it is striking that in their proposed realisations, the cellist is always instructed to play the printed bass note as the root of the chord except in very occasional cases of passing sevenths. This is a marked difference from Kauer, Fröhlich, Stiasny, Simmandl[28], Fischer and even (German and Italian influenced) Meyerbeer, where the cellist is often instructed to ignore the printed bass note and play other (usually easier) chordal voicings while the double bass plays the printed note. Through their words and their musical examples, it thus appears that French cellists did not view the cello and double bass as being as important a continuo team as did musicians elsewhere in Europe.

The double bass was not only perceived as less indispensable to recitative accompaniment in France, it was also viewed as less important and less deserving of respect generally, especially when compared to its image in other European countries at the same time. As Michael Greenberg has noted, in 1793 a double bass class existed at the Institut National de Musique, (the predecessor to the Conservatoire in Paris), but this class closed from 1798 through 1826 due to a lack of interested students and no professor. When a new bass professor was recruited in 1827, the hiring committee obliged him to teach with a bow model that he had never used before, an act of condescension that would be difficult to imagine being imposed on a new violin or cello professor[29].

Given the absence of a double bass class, most professional bassists in France during the early 19th century may well have been trained as cellists. Like their Italian counterparts, French double basses had only three strings at this time, but in France they were tuned in fifths, whereas in Italy, they were usually tuned in fourths, A^1-D^2-G^2. The larger interval between strings may have felt more familiar to ex-cellists, but it would have been more difficult to play fast scalar passages distinctly, because the fifth tuning requires significantly more shifting.

In any case, negative descriptions of orchestral double bass playing appear in France at this time, with this disrespectful attitude exemplified here in two editions of Justus Johann Friedrich Dotzauer's cello method published in the 1830s. Dotzauer was principal cellist in the Dresden court orchestra; most great German cellists throughout the 19th century studied either with him or with one of his students. In the entirely German version of his cello method published in Vienna c.1832, the paragraph on the role of the cello with respect to the bass reads as follows:

> In the orchestra, the cello serves to define more sharply the foundation from the double basses, which usually sound an octave lower, because the low tones from the double basses, especially when they follow one another in fast tempi, do not sound audible enough to the ear without other support. In addition to this function,

---

[28]. SIMMANDL 1890.
[29]. GREENBERG 2000, pp. 91-94, 108-113.

the cello is often on its own, and, without the double bass, serves as foundation for the melody or has its own melody. In the Quartet music of our best masters, the cello's role is similarly divided, in that it is sometimes playing the bass line and other times playing independent parts. As a solo instrument, like all other instruments in this category, it need only preoccupy itself with the principal line[30].

But in the 1838 French-German translation of Dotzauer's method, the version most often translated in the 19th century and the one commonly consulted by 'historically informed' cellists today, the roles of the cello and bass are described quite differently:

> The arpeggios, the double stops and the harmonics, among others, offer to cello players a great number of distinctive shades of nuances when they play as soloists. The compositions of Beethoven, Cherubini and others demonstrate the use of the cello in the orchestra. What little use would the muffled, scarcely audible sounds of the double basses have in fast movements if the cellos did not clarify their role? For this reason, it would be desirable if each double bass in the orchestra were seconded by two cellists[31].

The order of the roles for the cello is inverted between these different editions: the French translation puts the solo capacity of the cello first, while the German version places it last, possibly hinting that solo playing is less difficult than other roles. Most importantly, the German text implies that the actual bass line belongs to the double basses, with the cellists rendering it somewhat more audible whereas the French text, deriding the «muffled» and «scarcely audible sounds» emanating from double basses on fast notes, describes the cellos as furnishing the true bass line.

---

[30]. «Im Orchester dient das Violonzell meistentheils dazu, die Grundstimme des Contrabasses, welche gewöhnlich um eine Octave tiefer erklingt, schärfer zu markiren; weil die tieferen Töne des Contrabasses, besonders wenn sie im schnellen Zeitmass auf einander folgen, dem Ohr ohne anderweitige Unterstützung nicht vernehmlich genug erklingen. Neben dieser Funktion, tritt das Violonzell auch oft als für sich selbstständig auf, und dient ohne Contrabass als Unterstützung einer Melodie, oder führt selbst eine eigene Melodie. – In der Quartettmusik unserer besten Meister ist die Funktion des Violonzells ebenfalls getheilt, indem es bald die Grundstimme führt, bald ganz selbstständig auftritt. – Als Soloinstrument hat es, wie die übrigen Instrumente der Art, nur mit der Principalstimme zu thun». Dotzauer 1832, p. 14.

[31]. «Les arpèggios, les doubles cordes, les sons de Flageolet et de ponticelle offrent en-outre une grande quantité de nuances apréciables au [sic] joueurs de Violoncelle, lors qu'ils s'appliquent au solo. Les compositions de Beethoven, Cherubini et al. démontrent l'utilité du violoncelle pour l'orchestre. De combien peu serviroient les sons étouffés et sourds des contrebasses dans les mouvements précipités, si les violoncelles n'éclaircissoient pas leur marche! Il seroit désirable pour cet effet que chaque contrebasse fût secondé à l'orchestre par deux violoncelles». Dotzauer 1838, p. 1. These words appear in the Introduction of the bilingual edition where they are translated into German. In the German-only version, the words discussing the cello's role appear in the opening to the second section. The first section of the German edition, omitted in the French-German bilingual translation, is devoted to explaining musical notation.

The different language in the two texts also underscores a crucial aesthetic question, which is important to bassline playing in general: is the 'true' bassline what the cellos are playing at pitch, as the French 'translation' claims, and the basses then enhance or amplify that by playing the same notes an octave lower? Or is the 16-foot instrument playing the 'real' bassline, and the cellos are merely refining this part with added notes that sound an octave higher?

Most French orchestras in the 19th century had significantly more cellos than basses, though an examination of the personnel lists of various orchestras in Paris that played Italian repertoire during this period does show at certain times slightly more basses than cellos. This difference, however, was not nearly as significant in these French 'Italian' opera orchestras as it was in the truly Italian ones[32].

A comparison of the orchestral salaries at the Théâtre Italien in Paris from 1818 until 1827, shows further proof of the French double bass player's lower status: the principal double bass player always earned less than the principal cellist — sometimes markedly so. Despite his 'solo' accompanimental role in the secco recitatives, which were still common in comic Italian operas at this point, the principal bass's salary was often on par with the leader of the second violins[33]. At the Paris Opéra, where there were usually no secco recitatives to accompany, the discrepancy was even greater: in 1811, the highest paid cellist received 3000 francs, compared to only 1800 for the double bassist in the same position[34].

In Italy, the relationship between the cello and double bass was very different, with the latter instrument perceived to be more important. This reversal of accepted instrumental roles cannot be explained by differences in tessitura, as some writers have implied, for the cellos were tuned to the same notes in both countries and the lowest note on an Italian bass was usually only a step higher than the equivalent note on a French bass from the same period. Yet, in contrast to French ensembles, Italian opera orchestras usually had significantly more basses than celli and their ballet orchestras sometimes had no cellos at all[35].

The cello and double bass part in ILL. 2 comes from orchestral material for the opera, *Corrado d'Altamura* by Federico Ricci, found in the archives at the Pergola Theater in Florence and performed in 1841[36]. It not only demonstrates how the bass was considered more important than the cello in that setting, but also prompts the modern reader to examine current assumptions about the appropriate instrumental roles for these two instruments. First of all, the part is labelled for «Basso e Violoncello». Such a title is 'backwards' in today's world: shared material, which one still sometimes finds in orchestral settings, is always labelled for 'Cello and Bass'.

[32].   KELLY 2000, p. 198.

[33].   Archives Nationales AJ 13 130; AJ 13 131.

[34].   AUDEON – COLAS – DI PROFIO 2008, p. 222.

[35].   SPITZER – ZASLAW 2004, pp. 537-531.

[36].   Archivio dell'Accademia degli Immobili | Teatro della Toscana, document 1368.

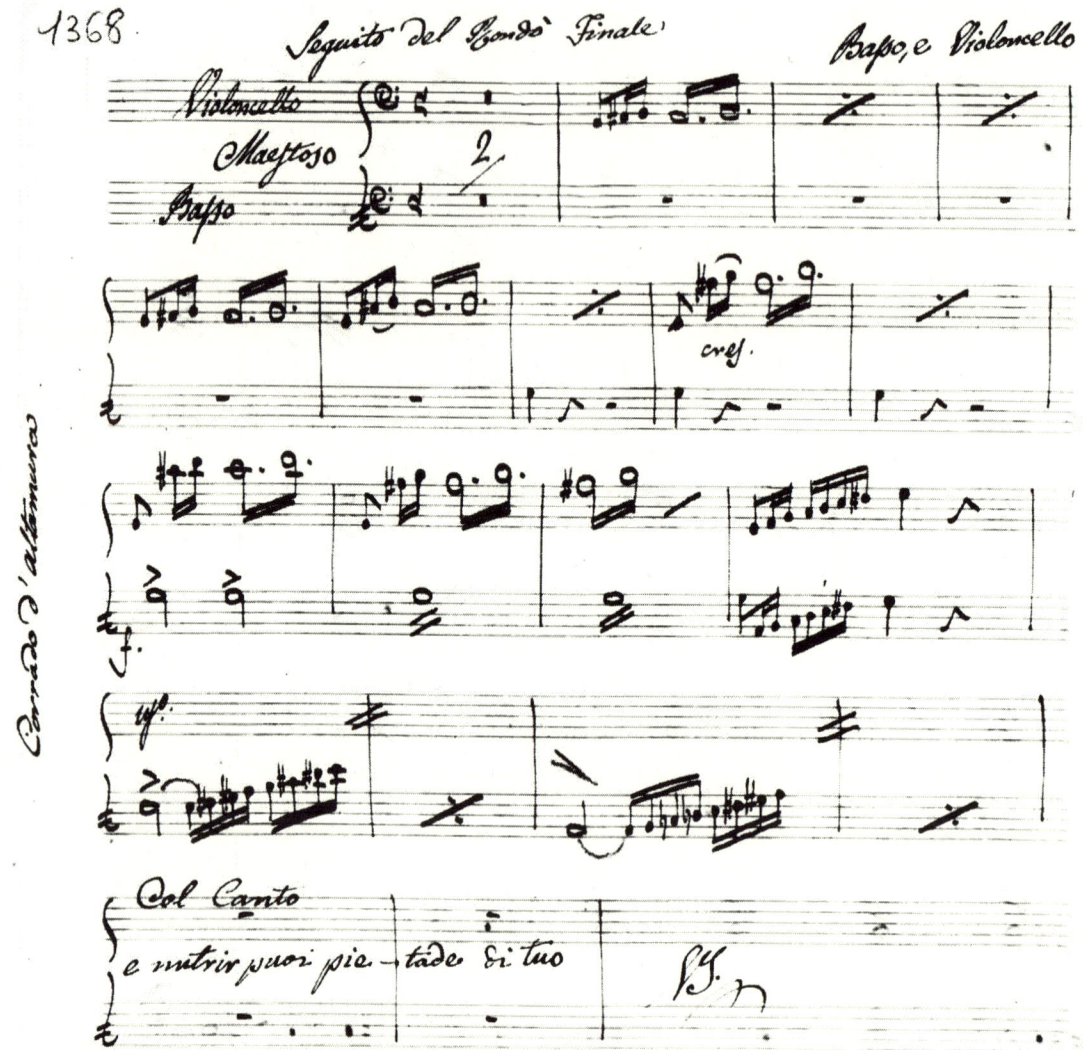

ILL. 2: RICCI 1841, cello and double bass part.

The Ricci opera excerpt begins with different parts for the two instruments. Nevertheless, in the fourth system, both the cellos and the basses must read the same notes. It is the cellist's eyes, however, that are required to change staves and read off another line. At the Paris Opera, at about the same time (and indeed, still today in shared cello/bass material), it is the double bass player, who must be more accommodating in such a situation (see ILL. 3).

This notational detail might mean that the Italian copyist viewed the 'real' bass line as coming from the double bass, or perhaps, that the double bassist's stature in the orchestra at that time demanded that he be less inconvenienced.

Ill. 3: Gioachino Rossini, *Le Siège de Corinthe*, 1826 BnF MAT-239 (342), p. 59.

In a libretto from a performance of Donizetti's *Lucia di Lammermoor* at La Fenice in 1836, the principal double bass is listed ahead of the principal cello in what is otherwise a list of high-to-low string instruments, demonstrating its greater importance[37].

This lower status of orchestral cellists in Italy continued into the later part of the 19th century. In 1854, Giuseppe Verdi rewrote a difficult passage for cellos and violas for a performance of his opera *Simon Boccanegra* in Reggio Emilia so that the inferior playing from this «pack of dogs» as he called them, would not be exposed[38]. As late as 1874, when Ercole Folegatti wrote about orchestral leadership, he recommended placing a «few skilled players» in the inner circle close to the conductor: a first violin, a second violin, a viola and a double bass. The cello was conspicuously absent[39]. It is not a coincidence that two 19th century virtuoso bass players, who also became known as leaders in orchestral situations, Domenico Dragonetti and Giovanni Paolo Bottesini, were from Italy. They had grown up in a culture where their instrument was viewed as a powerful orchestral entity[40].

National Styles
in 19ᵀᴴ-Century Recitative Accompaniment by Cellists

Probably, individual taste accounted for most of the differences in accompanying styles from recitative accompanying cellists, but when examined together, the evidence does point

---

37. <http://archiviostorico.teatrolafenice.it/scheda_0a.php?ID=3464>, accessed October 2023.

38. Harwood 1986, p. 111.

39. Folegatti 1874, p. 76; Meucci 2011, p. 134.

40. Bottesini became a conductor and Dragonetti was often described as leading the orchestra through the force of his playing. Palmer 1997, p. 85.

toward certain national tendencies about voicings, arpeggiation and asynchronous chordal placement. Above all, the number of sources listed here serves to remind the reader how ubiquitous cello chordal accompaniment was throughout Europe in earlier times.

The Paris Conservatory cello method from 1804[41] is an excellent starting point: it not only treats recitative accompaniment by cellists in some detail, but coming from the Conservatoire, the work had enormous influence on all French cellists (of course), and was also read throughout Europe. The words on recitative accompaniment in this method were translated into German by 1810[42], into English in 1827[43], and apparently even into Russian in 1840[44]. Furthermore, as some of the section on recitative realisation from this method found its way into the bilingual version of Dotzauer's cello method published by Schott in 1838 and since Dotzauer's method was also widely read and translated from this bi-lingual version, these recitative instructions maintained their influence throughout the entire century.

Like all instrumental methods published by the Paris Conservatory at this time, this work was written by committee: Pierre Baillot, the great violinist and pedagogue, was first in the list of authors. Also named were Charles-Simon Catel, the illustrious professor of harmony, and the two cello professors from the Conservatoire: Jean-Henri Levasseur, who was principal cellist at the Opéra, and his student, Charles Nicolas Baudiot. The latter two musicians were also to become first cellists of Napoleon's Imperial Chapel Orchestra where they often accompanied secco recitatives. Baudiot wrote his own cello method twenty years later.

---

41. BAILLOT *ET AL.* 1804.
42. FRÖHLICH 1810.
43. CROUCH 1827.
44. St Petersburg, Zotov, 1840, listed in ATANASOV 2018.

ILL. 4: BAILLOT *ET AL*. 1804, pp. 138-139.

After brief written instructions, the authors provide an example of cello accompaniment in recitative excerpts from *La Serva Padrona*, by Giovanni Battista Pergolesi[45]. Since this example is so important to recitative playing pedagogy throughout the 19th century, I include it here in its entirety (see ILL. 4). As with the other examples of realisation in recitatives provided by cellists, the upper line in bass clef was written by the composer; the lower line is what the cellist should play. In this example, there is no mention of a keyboard instrument or a double bass[46].

---

45. BAILLOT *ET AL*. 1804, pp. 138-139.
46. It is fascinating that these authors chose a work which had been composed over 70 years earlier, but which still carried notoriously strong Italian connotations for the Parisian public from its role during the *Querelle des*

It would be difficult for any cellist to imagine playing the realisation given here based on the instructions provided: there are four instances (mm. 2, 4, 9, 13) where the cellist is told to repeat the same harmony, even though this was against the authors' own rules. Similarly, the cellist does not always play the change of harmony where the composer has notated it, rather the new chord is rhythmically displaced, sometimes to a rest in the singer's part (mm. 8, 9, 11-12, 12, 13). Nor is the cellist obliged to play the seventh degree of the harmony, even when that note is written in the bass line (m. 7). Certainly the cellist should leave it out, even when indicated in the figures, if it is already in the singer's part, presumably in order to avoid doubling the dissonance (and its required resolution) causing parallel octaves (mm. 2, 9, 15)[47].

Chord Voicings

Not doubling the seventh was a well-known rule in harmony studies generally and the authors in their verbal instructions say the cellist must know how to 'save the dissonances' and avoid parallel fifths and octaves[48]. Many other cellists who wrote recitative accompaniment examples at this time, however, frequently violated these standard rules of voice leading and doubling. Jean Baumgartner, for example, who writes one of the earliest pedagogic texts for recitative realisation (c.1774), repeatedly flouts such rules in his exercises and examples of harmonic realisation in order to write harmonies that are more easily playable or more resonant on the cello[49]. Bernard Stiasny, first cellist at the Prague Opera, gives many examples of the cello doubling the leading tones and the sevenths that appear in the singer's part[50]. What seems to be more important in the voicing choices for these other, often German-speaking, sources, was making sure that the singer's first note was the highest note in the cellist's chord. No mention was made of the fact that this could potentially create parallel octaves with the voice[51].

The Paris Conservatory Method follows good voice leading principles more often than other sources, even going to lengths to avoid parallel fifths on V – I at cadences (m. 5). One imagines that Charles-Simon Catel had some influence here, as did, no doubt, the heavily theoretical component of a French musical education generally. In his own cello method written

---

bouffons. Secco recitative was also called 'Italian' recitative in France, due to the fact that it was much more common in Italian opera, particularly comic operas by this point.

[47]. In the bi-lingual version published the following year, these added sevenths of the vocal part are all indicated by figures. This first edition is missing the figures on the second page.

[48]. John GUNN 1802, was also very concerned with good voice leading in his heavily theoretical approach to harmonic cello playing, though he does not dwell directly on recitative accompaniment. My thanks to George Kennaway for pointing this out.

[49]. BAUMGARTNER 1774, p. 12.

[50]. STIASNY 1829, pp. 21-50.

[51]. FRÖHLICH 1810, p. 90.

twenty years later, Charles Nicolas Baudiot mentions his gratitude for Catel's teaching[52]. Here, Baudiot explains good voice leading principles in more depth, even with ninth harmonies. Baudiot usually follows these rules in his examples, but he too doubles the seventh occasionally[53].

The most rigorous application of voice leading rules in harmonic accompaniment is seen, however, in the later Italian methods, no doubt a reflection of their inherited partimento tradition. Guglielmo Quarenghi, the first cellist at La Scala as of 1850 and professor at the Milan Conservatory one year later, wrote a multi-volumed, exceedingly thorough cello method in 1877. He and his contemporary Gaetano Braga, who published a cello method four years earlier[54], give many exercises with polyphonic writing for the cello that contain excellent voice leading. Just before his discussion of recitative accompaniment, Quarenghi provides 27 pages of theoretical and practical harmonic writing, including the Rule of the Octave (Ill. 5) in several keys (with cellistic applications) and the preparation and resolution of many cadential formulas with various seventh, ninth and eleventh harmonies.

Ill. 5: Quarenghi 1877, part iii §i, p. 313.

Yet, as seen above, even Quarenghi includes parallel fifths in his rule-of-the-octave harmonisation for the cello, and he doubles the seventh in his recitative example! (On the same Ab as Baudiot, by a strange coincidence.) Perhaps we cellists are not as obliged as our keyboard colleagues players to have good voice-leading after all.

Text and Chordal Synchronicity

As shown above, the Paris Method also encourages the cellist to play harmony changes where they are not rhythmically indicated, though none of this interjectory behavior is mentioned in the verbal instructions.

---

[52]. Baudiot 1826, vol. ii, p. 192.

[53]. *Ibidem*, pp. 193-194.

[54]. Braga 1873.

Other sources also discuss the importance of such asynchronous chordal placement. In Italy, this usually occurred after the cadences. Giuseppe Scaramelli, concertmaster and director at the opera in Trieste, writes in 1811 that the cellist and bassist should always play after the end of the word so that the audience will not lose the last syllable[55]. In an article from 1882 on secco recitatives in *Il Teatro illustrato*, Amintore Galli laments the lost art of cello improvisations that occurred *after the end of the singer's sentence* (author's emphasis)[56]. In the one known early recording with solo cello chordal accompaniment of recitatives, (an excerpt from the Barber of Seville from Milan from about 1915), the cellist systematically plays every chord after the cadence, always during the singer's rests[57].

If Italian sources prefer the cellist to 'speak' after the cadence, sources outside of Italy, like the Paris Conservatory guidelines, give examples of asynchronous placement or re-iteration of the harmonies during rests that occur before the cadences (see ILL. 6).

ILL. 6: FISCHER 1891, p. 100.

Playing the harmonies in the rests — instead of synchronising them with the singer's words as the printed score indicates — not only avoids the risk of not being together with

---

55. «[...] la botta sempre dopo la parola, giacché altrimenti l'uditorio perderebbe ne' recitativi l'ultima sillaba». SCARAMELLI 1811, p. 44.

56. GALLI 1882, p. 131.

57. <https://youtu.be/8CiaAiCAOq0>, accessed October 2023.

the voice, it also allows the public to hear and understand the text more easily, and allows the singer to hear the harmonies better and to stay in tune. These moments of interjected double stops or re-voiced harmonies during the phrase are also similar to the words that people use as listeners to prove their interest and attentiveness: ('Really? Yes. Goodness!'). As such, they create a dialogue with the singer, and give the continuo group a more active supporting role.

Fascinatingly, many 19th-century sources even discuss cello recitative accompaniment to a vocal line that has no text! The following sources:
- Jean Baumgartner, 1774, La Haye (Augsburg);
- F. A. Kauer, 1788, Vienna;
- F. J. Fröhlich 1810, Bonn (Würzburg);
- J. G. C. Schetky, 1811, London (Darmstadt, Hamburg, Edinburgh);
- Ch. Baudiot, 1826, Paris (Text missing in preparatory exercise, not in example);
- Bernard Stiasny, c.1829, Mainz (Prague);

all give textless recitative excerpts. (The city after the date indicates where the work was published; the city in parenthesis indicates where the musician was educated or performed often). Note that these sources were primarily written by musicians who were educated or who performed in German-speaking places where the opera tradition had replaced secco recitative with spoken dialogue. Fröhlich's example is fascinating in this regard: he starts out by copying the famous example from Pergolesi's *La Serva Padrona*, which is found in the Paris Conservatory Method. He reproduces their realisation exactly but leaves out the text as well as the (relatively few) dynamic markings. He then adds, however, his own line of additional recitative with a German text, but this example is overflowing with dynamic and expressive instructions. Clearly, his reading and understanding of the words was affecting his accompaniment practice (see ILL. 7).

ILL. 7: FRÖHLICH 1810, p. 91.

153

It is worth noting that unlike Franz Joseph Fröhlich's example above, Frederick William Crouch's Cello Method (London, 1827) does retain the Italian text when copying the Pergolesi example from the Conservatory Method. Although Crouch and Schetky publish cello methods in London only 16 years apart, Schetky's method leaves out the words in his recitative example, probably due to his German heritage.

In all the recitative accompaniment examples for cellists, with text and without, the authors make no mention that knowing the text should influence the how the cellist should play; we must only ensure that the text can be heard and understood by the audience. This seems counterintuitive, perhaps heretical, to continuo cellists trained in earlier recitative performance practice. Instead of illustrating the text, the 19th-century cellist is urged to take into account only *what the singer is doing* with this text, that is, to not cover the singer by playing too loudly or adding too many ornaments and to help the singer when lost. The distinction is an important one: in these 19th century examples, cellists are not expected to interpret the words; they should help in furthering the textual or dramatic interpretation of someone else.

Arpeggiation

Written recitative instructions usually tell the cellist to play a 'short' or 'non-arpeggiated' chord or double stop. The Paris Conservatory Method states: «One should attack the chord without arpeggiation, and in general, in this manner»[58]:

Ill. 8: Baillot *et Al*. 1804, p. 138.

Most modern players would not call this execution to be 'without' arpeggiation, but for French string players in the 19th century the word 'arpeggiation' was used in connection with bowing technique, and one that involved many rapid string crossings. The drawing out of the notes of the chord as demonstrated above would be described as allowing the chord to sound ('*faire sonner*').

Interestingly, this spelling out of chords, even when no arpeggiation symbol was present, and describing such playing as 'non-arpeggiated' was also typical of keyboard players from the same time[59].

---

58. «On doit frapper l'accord sans arpéges et en général de cette manière». Baillot *et Al*. 1804, p. 138.
59. Peres Da Costa 2012, pp. 101-187.

After separating the lower notes in the chord, Charles Baudiot attaches much importance to finishing the chord with the top two notes sounding together, as demonstrated above in the example from the Paris Method that he helped to write. Twenty years later in his own Method, he specified this same approach more strongly:

> I will make the observation that the final chords which I placed in different scales and exercises are to be played down bow, beginning with the lowest note and ending, not as is often the case, with the last high note, but rather in letting the bow stay touching the last two high notes[60].

On the rare occasions when Baudiot wishes each note to sound separately in his recitative accompaniments, he indicates it precisely[61]. Nowhere is it implied that chords should be played quasi-simultaneously. Teaching at the Paris Conservatory for many years, Baudiot may well have persuaded other French cellists to execute their chords in his way, and this technique of separating the bass note(s) but ending the chord with a double stop, might have been a stylistic feature of French recitative accompaniment in the early 19th century[62].

Cellists in Great Britain did not engage in the partially separate and partially-simultaneous chordal execution that we see documented in France. They tended to execute all the notes of the chord separately and they were more likely to use the word 'arpeggiation' in harmonic or accompanimental contexts. The German born but Edinburgh-based cellist, J. G. C. Schetky, demonstrates chordal execution with each note played singly and his recitative example occurs just before his discussion of arpeggiated string crossings.

John Gunn, who wrote the one full work from the 19th century devoted entirely to harmonic cello playing[63], repeatedly writes out arpeggios in his harmonic progressions, clearly placing them in a harmonic role by including them in a book on that subject.

George Alexander Macfarren in an 1872 review of recitative accompaniment for *The Musical Times*, writes that «[...] Cervetto would fill up such otherwise moments of silence with arpeggios or like passages upon his instrument and his audience would be pleased with his feats of skill»[64].

---

[60]. «Je ferai observer que les accords finaux que j'ai mis dans différentes gammes et exercices, s'exécutent en tirant l'archet et en commençant par la note la plus grave, et en finissant, non pas comme cela arrive souvent, par la dernière note aigu [*sic*], mais en laissant l'archet appuyé sur le deux dernières notes aigus». BAUDIOT 1826, p. 13. The same idea is also reiterated on p. 195.

[61]. *Ibidem*, p. 200.

[62]. Jean-Marie Raoul, who also discusses recitative realisation in his *Méthode de Violoncelle* 1797, does space out each individual note of the chord, but he was an amateur cellist, for a long time not based in Paris and his technical approach to the instrument probably had little influence on other French players.

[63]. GUNN 1802.

[64]. MCFARREN 1872, p. 688.

The article on secco recitative in *Grove's Dictionary of Music and Musicians* written by William Smith Rockstro in 1883, depicts Lindley's playing as having many arpeggiated passages, including quite a few that lie on the same string (see Ex. 1).

Ex. 1: ROCKSTRO 1883, pp. 454-455.

Don Giovanni

Of course, these last two examples were written many years after the cellists in question stopped performing and are therefore of questionable reliability. Macfarren could not possibly have heard Giacobbe Cervetto, and says as much, but Rockstro, a music lover living in London who was thirty-two years old when Lindley died, probably did hear Lindley perform[65].

Nonetheless, he wrote this article, à la Muffat[66], many years after the fact. It is highly possible that the authors used the word 'arpeggio' differently from how a string player would have employed the term. Rockstro may not even have been aware that the notes of the arpeggios he imagined Lindley as playing often lie on one string. But these two English concert-goers clearly associated arpeggiated chordal cello playing as an appropriate, if virtuoso, part of recitative accompaniment by cellists.

At least one contemporaneous account confirms the more arpeggiated nature of Robert Lindley's harmonic accompaniments, certainly in comparison to the cellist at the Vienna Opera at the same time:

> [In Vienna,] [t]he chords are indeed struck upon the violoncello (without the *arpeggio* and brilliancy, the unique excellence of Robert Lindley), but their effect is tame[67].

---

65.   My thanks to Will Crutchfield for pointing out this fact, and for many other factual confirmations and sharing sources.

66.   Georg Muffat played under Lully but wrote about Lully's bowing and articulation preferences more than thirty years later.

67.   Edward Holmes, *A Ramble among Musicians of Germany, giving some Account of the operas of Munich, Dresden, Berlin, etc with Remarks upon the Church Music, Singers, Performers and Composers, and a Sample that Await the Lover of Art on a Similar Excursion, by a Musical Professor*, London, Hunt & Clark, 1828, p. 129, quoted in PALMER 1997, p. 116.

Regardless of how simultaneously the accompanimental chords were executed, most cello methods do indicate chord-voicings that lie across strings. Even here, however, cellists would be wrong to view one-string arpeggiation technique as completely 'anti-historical'. In Kauer's method from Vienna (1788), Bernard Stiasny's from Prague (1829), and occasionally in Baudiot's from Paris (1826), there are examples of 'one-string' arpeggiated chords.

Cellists in Italy do not appear to share the arpeggiation preferences of either the French or the British; even early in the 19th century, examples exist of more simultaneous and perhaps more abrupt execution of chords in recitatives. Pietro Rachele, first cellist at the excellent Ducal Court in Parma, defines 'arpeggio' in two ways, but for recitatives, the cellist should start from the lowest note, then proceed to each subsequent note until the entire chord is sounding in a single vibrating stroke[68].

Later Italian methods give even more support to this quasi-simultaneous approach to chordal playing in recitatives. Guglielmo Quarenghi claims that three and four note chords are to be executed with the *strappate* bow stroke, i.e., sounding virtually simultaneously, although the bow must hug the string not too harshly in order to create a robust sound.

The Neapolitan-trained solo cellist and opera composer, Gaetano Braga, published a cello method in 1873 that he claimed was an Italian translation of Dotzauer's Method. Unlike Vincenzo Merighi, whose method from 1838 truly does translate Dotzauer word for word, Braga's approach is much freer, and frequently his words and ideas are completely of his own invention. In this work, arpeggiation has many implications and contexts: arpeggiated string crossings are first introduced early on, in a harmonic context of triple-stop chordal progressions[69], and later as a «*bowstroke* which the cello seems created for»[70]. Nevertheless, eleven pages later he informs the reader that isolated chords of three of four notes should be played with full force as if the bow were a whip. This is similar to Quarenghi's advice, though Braga's words perhaps imply a more aggressively sounding execution[71].

Not only were these Italian cellists describing chord playing in recitatives as being abrupt and almost simultaneous, they were also employing many three and four note chords. This too may be an Italian characteristic, as it is not seen as often and even discouraged in other countries especially in earlier sources[72]. A copyist's version of Donizetti's opera *L'Ajo nell'imbarazzo*

---

[68]. Rachelle 1821, p. 32. It is interesting that this work is dedicated to a woman, Laudelia Giuseppina, who was «Suonatrice di tale Instrumento». It was not common to find female cellists in the early 19th century.

[69]. Braga 1873, Part I, p. 21.

[70]. *Ibidem*, Part II, p. 6.

[71]. *Ibidem*, Part II, p. 17: «Gli arpeggi quasi simultanei di tre o quattro corde, si battono con l'arco sulle corde con tutta la forza, come se l'arco fosse una frusta, specialmente quando quelli sono isolati».

[72]. The Paris Conservatory Method, 1804, has many two note chords and Baumgartner 1774, specifically encourages cellists to play only two notes in order to avoid intonation problems.

located in the Biblioteca del Conservatorio di musica 'S. Pietro a Majella' of Neaples, frequently proposes three- and four-note chords in its secco recitative accompaniments clearly conceived for a cellist[73]. In the 1915 recording from Milan cited earlier, the cellist is always playing such full chords (and executing them in a quasi-simultaneous fashion that Quarenghi and Braga might well have appreciated).

Melodic Ornamentation in Recitative Accompaniment

Discussion thus far has been limited to the placement and execution of chords and harmonies. What about melodic passages, or moments of more cadential-like improvisation? To what extent was this part of the cellist's 'accompanimental' role in recitatives? Here, much more than in the areas discussed above, personal taste must have been paramount in forming the cellist's decision, as it is today. To a certain extent, therefore, looking at historical sources for guidance in this area is, in itself, not historically accurate. As the occasion presents itself, and as continuo cellists today ask themselves these questions often, a brief summary is included here.

Several sources do discourage too much ostentatious playing from the cellist. Clearly, the audience's focus should be on the singers and the action on stage. The Paris Conservatory Method warns that the cellist should accompany simply, without embellishments, and should not spoil or cover the voice[74]. Perhaps most famous is Quarenghi's memorable admonition that the cellist should « not be a master, who wants to dominate the singer, but a friend who favours him »[75].

Even in these more conservative sources, however, the cellist is permitted some melodic ornamentation in recitative accompaniment. The Paris Method condones it in certain silences as long as one stays in the harmony. Quarenghi allows the cellist to add notes when the singer goes out of tune, which of course implies that on the spot, the cellist had enough experience and training to react to such a situation and improvise appropriately. Other sources go even

---

[73]. Biblioteca Identifier: IT\ICCU\MSM\0166201, <https://www.internetculturale.it/jmms/iccuviewer/iccu.jsp?id=oai%3Awww.internetculturale.sbn.it%2FTeca%3A20%3ANT0000%3AIT%5C%5CICCU%5C%5CMSM%5C%5C0166201&mode=all&teca=MagTeca+-+ICCU&viewType=onepage&mediaType=image&objectIndex=0>, accessed October 2023. See pages 33v, 34r, 44r, 44v, 77r, 77v, 78r. My thanks to Jakob Lehmann for this reference.

[74]. BAILLOT ET AL. 1804, pp. 137-138.

[75]. « In fine, non siate un padrone che vuol dominare il Cantante, ma un amico che lo sussidi ». QUARENGHI 1877, Part III/i, p. 331.

further: Stiasny writes in several upper and lower appoggiaturas to the top notes in his chords, Fröhlich suggests the cellist play passages between numbers, at scene changes, and even between harmonies. Amintore Galli in 1882 laments the loss of «elegant, playful and lively arpeggial interjections and modulations» from earlier cellists[76]. And obviously, Lindley was not restraining himself from adding flourishes most of the time.

A close reading of the sources, thus, proposes many avenues of exploration to the historically inquisitive cellist, including some that may challenge current assumptions about appropriate recitative accompaniment practice for late 18th and early 19th century secco recitatives. First of all, the presence of a double bass in the recitative accompaniment group was very common. This instrument was particularly important in Italy, the birthplace and centre of the secco recitative genre. Notably, some famous European opera houses employed no keyboard instrument, but rather used only cello and double bass for secco recitative accompaniment during this period[77]. The bass' presence gives the cellist more improvisatory freedom and a much wider range of possible chordal inversions. When choosing their harmonies, cellists probably tried to observe good voice leading rules, as French and Italian sources in particular advocated in their verbal instructions although these restrictions were by no means expected to be followed in every instance, as so many musical examples of cello harmonic playing from all over the continent demonstrated. Unlike earlier times, word painting and direct textual interpretation from the instrumentalists were not specifically encouraged in the sources from this period, but cellists were encouraged to help the singer express the drama and meaning of the text and were invited to use several techniques to further this goal. These included: not synchronising the placement of the harmonies with the text; using different degrees of arpeggiation (ranging from the quasi-synchronous triple and quadruple stops so common in Italy, to the heavy and spread-out arpeggiation, even along one string, which was often heard in England); and adding melodic or ornamental interludes. Above all, an awareness of the sheer number of sources that treat the subject of improvised harmonic cello recitative accompaniment in the late 18th and 19th century makes it difficult for musicians concerned with historical interpretation to continue to ignore this issue in performances of this repertoire today.

---

[76]. «La esecuzione del *recitativo secco*, come altra volta si denominava il *recitativo semplice*, era nell'opera giocosa leggiadra, vispa, aggraziata, interpolata dagli *accordi arpeggiati* del *violoncello* e del contrabasso detti al *cembalo* perché stavano accanto al maestro che sedeva a questo strumento. Il violoncellista e il contrabassista al *cembalo* erano addottrinati nello studio del *basso numerato*, il che loro permetteva di adornare le modulazioni ricorrenti al termine di ciascuna frase del recitativo, con eleganti fioriture [...]». GALLI 1882, p. 131.

[77]. Here is the author's proposed accompaniment recitative from Gioachino Rossini's *La gazza ladra* with such an instrumentation: <https://youtu.be/bYUW5GsefpQ>, accessed October 2023.

BIBLIOGRAPHY

ATANASOV 2018
ATANASOV, Boris. *A Complete List of Methods, Tutors, Treatises and A Complete List of Etudes, Caprices Exercises for the Violoncello in the XVIII and XIX Centuries*, 2018, <https://www.academia.edu/34449933/A_Complete_List_of_Methods_Tutors_Treatises_and_A_Complete_List_of_Etudes_Caprices_Exercises_for_the_Violoncello_in_the_XVIII_and_XIX_centuries>, accessed October 2023.

AUDEON – COLAS – DI PROFIO 2008
AUDEON, Hervé – COLAS, Damien – DI PROFIO, Alessandro. 'The Orchestras of Paris Opera Houses in the Nineteenth Century', in: *The Opera Orchestra in 18th- and 19th-Century Europe. 1: The Orchestra in Society*, edited by Niels Martin Jensen and Franco Piperno, Berlin, Berliner Wissenschafts-Verlag, 2008 (Musical Life in Europe 1600-1900: Circulation, Institutions, Representation), pp. 217-258.

BACCIAGALUPPI 2006
BACCIAGALUPPI, Claudio. '«Primo Violoncello al cembalo». L'Accompagnamento del recitativo semplice nell'ottocento', in: *Rivista Italiana di Musicologia*, XLI/1 (2006), pp. 101-134.

BAHN 2021
BAHN, Catherine. 'Partimento and Solfeggio Tradition on Bowed Bass Instruments', in: *The Hague Royal Early Music Conference Series*, 8 February 2021.

BAHN – BARBATI 2023
EAD. – BARBATI, Giovanna. 'The Partimento of Rocco Greco: Reconstructing the Pedagogical Tradition of the Early Violoncello', in: *Basso Continuo in Italy: Sources, Pedagogy and Performance*, edited by Marcello Mazzetti, Turnhout, Brepols, 2023 (Musica Incarnata: Pedagogy, Performance and Market, 1), pp. 187-210.

BAILLOT ET AL. 1804
BAILLOT, Pierre – LEVASSEUR, Jean-Henri – CATEL, Charles-Simon – BAUDIOT, Charles Nicolas. *Méthode de Violoncelle*, Paris, Imprimerie du Conservatoire, 1804.

BARBATI 2019
BARBATI, Giovanna. '«Il n'exécute jamais la basse telle qu'elle est écrite»: The Use of Improvisation in Teaching Low Strings', in: *Musical Improvisation in the Baroque Era*, edited by Fulvia Morabito, Turnhout, Brepols, 2019 (Speculum Musicae, 33), pp. 117-149.

BAUDIOT 1826
BAUDIOT, Charles. *Méthode de Violoncelle*, Op. 25, Paris, Pleyel, 1826.

BAUMGARTNER 1774
BAUMGARTNER, Jean. *Instructions de musique théorique et pratique à l'usage du violoncelle*, The Hague, Daniel Monnier, c.1774.

National Styles in Lower String Accompaniment of Secco Recitatives

Billé 1922
Billé, Isaia. *Nuovo Metodo per Contrabbasso*, Milan, Ricordi, 1922.

Braga 1873
Braga, Gaetano. *Metodo per Violoncello di J. J. Dotzauer*, Milan, Ricordi, 1873.

Crouch 1827
Crouch, Frederick William. *A Compleat Treatise on the Violoncello: Including besides the Necessary Preliminary Instructions, the Art of Bowing with Easy Lessons and Exercises in all the Keys, properly Fingered*, London, Chappell & Co., 1827.

Dotzauer 1832
Dotzauer, Justus Johann Friedrich. *Violoncell-Schule für den ersten Unterricht*, Op. 126, Vienna, Tobias Haslinger, c.1832.

Dotzauer 1838
Id. *Méthode de Violoncelle / Violoncell-Schule*, Mainz, Schott, 1838.

Fischer 1891
Fischer, Carl. *Method for the Violoncello: New and Revised Edition of Celebrated Tutors*, New York, Carl Fischer, 1891.

Folegatti 1874
Folegatti, Ercole. *Il violino esposto geometricamente nella sua costruzione*, Bologna, Fara e Garignani, 1874, BnF 8-B-1378.

Fröhlich 1810
Fröhlich, Franz Joseph. *Violoncell-Schule, nach den Grundsätzen der besten über dieses Instrument bereits erschienenen Schriften*, Bonn, Simrock, c.1810.

Galeazzi 1817
Galeazzi, Francesco. *Elementi teorico-pratici di Musica*, Ascoli, Francesco Cardi, 1817.

Galli 1882
Galli, Amintore. 'Forme liriche. Saggio storico e tecnologico: recitativo semplice', in: *Il teatro illustrato*, II (1882), pp. 131-132.

Gassner 1844
Gassner, Ferdinand S. *Dirigent und Ripienist, für angehende Musikdirigenten, Musiker und Musikfreunde* Karlsruhe, C. T. Groos, 1844.

Greenberg 2000
Greenberg, Michael. 'The Double Bass at the Paris Conservatory from 1826-62', in: *Journal of the American Musical Instrument Society*, XXIV (2000), pp. 83-140.

GUNN 1802
GUNN, John. *An Essay, Theoretical and Practical with Copious and Easy Examples on the Application of the Principles of Harmony, Thorough Bass and Modulation to the Violoncello*, London, by the author, 1802.

HARWOOD 1986
HARWOOD, Gregory. 'Verdi's Reform of the Italian Opera Orchestra', in: *Nineteenth Century Music*, X/2 (Autumn 1986), pp. 108-134.

HAUSE 1807
HAUSE, Wenzl. *Kontrabass Schule*, Dresden, Hilscher, c.1807.

KAUER 1788
KAUER, Ferdinand. *Kurzgefasste Anweisung das Violoncell zu spielen*, Vienna, Artaria, 1788.

KELLY 2000
KELLY, Thomas Forrest. *First Nights: Five Musical Premières*, New Haven, Yale University Press, 2000.

LUTTERMAN 2011
LUTTERMAN, John. 'Cet art est la perfection du talent: Chordal thorough Bass Realization and Improvised Solo Performance on the Viol and the Cello in the 18th Century', in: *Beyond Notes: Improvisation in Western Music of the Eighteenth and Nineteenth Centuries*, edited by Rudolf Rasch, Tournhout, Brepols, 2011 (Speculum Musicae, 16), pp. 111-128.

McFARREN 1872
McFARREN, G. A. 'The Accompaniment of Recitative', in: *The Musical Times and Singing Class Circular*, XV/358 (1 December 1872), pp. 687-689.

MEUCCI 2011
MEUCCI, Renato. 'Changes in the Role of the Leader in 19th-Century Italian Orchestras', in: *Spielpraxis der Saiteninstrumente in der Romantik. Bericht des Symposiums Bern, 18-19 November 2006*, editd by Claudio Bacciagaluppi, Roman Brotbeck and Anselm Gerhard, Schliengen, Edition Argus, 2011 (Musikforschung der Hochschule der Künste Bern, 3), pp. 122-137.

MEYERBEER 1836
MEYERBEER, Giacomo. *Les Huguenots*, Paris, Schlessinger, 1836, <http://ks4.imslp.net/files/imglnks/usimg/d/d7/IMSLP467645-PMLP39995-392988054.pdf>, accessed October 2023.

MUSICAL TIMES 1855
The Musical Times and Singing Class Circular, VII/148 (1 July 1855), p. 61.

MUSICAL WORLD 1837
'King's Theatre', in: *Musical World*, LX (5 May 1837), p. 126.

OLIVIERI 2021
OLIVIERI, Guido. 'The Early History of the Cello in Naples: Giovanni Bononcini, Rocco Greco and Gaetano Francone in a Forgotten Manuscript Collection', in: *Eighteenth-Century Music*, XVIII/1 (2021), pp. 65-97.

PALMER 1997
PALMER, Fiona. *Domenico Dragonetti in England (1794-1846): The Career of a Double Bass Virtuoso*, Oxford-New York, Clarendon Press, 1997.

PERES DA COSTA 2012
PERES DA COSTA, Neal. *Off the Record: Performing Practices in Romantic Piano Playing*, Oxford, Oxford University Press, 2012.

QUARENGHI 1877
QUARENGHI, Guglielmo. *Metodo di Violoncello*, Milan, Editore Musicale, 1877.

RACHELLE 1825
RACHELLE, Pietro. *Breve Metodo per imparare il Violoncello*, Trieste, Domenico Vicentini, c.1825.

RAOUL 1797
RAOUL, Jean. *Méthode de Violoncelle*, Op. 4, Paris, Pleyel, 1797.

RICCI 1841
RICCI, Federico *Corrado d'Altamura*, (1841), Archivio dell'Accademia degli Immobili, Teatro della Toscana, document 1368.

ROCKSTRO 1883
ROCKSTRO, William Smith. 'Secco recitative', in: *A Dictionary of Music and Musicians. 3*, edited by Sir George Grove, London, MacMillan & Co., 1883, pp. 454-455.

ROUSSEAU 1765
ROUSSEAU, Jean-Jacques. 'Harpègement', in: *Encyclopédie ou Dictionnaire Raisonné des Sciences, des Arts et des Métiers. 8 [H-IT]*, edited by Diderot, D'alembert et Jaucourt, Paris, Samuel Faulche et Cie, 1765, p. 58.

SCARAMELLI 1811
SCARAMELLI, Giuseppe. *Saggio sopra i doveri di un Primo Violino Direttore d'Orchestra*, Trieste, Weiss, 1811.

SIMMANDL 1890
SIMMANDL, FRANZ. *Neueste Methode des Contrabass-Spiels, Teil I: Vorbereitung zum Orchesterspiel*, Heilbrun, C. F. Schmidt, 1890.

SPITZER – ZASLAW 2004
SPITZER, John – ZASLAW, Neal. *The Birth of the Orchestra: History of an Institution, 1650-1815*, Oxford-New York, Oxford University Press, 2004.

STIASNY 1829
STIASNY, Bernard. *Violoncell-Schule*, Part II, Mainz, Schott, c.1829.

SUCKLING 2015
SUCKLING, Christopher Andrew. *The Realization of Recitative in Handellian Opera: Current and Historical Practices*, DMA Diss., London, City University London, 2015.

TE HAAR 2019
TE HAAR, Job. *The Playing Style of Alfredo Piatti: Learning from a Nineteenth-Century Virtuoso Cellist*, Ph.D. Diss., London, Royal Academy of Music, 2019.

VANSCHEEUWIJCK 2016
VANSCHEEUWIJCK, Marc. 'Cello Stories: The Cello in the 17th and 18th Centuries', CD Notes, Alpha Classics, Outhere Music France, 2016, pp. 25-72.

VANSCHEEUWIJCK 2020
ID. 'The Violoncello of the Bononcini Brothers', in: *I Bononcini da Modena all'Europa (1666-1747)*, edited by Marc Vanscheeuwijck, Lucca, LIM, 2020 (Studi e saggi), pp. 85-101.

WALDEN 1998
WALDEN, Valerie. *One Hundred Years of Violoncello: A History of Technique and Performance Practice 1740-1840*, Cambridge, Cambridge University Press, 1998 (Cambridge Musical Text and Monograph).

WATKIN 1996
WATKIN David. 'Corelli's Op. 5 Sonatas: «Violino e violone o cimbalo»?', in: *Early Music*, XXIV/4 (November 1996), pp. 645-663.

WHITTAKER 2012
WHITTAKER, Nathan H. *Chordal Cello Accompaniment: The Proof and Practice of Figured Bass Realization on the Cello (1660-1850)*, DMA Diss., Seattle (WA), University of Washington, 2012.

FROM THE PAGE TO THE PERFORMANCE
through Space and Time

PER OGNI TRADIZIONE IL SUO BASSO.
I BASSI SEGUENTI ITALIANI IN ALCUNE ANTOLOGIE
TEDESCHE DEL SEICENTO

Valeria Mannoia
(UNIVERSITÀ DI PAVIA, CREMONA)

È NOTO CHE GIÀ IN ETÀ tardo rinascimentale i compositori transalpini rivolsero con una certa costanza lo sguardo all'attività musicale sacra e profana italiana e che essa fu un punto di riferimento imprescindibile non solo per la definizione delle forme compositive locali ma principalmente per la formazione musicale scolastica. Il repertorio peninsulare fu accolto con un generale atteggiamento retrospettivo e ancora fino agli anni Venti del Seicento lo stile osservato continuò a suscitare l'interesse delle cappelle musicali tedesche. La circolazione del repertorio vocale italiano subì un inevitabile ritardo e, mentre nelle cappelle italiane comparivano le prime raccolte di *sacrae cantiones* da una a quattro voci con il basso d'organo, nei territori tedeschi settentrionali continuarono a essere eseguiti principalmente i mottetti per ampio organico vocale. Solo nel corso degli anni Trenta del Seicento la circolazione dei repertori italiani a poche voci raggiunse con successo tutte le aree transalpine, testimoniando l'uniformità della ricezione dei repertori sacri italiani.

Durante il corso del diciassettesimo secolo, la circolazione del repertorio liturgico e paraliturgico italiano nei territori a Nord delle Alpi fu veicolata attraverso tre canali di comunicazione: la vendita delle stampe italiane, principalmente veneziane e romane, presso le fiere librarie semestrali di Francoforte sul Meno e Lipsia[1], la redazione di nuove edizioni prodotte localmente, in primo luogo dall'editore Nikolaus Stein di Francoforte ma anche nelle Fiandre da parte della famiglia Phalèse, infine, la stampa locale di corpose antologie d'argomento sacro[2]. Se la redazione di nuove edizioni transalpine non tramandò particolari forme di intervento sul testo, la produzione antologica fu il luogo in cui si determinarono

---

[1]. ROSE 2005.
[2]. ROCHE 1974; BEER 1989; ROCHE 1998; GISELBRECHT 2012; MANNOIA 2019.

interessanti soluzioni di adattamento del testo musicale alle necessità pratiche delle diverse congregazioni religiose tedesche.

Tra il 1600 e il 1672 furono realizzate almeno trentacinque sillogi dedicate in prevalenza al concerto ecclesiastico italiano ma con una circoscritta presenza di composizioni di autori locali[3]. Tali antologie ebbero il raro pregio di sintetizzare intere tradizioni musicali, anche lontane nel tempo, e per tale ragione esse godettero di una propria autorità testuale pari a quella delle più comuni raccolte dei singoli autori[4]. Ogni antologia fu organizzata secondo parametri ben precisi, che furono determinati dal contesto storico, politico e socioeconomico in cui il volume fu progettato. I compilatori riservarono abitualmente una porzione del frontespizio o della lettera dedicatoria alla descrizione dell'opportuna spendibilità del testo stesso. L'ordinamento formale dei volumi seguiva il calendario liturgico ma in diversi casi fu osservata una pianificazione più semplice, secondo l'ordine alfabetico o secondo l'organico vocale. Ancor più di ogni catalogo librario, editoriale o fieristico, le sillogi furono e sono ancora oggi uno strumento prezioso per comprendere criticamente il processo di trasmissione e di ricezione del mottetto italiano.

La compilazione di ogni silloge si basò su un'attenta selezione dei mottetti già disponibili e assimilati nelle pratiche musicali locali, provenienti da stampe italiane o da ulteriori antologie tedesche, da cui furono scelti solo quei materiali più funzionali al contesto per cui l'antologia fu pensata. Ogni autore di antologie, nel guardare avanti per creare un nuovo prodotto editoriale, si rivolse puntualmente al passato con un approccio che, di norma, fu il riflesso del suo grado di conoscenza dei repertori musicali italiani. Pochi compositori proposero nelle loro raccolte dei concerti inediti o formalmente innovativi e che non rispecchiassero i comuni interessi del mercato musicale. Questo fu il caso di due antologie bavaresi: la *Siren cœlestis* (Monaco, 1616) di Georg Victorinus e la *Musica Romana* (Bamberga, 1665) di Spiridion à Monte Carmelo[5]. La prima silloge fu ideata per l'attività musicale del collegio gesuitico annesso alla chiesa di San Michele a Monaco nonché per la chiesa ducale dedicata a San Nicola; la seconda antologia propose diversi concerti romani a tre voci, con l'integrazione della coppia dei violini, per il monastero di San Teodoro a Bamberga. Non di rado le scelte di contenuto delle antologie furono i testimoni della presenza di reti culturali e musicali profonde e diramate in tutta Europa. L'indicizzazione nelle antologie gesuitiche dei repertori concepiti in seno al Collegio Germanico di Roma fu la dimostrazione dell'influenza che il Collegio stesso mantenne sulle università gesuitiche e sui collegi transalpini durante tutto il corso del Seicento[6].

Escluse tali eccezioni, i compilatori si concentrarono sull'osservazione e sull'adattamento dei repertori già cristallizzati nella prassi musicale delle chiese locali o delle cappelle scolastiche

---

[3]. MANNOIA 2019.

[4]. BENEDICT 1996; VAN ORDEN 2013; ROSE 2005.

[5]. MANNOIA 2019.

[6]. CULLEY 1970; KENNEDY 1982; GRENDLER 2017.

cui si rivolsero. La collana dei quattro *Promptuaria musices* (Strasburgo, 1611-1617) di Abraham Schade fu concepita per condensare in un formato pratico e funzionale il repertorio mottettistico più eseguito presso la Lateinschule di Spira; i tre *Florilegia Portensis* (Lipsia, 1603-1621), curati da Erhard Bodenschatz, furono raccolti per accompagnare i pasti refettoriali degli studenti del collegio di Pforta; i due volumi di *Geistliche Wolklingende Concerte* (Goslar, 1637-1638) per una, due e tre voci nacquero con l'intento di preservare la tradizione musicale della città di Nordhausen, alla luce dell'inasprimento delle tensioni provocate dalla guerra dei Trent'anni. In base al proprio contesto di appartenenza e alla generazione in cui ogni silloge fu ideata, si manifestò un maggiore interesse verso le soluzioni compositive più o meno tradizionali, come il concerto per ampio organico vocale, oppure il mottetto di transizione a poche voci.

ASPETTI METODOLOGICI

Da un punto di vista filologico, ognuno dei brani inseriti nelle antologie rappresenta un testo in movimento. Esso è autonomo, perché è dotato di una propria tradizione trasversale che coinvolge testimoni di diversa natura, ma allo stesso tempo è condizionato dai parametri del volume in cui è collocato. Per poter esprimere le multiple relazioni che sottostanno a un testo tratto da una miscellanea è necessario che l'analisi dei repertori segua incessantemente una doppia prospettiva, sincronica e diacronica. Si determina, così, una tensione continua tra il sistema dell'autore del brano e il sistema del compilatore della nuova antologia, ossia tra la lingua e lo stile fissati sulla carta all'atto della creazione del brano e la sua interpretazione proposta dal mediatore. Quando il codice stilistico e linguistico del compilatore si appone al testo, esso sviluppa una serie di diasistemi concettualmente tracciabili[7]. Tutti i diasistemi presenti sul testo detengono una propria autorità, tale da non poter essere destituiti, omessi o confusi all'interno dell'indagine critica[8].

Nella tradizione europea dei repertori italiani tardo rinascimentali e seicenteschi la presenza di precisi segni di tempo, la presenza o assenza del segno di battuta, l'indicazione delle pause, ma anche la cassazione o inserimento di una parte vocale o strumentale possono essere i tratti che determinano l'esistenza di uno specifico sistema linguistico-musicale secondario[9]. In generale, l'interpretazione del testo assume dei tratti di grande complessità poiché esso afferisce non solo

---

[7]. Il linguaggio di chi copia può rispondere a un 'macrosistema culturale' di appartenenza, ma può anche assumere degli atteggiamenti comportamentali unici nel suo genere. Perciò, il concetto di sistema cui si riferiva Cesare Segre poteva afferire al codice linguistico di una società, di una determinata area geografica, di una particolare epoca storica oppure essere proprio di uno unico individuo. In breve, esso detenava caratteristiche specifiche e variegate tali da non poter essere codificato in un assioma assoluto. SEGRE 1979.

[8]. Per sintetizzare la posizione di Segre, che tra i primi rifletté sulle ricezioni secondarie del testo e sul concetto del diasistema, ciò che accadeva in ogni opera era una «creolizzazione stilistica e formale del testo». *Ibidem*, p. 65.

[9]. Per un discorso musicale più ampio, CARACI VELA 2005, pp. 21-24, 61-62.

agli aspetti più pratici e meccanici della trascrizione del testo, ma coinvolge l'intera dimensione della sua comprensione. Cosa accade a un testo quando esso è recepito in un'area geografica nuova e tràdito secondo le esperienze culturali proprie di quel territorio? Cosa sopravvive del sistema originario, qualora la sua struttura di base non sia compresa e pienamente accettata? Si tratta di due interrogativi onerosi che impongono di affrontare con più cautela la diversità tra il sistema linguistico del testo iniziale e quello del ricevente, nonché il suo sostrato culturale di appartenenza[10]. Tutto ciò trova delle risposte indicative proprio nelle antologie di mottetti del Seicento. La loro organizzazione interna, le scelte operate dai loro compilatori, l'attenzione rivolta al singolo testo nell'atto della sua trascrizione all'interno del volume furono dei fattori altamente variabili nell'arco del secolo e sembrarono mutare considerevolmente in base alle condizioni culturali, sociali e storiche del preciso momento in cui ogni raccolta fu concepita. La scelta di aggiornare il testo, modificarne la struttura, adattarlo o mantenerlo inalterato furono operazioni necessarie per equiparare e uniformare il contenuto dell'antologia alle necessità pratiche dei suoi destinatari. Ogni qual volta che tutti i brani contenuti in una silloge furono sofisticati secondo un determinato parametro si verificò un diasistema uniformante, che si potrebbe definire un macro-diasistema[11].

LE ANTOLOGIE DEL PRIMO SEICENTO

Le prime antologie stampate agli albori del Seicento — ossia la serie antologica delle *Symphoniae Sacrae* (Norimberga, 1598-1613) di Kaspar Hassler, cui seguirono le *Reliquiae sacrorum concentuum* (Norimberga, 1615) di Georg Gruber e il *Florilegium Selectissimarum Cantionum* (Lipsia, 1603) di Erhard Bodenschatz — rispettarono i parametri formali, testuali e strutturali dei singoli brani, lasciando emergere le eventuali discontinuità del repertorio tràdito[12]. Diverse ragioni indussero l'organista Kaspar Hassler a non intervenire sull'organizzazione dei singoli brani oppure sull'eventuale parte per il basso seguente. Innanzitutto, i suoi volumi furono concepiti per una fruizione di tipo professionale. Kaspar Hassler trascorse l'intera

---

[10]. Questi quesiti, forse retorici, sono stati spesso dati per sottinteso. Ritornano alla mente le parole di Giorgio Pasquali in merito all'importanza dei criteri ambientali nella ricostruzione critica del testo. Il filologo si rifaceva certamente all'indagine della tradizione manoscritta classica e all'evidenza di fenomeni geografici laterali che talvolta permettevano la conservazione di lezioni più antiche. Prendere spunto da tali osservazioni potrebbe aiutare a riconsiderare il diasistema in una prospettiva più ampia. La trasmissione di un intero repertorio oppure di uno specifico testo o ancora soltanto di una sua piccola porzione al di fuori dell'ambiente culturale di provenienza non è indenne dall'affrontare certe difficoltà, quali la sua comprensione linguistica e l'interpretazione dei contenuti da parte dei riceventi, siano essi nuovi copisti o semplici lettori. PASQUALI 1988, Introduzione, pp. xv-xix.

[11]. MANNOIA 2019.

[12]. Se un simile atteggiamento può essere accettato per i primi volumi della serie, esso risulta certamente anomalo se si considera il volume stampato nel 1615, in cui è persino omessa la parte per l'organo prevista dall'autore.

carriera come organista delle principali chiese luterane di Norimberga[13] e mantenne una stretta relazione con diversi membri della famiglia Fugger[14]. Kaspar dedicò proprio il primo volume delle *Symphoniae Sacrae* (Norimberga, 1598) a Ottaviano II Fugger di Augusta, presso cui suo fratello Hans Leo fu a servizio come organista dal 1586. I volumi di Kaspar Hassler furono lo specchio degli interessi e delle pratiche musicali delle chiese e dei palazzi patrizi bavaresi (come la casa dei Fugger), nonché della cappella ducale a Monaco, ove circolavano abili organisti professionisti. Non era dunque, necessario fornire un supporto all'organista per la realizzazione della sua intavolatura.

Va anche considerato che nei *Länder* tedeschi la compilazione di raccolte già corredate dalle partiture per l'organo fu un fenomeno sporadico che inizialmente interessò solo i compositori vicini alla scuola centrosettentrionale italiana, come Gregor Aichinger, Johann Staden, Rudolph di Lasso, Urban Loth. La raccolta di *Cantiones ecclesiasticae* (Dillingen, 1607) a tre e quattro voci di Gregor Aichinger fu la prima con una parte di basso seguente per l'organo per i sedici mottetti a tre voci[15]. Nello stesso anno Bernhard Klingenstein stampò il suo primo libro di *Sacrae Symphoniae* (Monaco, 1607) con una parte di basso per l'organo anche per i mottetti a otto voci. Tre anni dopo Johann Stadlmayr diede alle stampe le *Missae octo vocum cum duplici basso ad organum accomodato* (Augusta, 1610). La presenza di un *basso seguente* divenne in breve tempo una prerogativa costante del repertorio mottettistico dei compositori dei *Länder* meridionali, a prescindere dalla tipologia di organico prescelta, ridotta a poche voci oppure più ampia[16].

In Italia, invece, già sul finire del Cinquecento la prassi di accompagnare i cantori con l'organo in forma quasi estemporanea o su intavolature redatte appositamente dall'organista fu progressivamente soppiantata dall'uso di partiture preparate dall'autore per coadiuvare l'organista alla realizzazione dell'accompagnamento[17]. Il primo esemplare significativo fu redatto nel 1594 dall'organista Giovanni Croce. Nel 1593 questi ricevette l'incarico dell'insegnamento della musica ai giovani del seminario annesso alla basilica di San Marco a Venezia e l'anno successivo diede alle stampe il suo primo libro di *Mottetti a otto voci* (Venezia, 1594) con una *Spartidura per l'organo*[18]. È probabile che i mottetti contenuti nel primo libro costituissero l'effettivo materiale di studio dei giovani cantori della scuola. In coda al volume

---

[13]. Nel 1586 Hassler fu assunto presso la chiesa di Sant'Egidio, nel 1587 passò alla chiesa di San Lorenzo e dal 1616 fino all'anno di morte fu organista presso la prestigiosa chiesa di San Sebaldo. BLANKENBURG 1980.

[14]. Sull'attività mecenatesca della famiglia Fugger si rinvia a WÖLFLE 2009 e al sito <https://www.fugger.de/it/storia>, visitato a ottobre 2023.

[15]. BEER 1989, pp. 247-250; CROOK 2006, p. 360.

[16]. Axel Beer ha individuato tra il 1607 e il 1632 ottantaquattro raccolte con una parte di basso seguente stampate nei centri della Germania meridionale. BEER 1989, pp. 165-170; HORSLEY 1977, pp. 466-471.

[17]. HORSLEY 1977.

[18]. CARABA 1985.

della *Spartidura delli Mottetti* fu inserita una nota ai lettori in cui fu dichiarata la volontà di facilitare le fatiche agli organisti. Non si può escludere che dietro questa sponsorizzazione non si celasse anche un'allusione alla sua attività didattica e agli allievi della sua classe[19]. Ciò che Croce propose ai suoi lettori fu una partitura a doppio rigo in cui riportò le voci più gravi dei due cori, senza inserire alcuna cifratura. Croce estese semplicemente la linea singola del basso secondo il numero delle formazioni polifoniche previste dal brano, due nel suo caso. Escluse le aree cadenzali, in cui i due bassi si sovrapponevano per alcune misure, le due parti si muovevano in relativa autonomia. Nelle successive edizioni dell'opera la *Spartidura* a doppio rigo fu soppressa[20]. Nell'edizione del 1607 apparve un volume, *Per sonar nell'Organo*, con una parte di basso a linea singola che seguiva la voce più grave puntualmente presente. Contestualmente all'operazione di Croce, il bolognese Adriano Banchieri allegò ai suoi *Concerti ecclesiastici a otto voci* (Venezia, 1595) una partitura per l'organo che intavolava le parti del canto e del basso. Di fatto, essa supportava esclusivamente il coro superiore (anche in questo caso senza indicare nessuna cifratura) e imponeva all'organista di realizzare le parti di canto e basso relative al secondo coro[21]. Croce e Banchieri proposero due modelli di basso seguente concettualmente diversi ma che furono immediatamente oggetto di interessanti repliche[22].

Le antologie tedesche che furono stampate tra gli anni Dieci e Venti del Seicento dimostrarono che il modello organistico italiano fu progressivamente assimilato e che anche in Germania fu necessario facilitare il compito degli organisti. I compilatori delle sillogi per ampio organico vocale aggiornarono i brani formalmente desueti, li resero coerenti con la produzione più moderna e più facilmente fruibili dalle comunità religiose. Tale approccio interessò, in particolare, i quattro *Promptuaria musices* (Strasburgo, 1611-1617) di Abraham Schade e Caspar Vincentius e i due *Florilegia Portensis* (Lipsia, 1618-1621) di Erhard Bodenschatz che furono interamente dedicati al mottetto per ampio organico da cinque a otto voci, con particolare attenzione alle composizioni suddivise in due cori. Le due collane ospitarono tanto

---

[19].   «Aspettate honorati Virtuosi da me continuamente nove inventioni per facilitarvi la strada alle fatiche, con Intavolature, Passaggi, & Paritdure [*sic*]: delle quali già ne ho fatte alquante forte, & ne andrò tuttavia facendo, come vegga che voi ve ne serviate, & che vi sia grata l'opera mia. Vivete felici». CROCE 1594, «A' Lettori Giacomo Vincenti». La nota ai lettori reca la firma di Giacomo Vincenti. Non è chiaro, dunque, se la partitura sia stata redatta per volontà dello stesso Croce oppure per soddisfare l'esigenza di un editore in cerca di soluzioni commerciali più appetibili per il mercato musicale. KINKELDEY 1910; HORSLEY 1977, p. 468.

[20].   Non sopravvivono eventuali testimoni della *Spartidura* nelle edizioni del 1596 (RISM A/I C 4430), del 1599 (A/I C 4431) e del 1603 (A/I C 4432) per cui è lecito supporre che Croce o l'editore Vincenti abbiano deciso di sopprimerla.

[21].   «Volendo la Spartitura di tutti due Chori, sarà facil cosa accomodarla prestissimo, pigliando la parte acuta e grave del Secondo Choro, & dove in questa dice à 8 lasciarlo, & aggiungendo quella à questa, vi saranno tutti e due: ma l'Autore non l'ha fatta, atteso che l'intentione sua è per concertarla à Chori separati. Intanto vivete felici». BANCHIERI 1595, «A gli Sig. Organisti».

[22].   Per uno sguardo d'insieme si veda HORSLEY 1977.

il repertorio tardo rinascimentale quanto il mottetto a molte voci, ancora in stile osservato, ma già corredato di una propria partitura e diedero spazio anche al repertorio locale, con maggiore enfasi su quei compositori che si formarono in Italia o che applicarono il modello compositivo peninsulare, come Hans Leo Hassler, Gregor Aichinger, Christian Erbach e Christoph Thomas Walliser.

L'aggiornamento dei mottetti a molte voci, antologizzati da Schade e Bodenschatz, non fu solo un espediente per mantenere in uso un repertorio che altrimenti sarebbe scomparso, ma fu un'operazione giustificata dalla destinazione delle due collane. Entrambe furono concepite per la formazione corale dei giovani studenti dei collegi di Spira (nel Palatinato) e di Pforta (in Sassonia). La funzione originariamente didattica delle raccolte, che fungevano da eserciziario per lo studio della polifonia su testo latino, imponeva di fornire un supporto pratico all'organista che avrebbe accompagnato i cantori.

Sebbene i compilatori abbiano seguito due differenti pratiche, essi furono mossi da un'intenzione comune: uniformare i brani secondo un preciso modello di basso seguente. La scelta di adoperare un determinatore comune affine a un linguaggio musicale più moderno permette di considerare queste antologie come dei macro-diasistemi. Nel complesso, i compilatori agirono secondo due diverse modalità:

1. in mancanza di una parte per l'organo preesistente, i curatori composero un nuovo basso seguente, generalmente pedissequo alla voce più grave presente nel brano.

2. in presenza di una parte per il basso d'organo già scritta, il testo fu aggiornato secondo la prassi locale più diffusa. Ciò interessò il piano esclusivamente formale, come l'impostazione o impaginazione delle parti, oppure il piano concettuale, come la rielaborazione della veste melodica e/o ritmica, infine, l'inserimento di una cifratura del basso diversa da quella originale e tipica di una prassi organistica locale.

Le tipologie di basso adoperate si dimostrano fedeli a quanto descritto da Imogene Horsley[23]. Nel complesso, i compilatori alternarono la redazione di bassi a linea singola, la partitura ridotta con le parti più gravi dei mottetti policorali, infine, la partitura ridotta a canto e basso per i mottetti polifonici.

I *PROMPTUARIA MUSICES*

I volumi per l'organo dei quattro *Promptuaria musices* (Strasburgo, 1611-1617) di Spira furono affidati a Caspar Vincentius, organista della chiesa principale di Spira. Di origini

---

23. Imogene Horsley dedicò la conclusione del suo studio a descrivere brevemente le tipologie di partiture per l'organo maggiormente diffuse nei paesi di lingua tedesca e individuò alcuni atteggiamenti editoriali costanti. Essi sono la dimostrazione del forte ascendente del modello italiano sulle abitudini locali tedesche, fino a quel momento avvezze solo all'uso della tradizionale intavolatura. *Ibidem*, p. 497.

fiamminghe, Vincentius fu cantore presso la cattedrale di Saint Omer, successivamente presso la cappella della corte imperiale dell'arciduca Ernesto a Bruxelles e dal 1595 fu assunto presso la cappella della corte imperiale di Vienna dove seguì l'insegnamento musicale dell'anziano Philippe de Monte. Vincentius giunse a Spira nel 1602 circa[24]. Durante i sette anni alla corte imperiale Vincentius assorbì i modelli compositivi italiani tradizionali e divenne ricettivo verso le novità proposte in Italia e che circolavano oltralpe nelle librerie musicali e anche attraverso le ristampe degli editori locali. Nel volume per l'organo del *Promptuarium musicum I* (Strasburgo, 1611), Caspar Vincentius dichiarò di voler risparmiare agli organisti la redazione occasionale dell'intavolatura delle parti vocali, per permettere loro di progredire più facilmente nella lettura delle *sacrae cantiones* e per proporre un'organizzazione sistematica della parte dell'organo: «[...] more denique pluribus in locis receptum & confirmatum, ut Organorum Symphonia cum musicorum commisceatur vocibus, ut Organistas transcribendi inque sua tempora cantiones redigendi labore taedioso sublevarem: Basin quam vocant generalem Cantionum harum conficere, & huic operi annectere conatus sum».

Vincentius indicò espressamente di voler seguire il modello proposto da Lodovico Viadana, così come fece precedentemente anche Aichinger nel suo volume di *Sacrae cantiones* (1607). Vincentius fece un chiaro riferimento alla guida per gli organisti che Viadana stampò all'interno dei *Cento concerti ecclesiastici* (Venezia, 1602), di cui dimostrò di conoscere non solo l'edizione veneziana ma anche la nuova edizione stampata a Francoforte da Nikolaus Stein nel 1609. Se il basso seguente di Viadana fu ideato per accompagnare i concerti ecclesiastici da una a quattro parti, Vincentius dovette adattare questo modello anche alle composizioni per ampio organico, seguendo un approccio affine alla prima *Spartidura per l'organo* che Giovanni Croce propose nei suoi *Mottetti a otto voci* (Venezia, 1594). È possibile che Vincentius abbia avuto modo di studiare la prima edizione dei mottetti di Croce. Il manoscritto Mus. 16703 redatto intorno al 1598 per la corte dell'imperatore Ferdinando II a Graz tramanda quattro brani tratti da quella raccolta (*Percussit Saul mille, Benedictus Dominus Deus, Audite verbum Domini e Factum est silentium*)[25]. Il *Benedictus Dominus Deus* fu inserito da Vincentius anche nel *Promptuarium musicum IV* (Strasburgo, 1617). L'organista non copiò esattamente quanto realizzato da Croce ma realizzò un nuovo basso seguente. Mentre Croce cercò di ridurre al minimo le sovrapposizioni tra i due bassi, tese a mantenere i valori larghi ed evitò di inserire la numerica, Vincentius segnalò con maggior anticipo gli ingressi delle voci, spezzò i valori larghi per imitare il dettato verbale e segnalare con più agio i ritardi oppure, al contrario, i movimenti ascendenti sul basso.

Si evidenzia, in generale, un approccio prudente volto a chiarire il più possibile le formule delle edizioni originali per aiutare gli organisti a orientarsi nell'accompagnamento. Per i mottetti

---

24. KIRWAN 2001.
25. CARVER 1988, pp. 251-252; BENNETT – SAUNDERS – WEAVER 2021, p. 181; MECONI 2021, p. 387; GLIXON – KURTZMAN – SAUNDERS 2021, p. 537.

da cinque a sette voci predispose un basso seguente a linea singola[26]. Per i mottetti a otto voci, specialmente per quelli composti da due semicori, predispose una partitura a linea doppia, una per l'accompagnamento di ogni coro[27]. Il basso seguente era costruito sulla voce più grave progressivamente disponibile. Vincentius ridusse al minimo le proprietà (♯ e ♭) ma fornì almeno la cifratura per i ritardi (9-8, 7-6, 6-5 e 4-3) aggiungendo al secondo punto della guida agli organisti che «diligentem Organista habeat numerorum supra notulas positorum, signorumque ♯ e ♭ rationem: ne sexta pro Quinta, Quartave pro tertia in concentu absque discrimine utatur: Tertiave major cum Tertia minore, & pari modo ipsae Sextae confundantur». La collana dei *Promptuaria musices* fu concepita in un ambiente scolastico e si rivolse principalmente a un'utenza giovanile, non necessariamente esperta nella lettura della partitura; perciò, pare naturale che Vincentius abbia suggerito una guida per la numerica. Questa era sempre limitata all'interno dell'ottava ma, al terzo punto della premessa, Vincentius indicò la possibilità di muoversi oltre le tre ottave (3a. 10a. 17a. e 5a. 12a. 19a.), facendo attenzione a non causare involontari moti paralleli e agendo secondo il buon senso dell'*artifex peritus auribus industrie*. L'uso della numerica contenuta all'interno dell'ottava e le generali indicazioni di Vincentius riflettono la conoscenza delle raccolte di Agostino Agazzari e del suo trattato *Del Sonare sopra 'l basso con tutti li stromenti e dell'uso loro nel Conserto* (Siena, 1607). Il teorico di Wolfenbüttel Michael Praetorius rimarcò, alcuni anni dopo, l'importanza del trattato di Agazzari la cui autorità era pari alla *Prefazione* dei *Cento concerti ecclesiastici* (Venezia, 1602) di Lodovico Viadana e nel *Syntagma musicum III* (Wolfenbüttel, 1619) dedicò il capitolo VI a riassumere le posizioni di entrambi i compositori-teorici[28]. In sintesi, Praetorius appoggiò la posizione di Agazzari in favore di un uso saggio e attento della numerica per indicare all'organista — esperto, studente o dilettante che fosse — la precisa intenzione del compositore[29]. Sulle abitudini consolidate dai compositori italiani, aggiunse:

> Qualcuno preferisce essere più preciso e indicare la completa disposizione degli intervalli ricorrendo ai numeri 10, 11, 12, 13 sulle note. Ma poiché ciò è troppo complicato e serve solo a rendere il brano più difficile, probabilmente è meglio aderire ai numeri semplici. Un organista deve avere un buon orecchio, essere attento e ascoltare con cura per capire se sia meglio suonare la terza, la quarta, la quinta all'ottava bassa oppure se suonare la decima, undicesima o dodicesima all'ottava più acuta[30].

---

[26]. Si trattò di trentasette interventi nel primo volume, cinquanta nel secondo volume, cinquantanove nel terzo volume e cinquantadue nell'ultimo volume.

[27]. Si trattò di quarantasei interventi nel primo volume, di cinquantuno nel secondo volume, di sessantadue nel terzo volume e di ottanta nell'ultimo volume.

[28]. PRAETORIUS 2004, pp. 133-151.

[29]. *Ibidem*, pp. 135-136.

[30]. PRAETORIUS 2004, pp. 139-140. Praetorius si riferiva alle composizioni dei bolognesi Adriano Banchieri e Girolamo Giacobbi. Nella *Prima parte de i salmi concertati a due e più chori, commodi da concertare in diverse maniere* (Venezia, 1609) Giacobbi ricorse abitualmente all'11-10 per i ritardi di terza.

Nel *Promptuarium musicum I* (Strasburgo, 1611) Vincentius compose un nuovo basso seguente per almeno ventisette mottetti che originariamente ne erano privi e adattò il basso seguente preesistente in almeno ventuno mottetti italiani, alternando tra il basso a linea doppia e il basso a linea singola.

TABELLA 1: COMPOSIZIONI PRESENTI NEL *PROMPTUARIUM MUSICUM I* (STRASBURGO, 1611) ORIGINARIAMENTE PRIVE DI UN BASSO PER L'ORGANO

Francesco Bianciardi	*Hierusalem citò veniet salus tua (5), Surgite pastores (5), Ave gratia plena: quae est ista salutatio? (6), Extollens vocem quædam mulier (6), Hei mihi Domine quia peccavi nimis (8), Omnia quæ fecisti nobis (8), Ave rex noster tu solus nostros es miseratus (8).*	FRANCISCI|BIANCIARDI|CASVLANI|Metropolitana Senenſis Eccleſiæ Cantorum Moderatoris | SACRARVM MODVLATIONVM, | Quæ vulgo Moteêta, & Quattuor, Quinis, Senis, | & Oêtonis vocibus concinuntur. | LIBER SECVNDVS | Nunc primum in lucem editus. VENETIIS, APVD ANGELVM GARDANVM | 1601
Curzio Valcampi	*Canite tuba Sion (6), Tribus miracolis ornatum diem (6), Senex puerum portabat (6).*	SACRARUM CANTIONUM QUAE VULGO MOTECTA APPELLANTUR SENIS VOCIBUS CONCINNATUS [...] liber primus [...] Venezia, Amadino, Ricciardo 1602
Giovanni Gabrieli	*Miserere mei Deus (6), Domine exaudi orationem meam (6 op 8), O Jesu mi dulcissime (8)*	SACRÆ | SYMPHONIÆ, | IOANNIS GABRIELII. SERENISS. REIP. VENETIAR. ORGANISTÆ | IN ECCLESIA DIVI MARCI. | Senis, 7, 8, 10, 12, 14, 15, & 16, Tam | vocibus, Quam Inſtrumentis. | Editio Noua. CVM PRIVILEGIO. VENETIIS, Apud Angelum Gardanum. 1597
Orfeo Vecchi	*Gloria in excelsis Deo (6)*	ORPHEI VECCHI| MEDIOLANENSIS| IN ECCLESIA D. MARIÆ SCALEN| reg. duc. Musicæ, & Chori Magistri, | MOTECTORUM | Sex Vocibus | LIBER TERTIUS.| MEDIOLANI, | Apud Hæredem Simonis Tini, & Io. Franciscum Besutium, | 1598
Floriano Canale	*Quem vidistis pastores ? secuna pars: Dicite quidam vidistis? (6)*	SACRAE CANTIONES | SEX VOCIBVS | CONCINENDÆ, | Tum viua voce, tum Inſtrumentis cuiuſuis generis | cantatu accommodiſſimæ. | A D. FLORIANO CANALI IN ECCLESIA | Diui Ioannis Euangeliſtæ de Brixia Organiſta, | Nouiter compoſitæ. | LIBER PRIMVS. | *Ad Illuſtriſſ. & Reuerendiſſ. Marinum Georgium* | *Epiſcopum Brixienſem.* | VENETIIS, Apud Iacobum Vincentium. MDCIII.
Vincenzo Bertolusi	*Domine ante te (6), Lætare Hierusalem et conventum facite (8)*	SACRARVM | CANTIONVM | VINCENTII BERTHOLVSII MVRIANENSIS SERENISSIMI REGIS POLONIAE, ET SVETIAE Organiſtæ, Sex, Septem, Oêto, & Decem vocibus | LIBER PRIMVS Venetijs, Apud Angelum Gardanum 1601
Flaminio Nocetti	*O suavitas et dulcedo (6)*	PRIMVSCONCENTVS|SIVESACRAECANTIONES| FLAMINII NVCETI | PARMENSIS, | Organi (vt vocant) Modulatoris in Aede D. Io. Euang. | Parmæ, ex Quinis, Senis, Septenis, Oêtonis, | & Nouenis vocibus confeêtæ, | VENETIIS, APVD ANGELVM GARDANVM | 1602

176

Guglielmo Lipparino	*Hodie nobis cælorum rex (7)*	IL PRIMO LIBRO | DE MOTETTI. | A Sette, Otto, & vuo à Quindici voci. | DI F. GVGLIELMO LIPARINO | Bolonefe Aguftiniano dell'Offer-|uanza di Lombardia. | Nouamente compofto, & dato in luce. | IN VENETIA| Appreffo Aleffandro Rauerij. 1609
Tiburzio Massaini	*Gabriel Angelus, locutus est Mariæ (8), Conserva me Domine, secunda pars: Benedicam Dominum (8)*	TIBVRTII MASSAINI| AVGVSTINIANI OBSERVANTIS| Sacri modulorum Concentus 8. 9. 10. 12. 15. | ac 16. vocum concinendi: | Studio elaborati. | Opus 31. Nunc primum in lucem editum. VENETIIS. |1606
Tiburzio Massaini	*Intelligite insipientes (7)*	TIBVRTII MASSAINI CREMONENSIS, | SACRARVM CANTIONVM | SEPTEM VOCIBVS. | LIBER PRIMVS. | Nunc Primum in lucem editus. | Cum Baffo ad Organum. | OPVS TRIGESIMVM TERTIVM| VENETIIS, | Apud Alexandrum Rauerium 1607˙
Lodovico Viadana	*Hodie nobis cælorum Rex (8)*	LVDOVICI | VIADANÆ, |ECCLESIAE CATHEDRALIS MANTVAE | Musices Præfecti | MOCTETA FESTORVM TOTIVS ANNI | OCTONIS VOCIBVS. | McHORVS SECVNDVS. | Nunc primum in lucem edita. | Opera X. | Venetijs, apud Ricciardum Amadinum, 1597
Girolamo Giacobbi	*Parvulus hodie natus est (8)*	HIERONYMI | IACOBII | BONONIENSIS | D. PETRONII IN CHORO | MVSICO PROMAGISTRI | MOTECTA | *Multiplici vocum numero concinenda.* | LIBER PRIMVS | Nunc primum in lacem editus. | | VENETIIS| APVD ANGELVM GARDANVM 1601
Simon Gatto	*Obsecro vos fratres (8)*	MOTECTORVM| IIII. V. VI. VII. VIII. X. & XII.| VOCIBVS| Simonis Gatti Ser. Principis ac Domini D. Caroli| Archiducis Austriæ, Musicorum Præfecti:| Tum Annibalis Perini, eiusdem Serenitatis, felicissimæ recordationis,| Organorum præfecti: insequens opus hoc Levidenfe| noviter Collectorum,| Autore Horatio Sardena, Serenissimi Principis ac Domini| D. FERDINANDI Archiducis Austriæ, Musico| Venetiis, Apud Ricciardum Amadinum| 1604
Honorio Naldi	*Cum turba plurima conveniret ad Jesum (8)*	MOTTECTORVM | DVOBVS CHORIS | DOMINICIS DIEBVS CONCINENDORVM | PARTIS HYEMALIS. LIBER PRIMVS. | ROMVLO NALDIO CLERICO BONONIENSI AVCTORE | VENETIIS APVD ANGELVM GARDANVM. 1600
Francesco Soriano	*Adorna thalamum tuum Syon (8)*	FRANCISCI SVRIANI | ROMANI | MOTECTORVM | QVAE OCTO VOCIBVS | CONCINVNTVR. | SVPERIORVM PERMISSV| ROMAE, *Per Nicolaum Mutium.* 1597

˙ Il mottetto in questione è uno dei tre a non avere una parte per il basso generale, sebbene la raccolta del 1607 preveda un volume di basso per l'organo.

Nel mottetto a cinque parti *Hierusalem cito veniet salus tua* di Francesco Bianciardi, la linea del basso seguente è interamente aggiunta raddoppiando la parte vocale più bassa progressivamente a disposizione per cui esso procede senza alcuna forma di autonomia. Superato l'*incipit* del canto I, l'organo è indotto a seguire l'alto per poi stabilizzarsi sul basso vocale e ancora, al breve *tacet* del basso, raddoppia il tenore e salta di posizione di settima.

Es. 1: F. Bianciardi, *Hierusalem cito veniet*, incipit.

Nel caso del mottetto a cinque parti, *Hierusalem plantabis vineam* di Agostino Agazzari, tratto dal primo libro di *Sacrae cantiones quæ quinis, senis, septenis, octonisque vocibus concinuntur* (Roma, 1602), Vincentius propose un basso seguente discretamente fedele al modello originale e intervenne esclusivamente sulla ritmica, allo scopo di rendere il basso a valori larghi di Agazzari più aderente all'articolazione vocale e integrò la numerica, che era totalmente assente nella stampa romana.

Es. 2: A. Agazzari, *Hierusalem plantabis vineam,* frammento.

In alcuni casi la diversa interpretazione di un concerto comportò l'uso di una diversa tipologia di basso seguente per l'organo. Ciò accadde nel mottetto a sette parti *Beata es virgo Maria* di Giovanni Battista Stefanini, maestro di cappella presso la chiesa di Santa Maria della Scala a Milano, e apparso precedentemente nel *Secondo libro di motetti a cinque, sei, sette e otto voci* [...] (Venezia, 1608). Vincentius sostituì il basso seguente a linea singola con una partitura a doppia linea. È plausibile che l'organista abbia interpretato il mottetto come un brano a doppio coro: un coro superiore composto da tre parti acute (due canti e un alto) e un coro inferiore grave (composto da un alto, due tenori e un basso). Osservando la condotta del nuovo basso seguente si nota che esso è costruito seguendo principalmente la voce del contralto secondo e quella del basso primo, ossia le parti più gravi dei due cori.

Es. 3: G. B. Steffanini, *Beata es virgo Maria*, incipit.

Nel *Promptuarium musicum II* (Strasburgo, 1612) Vincentius trattò un ulteriore mottetto a sette voci di Stefanini, *O sacramentum pietatis*, secondo il medesimo atteggiamento e suddivise la formazione polifonica in due semicori: un coro acuto (due canti e tenore) e un coro grave (alto, due tenori e basso). La primigenia linea singola del basso seguente, costruita seguendo alternativamente le parti vocali del basso e del tenore, è semplicemente suddivisa su due linee, ognuna lievemente integrata e attinente a uno specifico semicoro.

Nel caso del mottetto *Ave verum corpus* di Domenico Brunetti — tratto dal volume *Unica voce, Binis, Ternis, Quaternis, & pluribus ad usum Ecclesię varij Concentus, Cum Gravi, & Acuto ad Organum* (Venezia, 1609) — Vincentius sostituì la partitura ridotta canto-basso con una a doppio rigo per le due voci gravi (tenore per il primo coro e basso per il secondo coro). Anche in questo caso, l'impostazione delle parti rivela un trattamento a due semicori del brano.

Es. 4: D. Brunetti, *Ave verum corpus*, confronto tra i bassi seguenti.

Valeria Mannoia

I *Florilegia Portensis*

L'inserimento della parte di basso generale interessò anche il primo *Florilegium Portense* (Lipsia, 1618), un'antologia a cura di Erhard Bodenschatz. Se nei quattro *Promptuaria musices* l'intervento integrativo avvenne in fase di concepimento dell'antologia, nel caso del *Florilegium* di Pforta l'aggiornamento testuale interessò una silloge già stampata e ampiamente circolante da tempo. Il *Florilegium Portense* era, infatti, la seconda edizione corretta e aggiornata del *Florilegium Selectissimarum cantionum* (Lipsia, 1603) che lo stesso Bodenschatz compilò al tempo del suo incarico di Kantor alla *Schulpforte*[31]. Originario di Lichtenberg (in Baviera), Erhard Bodenschatz ricevette una formazione musicale di alto livello presso alcune delle più importanti istituzioni protestanti della Sassonia: nel 1586 entrò come giovane cantore alla cappella di corte a Dresda, sotto la guida di Michael Rogier, nel 1591 fu ammesso a studiare al collegio di Pforta (nei pressi di Naumburg) sotto la guida dell'illustre Kantor Seth Calvisius (Kalwitz) e nel 1595 intraprese gli studi di Giurisprudenza all'Università di Lipsia. Tra il 1601 e il 1603 rientrò a Pforta per ricoprire l'incarico di Kantor, successivamente fu il pastore della vicina comunità di Groß-Osterhausen. I tre *Florilegia Portensis*, stampati nel 1603, 1618 e nel 1621, furono concepiti per l'ambito scolastico di formazione dello stesso Bodenschatz e furono il riflesso delle pratiche musicali della scuola che furono introdotte al tempo del Kantor Calvisius. Il primo *Florilegium Selectissimarum cantionum* (Lipsia, 1603) raccolse proprio il repertorio più praticato sotto la direzione di Calvisius: si trattava principalmente di *Choralmotette* e *sacrae cantiones* composti localmente e in stile osservato per il contesto devozionale luterano. La nuova edizione fu concepita per sostituire i brani della tradizione locale — come le *rotulae* natalizie — con *sacrae cantiones* su testo latino di autori italiani e aggiornare formalmente il resto del repertorio. L'intervento più significativo riguardò la compilazione di un libro parte di basso seguente per l'organo, originariamente non previsto. Bodenschatz seguì un unico modello formale e per tutti i brani della raccolta compilò un basso a linea singola che replicava la voce più grave della composizione. Nell'uso della numerica si limitò a segnalare i ritardi principali e qualche settima, lasciando una certa libertà di movimento all'organista. Le parti del basso furono, inoltre, corredate da elementi di supporto come la sottoposizione del testo-guida e una regolare indicazione del segno di battuta, alla breve.

Il secondo volume del *Florilegium Portense* (Lipsia, 1621), che fu compilato dallo stesso Bodenschatz contestualmente al volume del 1618, fu dedicato principalmente a raccogliere un ricco repertorio di *sacrae cantiones* italiane da cinque a otto voci. L'atteggiamento compilativo fu profondamente ispirato dai quattro *Promptuaria musices* (Strasburgo, 1611-1617) del collegio di Spira, con cui esiste un livello di parentela diretta. Almeno ottantatré brani del *Florilegium Portense* furono copiati dalla serie antologica di Schade e Vincentius. Bodenschatz,

---

[31]. MANNOIA 2019.

però, sostituì la partitura mista di Vincentius — a doppio rigo per i brani per due semicori e a rigo singolo per i mottetti polifonici semplici — con una parte di basso seguente a linea singola, analoga a quella adoperata per il primo *Florilegium Portense* (Lipsia, 1618). Nel caso del mottetto *Beata es virgo Maria* di Giovan Battista Stefanini, già individuato nel *Promptuarium musicum II* (Strasburgo, 1612), il confronto tra i tre bassi d'organo tradisce una concordanza tra le antologie. Bodenschatz si limitò a collocare la parte seguente su un unico rigo e aggiunse una numerica più articolata.

Es. 5: G. B. Steffanini, *Beata es virgo Maria*, confronto tra i bassi seguenti.

TRADIZIONI TARDE

Successivamente alla stampa delle due collane di Spira e Pforta comparvero altri sporadici interventi e integrazioni della parte del basso d'organo. Diversi casi interessanti riguardarono la collana di *Promptuaria musices* (Strasburgo, 1622-1627) di mottetti per due, tre e quattro voci compilata da Johann Donfrid per la cattolica Lateinschule di Rottenburg am Neckar (nel Baden-Württemberg). L'intervento di adattamento riguardò quei mottetti a quattro voci di stampo tardorinascimentale ma che erano ancora praticati presso le congregazioni religiose cattoliche. Donfrid inserì nel *Promptuarium musicum I* (Strasburgo, 1622) un mottetto a quattro parti, *O magnum mysterium*, di Tomás Luis de Victoria[32]. La struttura formale del brano è del tipo AB, con una breve coda alleluiatica conclusiva e la scrittura imitativa è a quattro parti piene. Donfrid inserì una parte di basso seguente per uniformarlo ai criteri generali della raccolta. Il basso d'organo su linea singola segue principalmente la parte del basso vocale, assecondando, ove necessario, anche tutti gli ingressi significativi delle altre tre voci. Nel complesso, lo stile compositivo del brano discorda dagli altri mottetti a poche voci, la cui scrittura era principalmente concertata.

L'inserimento dell'*O magnum mysterium* di Victoria, però, non fu casuale. Johann Donfrid concepì la sua collana di *Promptuaria musices* per una comunità cattolica dallo spirito profondamente contro-riformista. Proprio nel 1623 l'arciduca Leopoldo diede l'autorizzazione all'ordine gesuitico di fondare a Rottenburg am Neckar un proprio collegio che gli permise di stabilire progressivamente la propria autorità sul territorio[33]. Donfrid, che si era formato presso l'Università gesuitica di Dillingen, diede particolare risalto all'attività musicale di numerosi compositori formatisi presso il Collegio Germanico di Roma[34], come Agostino Agazzari, Antonio Cifra, Giovanni Francesco Anerio, Abbondio Antonelli e Gregorio Allegri. La presenza di Victoria, che dal 1571 al 1576 circa fu maestro di musica e successivamente maestro di cappella del Collegio germanico, fu un chiaro omaggio al suo ruolo all'interno della cerchia gesuitica romana.

La necessità di integrare le composizioni con una parte d'organo, arricchita di guide per il musicista (come il segno di battuta oppure il testo sottoposto alla musica) e di una numerica più semplice da gestire, testimonia la natura didattica di questi volumi, che si rivolgevano principalmente a un'utenza poco pratica nella lettura rapida della partitura.

La volontà di riproporre un repertorio obiettivamente obsoleto tradisce la mancanza di aggiornamento dei centri periferici tedeschi e in primo luogo delle biblioteche scolastiche e delle cappelle musicali.

---

[32]. Il brano fu stampato per la prima volta nei *Motecta, que partim, quaternis, partim, quinis, alia, senis, alia Octonis, Alia Duodenis, Vocibus, concinnuntur* (Roma, 1583). All'edizione romana di Gardano seguirono l'edizione milanese del 1589 di Francesco ed eredi di Simon Tini e l'edizione veneziana di Angelo Gardano del 1603. Non è possibile capire quale delle tre edizioni fu in possesso di Johann Donfrid. La *Bibliotheca classica sive Catalogus officinalis* di Georg Draud (1611, n. 1225) segnala anche un'edizione pubblicata da Nikolaus Stein nel 1602 a Francoforte ma non è pervenuta.

[33]. DUHR 1913, pp. 277-278.

[34]. L'istituto gesuitico fu l'organo preposto alla formazione dei giovani sacerdoti che avrebbero costituito il clero tedesco. KENNEDY 1982.

Infine, la riorganizzazione della partitura del basso d'organo per quei brani che ne erano già corredati ci conferma l'esistenza di più abitudini pratiche nella formalizzazione del testo per il basso d'organo.

Per cui, le sei antologie stampate a Pforta e Spira rappresentano una fase transitoria nella storia della ricezione del mottetto italiano in cui lo sguardo alla tradizione convive con la necessità di rendere più pratico e più facilmente spendibile un repertorio di tradizione.

BIBLIOGRAFIA

BANCHIERI 1595
BANCHIERI, Adriano. *Concerti Ecclesiastici a otto voci* [...] *Aggiuntovi nel Primo Choro la spartitura per sonare nell'Organo commodissima, Nuouamente Composti, et dati in luce*, Venezia, Giacomo Vincenti, 1595.

BEER 1989
BEER Axel. *Die Annahme des «Stile nuovo»*, Tutzing, Verlegt Bei Hans Schneider, 1989.

BENEDICT 1996
BENEDICT, Barbara M. *Making the Modern Reader: Cultural Mediation in Early Modern Literary Anthologies*, Princeton, Princeton University Press, 1996.

BENNETT – SAUNDERS – WEAVER 2021
BENNETT, Lawrence – SAUNDERS, Steven – WEAVER, Andrew. 'The Court Chapels of the Austrian Line (II): From Archduke Charles II to Emperor Leopold I', in: *A Companion to Music at the Habsburg Courts in the Sixteenth and Seventeenth Centuries*, a cura di Andrew H. Weaver, Leida-Boston, Brill, 2021 (Brill's Companions to the Musical Culture of Medieval and Early Modern Europe, 4), pp. 176-219.

BLANKENBURG 1980
BLANKENBURG, Walter. 'Hassler Kaspar', in: *The New Grove Dictionary of Music and Musicians*, a cura di Stanley Sadie, 20 voll., Londra, Macmillan, ⁶1980, vol. VIII, p. 297.

CARABA 1985
CARABA, Piero. 'Croce, Giovanni', in: *Dizionario Biografico degli Italiani. 31*, Roma, Istituto dell'Enciclopedia Italiana, 1985, <https://www.treccani.it/enciclopedia/giovanni-croce_(Dizionario-Biografico)/>, consultato a novembre 2023.

CARACI VELA 2005
CARACI VELA, Maria. *La Filologia musicale. Istituzioni, storia, strumenti critici. 1*, Lucca, LIM, 2005.

CARVER 1988
CARVER, Anthony F. *Cori spezzati. The Development of Sacred Polychoral Music to the Time of Schütz*, 2 voll., Cambridge, Cambridge University Press, 1988.

CROCE 1594
CROCE, Giovanni. *Motetti a otto voci* [...], Venezia, Giacomo Vincenti, 1594.

CROOK 2006
CROOK, David. 'Germany and Central Europe: 1660-1640', in: *European Music 1520-1640*, a cura di James Haar, Woodbridge, The Boydell Press, 2006 (Studies in Medieval and Renaissance Music, 5), pp. 353-370.

CULLEY 1970
CULLEY, Thomas D. *Jesuits and Music: A Study of the Musicians Connected with the German College in Rome during the XVII Century and of their Activities in Northern Europe*, Roma, Jesuit Historical Institute, 1970 (Sources and Studies for the History of the Jesuits, 2).

DUHR 1913
DUHR, Bernhard. *Geschichte der Jesuiten in den Ländern deutschen Zunge in der ersten Hälfte des XVII Jahrhunderts*, 2 voll., Freiburg im Breisgau, Herdersche Verlagshandlung, 2013.

GISELBRECHT 2012
GISELBRECHT Elisabeth. *Crossing Boundaries: The Printed Dissemination of the Italian Sacred Music in German Speaking-Areas (1580-1620)*, Ph.D. Diss., Cambridge, King's College, University of Cambridge, 2012.

GLIXON – KURTZMAN – SAUNDERS 2021
GLIXON Beth L. – KURTZMAN Jeffrey – SAUNDERS Steven. 'Musical Connections between the Austrian Habsburgs and Venice in the Late Sixteenth and Seventeenth Centuries', in: *A Companion to Music at the Habsburg Courts in the Sixteenth and Seventeenth Centuries*, op. cit., pp. 534-570.

GRENDLER 2017
GRENDLER, Paul. *The Jesuits and Italian Universities 1548-1773*, Washington (DC), Catholic University of America Press, 2017.

HORSLEY 1977
HORSLEY, Imogene. 'Full and Short Scores in the Accompaniment of Italian Church Music in the Early Baroque', in: *Journal of the American Musicological Society*, XXX/3 (1977), pp. 466-499.

KENNEDY 1982
KENNEDY, T. Frank. *Jesuits and Music: The European Tradition (1547-1622)*, Ph.D. Diss., Santa Barbara (CA), University of California, 1982.

KINKELDEY 1910
KINKELDEY, Otto. *Orgel und Klavier in der Musik des 16. Jahrhundert; Ein Beitrag zur Geschichte der Instrumentalmusik*, Lipsia, Breitkopf & Härtel, 1910.

KIRWAN 2001
KIRWAN, A. Lindsey. 'Vincentius [Vincent], Caspar', in: *Grove Music Online*, 2001, <www.oxfordmusiconline.com/grovemusic>, consultato a novembre 2023.

Mannoia 2019
Mannoia, Valeria M. R. *La ricezione del motetto italiano nelle antologie tedesche del Seicento. Con un approfondimento sulla teoria dei diasistemi di Cesare Segre*, Tesi di dottorato, Cremona, Università degli studi di Pavia, 2019.

Meconi 2021
Meconi, Honey. 'Manuscript Culture: The Habsburg-Burgundian Scriptorium and Some Successors', in: *A Companion to Music at the Habsburg Courts in the Sixteenth and Seventeenth Centuries*, a cura di Andrew H. Weaver, Leida-Boston, Brill, 2021 (Brill's Companions to the Musical Culture of Medieval and Early Modern Europe, 4), pp. 347-396.

Pasquali 1988
Pasquali, Giorgio. *Storia della tradizione e critica del testo*, Firenze, Casa editrice Le Lettere, 1988 (Collana Bibliotheca).

Praetorius 2004
Praetorius, Michael. *Syntagma musicum III: Termini musici*, (1619), a cura di Willibald Gurlitt, Kassel, Bärenreiter Verlag, 2004 (Documenta Musicologica. Erste Reihe, Druckschriften-Faksimiles, 21).

Roche 1974
Roche, Jerome. 'Anthologies and the Dissemination of Early Baroque Sacred Music', in: *Soundings*, IV (1974), pp. 6-12.

Roche 1998
Id. 'Aus den berühmbsten italiänischen Autoribus: Dissemination North of the Alps of the Early Baroque Italian Sacred Repertory through Published Anthologies and Reprints', in: *Claudio Monteverdi und die Folgen: Bericht über das Internationale Symposium, Detmold 1993*, a cura di Silke Leopold e Joachim Steinheuer, Kassel, Bärenreiter, 1998, pp. 13-28.

Rose 2005
Rose, Stephen. 'The Mechanisms of the Music Trade in Central Germany, 1600-1640', in: *Journal of the Royal Musical Association*, CXXX/1 (2005), pp. 1-37.

Segre 1979
Segre, Cesare. *Semiotica filologica. Testo e modelli culturali*, Torino, Einaudi, 1979.

Van Orden 2013
Van Orden, Kate. *Music, Authorship and the Book, in the First Century of Print*, Berkeley (CA), University of California Press, 2013.

Wölfle 2009
Wölfle, Sylvia. *Die Kunstpatronage der Fugger (1560-1618)*, Augusta, Wißner-Verlag, 2009.

Il basso continuo nelle composizioni per i defunti di Pierre-Louis Pollio (1724-1796). Uso, notazione e problematiche relative all'edizione moderna della partitura

Francesca Mignogna
(Sorbonne Université/IReMus, Paris)

La notazione della musica cosiddetta 'occidentale', dal Medioevo a oggi, si è sviluppata, anche se non necessariamente in modo lineare, da *descrittiva* a *prescrittiva*[1]. Questa trasformazione funzionale accompagna, favorisce, influenza e supporta non solo l'evoluzione delle tecniche compositive, ma anche il concetto stesso di opera musicale. Quest'ultima, infatti, è stata per lungo tempo il risultato di una pratica collettiva ed è soltanto a partire dal XIX secolo che, parallelamente alla trasformazione dello status sociale del compositore e l'emergenza del concetto di proprietà artistica, la scrittura serve a comunicare una composizione personale da riprodurre senza alterazioni, rendendo così la partitura un oggetto finito in sé, fedele alle intenzioni del suo autore, e/o affermazione di un sistema musicale iper-normatizzato (come nel caso, ad esempio, dello strutturalismo). Pierre-Louis Pollio, compositore francese del periodo barocco, le cui opere per i defunti sono oggetto di questo studio, si colloca circa a metà della linea temporale evocata, e le fonti che hanno tramandato la sua musica permettono di evidenziare l'apertura della notazione musicale verso i contesti della musica sacra tardo-barocca, in particolare per ciò che riguarda il basso continuo.

Nato a Digione il 15 giugno 1724, Pierre-Louis Pollio rimase per molto tempo un compositore negletto ai musicisti e alla musicologia[2]. Due programmi di ricerca condotti dal

---

[1]. Questa affermazione si riferisce solo alla notazione in quanto *tonschrift*, e non tiene conto delle *grifschrift*, ossia dei vari tipi di messa in intavolatura, il cui carattere è prescrittivo. *Cfr.* APEL 1953, p. 54.

[2]. Pollio è stato oggetto, a partire dalla metà del XX secolo, di alcuni studi, principalmente biografici, tra cui: WANGERMÉE 1945; GURLITT 1961; LORETTE 1989.

2014 all'Institut de recherche en musicologie (IReMus)[3] costituiscono il primo e più importante progetto collettivo dedicato alla riscoperta delle opere di questo compositore. Figlio di un sarto e probabilmente allievo, alla Sainte-Chapelle du Roi a Digione, del maestro Joseph Michel e dell'abbé Doriot, Pierre-Louis Pollio servì durante tutta la sua carriera come maestro di coro e di musica in istituti ecclesiastici situati nel nord-est della Francia e fino all'Hainaut belga, in particolare la collegiata di Saint-Fursy a Péronne (174?-1751?), la Sainte-Chapelle du Roy a Digione (1751?-1762?), la cattedrale di Saint-Pierre a Beauvais (1762?-1767) che, nel 1767, lasciò per la collegiata di Saint-Vincent a Soignies (Belgio), dove rimase fino alla sua morte sopraggiunta nel 1796. Per quarant'anni fu responsabile della composizione della musica per le varie chiese in cui prestò servizio, in particolare a Digione, Beauvais e Soignies. Se la vita di Pollio risulta scarsamente documentata nelle fonti dell'epoca, la sua opera, al contrario, si rivela una fonte preziosa per lo studio della musica sacra tardo barocca: ne emerge un *corpus* tràdito decisamente copioso, frutto della convivenza di due diverse concezioni musicali, quella del contrappunto tradizionale e quella dell'armonia ramista (il cosiddetto stile barocco). I circa milleduecento numeri d'opera giunti fino a noi, che sono tutti (con una sola eccezione, *cfr. infra*) rimasti inediti, fanno di Pollio l'unico compositore dell'*ancien régime* francese — oltre a Marc-Antoine Charpentier — la cui opera è stata preservata nella sua quasi totalità. È anche autore di diversi scritti didattici e teorici, tuttora inediti, tra cui un trattato di *chant sur le livre*[4]. Le opere di Pollio per la liturgia dei defunti, oggetto di questo studio, consistono in sessantanove composizioni databili tra il 1765 e il 1776, le quali possono essere suddivise in due gruppi principali: opere del periodo beauvaisiano e quelle del periodo soigniniano. Le opere del periodo beauvaisiano (tre messe per i morti) sono contenute esclusivamente in un *livre de chœur* realizzato con la tecnica dello stencil[5] (equivalente del *pochoir* francese), mentre le opere per i morti del periodo di Soignies sono conservate esclusivamente in forma manoscritta, principalmente in volumi di partiture autografe che Pollio copiò e classificò tra il 1770 e il 1790 circa, ai quali si aggiungono numerose copie di parti separate per lo più autografe[6]. Il numero e le caratteristiche delle fonti disponibili per il *corpus* studiato sono rari nel campo della musica liturgica francese dell'*ancien régime*. Fra XVII e XVIII secolo, se la maggior parte delle composizioni polifoniche furono pubblicate in forma di *livre de choeur* principalmente da Pierre e Robert Ballard[7], le partiture, specialmente quelle redatte direttamente dal compositore,

---

[3]. '*Autour du lutrin*' (2020-in corso); 'Pierre-Louis Pollio (1724-1796)' (2014-2019).

[4]. Pollio 1770. *Cfr.* Wangermée 1945 e Montagnier 1995.

[5]. Pollio 1765. Si tratta dell'unica raccolta edita contenente musica di Pollio e pervenuta fino a noi.

[6]. Le fonti relative al periodo di Soignies provengono dagli archivi musicali della collegiata di Saint-Vincent a Soignies (B-Ssv), dal museo del Capitolo di Soignies (B-Smc) e dalla collezione musicale della chiesa di Saint-Elisabeth a Mons (B-Mse); il *livre de chœur* contenente le messe per i morti composte a Beauvais è conservato nel tesoro della cattedrale di Saint-Pierre.

[7]. *Cfr.* Guillo 2023.

sono assai rare. Per quanto concerne, invece, il formato a parti separate — piuttosto comune fra le edizioni a stampa e fra i manoscritti che riportano preziose informazioni sulla pratica musicale —, esso mostra diverse carenze ai fini di uno studio oggettivo dell'opera, non soltanto per la quasi impossibilità nel determinare l'esistenza di parti perdute ma soprattutto perché non permette uno studio dell'opera nella sua manifestazione 'assoluta', essendo i manoscritti concepiti per un determinato contesto esecutivo: in assenza di altre fonti di confronto, la loro natura fortemente prescrittiva (dovuta alla preoccupazione di fornire all'esecutore 'istruzioni per suonare' le più precise possibili) rende difficile l'identificazione degli elementi strutturali della composizione[8].

La comparazione fra le diverse fonti della musica per i defunti di Pierre-Louis Pollio ha evidenziato la differenza ontologica tra esse. Le parti separate destinate all'uso di cantanti e strumentisti sono, per loro stessa natura, *prescrittive*, in quanto vi sono annotati tutti gli elementi ritenuti necessari per l'esecuzione. Le partiture, invece, sono tutt'altro che esaustive dal punto di vista della notazione e delle informazioni fornite e sono quindi *descrittive*: redatte dal compositore per la conservazione e come riferimento per la copiatura delle parti separate, l'apertura della notazione non si limita a quegli elementi che, per loro natura, erano legati a una pratica estemporanea. Un confronto tra le fonti citate mostra, in particolare, che la linea melodica del basso continuo è generalmente molto più dettagliata e sviluppata nelle parti separate che nelle partiture. Inoltre, quando sono disponibili diverse copie della parte separata del basso continuo, esse forniscono, nella maggior parte dei casi, versioni più o meno divergenti l'una dall'altra in termini di configurazione melodica. L'osservazione di tali divergenze, apparentemente aleatorie, oltre che l'esistenza di composizioni parodia e di autoimprestiti all'interno del *corpus* in oggetto, suggerisce che le differenti versioni che le fonti trasmettono siano delle *attualizzazioni* di un'opera *virtuale*[9]. Le fonti di Pollio mostrano, in modo evidente, che «la sostanza dell'opera, di per sé non afferrabile, è presente esclusivamente nell'insieme di tutte le varianti»[10]; all'opposizione tra opera ideale (propria del pensiero romantico) e opera empirica[11], si interpone quella che potremmo definire *opera virtuale* e che, pur essendo

---

8. *Cfr.* Leon 2000.

9. *Cfr.* Deleuze 1968.

10. Dahlhaus 2009, p. 152.

11. «L'affermazione secondo cui "la sostanza dell'opera sia presente esclusivamente nell'insieme di tutte le varianti" detiene una problematicità intrinseca nella misura in cui essa risulta in contrasto con il concetto di "opera d'arte musicale" generalmente diffuso presso la comunità musicologica e musicale d'oggidì, e non sostanzialmente diverso rispetto a quello codificato in Europa, prioritariamente in area germanica, tra la fine del Settecento e l'inizio dell'Ottocento. Secondo tale concettualizzazione, l'opera d'arte si pone quale entità ideale, corrispondente alla formalizzazione di un pensiero autoriale, ossia dell'attività creativa di un soggetto che, libero da condizionamenti materiali e in ossequio esclusivo alla propria volontà, ha generato un'entità, scegliendo e plasmando una materia cui ha conferito perfezione interna. [...] Quanto mai lungi dall'essere un oggetto ideale, essa [l'opera, NDA] si pone

rappresentazione dell'intenzione autoriale del compositore, può assumere una forma differente secondo le contingenze di esecuzione, nutrendosi della mutazione continua. Tale lettura 'aperta' dell'opera di Pollio, e più in generale della musica sacra barocca, solleva numerose questioni di ordine analitico e, conseguentemente, editoriale; in particolare, l'editore moderno è portato a interrogarsi sulla maniera di produrre un'edizione moderna che non alteri il valore ontologico originale della notazione e che rifletta la pluralità del *testo*[12] trasmesso. Per fare questo, è necessario identificate quali siano gli elementi 'strutturali' dell'opera e determinare se le varianti disponibili, in particolare per il basso continuo, appartengano a una classe di elementi equivalenti e interscambiabili o se esistano, al contrario, delle logiche implicite e indipendenti dal sistema normativo adottato dal compositore che ne determinano l'occorrenza.

LE FONTI

Due dei venti volumi di partiture manoscritte[13] che costituiscono i dieci numeri d'*opus* raccolti da Pollio durante la sua carriera sono interamente dedicati alle composizioni per la liturgia dei morti. Si tratta dei manoscritti numero 12 e 18 della collezione del Musée du Chapitre de Soignies (B-Smc). I due volumi contengono un totale di sessantatre delle sessantanove composizioni di Pollio per i defunti[14]. Le partiture contenute in questi due volumi non contengono alcuna indicazione relativa all'orchestrazione strumentale e vocale[15]; la tipologia di ogni voce o strumento può essere dedotta solo sulla base della chiave utilizzata e, eventualmente, confermata dal confronto con le parti separate. Di norma, se lo spazio disponibile sulla pagina è ottimale, oltre alle parti vocali sono presenti uno (basso continuo) o due (basso continuo e strumento obbligato) righi strumentali; tuttavia, la variabilità del numero di parti vocali nei cori (che varia da 4 a 6) fa sì che in alcuni punti la parte strumentale non abbia un pentagramma

---

[...] quale entità propriamente empirica. Il riconoscimento dell'opera nei termini di concetto empirico comporta alcune implicazioni, prima fra tutte quella secondo cui l'opera musicale sia un'entità plurale che, a ragione, risulta unicamente dall'insieme di tutte le varianti». DI CINTIO 2017.

[12]. «The Text is plural. This does not mean only that it has several meanings but that it fulfills the very plurality of meaning: an irreducible (and not just acceptable) plurality. The text is not coexistence of meaning, but passage, traversal; hence, it depends not on interpretation, however liberal, but on an explosion, on dissemination. The plurality of the Text depends, as a matter of fact, not on the ambiguity of its contents, but on what we might call the stereographic plurality of the signifiers which wave it [...]». BARTHES 1989, pp. 59-60.

[13]. *Cfr.* GUILLOUX 2016, pp. 252-256.

[14]. Il manoscritto 18 (POLLIO 1769-1776) contiene le messe per i morti (4), le elevazioni (17) e i *Libera me* (2). Il manoscritto 12 (POLLIO 1771-1776) contiene i *De Profundis* (4+8), i mottetti (24) e i *Genitori* (penultima strofa dell'innno *Pange lingua*) (4).

[15]. L'unica eccezione si trova nella prosa della messa n. 1 *Si iniquitates* (POLLIO 1769-1776, p. 19), dove figura l'indicazione «Basson» in corrispondenza del rigo dello strumento concertante.

dedicato, ma condivida il pentagramma con una delle voci (solitamente con la voce di basso). Ad esempio, spesso lo strumento obbligato non ha un pentagramma dedicato, ma viene annotato sul pentagramma del basso, lì dove quest'ultimo tace (e il ruolo di questo strumento nel *tutti* può quindi essere stabilito solo dal confronto con le parti separate). Il basso continuo, invece, è spesso privo di un rigo dedicato; ciò accade soprattutto quando è *seguente* del basso vocale. Inoltre, queste *mises en page* difettive, dovute principalmente alla mancanza di spazio sulla pagina e che non mancano di interessare le parti vocali (soprattutto in corrispondenza dei cori a sei voci), variano non solo da un brano all'altro ma anche, in alcuni casi, all'interno dello stesso brano[16]. Le partiture autografe di Pierre-Louis Pollio sono caratterizzate, più in generale, da una notazione 'essenziale', comportante numerosi segni di abbreviazione o elementi di notazione arcaicizzanti (come, ad esempio, l'uso del punto di valore a cavallo di misura o come segno generico di prolungamento del valore di una nota). Le legature sono uno degli elementi della partitura che più risentono di questo tipo di notazione, soprattutto per quanto riguarda l'uso delle legature sui melismi, molto irregolare in Pollio. In contrasto con questo stile di notazione 'sintetico', vi sono alcuni elementi di notazione che potrebbero essere considerati 'accessori': ad esempio, sono presenti alcune rare numerazioni di misura che aiutano, in alcuni casi, a comprendere la concezione dell'autore sulla divisione strutturale del brano.

Per le opere funebri di Pollio sono disponibili numerose parti separate che si trovano perlopiù in buono stato di conservazione[17]. Se la maggioranza di esse costituisce una fonte ulteriore per le composizioni contenute nei volumi di partiture, alcune parti separate contengono invece ulteriori 'attualizzazioni' delle opere presenti nei volumi di partiture, che possono quindi essere considerate come composizioni a sé stanti. Al contrario, per molte delle composizioni raccolte da Pollio nei volumi di partiture, non sono oggi disponibili parti separate. Le parti separate tuttora esistenti si dividono principalmente in due categorie: le copie autografe di Pollio e le copie realizzate da altri copisti; ciò nonostante, possono essere considerate tutte fonti autorevoli, in quanto non solo tutte le copie disponibili sono contemporanee a Pollio ma, essendo state redatte con ogni probabilità da studenti della *maîtrise* (come mostrato da alcune annotazioni presenti), sono state indubbiamente oggetto di 'convalida' da parte di Pollio[18]. Il numero e il tipo di parti disponibili per ogni numero d'*opus* è variabile. Nella maggior parte dei casi disponiamo di almeno una copia per ciascuna delle parti vocali, oltre che per il serpentone, il basso continuo e, eventualmente, lo strumento obbligato. L'unica parte strumentale presente in tutte le composizioni di cui possediamo materiale d'esecuzione è

---

[16]. Questa variabilità nel numero di righi è spesso legata alla mobilità della voce di *basse-taille*, che costituisce la quinta parte vocale che si aggiunge ai cori a quattro parti.

[17]. Provenienti dai fondi del Capitolo di Saint-Vincent a Soignies (B-Ssv) e della Chiesa di Saint-Elisabeth a Mons (B-Mse).

[18]. La questione riguardante lo statuto ontologico di ognuna delle fonti disponibili è affrontato in modo più approfondito in Mignogna 2024 (tesi di dottorato depositata a ottobre 2023).

quella del serpentone, che era considerato uno strumento di rinforzo del coro; infatti le parti del serpentone, che raddoppiano il basso vocale in quasi tutte le opere (con un'eccezione, *cfr. infra*), sono integralmente munite di testo. Le parti del basso continuo, invece, sono disponibili per la maggior parte delle composizioni (mancano solo per i *Nouveaux De profundis*), ma in alcuni casi sono usurate o incomplete. Al contrario, esistono fascicoli di parti di strumento concertante (indicato come 'fagotto o violoncello', 'fagotto' o 'violoncello', a seconda dei casi) solo per tre delle otto messe da requiem[19] e per le elevazioni.

In particolare, le parti separate consentono di integrare le informazioni sulla strumentazione e sull'orchestrazione dei brani, che mancano nei volumi delle partiture. Questo è particolarmente utile per determinare il ruolo della voce di *basse-taille* nei cori, ed è ancora più prezioso per completare le informazioni sulle parti strumentali. Come già detto, nelle partiture manoscritte spesso manca il rigo di basso continuo. Solo il confronto con le parti separate ha permesso di confermare l'ipotesi che, in questi casi, il basso continuo non sia assente ma *seguente* dalla parte più bassa del complesso vocale. Ad esempio, il confronto tra la partitura e le parti separate ha mostrato che, nei trii della sequenza della messa da requiem n. 3, contenuta nel manoscritto 18, il basso continuo (che non è annotato nella partitura) è *seguente* dalla voce più grave del coro, vale a dire il basso (nei trii costituiti da *haute-contre*, *taille* e *basse*) o il tenore (nei trii costituiti da *premier dessus*, *deuxième dessus* e *taille*). Inoltre, sebbene nell'esempio appena citato la parte raddoppiata dal basso continuo nei trii corrisponda anche al *cantus firmus*, il confronto con le parti separate ha permesso di escludere un legame sistematico tra i due elementi. Lo stesso vale per il serpentone, di cui non c'è traccia in partitura, e le cui parti separate mostrano che pedissequamente (con la sola presenza di un già menzionato *hapax*) raddoppia il basso e non (quando presente) il *cantus firmus*. Inoltre, le parti separate permettono di determinare il ruolo dello strumento obbligato nei cori (che spesso non è notato nelle partiture): nella maggior parte dei casi, e con alcune variazioni idiomatiche minori, esso raddoppia il basso continuo.

ORGANICO STRUMENTALE

Come già ricordato, nelle fonti contenenti le composizioni di Pollio per la liturgia dei morti sono menzionati esplicitamente soltanto tre strumenti musicali: il serpentone, il fagotto e il violoncello. La lettera di Pollio risalente al 1788 e indirizzata all'Abbé Doriot, presenta un elenco minuzioso delle caratteristiche specifiche del pezzo per il concorso di *maître de chapelle* alla collegiata di Soignies, dal quale possiamo ricavare utili informazioni sull'organico strumentale disponibile e sui precetti diocesani relativi all'impiego degli strumenti musicali:

---

[19]. Si tratta delle messe da requiem n. 1 e n. 2 contenute nel manoscritto 18, e della *Messe des morts à cinq*, parodia della messa n. 1, disponibili solamente sotto forma di parti separate.

[...] la pièce pour l'éprouve doit être sans simphonie; mais à deux ou trois Violonchels y compris la Basse Continue ou Contre Basse; [...] l'usage de l'Eglise n'admet point de Simphonie; mais que les chœurs à cinq voix sont bien remplis, qu'on y rend bien aussi les Solo, Duo, Trio dans le goût François, et non dans le genre italien, qui ne feroit point fortune à Soignies[20].

In compenso, le partiture manoscritte del periodo di Beauvais di Pollio[21] mostrano che egli aveva a disposizione una gamma più ampia di strumenti[22]. A Beauvais, come a Soignies, le parti del basso continuo (non cifrate) non contengono alcuna informazione sullo strumentario utilizzato; la comparazione delle partiture e parti separate con elementi prosografici relativi ai musicisti presenti a Beauvais e a Soignies durante il mandato di Pollio lasciano supporre che il *continuum* fosse assicurato dall'organo e rafforzato in precise circostanze (dipendenti dal livello di solennità della celebrazione) dal fagotto o dal violoncello e, a Beauvais soltanto, da un secondo serpentone[23]. La presenza dell'organo che accompagna il serpentone e il fagotto (o violoncello) renderebbe le composizioni di Pollio perfettamente compatibili con l'organico strumentale disponibile sia nella Cattedrale di Beauvais che nella Collegiata di Soignies.

A partire dal XVII secolo, il serpentone è lo strumento d'elezione in Francia per l'accompagnamento del canto piano, al quale dovrebbe apportare una nuova sonorità e un nuovo gusto[24]; privo di chiavi, la sua esecuzione dipende dalla combinazione di diteggiature e lingue (ossia articolazioni) che consentono la modulazione dell'intonazione[25]; pur essendo uno strumento musicale, le sue caratteristiche organologiche lo portano a mantenere un particolare legame con il canto, come testimonia la presenza del testo in tutti i libri parte analizzati in questo studio[26]. Durante la sua prolungata presenza nella Chiesa di Francia, il serpentone ha ricoperto diverse funzioni nei diversi dispositivi di scrittura musicale:

---

[20]. B-Mse, Archives du Chapitre Saint-Vincent à Soignies, n. 6 (Registre aux résolutions Capitulaire, 1787-1794), ff. 72-73 (riprodotto in Lorette 1989, p. 106): «il brano per la prova deve essere senza sinfonia; ma con due o tre violoncelli, compreso il basso continuo o il contrabbasso; [...] la consuetudine della Chiesa non ammette punto la sinfonia; ma che i cori a cinque voci siano ben riempiti, che i soli, i duo e i trii siano ben resi nello stile francese, e non in quello italiano, che non farebbe fortuna a Soignies». Le traduzioni, dove non ulteriormente specificato, sono dell'autore del presente saggio.

[21]. *Cfr.*, ad esempio, la prima pagina della partitura manoscritta del motetto *Benedictus Dominus Deus meus*, composto nel 1764 (riprodotto in Lorette 1989).

[22]. Riguardo alla effettiva presenza di strumenti non notati nelle fonti, si veda Montagnier 2019, capitoli 'The Use of Instruments' e 'A Hidden Polychorality? A Hidden Orchestra?'.

[23]. *Cfr.* Mignogna 2024, cap. 2.4.

[24]. Morley-Pegge – Bate – Weston 2001; Davy-Rigaux – Gétrau 2005.

[25]. Davy-Rigaux – Gétrau 2005, p. 4.

[26]. Con un'unica eccezione, *cfr. infra*.

Métoyen [*Méthode de serpent* (ms., c1810, F-Pc)] souligne de son côté que le serpentiste pouvait parfois improviser une variation mélodique à partir de la ligne de plain-chant, ou en proposer une basse d'accompagnement, ces deux dernières pratiques concernant surtout les hymnes et proses ou certains chants exceptionnels [...]. Le serpent assurait aussi son rôle de soutien dans les formes développées traditionnelles du chant ecclésiastique qu'étaient le faux-bourdon et le chant sur le livre. Il était employé en doublure de la partie de basse (effectuant la ligne de plain-chant) dans les faux-bourdons à quatre ou cinq parties, ou pour exécuter la mélodie en plain-chant au-dessus de laquelle les chantres improvisaient le chant sur le livre. [...] Comme le sous-entend Mersenne [*Harmonie universelle...*, Paris, 1636, *Traité des instruments*, Livre cinquième], le serpent fut par ailleurs vraisemblablement utilisé dès sa création, en tant que basse de la famille des cornets, pour la réalisation des doublures des voix de basses ou celle des parties de basses instrumentales dans le cadre des messes ou motets polyphoniques[27].

Nelle opere per i defunti di Pollio conservate a Soignies, il serpentone raddoppia, nella stragrande maggioranza dei casi, il basso vocale nei cori, rimanendo invece silenzioso in occasione di tutti i soli, duetti, terzetti o quartetti: è il caso di tutte le composizioni in forma di mottetto, sia che il coro esegua in stile contrappuntistico (*chant sur le livre*) che omoritmico[28]. Nel caso dei cori in stile di *faux-bourdons*, il serpentone raddoppia, nella maggior parte dei casi, al tempo stesso il basso vocale e il basso continuo, quest'ultimo raddoppiando a sua volta il basso vocale (con l'eccezione di alcune varianti idiomatiche); in sintesi, nell'intero *corpus* studiato, emerge un rapporto più stretto del serpentone con i bassi che con il *plain-chant*. Questa ipotesi è confermata anche da una particolarità dell'intonazione dell'*Agnus Dei* nella versione beauvaisiana della messa *Parce mihi, Domine*: qui, a differenza di tutte le altre intonazioni in canto piano presenti nei *faux-bourdons*, il rigo di *Bassus II* comporta non l'intonazione in sé, ma anche una melodia che costituisce una sorta di basso fondamentale; è probabile che questa parte fosse affidata al serpentone, che accompagna gli incipit ma come 'basso continuo'; ciò confermerebbe anche l'ipotesi della presenza di due serpenti (*cfr. infra*).

---

[27]. DAVY-RIGAUX – GÉTRAU 2005, pp. 5-6: «Métoyen [Méthode de serpent (ms., c.1810, F-Pc)] sottolinea che il suonatore di serpente poteva a volte improvvisare una variazione melodica a partire dalla linea di canto piano, o suggerire un accompagnamento di basso; queste due ultime pratiche erano utilizzate principalmente per gli inni e le prose o per alcuni canti eccezionali [...]. Il serpente svolgeva anche un ruolo di supporto nelle forme tradizionali sviluppate di canto ecclesiastico, come il faux-bourdon e il chant sur le livre. Nel faux-bourdon a quattro o cinque parti, il serpente veniva usato per raddoppiare la parte del basso (che suonava la linea del canto piano), o per suonare la melodia del canto piano su cui i cantori improvvisavano il chant sur le livre. [...] Come suggerisce Mersenne [*Harmonie universelle...*, Paris, 1636, *Traité des instruments*, Livre cinquième], il serpente fu probabilmente utilizzato fin dall'inizio, come basso della famiglia dei cornetti, per raddoppiare le voci basse o per eseguire le parti di basso strumentale nelle messe polifoniche o nei mottetti».

[28]. Con la sola eccezione del coro, in stile di *chant sur le livre*, dell'introito della *Messe des morts à cinq*, dove il serpentone si comporta come una voce indipendente del tessuto polifonico. *Cfr.* MIGNOGNA 2024.

A questo proposito, è interessante notare quanto osservato nell'Ottocento nella *Méthode de plain-chant, principalement destinée au diocèse de Beauvais* dell'abbé Devergie, riguardo al ruolo del serpente in relazione al canto piano:

> Un avis essentiel à donner à tous les *serpens*, mais surtout à ceux de la campagne, c'est qu'il faut jouer le plain-chant purement et simplement, tel qu'il est noté; tous ces fredons, toutes ces additions de notes superflues, sont du plus mauvais goût et souvent du plus parfait ridicule; elles défigurent le chant, au lieu de l'orner; elles gênent et dérangent le chœur, au lieu de le soulager et de le soutenir; [...] Par là, nous ne prétendons point interdire les accords avec le serpent; que l'on fasse une basse bien juste dans un psaume, dans un hymne, dans un motet, rien de plus beau, rien qui relève mieux le chant de l'église; c'est un des grands avantages que procure l'usage de cet instrument[29].

Il fagotto o il violoncello, strumenti esplicitamente attestati solo in alcune delle fonti studiate, sembrano essere strumenti accessori, la cui presenza riflette probabilmente il grado di solennità attribuito a ciascuna occasione e, di conseguenza, gli sforzi finanziari impiegati[30]. La presenza, nelle fonti, di una parte obbligata indipendente è piuttosto eterogenea. Non troviamo alcuna parte indipendente di fagotto o violoncello nella totalità dei *Saluts des morts* (ossia tutte le opere del Ms. 12: mottetti, *De profundis* e *Nouveaux de profundis*, *Genitori genitoque*) e nei due *Libera me*; nelle diciassette elevazioni contenute nel Ms. 12, troviamo una parte obbligata di fagotto o violoncello nella maggior parte dei *récits* ma mai nei duetti o nei terzetti, o quartetti; la parte separata di fagotto o violoncello, disponibile per la totalità delle elevazioni, indica che, quando non c'è una parte indipendente, questi strumenti raddoppiano la parte di basso continuo. Le cinque messe per i defunti ci forniscono almeno tre casi diversi:

---

29.   DEVERGIE 1840, pp. 65-66: «Un consiglio essenziale da dare a tutti i suonatori di serpentone, ma in particolare a quelli di campagna, è che il canto piano, puro e semplice, deve essere suonato così come è annotato; tutti questi ornamenti, tutte queste aggiunte di note superflue, sono di pessimo gusto e spesso sortiscono l'effetto del più perfetto ridicolo; deturpano il canto, invece di ornarlo; ostacolano e disturbano il coro, invece di alleggerirlo e sostenerlo; [...]. Con questo non intendiamo proibire gli accordi con il serpentone; che si faccia un basso ben intonato in un salmo, in un inno, in un mottetto, nulla è più bello, nulla che valorizzi di più il canto della chiesa; questo è uno dei grandi vantaggi dell'uso di questo strumento».

30.   A tale poposito, è interessante sottolineare quanto osservato da Audéon e Davy-Rigaux: «L'emploi alternatif ou concomitant, par Métoyen, des termes "basse continue" et "basses" pour désigner la même partie notée de ses partions [...], qui dans tous les cas ne comportent jamais de chiffrages, nous invite à les considérer comme synonymes. Doit-on pour autant en déduire que cette ligne grave réclame toujours le même type d'instrumentation reposant sur les violoncelles, bassons et contrebasses? C'est ce que nous convie à conclure Métoyen lui-même par ses considérations sur les "musiques cathédrale"; si ce n'est que, selon l'effectif vocal et le caractère de la pièce, il peut être amené à alléger cette instrumentation (le trio de la messe des morts du vol. v, p. 127, est par exemple "sans contrebasse"). Les deux messes des morts du volume 1 doivent donc probablement requérir ce type d'instrumentation pour l'exécution de la partie dite de "basse continue"». AUDÉON – DAVY-RIGAUX 2008.

1) la totale assenza di uno strumento obbligato nelle partiture e nessuna parte separata giunta fino a noi (messe n. 3 e n. 4); 2) il fagotto o il violoncello che suonano una parte obbligata nei soli ma non nei duetti, nei trii, o nei cori, dove questi strumenti raddoppiano, invece, il basso continuo (messa n. 2); 3) il fagotto o il violoncello svolgono una parte obbligata nei soli, nei duetti e nei trii; nei cori, invece, raddoppia il basso continuo (messe n. 1 e *Messe des morts à cinq*). In conclusione, l'unica costante osservata in relazione alla parte strumentale obbligata è che, se presente, essa raddoppia il basso continuo nei cori.

Per quanto riguarda le composizioni del periodo di Beauvais, le tre messe per i defunti contenute nel *livre de chœur* della Cattedrale di Beauvais non prevedono righi strumentali oltre a quello del basso continuo. Tuttavia, la parte strumentale della messa quotidiana *Parce mihi, Domine* presenta caratteristiche particolari: denominata *'Bassus continuus aut Serpens'*, presenta, in corrispondenza della prima misura, l'indicazione *basson*. La congiunzione *aut* suggerisce, tra le varie ipotesi possibili, l'opzione di orchestrare questa messa in due modi diversi, probabilmente in relazione alla presenza di due serpentoni[31]. A tale proposito, ci sarebbero due possibilità: una prima opzione è che uno dei due serpenti raddoppi la parte del basso vocale e che l'altro suoni la parte strumentale; in alternativa, la parte strumentale potrebbe essere suonata dagli strumenti che costituiscono il continuo (tra cui il fagotto).

'ATTUALIZZAZIONI'

Come evocato, il confronto tra le fonti citate mostra che la linea melodica del basso continuo è generalmente molto più dettagliata e sviluppata nelle parti separate che nelle partiture. Le discrepanze tra le fonti possono essere piccole, come lievi cambiamenti nel disegno melodico o cambiamenti di ottava o di ritmo, oppure possono essere più significative. Inoltre, quando sono disponibili più copie della parte separata del basso continuo, esse forniscono, nella maggior parte dei casi, versioni che differiscono in misura maggiore o minore l'una dall'altra in termini di configurazione melodica. E tali osservazioni si intersecano con un altro aspetto fondamentale del *corpus* di opere per i morti di Pollio: la presenza di autoimprestiti e, più precisamente, di composizioni parodia, nelle quali il prestito non si limita ad assorbire un elemento melodico preesistente (parafrasi), ma è la sostanza stessa della composizione (melodie, ritmo, configurazione armonica) ad essere assorbita nella nuova composizione e soggetta a manipolazioni su diversi parametri. In effetti, alcune delle osservazioni finora fatte sull'apparente assenza di una parte di strumento concertante in alcune composizioni non tengono conto della circolazione e del riutilizzo di alcune di esse (in particolare i mottetti) all'interno del *corpus*; tra una versione e l'altra, infatti, si riscontrano divergenze per quanto riguarda la presenza di un fagotto o di un violoncello, sia esso obbligato o in raddoppio del basso continuo.

---

[31]. Tale ipotesi è compatibile con il l'organico di musicisti presenti nella cattedrale di Beauvais in quegli anni. Tale aspetto è dettagliato in MIGNOGNA 2024.

Le caratteristiche del *corpus* in esame permettono di interrogarsi sull'apertura' di questa musica non solo in relazione agli aspetti interpretativi, ma anche per quanto riguarda il rapporto tra il modo in cui il compositore ha rappresentato la propria idea musicale e l'*attualizzazione* di quest'ultima. Nel suo saggio *Difference et répétition*, Gilles Deleuze sostiene che:

> *"Le virtuel ne s'oppose pas au réel, mais seulement à l'actuel. Le virtuel possède une pleine réalité, en tant que virtuel... Le virtuel doit même être défini comme une stricte partie de l'objet réel* [...]*"* (G. Deleuze, *Difference et répétition*, Ed. P.U.F., 1968, p. 269.) Actuel et virtuel sont deux phases du réel qui ont une valeur égale et existent solidairement, mais jamais simultanément. Cela ne signifie pas que le virtuel soit destiné à se résoudre par l'actualisation, l'actuel supprimant dès lors le virtuel, mais que virtuel et actuel sont échangeables: ils sont des "phases adverses et réversibles", envers et endroit du réel. Ainsi, réalisation et actualisation ne sont pas équivalentes: la réalisation désigne *"l'occurrence d'un possible prédéfini"*, tandis que l'actualisation est *"l'invention d'une solution exigée par un complexe problématique"*[32].

L'osservazione delle discrepanze apparentemente aleatorie tra le fonti e l'esistenza di composizioni parodiate nel *corpus* in questione suggeriscono che le diverse versioni trasmesse dalle fonti non siano, dunque, le realizzazioni ma le *attualizzazioni* di un'opera *virtuale*: le parti separate, che rappresentano più dettagliatamente il prodotto sonoro, costituiscono la trascrizione di un'attualizzazione tra tutte quelle possibili; esse non rappresentano quindi il «verificarsi di un possibile predefinito», ma una delle «soluzioni richieste» dai numerosi complessi problematici latenti nella partitura.

La suddetta differenza tra la versione del basso continuo scritta in partitura e quella risultante dalle parti separate suggerisce, inoltre, la necessità, in caso di mancanza di parti separate, di ripristinare una versione ampliata della melodia annotata in partitura. Inoltre, l'idea dell'opera musicale barocca come *opera virtuale* permetterebbe di estendere il concetto stesso di restituzione; infatti, se si considera ogni versione disponibile non come una *realizzazione* ma piuttosto come un'*attualizzazione*, l'atto di restituzione non sarebbe più riservato solo a colmare le lacune delle fonti, ma potrebbe anche mirare a fornire nuove attualizzazioni dell'opera, attualizzazioni possibili ma non ancora esplorate. Ci si chiede allora: in questo processo di restituzione delle parti del basso continuo c'è il rischio che, pur rispettando gli stessi

---

32.   Roussel 2012: «"Il virtuale non si oppone al reale, ma solo all'effettivo. Il virtuale possiede una realtà piena, nella misura in cui è virtuale... Il virtuale deve addirittura essere definito come una parte stretta dell'oggetto reale [...]". (Deleuze 1968, p. 269.) L'effettivo e il virtuale sono due fasi del reale che hanno lo stesso valore ed esistono insieme, ma mai contemporaneamente. Questo non significa che il virtuale sia destinato a risolversi con l'attualizzazione, con l'effettivo che poi sopprime il virtuale, ma che il virtuale e l'effettivo sono scambiabili: sono "fasi opposte e reversibili", l'altra faccia e l'altro lato del reale. Così, realizzazione e attualizzazione non sono equivalenti: la realizzazione designa "il verificarsi di un possibile predefinito", mentre l'attualizzazione è "l'invenzione di una soluzione richiesta da un complesso problematico"».

Es. 1a: comparazione di un estratto dell'introito delle due versioni della messa *Parce mihi, Domine*: versione del periodo di Beauvais (POLLIO 1766).

precetti normativi espliciti adottati dal compositore, il musicologo commetta errori in relazione a una logica implicita all'opera? Infatti, le varianti a cui ci riferiamo riguardano per lo più elementi della scrittura musicale (in particolare, le scelte melodiche, per così dire, 'riempitive') la cui granularità sfugge alle maglie normative del sistema teorico-pedagogico dell'epoca; in altre parole, si tratta di scelte su cui le regole della scrittura non si esprimono esplicitamente e

Es. 1b: comparazione di un estratto dell'introito delle due versioni della messa *Parce mihi, Domine*: versione del periodo di Soignies (POLLIO 1769-1776).

categoricamente. L'Ex. 1ab mostra gli estratti dello stesso passaggio in due versioni esistenti di una messa oggetto di parodia (messa *Parce mihi, Domine*). L'esempio indica che, parallelamente alle divergenze nella parte di basso continuo, la realizzazione contrappuntistica del coro è differente nelle due versioni. La presenza dell'una o dell'altra versione del basso continuo dipende in qualche modo dalla configurazione polifonica della battuta successiva oppure, al contrario, le due versioni del basso continuo sono idealmente interscambiabili? O ancora: la scelta di una determinata configurazione melodica del basso nella prima battuta è in qualche modo legata alle scelte melodiche effettuate in seguito? È evidente che nei due casi discussi le due versioni del basso continuo sono *a priori* interscambiabili, poiché l'uso dell'una o dell'altra non comporterebbe alcun errore rispetto alle norme di scrittura.

Un tentativo di rispondere a tali domande potrebbe passare per l'adozione di un approccio analitico neutro. Un approccio possibile sarebbe quello di adottare una metodica analitica simile a quella che è generalmente riservata all'analisi delle musiche cosiddette di tradizione orale, che sia in grado di operare sulle emanazioni *linguistiche* dell'opera per arrivare ai processi impliciti (o inconsci) che le determinano. In linea teorica, sarebbe possibile adattare alle esigenze di un contesto polifonico la distinzione tra *paradigmatico* e *sintagmatico* presa in prestito alla linguistica dal metodo paradigmatico di Nicolas Ruwet[33]. Applicati alla nostra problematica, tali concetti potrebbero servire a determinare se le varianti del basso continuo osservate abbiano un semplice rapporto paradigmatico tra loro (cioè se costituiscano classi di elementi equivalenti e intercambiabili) o se, al contrario, la presenza dell'una o dell'altra sia legata da un rapporto sintagmatico all'occorrenza di altre varianti, anche se distanti tra loro e relative a parametri diversi da quelli melodici (armonici, prosodici, ecc.). Evochiamo le definizioni di relazioni sintagmatiche e paradigmatiche (che egli chiama «relazioni associative») formulate da Ferdinand de Sassure nel suo *Cours de linguistique générale*, del 1916[34]:

> D'une part, dans le discours, les mots contractent entre eux, en vertu de leur enchaînement, des rapports fondés sur le caractère linéaire de la langue, qui exclut la possibilité de prononcer deux éléments à la fois. Ceux-ci se rangent les uns à la suite des autres sur la chaîne de la parole. Ces combinaisons qui ont pour support l'étendue peuvent être appelées syntagmes. Le syntagme se compose donc toujours de deux ou plusieurs unités consécutives[35].
>
> D'autre part, en dehors du discours, les mots offrant quelque chose de commun s'associent dans la mémoire, et il se forme ainsi des groupes au sein desquels règnent des rapports très divers. [...] On voit que ces coordinations sont d'une tout autre espèce que les premières. Elles n'ont pas pour support l'étendue; leur siège est dans le cerveau; elles font partie de ce trésor intérieur qui constitue la langue chez chaque individu. Nous les appellerons rapports associatifs[36].

---

[33]. RUWET 1966, pp. 65-90.

[34]. SASSURE 1916.

[35]. *Ibidem*, p. 171: «Da una parte, nel discorso, le parole contraggono tra loro, in virtù del loro concatenarsi, dei rapporti fondati sul carattere lineare della lingua, che esclude la possibilità di pronunciare due elementi alla volta. Esse si schierano le une dopo le altre sulla catena della parole. Queste combinazioni che hanno per supporto l'estensione possono essere chiamate sintagmi. Il sintagma dunque si compone sempre di due o più unità consecutive». Traduzione in SASSURE 2005, p. 149.

[36]. SASSURE 1916: «D'altra parte, fuori del discorso, le parole offrenti qualche cosa di comune si associano nella memoria, e si formano così dei gruppi nel cui ambito regnano rapporti assai diversi. [...] Ognuno vede che queste coordinazioni sono d'una specie affatto diversa rispetto alle prime. Esse non hanno per supporto l'estensione;

Egli osserva, inoltre, che «Le rapport syntagmatique est *in praesentia*; il repose sur deux ou plusieurs termes également présents dans une série effective. Au contraire le rapport associatif unit des termes in absentia dans une série mnémonique virtuelle»[37]. Tali concetti potrebbero essere sfruttati al fine di determinare se alcune varianti del basso continuo — che, in base alle norme di scrittura applicate dal compositore, risulterebbero equivalenti e intercambiabili — mantengano in realtà una relazione sintagmatica con altre varianti appartenenti ad altri parametri o altri livelli della composizione (in particolare, con la configurazione polifonica del coro). In altre parole, si tratterebbe di analizzare i processi inconsci operati dal compositore per cercare di portare alla luce una possibile correlazione implicita che determina la compresenza, in un 'enunciato' musicale, di due elementi. Il tutto, con l'obiettivo finale di fornire strumenti per la restituzione (o *riattualizzazione*) di parti di basso continuo mancanti o carenti. Tali concetti porterebbero a produrre un metodo di analisi 'paradigmatica *aumentata*' in quanto, pur avendo come oggetto il basso continuo e la sua configurazione melodica, finalizzata a esplorare le possibili relazioni che quest'ultimo intrattiene con il contesto polifonico. La relazione sintagmatica andrebbe quindi ricercata non solo sul piano lineare né solo tra elementi adiacenti dello stesso tipo. La multidimensionalità della composizione polifonica impone, conseguentemente, di adattare i concetti di sintagma e paradigma. In linguistica, le relazioni sintagmatiche riguardano unità dello stesso tipo: tradotto in termini musicali, ciò significherebbe che un elemento melodico può essere in relazione sintagmatica solo con un altro elemento melodico. Al nostro scopo, sarebbe necessario estendere questo discorso agli altri parametri della composizione polifonica. Per relazione sintagmatica andrebbe dunque intesa, per i nostri scopi, una relazione che condiziona la compresenza di due (o più) elementi, sia che questi appartengano allo stesso parametro musicale sia che appartengano a due parametri diversi. Questo adattamento del concetto implica anche che è possibile riconoscere il carattere di sintagma non solo a una coppia di due unità melodiche, ma anche, ad esempio, a coppie costituite da un'unità melodica del basso continuo e ad una determinata configurazione armonica o contrappuntistica del coro, e questo sia che i due elementi siano adiacenti o meno. Inoltre, la configurazione della composizione polifonica richiede anche un altro adattamento del concetto dalla linguistica: la linguistica, avendo come oggetto il discorso che si dispiega in un'unica direzione nel tempo «non riconosce altro ordine che quello della successione»; invece, nel caso di una composizione polifonica, che è di per sé costituita da più livelli sovrapposti, una frase come l'ho appena definita può essere costituita anche da due elementi simultanei. Il concetto di paradigma rimane, altresì, pressoché invariato, ove per paradigma si intende una classe di elementi musicali intercambiabili tra loro

---

la loro sede è nel cervello; esse fanno parte di quel tesoro interiore che costituisce la lingua in ciascun individuo. Noi le chiameremo rapporti associativi». Traduzione in Sassure 2005, pp. 149-150.

[37]. Sassure 1916: «Il rapporto sintagmatico è *in praesentia*; esso si basa su due o più termini egualmente presenti in una serie effettiva. Al contrario il rapporto associativo unisce dei termini *in absentia* in una serie mnemonica virtuale». Traduzione in Sassure 2005, p. 150.

in un enunciato. Applicando tale idea all'Es. 1 mostrato, si tratterebbe di cercare di determinare se la variante del basso continuo che abbiamo osservato nelle due versioni della composizione parodiata costituisca un sintagma (cioè se la sua presenza sia in relazione): 1) con la particolare configurazione melodica del basso continuo nella battuta successiva (il che costruirebbe un sintagma tra elementi dello stesso tipo, successivi e adiacenti); 2) con la particolare configurazione melodica del basso continuo due battute più avanti (che costruirebbe un sintagma tra elementi dello stesso tipo, successivi e non adiacenti); 3) con la particolare configurazione polifonica del coro nella stessa battuta (che costruirebbe una frase tra elementi di tipo diverso, non successivi e adiacenti); 4) con la particolare configurazione polifonica del coro alla battuta successiva (che costruirebbe una frase tra elementi di tipo diverso; 5) con la particolare configurazione polifonica del coro due battute dopo (che costruirebbe una frase tra elementi successivi non adiacenti di tipo diverso).

Come facilmente intuibile, la messa in opera di un tale tipo di analisi, affinché conduca a risultati coerenti, richiede uno spoglio sistematico dell'integralità dell'opera di Pollio, e necessita di automatizzazione e di lavoro collaborativo. La complessità degli elementi e dei parametri coinvolti implica, infatti, l'inevitabile utilizzo di strumenti digitali per un'analisi automatizzata che comprenda la codifica del *corpus* musicale in un linguaggio interpellabile dalla macchina[38] e la progettazione di un software per la segmentazione e l'analisi dei dati che sia istruito ad analizzare le manifestazioni linguistiche delle opere per arrivare ai gesti inconsci del processo compositivo, e questo in un contesto polifonico[39]. Lo stato di avanzamento degli studi sull'opera di Pollio non rende possibile la messa in atto, a breve termine, di tale progetto analitico. Nell'attesa della realizzazione di tale progetto, si rende dunque necessario progettare un'edizione moderna di tipo 'tradizionale' che permetta, nella misura possibile, di rispettare la polivalenza del testo trasmesso dalle fonti.

STRATEGIE DI EDIZIONE MODERNA

Quanto osservato rende manifesta la necessità di un'edizione 'virtuale', che permetta di superare i limiti di un'edizione tradizionale e di manipolare il materiale delle fonti, al fine di

---

[38]. A questo scopo, lo standard oggi più utilizzato nel mondo accademico è il MEI, acronimo di Music Encoding Initiative; formalismo per la notazione e i metadati musicali, basato su un dialetto XML. *Cfr.* <https://music-encoding.org/>, visitato a novembre 2023.

[39]. Il software deve quindi essere in grado di identificare le occorrenze di coppie di unità, coppie che sono costituite da un elemento melodico del basso continuo e da qualunque altro elemento della composizione polifonica derivato da un qualsiasi parametro musicale. Allo stesso tempo, dovrebbe essere in grado di fare un lavoro di 'segmentazione', per così dire, delimitando le 'unità' stesse. Inoltre, sarebbe interessante poter elaborare i risultati ottenuti ed effettuare lo stesso approccio analitico a un livello superiore, alla ricerca di possibili 'sintagmi di sintagmi'.

rendere visibili le diverse 'attualizzazioni' esistenti di una stessa opera. Mentre una 'edizione virtuale', manipolativa e non gerarchica, è pienamente realizzabile solo nel contesto digitale[40], l'edizione a stampa potrebbe essere orientata verso una configurazione 'aperta' attraverso l'implementazione di alcuni elementi, in particolare la visualizzazione sinottica. Il filologo Gianluca Valenti aveva già proposto, in un articolo del 2013, di implementare le nuove edizioni critiche con l'uso 'ponderato' (*cit.*) dei colori, o delle sfumature di colore. La strategia in questione si basa sull'uso delle sfumature di grigio ed è particolarmente adatta per i *corpora* con filiazione semplice delle fonti, come per il caso dell'*opus* di Pollio. Tale strategia si configura come segue: le sfumature di grigio significano, passando dal nero al grigio chiaro: concordanza di tutte le fonti, concordanza di tutte le fonti tranne una, discordanza di tutte le fonti. Tale strategia permette di individuare immediatamente i passaggi divergenti ma, come nota Valenti, non sostituisce le note critiche (la cui ragion d'essere e le cui modalità di redazione rimangono inalterate). Come nota l'autore, questa strategia ha il vantaggio di mostrare a prima vista non solo la disponibilità di più fonti per il brano in questione, ma anche il numero di varianti; allo stesso tempo, permette di valutare intuitivamente il grado di stabilità di ciascun elemento. Come sottolinea Valenti, tale approccio editoriale

> è uno strumento di complemento alle moderne edizioni critiche. È un procedimento a costo zero per il filologo-lettore, nel senso che è un aiuto al lettore il quale, senza ulteriore dispendio di tempo o energie, potrà grazie ad esso ottenere in modo intuitivo una panoramica della tradizione manoscritta del testo che ha sotto gli occhi. È un procedimento pensato soprattutto per edizioni digitali di testi medievali, ma può essere estensibile in linea di principio anche a edizioni a stampa o ad altre tipologie testuali, come ad esempio edizioni critiche di testi moderni. [...] Di contro, questo procedimento non è un nuovo metodo per l'elaborazione di edizioni critiche. Non è dunque in alcun modo un'alternativa ai metodi lachmanniano e bédieriano, né alle loro successive implementazioni. Non è un procedimento a costo zero per filologo-editore, al quale, di contro, è richiesto un ulteriore sforzo in fase di allestimento del testo critico[41].

Le diverse strategie previste da Valenti si basano su *corpora* la cui tradizione è molto più complessa di quella del nostro *corpus*, il che ci rassicura in termini di fattibilità e leggibilità. Tuttavia, le differenze sostanziali del nostro *corpus* di studio in termini di materiale (musicale

---

40. Il MEI consentirebbe di codificare le varianti dalle fonti come *ossia* e quindi di sottoporre l'intero insieme delle varianti all'analisi automatizzata e di visualizzare in modo sinottico e/o di gerarchizzare le diverse attualizzazioni dell'opera, oltre che le eventuali restituzioni editoriali del basso continuo. Inoltre, alcune applicazioni per la visualizzazione di partiture codificate in MEI, come meiView, consentono di creare una partitura dinamica, in cui il lettore può scegliere quale variante visualizzare, permettendo così la creazione di edizioni personalizzabili.

41. Valenti 2013.

anziché letterario) e di obiettivo ci obbligano a una maggiore prudenza e a una dettagliata rivalutazione di ogni parametro.

***

Valenti non manca di sottolineare i limiti della strategia che propone. In particolare, egli nota che questa strategia non è adatta alla rappresentazione immediata di inversioni di versi e strofe, un problema che corrisponde, in un certo senso, alla 'mobilità' delle voci che si può osservare nel *corpus* e, più in generale, alle varianti maggiori esistenti tra le due versioni di un opera parodiata. Tuttavia, la complessità delle divergenze tra le diverse versioni delle composizioni di Pollio, in particolare nei casi di parafrasi e autoimprestito, ci induce a ritenere che, nel contesto dell'edizione a stampa, non sarebbe possibile una rappresentazione completa dei numerosi aggiornamenti esistenti dell'opera. La loro presentazione sinottica resta quindi realizzabile solamente nel contesto di un'edizione digitale. La soluzione parziale offerta da un'edizione tradizionale implementata, quale è quella proposta da Valenti, conferma che, come già suggerito da Nattiez, è necessario rivalutare radicalmente il tipo di approccio analitico adottato per le musiche dette 'occidentali':

> [...] perché non dovremmo affrontare aspetti fondamentali, "non chiari" o ignorati delle "nostre" musiche come se avessimo a che fare con musiche di tradizione orale, come se ci fossero estranee, come se le teorie consolidate rischiassero di occultarne proprietà specifiche e importanti? Certo, le teorie trasmesse dall'insegnamento accademico riflettono una "pratica comune" di cui difficilmente si può negare il ruolo nella creazione e nella percezione delle opere; ma proprio nel momento in cui si formula l'ipotesi che le musiche, in virtù della loro complessità parametrica, non vengano necessariamente percepite per come sono state ideate, ecco che torna a essere urgente dotarsi di strumenti empirici di descrizione, e chiarire la differenza tra le norme pedagogiche dei trattati e ciò che i compositori hanno effettivamente fatto, cosa che dovrebbe anche permettere di interrogarsi sulle strategie compositive seguite e sulle strategie percettive messe in atto da queste opere[42].

Una rivalutazione totale dell'approccio analitico diviene, dunque, l'unica soluzione per poter individuare e rappresentare opportunamente nell'edizione moderna tutti quegli elementi appartenenti sia alla *definizione* stessa dell'opera — ciò che è trasmesso in partitura quale elemento strutturale — sia al *proprio*[43] di ciascuna attualizzazione.

---

[42]. NATTIEZ 2000, p. 348.
[43]. *Cfr.* ECO 2017, pp. 20-21.

Bibliografia

Apel 1953
Apel, Willi. *The Notation of Polyphonic Music, 900-1600*, Cambridge (MA), Mediaeval Academy of America, 1953.

Audeon – Davy-Rigaux 2008
Audéon, Hervé – Davy-Rigaux, Cécile. 'Jean-Baptiste Métoyen (1733-1822): Parcours et œuvre d'un musicien de la Chapelle royale, de l'Ancien Régime au début de la Restauration', in: *Revue de Musicologie*, xciv/2 (2008), pp. 347-385.

Barthes 1989
Barthes, Roland. 'From Work to Text', in: *The Rustle of Language*, Berkley-Los Angeles, University of California Press, 1989.

Dahlhaus 2009
Dahlhaus, Carl. 'Filologia e storia della ricezione. Osservazioni sulla teoria dell'edizione', in: «*In altri termini». Saggi sulla musica*, a cura di Alberto Fassone, Roma, Accademia Nazionale di Santa Cecilia, 2009, pp. 143-161.

Davy-Rigaux – Getrau 2005
Davy-Rigaux, Cécile – Gétrau, Florence. 'La méthode de serpent de Jean-Baptiste Métoyen: héritages et évolutions', in: *Jean-Baptiste Métoyen, Ouvrage complet pour l'éducation du le Serpent d'après les manuscrits conservés à la Bibliothéque nationale de France*, a cura di Benny Sluchin, Parigi, Éditions Musicales Européennes, 2005 (Brass Urtext), pp. vii-xii (versione inglese alle pp. xxv-xxx).

Deleuze 1968
Deleuze, Gilles. *Différence et répétition*, Parigi, P.U.F, 1968.

Devergie 1840
Devergie, Abbé. *Méthode de plain-chant, principalement destinée au diocèse de Beauvais et utile à tous les diocèses* [...], Beauvais, chez Bocquillon-Porquier, 1840.

Di Cintio 2017
Di Cintio, Eleonora. 'Alcune riflessioni sull'ontologia e la filologia di un'opera empirica', in: *Bollettino del Centro Rossiniano di Studi*, lvii (2017), pp. 33-52.

Eco 2017
Eco, Umberto. *Dall'albero al labirinto. Studi storici sul segno e l'interpretazione*, Milano, La nave di Teseo, 2017.

Guillo 2003
Guillo, Laurent. *Pierre i Ballard et Robert iii Ballard, Imprimeur du roy pour la musique (1599-1673)*, 2 voll., Sprimont, Mardaga, 2003 (Musique, Musicologie).

GUILLOUX 2016
GUILLOUX, Fabien. *Inventaire des archives musicales de la Collégiale Saint-Vincent de Soignies: (1611) 1700-1890 (1945)*, Bruxelles, Archives générales du Royaume, 2016 (Archives de l'État à Mons. Inventaires, 132).

GURLITT 1961
GURLITT, Wilibald. 'Pollio P. L.', in: *Riemann Musik-Lexikon, Personenteil. 2*, Magonza, B. Schott Söhne, 1961, p. 425.

LEON 2000
LÉON, Jean-Charles. 'L'Art du maître de musique: Essai sur la fonction des sources musicales de la messe polyphonique en France aux XVIIe et XVIIIe siècles', in: *Revue de Musicologie*, LXXXVI/2 (2000), pp. 193-216.

LORETTE 1989
LORETTE, Myriam. *P. L. Pollio (1724-1796). Maître de musique à la collégiale Saint-Vincent de Soignies. 3*, mémoire de Licence, Bruxelles, Université Libre de Bruxelles, 1989.

MIGNOGNA 2024
MIGNOGNA, Francesca. *Écriture(s) et réécriture(s) dans l'œuvre pour les défunts de Pierre-Louis Pollio (1724-1796): un exemple d'œuvre ouverte au XVIIIᵉ siècle. Étude et édition critique*, Parigi, Sorbonne Université, 2024.

MONTAGNIER 1995
MONTAGNIER, Jean-Paul. 'Les sources manuscrites françaises du «Chant sur le livre» aux XVIIᵉ et XVIIIᵉ siècles', in: *Revue belge de Musicologie / Belgisch Tijdschrift voor Muziekwetenschap*, XLIX (1995), pp. 79-100.

MONTAGNIER 2019
ID. *The Polyphonic Mass in France, 1600-1780: The Evidence of the Printed Choirbooks*, Cambridge-New York, Cambridge University Press, 2019.

MORLEY-PEGGE – BATE – WESTON 2001
MORLEY-PEGGE, Reginald – BATE, Philip – WESTON, Stephen J. 'Serpent', in: *Grove Music Online*, 2001, <https://www.oxfordmusiconline.com/grovemusic>, consultato a novembre 2023.

NATTIEZ 2000
NATTIEZ, Jean-Jaques. 'Modelli linguistici e analisi delle strutture musicali', in: *Rivista Italiana di Musicologia*, XXXV/1-2 (2000), pp. 321-377.

POLLIO 1765
POLLIO, Pierre-Louis. *Opera Domini Petri-Ludovici (Mariae) Pollionis. Pars Prima*, Bellovaci, Petrus-Joannes le Coutre, 1765.

POLLIO 1769-1776
POLLIO, Pierre-Louis. *Opera 6a [...] Liber unicus. Pars 3a*, ms., B-Smc MS 18 [1769-1776].

IL BASSO CONTINUO NELLE COMPOSIZIONI PER I DEFUNTI DI PIERRE-LOUIS POLLIO

POLLIO 1770
ID. *Traité / Du / chant sur le livre*, 1790, ms., B-Smc MS 25, 1770.

POLLIO 1771-1776
ID. *Opera 4 [...] Liber Quintus*, ms., B-Smc MS 12, [1771-1776].

ROUSSEL 2012
ROUSSEL, Marion. 'Actuel/virtuel: Introduction a une problématique architecturale', in: *DNArchi*, 15 giugno 2012, <http://dnarchi.fr/culture/actuelvirtuel-introduction-une-problematique-architecturale/>, consultato a novembre 2023.

RUWET 1966
RUWET, Nicolas. 'Méthodes d'analyse en musicologie', in: *Revue belge de Musicologie / Belgisch Tijdschrift voor Muziekwetenschap*, , XX (1966), pp. 65-90.

SASSURE 1916
SASSURE, Ferdinand de. *Cours de linguistique générale*, Parigi, Payot et Rivages, 1916.

SASSURE 2005
ID. *Corso di linguistica generale. Introduzione, traduzione e commento di Tullio De Mauro*, Bari, Laterza, 2005.

VALENTI 2013
VALENTI, Gianluca. 'Una proposta per la pubblicazione (e la lettura) intuitiva delle edizioni di testi a tradizione manoscritta', in: *Cognitive Philology*, no. 6 (2013), n.p.

WANGERMÉE 1945
WANGERMÉE, Robert. 'Le traité du chant sur le livre de P. L. Pollio, maître de musique à la collégiale Saint-Vincent à Soignies dans la seconde moitié du XVIIIe siècle', in: *Hommage à Charles van den Borren: Mélanges*, Anvers, N. V. de Nederlandsche Bokhandel, 1945, pp. 336-350.

The Principles of Partitura Playing:
An Introduction to Basso Continuo Instruction
and Practice in Eighteenth-Century Salzburg

Anthony Abouhamad
(Sydney Conservatorium of Music – The University of Sydney)

T HE PRACTICE OF BASSO CONTINUO accompaniment in eighteenth-century Austrian church music has received little attention in historical performance research[1]. Yet, it plays an integral role in performing Austrian church music including compositions by Johann Joseph Fux, Joseph and Michael Haydn as well as Leopold and Wolfgang Mozart. The present study examines the principles of basso continuo pedagogy in Salzburg to highlight elements of its practice in eighteenth-century Austrian church music. In Salzburg, five court organists documented their methods for realising a figured bass in instructional manuals, which refer to the practice of basso continuo accompaniment as 'partitura'. The manuals span a period of almost a century, from the time of Georg Muffat to that of Michael Haydn; nonetheless, they follow a similar method of instruction, which attests to a tradition of basso continuo pedagogy in Salzburg. The Salzburg method for playing a partitura sheds light on its practice both in that city and, potentially, in the broader Habsburg sphere of influence.

A noteworthy feature of the Salzburg method is that it instructs partitura playing through illustrations of musical patterns composed of voice-leading formulas. Such patterns are defined in the academic literature as schemata[2]. Notating the exact movement of each upper part in the schema with figures, the manuals place particular emphasis on proper voice leading. The centrality of schemata in the manuals highlights a common feature between Salzburg partitura instruction and those in eighteenth-century north German basso continuo treatises as well as

---

[1]. An overview of this broad topic is given in PRASSL 2010.

[2]. For a detailed explanation of schemata and their role in eighteenth-century music, see GJERDINGEN 2007. Further descriptions and analyses can be found in SHERILL – BOYLE 2015 and RABINOVITCH 2018.

Italian partimento sources. However, it is distinct from these two traditions. Unlike Italian partimento instruction, the Salzburg manuals do not directly address realising an unfigured bass. Voice-leading principles in Italian partimento, particularly in Naples, were issued orally by masters to the pupil at the keyboard[3]. In reference to voice leading in basso continuo practice, therefore, the Salzburg manuals provide more detail than partimento sources.

Unlike north German basso continuo treatises, the Salzburg manuals do not begin their partitura instruction with four-part accompaniment[4]. Instead, they illustrate that a four-part accompaniment develops by adding voice-leading formulas to a schema in two-part counterpoint. By analysing the manuals' process of combining voice-leading formulas with a two-part framework, I derive two principles — disposition and exchange — that underpin their mode of realising a partitura from a figured bass. I label the first 'disposition', which describes the process of combining voice-leading formulas above a bass motion. The second principle details the manuals' method of inverting those voice-leading formulas that sit above the bass. The manuals term this principle «Verwechslung», which I translate as 'exchange'. The focus of the analysis will be examples of schemata from Matthäus Gugl's *Fundamenta Partiturae* because his descriptions are clearer and more succinct than in the other manuals[5].

In addition to instructing students in voice-leading principles, the schemata in the manuals also illustrate the formation of chords. Like their structural illustrations of schemata, the manuals define chords as combinations of intervals and label them *Griffe*. The term *Griffe* (singular: *Griff*), is a German noun that probably derives from the verb 'to grip' (zu greiffen). Determining the combination in a *Griff* is the interval that sits at its core. The three-part combination 4-2 and the four-part combination 6-4-2, for instance, are examples of 2-*Griffe*. The manuals catalogue far more than two types of 2-*Griffe*, however. Gugl lists no less than twelve possible combinations. Using the disposition and exchange principles, I will show that the 2-*Griffe* combinations Gugl lists are vertical constructs that arise from the complex of voice-leading formulas that constitute a schema.

Demonstrating the application of the disposition and exchange principles, as well as examples of the 2-*Griffe* in Gugl's catalogue, are two proposed partitura solutions to a song written by Salzburg organist Johann Ernst Eberlin. The song, composed for a soprano voice and a figured bass accompaniment, comes from Eberlin's *Fundamenta Partitura* and concludes

---

[3]. SANGUINETTI 2012, p. 116. For a detailed examination of partimento training in Naples in particular, see VAN TOUR 2015.

[4]. The primary instruction of chords in Johann David Heinichen's *Grundliche Anweisung*, for instance, begins with accompaniment in a four-part setting, see MONGOVEN – BRILMAYER 2012, pp. 17-27 and TELEMANN 1983. Later in the eighteenth century, Carl Philipp Emanuel Bach also advocates beginning accompaniment in four parts, BACH 1944, pp. 176-177. The importance of four-part accompaniment in German basso continuo practice is also described in CHRISTENSEN 2002, pp. 62-64.

[5]. GUGL 1719.

his description of the 2-*Griff*[6]. The two solutions highlight that Salzburg partitura practice preferences a linear and melodic, rather than a strictly chordal, approach to basso continuo playing. Furthermore, in light of the Salzburg manuals' method of instruction, the two partitura solutions make salient the significance of schema theory in the practice of partitura playing.

While not a cosmopolitan musical centre, the Archbishopric of Salzburg maintained an active court chapel throughout the eighteenth century[7]. Attesting to its strong musical culture are the pedagogical resources written by generations of the Archbishopric's musicians. These range from a sixteenth-century tract on singing by Johannes Stomius (Augsburg, 1537) through to Leopold Mozart's essay on violin playing (Augsburg, 1756). Less known than Mozart's essay are six instructional manuals on basso continuo playing written by five of Salzburg's court organists. Because many of the manuals' authors shared a teacher-student relationship, the methods of instruction across all six are alike. Austrian musicologist Hellmut Federhofer places them within the broader context of Salzburg's musical history in addition to analysing the similarities between the manuals. He explains that the manuals' authors fall within a larger 'Salzburg group' of musicians and theorists that contributed to defining the city's musical landscape[8]. TABLE 1 provides an overview of the Salzburg manuals, including authors as well as manuscript or publication details.

TABLE 1: THE SALZBURG MANUALS, THEIR AUTHORS AND MANUSCRIPT/PUBLICATION DETAILS

ORGANIST	NAME OF DOCUMENT	MANUSCRIPT/PUBLICATION DETAILS
Georg Muffat	«Regulae Concentuum Partiturae»*	One manuscript copy, Passau, c.1699
Johann Baptist Samber	*Manaductio ad Organum* (1704); *Continuatio ad Manaductionem Organicam* (1709)**	Both published in Salzburg
Matthäus Gugl	*Fundamenta Partiturae****	First published in Augsburg, 1719, followed by five subsequent editions
Johann Ernst Eberlin	«Fundamenta Partitura»****	One manuscript copy, Salzburg, 1766
Anton Cajetan Adlgasser and Johann Michael Haydn	«Partiturfundament»*****	Five manuscript copies, Salzburg, n.d.

*. MUFFAT 1699. A modern transcription of the original has been undertaken by FEDERHOFER 1961.

**. SAMBER, 1704; SAMBER, 1707.

***. GUGL 1719, GUGL 1727, GUGL 1757, GUGL 1762, GUGL 1777, GUGL 1805. Citations refer to the fifth edition (1777).

****. EBERLIN 1766.

*****. ADLGASSER – HAYDN n.d.

---

6. EBERLIN 1766, pp. 10-11.

7. HOCHRADNER 2005; EISEN 1989.

8. FEDERHOFER 1964.

In addition to Federhofer, Thomas Christensen and Felix Diergarten have noted that the Salzburg manuals bespeak a tradition of basso continuo instruction in Salzburg, which changed little from the time of Muffat to that of Mozart[9]. Attesting to the partitura tradition is the similarity of the manuals' titles, each of which indicates an intention to provide the rules (*Regulae*) and/or the foundations (*Fundamenta*) of playing a partitura. The term 'partitura' also appears in all the manuals' titles. It is a term that Austrian musicians used interchangeably with basso continuo and General-Bass. While the terms General-Bass, basso continuo and partitura were often used interchangeably, they do in fact hold distinct meanings according to Samber's definition in his *Manaductio*. After describing the history of the «*General-Bass, Partiturâ* or *Basso Continuo*», he defines each of these terms in more explicit detail:

> It is [...] called *Bassus Generalis* because it contains all, and especially the *fundamental* voices of each song. It is called *Bassus Continuus* because it goes through the song from beginning to end without large breaks and continues. It is, therefore, called Partitura because each and every voice originates in the *General Bass* and the very same, as it were, gives birth to them[10].

Writing in 1704, Samber's description of *Bassus Continuus* points out that the bass is generally present throughout the course of a composition. Conversely, the *General-Bass* carries the fundamental parts of a composition, encoded with figures. Partitura refers to realising these parts from the information provided in the *General-Bass*. Samber's description seems to indicate that the partitura is the result of unpacking or laying out the parts encoded in the *Bassus Generalis*.

In addition to Samber, other Austrian and south German sources define partitura in similarly practical terms. In his organ treatise of 1676, for instance, Alessandro Poglietti explains partitura as playing both «notes and numbers»[11]. Likewise, in his 1766 treatise on singing and playing the violin, Ignaz Franz Kurtzinger defines partitura as the part from which an organist performs[12]. Wolfgang Mozart also uses the term in a letter to Maria Anna, in which he praises his sister's diligence in learning partitura playing, a course of study she undertook with her father[13]. In Leopold Mozart's accounts of instructing partitura to Maria Anna, he explains that

---

[9]. DIERGARTEN 2015, pp. 59-63; CHRISTENSEN 2008.

[10]. «*Bassus Generalis* wird er also genennet / weil solcher alle / und sonderlich die *Fundamental*-Stimmen eines jeden Gesangs in sich begreifft. *Bassus Continuus* wird er genennet / weilen er von Anfang biß zum End deß Gesangs ohne grosse Pausen fort gehet / und *continuirt*. *Partitura*, wird es darumben genennet / an weilen jede / und alle Stimmen von dem *General Bass* entspringen / und gleichsamb von selbigen gebohren werden». Many thanks to Goetz Richter, who helped me refine the translation of this very poetic text in SAMBER 1704, p. 99.

[11]. POGLIETTI 2007, p. 53.

[12]. KÜRTZINGER 1763, p. 86.

[13]. Wolfgang Amadeus Mozart to his father, postcript to his sister, 7 March 1778, MOZART 2005, p. 320.

she practised accompanying compositions from the cathedral library, which included vocal genres as well as symphonies[14]. After months of instruction, Leopold writes in a letter to his son that Maria Anna can accompany «like a Capellmeister»[15]. She had the opportunity to display her skills in an ensemble organised by Count Czernin, in which she accompanied symphonies and an aria at the harpsichord in concert[16].

Leopold's letters imply that his partitura instruction had a strong practical focus. This may shine light on the course of instruction that lies behind the texts in the Salzburg manuals because, like Leopold, their authors were also instructors. In fact, the court required many of its musicians to teach the choir boys under its care. Official court records and employment contracts specify that as a part of their duties as court organists, both Adlgasser and Haydn, were to instruct the choir boys[17]. These boys lived in the court-funded *Capellhaus* (chapel house) and performed regularly in church, chamber and theatre music[18]. Keyboard playing formed a part of their instruction, according to Leopold Mozart, and it may have been for this reason that Salzburg's court organists composed manuals on partitura playing[19]. While it cannot be proven unequivocally, the circumstantial evidence suggests that this may have been the case. If so, then the Salzburg manuals reflect the pedagogical methods Salzburg's professional court organists used to teach youths basso continuo accompaniment. Examining these manuals may then shine light on this method and, furthermore, their authors' own professional practices as basso continuo accompanists.

All of the Salzburg manuals introduce students to partitura playing with a description of intervals and their qualities. Following the description of intervals, the manuals then illustrate how these combine to form *Griffe*. The authors use a combination of three- and four-part schemata to illustrate the formation of *Griffe* and, using either a figured bass or a realised partitura on two staves, indicate the voice-leading in their upper parts[20]. While the manuals do not give explicit instructions, the schemata may act as voice-leading models that students were required to replicate in a series of figured bass exercises that follow. By practising these exercises, students would be trained to internalise a body of schemata. The exercises in the Salzburg manuals are not organised by bass motion as one would expect in partimento sources. Rather,

---

[14]. Leopold Mozart to his wife and son, 25 and 26 February 1778, *ibidem*, p. 300.

[15]. «[...] die Nannerl accompagniert wie ein ieder Capellmeister». Leopold Mozart to his son, 6 April 1778, *ibidem*, p. 337.

[16]. Leopold Mozart to his wife and son, 12 April 1778, *ibidem*, p. 338.

[17]. For information outlining these organists' courtly duties, see HINTERMAIER 1972, pp. 3 and 66.

[18]. *Ibidem*, pp. xxvii-xviii.

[19]. MOZART 1757, p. 194.

[20]. Muffat also includes examples of full-voiced accompaniment. A description of Muffat's examples contextualised within the practice of early eighteenth-century Italian basso continuo practice is in MORTENSEN 1996.

more akin to north German basso continuo treatises, the Salzburg manuals divide their corpus of schemata into chapters organised by *Griff*-type.

Following the *Griff* chapters, Eberlin's as well as Adlgasser's and Haydn's manuals conclude; however, those by Muffat, Samber and Gugl continue with two further topics: cadences and bass motions. The introduction of the cadence and bass motion topics attests to the influence of partimento instruction on the Salzburg manuals. Their cadential taxonomy, for instance, is like that in Roman partimento sources. According to Diergarten, the Italian influence most probably results from Muffat's studies with the Roman keyboardist Bernardo Pasquini[21]. The bass motions, on the other hand, differ from partimento instruction because they do not attempt to provide systematic rules for the accompaniment of unfigured basses. Gugl claims, for example, that he can provide «no specific rule» («keine gewisse Regul») that summarises the contrapuntal solutions possible for a bass motion. In addition to the twenty-two pages of examples in the *Fundamenta Partiturae*, Gugl states that many more options are possible[22]. This may explain why Samber, perhaps attempting to account for all the possibilities, catalogues 106 pages of figured bass motions in his *Continuatio*[23].

It is impossible to say with certainty why the manuals do not discuss the accompaniment of unfigured basses. Considering the fact that Nannerl was explicitly instructed to accompany without figures by her father, it would be inaccurate to state that Salzburg organists were unaware or even apprehensive of this skill[24]. Research tells us that Italian conservatory teaching convention employed oral instruction for accompaniment of unfigured basses[25]. While there is no explicit evidence to prove this, Salzburg maestros may have employed similar techniques. Nonetheless, the absence of written instructions highlights the importance of the chapters on *Griffe* in the Salzburg manuals. These chapters provide more detail on basso continuo accompaniment than any other topic, thereby highlighting the key roles that *Griffe* and schemata play in Salzburg partitura instruction. It is for this reason that the following analysis focuses on the schemata and figured bass exercises that the manuals document in their chapters on *Griffe*.

The manuals define a *Griff* by its core interval. The core determines the other interval or intervals that may combine to it to form a *Griff* in three- or more respective parts. Based on their core intervals, the Salzburg manuals identify six types of *Griff*: *2-Griff*, *4-Griff*, *5-Griff*, *6-Griff*, *7-Griff* and *9-Griff*. The structure of each *Griff* type includes subtypes, which the manuals distinguish from one another based on the quality of their core interval. There are

---

[21].   DIERGARTEN 2015, pp. 59 and 66-70.

[22].   GUGL 1777, p. 44.

[23].   SAMBER 1707, pp. 1-106.

[24].   C. P. E. Bach takes a rather dismissive attitude towards accompaniment from an unfigured bass, see BACH 1944, p. 411.

[25].   A detailed analysis of the practice of realising an unfigured bass can be found in SANGUINETTI 2012, pp. 174-182.

distinctions, therefore, between the *Griffe* of the Major-, Minor- and Augmented-second, all of which are subtypes of the main 2-*Griff* type. Additionally, the manuals describe the Perfect-*Griff*, composed of the intervals 5 and 3. Unlike other *Griffe*, however, the Perfect-*Griff* is not a combination of intervals but a predefined chord structure.

The subject of the following analysis focuses on chapter six from Gugl's *Fundamenta Partiturae*, titled «on the second» («Von der Secund»), in which he describes the 2-*Griff*. An analysis of the schemata in Gugl's chapter on the 2-*Griff* demonstrates that the disposition and exchange principles underpin the fundamental rules of partitura playing. Beginning the analysis is a description of the valid interval combinations Gugl catalogues at the beginning of his sixth chapter on the 2-*Griff*. The catalogue of combinations accounts for the forms of the *Griff* in both three and four parts. In ILL. 1 is Gugl's catalogue of 2-*Griffe* as it appears in his *Fundamenta Partiturae*. He notates the *Griffe* using vertical stacks of intervals reckoned from a bass note along with a brief description of the twelve combinations he catalogues. To the left of ILL. 1 are seven combinations in four parts whereas the five others on the right illustrate the 2-*Griff* in three parts.

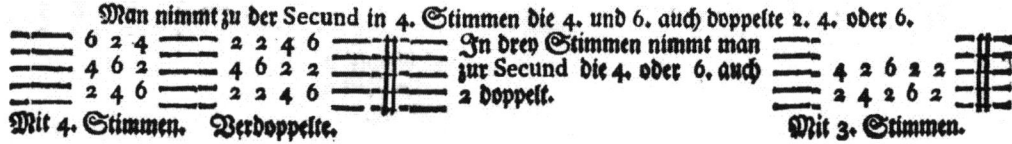

ILL. 1: Catalogue of 2-*Griffe* in Gugl's *Fundamenta Partiturae*[26].

The catalogue of 2-*Griffe* includes a conventional four-part combination of 6-4-2, the intervals of which Gugl inverts to form two other *Griffe*: 2-6-4 and 4-2-6. The four other four-part 2-*Griffe* that Gugl catalogues, which are comparatively irregular, are examples of combinations in which one interval above the bass is doubled. In the first two of these 'doubled' combinations, Gugl doubles the second (2-4-2 and 2-6-2), the third includes two fourths (4-2-4) and the fourth has two sixths combined with a second (6-2-6). Gugl explains that in a three-part 2-*Griff* one combines either the fourth to the second (4-2 and 2-4), the sixth with the second (6-2 and 2-6) or the core interval is doubled (2-2).

Although Gugl includes twelve possible combinations in his catalogue, his exercises for the 2-*Griff* only include the three-part combinations 4-2 and 2-4 as well as the four-part combinations 6-4-2, 2-6-4 and 4-2-6. Illustrations of the three-part combinations 6-2 and 2-2, on the other hand, do appear in Muffat's description of the 2-*Griff* in his *Regulae*; however, none of the manuals provide voice-leading models that demonstrate the construction of the four-part 2-*Griff* combinations that Gugl describes as having doubled intervals. These are 2-4-2,

---

[26]. GUGL 1777, p. 9.

2-6-2, 6-2-6 and 4-2-4. I will address the construction of the two three-part 2-*Griffe* 6-2 and 2-2 in Muffat's *Regulae* as well as the combinations with doubled intervals following an analysis of those Gugl provides in his *Fundamenta Partiturae*.

Gugl's catalogue of 2-*Griffe* does not provide a complete picture of Salzburg partitura instruction; however, it does highlight two key structural elements of *Griffe*. Firstly, *Griffe* form through a process of adding one or two intervals to a core interval to form three- or four-part combinations respectively. Gugl does not stipulate, secondly, that a *Griff* requires four parts to be complete as he provides both three- and four-part combinatory options in his catalogue of 2-*Griffe*. The combinatory approach to constructing *Griffe* is not distinct to Salzburg partitura instruction. Rather, it reflects what Ludwig Holtmeier describes as an «Italian morphology of chords», which he argues is evident in Johann David Heinichen's writings on basso continuo accompaniment and stands in opposition to Jean-Philippe Rameau's theory of inversion[27]. Like Heinichen's description of chord construction, Gugl's catalogue in ILL. 1 suggests that the structure of *Griffe* is fluid; it contains both three- and four options for the 2-*Griff*, some of which appear irregular.

Unlike Heinichen and other German theorists of his generation who focus on four-part accompaniment, Gugl gives equal attention to constructing *Griffe* in three parts as well. He demonstrates the construction of three- and four-part *Griffe* in schemata illustrations that specify the exact voice-leading patterns above a bass motion. To understand the morphology of *Griffe* in the Salzburg manuals, therefore, one must look beyond catalogues like Gugl's in ILL. 1 and examine the schemata he illustrates in the *Griff* chapters. The schemata show that *Griffe* are not predefined structures but abstractions from a contrapuntal complex composed of voice-leading patterns. Moreover, an examination of the voice-leading patterns in the schemata bring to light two principles for playing a partitura: disposition and exchange.

As outlined in the introduction, I use the terms disposition and exchange to describe the construction of schemata in the Salzburg manuals. Exchange («Verwechslung») is a term found in the manuals themselves to refer either to inverting layers of counterpoint above a bass, or to describe the arrangements of figures within a *Griff*. Using Gugl's catalogue in EX. 1 as an example, the figures 2-4 are an exchange of 4-2. To describe the process of layering melodies above the bass, the manuals do not use a specific term. Rather, they refer to schemata realised in two-, three- and four-parts with the respective abbreviations à 2, à 3 and à 4. Because the manuals do not use a specific term to describe the process of realising schemata using different numbers of parts, I have adopted the expression *disposizione* from Italian partimento-fugues. These fugues often indicate the number of parts in which they are composed. For instance, *disposizione à 3* refers to a three-part fugue; *disposizione à 4* describes a four-part fugue, etcetera[28]. While not

---

27. HOLTMEIER 2007, pp. 31-38.
28. SANGUINETTI 2012, p. 50.

describing partimento-fugues, the term disposition here likewise refers to the number of parts used in a schema.

In order to demonstrate that the disposition and exchange principles are fundamental to partitura instruction, an analysis of the voice-leading patterns in three 2-*Griff* schemata from Gugl's manual follows. The schemata in the analysis are realisations of the same bass motion, however, each is set in a different disposition. Gugl's realisations begin with a 2-*Griff* schema set in two parts (à 2), the next is in three parts (à 3) and the final model realisation contains four parts (à 4). The figured bass in each dispositional setting makes clear Gugl's method of constructing schemata, which involves stacking layers of voice-leading patterns above a bass motion. To construct the three-part setting of the 2-*Griff* schema, for example, Gugl adds a layer of counterpoint to that set in two parts. Likewise, the voice leading in the 2-*Griff* schema à 4 includes another layer of counterpoint to the setting in three parts. Therefore, underpinning the voice-leading patterns in both Gugl's three- and four-part figured bass realisations of 2-*Griff* schemata is the first progression in two-part counterpoint that he illustrates; the two-part progression is present in each of the realisations and acts as its structural framework.

The two-part structural framework of the three- and four-part 2-*Griff* schemata is composed of a syncopated lower part against which an upper part moves on the beat. Gugl illustrates two possible two-part frameworks for 2-*Griff* schemata using only a figured bass. Both have the same lower part whereas the upper part of each varies slightly. Along with Gugl's figured bass, Ex. 1 includes realisations of the two possible upper parts in the two-part framework. The first, marked (a), begins on the bass note C. Over the same bass motion transposed up a fifth to G, marked (b), the figures indicate the alternative upper framework part.

Ex. 1: Realisations of a figured bass by Gugl illustrating two possible framework parts for the 2-*Griff* schema[29].

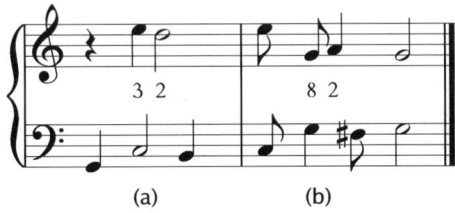

(a)   (b)

The figured bass in Ex. 1 indicates that the upper framework part in framework (a) approaches the second from the third (3-2) whereas that in (b) moves to the second from the octave (8-2). My realisation of the figured bass assumes that the dissonant second in both instances resolves to the third. In both (a) and (b), the lower framework part moves against the beat. In a classic case of Fuxian fourth-species counterpoint, the syncopation in the lower of the two framework parts prepares the dissonant second with a consonance and subsequently resolves by stepwise descent.

---

29.   Gugl 1777, p. 9.

To realise the same bass motion in three-parts, Gugl adds a layer of counterpoint to the two-part framework labelled (a) in Ex. 1, in which a third prepares the dissonant second. The third layer of counterpoint includes the interval of a fourth, which combines with the second in the schema's upper framework part to form the *Griff* combinations 4-2 and 2-4. Rectangles highlight the two combinations in the figured bass of Ex. 2, which contains two 2-*Griff* schemata. The letters (a) and (b) distinguish the two schemata from each other in Ex. 2. In addition to Gugl's figured bass, Ex. 2 includes my three-part realisation of the 2-*Griff* schemata (a) and (b).

Ex. 2 Realisations of a figured bass by Gugl illustrating 2-*Griff* schemata à 3[30].

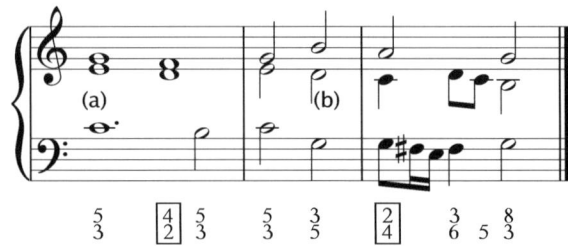

In the first schema, labelled (a), the third layer of counterpoint moves in parallel thirds against the upper framework part of the 2-*Griff* schema and forms the 2-*Griff* combination 4-2. In the following schema on G, labelled (b), Gugl exchanges the thirds to make sixths and thus illustrates the 2-*Griff* combination 2-4. Proceeding the 2-*Griff* in schema (a) is a combination of a diminished fifth and a minor third over the bass note B. Together, the parts form the combination ♭5-3, which the manuals classify as one of two options for constructing a three-part ♭5-*Griff*, that is a chord built on the core interval of a diminished fifth[31]. In three-parts, as Gugl's figured bass in schema (a) indicates, the diminished fifth in the ♭5-*Griff* may ascend by step as a consonance[32]. Alternatively, the diminished fifth may descend by step as it does in schema (b). As will be discussed in relation to Ex. 3 below, Gugl treats the diminished fifth strictly as a dissonance in the four-part setting of the 2-*Griff* schema.

In a four-part disposition, Gugl combines another layer of counterpoint to the three-part schemata (a) and (b) presented in Ex. 2. Ex. 3 illustrates schemata (a) and (b) in four-parts and includes a third 2-*Griff* schema, which begins on the bass note D and is labelled (c). Around the figured bass in Ex. 3 are three rectangles, each of which highlight the upper framework part within each of the schemata. Along with Gugl's figured bass, Ex. 3 includes my realisations of the three 2-*Griff* schemata set in a four-part disposition.

---

[30]. *Ibidem*, p. 10.

[31]. The other possible combination is 6-♭5.

[32]. Johann Joseph Fux also treats the diminished fifth in the *Griff* combination ♭5-3 as a consonance in a three-part setting of a fugue, see FUX 1725, p. 159.

Ex. 3: Realisations of a figured bass by Gugl illustrating the 2-*Griff* schema à 4[33].

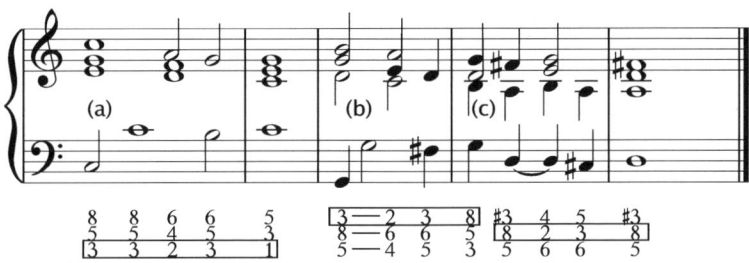

In schema (a), the upper framework part of the 2-*Griff* schema lies in the tenor, then in the soprano in the schema (b) and finally in the alto in schema on (c). The soprano provides a fourth layer of counterpoint in schema (a) to the three-part model labelled (a) in Ex. 2. Moving with the intervals 8 - 6 - 6 - 5 against the bass, the soprano combines with the alto and tenor to form the four-part *Griff* combination 6-4-2. In the two schemata that follow, Gugl exchanges the upper parts to produce the four-part 2-*Griff* combination 2-6-4 in schema (b) and 4-2-6 in schema (c). As Gugl's figured bass in Ex. 3 illustrates, the diminished fifth combines with a sixth and a third to form the four-part ♭5-*Griff* 6-♭5-3. Unlike in his three-part setting of the 2-*Griff* schema, Gugl treats the diminished fifth in the four-part ♭5-*Griff* exclusively as a dissonance.

The dual consonant-dissonant quality of the diminished fifth in the ♭5-*Griff* initially appears perplexing. It highlights, however, that the structure of a *Griff* determines the quality of certain intervals. In Jean-Philippe Rameau's theory of fundamental bass, intervals are defined as consonant or dissonant through the concept of inversion. With regards to the four-part ♭5-*Griff*, the diminished fifth is dissonant because it is the chordal seventh in a root-position 7-chord. Rameau's theory is not applicable to the Salzburg manuals, however, because they do not generate *Griffe* through the principle of inversion. Instead, the manuals classify intervals as consonances or dissonances based on those they are paired with within a specific *Griff* combination. In the three-part ♭5-*Griff* combination ♭5-3, for example, the diminished fifth and the third lie a third apart and are therefore both consonances. Whereas in four-part ♭5-*Griff* combination 6-♭5-3, the diminished fifth is dissonant because it forms a second with the sixth.

The analysis of the figured basses in Exs. 2 and 3 demonstrates the disposition principle; that is, the procedure of adding one or two layers of counterpoint to a two-part framework to form schemata in three or four respective parts. The combination of contrapuntal voice-leading formulas results in the formation of *Griffe*. Ex. 2 demonstrates the formation of the three-part 2-*Griffe* 4-2 in schema (a) and, as a result of exchanging its upper parts, 2-4 in schema (b). In Ex. 3, schema (a) includes the four-part 2-*Griff* combination 6-4-2, which results from adding a fourth layer of counterpoint to schema (a) in Ex. 2. By exchanging the upper parts of schema (a)

33. GUGL 1777, p. 10.

in Ex. 3, Gugl illustrates the formation of the four-part 2-*Griffe* combinations 2-6-4 in schema (b) and 4-2-6 in schema (c)

Using the disposition and exchange principles to analyse the schemata in Exs. 3 and 4 highlights the manuals' definition of *Griffe* as combinations of intervals. Furthermore, the principles show that *Griffe* form through a combination of voice-leading formulas within the context of a schema. With the same two principles, I will now account for the 2-*Griffe* combinations Gugl includes in his catalogue but does not demonstrate in his schemata. I begin with the three-part combinations 2-2 and 6-2, examples of which Muffat includes in his *Regulae*.

The letters (a) and (b) distinguish the two 2-*Griff* schemata in Ex. 4. The first schema, marked (a), contains the combination 2-2 whereas schema (b) includes the combination 6-2. As in Muffat's *Regulae*, both schemata in Ex. 4 are notated in partitura on two staves; however, I have substituted Muffat's shorthand figuring with a fully figured bass to indicate the precise voice-leading in the upper parts. Rectangles in the figured bass highlight the upper framework part of the 2-*Griff* schema in both letters (a) and (b).

Ex. 4: Two three-part 2-*Griff* schemata from Muffat's *Regulae*[34].

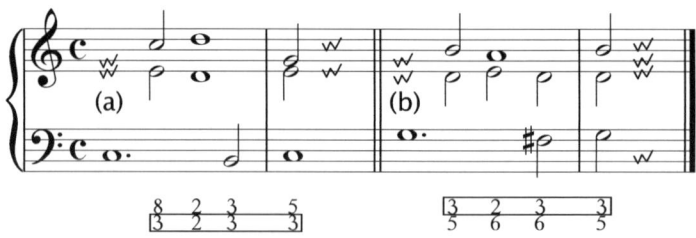

Underpinning the counterpoint of schemata (a) and (b) in Ex. 4 is the two-part framework for the 2-*Griff* schema marked (a) in Ex. 1. Against the syncopated bass in Ex. 4, the schema's upper framework part lies in the alto in schema (a) and the soprano in schema (b). Accompanying the two-part framework in schema (a) is the soprano, which moves against the bass with the intervals 8 - 2 - 3. Together, all three parts form the 2-*Griff* combination 2-2. In schema (b), it is the alto that accompanies the schema's framework parts and combines with them to form the 2-*Griff* combination 6-2.

Ex. 5 illustrates the four four-part 2-*Griffe* with doubled seconds from Gugl's catalogue. Using the disposition principle, I reconstruct the four-part 2-*Griffe* by adding a layer of counterpoint to selected three-part 2-*Griff* schemata from Muffat's and Gugl's manuals. Like in

34.   FEDERHOFER 1961, p. 54. For the sake of clarity, Ex. 4 contains only those notes from Muffat's examples that belong to schemata (a) and (b). The custodes indicate the notes that pre- and proceed those notated in the excerpt above.

Muffat's and Gugl's exemplars, those in Ex. 5 include the 2-*Griff* schema's two-part framework illustrated in Ex. 1. Schemata (a) and (b) in Ex. 5 include 2-*Griffe* with doubled seconds; schema (a) demonstrates the formation of the combination 2-4-2 whereas schema (b) contains the combination 2-6-2. The schema in (c) illustrates the doubled fourth combined with the second (4-2-4) and schema (d) shows the doubled sixth combined with the second (6-2-6).

Ex. 5: Four reconstructed 2-*Griff* schemata demonstrating the formation of four-part 2-*Griffe* with doubled intervals.

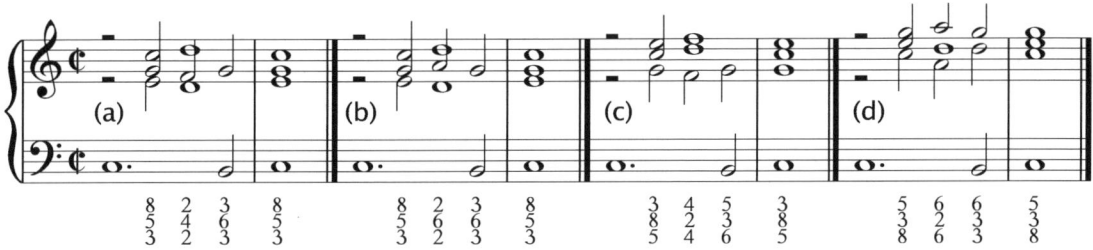

The soprano and tenor parts in the four-part schemata (a) and (b) in Ex. 5 replicate the voice-leading formulas of the soprano and alto parts in schema (a) from Ex. 4. In schema (a) from Ex. 5, the alto progresses with the intervals 5-4-6-5 against the bass and combines with the other parts to form the four-part 2-*Griff* 2-4-2. The alto in schema (b) moves 5-6-6-5 against the bass and, with the three other parts, makes the 2-*Griff* combination 2-6-2. In both cases, the 2-*Griffe* resolve to the four-part 6-*Griff* combination 3-6-3.

To form the 2-*Griff* combination 4-2-4 in schema (c), I have added a tenor part to the three-part 2-*Griff* schema Gugl illustrates in Ex. 2 (a); however, because the tenor in schema 6 (c) moves to the sixth over the bass note B, the diminished fifth in the soprano is dissonant in the ♭5-*Griff* and must therefore resolve to the third over the final bass note. In schema 6 (d), I have used Muffat's three-part model for the 2-6 *Griff* in schema 5 (b) to illustrate the formation of the four-part 2-*Griff* 6-2-6. Here, I exchanged Muffat's 2-6 to form the combination 6-2 in the soprano and alto. I added a tenor, which moves 8-6-3-8 against the bass, to the soprano and alto parts in schema 5 (b) to form the 6-2-6 2-*Griff*. Like in schemata 6 (a) and (b), the 6-2-6 in schema 6 (d) resolves to a 6-*Griff* with a doubled third (6-3-3).

Exs. 2 to 5 demonstrate the form of each 2-*Griff* combination in Gugl's catalogue within a schema based on either the two-part frameworks labelled (a) or (b) in Ex. 1. To illustrate the 2-*Griff* beyond the context of isolated schemata and within an accompaniment, I have constructed two partitura solutions — the first à 3 and the second à 4 — to a song by Eberlin. Eberlin's song, composed for a solo voice set in the soprano clef accompanied with a figured bass, concludes the chapter on the 2-*Griff* in his *Fundamenta Partitura*. The two-partitura solutions along with the vocal part and figured bass in Eberlin's song are presented in Ex. 6. It also includes an analysis of the figured bass in Eberlin's song, which indicates that it contains five 2-*Griff* schemata. A square bracket below the figured bass shows the beginning and end of the schemata, each of which are numbered (i) through to (v).

Ex. 6: Three- and four-part partitura solutions to a song in *Fundamenta Partitura* by Johann Ernst Eberlin[35].

35. EBERLIN 1766, pp. 10-11. Due to water damage, it was not possible for me to accurately transcribe all the lyrics in Eberlin's song. Where the text was illegible, I have included the notes of the vocal part alone without lyrics.

The realisation of schemata (i) - (iii) and schema (v) follow the voice-leading models in Muffat's and Gugl's manuals as well as those reconstructed in Ex. 5. TABLE 2 documents the voice-leading models that underly their partitura solutions and details the constituent *Griffe* of schemata (i), (ii) (iii) and (v). Schema (iv), on the other hand, may be considered a variant of the standard 2-*Griff* schema because its bass approaches the dissonant second by step rather than through a consonant preparation. Because of its bass motion and considering that the Augmented second is at the core of its 2-*Griff*, the partitura solutions to schema (iv) cannot follow any of the voice-leading models illustrated in ILLS. 3 to 6. Its structure will be discussed in further detail below.

Table 2: Details of *Griffe* Construction in the
Three- and Four-Part Partitura Solutions in Ex. 6

2-*Griff* schema	Bar(s)	2-*Griff* combination (à 3) and resolution	Voice-leading model	2-*Griff* combination (à 4) and resolution	Voice-leading model
(i)	1-2	2-2 resolving to 3-3	Ex. 4 (a)	4-2-4 resolving to ♭5-3-6	Ex. 5 (c)
(ii)	2-3	2-6 resolving to 3-6	Ex. 4 (b)	6-2-6 resolving to 6-3-3	Ex. 5 (a)
(iii)	5	4-2 resolving to 5-3	Ex. 2 (a)	2-6-4 resolving to 3-8-5	Ex. 3 (b)
(iv)	7	2-4 resolving to 3-5	–	2-6-4 resolving to 3-8-5	–
(v)	8-9	2-4 resolving to 3- ♭5	Ex. 2 (b)	4-2-6 resolving to ♭5-3-6	Ex. 3 (c)

As documented in Table 2, Ex. 6 includes eight of the twelve 2-*Griff* combinations Gugl catalogues. Like in Muffat's and Gugl's voice-leading models, the resolutions of the 2-*Griffe* in Ex. 6 vary depending on the 2-*Griff* combination itself. In the three-part partitura, for instance, the combination 2-4 in schema (v) resolves to the ♭5-*Griff* combination 3-♭5 whereas the 2-6 in schema (i) resolves to the 6-*Griff* combination 3-6. In the four-part partitura, two of the five 2-*Griffe* resolve to a ♭5-*Griff* — schemata (i) and (v) — whereas the 2-*Griff* in schema (ii) resolves to a 6-*Griff*. On the other hand, the figured basses in both schemata (iii) and (iv) specify that the 2-*Griffe* resolve to Perfect-*Griffe*.

Although they contain different *Griffe*, either the two-part framework in Ex. 1 (a) or 2 (b) underpins the voice-leading in each schema in Ex. 6 — apart from schema (iv). The variant of the 2-*Griff* schema in schema (iv), on the other hand, requires a modification of the voice-leading in the partitura solutions. Muffat accounts for the variant presented in schema (iv), in which he describes the 2-*Griff* as «struck freely by upward step» («freÿ graditam geschlagen»[36]). He explains further that this 2-*Griff* schema variant is particular to a 2-*Griff* with an Augmented second. Following Muffat's voice-leading model, the partitura solutions for schema (iv) approach the Augmented second in the 2-*Griff* by oblique motion.

Research in the field of eighteenth-century composition and improvisation highlights the key role schemata play in these two practices. Partitura playing is no exception; it is through the medium of schemata that the Salzburg manuals instruct basso continuo accompaniment. In essence, the Salzburg manuals instruct readers to identify schemata in a figured bass and to reproduce their constituent parts into partitura. The disposition and exchange principles attempt to codify the Salzburg method of decoding schemata from a figured bass. The two principles make salient that voice leading is of primary significance in partitura instruction and consequently highlight the contrapuntal emphasis on basso continuo practice in Salzburg.

As the partitura solutions to Eberlin's song suggest, the disposition and exchange principles lend a melodic style to basso continuo realisations. Nonetheless, the focus on voice leading in the

---

36. Federhofer 1961, p. 62.

partitura solutions does not diminish the significance of proper chord construction; the twelve 2-*Griff* combinations in Gugl's manual attest to the wide harmonic vocabulary in Salzburg partitura practice. Acting as a mnemonic aid for keyboardists, *Griffe* translate the combination of voice-leading formulas in a schema into a series of tangible hand positions. As such, the manuals synthesise the instructions of harmony and voice leading rather than treating them as separate components. This, in essence, allows us to understand the particularity of the Salzburg method of partitura instruction. The instruction, however, holds significance beyond the walls of the *Cappelhaus*. A choir boy instructed in the Salzburg method would proceed to apply the disposition and exchange principles to professional practice. Therefore, the Salzburg method has the potential to show us how court organists, such as Muffat and Mozart, approached playing a complex partitura in the performance of church music characteristic of their times.

BIBLIOGRAPHY

ADLGASSER – HAYDN n.d.
ADLGASSER, Cajetan Anton – HAYDN, Michael. 'Partiturfundament', ms., Salzburg, Ertzabtei St. Peter, Hay 2120.1-5.

BACH 1944
BACH, Carl Philipp Emanuel. *Essay on the True Art of Playing Keyboard Instruments*, edited by William J. Mitchell, New York-London, W. W. Norton & Company, 1944.

CHRISTENSEN 2002
CHRISTENSEN, Jesper Bøje. *18th-Century Continuo Playing: A Historical Guide to the Basics*, Basel, Bärenreiter, 2002.

CHRISTENSEN 2008
CHRISTENSEN, Thomas. 'Fundamenta Partiturae: Thorough Bass and Foundations of Eighteenth-Century Composition Pedagogy', in: *The Century of Bach and Mozart: Perspectives on Historiography, Composition, Theory, and Performance*, edited by Sean Gallagher and Thomas Forrest Kelly, Cambridge (MA), Harvard University Press, 2008, pp. 17-40.

DIERGARTEN 2015
DIERGARTEN, Felix. 'Beyond «Harmony» the Cadence in the Partitura Tradition', in: *What Is a Cadence?*, edited by Markus Neuwirth and Pieter Bergé, Leuven, Leuven University Press, 2015, pp. 59-83.

EBERLIN 1766
EBERLIN, Johann Ernst. *Fundamenta Partitura del Signor Giovanni Ernesto Eberlin, gentil uomo e maestro di Capella Di S: A: R:Ma Arcivescovo etc. e Prencipe di Salisburgo. 1766*, ms., Salzburg, Musikalien-Archiv Ertzabtei St. Peter.

EISEN 1989
EISEN, Cliff. 'Salzburg under Church Rule', in: *The Classical Era*, edited by Neal Zaslaw, Houndmills, Macmillan Press, 1989, pp. 166-187.

FEDERHOFER 1961
FEDERHOFER, Hellmut. *Georg Muffat an Essay on Thoroughbass*, edited by Armen Carapetyan, Tübingen, C.L. Schlutheiß and Chr. Gulde, 1961.

FEDERHOFER 1964
ID. 'Ein Salzburger Theoretikerkreis', in: *Acta Musicalogica*, XXXIV/2-3 (1964), pp. 50-79.

FUX 1725
FUX, Johann Joseph. *Gradus ad Parnassum*, Vienna, Joannis Petri Van Ghelen, 1725.

GJERDINGEN 2007
GJERDINGEN, Robert O. *Music in the Galant Style*, Oxford-New York, Oxford University Press, 2007.

GUGL 1719
GUGL, Matthäus. *Fundamenta Partiturae in Compendio Data*, Augsburg, Joseph Wolf, 1719.

GUGL 1727
GUGL, Matthäus. *Fundamenta Partiturae in Compendio Data*, Augsburg, Joseph Wolf, ^{2}1727.

GUGL 1757
GUGL, Matthäus. *Fundamenta Partiturae in Compendio Data*, Augsburg, Joseph Wolf, ^{3}1757.

GUGL 1762
GUGL, Matthäus. *Fundamenta Partiturae in Compendio Data*, Augsburg, Joseph Wolf, ^{4}1762.

GUGL 1777
GUGL, Matthäus. *Fundamenta Partiturae in Compendio Data*, Augsburg, Joseph Wolf, ^{5}1777.

GUGL 1805
GUGL, Matthäus. *Fundamenta Partiturae in Compendio Data*, Augsburg, Lotter, ^{6}1805.

HINTERMAIER 1972
HINTERMAIER, Ernst. *Die Salzburger Hofkapelle von 1700 Bis 1806: Organisation und Personal*, unpublished Ph.D. Diss., Salzburg, University of Salzburg, 1972.

HOCHRADNER 2005
HOCHRADNER, Thomas. '«Zwischen Höhenpunkten» Die erste hälfte des 18. Jahrhunderts', in: *Salzburger Musikgeschichte vom Mittelalter bis ins 21. Jahrhundert*, edited by Jürg Stenzl, Ernst Hintermaier and Gerhard Walterskirchen, Salzburg, Verlag Anton Pustet, 2005, pp. 228-254.

HOLTMEIER 2007
HOLTMEIER, Ludwig. 'Heinichen, Rameau, and the Italian Thoroughbass Tradition: Concepts of Tonality and Chord in the Rule of the Octave', in: *Journal of Music Theory*, LI/1 (2007), pp. 5-49.

KÜRTZINGER 1763
KÜRTZINGER, Ignaz Franz Xaver. *Getreuer Unterricht zum Singen mit Manieren, und die Violine zu spielen*, Augsburg, Lotter, 1763.

MONGOVEN – BRILMAYER 2012
MONGOVEN, Casey – BRILMAYER, Benedikt. *Johann David Heinichen's Grundliche Anweisung (1711): Comprehensive Instruction on Basso Continuo, with Historical Biographies*, Hillsdale (NY), Pendragon Press, 2012.

MORTENSEN 1996
MORTENSEN, Lars Ulrik. '«Unerringly Tasteful»?: Harpsichord Continuo in Corelli's Op. 5 Sonatas', in: *Early Music*, XXIV/4 (1996), pp. 665-679.

MOZART 1757
MOZART, Leopold. 'Nachricht von dem gegenwärtigen Zustande der Musik Sr. Hochfürstl. Gnaden des Erzbischoffs zu Salzburg im Jahr 1757', in: *Historich-Kritische Beyträge zur Aufnahme der Musik*, III/3 (1757), pp. 183-198.

MOZART 2005
MOZART, Wolfgang Amadeus. *Briefe Und Aufzeichnungen: Gesamtausgabe*, edited by Wilhelm A. Bauer, Otto Erich Deutsch, Leopold Mozart, Joseph Heinz Eibl and Ulrich Konrad, Kassel, Bärenreiter, 2005.

MUFFAT 1699
MUFFAT, Georg. *Regulae Concentuum Partiturae*, ms., Vienna, Musikarchiv Minoritenkonvent, I H1699.

POGLIETTI 2007
POGLIETTI, Alessandro. *Compendium: oder kurzer Begriff und Einführung zur Musica, sonderlich einem Organisten dienlich, 1676*, facsimile edition, Kremsmünster-Stuttgart, Cornetto-Verlag, 2007, pp. 209-233.

PRASSL 2010
PRASSL, Franz Karl. 'Zur Generalbasspraxis in der Kirchenmusik des Späten 18. Jahrhunderts', in: *Mozart und die Geistliche Musik in Süddeutschland. Die Kirchenwerke von Leopold und Wolfgang Amadeus Mozart im Spannungsfeld zwischen Klösterlicher Musiktradition und Aufklärerischem Staatskirchentum*, edited by Friedrich Wilhelm Riedel, Sinzig, Studiopunkt-Verlag, 2010.

RABINOVITCH 2018
RABINOVITCH, Gilad. 'Gjerdingen's Schemata Reexamined', in: *Journal of Music Theory*, LXII/1 (2018), pp. 41-84.

SAMBER 1707
SAMBER, Johann Baptist. *Continuatio Ad Manuductionem Organicam*, Salzburg, Johann Baptist Mayrs seel. Wittib und Sohn, 1707.

SAMBER 1704
ID. *Manaductio Ad Organum*, Salzburg, Johann Baptist Mayr, 1704.

SANGUINETTI 2012
SANGUINETTI, Giorgio. *The Art of Partimento: History, Theory and Practice*, Oxford-New York, Oxford University Press, 2012.

SHERILL – BOYLE 2015
SHERILL, Paul – BOYLE, Matthew. 'Galant Recitative Schemas', in: *Journal of Music Theory*, LIX/1 (2015), pp. 1-61.

TELEMANN 1983
TELEMANN, Georg Philipp. *Singe-, Spiel-, Und Generalbass-Übungen*, edited by Günter Fleischhauer, Leipzig, Zentralantiquariat der Deutschen Demokratischen Republik, 1983.

VAN TOUR 2015
VAN TOUR, Peter. *Counterpoint and Partimento: Methods of Teaching Composition in Late Eighteenth-Century Naples*, Uppsala, Acta Universitatis Upsaliensis, 2015 (Studia musicologica Upsaliensia. Nova Series, 25).

«Quod licet Bacho non licet Francisco»: A New Perspective on the Continuo Realisations of Johannes Brahms and Robert Franz

Martin Ennis
(University of Cambridge)

WRITING IN THE *Neue freie Presse* in September 1871, the critic Eduard Hanslick did not stint on invective. The composer pilloried in his article was guilty of: «the most hair-raising technical errors»; «an absolutely devastating catalogue of musical sins»; «schoolboy errors of the most elementary nature [...]».[1] Which hapless amateur could merit such an onslaught? The answer, remarkably, is Johannes Brahms, the very composer whom Hanslick had been championing for the best part of a decade as the acceptable face of contemporary music — someone who, moreover, had been a close friend since 1863.

To explain, we must trace the history of a controversy that raged in the 1860s and 1870s over the most appropriate way of realising figured bass. The main actors, apart from Hanslick, included Friedrich Chrysander (1826-1901) and Philipp Spitta (1841-1894) — respectively, the preeminent Handel and Bach scholars of their age. However, scholarly attention has tended to focus on the two composers who produced most of the realisations at the heart of the dispute: Robert Franz (1815-1892) and Johannes Brahms (1833-1897). Nowadays, Franz and Brahms are usually viewed as polar opposites, at least insofar as their approach to the performance of early music is concerned[2]. Brahms is typically associated with the purists, including Chrysander

---

[1]. «[...] haarsträubendsten Satzfehler»; «ein musikalisches Sündenregister, das geradezu vernichtend ist»; «Schulfehler gröbster Art». HANSLICK 1871, p. 2.

[2]. Most treatments of the theme are very cursory, but the same message shines through almost all of them. Christian Martin Schmidt's verdict on a concert Brahms directed in 1864 is representative: «Brahms handled [...] the realisation of the figured bass with the greatest possible reserve, with the aim of leaving the works' historical style untouched. In so doing, he distinguished himself clearly from the arrangements [...] of, say, R. Franz». («Die praktische Einrichtung der Kompositionen, vor allem die Generalbaß-Aussetzung, nahm Brahms mit größter

and Spitta, who saw it as their mission to recreate as accurately as possible the practices of earlier ages. Franz, on the other hand, is identified with those who took their lead from Hegel's concept of «necessary anachronism», arguing that different instruments, different social environments — different sensibilities, even — demanded new approaches. Elaine Kelly, the author of the most recent study of Brahms and Franz, maintains the customary dichotomy, going so far as to stress the «extreme disparity» between the two composers' styles of continuo realisation[3]. Franz's highly inventive approach is set in stark contrast to that of Brahms. As Kelly puts it, «continuo for Brahms was not a forum for his compositional creativity, but a puzzle from the past that needed to be solved in as artistic and authentic a manner as possible»[4]. Franz, we are given to understand, is very different. He allowed his compositional instincts to override musicological proprieties; indeed, he believed it to be «absolutely essential that the act of reconstruction draw on truly creative powers»[5].

The primary purpose of the following pages is to question this binary interpretation. As will be demonstrated, the approaches of Brahms and Franz to the realisation of basso continuo could at times be surprisingly similar. In fact, both aesthetics and practice reveal far more similarities than differences.

THE CONTROVERSY

A full account of the controversy over figured bass has yet to be written[6], and space allows only a summary here, but the story reaches back at least as far as Otto Jahn's Mozart biography of 1856-1859; here, the question of continuo realisation is broached with reference to Mozart's version of Handel's *Messiah*[7]. However, the first milestone in the controversy was Robert

---

Zurückhaltung und dem Bestreben vor, den historischen Stil der Werke unangetastet zu lassen. Er setzte sich damit deutlich ab von den Bearbeitungen, wie sie etwa R. Franz mit der Tendenz hergestellt hatte, die alten Werke der neuen Zeit anzupassen»). SCHMIDT 1983, p. 69. The sole exception appears to be a passing comment added by Wilhelm Altmann to the correspondence between Brahms and Karl Reinthaler: «Brahms does not therefore appear to have been an opponent of Rob. Franz's Bach arrangements». («Brahms scheint also kein Gegner der Bach-Bearbeitungen von Rob. Franz gewesen zu sein»). ALTMANN 1907, p. 70. However, this comment has gone unnoticed in later scholarship.

   [3]. KELLY 2006, p. 191.

   [4]. *Ibidem*, p. 203.

   [5]. «[Es ist] durchaus nothwendig, dass die reconstruirende Thätigkeit auf einer wirklich produktiven Kraft [...] ruhe». FRANZ 1871, p. 35.

   [6]. Apart from KELLY 2006, the most thorough accounts to date are SCHARDIG 1986 (especially pp. 79-109 and 140-160); GUTKNECHT 1993; and HINRICHSEN 1999.

   [7]. SCHÄFFER 1875, p. 437. A letter dated 8 July 1877 confirms the connection; here, Franz criticises Jahn for praising Julius Rietz's arrangement of *Messiah*: «Jahn must have had no ears at all; he would never otherwise have failed to spot the flagrant howlers running right through Rietz's piano reduction». («Jahn muß gar keine Ohren

Franz's 1863 *Mittheilungen über J. S. Bach's 'Magnificat'* (Communications about J. S. Bach's 'Magnificat'), one of the earliest attempts to set out guiding principles for the performance of eighteenth-century choral music (and, incidentally, the first significant analytical study of the *Magnificat*)[8]. Franz tackles the issue of continuo realisation from several angles — some historical, some aesthetic — but the essay culminates in a disquisition on motivic consistency in Bach's counterpoint, a theme that would preoccupy him in later writings. It is striking, however, that the one aria in the *Magnificat* in which only a bass line supports the voice, 'Quia fecit mihi magna', did not give rise to guidance on how to realise continuo parts. Arias such as this would soon lie at the eye of the storm. What's more, Franz was particularly proud of his 'Quia fecit' arrangement; years later, he claimed it would serve as an eternal monument to his art[9].

Franz's pamphlet may have caused hackles to rise, but it failed to spark a war of words. The same cannot be said of the editions of eighteenth-century compositions that Franz published from 1860 onwards. Anthologies of Bach arias appeared that year, followed in 1862 by three cantatas — *Es ist dir gesagt, Mensch, was gut ist*, BWV 45; *Gott fähret auf mit Jauchzen*, BWV 43; and *Ich hatte viel Bekümmernis*, BWV 21 — and an edition of the *Magnificat* in 1863, the year of the *Mittheilungen*. Though critics generally comment positively on the pioneering nature of Franz's work — at the time, the cantatas were largely unknown — the polyphonic web he often built round the spare lines of Bach's scores alarmed many. As early as July 1862, Selmar Bagge was able to write that «opinion on the whole direction of Franz's artistic activities [...] is *still* divided»[10].

While Franz demonstrated his position on continuo realisation primarily through his arrangements, Julius Schäffer (1823-1902), a choral conductor who worked in Breslau, latterly as *Universitäts-Musikdirektor*, advanced Franz's cause in prose that could be trenchant[11]. In 1863, Schäffer issued a pamphlet with the typically provocative title *Two Reviewers of Robert Franz: A Contribution to Clearing up the Dreadful State of Music Criticism in Newspapers and Brochures*[12]. Though the focus here is on *Lieder*, Schäffer's unswerving loyalty to Franz is already apparent.

Arguments rumbled on through the 1860s, but the storm finally broke in 1868. On the occasion of a performance of Bach's *St Matthew Passion* using Franz's edition, Schäffer wrote

---

gehabt haben, sonst würden ihm doch die handgreiflichen Plumpheiten, von denen der Rietz'sche Clavierauszug wimmelt, nicht entgangen sein»). Golther 1907, p. 271.

[8]. Franz 1863.

[9]. Waldmann 1895, p. 111. For a study of Franz's role in one aspect of the *Magnificat*'s performance history, see Cammarota 2001.

[10]. «[...] die Stimmen über die Gesammtrichtung der Franz'schen Kunstthätigkeit [...] noch immer getheilt sind». Bagge 1862, p. 225. My emphasis.

[11]. The author's name appears variously as 'Schäffer' and 'Schaeffer'; here, the first form is used throughout.

[12]. Schäffer 1863.

a lengthy justification of Franz's approach to continuo realisation[13]. This polemic, based on a lecture Schäffer had given for the Schlesische Gesellschaft für vaterländische Cultur, was published in the Leipzig *Allgemeine musikalische Zeitung* in four instalments, beginning on 1 January 1868. Each of the four parts appeared as the main feature of its issue — by no means a given for multi-part articles at the time.

Schäffer's critique appeared during the last months of the editorship of Selmar Bagge, who had moved from the *Deutsche Musik-Zeitung* in 1863. Bagge was an astute critic who used his time as editor of the *Allgemeine musikalische Zeitung* to support Franz — and to highlight the achievements of Schumann's acolytes, not least Brahms whom he championed vigorously. Bagge was replaced in July 1868 by Arrey von Dommer, but by the end of October 1868 the editorship had passed to Friedrich Chrysander. Chrysander held an ultra-conservative position on the realisation of continuo parts — Dieter Gutknecht termed him Franz's «most exacting opponent» — and he soon reversed the journal's line[14].

Meanwhile, Vienna became embroiled in the spat. In an article on Gluck's *Armida* published on 1 December 1869, Eduard Hanslick took a swipe at unnamed «art zealots» who decried even the tiniest intervention in eighteenth-century scores. Some modernisation, Hanslick insisted, served the interests of the works themselves, and he argued that purists were all too willing to sacrifice the effect of artworks on the altar of «philological literality»[15]. Chrysander responded in the *Allgemeine musikalische Zeitung* one week later with a tart piece entitled 'What Herr Prof. Hanslick understands by «art zealots»'. Here, Hanslick's words are turned back on him, and Chrysander ends his article with the assertion that he, Chrysander, is «*no* pedant» — adding, rather lamely, that those in the know support this view[16]. The gloves were off, and in his next column, a summary of recent concert and operatic activity in Vienna, Hanslick begged his readers' indulgence as he launched a sharply personal attack. Hanslick's description of Chrysander behaving like «puffed-up small-town people who believe that everyone is thinking and talking only about them» can only have fanned the flames[17].

Up to this point, most of the debate had been conducted in the pages of music journals. However, the controversy took a new turn in 1870 with the appearance of Volume 32 of Chrysander's complete Handel edition, published by the Deutsche Händelgesellschaft (the German Handel Society) under the title *G. F. Händel's Werke*. Volume XXXII contained

---

13.   SCHÄFFER 1868.

14.   «In Friedrich Chrysander [...] erwuchs der "Bearbeitungsmode" der strikteste Widerpart». GUTKNECHT 1993, p. 230.

15.   «Kunstzeloten»; «der philologischen Buchstabentreue». HANSLICK 1869a, p. 1.

16.   «[...] *kein* Pedant». CHRYSANDER 1869, p. 389.

17.   «Nach Art kleinstädtisch eingebildeter Leute, welche glauben, es werde überall nur an sie gedacht und von ihnen gesprochen». HANSLICK 1869b, p. 3. Only three months later, Ludwig Meinardus offered another weighty contribution to the debate; see MEINARDUS 1870.

thirteen duets and two trios for voices and basso continuo — in other words, pieces without obbligato instrumental parts. Chrysander attempted to confer respectability on his edition by assigning nine of the continuo realisations to Brahms and one to Joseph Joachim[18]. Indeed, a letter of early 1870 suggests a degree of cynicism on Chrysander's part in employing Brahms; the reader is left wondering whether he fully trusted the composer's instincts when realising continuo parts[19].

The publication of the Handel volume stirred Franz to action. In an *Offener Brief an Eduard Hanslick* (Open Letter to Eduard Hanslick), he laid out the principles to be employed when arranging Baroque scores for performance[20]. For Franz, there were, essentially, two issues. The first concerned the instruments to be used for 'modern' performances of eighteenth-century music — a topic that is not explored at length in this study. The second and more significant issue was how to realise figured bass when the bass line is the only instrumental part provided by the composer. This was the principal challenge faced by those responsible for the 1870 volume: most of the Handel sources contained only the voice parts and an unfigured bass, a configuration that allowed performers and arrangers considerable latitude.

Franz used the *Offener Brief* to point out many inadequacies in Chrysander's edition of the duets and trios, including a series of basic errors in the continuo realisations. He provides brutally explicit illustrations of parallel fifths and octaves (Ex. 1), suggesting these were the tip of an iceberg[21]. Franz claimed the polemics of the *Offener Brief* were «directed only at the miserable keyboard accompaniments of the German Handel Society», but it is clear from a letter to his ardent supporter Arnold Freiherr Senfft von Pilsach that the main target of the section with parallel intervals was Chrysander, whose constant carping Franz blamed for the difficulties he had securing publishers for his work[22].

---

18.   Brahms was responsible for the following numbers (see HANDEL 1870 and HANDEL 1880): first edition (1870): Duets 7-12 and the two Trios / revised and extended edition (1880): Duets 1b and 9-22 and the two Trios. For more on the origins of these works and on Chrysander's editions, see the 'Vorwort' of HANDEL 2011, pp. xi-xii.

19.   RACKWITZ 1999, p. 48.

20.   FRANZ 1871. Franz also used the *Offener Brief* to respond to fresh barbs from Chrysander. In a review of Handel's '*L'Allegro, ed il Pensieroso*' [sic] that appeared in the *Allgemeine musikalische Zeitung* on 10 May 1871, Chrysander encouraged future performers of the work to refrain from using «wretched modern "arrangements"» («leidigen modernen "Bearbeitungen"») — a clear attack on Franz who regarded his version of *L'Allegro* as his crowning achievement. Chrysander concluded by asking, «Would it be anything but barbaric tastelessness, if one were to paint over old paintings?» («Was wäre es anders, als barbarische Geschmacklosigkeit, wollte man alte Gemälde neu überpinseln?») CHRYSANDER 1871, col. 299. Franz returns obsessively to the concept of «painting over» in the *Offener Brief*.

21.   The music examples were prepared by Sasha Valeri Millwood. Please note that, for reasons of space, blank and duplicated staves have been omitted from some examples.

22.   «[...] trifft nur die erbärmlichen Klavierbegleitungen der deutschen Händelgesellschaft, für welche die Redaction ganz allein verantwortlich gemacht werden muß». GOLTHER 1907, p. 100.

Ex. 1: Examples of faulty voice-leading taken from Volume 32 of the Handel Complete Edition. FRANZ 1871, p. 18.

Seite 53, Zeile 5, Takt 1–2, Quinten
zwischen Mittelstimme und Bass:

Seite 58, Zeile 4, Takt 5, Quinten
zwischen den beiden äusseren Stimmen:

Seite 61, Zeile 4, Takt 2, der Abwechslung
wegen Octaven zwischen Tenor und Bass:

Hanslick soon weighed in. Under the pretext of a review of the *Offener Brief*, he offered a wide-ranging discussion of continuo realisation that culminated in a diatribe against Chrysander and his Handel edition. Some of Hanslick's most pointed comments were quoted at the start of this study. However, the tone is unrelentingly negative, and the review's harshest invective is reserved, once again, for Chrysander. According to Hanslick, the latter delighted in seeing himself «in the role of Germany's infallible musical pope, whose frequent anathema inevitably resulted in eternal damnation for those involved» — a reference to the recent declaration of papal infallibility[23]. We cannot be certain that Hanslick had access to the Handel volume when writing his review. If he did, he could easily have worked out that nine of Franz's ten examples of parallels, including the three illustrated in Ex. 1, stemmed from Brahms's rather than Chrysander's pen. Even if he did not, he must have known of Brahms's involvement in the project. The sharpness of his critique is therefore all the more remarkable[24].

The public dressing-down from both Franz and Hanslick will surely have irked Brahms. From the 1860s onwards he built up a «collection of interesting passages from early masters» consisting of over 100 examples of so-called forbidden intervals[25]. Brahms concluded, almost certainly unbeknownst to Franz, that great composers do not write bad parallels: either the parallels are used deliberately for expressive effect — and are therefore perfectly justifiable — or they are so incidental as to be of no consequence. However, some

23.   Hanslick described the examples of parallels as «a small bouquet of the most hair-raising technical errors in Chrysander's arrangements» («eine kleine Blumenlese der haarsträubendsten Satzfehler in Chrysander's Bearbeitungen»). «[...] in der Rolle eines unfehlbaren Musikpapstes, dessen fleißig geübter Bannfluch unausweislich die ewige Verdammniß für den Betroffenen nach sich zieht». HANSLICK 1871, p. 2.

24.   It emerges from a letter dated 15 December 1870 that Franz was fully aware of the distribution of the labour in Volume XXXII. GOLTHER 1907, p. 87. However, I can find no evidence that Hanslick shared this knowledge. Elaine Kelly makes the intriguing point that all the excerpts Franz criticised on aesthetic grounds are taken from duets arranged by Chrysander, while examples of technical shortcomings are almost all taken from Brahms's contributions; in other words, Franz used the *Offener Brief* to call into question «Chrysander's creativity and Brahms's scholarly abilities». KELLY 2006, p. 188.

25.   «Sammlung interessanter Stellen aus alten Meistern». See McCORKLE 1984, pp. 728-732; and MAST 1980. According to McCorkle (*ibidem*, p. 728), Brahms began the collection in the first half of the 1860s, resumed work in the mid 1870s, carrying on until the early 1890s. The collection contains examples from the work of 32 composers ranging from Clemens non Papa to Bizet.

of Franz's examples fall well outside these categories and must, therefore, have resulted from ignorance or lack of attention.

Brahms kept his council, at least in public. However, he appears to have taken heed of Franz's censure, for most of the technical errors were removed in the revised and expanded edition of the duets and trios, Volume XXXIIa, that appeared in 1880. A letter from Franz dated 1 January 1881 casts fascinating light on the changes in the new edition. Here, Franz launches into a devastating critique of Chrysander's rationale for the edition. According to Chrysander, Joachim prepared the first version of 'his' duet using an incorrect source; however, as Franz delights in pointing out, Handel's voices are identical in the two volumes, and the errors occurred only in the added parts. Franz also mocks Chrysander's explanation for Brahms's errors: apparently, Brahms failed to receive proofs for his arrangements and, as a result, could not make the necessary adjustments. Franz acknowledges that Brahms used the new edition to remove faulty progressions — not all of them, it should be observes — but notes that he introduced further errors in the newly added duets: these realisations «teem with the vermin». Franz ends by claiming a new Open Letter will be needed «to clear out the dung»[26]. As for Brahms, he decided to take advantage of the work involved in producing the continuo parts by choosing six of the best duets for a Peters Edition volume that appeared in 1881[27]. Brahms's Handel arrangements thus appear in three separate publications: Volume XXXII and Volume XXXIIa of Chrysander's complete Handel edition and the afore-mentioned Peters edition.

Today, most of the protagonists mentioned so far are thought to be opposed to the innovations of the *neudeutsche Schule* (New German School). However, the traditional dichotomy between conservative 'authenticists' and radical modernisers, sketched out at the beginning of this study, scarcely holds up against the evidence of the essays that fuelled the controversy. It might be thought the situation changed with the publication in 1872 of Franz Liszt's *Robert Franz*, a short monograph containing highly positive reviews of Franz's continuo arrangements[28]. In truth, however, the basso continuo controversy was conducted largely without regard to the principal musico-political dispute of the age.

By the early 1870s, the main arguments for and against individual styles of continuo realisation were well established. However, the absence of radically new perspectives did not prevent further rounds of attack and counterattack. In 1872, Heinrich Bellermann, a musicologist with a particularly intense attachment to *a cappella* music, took Franz to task for his arrangements, arguing at the same time that Chrysander's suggestions for performing

---

[26]. «[...] deren Begleitungen wieder von diesem Ungeziefer wimmeln. Es wird also eines neuen "offenen Briefes" bedürfen, um den Mist ausgeräumt zu sehen». GOLTHER 1907, p. 309.

[27]. Brahms claimed that 'Beato in ver chi può', was his «favourite number» («Lieblingsnummer»). FOCK 1956, p. 67.

[28]. LISZT 1872. According to Franz, Liszt promised to use Franz's arrangements for future performances of Bach cantatas. GOLTHER 1907, p. 102.

Handel — harpsichord to accompany arias and organ for large ensembles and choruses — were equally applicable to Bach[29]. Shortly afterwards, Philipp Spitta devoted a substantial section of the first volume of his Bach biography, published in 1873, to a polemical treatment of the issue of 'Accompagnement'[30]. This was the first systematic attempt to apply knowledge gained from eighteenth-century sources to the performance of Bach's sacred music. Spitta's conclusion — that the organ was used for sacred and the harpsichord for secular music — was different from Bellermann's[31]. However, the fundamental divide between a purist approach and practices governed by aesthetics clearly overrode any divergences of opinion within the historical camp.

In May 1875, Spitta took to the *Allgemeine musikalische Zeitung* once more[32]. The immediate stimulus for his new article, 'Der Bach-Verein zu Leipzig', was the founding of an ensemble devoted to the performance of cantatas using the texts of the Leipzig Bach-Ausgabe. Soon, however, Spitta turned his attention to the challenges of recreating an «artistic world completely lost from sight», and it rapidly became clear that his main interest lay in rehearsing arguments for a historically informed approach to continuo realisation. Unusually, the article was reproduced only a few weeks later in the *Musikalisches Wochenblatt*[33].

In the article, Spitta focused on what he appears to have seen increasingly as *the* fundamental divide in basso continuo realisation. He dismissed «an independent and polyphonically rich treatment» of the continuo part, the approach favoured by Franz and his supporters, claiming that this «cannot be justified either outwardly or inwardly» — i.e., through historical evidence or through the music itself[34]. Spitta then turned to a significant eighteenth-century source:

> Bach himself certainly favoured a full realisation but found a simple chordal accompaniment perfectly adequate [...] as is indisputably seen in the accompaniment prepared by his pupil Kirnberger for the Trio from the *Musical Offering*[35].

29. BELLERMANN 1872. Bellermann's attitude to Brahms's music was highly dismissive; in 1872 he described one work — probably, the String Sextet, Op. 18 — as «pitiful stuff» («jammervolles Zeug»). RACKWITZ 1999, p. 48.

30. SPITTA 1873-1880.

31. As Laurence Dreyfus among others has demonstrated, Spitta's conclusions rest on dubious foundations; nonetheless, his arguments were influential for decades to come. DREYFUS 1987, pp. 12-17.

32. SPITTA 1875A. Around the same time, August Saran, a Lutheran priest and pupil of Franz, provided a riposte to Spitta; however, his contribution seems to have fallen largely on deaf ears. SARAN 1875.

33. «[...] vollständig versunkene Kunstwelt». SPITTA 1875A, col. 305. See also *Musikalisches Wochenblatt*, VI/25 (18 June 1875), pp. 307-311.

34. «[...] dass dem Orgel-Continuo eine selbstständige, polyphonisch reiche Ausführung zugedacht gewesen sei, ist weder äusserlich noch innerlich begründet». SPITTA 1875A, col. 309. As Dieter Gutknecht points out, Spitta's early writings show some respect for Franz's achievements; however, little trace of this is evident by the mid 1870s. GUTKNECHT 1993, pp. 241 and 253.

35. «Bach liebte für seine Person allerdings ein volles Accompagnement, es genügte ihm aber [...] eine einfache accordische Begleitung durchaus, wie dies unwiderleglich hervorgeht aus einer von seinem Schüler Kirnberger

In short, Spitta's ideal accompaniment was one devoid of counterpoint. As the controversy reached its peak in 1875 and 1876[36], the two camps dug in, with one advocating simple chordal realisations and the other favouring textures enlivened by motivic parallels and independent counterpoints.

It is not known what Franz made of Spitta's 'Bach-Verein' article. Later in life, however, he delivered a damning verdict on Kirnberger's continuo part, suggesting that the realisation should be seen as a compositional exercise rather than as an illustration of what a keyboard player did — or should do — in performance. In characteristically caustic prose, he described Kirnberger's approach as «pure garbage», adding that «Kirnberger's harmonies [...] very often punch the melody right in the face»[37]. Franz's comments are not illustrated with music examples, but it is worth noting that the first seven bars of Kirnberger's continuo part contain no fewer than three inaccuracies (Ex. 2)[38].

Ex. 2: Johann Philipp Kirnberger's realisation of the continuo part of the trio sonata from J. S. Bach's *Musical Offering*, with inaccurate chordings highlighted.

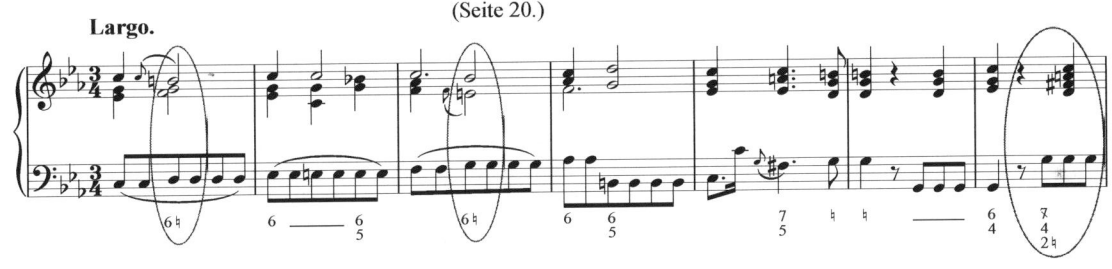

Spitta's attempts at continuo realisation are equally dubious[39]. The style is lumpy, and he allows himself frequent liberties with the harmony — mostly, as with Kirnberger, involving

gefertigten Begleitung zu dem Trio des *Musikalischen Opfers*». SPITTA 1875a, col. 309.

[36].   In a letter dated 7 April 1876, Franz noted «that the feud has finally broken out» («daß die Fehde endlich ausgebrochen ist»). GOLTHER 1907, p. 229.

[37].   «[...] der reine Schund»; «Kirnberger's [...] Accorde schlagen sehr häufig der Melodie geradezu ins Gesicht». WALDMANN 1895, p. 72.

[38].   Franz addressed Kirnberger's shortcomings also in the 'Vorbemerkung' to his own edition of the Sonata from Bach's *Ein musikalisches Opfer*, claiming that Kirnberger constantly obscured the obbligato voices with sounds that either contradict them directly or crush them under a dead weight of noise («indem es die obligaten Stimmen unaufhörlich mit Klängen bedeckt, die denselben entweder direkt ins Gesicht schlagen oder gleichgültig als lebloses Getön auf ihnen lasten»). BETHGE 1910, p. 83.

[39].   Spitta edited the *Musikalische Werke Friedrichs des Großen* for Breitkopf & Härtel (1889). The Ex. 3 is taken from the first of the 121 flute sonatas, and we might therefore expect it to be particularly carefully edited. As

seventh chords. In this extract from the finale of a C major flute sonata by Frederick the Great (Ex. 3), Spitta converts three pure G major triads into seventh chords for no obvious reason. The third case is particularly reprehensible, as the following bar, which *is* figured with a seventh chord, appears to be a deliberate intensification, presumably in support of the highest note in the flute. Purists, we must conclude, are not always pure; zealots reinterpret scripture when it suits them.

Ex. 3: Finale of a sonata in C major for flute and keyboard by Frederick the Great, in an edition by Philipp Spitta (Leipzig, Breitkopf und Härtel, 1889).

Within a few weeks of Spitta's 'Bach-Verein' article appearing, Franz's supporters demonstrated that they too could deploy historical evidence. Julius Schäffer responded to Spitta with a four-part article in the *Musikalisches Wochenblatt* in which he married rhetorical flourishes with carefully chosen examples from two eighteenth-century volumes, Heinichen's *Der General-Bass in der Composition* and Mattheson's 'General-Bass' in his *Exemplarische Organisten-Probe*[40]. Schäffer draws particular attention to the idea of using imitation in

---

for Franz, he never tired of decrying his opponents' abilities. In the *Offener Brief*, for example, he claimed the leading figures among the musicologists «arrived on the scene with a strong sense of self-confidence but, unfortunately, with only very limited musicianship» («traten mit starkem Selbstgefühl, aber leider nur sehr mässiger Kunstbegabung auf»). FRANZ 1871, p. 10.

[40]. SCHÄFFER 1875. Brahms was familiar with Mattheson's *Exemplarische Organisten-Probe*, first published in Hamburg in 1719: in 1856, Brahms's relatives clubbed together to buy him a copy for his birthday. FOCK 1956, p. 46.

keyboard realisations, a device described by Heinichen as «a particular idiom»[41]. Clearly, the situation was not as clear-cut as Spitta would have his readers believe.

Schäffer went on to republish his articles as a pamphlet in early 1876[42]. Franz was exultant, writing: «at least we've now forced the historians to shut up — they'll certainly have to be rather more careful with their entitled pronouncements in future»[43]. He was wrong. By this point, Spitta had already published a riposte to Schäffer[44]. It is a mark of the significance attached to the debate over continuo realisations that Schäffer's essays were reproduced as a *Beilage* to Spitta's article. The *Allgemeine musikalische Zeitung* ran two more articles on the same theme in 1876 by one Count Waldersee. Franz viewed these as an important demonstration of the validity of his approach[45]. However, none of the arguments is substantially new, and writers and readers must have sensed by now that neither reconciliation nor victory was to be reached through columns in music journals.

It is difficult to say exactly when the controversy ended, but the appearance in 1880 of Volume 32a of the Handel Edition was the last significant flashpoint. The heat was going out of the argument, and when two of the main actors, Brahms and Schäffer, met in Breslau in early 1881 — Brahms had travelled there for the premiere of his *Akademische Fest-Ouvertüre*, Op. 80 — they managed to discuss the new Handel edition without losing their tempers. However, in the course of the meeting it became clear just how much Franz's *Offener Brief* and Schäffer's most recent publications rankled with Brahms. According to an account sent to Franz, Schäffer «pulled no punches» when listing the deficiencies of the Handel realisations, and Brahms made little attempt to defend himself, claiming he had no interest in the sort of critique offered by Franz and Schäffer[46]. Tellingly, Brahms appears not to have challenged the validity of Franz's approach to continuo realisation.

Realising Continuo Parts

Why did Brahms choose not to engage in the public debate about continuo realisations? Various reasons can be advanced. Perhaps Brahms was conscious of the fact that, despite the enormous effort he had invested in the Handel editions, not all details bore scrutiny. Perhaps he was still smarting from the disaster of the 1860 Manifesto. This document, directed against what

---

41. «[...] eine besondere Manier». SCHÄFFER 1875, p. 450.

42. SCHÄFFER 1876.

43. «Jedenfalls ist jetzt den Historikern der Mund gestopft worden — sie werden in Zukunft mit ihren Machtsprüchen wohl etwas vorsichtiger sein». GOLTHER 1907, p. 230.

44. SPITTA 1875b.

45. WALDERSEE 1876. For Franz's delighted response, see GOLTHER 1907, pp. 245-246. For more on Waldersee and Franz, see GUTKNECHT 1993, pp. 238-242.

46. «Ich habe dabei kein Blatt vor den Mund genommen». GOLTHER 1907, p. 309.

Brahms and his friends saw as the excesses of the *neudeutsche Schule*, was released prematurely with only four signatories[47]. Brahms appears to have taken a vow of silence on musical politics; as he confessed to Clara Schumann in 1868, «I speak though my music»[48].

Another factor seems to have been deep-seated ambivalence about printed continuo realisations. Brahms argued repeatedly that a printed realisation cannot be the same as a realisation produced *extempore* by an experienced musician. He wrote as follows to Chrysander:

> When playing from a score or a bass line, I accompany quite differently from how I would write it out; in particular, I have the freedom to play differently every day. I wouldn't choose to write down the most inspired ideas that occur to me — I'd never be done with that, if only because of [the need to think about] "tomorrow". But in general, and especially for your purposes, I find the simplest solution both appropriate and sufficient. Now, by providing a printed realisation I don't mean to imply that *I* would play in precisely that fashion; I only wish to throw a lifeline to the unversed (and to the inexperienced player). However, there is so much nonsense spoken on the subject these days — indeed, the customary politeness that has long been shown to Robert Franz has blurred everything to such an extent — that I'd prefer not to get involved[49].

Brahms seems to have found little joy producing the simple harmonic realisations requested by Chrysander for Volume XXXII. His correspondence reveals reluctance and, occasionally, horror at the magnitude of the undertaking. On one occasion, Chrysander replied to a (missing) letter from Brahms with the following calming words:

> I'm not surprised that the task — following so closely in the footsteps of others — seems sterile to you, and I'd be glad to obviate the need to provide two different types of material, for household use and publication, by printing no realisations whatsoever for all these works, were it not for the fact that for the vast majority of amateurs the works would clearly be locked away with seven seals[50].

---

[47]. MOSER 1912, vol. I, p. 262.

[48]. «In meinen Tönen spreche ich». LITZMANN 1927, vol. I, p. 595.

[49]. «Ich begleite aus der Partitur oder der Baßstimme ganz anders, als ich es aufschreiben würde, namentlich aber habe ich die Freiheit, jeden Tag anders zu begleiten. Ich möchte nicht versuchen, das Geistreichste aufzuschreiben, das mir einfallen könnte — würde auch, eben des "Morgen" wegen, niemals fertig damit. Überhaupt aber und insbesondere für Ihren Zweck finde ich auch das Einfachste so angemessen als genügend. Nun will ich aber doch mit einer gedruckten Begleitung nicht sagen, daß *ich* eben so begleite, ich will nur dem Ungeübten (auch dem ungeübten Spieler) einen Notbehelf liefern. Heute aber wird so viel über die Sache gekohlt — namentlich die langgeübte und gewohnte Höflichkeit gegen Robert Franz hat alles so unklar gemacht — ich möchte nicht mitmachen». Letter of 15 May 1877; FOCK 1956, p. 64; text corrected according to MARX 2007, p. 240. Brahms made a very similar comment to Schäffer when they met in Breslau in 1881. GOLTHER 1907, p. 310.

[50]. «Daß Ihnen die Arbeit — dieses enge Nachtreten der Pfade Anderer — steril vorkommt, kann mich nicht wundern, und ich würde gern bereit sein, jenes Dilemma, daß die Arbeit für den Hausgebrauch und für den Druck

Despite his reservations, Brahms persisted with the Handel arrangements. It should be stressed, however, that the realisations he provided for Chrysander were not entirely his own work. When commissioning the realisations, Chrysander sent Brahms a copy of the edition of the duets and trios that Henry Smart had produced in 1852 for the London Handel Society, and this served as an *Arbeitsvorlage* for Brahms[51]. In his covering letter, Chrysander was scathing about the elaborate nature of Smart's arrangements, noting that he «had completely lost himself in figurative and contrapuntal writing»[52]. It is true that Smart's realisations are sometimes elaborate, but Smart justified this by arguing he had merely introduced «some of those features of contrapuntal garniture in which Handel is recorded to have extemporaneously indulged when accompanying his own music»[53].

Ex. 4a: Contrasting realisations of Handel's 'A mirarvi io son intento'.

HANDEL 1852 (Smart)

HANDEL 1870 (Brahms)

For his part, Brahms retained significant elements of Smart's work in his realisations. Sometimes, he took over the outline of Smart's realisation, simplifying or — as in the case of

zweierlei ist, mit Ihnen herzhaft zu überspringen und gar keine Begleitungen zu all diesen Werken zu geben, wenn dieselben für die übergroße Mehrzahl der Liebhaber dadurch nicht offenbar siebenfach versiegelt würden.» Letter of 24 January 1870; FOCK 1956, p. 63. Hans Joachim Marx transcribes «steril» (sterile) as «steil» (steep). MARX 2007, p. 234.

[51]. HANDEL 1852. Curiously, Smart's daughter Ellen was married to Joseph Joachim's brother Henry (originally, Heinrich). It is unlikely, however, that there was any direct contact between Brahms and Smart.

[52]. «[...] die Begleitung [...] so ganz in das Figuriren und Contrapunktiren sich verirrt hat». NEUBACHER 1998, p. 210. For more on the relationship between Brahms's realisations and those of Smart, see SERWER 1993.

[53]. HANDEL 1852, 'Introduction', [p. 2].

Ex. 4a — elaborating on his voice-leading. At times, he repositioned the harmonies but retained Smart's gestures (Ex. 4b). (Would Brahms have come up with the right-hand part here, had he not already seen Smart's solution?) And occasionally Brahms out-Smarted Smart. One shudders to think what Chrysander made of the florid right-hand writing of Ex. 4c; Brahms's «figurative and contrapuntal writing» is clearly even more «lost» than Smart's. Indeed, the accompaniments Brahms provided for the six new duets of Volume XXXIIa — duets for which Smart left no realisations — are, in general, more elaborate than those based on the 1852 *Vorlagen*. The most extreme is probably 'Quel fior che all'alba ride', the fifteenth duet of Volume XXXIIa. According to Howard Serwer, the textures here «fairly scream "nineteenth-century"»; one could just as well say they scream «contrapuntal»[54].

Ex. 4b: Contrasting realisations of Handel's 'Se tu non lasci amore'.

HANDEL 1852 (Smart)

HANDEL 1870 (Brahms)

Brahms's contributions to the revised Handel edition of 1880 mark the end of his work on basso continuo. Earlier in his career, however, he had numerous opportunities to produce realisations unfettered by purists' admonitions or pre-existing arrangements. Indeed, as an

---

54. SERWER 1993, p. 155.

Ex. 4c: Contrasting realisations of Handel's 'Quando in calma ride il mare'

HANDEL 1852 (Smart)

HANDEL 1870 (Brahms)

enthusiast for Bach's cantatas, Brahms couldn't escape the task of providing realisations for works where the available performing materials, instruments and, occasionally, performers were inadequate[55]. It is in the arrangements Brahms made for his own Bach performances that we can best assess the relationship between his practice and Franz's. For the purposes of comparison, two realisations from the same period will be juxtaposed.

First, Brahms's version of a movement from *Ich hatte viel Bekümmernis*, BWV 21, one of the best-known Bach cantatas in mid nineteenth-century Germany. Brahms first tried to perform the work at Detmold in 1857 but gave up owing to practical difficulties. *Ich hatte viel Bekümmernis* was, however, the first of three Bach cantatas Brahms performed with the Vienna Singakademie during his one season as director (1863-1864); indeed, this was the very first piece of choral music he directed in Vienna[56]. The movement in question, 'Komm, mein Jesu, und erquicke', is a duet in which the soprano represents a soul begging for succour, while the bass impersonates Christ.

In the Bach-Gesellschaft score, the only instrumental voice is a carefully figured continuo line. For his performance of the duet, Brahms dispensed with a keyboard realisation and, instead, used a quartet of strings — two violins and two violas — supported on the bass line by cello and double bass. Even a cursory examination of the opening bars (Ex. 5) reveals the elegant nature of Brahms's writing: two one-bar phrases are followed by a variation on the same shapes[57]. The realisation makes clear use of motivic parallels within the string parts: the first three bars present two (arguably three) versions of a motif loosely related to the first soprano phrase (see the rectangular shapes); and in bb. 4-6 we find three (arguably four) versions of a motif that derives its conclusion from the soprano phrase of b. 5 (see the rounded shapes)[58]. Robert Pascall characterised Brahms's realisation as «distinctly creative», pointing out that his additions are «worked out in imitation, inversion, antiphony, and voice-exchange, all this without overshadowing the vocal parts». Though Pascall does not connect the realisation to the basso continuo controversy, his account of Brahms deploying «his full composerly powers» stands in stark contrast to Kelly's idea of continuo realisation as a «puzzle»[59].

55.   Some of the realisations appear to have resulted from the inadequacies of Detmold's keyboard player; as Brahms put it, «My pianist is of little use» («Mein Pianist nützt wenig»). MOSER 1912, vol. I, p. 221.

56.   For details of the surviving performance materials for choral works by Bach, see MCCORKLE 1984, pp. 648-649.

57.   This example is taken from a score prepared for a forthcoming volume in the new Brahms complete edition (G. Henle Verlag). The volume has been much delayed, not least because of the sad death in 2018 of the volume's editor, Robert Pascall. This example reproduces a draft of Pascall's edition of the duet used for the UK premiere of Brahms's arrangement, which the present author had the privilege of conducting in the Music Faculty of the University of Cambridge on 4 February 2015. For further details of the materials Brahms prepared for performances of vocal works by Bach, see PASCALL 2013.

58.   For more on Brahms's continuo realisations — and, in particular, for descriptions of arrangements far removed from Spitta's simple chordal ideal — see STOCKMANN 1999.

59.   PASCALL 2013, p. 4. See also fn. 4.

Ex. 5: J. S. Bach: *Ich hatte viel Bekümmernis*, BWV 21, movement 8, as arranged by Brahms.

Compare this with Franz's version of the tenor aria 'Der Glaube ist das Pfand der Liebe'. This is taken from the Ascensiontide cantata *Wer da gläubet und getaufet wird*, BWV 37, an arrangement of which Franz published in 1864[60]. One of only two Bach-Franz movements included in Robert Bethge's *Gesammelte Schriften über die Wiederbelebung Bach'scher und Händel'scher Werke*, this realisation can be regarded as typical of Franz's approach[61].

The Bach-Gesellschaft edition of the aria contains only the tenor line and a richly figured continuo part[62]. Franz observes the figuring punctiliously throughout. The continuo part is realised initially in the strings (with a little help from a horn), but in the third bar Franz introduces a quartet of two clarinets and two bassoons, the combination of instruments that, he believed, offered the closest alternative within a mid-nineteenth-century orchestra to the sound of an organ (Ex. 6). Franz is careful to distinguish Bach's lines from his additions (note the lines marked 'F.').

Ex. 6: J. S. Bach: *Wer da gläubet und getauft wird*, BWV 37, movement 2, as arranged by Robert Franz.

---

60. Franz's edition was published by F. E. C. Leuckart of Leipzig under the title 'Wer da glaubet und getauft wird'.
61. BETHGE 1910.
62. That Franz used the Bach-Gesellschaft score is clear from *ibidem*, 'Notenbeilagen', p. 21.

Franz constructs a sophisticated contrapuntal web nourished by motivic parallels. The figures isolated in rectangular shapes are derived, we must assume, from the neighbour-note figures and upwards fourth leaps of Bach's bass part (see the rounded shapes). In other words, Franz's added voices are cut from the same cloth as Bach's bass.

In creating his version of the aria, Franz followed a *modus operandi* first articulated in the *Offener Brief*:

> Both in the make-up of the bass and in the figurations of the melody line, elements presented themselves that could be used to form motifs and were susceptible to development; as soon as they had been identified, the working out [of the realisation] took its course quite naturally[63].

The same delicate balance between meticulous preliminary study and free-flowing inspiration informs a comment Franz made years later to Wilhelm Waldmann:

> People talk of inspiration and write down anything that happens to come into their head; after all, it's inspiration! [...] But the dear Lord didn't just give us a heart, he also gave us a mind, and that's what we need to *correct* our inspirations and develop them[64].

Brahms was similarly suspicious of the idea of inspiration, and in one of his most famous statements on the compositional process, he provided a near paraphrase of Franz's words:

> There is no real creating without hard work. That which you would call invention, that is to say, a thought, an idea, is simply an inspiration from above, for which I am not responsible, which is no merit of mine. Yea, it is a present, a gift, which I ought even to despise until I have made it my own by right of hard work[65].

Given this, we might ask whether Franz's realisation of the tenor aria from *Wer da gläubet und getaufet wird*, is fundamentally different, in either method or philosophical standpoint,

---

[63]. «Sowohl in der Struktur des Basses, als in dem Figurenwerk der Cantilene stellten sich Momente dar, die sich zu Motivbildungen eigneten und mit denen gearbeitet werden konnte — waren sie nur erst aufgefunden, dann entwickelte sich der weitere Verlauf wie von selbst». Franz 1871, p. 5. A few years later, Count Waldersee reduced the task of realising figured bass to a quasi-mechanistic process: «I'd compare these arias with a mathematical equation; once x has been found, the remaining unknowns appear of their own accord» («Ich möchte diese Arien mit einer arithmetischen Gleichung vergleichen, ist x gefunden, so ergeben sich die übrigen Unbekannten von selbst»). Waldersee 1876, p. 502.

[64]. «Da reden die Leute von Inspiration und schreiben Alles, was Ihnen gerade in den Kopf kommt, hin, denn es ist ja Inspiration! [...] aber der liebe Gott hat uns nicht bloß ein Herz gegeben, er hat uns auch den Verstand gegeben, damit sollen wir das, was uns einfällt, *korrigieren*, ausarbeiten». Waldmann 1895, p. 4.

[65]. Henschel 1907, pp. 22-23.

from Brahms's arrangement of the duet from *Ich hatte viel Bekümmernis*. In both scores the composers derive highly sophisticated textures from Bach's 'skeleton', favouring loosely imitative procedures within their instrumental parts.

As it happens, we also possess an arrangement of *Ich hatte viel Bekümmernis* by Franz. This was published in 1862, two years before *Wer da gläubet und getaufet wird*. Most relevant to the present discussion, significant independent counterpoints are almost totally absent here (Ex. 7). In the opening bars, the textural richness of the accompaniment derives almost entirely from doublings of the vocal parts at the unison and octave. The arrangement continues in a similar vein, with further doublings in thirds, a frequent feature of Franz's accompaniments. We might reasonably conclude that Brahms's approach to BWV 21 is, in fact, more rigorously contrapuntal that Franz's. Or, to put it another way, on the issue that lay at the core of the basso continuo controversy, Brahms applies Franz's precepts more rigorously than Franz himself. Once again, we are forced to query the traditional narrative about Franz and Brahms as opposites.

Ex. 7: J. S. Bach: *Ich hatte viel Bekümmernis*, BWV 21, movement 8, as arranged by Robert Franz.

There is, of course, one significant difference between Brahms's realisation for 'Komm, mein Jesu, und erquicke' and Franz's various arrangements. The latter were intended for public use, while Brahms's accompaniment for *Ich hatte viel Bekümmernis* was put together for performances under his direction (and remains unpublished at the time of writing). That said, all of Brahms's surviving realisations — including those that betray the pressures of limited time and, perhaps, commitment — are marked by a close attention to line. Even the Handel arrangements, completed under Chrysander's demand for non-contrapuntal realisations, are constantly enlivened by cross-rhythms, answering phrases and filling parts where the voices are silent.

That Brahms adopted a motivically determined approach in 'Komm, mein Jesu, und erquicke' is incontestable. However, it is hard to see how many passages in Brahms's realisations of Handel's duets and trios — for instance, Ex. 4c above — can reasonably be described as anything other than contrapuntal. Yet, the continuo realisations of Volumes 32 and 32a are often described bluntly as «homophonic»[66]. This is misguided. Indeed, it could be argued that the decision to equate Brahms's Handel realisations with the dry-as-dust accompaniments of Chrysander and Spitta lies at the root of many misunderstandings about Brahms and Franz. It was Franz who coined the phrase «historisch-archäologisch» to describe the realisations of the principal musicologists of his age[67]. However, the evidence of the realisations Brahms produced over some two decades suggests he felt no more sympathy than Franz for a musicologically conditioned approach to continuo realisation.

Conclusion

Perhaps we should not be surprised that the aesthetics of Brahms and Franz are more similar than is usually thought[68]. The first time Brahms's name appeared in a major publication — Robert Schumann's 'Neue Bahnen' (New Paths) essay of 1853 — he is presented as a figure very much in Franz's mould, as part of «the progressive avant garde», a cadre of composers to which Schumann assigned both Franz and Brahms[69]. Seven years later, at the time of the

---

[66]. See, for example, KELLY 2006, p. 187. For details of Brahms's highly figurative realisation of 'Ach Gott, wie manches Herzeleid' from the cantata *Sie werden euch in den Bann tun*, BWV 44, see HORNE 2012.

[67]. FRANZ 1871, p. 10.

[68]. In several respects, the careers and *Lebensanschauungen* of the two composers were remarkably similar: both saw themselves as autodidacts who were set on the road to artistic maturity by Robert Schumann; both withdrew from free composition for a lengthy period to devote themselves to the study of counterpoint; both were steeped in chorales and German folksong; both were religious sceptics who derived what comfort they could from the philosophy of Schopenhauer; neither had much interest in dramatic music.

[69]. The translation is taken from MACDONALD 1990, p. 24 (see also p. 18). Schumann lists a dozen composers, including Franz, Gade, Joachim and Schäffer, as examples of «rüstig schreitende Vorboten». For the full list, see KALBECK 1904-1914, vol. I, p. 126.

1860 Manifesto, Brahms was enthusiastic enough about Franz and Schäffer to suggest they be added to the list of signatories[70]. Franz refused to sign, largely because of concern for Liszt[71], but Brahms stressed in a letter to Joseph Joachim the importance of ensuring no one could interpret the Manifesto as directed against Franz[72].

Admittedly, not all of Brahms's later statements about Franz suggest a similar level of respect. However, most of his disparaging remarks are directed not at Franz the composer and arranger, but at Franz the man. In an 1888 conversation with Richard Heuberger, for example, Brahms described Franz as «inwardly vain for all his outward show of modesty»[73].

Modesty also lies at the heart of Brahms's most extended critique of Franz's work. Responding to Max Kalbeck's enthusiasm for Franz's arrangements, Brahms referred repeatedly to the principle of modesty, suggesting that Franz failed to show this essential quality. Kalbeck continues as follows:

> They [Franz's modernisations in instrumentarium and the luxuriant polyphony he drew from figured basses] struck [Brahms] as brazen and reprehensible infringements. When I remarked how feeble the orchestra of Bach and Handel sounds today, he replied that we have no inkling of how splendid the original instruments would have sounded in church, with those incredible doubled wind parts combined with harpsichord and organ. Do you believe, I asked him, that Bach would have been content with a simple harmonic realisation of the figured bass when he accompanied arias on the organ? Brahms replied, quick as a flash, "Quod licet Bacho non licet Francisco" [What is permissible for Bach is not permissible for Franz][74].

---

[70].   MOSER 1912, vol. I, p. 262.

[71].   Letters of 21 and 23 March 1860. JOACHIM – MOSER 1911-1913, vol. II, pp. 79-83. For more on Franz's debt to Liszt, see CLIVE 2006, p. 150.

[72].   Letter of 5 May 1860; MOSER 1912, vol. I, p. 273.

[73].   «[Franz], den er aber bei aller scheinbaren Bescheidenheit für innerlich eitel hält». HEUBERGER 1976, p. 159. Curiously, Franz's complaints about Brahms's music are not unlike Brahms's about Franz. In 1877, Franz claimed that the musical quality he revered above all others was «chasteness» (Keuschheit), a characteristic sorely lacking in Brahms's music. And in a letter dated 12 July 1885, Franz refers to Brahmsian «Schwulst», a term usually translated as bombast or fustian. See GOLTHER 1907, pp. 271 and 337. Peter Clive put it succinctly: Franz «never ceased to be revolted by Brahms's music». CLIVE 2006, p. 151.

[74].   «[...] sie schienen ihm dreiste und tadelnswerte Übergriffe zu sein, und als ich ihm einwarf, das Orchester Bachs und Händels klinge uns doch gar zu dürftig, entgegnete er, wir hätten gar keine Vorstellung davon, wie herrlich es in der alten Besetzung mit seinen unglaublich vervielfachten Bläserstimmen und in der Verbindung mit Klavier und Orgel in der Kirche geklungen habe. Glauben Sie, fragte ich ihn, daß Bach, wenn er an der Orgel saß und Arien begleitete, sich mit der einfachen harmonischen Auflösung des bezifferten Basses begnügt haben würde? "Quod licet Bacho non licet Francisco" replizierte er schlagfertig». KALBECK 1904-1914, vol. I, p. 281. In making his case, Kalbeck seems to pick up Franz's arguments as transmitted by Ludwig Meinardus: «are we to believe that these masters [Handel and Bach] were content with a desiccated, spindly accompaniment for the voice [...]?! That

It should be clear by now that simple binaries are inadequate in this sphere. Perhaps Kalbeck was right to express enthusiasm for Franz *and* Brahms. After all, they approached basso continuo in strikingly similar ways: the only significant difference between them was one of scale, an issue encapsulated in the concept of 'modesty'. In Robert Schumann's resonant phrase, Brahms and Franz, in their continuo realisations, both aspired to create a «higher echo of the past»[75].

BIBLIOGRAPHY

ALTMANN 1907
Johannes Brahms im Briefwechsel mit Karl Reinthaler, Max Bruch, Hermann Deiters, Friedr. Heimsoeth, Karl Reinecke, Ernst Rudorff, Bernhard und Luise Scholz, edited by Wilhelm Altmann, Berlin, Deutsche Brahms-Gesellschaft, 1907 (Brahms-Briefwechsel, 3).

BAGGE 1862
BAGGE, Selmar. 'Drei Kantaten von J. S. Bach, in Clavierauszug bearbeitet von Rob. Franz', in: *Deutsche Musik-Zeitung*, no. 3 (1862), pp. 225-229.

BELLERMANN 1872
BELLERMANN, H. 'Robert Franz' Bearbeitungen älterer Tonwerke', in: *Allgemeine musikalische Zeitung*, VII (1872): 31 July, cols. 489-495; 7 August, cols. 505-510; 14 August, cols. 521-526.

BETHGE 1910
Gesammelte Schriften über die Wiederbelebung Bach'scher und Händel'scher Werke, edited by Robert Bethge, Leuckart, Leipzig, 1910.

CAMMAROTA 2001
CAMMAROTA, Robert M. 'On the Performance of «Quia respexit ... omnes generationes» from J. S. Bach's *Magnificat*', in: *The Journal of Musicology*, XVIII/3 (2001), pp. 458-489.

CHRYSANDER 1869
CHRYSANDER, Friedrich. 'Was Herr Prof. Hanslick sich unter «Kunstzeloten» vorstellt', in: *Allgemeine musikalische Zeitung*, IV (1869), pp. 387-389.

CHRYSANDER 1871
[ID]. 'Berichte. Nachrichten und Bemerkungen', in: *Allgemeine musikalische Zeitung*, VI (1871), col. 299.

---

is unthinkable!» (sollten diese Meister sich mit einer spindeldürren Begleitung der Singstimme begnügt haben [...]?! Das ist undenkbar!) MEINARDUS 1870, p. 248.

75. «Die Zukunft soll das höhere Echo der Vergangenheit sein». SCHUMANN 1971, p. 304.

Clive 2006

Clive, Peter. *Brahms and His World: A Biographical Dictionary*, Lanham (MD), Toronto-Oxford, The Scarecrow Press, 2006.

Dreyfus 1987

Dreyfus, Laurence. *Bach's Continuo Group: Players and Practices in His Vocal Works*, Cambridge (MA), Harvard University Press, 1987.

Fock 1956

Fock, Gustav. 'Brahms und die Musikforschung, im besonderen Brahms und Chrysander', in: *Beiträge zur hamburgischen Musikgeschichte: Festgabe des Musikwissenschaftlichen Instituts der Universität Hamburg an die Teilnehmer des Internationalen Musikwissenschaftlichern Kongresses, Hamburg 1956*, edited by Heinrich Husmann, Hamburg, Musikwissenschaftliches Institut der Universität Hamburg, 1956, pp. 46-69.

Franz 1863

Franz, Robert. *Mittheilungen über J. S. Bach's 'Magnificat'*, Halle, Heinrich Karmrodt, 1863 [²1889].

Franz 1871

Id. *Offener Brief an Eduard Hanslick. Über Bearbeitungen älterer Tonwerke namentlich Bach'scher und Händel'scher Vocalmusik*, Leipzig, F. E. C. Leuckart, 1871.

Golther 1907

Robert Franz und Arnold Freiherr Senfft von Pilsach. Ein Briefwechsel, 1861-1888, edited by Wolfgang Golther, Berlin, Alexander Duncker, 1907.

Gutknecht 1993

Gutknecht, Dieter. 'Robert Franz als Bearbeiter der Werke von Bach und Händel und die Praxis seiner Zeit', in: *Robert Franz (1815-1892). Bericht über die wissenschaftliche Konferenz anläßlich seines 100. Todestages am 23. und 24. Oktober 1992 in Halle (Saale)*, edited by Konstanze Musketa and Götz Traxdorf, Halle an der Saale, Händel-Haus, 1993, pp. 219-247.

Handel 1852

Handel, George Frederic. *Chamber Duets and Trios*, edited by Henry Smart, London, The Handel Society, 1852.

Handel 1870

Id. *Italienische Duette und Trios*, edited by Friedrich Chrysander, Leipzig, Deutsche Händelgesellschaft, 1870.

Handel 1880

Id. *Italienische Duette und Trios*, edited by Friedrich Chrysander, Leipzig, Deutsche Händelgesellschaft, 1880.

Handel 2011

Id. *Kammerduette, HWV 178-181, 182[a,b], 184-194, 196-199, Kammerterzette, HWV 200, 201[a,b]*, edited by Konstanze Musketa, Kassel, Bärenreiter, 2011 (Hallische Händel-Ausgabe, v/7).

HANSLICK 1869A
HANSLICK, Eduard. 'Feuilleton: Hofoperntheater (Gluck's *Armida*)', in: *Neue freie Presse*, no. 1889 (1 December 1869), pp. 1-2.

HANSLICK 1869B
ID. 'Feuilleton: Musik (Concerte. – «Figaro's Hochzeit.» – «Der Prophet.» – Ein Wort an Herrn Chrysander.)', in: *Neue freie Presse*, no. 1903 (15 December 1869), pp. 1-3.

HANSLICK 1871
ID. 'Feuilleton: Musikalische Neuigkeiten', in: *Neue freie Presse*, no. 2546 (26 September 1871), pp. 1-2.

HENSCHEL 1907
HENSCHEL, George. *Personal Recollections of Johannes Brahms: Some of His Letters to and Pages from a Journal Kept by George Henschel*, Boston, Badger, 1907.

HEUBERGER 1976
HEUBERGER, Richard. *Erinnerungen an Johannes Brahms*, edited by Kurt Hofmann, Tutzing, Hans Schneider, ²1976.

HINRICHSEN 1999
HINRICHSEN, Hans-Joachim. 'Die Bach-Gesamtausgabe und die Kontroversen um die Aufführungspraxis der Vokalwerke', in: *Bach und die Nachwelt II (1850-1900)*, edited by Michael Heinemann and Hans-Joachim Hinrichsen, Laaber, Laaber-Verlag, 1999, pp. 227-297.

HORNE 2012
HORNE, William. 'Brahms and Karl Grädener's *Harmonielehre*', in: *Newsletter of the American Brahms Society*, XXX/2 (Fall 2012), pp. 6-8.

JOACHIM – MOSER 1911-1913
Briefe von und an Joseph Joachim, edited by Johannes Joachim and Andreas Moser, 3 vols., Berlin, Bard, 1911-1913.

KALBECK 1904-1914
KALBECK, Max. *Johannes Brahms*, 4 vols., Berlin, Deutsche Brahms-Gesellschaft, 1904-1914.

KELLY 2006
KELLY, Elaine. 'Evolution versus Authenticity: Johannes Brahms, Robert Franz, and Continuo Practice in the Late Nineteenth Century', in: *19ᵗʰ-Century Music*, XXX/2 (2006), pp. 182-204.

LISZT 1872
LISZT, Franz. *Robert Franz*, Leipzig, F. E. C. Leuckart, 1872.

Litzmann 1927
Clara Schumann, Johannes Brahms. Briefe aus den Jahren 1853-1896, edited by Berthold Litzmann, 2 vols., Leipzig, Breitkopf & Härtel, 1927.

MacDonald 1990
MacDonald, Malcolm. *Brahms*, Oxford, Oxford University Press, 1990.

Marx 2007
Marx, Hans Joachim. 'Johannes Brahms im Briefwechsel mit Friedrich Chyrsander', in: *Musik und Musikforschung. Johannes Brahms im Dialog mit der Geschichte*, edited by Wolfgang Sandberger and Christiane Wiesenfeldt, Kassel, Bärenreiter, 2007, pp. 221-274.

Mast 1980
Mast, Paul. 'Brahms's Study «Octaven u. Quinten u.a.» with Schenker's commentary translated', in: *Music Forum*, v (1980), pp. 1-196.

McCorkle 1984
McCorkle, Margit. *Johannes Brahms. Thematisch-Bibliographisches Werkverzeichnis*, Munich, G. Henle Verlag, 1984.

Meinardus 1870
Meinardus, Ludwig. 'Robert Franz', in: *Musikalisches Wochenblatt*, i (1870): 1 April, pp. 211-213; 8 April, pp. 228-231; 15 April, pp. 247-249.

Moser 1912
Johannes Brahms im Briefwechsel mit Joseph Joachim, edited by Andreas Moser, 2 vols., Berlin, Deutsche Brahms-Gesellschaft, ²1912 (Brahms-Briefwechsel, 5, 6).

Neubacher 1998
Neubacher, Jürgen. 'Ein neuer Quellenfund zur Mitarbeit Johannes Brahms' an Friedrich Chrysanders Ausgabe von Händels «Italienischen Duetten und Trios» (1870)', in: *Die Musikforschung*, li (1998), pp. 210-215.

Pascall 2013
Pascall, Robert. '«In Concert-Life, the Most Striking, Most Pleasing of Adventures» – Brahms's Arrangements of Bach Cantatas', in: *Newsletter of the American Brahms Society*, xxxi/2 (Fall 2013), pp. 1-8.

Rackwitz 1999
Rackwitz, Werner. 'Anmerkungen zum Verhältnis Friedrich Chrysanders zu Johannes Brahms und Joseph Joachim', in: *Brahms-Studien*, xii (1999), pp. 41-60.

Saran 1875
Saran, August. *Robert Franz und das deutsche Volks- und Kirchenlied*, Leipzig, F. E. C. Leuckart, [1875].

SCHÄFFER 1863

SCHÄFFER, Julius. *Zwei Beurteiler Robert Franz's. Ein Beitrag zur Beleuchtung des Unwesens musikalischer Kritik in Zeitungen und Broschüren*, Breslau, F. E. C. Leuckart, 1863.

SCHÄFFER 1868

ID. 'Ueber die Bearbeitung der Bach'schen Matthäus-Passion durch Rob. Franz', in: *Allgemeine musikalische Zeitung*, III (1868): 1 January, pp. 1-4; 15 January, pp. 17-19; 22 January. pp. 25-28; 29 January: pp. 33-36.

SCHÄFFER 1875

ID. 'Robert Franz in seinen Bearbeitungen älterer Vocalwerke', in: *Musikalisches Wochenblatt*, VI (1875): 3 September, pp. 437-439; 10 September, pp. 449-454; 17 September, pp. 461-462; 24 September, pp. 473-476.

SCHÄFFER 1876

ID. *Friedrich Chrysander in seinen Klavierauszügen zur deutschen Händel-Ausgabe*, Leipzig, F. E. C. Leuckart, 1876.

SCHARDIG 1986

SCHARDIG, Waltraut. *Friedrich Chrysander. Leben und Werk*, Hamburg, Verlag der Musikalienhandlung Karl Dieter Wagner, 1986 (Hamburger Beiträge zur Musikwissenschaft, 32).

SCHMIDT 1983

SCHMIDT, Christian Martin. *Johannes Brahms und seine Zeit*, Laaber, Laaber-Verlag, 1983.

SCHUMANN 1971

SCHUMANN, Robert. *Tagebücher, Band 1: 1827-1838*, edited by Georg Eismann, Leipzig, VEB Deutscher Verlag für Musik, 1971.

SERWER 1993

SERWER, Howard. 'Brahms and the three Editions of Handel's Duets and Trios', in: *Händel-Jahrbuch* XXXIX (1993), pp. 134-160.

SPITTA 1873-80

SPITTA, Philipp. *Johann Sebastian Bach*, 2 vols., Leipzig, Breitkopf & Härtel, 1873-1880.

SPITTA 1875A

ID. 'Der Bach-Verein zu Leipzig', in: *Allgemeine musikalische Zeitung*, X (1875), cols. 305-312.

SPITTA 1875B

ID. 'Ueber das Accompagnement in den Compositionen Seb. Bach's', in: *Allgemeine musikalische Zeitung*, X (1875): 17 November, cols. 721-729; 24 November, cols. 740-745.

STOCKMANN 1999

STOCKMANN, Bernhard. 'Brahms und der Generalbaß', in: *Johannes Brahms. Quellen – Text – Rezeption – Interpretation. Internationaler Brahms-Kongreß, Hamburg 1997*, edited by Friedhelm Krummacher and Michael Struck, in collaboration with Constantin Floros and Peter Petersen, Munich, Henle, 1999, pp. 305-313.

WALDERSEE 1876

WALDERSEE, Paul G. 'Ueber Bearbeitung und Ausführung Bach'scher Werke', in: *Allgemeine musikalische Zeitung*, XI (1876): 24 May, cols. 328-331; 9 August, cols. 501-505.

WALDMANN 1895

WALDMANN, Wilhelm. *Robert Franz. Gespräche aus zehn Jahren*, Leipzig, Breitkopf & Härtel, 1895.

Basso Continuo and Partimento as a Pedagogical Tool Then and Now

Figured Bass: Then and Now[1]

Thomas Christensen
(The University of Chicago)

WITHIN JUST THE PAST FEW YEARS, there seems to have been an explosion of scholarship in the field of thoroughbass, with unprecedented numbers of books and articles by musicologists, theorists, and performers of early music treating the history and practice of the figured bass. At the same time, one can scarcely surf the internet without seeing uncountable websites, blog posts, interest groups, and YouTube videos that deal with some aspect or another of thoroughbass realization — whether figured or unfigured. And then there are all those classes, workshops, seminars, and yes, even conferences, about the *basso continuo*. Never since its heyday in the eighteenth century, it seems, have more musicians been studying the thoroughbass, talking about it, and most of all playing it. Something new is clearly happening in the world of the figured bass[2].

And what is that? Why is there such an apparent surge of interest in an antiquated and, for many musicians, a rather esoteric performance practice that has been largely dormant for over two centuries, at least as a meaningful part of contemporaneous music making?

I suppose the first answer to this question might be simply this: there are more and more musicians who are interested in performing early music — or let's be more specific — in performing a repertoire of music in which a continuo component is demanded. Historically informed music performance seems to be attracting a new generation of performers, and this means performers who can read and play in a continuo ensemble.

But all this still begs the question, why now? It is not that there was no interest in early music among previous generations of musicians. After all, the first major stirrings of the

---

[1].   This chapter is a revised version of the Keynote Address I gave at the international virtual conference: *The Figured Bass Accompaniment in Europe*, 9-12 September, 2021.

[2].   In this paragraph, I have deliberately conflated the terms figured bass, basso continuo, and thoroughbass (not to mention other related terms we might use: *Generalbass, basso seguente, partitura*, etc.). Historians of Baroque performance practice will be well aware that these are all not equivalent terms. Later in this paper I will have much more to say about the various uses and meanings of figured bass and what their lessons were for musicians.

historical-informed performance movement began already in the 1960s and 70s in a few urban centers such as Amsterdam, London, and Boston. (Back then, some of you may remember, we could use the term 'historically authentic performance practice' without flinching). Yet, while there was certainly much concomitant scholarship and pedagogy about the figured bass to go along with this nascent performance movement, it hardly approached the frothy waters we see today.

So let me suggest a second, perhaps more significant catalyst to the renewed interest in figured bass realization today. And that is the recognition and interest in Neapolitan partimento. We might date the beginnings of this story with the publication of Robert Gjerdingen's important book on Galant music[3], followed by Giorgio Sanguinetti's marvelous study on the history of partimento[4]. Wherever we may wish to date the beginnings of this Renaissance, it is not hard to see why the partimento proved so bracing for so many musicians.

First of all, partimenti studies seemed to have unlocked the studios of numerous composers and performers from the eighteenth century, revealing secrets of performance and pedagogy that had long remained hidden from us. Not only was the partimento a means for a student to learn to realize a continuo bass line — whether figured or not — it also was a stimulus for solo improvisation. Once mastered, a keyboardist (or perhaps even a guitarist or lutenist) had a thesaurus of stylistically idiomatic progressions that could be employed and elaborated at will. Best of all, this knowledge proved to be transferable to today. Although it was originally transmitted orally by a master hovering over the should of his adolescent orphan boys sitting at a keyboard, it turns out that we have been able to reconstruct much of this pedagogy and thereby learn to realize partimento exercises in a stylistically coherent language with a fluency that seems almost uncanny.

This recovery of a hitherto lost, or at least little recognized, pedagogical tradition has had seismic reverberations extending well beyond aiding historically informed musical performance. We can see how knowledge of the Neapolitan partimento schools has helped to reshape our own teaching of music history and theory.

Consider how our understanding of the eighteenth century has changed in just about one generation. Until quite recently most textbooks of music history (or at least those that I know in North America) would tell us that there was a radical caesura in the middle of the eighteenth century that marked the boundary between two differing, and really almost irreconcilable musical periods: In Anglo-American traditions, we called those periods Baroque and Classical, respectively. 1750 proved to be a convenient terminus for the Baroque era coinciding with the death of Bach, while also the advent of Viennese classicism with the very first compositions

---

[3]. GJERDINGEN 2007.

[4]. SANGUINETTI 2012. Then again, there were some earlier discussions of partimento found in scattered musicological literature such as the pioneering studies of FELLERER (1930), BORGIR (1987), or even my own historical essay on the Rule of the Octave (CHRISTENSEN 1992).

composed by Joseph Haydn. While it is easy for us to ridicule the obvious over-simplification of this artificial historical boundary, the date seemed irresistible when teaching young students music history, at least as long as we adhered to a history that focused on a largely Austro-Germanic model dominated by a few canonical composers like Bach, Handel, Haydn and Mozart[5].

What the partimento revolution has done is to highlight Italian musical practices and pedagogies that continued seamlessly through the entire eighteenth century and even into the nineteenth century, whether the music was secular or sacred, instrumental or vocal. The Neapolitan conservatories were central, as we know, in codifying and disseminating this practice by sending hundreds of their most successful pupils throughout Europe as Kapellmeisters, Church organists, singers, and private music instructors[6]. And they in turn would pass on this guild knowledge to their students. In so doing, a common vocabulary and grammar of musical practice that we have come to call galant became a lingua franca among musicians across Europe, a style that connected music in all genres in the long eighteenth century, and thus confirming the sense of stylistic unity in the eighteenth century that historians such as Carl Dahlhaus long ago suggested[7].

Another area in which the partimento has proven catalytic — and might thereby explain part of its resurgence today — is in the reforms of music theory instruction. Most music students in the twentieth century have learned to analyze and perhaps to compose simplified models of tonal music using theories of Roman numeral scale-degree theory based on principles drawn from Rameau, or if you studied in Germany, perhaps a version of Riemannian functional theory. What the partimento did is offer an alternative approach that emphasized the learning of musical style and keyboard skills using many of the same common figured-bass patterns, progressions, scale harmonizations, schemata, and topics that would have been taught in the Neapolitan conservatories. (German music theorists often term this *Satzlehre*.) This knowledge was one gained by a Neapolitan student not by memorizing rules read in a text or composing species counterpoint exercises. Rather, it was gained by demonstration, imitation, and iteration. Today, the partimenti has found its way into a few school textbooks of music harmony and counterpoint — and thereby into our classrooms — by such authors as Job Ijzerman in the Netherlands and Michael Callahan in the United States[8]. In my own institution at the University of Chicago, my colleague Olga Sánchez-Kisielewaska has been incorporating partimenti into our tonal theory courses, beginning with our students memorizing and playing the Rule of the Octave[9].

---

[5]. WEBSTER 2004.
[6]. GJERDINGEN 2020.
[7]. DAHLHAUS 1985.
[8]. IJZERMAN 2018 and CALLAHAN 2017.
[9]. SÁNCHEZ-KISIELEWASKA 2017.

Partimento has also stimulated a resurging interested in improvisation among keyboardists. Of course the ubiquity of improvisational genres in the eighteenth century has long been well known by historians; we know that 'Preluding' or 'Fantasizing' (to give only their English cognates) was widely practiced in the Baroque and Classical periods. Yet too often, this practice has been mystified as an almost occult skill within the grasp of only a few musical geniuses or cognoscenti of the time. Partimenti has pulled the veil off this practice, so to speak, by showing us how our Neapolitan orphans could become wizards of improvisatory skill by learning how to combine and manipulate the hundreds of various schema, figurations, topics, divisions, embellishments and other similar patterns and figures. The ability to realize an unfigured-bass by finding idiomatic and appropriate harmonies to play leads logically — and almost effortlessly, it seems — to the next stage of musical development in which a keyboardist can simply improvise those progressions with a bass they invent themselves[10].

There is one final aspect of the partimenti that I would say has had fascinating, if perhaps unexpected repercussions. It has raised increased awareness that much musical training has historically been inculcated as embodied knowledge. Keyboardists memorized all those idiomatic musical progressions viscerally — like the Rule of the Octave — such that they became lodged in the fingers, thus helping to explain how they could undertake remarkable feats of improvisation. In turn, this has helped to connect eighteenth century performance practice with other orally-transmitted improvisatory pedagogies to be found in Medieval and Renaissance music, jazz, and even non-Western practices from the Middle East and South Asia. Suddenly the thoroughbass was not just some mechanical and musty old orthography of eighteenth-century music, but a vibrant, creative musical practice that was a piece of a common heritage of improvisatory and artisanal skills that linked diverse musical cultures across time and place.

All of this is a wonderful, and I would even say, breathtaking result of the collective efforts of numerous scholars and musicians of our generation. We can rightly be proud of what we have accomplished today. I have elsewhere said that the partimento is one of the most consequential revolutionary discoveries of musicology over the past two decades, whose importance far transcends the mere pedagogy of Baroque continuo practice[11]. And I mean that. But it is not just performers of early music who are studying and playing the figured bass today. A whole new generation of keyboardists seem to have joined the fun, the majority of whom would probably not identify themselves as professional musicians. Whether this is a coincidence or a consequence of the partimenti revolution, it seems clear that the figured bass is enjoying a new renaissance, one that seems to be opening up ever more doors into the

---

[10]. The literature on improvisation for early-music performance has become a deluge in recent years. For a helpful stock-taking of where we are at the moment in this rapidly evolving field, see the studies collected in GUIDO 2017.

[11]. CHRISTENSEN 2017.

practice and theory of early music that is proving creative, rich, diverse, and popular. Maybe it is time to uncork some champagne and celebrate.

Before we do, though, I am going to now throw a little cold water on our party and suggest some contrarian evidence to this pleasant picture I just drew. It is not that this picture is completely wrong. Far from it. But our emphasis on the performative elements of the figured bass may conceal some of the other ways it was understood and used by musicians in the past, ways that have not always enjoyed unwavering consent and admiration. And these stories are also a part of its history and reception. It is not that we are necessarily mistaken in our eager embrace of the basso continuo or partimento, but to see that our perspective is perhaps an incomplete one.

Let me explain what I mean with an example and consider the Viennese music theorist Heinrich Schenker (1868-1935). Schenker probably knew nothing about Neapolitan partimento practices. For that matter, he really had little interest himself in the actual practice of continuo realization. Who did in the first decades of the twentieth century when he began to write about the thoroughbass? But he did know well many of the theoretical publications of eighteenth-century German *Generalbass* tradition, above all that of C. P. E. Bach. And he saw Bach's *Versuch* as confirming his growing understanding of tonality as multiply embedded contrapuntal lines articulating a tonic triad over time and space, all controlled by common rules of voice-leading. Schenker came to view figured bass as taught in C. P. E. Bach's *Versuch* to be perhaps the purest representation of his theory of hierarchical scale degree (*Stufen*) and tonal voice leading. On the other hand, the harmonic theory of Rameau, he would tartly remind us, falsely conflated many figured-bass signatures through the theory of chordal inversion and the fundamental bass, marking an errant turn in the history of harmonic theory[12].

More recently, Ludwig Holtmeier made something of a similar argument[13]. Holtmeier sees the systematic theorizing of musicians such as Rameau or Riemann as obscuring — and often distorting — the real insights of theorists who remained true to the spirit of thoroughbass such as Heinichen or Sorge[14]. For observers such as Schenker and Holtmeier, the thoroughbass perspective revealed and reveled in the rich vocabulary of chord signatures it taught along with its almost infinitely nuanced sensitivity to chordal voicing and counterpoint, features that risked being lost in the more abstract, systematic strains of speculative harmonic theory. In short, the figured bass was valued not because of any performance element, but as an idealized representation and notation of musical structure, one that was held in opposition to other more speculative strains of harmonic abstraction by Rameau and his followers.

---

12. SCHENKER 1930.

13. HOLTMEIER 2017, pp. 99-107.

14. For that matter, of Rameau as well. As Holtmeier points out (*ibidem*), so much fuss has been made by historians of theory concerning Rameau's 'systematic' theory of the *basse fondamentale*, that we too often overlook the primary role figured bass plays in his pedagogy and theory.

It is all very ironic since Rameau's theory of the fundamental bass can actually be seen as a theory of the thoroughbass, explaining the logic by which chord signatures succeed one another in any continuo progression, and even using the same nomenclature of the figured bass to model the *basse fondamentale*. His theory of chordal inversion was a means of clarifying a harmonic syntax that was obscured by the rote empiricism of the figured bass, with its plethora of signatures. Arguing that a smaller number of fundamental harmonies unify many figured-bass signatures (for instance, that the 6/3 or 6/4 chords were but inversions of a fundamental, root-positioned 5/3 triad), Rameau believed his theory of the fundamental bass demonstrated the logic behind harmonic succession[15].

This was not the view of Hugo Riemann. In his Handbook of music history[16], Riemann eschewed the label of 'Baroque' (recently made famous by the art historian, Heinrich Wölfflin) to encompass music of the seventeenth and early eighteenth centuries in favor of a more prosaic term to describe its most characteristic ensemble component: «Das Generalbass-Zeitalter» — the Age of the Thoroughbass. It was a designation he bestowed with some prejudice. For Riemann, as practical and widespread as the *Generalbass* was for accompaniment during the seventeenth and eighteenth centuries, it was marked by a patently anti-intellectualist approach in treating harmony as a purely empirical practice, one that inaugurated a catastrophic turn away from the brilliant insights of Zarlino[17]. Of course, Riemann was considering the thoroughbass unfairly as a deficient theory of harmony — something it never claimed to be. Nevertheless, by failing to acknowledge elements such as functional harmony, inversional equivalence, harmonic dualism, or scale-degree hierarchies, the thoroughbass was condemned by Riemann as useless to musicians who would wish to understand the harmonic logic underlying the new tonality. The figured bass was a neutral and completely unrevealing orthography. He would have found it preposterous to think that it could in any way have anything useful to teach us about musical composition.

Riemann had allies in the eighteenth century who also took a dubious view of figured bass. No one was more rudely dismissive of the practice than the polyglot music critic from Hamburg, Johann Mattheson. This may sound strange given that Mattheson wrote a number of important *General-Bass* treatises, and he was actually aware of the partimento tradition from Italy that he even adopted — if in a rather North German manner — in one of his own treatises of the thoroughbass[18]. But despite all that — and maybe because of it — Mattheson simply could not accept the proposition that knowledge of the thoroughbass could be equated with the exalted mastery of composition. On the contrary, it was menial finger work (*Handsachen*

---

[15]. Christensen 1992.
[16]. Riemann 1922.
[17]. *Ibidem*, p. 76.
[18]. Mattheson 1731.

was his term) that was not worthy of a true *musicus*. Mattheson was here taking issues with the claim of Friedrich Niedt, who had called the *Generalbass* the «fundamentum» of musical composition — a pairing that would be taken up by subsequent generations of musicians throughout Europe — who famously described the *Generalbass* as «the most perfect foundation of music» (*Das volkommenste Fundament der Musik*)[19].

Mattheson could never accept this analogy. In his view, the true art of composition lay not in harmony, but in melody. And no treatise on thoroughbass, let alone reams of figured and unfigured basses for the student to realize, could ever teach that skill. Anticipating language that Rousseau would use several decades later in his argument with Rameau, Mattheson extolled melody as «...the true *fundamentum* of music...»[20]. For a composer to place harmony in importance before melody, he quipped, was like putting the cart before the horse[21].

It is not that the teachers of the thoroughbass in the eighteenth century were oblivious to melody — even the partimenti maestros recognized the value of melody. It would be strange, indeed, if musicians from the land that is often credited with the development and dissemination of opera across Europe were deaf to the beauty of melody in music. But Mattheson was evidently not familiar with the tradition of solfeggio pedagogy that Nicholas Baragwanath has recently brought to light by which singers — and composers — learned to sing, improvise and write down melodic lines against some fixed cantus or over those figured and unfigured basses[22].

But to return for a moment to the criticisms of Riemann, I have to say I think our Leipzig theorist was profoundly wrong about the thoroughbass. (Well, he was profoundly wrong about a lot of things, but that's a story for another time). Riemann posited the empiricism of the figured bass as the intellectual opposite of what a *Harmonielehre* attempts to due in rationalizing harmonic practice theoretically. But what Riemann does not seem to see is how the figured bass was in fact the very foundation — the *fundamentum* — of that kind of theorizing. It was precisely the means by which theorists in the eighteenth and early nineteenth century conceived their various insights into tonal harmony. Think of the challenges thoroughbass posed to musicians attempting to understand the logic of dozens upon dozens of baffling signatures. How to learn, memorize and categorize them? By challenging pedagogues to think about the grouping of chords based on intervallic content, dissonance, and scale degree placement, the thoroughbass became the incubator of the most progressive harmonic theories of the day: defining chordal roots, inversional equivalence of chords, *Stufentheorie* and scale-degree theory, and hierarchies of harmonic function.

---

[19]. See the full quote NIEDT 1700, f.A 3'. The genealogy of this definition of the *Generalbass* as a «foundation» of musical composition is a deep one that can be traced back to the early seventeenth century. See CHRISTENSEN 2004, esp. pp. 16-17.

[20]. MATTHESON 1722, p. 340.

[21]. MATTHESON 1735, pp. 48-51.

[22]. BARAGWANATH 2020.

Of course, this does not mean that theory and the continuo were always twinned. Mattheson had a point that we should not dismiss out of hand. A great deal of continuo playing — and its pedagogy — he wrote, was quite awful; many teachers and tutors simplified the realization of a figured bass to something of a children's game, blanching the richness of musical harmony for the sake of pedagogical expediency[23]. It really was as often as not a mechanical routine in which a not particularly skilled keyboardist would learn to pound out chords with little understanding or instinct for harmony or tasteful elaboration. And no wonder. Just look at the way many eighteenth-century musicians learned the figured bass. Few of them had the luck to study with a Durante, a Leo, a Sala — or any of their students for that matter.

Well, you might counter, at least they could pick up a good treatise or two by Henichen, Saint-Lambert, C. P. E. Bach, and a few others that would teach them the skill of signature realization with particular Italian brio, French *beinseance*, or perhaps some North German *Empfindsamkeit*. Maybe they could even pick up a bit of theory along the way. Yet, because we today canonize a few of these treatises — monumental works that seem almost impeccable in their sophistication and excellence — it is by no means the case that they were received that way in their own generation. Let us be honest, most keyboard students learning to play the keyboard on their own would not have had the patience — or probably even the means — to work through these difficult publications. Instead, they would have turned to any number of short and cheap manuals of accompaniment that promised to teach them this skill in just a matter of months[24].

These may not be texts that many of us today would probably assign — and for good reason. Yet, we must not forget that these were the works in which legions of amateur keyboardists learned to play the continuo during the eighteenth century. Students would learn mechanical fingerings and rigid mnemonics for realizing chord signatures, simple cadential models, sequences, and harmonic progressions such as, well, the Rule of the Octave[25]. It must have been a desolate soundscape. After all, why would so many musicians complain about the poor state of continuo playing again and again, railing against incompetent organists and harpsichordists who were unable to read the simplest figured bass without botching it if the problem was not ubiquitous? In his *Musikalische Handleiturn* from 1700, Niedt lamented how so many keyboardists did not really understand the true art — *die Wahre Fundament* — of the thoroughbass but could only read figures in tablature to pound out with one's fingers[26].

---

[23]. MATTHESON 1735, pp. 49-50.

[24]. Such examples might be those pocket-sized instructions by [VON FREUDENBERG] 1733, KELLNER 1732, DUBUGRARRE 1754, PIXNER 1789.

[25]. The *Règle de l'octave*, we should not forget, had almost as many opponents and critics as it did advocates for teaching accompaniment in the eighteenth century. Those critics thought it would lead to a mechanical routine of chordal realization and improvisation, along with an impoverished chordal vocabulary. See CHRISTENSEN 1992, esp. pp. 102-106.

[26]. NIEDT 1710, 'Preface'.

Figured Bass: Then and Now

It is no wonder that right through the eighteenth century, we can find countless publications that appealed to the lowest dominator of keyboard competence with simplistic, mechanical suggestions for making the playing of the figured bass quick and easy. No better example exists of this pedagogical genre than the one by Lorenz Mizler. A contemporary and acquaintance of Sebastian Bach, Mizler published a small treatise that described a machine, which would teach a student the correct chord to realize for any scale degree of any key «in a mathematical manner»[27]. Essentially, it started as a volvelle, which transposed the common chords of the rule of the octave to every possible key transposition. Figured bass was no longer an art; it was not even a science; With Mizler's machine, it was a repetitive, rote, quite literally a mechanical activity.

This is not to say that understanding and playing the thoroughbass well needed to be an overly complicated, painstaking and cerebral affair. I remember when I was first learning to read the figured bass as a music student in Boston in the 1970s turning to the magnificent history of the thoroughbass by Franck T. Arnold[28]. It still is a magnificent work, and one that I think deserves a place in the library of any serious student of the thoroughbass. But as a practical tutor, it fails miserably. The detail by which Arnold inventories and analyzes the dizzying array of signatures treated by dozens of individual theorists over the course of the long eighteenth century became overwhelming to me. Reading Arnold, figured bass realization seemed to be a fussy, persnickety rule of spacing, doubling, and voice-leading. How to possibly remember all the nuance and variants of these rules, let alone to decide which theorist to follow, especially in the heat of performance?

Arnold, some of you may know, ultimately chose C. P. E. Bach — as had Schenker — as the final arbiter of good taste in deciding the best and final solution for realization. And who would blame him? As Scheibe already noted in 1773, C. P. E. Bach's *Versuch* was probably the most detailed *Kompositionslehre* of the eighteenth century.

> Whether or not Herr Bach wrote his book for composers, since it is properly about keyboard performance and accompaniment, it nonetheless contains a great quantity of tasteful and sound observations about a large number of harmonic progressions and the proper employment of consonance and dissonance, observations unequaled by any other treatise aimed specifically at the teaching of composition[29].

We can get a sense of what Scheibe (and presumably Schenker) meant simply by observing the detail he goes into about one single signature. For the «chord of the second» (4/2), his

---

[27]. MIZLER 1739.
[28]. ARNOLD 1931.
[29]. SCHEIBE 1773, p. 14.

discussion takes up thirteen full pages along with almost fifty separate examples[30]. Virtually every imaginable voicing, chromatic alteration, and irregular preparation or resolution of the 4/2 chord is itemized and illustrated. The result is one of the most exhaustive and nuanced descriptions of North German *Empfindsam* practice to be found in the entire corpus of pedagogical writings for the time. No other thorough-bass treatise in subsequent generations comes close to the detail and variety Bach offers.

But as a text to learn accompaniment, it is a formidable challenge. It is no wonder, then, that Arnold's rules for realizing chord signatures proves so frustrating as a pedagogical text, based as they are on Bach's treatise. As I began to learn to read and translate those thickets of signatures into actual sounds on my harpsichord (built at home as many of us did in the 1970s from a Zuckerman kit), I was continually anxious that I was committing some inappropriate doubling, hidden parallel fifth, or unresolved dissonance that C. P. E. Bach would surely have disapproved.

Of course, not everyone agreed that thoroughbass and composition were equivalent, as we have already seen in the case of Johann Mattheson. Georg Michael Telemann (the Grandson of Georg Philipp) was another critic who objected to the complexity of Bach's magnum opus, reminding readers that «thoroughbass does not deal with composition, but above all, simple accompaniment»[31].

Still, the conflation is not without some justification. After all, in the eighteenth century, it was common to pair the skills of composition and harmony with accompaniment as being virtually identical. Countless treatises of the time are entitled (with adjustments in language) as 'Treatise of Harmony and Accompaniment' or 'Manual of the Thoroughbass and Composition'[32]. But in most of these treatises (particularly towards the end of the century), figured bass meant less a means of accompaniment than a shorthand notation for harmony. These authors would argue that 'accompaniment' (or *Generalbass* for the Germans) was simply another name for composition and harmony. You remember those repeated designations I mentioned of the thoroughbass as the 'fundamentum' of compositional knowledge. By the later eighteenth century, 'accompaniment' had far less to do with realizing a continuo part than the learning of harmony.

The treatises of Marpurg and Kirnberger are illustrative. Both authors were active in Berlin with a circle of musicians associated with J. S. Bach. (Ironically, both actually claimed to be authorative heirs of Bach the teacher, even if there is no evidence either one every studied

---

30. BACH 1762, pp. 97-109.

31. TELEMANN 1773, 'Preface'.

32. CAMPION 1716, RAMEAU 1722, HEINICHEN 1728, GERVAIS 1733, MARPURG 1755-1758, LE BŒUF 1766, HECK 1780, KIRNBERGER 1781, RODOLPHE 1785, MILLER 1787. Interestingly, a number of Italian pedagogues often conflated accompaniment not with harmony, but rather with counterpoint in their treatise titles: BRUSCHI 1711, FENAROLI 1775, SACCHI 1780.

directly with the Leipzig Master.) But both their treatises on the *Generalbass*[33] are more about harmony than they are about continuo practice, despite their titles. I think you'd get a very misleading idea about Bach's pedagogy of the thoroughbass through the texts of either Marpurg or Kirnberger.

It is not that we do not know much about Bach's continuo playing. We actually have surprisingly detailed reports that describe it. One by Johann Christian Kittel, evidently the last of Bach's students, and one who lived into the nineteenth century, is especially interesting. He reported that:

> One of his most capable pupils always had to accompany on the harpsichord. It will easily be guessed that no one dared to put forward a meager thorough-bass accompaniment. Nevertheless, one always had to be prepared to have Bach's hands and fingers intervene among the hands and fingers of the player and, without getting in the way of the latter, furnish the accompaniment with masses of harmonies that made an even greater impression than the unsuspected close proximity of the teacher[34].

One might suspect based on Kittel's report that Bach's own realizations of the figured-bass would have been as complex as, say, one of his chorale harmonizations, with intricate four-part counterpoint or something that we could find in C. P. E. Bach's *Versuch*, with its obsessive focus on voice leading details.

Yet, a very differing picture of Bach's figured-bass pedagogy comes from a more recent study led by Robin Leaver and Derek Remeš. Both these scholars have discovered convincing documentation that the realization of chorales in the circle of Bach's students could be actually quite a simple matter. Based on their recent analysis of a manuscript now in the Sibley Library at the Eastman School of Music, it seems that Bach's students may have begun learning the figured bass with a simplified two voiced skeleton of a choral melody and bass line that would then be filled in by the right hand ex tempore, whether figured or not[35]. Later lessons, it seems, would have the student invent his own bass under the choral melody and then fill that in. The *Choralbuch*, as this method is called, was perhaps something of a North-German version of the Neapolitan partimento. In both cases, the realization by the keyboardist was something inculcated viscerally as finger knowledge — and not necessarily laden with too much complexity or over-rationalization[36].

---

[33]. MARPURG 1755-58, KIRNBERGER 1781.

[34]. *BACH READER* 1998, p. 323.

[35]. LEAVER – REMEŠ 2018.

[36]. See also REMEŠ 2021 for a good summary of these recent discoveries and their implications for future Bach scholarship.

But luckily for us, it is not a question of choosing between one or the other. Obviously, there have been multiple styles of figured bass realization in the past, and as well as multiple ways to learn these styles. And it is not always possible to reconcile these differences into a single uniform style or pedagogy.

This was true even in the partimento tradition. In his brilliant dissertation that was published in 2015, Peter van Tour has laid out for us two competing schools of partimento stemming from the respective teaching of Francesco Durante and Leonardo Leo, with students emerging from each atelier with differing skills and styles leading to professions in the court and Church, respectively[37]. In some ways, it was the eighteenth-century equivalent of premier league rivalries.

But why should we be surprised? Since when were teachers of music not a bickering lot possessing strong egos and holding righteously to their own approach in the classroom? Marpurg and Kirnberger, as I have just eluded, fought viciously over which one was the true torch bearer of Bach's legacy (while at the same time arguing just as viciously over the question of Rameau's music theory and its value for the understanding of Bach's music.)

Then there is the Paris Conservatory. Founded shortly after the Revolution, the *Conservatoire national de musique et de declamation* quickly became the most celebrated and influential musical institution in all of Europe. As Robert Gjerdigen has laid out in his most recent book, many teachers there became guardians of the partimento inheritance, faithfully teaching its practice well into the twentieth century[38]. But we should not presume that all composition instruction in those hallowed halls followed in lock step.

While there were indeed instructors in the first century of the institution who promoted partimento instruction — including Tomeoni, Catel, Choron, Cherubini, Berton, Fétis, and Vidal — there were those were adamantly opposed to this pedagogy as hopelessly regressive. No one was more critical of this partimenti instruction than was the Bohemian emigre, Anton Reicha. Teaching classes of counterpoint, harmony, and composition in the Paris Conservatory between 1818 and his death in 1836, Reicha fought a continuing battle to drag composition instruction fully into the nineteenth century. And this meant rejecting the partimenti pedagogy he saw his colleagues teaching down the hallways, which he criticized as indoctrinating students to replicate the most conservative and out-moded styles of music from the previous century. Why in the world would a composer want to imitate the powdered-wig galant music of the eighteenth-century court in a post-revolutionary century?

Reicha was also concerned with aspects of the compositional craft to which partimenti had nothing to say: To begin with, there was the craft of writing melodies (something he addressed in his first treatise on melody in 1814); but there was also questions of technique, genre, and

---

[37]. VAN TOUR 2015.
[38]. GJERDINGEN 2020.

style, all topics he addressed by having students undertake a relatively new type of musical study: score analysis! In his major treatises — and presumably in his classes as well — Reicha would ask his students to look at excerpts of music by composers such as Haydn, Mozart, Gluck, Dalayrac and Cimarosa, all as models for inspection and emulation. In addition, he would have those same students study and imitate countless model examples of his own pen that illustrated the most up-to-date harmonies and textures — a pedagogy I have elsewhere called obsessive exemplification and iteration[39].

Musical Form was another concern for Reicha, a topic he addressed in his treatise from 1824, the *Traité de haute composition musicale*. Some of you may know this is where Reicha laid out his famous schematic of sonata form — what he called the *grande coupe binaire*. That is something few teachers of the partimento probably worried about. And then, there was knowledge of orchestration, which he noted had never been part of any compositional curriculum, yet surely was essential for any composer hoping to make a mark in the nineteenth century. You will not be surprised to learn, then, that we can find countless reports of the bad blood that ran between Reicha and his colleagues in the Conservatory, with groups of students aligning in opposition depending on who their teachers were.

I bring up the example of Reicha in the Paris Conservatory not to denigrate the coalition in the conservatory who continued to champion partimento. After all, they constituted a formidable and resilient faction that survived into the twentieth century. Their legacy can be seen in the annual competitions composition students faced in realizing figured bases, fugue subjects, or solfeggio melodies of hair-raising complexity shut in a room with just a few hours to finish a polished realization in four voices. The point I want to make, though, is that this was not all students could learn in the conservatoire. And there were alternative paths an aspiring composer could — and would — take in the nineteenth century that had nothing to do with realizing a figured or unfigured bass. As in music Departments today, there could be many approaches to teaching topics of harmony, counterpoint, and composition, each with its own textbook.

We can hear voices of disapproval regarding the figured bass through the nineteenth century as numerous theorists and composers called out the thoroughbass as an antiquated and stultifying remnant of the ancient regime that was long overdue for a revolutionary overthrow. Berlioz was one such composer. We will not be surprised to learn his composition teacher in the conservatory was Reicha. And like his teacher, he saw nothing of virtue in those competitions in which he was forced to realize a complex figured bass or fugue in four voices.

Others were coming to the same opinion. Heinrich Joseph Vincent published a tract in 1860 entitled *Kein Generalbass Mehr* (in English it would be 'No More Thoroughbass!' — or

---

39. CHRISTENSEN 2021.

maybe even more accurately, 'To Hell with the Thoroughbass!')[40] His objection, it turns out, was precisely the concern of Reicha regarding the continued dominance of the thoroughbass in conservatory teaching that he believed was retarding the progress of music students who were languishing in an outmoded and regressive pedagogical model. It was an «old and uninhabitable building» for the new spirit of unity that he felt his own theory of music offered. To be sure, Vincent was not thinking of partimento style of thoroughbass, which had made relatively little inroads in Germany during the nineteenth century. For that matter, he was not thinking of figured-bass accompaniment. Who would have been? In the middle of the nineteenth century, very few musicians thought it important to learn how to realize a figured bass in a continuo ensemble. Vincent was rather thinking of the persistence of figured bass as an orthography used by harmony teachers (along with Roman numerals) to label and classify ever-increasing numbers of complex harmonies that had come into use by composers.

With voracious opponents like Reicha, Vincent, and Riemann succeeding in their attempts to suppress the study of thoroughbass, it's not a surprise to find that when the first volumes of the Bach Gesellschaft edition started to appear in the second half of the century, many musicians complained that they had no idea how to read and realize the figured bass notations it contained. Along with figured bass, keyboard improvisation had also taken a drastic downward turn in the second half of the nineteenth century as we can read in Dana Gooley's fabulous book on the history of Romantic improvisation[41]. Robert Schumann illustrates this rapid change clearly. While he began his compositional career as an inveterate improviser on the piano which he claimed inspired some of his best piano works, at some point in the 1840s, Schumann had a change of heart. He began to regret the hours he had wasted meandering at the keyboard or in salon showcases. Instead, he gave up improvising and embraced a more conservative ethic in which crafting a composition required thought, reflection, and constant revision while sitting at a desk. It is not a coincidence, I think, that the general decline of improvisation as a cultural phenomenon in Biedermeier society coincided with the precipitous decline of partimento as a living practice, along with the rise of a *Werktreue* esthetic — the vaunted Work Concept.

By the end of the nineteenth century, then, figured bass really had become something of a lost art save for a tenuous hold among a handful of conservative instructors. All you need do is look at some of the first editions of the operas of Rameau or Monteverdi published in the early twentieth century to realize how little editors actually knew about the *basso continuo*—even if edited by the likes of d'Indy or Saint-Saëns.

It was only as the twentieth century progressed that we begin to see a slow recovery and rehabilitation of figured-bass pedagogy, one that comes in tandem with the first stirrings of

---

40. VINCENT 1860.
41. GOOLEY 2018.

professional musicology. Studies by Otto Kinkeldey, Arnold Dometsch, and Max Schneider all began the slow process of resuscitating this lost practice of continuo realization. But even then, widespread understanding and practice of the continuo took time to take root in the post war era as the first major stirrings of an early — music performance revival began to take root. Well, we know the rest of that history.

The conclusion to my ruminations on the peregrinations of figured bass and its many ups and downs over the centuries is that a wide gap seems to have always existed between the messy and gloriously diverse historical practices of this skill and the later appropriations — and sometimes distortions — of that practice as theoretical and even aesthetic ideals. It is all too convenient today to equate the figured bass with any variety of apparently synonymous or derivative practices and skills: *partitura*, the basso continuo, thoroughbass, accompaniment, partimenti, *fundamenta*, and even 'harmony' or 'composition'. Yet, this conflates — and thereby diminishes — the miraculous flexibility of these Arabic numbers when attached to a musical bass staff.

Those bass lines with figures above them are more than just inert signs waiting to be mechanically translated into sounds; they are ciphers waiting to be interpreted, used and reimagined in a multitude of possibilities. After all, if that was not the case, we would have nothing to talk about in this book. Just as there is no single, uniform and homogenized kind of figured-bass realization that we can impose upon all eighteenth-century practice in all places, styles, and genres, so too is there no single meaning for us today of the figured bass. For each generation, it seems, figured bass has something new to say, though it rarely gives up its secrets without a fight. So here is hoping we have many more interesting battles ahead. Our lessons on the figured bass may not be over just yet.

BIBLIOGRAPHY

ARNOLD 1931
ARNOLD, Franck T. *The Art of Accompaniment from a Thorough-Bass as Practiced in the XVIIth & XVIIIth Centuries*, (1931), New York, Dover Publications, 1970.

BACH 1762
BACH, Carl Philipp Emanuel. *Versuch über die wahre Art das Clavier zu spielen. Zweite Teil*, Berlin, George Ludewig Winter, 1762.

BACH READER 1998
Bach Reader, edited by Hans David and Arthur Mendel, New York, Norton, ²1998.

BARAGWANATH 2020
BARAGWANATH, Nicolas. *The Solfeggio Tradition: A Forgotten Art of Melody in the Long Eighteenth Century*, Oxford-New York, Oxford University Press, 2020.

BORGIR 1987
BORGIR, Taraldh. *The Performance of the Basso Continuo in Italian Baroque Music*, Ann Arbor (MI), UMI, 1987.

BRUSCHI 1711
BRUSCHI, Antonio. *Regole per il contrapunto, e per l'accompagnatura del basso continuo*, Lucca, Venturini, 1711.

CALLAHAN 2017
CALLAHAN, Michael. 'Learning Tonal Counterpoint through Keyboard Improvisation in the Twenty-first Century', in: GUIDO 2017, pp. 185-204.

CAMPION 1716
CAMPION, François. *Traité d'accompagnement et de composition selon la règle des octaves de musique*, Paris, G. Adam, 1716.

CHRISTENSEN 1992
CHRISTENSEN, Thomas. 'The *Règle de l'octave* in Thorough-Bass Theory and Practice', in: *Acta Musicologica*, LXIV/2 (1992), pp. 91-117.

CHRISTENSEN 2004
ID. 'Fundamentum, fundamental, basse fondamentale', in: *Handwörterbuch der musikalischen Terminologie, im Auftrag der Kommission fur Musikwissenschaft der Akademie der Wissenschaften und der Literatur zu Mainz*, edited by Hans Heinrich Eggebrecht *et. al.*, vol. XXXVII, Stuttgart, Steiner, 2004.

CHRISTENSEN 2017
ID. 'The Improvisatory Moment', in: GUIDO 2017, pp. 9-24.

CHRISTENSEN 2021
ID. 'Reicha's *Cours de composition musicale*: a Textbook for the New Century', in: *Antoine Reicha and the Making of the Nineteenth-Century Composer*, edited by Fabio Morabito and Louise Bernard de Raymond, Bologna, Ut Orpheus Edizioni, 2021 (Quaderni Clementiani, 5), pp. 291-316.

DAHLHAUS 1985
DAHLHAUS, Carl. 'Das 18. Jahrhundert als Musikgeschichtliche Epoche', in: *Die Musik des 18. Jahrhunderts*, Laaber, Laaber Verlag, 1985, pp. 1-8.

DUBUGRARRE 1754
DUBUGRARRE. *Méthode plus courte et plus facile que l'ancienne pour l'accompagnement du clavecin*, Paris, L'auteur, [1754].

FELLERER 1930
FELLERER, Karl G. 'Das Partimentospiel, eine Aufgabe des Organisten im 18. Jahrhundert', in: *International Society for Musical Research: First Congress*, edited by Peter Wagner and Wilhelm Merian, Guildford, Billing, 1930, pp. 109-112.

FIGURED BASS: THEN AND NOW

FENAROLI 1775
FENAROLI, Fedele. *Regole musicali per i principianit di cembalo nel sonar coi numeri e per i principianti di contrapunto*, Naples, Massola, 1775.

GERVAIS 1733
GERVAIS, Laurent. *Méthole pour l'accompagnement du clavecin*, Paris, Boivin, 1733.

GJERDINGEN 2007
GJERDINGEN, Robert O. *Music in the Galant Style*, Oxford-New York, Oxford University Press, 2007.

GJERDINGEN 2020
ID. *Child Composers in the Old Conservatories: How Orphans Became Elite Musicians*, Oxford-New York, Oxford University Press, 2020.

GOOLEY 2018
GOOLEY, Dana. *Fantasies of Improvisation*, Oxford-New York, Oxford University Press, 2018.

GUIDO 2017
GUIDO, Massimiliano. *Studies in Historical Improvisation from «Cantare super Librum» to «Partimenti»*, Abingdon-New York, Routledge, 2017.

HECK 1780
HECK, John Caspar. *A Complete System of Harmony, or a Regular and Easy Method to Attain a Fundamental Knowledge and Practice of the Thorough Bass*, London, the Author, 1780.

HEINICHEN 1728
HEINICHEN, Johann. *Der General-Bass in der Composition*, Dresden, the Author, 1728.

HOLTMEIER 2017
HOLTMEIER, Ludwig. *Rameaus langer Schatten. Studien zur deutschen Musiktheorie des 18. Jahrhunderts*, Hildesheim, Georg Olms Verlag, 2017.

IJZERMAN 2018
IJZERMAN, Job. *Harmony, Counterpoint, Partimento: A New Method Inspired by Old Masters*, Oxford, Oxford University Press, 2018.

KELLNER 1732
KELLNER, David. *Treulicher Unterricht im General-Bass*, Hamburg, Kissner, 1732.

KIRNBERGER 1781
KIRNBERGER, Johann Philipp. *Grundsätze des Generalbasses als erste Linien zur Composition*, Berlin, Hummel, 1781.

Le Bœuf 1766
Le Bœuf, Francois-Henry. *Traité d'harmonie et règles d'accompagement servans à la composition*, Paris, Bureau musical, 1766.

Leaver – Remeš 2018
Leaver, Robin – Remeš, Derek. 'J. S. Bach's Chorale-Based Pedagogy: Origins and Continuity', in: *BACH: Journal of the Riemenschneider Bach Institute*, xlviii-xlix/1-2 (2018), pp. 116-150.

Marpurg 1755-1758
Marpurg, Friedrich Wilhelm. *Handbuch bey dem Generalbasse und der Composition*, Berlin, J. J. Schutzens, 1755-1758.

Mattheson 1722
Mattheson, Johann. *Critica Musica*, Hamburg, Kissner, 1722.

Mattheson 1731
Id. *Grosse General-Bass Schule*, Hamburg, Kissner, 1731.

Mattheson 1735
Id. *Kleine General-Bass Schule*, Hamburg, Kissner, 1735.

Miller 1787
Miller, Edward. *Elements of Thorough Bass and Composition*, London, Longman, 1787.

Mizler 1739
Mizler, Lorenz Christoph. *Anfangs-Gründe des General Basses, nach mathematischer Lehr-Art abghandelt*, Leipzig, the Author, 1739.

Niedt 1710
Niedt, Friedrich Erhardt. *Musikalische Handleitung*, Hamburg, Spieringk, 1710.

Pixner 1789
Pixner, Sebastian. *Kann man nicht in zwei oder drei Monaten die Orgel gut und regelmäßig schlagen lernen?, Mit Ja beantwortet und dargethan vermittelst einer Einleitung zum Generalbasse*, Landshut, Hagen, 1789.

Rameau 1722
Rameau, Jean-Philippe. *Traité de l'harmonie*, Paris, Ballard, 1722.

Remeš 2021
Remeš, Derek. 'Bach's Chorale Pedagogy', in: *Rethinking Bach*, edited by Bettina Varwig, Oxford-New York, Oxford University Press, 2021, pp. 271-288.

Riemann 1922
Riemann, Hugo. *Handbuch der Musikgeschichte. 1, Part 2: 'Das Generalbasszeitalter'*, Leipzig, Breitkopf und Härtel, [2]1922.

FIGURED BASS: THEN AND NOW

RODOLPHE 1785
RODOLPHE, Jean Joseph. *Théorie d'accompagnement et de composition*, Paris, Richault, 1785.

SACCHI 1780
SACCHI, Giovenale. *Delle Quinte Successive nel Contrappunto e delle regole degli Accompagnamenti*, Milan, per C. Oresta stamperia Malatesta, 1780.

SÁNCHEZ-KISIELEWASKA 2017
SÁNCHEZ-KISIELEWASKA, Olga. 'The Rule of the Octave in First-Year Undergraduate Theory; Teaching in the Twenty-First Century with Eighteenth-Century Strategies', in: *Journal of Music Theory Pedagogy*, XXXI (2017), pp. 113-134.

SANGUINETTI 2012
SANGUINETTI, Giorgio. *The Art of Partimento: History, Theory, and Practice*, Oxford-New York, Oxford University Press, 2012.

SCHEIBE 1773
SCHEIBE, Johann. *Über die musikalische Composition*, Leipzig, Schwickert, 1773.

SCHENKER 1930
SCHENKER, Heinrich. 'Rameau oder Beethoven? Erstarrung oder Geistiges Leben in der Musik?', in: *Das Meisterwerk in der Musik. 3*, Vienna, Drei Masken Verlag, 1930, pp. 11-24 [Translated by Ian Bent *The Masterwork in Music: A Yearbook. 3*, edited by William Drabkin, Cambridge, Cambridge University Press, 1997, pp. 1-8].

TELEMANN 1773
TELEMANN, Georg Michael. *Unterricht im Generalbass-Spielen*, Hamburg, Bock, 1773.

VAN TOUR 2015
VAN TOUR, Peter. *Counterpoint and Partimento: Methods of Teaching Composition in Late Eighteenth-Century Naples*, Uppsala, Acta Universitatis Upsaliensis, 2015 (Studia musicologica Upsaliensia. Nova Series, 25).

VINCENT 1860
VINCENT, Heinrich Josef. *Kein Generalbass mehr! Dafür: der Geist der Einheit*, Vienna, Wallishausser, 1860

[VON FREUDENBERG] 1728
[VON FREUDENBERG, (Fraulein) ?]. *Kurtze Anführung zum General-Bass darinnen die Regeln, welche bey Erlernung des General-Basses zu wissen nöthig, kürtzlich und mit wenig Worten enthalten. Allen Anfängern des Claviers zu nützlichen Gebrauch zusammen gesetzet*, Leipzig, A. Martini, 1733.

WEBSTER 2004
WEBSTER, James. 'The Eighteenth Century as a Music-Historical Period?', in: *Eighteenth-Century Music*, I/1 (March 2004), pp. 47-60.

«With Regard to the Now Prevailing Taste in Music»: The Music Theoretical Work of Johann Gottfried Vierling (1750-1813)

Stephan Lewandowski

(Brandenburg University of Technology Cottbus-Senftenberg)

Johann Gottfried Vierling *is a child of the Thuringian mountains*[1] — with these words begins a biography of Vierling written in 1922 by Karl Paulke. This statement points out right at the beginning that the organist, composer and music theorist — who was born in 1750 in the small south-western Thuringian village of Metzels near Meiningen — was a local hero, who remained true to his home region throughout his life, and whose stations in life were limited to a narrow geographical radius.

At the age of 13, Vierling became a pupil at the Lyceum in Schmalkalden. Just five years later, in 1768, he was appointed there to succeed the Schmalkalden cantor Johann Nikolaus Tischer (1707-1774), who was in poor health. Later publications also identify Vierling as a student of Carl Philipp Emanuel Bach (1714-1788) and Johann Philipp Kirnberger (1721-1783)[2]. However, neither of these is regarded as certain at the present time. The early recognition of the very high musical quality of Vierling's works may have led to the assumption that an author of such excellent compositions must have been apprenticed to a Bach son and/or an important Bach student.

Vierling published several works on music theory and composed several collections of educational pieces for organ, all of which were printed during his lifetime. Additionally, several sonatas for piano, works for chamber music ensembles and songs were published. In addition to the printed works, Paulke lists numerous handwritten cantatas, further vocal works, an opera and two symphonies[3].

---

[1]. Paulke 1922, p. 439: «Johann Gottfried Vierling ist ein Kind der Thüringer Berge».

[2]. See Kretzschmar 1895, p. 678.

[3]. Paulke 1922, pp. 452ff. Stefan Garthoff deals with Vierling in an essay on forgotten symphonic composers of the 18th and 19th centuries, Lewandowski 2016, pp. 118-125.

In 2008, Folker Froebe brought about a small renaissance of Vierling's music theory within the German-speaking scene of music theory when he published a new edition of his theoretical-practical textbook *Attempt at a Guide to Preluding for the Untrained, Explained with Examples by Johann Gottfried Vierling | Organist in Schmalkalden*[4]. Froebe explained and commented on the theories contained in the textbook, which is as short as it is dense in content, in two essays[5]; he also placed these theories in their contemporary historical contexts and proposed the use of Vierling's writing for the present historically informed teaching of music theory.

Nevertheless, Vierling's music-theoretical œuvre is far more diverse and comprehensive. The following theoretical-practical textbooks have been rediscovered and made easily accessible today:

• *Short Introduction to Thoroughbass*, Kassel, [1789][6];

• *Attempt at a Guide to Preluding for the Untrained, Explained with Examples by Johann Gottfried Vierling | Organist in Schmalkalden*, Leipzig, [1794][7];

• *General Instruction in Thorough Bass with Regard to the Now Prevailing Taste in Music, Explained by Apt Examples*, 2 vols., Leipzig 1805 and 1807[8].

The earliest of these writings is the *Short Introduction to Thorough Bass*[9]. In the preface to this manual, the author explains that the work «was not actually intended for printing»[10], but was originally intended for his students as supplementary literature for personal private lessons. It goes on to say that the publication «is admittedly only an excerpt from larger works»[11]. In a footnote, it is pointed out that these are works by «S. Bach, Kirnberger, and Marpurg»[12], from which quotations are made (obviously in terms of content, but not literally). Exactly which works these are must remain speculation, yet the selection of music-theoretical textbooks in question is a manageable one. Vierling probably refers to

• Bach, Johann Sebastian. *Regulations and Principles for Four-part Playing of Thorough Bass or Accompagnement for His Scholars in Music*, Leipzig, 1738[13];

• Kirnberger, Johann Philipp. *Principles of Thorough Bass as First Guidelines to Composition*, Berlin, 1781[14];

---

[4]. VIERLING 2008.

[5]. FROEBE 2008, FROEBE 2010.

[6]. VIERLING [1789].

[7]. VIERLING [1794], see also FROEBE 2008.

[8]. VIERLING 1805-1807. A list of Vierling's theoretical textbooks can also be found in LEWANDOWSKI 2020, p. 132.

[9]. VIERLING [1789].

[10]. *Ibidem*, Vorbericht [foreword]: «eigentlich nicht zum Druck bestimmt war».

[11]. *Ibidem*: «freilich nur Auszug aus größeren Werken ist».

[12]. *Ibidem*, footnote: «S. Bach, Kirnberger und Marpurg».

[13]. BACH 1738.

[14]. KIRNBERGER 1781.

• Marpurg, Friedrich Wilhelm. *Manual for Thorough Bass and Composition*, 3 vols., Berlin, 1755-1762[15].

That Vierling's writing is a modern theoretical treatise of the late 18th century, by a well-read and informed author who is absolutely up-to-date, is proven, among other things, by the coexistence of 'old' thorough bass theory and a thought process based on chord inversions. For example, the arrangement of the rules (paragraphs) differs significantly from that of a thorough bass school from the first half of the 18th century. In order to illustrate such a difference, the following discussion briefly highlights essential features of older textbooks on thorough bass, which at the end of the 18th century could be considered conventional and partly outdated both in terms of content and didactic approaches.

After the root position chord, the sixth chord is usually introduced in these older textbooks. It represents an independent type of chord and has numerous variants — depending from its position on certain scale degrees of the major or minor scale — and is explicitly not understood as the first inversion of the preceding root position chord (see Ex. 1a). The six four chord (which can be interpreted as the second inversion of the root position chord) appears much later. It is understood as a combination of the *quarta syncopata* with the *sexta syncopata*, the latter being the enrichment with thirds of the former. The chord usually is placed either on the I or on the V scale degree (Ex. 1b).

The difference between traditional and newer arrangements becomes even clearer with regard to the seventh chord. Its inversions are usually understood as representatives of the sixth chord family in the thorough bass theory of the first half of the 18th century and are introduced accordingly early on. The three four chord, explained already in the third exercise of the text book, is understood as a sixth chord of the second scale degree enriched with a fourth (in French treatises often named *petite sixte*, see Ex. 1c). The five six chord is the most common representative of the IV scale degree, provided that the bass line is led stepwise upwards subsequently (Ex. 1d). The four two chord is placed either on the IV scale degree, if the bass line continues stepwise downwards (Ex. 1e), or on the I scale degree within a typical Baroque opening model, commonly known as *initial cadence* (Ex. 1f).

All of the latter chords, the four three chord on the II scale degree, the five six chord on the VII scale degree, and the four two chord either on the V or on the I scale degree, are not related to their root position form, the seventh chord, which itself is usually introduced relatively late, not uncommonly in the context of a sequence of falling fifths, to be explained as chain of dominant chords (Ex. 1g).

The following exercises from Jean-François Dandrieu's (1682-1738) teaching book on thorough bass (Ex. 1a-g) may serve as an example to illustrate these facts[16]. Although

---

15. Marpurg 1755-1762.

16. Dandrieu 1719, excerpts reprinted in Christensen 1997.

Dandrieu belongs to the great masters of the French thorough bass tradition, which must be fundamentally distinguished from the German and Italian ones, the fact remains that French textbooks written at the beginning of the 18th century represent pedagogical models whose influences are also to be seen in numerous German-language textbooks of the time and the immediately following period.

Ex. 1a-g: Excerpts from exercises after DANDRIEU 1719, reproduced after CHRISTENSEN 1997.

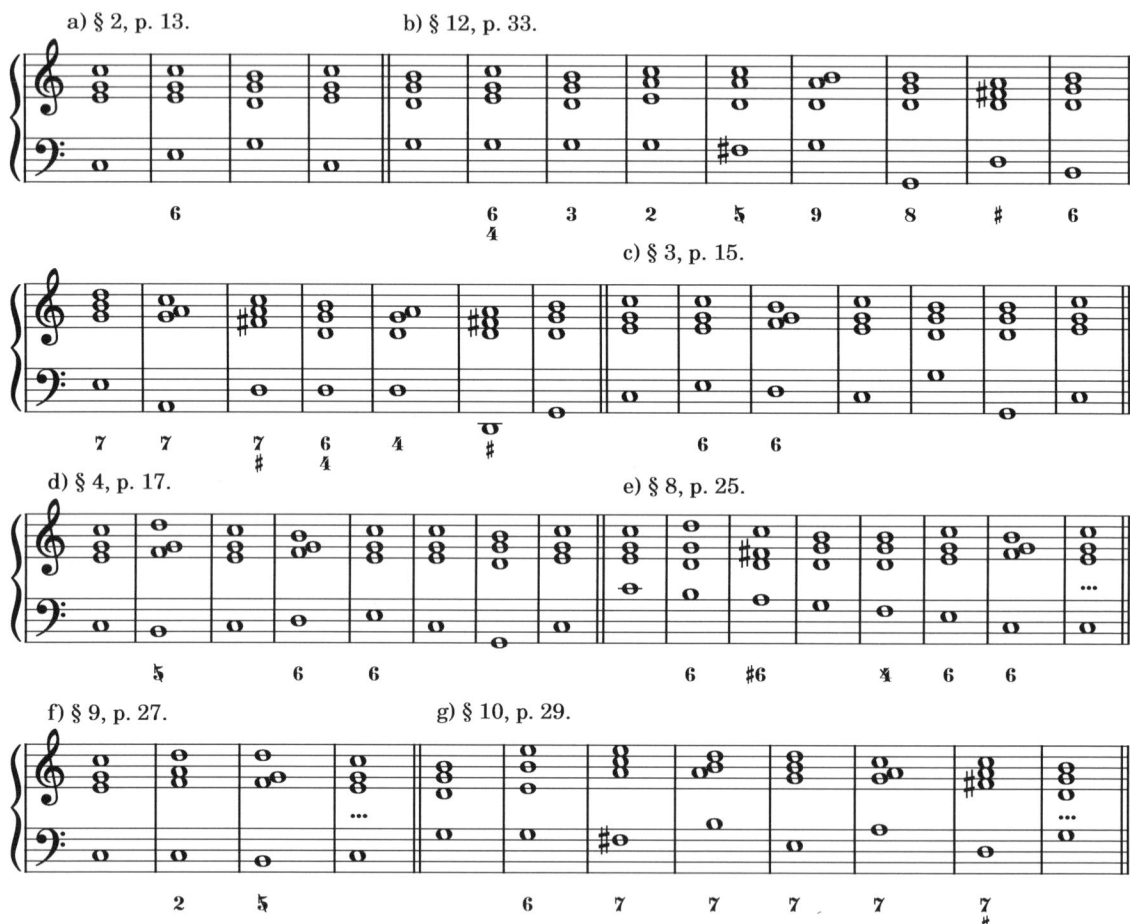

In comparison, the sequence of exercises in Vierling's textbook is typically different in the context of a more modern arrangement: the root position chord («proper triad, or chord»[17]) is followed by the sixth chord as its first inversion. The seventh chord that follows is then also presented in all its various inversions. The fact that the six four chord is introduced as late as in

---

17.   VIERLING [1789], p. 5: «ordentlichen Dreiklang, oder Accord».

a traditional textbook, is even pointed out by the author as an oversight[18]. All in all, Vierling's earlier and shorter treatise on thorough bass otherwise presents itself as a typical textbook with typical contents for its time.

The later two-volume treatise on thorough bass (the first volume appeared in 1805, the second in 1807[19]) was originally intended as an expanded version of the *Short Introduction to Thorough Bass*. The work on this, however, evidently led to the creation of a completely new comprehensive book. The addition to the title «With Regard to the Now Prevailing Taste in Composition» indicates the book's ambition: on the one hand, it wants to preserve conservative theoretical-practical education with the help of thorough bass, but on the other, it also wants to show ways in which traditional teaching methods can continue to serve contemporary stylistic developments in music or how musical innovations are rooted in tradition. Thus, according to Vierling's approach, modern stylistic elements do not necessarily require new music-theoretical systems. Nevertheless, Vierling's later thorough bass teaching is, in comparison to the earlier one, an educational book of a completely different character. Not only are rules presented and explained in individual progressively advancing paragraphs and illustrated with examples, but concrete tasks for practicing and applying the rules are also given. The first such exercise appears on p. 15f., where several short given bass lines are printed, preceded by the following: «The learner should now set the following short examples in chords, in three positions, transpose them into several keys and observe the following rules»[20]. The training material is comprised of written exercises in compositional technique and performance of them on the instrument, as well as transposing these exercises. In this way, the material is already completely foreshadowing the tradition of 19th century textbooks that were published to accompany lessons at conservatories or comparable institutions as well as those used for self-study.

While the content of the first volume of *General Instruction in Thorough Bass* hardly goes beyond the *Short Introduction to Thorough Bass*, the second volume contains music-theoretical constructs that seem almost futuristic. At the beginning of the second volume, Vierling gradually creates a large number of chords whose root positions consist of all possible combinations of diminished, minor, major and augmented thirds as well as diminished, major and minor fifths over a fundamental tone. In ch. 18, the resulting combinations are listed in a diagram, whereby the author points out that «no use is to be made of the triad at 7 and 12»[21]. Ten chord types remain; chords no. 4 and 8 can only be performed in three parts.

---

[18]. *Ibidem*, p. 12.

[19]. Vierling 1805-1807.

[20]. *Ibidem*, vol. i, pp. 15ff.: «Folgende kurze Beispiele setze nun der Lernende in Akkorden, in dreien Lagen aus, versetze sie in mehrere Tonarten und beobachte folgende Regeln».

[21]. *Ibidem*, vol. ii, p. 15: «vom Dreyklang bei 7 und 12 kein Gebrauch zu machen».

Ex. 2: Chord types after VIERLING 1805-7, vol. II, ch. 18, p. 15.

Although it becomes apparent through given musical examples that the chord types that Vierling defines as such are mainly vertical snapshots of emerging harmonies in the course of linear-contrapuntal procedures (mostly syncopations), their musical-practical relevance nevertheless remains questionable at times. Without giving a concrete example, however, Vierling is of the opinion: «The fact that the [chords] in this supplement [...] [meaning the second volume] are all usable and applicable is shown by the compositions of the present best masters»[22].

The foregoing considerations place Vierling's *Attempt at a Guide to Preluding for the Untrained*[23] as both the most traditional as well as by far the shortest of his music-theoretical writings. Strictly speaking, the author's efforts to preserve the tradition of preluding, which was gradually losing importance towards the end of the 18th century, are only a very small part of a considerable body of music-theoretical work. What further sets this educational book apart from Vierling's other writings is its extraordinarily practice-oriented treatment of music-theoretical craft. With only a few rules (and correspondingly little text), the author explains how to improvise organ preludes within only 25 paragraphs, which extend over only 31 pages. With regard to Vierling's teaching pace, the addition in the title of the textbook «for the Untrained» must be put into perspective.

The harmonic-contrapuntal basis for Vierling's explanations is a version of the rule of the octave, which the author presents in the third paragraph[24]. In connection to this, several variants are described: on the II scale degree, for example, one has the option of using either the sixth chord or the four three chord; on the V scale degree, either the root position chord or the seventh chord is indicated, at least in the case of the ascending major scale, according to the given graph (see Ex. 3).

Furthermore, ch. 2 is of some interest. Even before the rule of the octave is described (which Vierling calls the «seat of the chords»[25]), modulation is dealt with. Instructions on how

---

22. *Ibidem*, p. 16: «Dass die [Akkorde] in diesem Nachtrage [...] [gemeint ist der zweite Band] alle brauchbar und anwendbar sind, zeigen die Kompositionen der jetzigen besten Meister».

23. VIERLING [1794].

24. *Ibidem*, ch. 3, pp. 4ff.

25. *Ibidem*, p. 4: «Sitz der Akkorde».

Ex. 3: Rule of the octave after Vierling [1794], ch. 3, p. 5.

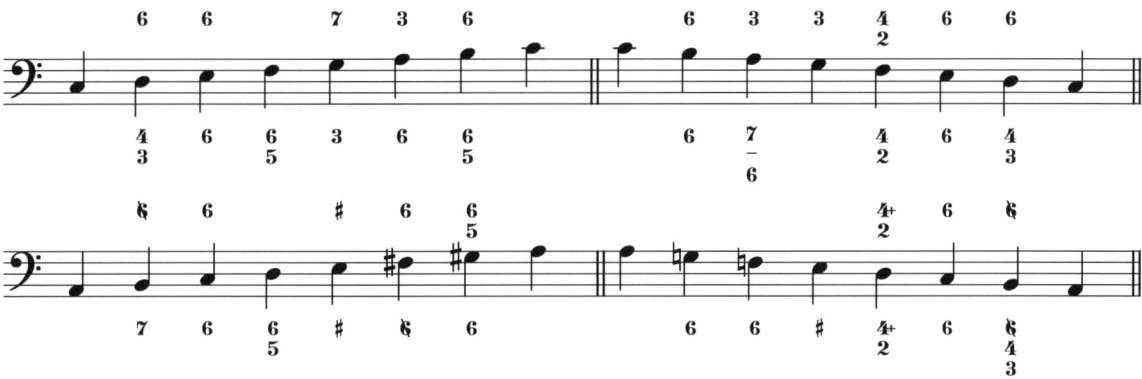

to modulate «from one key to another in a regular manner»[26] are initially given abstractly and without concrete note examples in only a few words:

> In a piece, one modulates in a proper manner only in the most related tones,
> and these are
>   a) in the hard key [major]: the fifth, sixth, third, fourth, and second.
>   b) In the soft key [minor]: the third, fifth, fourth, sixth, and seventh[27].

What at first appears to be a conventional set of rules for modulation contains, on closer inspection, a special feature in contrast to numerous other music theory textbooks: Vierling gives a hierarchy of key relationships. The most closely related keys are mentioned first (the v scale degree in major, then the iii scale degree in minor etc.), after that the degree of relationship decreases steadily as one moves to the right in the two lines.

Other representations of the same modulation technique do not contain such a hierarchy or only give an example of a possible modulation sequence. The basis of some graphic representations are scale sections to which thirds are added to define the mode (major or minor) of the respective target key. An example of this can be found in the illustration from Ambros Rieder's (1771-1855) treatise on the art of preluding (see Ex. 4)[28].

Vierling's modulation rules do not remain abstract. The author provides musical examples showing how to modulate from C major to G major, A minor, E minor, F major, and D minor[29]. At the end, there is an example in which «tones from other keys are added without

---

26. *Ibidem*, p. 3: «von einem Ton in den anderen auf eine regelmäßige Weise».

27. *Ibidem*: «Man weiche in einem Stücke ordentlicher Weise nur in den verwandtesten Tönen aus, und dieses sind a) in der harten Tonart [Dur]: die Quinte, die Sechste, Terz, Quarte und Sekunde. b) In der weichen Tonart [Moll]: die Terz, Quinte, Quarte, Sechste und Septime».

28. Rieder [1826], p. 12.

29. Vierling [1794], p. 4.

Ex. 4: Rules for modulating after RIEDER [1826], p. 12.

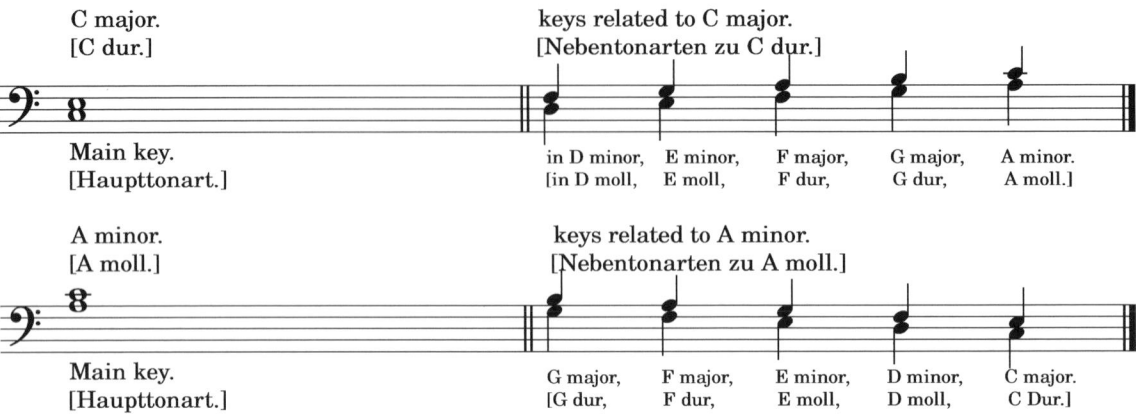

a modulation, because they can be followed by tones that belong to the main tone»[30]. Vierling creates such a case by means of a sequence of sixth chords or six five chords alternating with root position chords over an ascending chromatic bass line, commonly known as the monte sequence.

After giving instructions on diminutions and chord breaks in ch. 18[31], the author very quickly arrives at numerous examples of preludes, which are the result of implementations of the rules presented in the preceding paragraphs. It is worthy of note that the majority of them are written in three parts. Another noteworthy aspect with regard to compositional technique and improvisation is found without comment towards the end of the short manuscript: In ch. 21 and 22, Vierling first gives abstract thorough bass lines, which are then developed into a prelude[32]. It is noticeable that the durations of the bass notes can vary in the arrangement when compared to the thorough bass template: If the note *e* on the second beat of bar 1 is a crotchet in the original, the *e* in the prelude lasts half a bar. The following quaver *d* in the original is even stretched fourfold and takes up the entire space of the first half of bar 2 in the prelude.

Ex. 5: Opening bars of thoroughbass template and prelude after VIERLING [1794], p. 22.

---

[30]. *Ibidem*: «Töne aus anderen Tonarten angebracht werden, ohne daß eine Ausweichung geschiehet, weil wieder Töne darauf folgen können, die dem Hauptton zugehören».

[31]. *Ibidem*, p. 12.

[32]. *Ibidem*, pp. 21ff.

This process, which Vierling apparently takes for granted as he does not bother to give any explanation, provides an important insight into the author's conceptualisation of compositional material and perhaps to what was quite common, or at least possible, in the late 18th century with regard to musical realisations of given thorough bass lines. The sequence of individual bass notes in their succession is obviously of a higher priority and a fixed, unchangeable criterion in comparison to the rhythmic-metrical integration of the bass notes, which allows for numerous variations.

The preceding reflections on Vierling's treatise on the art of preluding are to be the basis for the following analysis of selected passages from his *xxx Easy Three-Part Organ Pieces*[33]. The pieces were published by the Leipzig publishing house Kühnel without a date. Paulke does not include such a collection in his list of printed works, but a collection of three-part organ pieces is mentioned. However, it is stated that it was published by Blatschek in Fulda and that a second edition by Peters in Leipzig exists[34]. Unfortunately, it was not possible for me to find these editions, so it remains open whether these are the same compositions or a different collection is being referred to.

The Sächsische Landes-, Staats- und Universitätsbibliothek has made a collection of three-part organ pieces by Johann Gottfried Vierling, which originates from the Bach Archive in Leipzig, freely available in digital form[35]. This is a copy of Vierling's compositions, which appear in a different order and are attributed to Johann Valentin Bach (1787-1875). TABLE 1 shows a comparison of the arrangements of the pieces in the aforementioned printed editions by the publishers Kühnel and Sonat (left column) and Bach's copy (right column).

---

33. VIERLING n.d., reprint, VIERLING 2015.
34. PAULKE 1922, p. 451.
35. VIERLING [1810].

TABLE 1: ARRANGEMENTS OF THE PIECES WITHIN THE COLLECTION
XXX EASY THREE-PART ORGAN PIECES IN DIFFERENT SOURCES
(VIERLING n.d. and VIERLING 2015 in comparison to VIERLING [1810]).

VIERLING n.d. (publishing house Kühnel) / VIERLING 2015 (Sonat)		VIERLING [1810]
No. 1 in C major	=	No. 10
No. 2 in C major	=	No. 11
No. 3 in C minor	=	No. 12
No. 4 in C minor	=	No. 13
No. 5 in D major	=	No. 14
No. 6 in D major	=	No. 6
No. 7 in D minor	=	No. 15
No. 8 in D minor	=	No. 16
No. 9 in E-flat major	=	No. 17
No. 10 in E-flat major	=	No. 18
No. 11 in E major	=	No. 19
No. 12 in E major	=	No. 20
No. 13 in E minor	=	No. 7
No. 14 in E minor	=	No. 21
No. 15 in F major	=	No. 8
No. 16 in F major	=	No. 22
No. 17 in G major	=	No. 9
No. 18 in G major	=	No. 23
No. 19 in G minor	=	No. 24
No. 20 in G minor	=	No. 25
No. 21 in A major	=	No. 26
No. 22 in A major	=	No. 27
No. 23 in A minor	=	No. 28
No. 24 in A minor	=	No. 29
No. 25 in B-flat major	=	No. 5
No. 26 in B-flat major	=	No. 30
No. 27 in C major	=	No. 1
No. 28 in D minor	=	No. 2
No. 29 in F major	=	No. 3
No. 30 in G major	=	No. 4

The comparison reveals that the printed editions are ordered by key; a feature that is not present in Bach's handwritten copy. The collection begins with two pieces in C major, followed by the variant key of C minor, after which the fundamental tones gradually increase, with only keys that have a maximum of four accidentals (four sharps or three flats). In this way, a logical arrangement is created within the boundaries of the canon of common keys, whereby an additional emphasis is placed on the keys of C major, D minor, F major and G major by giving each of them a third prelude after passing through the regular key sequence — as it were in an appendix (nos. 27-30). The reason for this appendix could lie in the instructive intention of the pieces: «They are only meant to be practice pieces for learners», Vierling writes in the preface to the Kühnel edition[36]. He recommends practising precisely these pieces first (together with no. 25), then proceeding to preludes nos. 6, 13, 15 and 17, and then playing all the remaining pieces[37].

Stefan Rauh, editor of the new edition of Vierling's *xxx Easy Three-Part Organ Pieces*, published by Sonat in 2015, refers to the collection published by Kühnel as the first edition, which served as the source for the new edition and which will also be the basis for the following analytical considerations[38].

The fact that both Vierling's educational book and his organ pieces concentrate on three-part textures seems to testify to the fact that this type of composition was regarded as an aesthetic ideal, the mastery of which was highly desirable both on the instrument and compositionally or improvisationally. In the foreword to the *xxx Easy Three-Part Organ Pieces*, Vierling writes: «The TRIO is one of the most beautiful and pleasant, but also one of the most difficult in execution and performance on the organ»[39]. Such difficulties are then also listed: «Noble and flowing singing, ties and imitations of the voices among themselves are the peculiarities of the same. This peculiarity also makes that texture difficult, just as the performance tends to be made more difficult by the habit of playing the notes of the pedal with the little finger in chorales and other full-voiced pieces»[40]. As the logical result of these characteristics and circumstances, Vierling describes that there are numerous organists who, despite their good improvisational skills, have difficulties in sight-reading even simple trios[41].

Nevertheless, Vierling's organ pieces represent more than a collection of preludes for use by aspiring organists; they provide equally instructive examples both on the level of improvisational and compositional technique. The intention expressed by the composer in the

---

36. Vierling n.d., foreword: «Nur Übungsstücke für Lernende sollen sie sein».

37. *Ibidem.*

38. *Ibidem.*

39. *Ibidem*: «Das TRIO ist eins der schönsten und angenehmsten, aber auch eins der schwersten in der Ausführung und im Vortrag auf der Orgel».

40. *Ibidem*: «Edler und fliessender Gesang, Bindungen und Nachahmungen der Stimmen unter sich sind das Eigenthümliche desselben. Dieses Eigenthümliche macht zugleich die Schwierigkeit im Satze, so wie der Vortrag durch die Gewohnheit, bei Chorälen und andern vollstimmigen Sachen, immer oder mehrentheils die Noten des Pedals mit dem kleinen Finger mitzuspielen, erschwert zu werden pflegt».

41. *Ibidem.*

preface, that he does not wish to provide «models of three-part texture»[42] with these works, is in complete contradiction to their technical sophistication. Several of the pieces have the characteristic that their two upper voices are interchangeable, i.e. they are composed in double counterpoint of the octave. In the Kühnel edition, there are notes on this before the individual pieces; in the new edition, these are summarised on the last page. Three categories of alternative versions of the pieces can be observed. These are listed in the following table together with the pieces in which they are applicable.

Table 2: Categories of Alternative Performance Versions
by Interchangeable Upper Voices in Vierling n.d.

A   first voice one octave lower, second voice one octave higher (nos. 1, 11, 19, 23 and 24)

B   first voice an octave lower, second voice as notated (nos. 3, 16 and 20)

C   first voice as notated, second voice an octave higher (nos. 4, 7, 8, 14, 15, 16 and 20)

It is noticeable that pieces 16 and 20 offer, in addition to their printed version, two further possibilities for their playability by means of octave transpositions of the upper voices. Preludes 2, 5, 6, 9, 10, 12, 13, 17, 18, 21 and 25-30, on the other hand, do not seem to offer any good prospects of playability with octave transpositions of one or both upper voices, or are not composed in double counterpoint. This applies to 16 out of the 30 pieces, which makes the statement in the preface that «most of these pieces are set in octave counterpoint»[43] seem incorrect.

Pieces no. 27-30 are the aforementioned appendices, each of which uses a key previously represented in the collection for the third time, thereby going beyond what was considered normal, and which, moreover, according to the composer's recommendation, should be practised first, thus representing the supposedly easiest introductory exercises; an absence of exercises on octave transpositions of at least one upper voice in them is therefore not surprising. Of the other pieces without immanent (or at least with difficult or impossible to execute) double counterpoint, two subcategories stand out above all: compositions in which two voices (the two lower ones) take on the function of accompaniment, as in No. 9 and in No. 17, and compositions that go beyond a three-part texture, as is the case in No. 10 and No. 12[44]. In addition, Vierling seems to provide an overall collection of instructive organ compositions in which alternative realisations by means of octavation of upper voices are possible or not. Both groups — pieces with the possibility of voice octavation and pieces without this possibility — are represented in roughly equal numbers in the collection.

---

[42].   *Ibidem*: «gerade nicht Muster des dreistimmigen Satzes».

[43].   *Ibidem*: «die mehresten dieser Stücke sind im Contrapunkt der Octave gesetzt».

[44].   Piece No. 2 in C major also goes beyond a three-part texture, though here this is limited only to occasional notated octavations in the bass part, not to genuinely new tonal material or additional parts.

The following is an attempt to compare the rules and musical examples contained in Vierling's educational book on the art of preluding with the composer's own practice. Selected passages from individual pieces from the previously considered collection will be the subject of the investigations. The starting point for such a comparison shall be schemata theory, which has been a focus of musical analysis in music-theoretical scholarship at least since Robert O. Gjerdingen's groundbreaking publication *Music in the Galant Style*[45]. In a review of Gjerdingen's book, Markus Neuwirth describes the path taken by German-language music theory in this field, especially in comparison to North American music theory: «In many cases, one and the same model has been given divergent descriptions and conceptual coinages in the German-speaking world and in the USA. The English translation by Robert O. Gjerdingen (1990) of Carl Dahlhaus' habilitation thesis *Untersuchungen über die Entstehung der harmonischen Tonalität*, published in 1967, is one of the exceptional cases of a reception of German-language research by American music theory»[46].

The present contribution does not attempt to work out further terminological and textual differences or differentiations of individual models, as they undoubtedly arose in Europe and in America in the wake of the standard works of Dahlhaus and Gjerdingen; rather, the purpose here is to analyse the musical works of a composer with regard to the rules of his own theoretical textbooks and thus to examine the degree of identity or divergence between what is theoretically taught and musical practice. This seems to be a path that has not been taken very far yet, at least with regard to the late 18th and early 19th centuries. The reasons for this may be obvious. A specialisation or differentiation of the profession of a composer and a music theorist had basically been long since taking place in the late 18th century. A musical work that merely satisfies the rules conveyed in theoretical works is all too easily regarded as uninspired and does not necessarily seem worthy of analytical attention. Finally, even in cases of masters who are productive in the fields of both music theory and composition, there is often not necessarily a high degree of congruence between theory and practice, but rather the contrary: the attempt to consciously go beyond typically taught harmonic and contrapuntal rules in artistic works appears to occur frequently.

Over the course of the emergence of historically informed music theory in recent decades, numerous writings and instructional works that were popular in their time — as well as compositions — have been made accessible again, and in some cases rediscovered for modern educational purposes due to a high degree of interlocking between theory and practice

---

[45]. Gjerdingen 2007.

[46]. Neuwirth 2008, p. 401: «Vielfach haben ein und dieselben Modelle im deutschsprachigen Raum und in den USA divergierende Beschreibungen und begriffliche Prägungen erfahren. Die englische Übersetzung von Carl Dahlhaus' 1967 publizierter Habilitationsschrift *Untersuchungen über die Entstehung der harmonischen Tonalität* durch Robert O. Gjerdingen (1990) zählt zu den Ausnahmefällen einer Rezeption der deutschsprachigen Forschung durch die amerikanische Musiktheorie». Neuwirth refers to Dahlhaus 1966 and Dahlhaus 1990.

to the extent that such an approach seems both possible and valuable today. Analysing Vierling via Vierling promises to be rich in content in this respect, since the Schmalkalden organist, composer and music theory teacher can be counted among the few personalities who comment intensively, openly and with great matter-of-factness on their own compositional practice.

As a *point de départ* for this approach, ch. 7-15 in the *Attempt at a Guide to Preluding* are particularly suitable[47], since they provide musical schemata as material for improvisation, for which not only are examples provided within the textbook from ch. 19 onwards for their compositional-practical implementation, mainly in three part setting[48], but which also form the basis for numerous passages in the *xxx Easy Three-Part Organ Pieces*.

The very first piece in the collection (according to the order of the printed editions) may serve to illustrate these facts. It begins with a sequence of ascending fifths, which are recognisable on the accented beats in bars 1-4. The opening bars can be understood as ornamentation of the schema that Vierling introduces in his textbook in ch. 14[49] (see Ex. 6a). A little later, a sequence of falling fifths is heard in the same piece from bar 9 onwards, which corresponds with ch. 8[50] (Ex. 6b).

The fact that thinking in chord inversions is also present in Vierling's treatise on preluding is shown by the fact that in ch. 9 the author presents inversions of the sequence of falling fifths; harmonic-contrapuntal structures, which he obviously conceives as related[51]. Mostly these chord structures and their musical character lead to their conception as independent schemata. The inversions of sequences of falling fifths introduced by Vierling essentially fall into two categories: the sequence of falling thirds, which is created by sixth chords or six five chords alternating with root position chords, and the sequence of alternating sixth chords and four two chords, which has a gradually descending bass line. In Exs. 6c and 6d, the fundamental tones of the respective models are each connected by lines to illustrate their relationship based on chord inversions. These schemata are also found in the *xxx Easy Three-Part Organ Pieces*: Bars 9-13 in No. 2 in C major may be cited as a representative example of a sequence of falling thirds; No. 23 in A minor contains a sequence of sixth chords and four two chords in bars 11-13.

Three other categories of well-known musical schematas, which can already be described as traditional at the time of the composition of Vierling's organ pieces, are included in Vierling's

---

[47]. VIERLING [1794], pp. 6-11.

[48]. *Ibidem*, pp. 13ff.

[49]. *Ibidem*, p. 10.

[50]. *Ibidem*, p. 7.

[51]. *Ibidem*, pp. 7ff., see above all the musical examples a and b on p. 8. Vierling presents here not only variants of the inversions of a sequence of falling fifths, but also its use for modulating. In ch. 10 on p. 9, further, more complex variants of sequences of falling thirds are presented, including one with two successive falling thirds in the bass followed by a second step upwards (see Ex. 6c).

treatise on preluding: ch. 13 describes a romanesca[52], and ch. 15 presents different variants of an opening structure with a pedal point[53]. For each of these categories, Ex. 6e and f gives a musical example from Vierling's compositional practice.

Ex. 6a-f: Musical schemata in den Vierling's *xxx Easy Three-Part Organ Pieces* (Vierling 2015) and their corresponding passages in Vierling's treatise on preluding (Vierling [1794]).

---

52. *Ibidem*, p. 10.
53. *Ibidem*, p. 11.

In this text, only the sequential models presented in Vierling's instructions (and additionally one opening chord structure that is not accompanied by motivic sequencing) have been singled out as musical topoi. Harmonic segments based on the rule of the octave and cadences, are disregarded in the present analytical considerations. If they were included, most of the *xxx Easy Three-Part Organ Pieces* would be completely or almost completely explainable by means of the compositional 'building blocks' and rules taught on only a few pages. To exaggerate, the collection could be seen as an extension of the musical examples provided in the last part of Vierling's textbook[54].

The fact that Vierling's *Attempt at a Guide to Preluding* is by far the most popular of his theoretical instructional works to this day may seem a curiosity at first glance, given that it is a book only 31 pages long and that it was written by a full-time organist from the Thuringian province. However, its popularity is obvious for several reasons. Firstly, it is the compact nature of the text that makes it so valuable: On only a few pages, a complex set of rules is created step by step, mostly without commentary and without extensive derivations, which is intended to serve as a guide to improvisation and the composition of organ preludes. Secondly, it provides an excellent picture of the rules and aesthetic premises that were particularly relevant in practice in Central Germany at the time. Thirdly, it swims against the tide in terms of content: it represents an attempt to preserve a tradition that was dying out at the time it was written — the tradition of preluding — and to pass it on to future generations.

In the latter respect, the textbook was more successful than one might initially assume. In any case, the time span between when it was presumably forgotten and its renaissance in the context of current university research and teaching, at least in the German-speaking world, does

---

54. *Ibidem*, pp. 12ff.

not span the period between Johann Gottfried Vierling's death in 1813 and Folker Froebe's research in the first decade of the new millennium[55]. The treatise found its way out of Thuringia into the English-speaking world: in 1827 it was translated into English by James Alexander Hamilton (1785-1845)[56]. As short and concise as it may be, it is precisely because of its compactness that it represents a weighty contemporary testimony to compositional-practical thinking and music-theoretical teaching around 1800 — a contemporary testimony that proves that even in provincial places, remarkable and noteworthy things can be created.

Bibliography

Bach 1738

Bach, Johann Sebastian. *Vorschriften und Grundsätze zum vierstimmigen Spielen des General-Bass oder Accompagnement für seine Scholaren in der Music*, Leipzig, 1738.

Christensen 1997

Christensen, Jesper Bøje. *Die Grundlagen des Generalbaßspiels im 18. Jahrhundert. Ein Lehrbuch nach zeitgenössischen Quellen*, Kassel, Bärenreiter, ²1997.

Dahlhaus 1966

Dahlhaus, Carl. *Untersuchungen über die Entstehung der harmonischen Tonalität*, Univ. Habil.-Schr., Kiel, Christian-Albrechts-Universität, 1966.

Dahlhaus 1990

Id. *Studies on the Origin of Harmonic Tonality*, translated by Robert O. Gjerdingen, Princeton, Princeton University Press, 1990.

Dandrieu 1719

Dandrieu, Jean-François. *Principes de l'accompagnement du clavecin*, Paris, l'auteur, 1719.

Froebe 2008

Froebe, Folker. '«...so kommt es blos darauf an, dass er [die Gänge] gehörig verbinden lerne». Anmerkungen zu Johann Gottfried Vierlings Versuch einer Anleitung zum Präludieren', in: *Zeitschrift der Gesellschaft für Musiktheorie*, v/2-3 (2008), pp. 371-374.

---

[55]. Froebe's earliest publication of his research on Vierling that I know of was at the 8th Annual Congress of the Gesellschaft für Musiktheorie, held at the University of Music and Performing Arts in Graz from 9-12 October 2008. There, on 10 October 2008, Froebe gave a lecture entitled 'Johann Gottfried Vierling's «Versuch einer Anleitung zum Präludieren für Ungeübtere»: Eine Improvisationslehre um 1800 auf Grundlage der Oktavregel und ihre Potentiale für die gegenwärtige Lehre' in a section chaired by Ludwig Holtmeier. The lecture should essentially correspond to the publication with the identical title in the post-conference book, Froebe 2010.

[56]. Vierling 1827, see also Lewandowski 2020, p. 141.

Froebe 2010
Id. 'Johann Gottfried Vierlings «Versuch einer Anleitung zum Präludieren für Ungeübtere»: Eine Improvisationslehre um 1800 auf Grundlage der Oktavregel und ihre Potentiale für die gegenwärtige Lehre', in: *Musiktheorie als interdisziplinäres Fach*, edited by Christian Utz, Saarbrücken, Pfau, 2010, pp. 49-66.

Gjerdingen 2007
Gjerdingen, Robert O. *Music in the Galant Style*, Oxford, Oxford University Press, 2007.

Kirnberger 1781
Kirnberger, Johann Philipp. *Grundsätze des Generalbasses als erste Linien zur Composition*, Berlin, J. J. Hummel, 1781.

Kretzschmar 1895
Kretzschmar, Johannes. 'Vierling, Johann Gottfried', in: *Allgemeine Deutsche Biographie. 39*, Leipzig, Deutsche Nationalbibliothek, 1895.

Lewandowski 2020
Lewandowski, Stephan. 'Adolph Friedrich Hesse Going West. Influences of the Theoretical School of Johann Christian Heinrich Rinck and Beyond', in: *Tradycje Ślaskiej Muzycznej XV*, edited by Anna Granat-Janki, Wrocław, Akademia Muzyczna im. Karola Lipińskiego we Wrocławiu, 2020, pp. 129-146.

Lewandowski 2016
Lewandowski, Stephan. 'Vergessene Sinfoniker', in: *Warum ist Musik erfolgreich?*, edited by Jörn Arnecke, Hildesheim, Georg Olms, 2016, pp. 117-136.

Marpurg 1755-1762
Marpurg, Friedrich Wilhelm. *Handbuch bey dem Generalbasse und der Composition*, 3 vols. and an Appendix, Berlin, Lange, 1755-1762.

Neuwirth 2008
Neuwirth, Markus. 'Robert O. Gjerdingen, *Music in the Galant Style*, Oxford University Press 2007', in: *Zeitschrift der Gesellschaft für Musiktheorie*, v/2-3 (2008), pp. 401-408.

Paulke 1922
Paulke, Karl. 'Johann Gottfried Vierling', in: *Archiv für Musikwissenschaft*, IV/4 (1922), pp. 439-455.

Rieder [1826]
Rieder, Ambros. *Anleitung zum Präludiren auf der Orgel oder dem Piano-Forte*, Op. 84, Vienna, Diabelli, [1826].

Vierling [1789]
Vierling, Johann Gottfried. *Kurze Anleitung zum Generalbaß*, Kassel, gedruckt in der Waisenhaus-Buchdruckerei, [1789].

Vierling [1794]
Vierling, Johann Gottfried. *Versuch einer Anleitung zum Präludieren für Ungeübtere mit Beispielen erläuter von Johann Gottfried Vierling | Organist zu Schmalkalden*, Leipzig, Breitkopf, [1794].

Vierling 1805-1807
Id. *Allgemeinfasslicher Unterricht im Generalbass mit Rücksicht auf den jetzt herrschenden Geschmack in der Komposition durch treffende Beispiele erläutert*, 2 vols., Leipzig, Johann Friedrich Gleditsch, 1805-1807.

Vierling [1810]
Id. *Sammlung dreistimmiger Orgelstücke*, manuscript, n.p., undated [c.1810], online: <http://sachsen.digital/werkansicht?tx_dlf[id]=6537&tx_dlf[page]=1>, accessed November 2023.

Vierling 1827
Id. *An Instruction to the Art of Preluding and of Extratemporaneous Performance in General: Illustrated by Numerous Examples and Designed for the Use of Students in Harmony & Composition*, translated by James Alexander Hamilton, London, 1827.

Vierling 2008
Id. 'Versuch einer Anleitung zum Präludieren für Ungeübtere, mit Beispielen erläutert von Johann Gottfried Vierling | Organist zu Schmalkalden', in: *Zeitschrift der Gesellschaft für Musiktheorie*, v/2-3 (2008), pp. 375-394, <https://www.gmth.de/zeitschrift/artikel/313.aspx>.

Vierling 2015
Id. *30 leichte dreistimmige Orgelstücke*, edited by Stefan Rauh, Kleinmachnow, Sonat-Verlag, 2015.

Vierling n.d.
Id. *xxx leichte dreystimmige Orgelstücke*, Leipzig, n.d.

Improvisation Pedagogy in Nineteenth-Century Guitar Education

Matthew Paul Mazanek
(Royal Irish Academy of Music, Dublin)

The Rise of Dilettante Education

As commerce grew in late eighteenth-century Europe, working-class and aristocratic families began learning music for recreation. This growing *petite-bourgeois* created a sizeable market in Paris, London, Vienna and other European urban centres, which created a demand for music education aimed towards dilettantes. This movement has its origins with the writings of Johann Friedrich Daube who published several treaties with dilettantes as the intended audience[1]. The guitar, harp and the piano were the three most common instruments for amateurs to learn and the educational materials published between 1760 and 1869 for these instruments can be seen as a distinct contribution to the dilettante educational movement. Publications with dilettantes in mind increased substantially and the methods for guitar were the most abundant[2]. This increased access to educational materials created an educational environment in which the typical concerns of professional musicians could be disregarded in exchange for those specific to leisure learners. Many more treatises incorporated training in figured bass harmonisation, and for the guitar they were indelibly instrument specific, but training in figured bass receded as the cornerstone of music education as arias with printed accompaniments for piano, harp and guitar became more prevalent. The guitar, due to its portability, was still seen as the most useful instrument for accompanying the voice and since the desire to accompany never fell out of fashion, the typical tools to teach harmony from a figured bass began to shift to fit this new format for accompaniment. This shift created a new set of tools to teach accompaniment, which incorporated figured-bass instruction but also included unique devices used to teach spontaneous variation upon existing songs and improvising preludes with modulations. Often this instruction was implicit, a seemingly unremarkable facet of learning an instrument, but slowly it became more explicitly taught before steadily declining around 1860.

---

[1]. Daube 1773, Daube 1797-1798.
[2]. Stenstadvold 2010.

Attitudes on improvisation in the early nineteenth century were conflicted, especially in their relation to amateurs and their private activities. The public commentary on amateur music-culture was rife with allusions to the improvised activities of those learning the guitar and the harp. These two instruments appeared to have the most popular appeal and thus attracted more public remark. The harp and the piano were less likely to acquire such negative connotations, perhaps because of the public reverence for improvised fantasias by touring professionals. The piano was the most common instrument to hear an improvised fantasia, but harpists were known to improvise as well, and this created a documentable public perception towards improvisation[3]. Dana Gooley suggests the term «improvisation imaginary» for the unique attitude and reverence that seemed to be held by critics towards improvised fantasias — it was a sign of sophistication in a musician and seen as a type of perfect performance[4]. Nevertheless, improvising on the guitar was more often derided as a thing amateurs did for enjoyment when gathered among friends and family[5]. This contrast, between the idealised, often romanticised, free expression of the virtuoso and the implicitly criticised, mundane ramblings of amateur 'tinkling', created a conflicted pedagogical space. It was commonly asserted in magazines and newspapers that amateurs were incapable, or at least not expected to improvise their own preludes[6]. One writer in the *Bombay Gazette*, using the pseudonym «Il Fanatico, per la musica», summed up some of the popular ideals regarding dilettantes and improvisation, and described quite clearly his views, stating that improvisation was a sign of a more competent amateur:

> It is right I should so far qualify it as to confine my belief to the great class of untaught men, and the very small class of thoroughly taught, Musicians. The middle class, the amateurs (among whom, I fear, I must be ungallant enough to include nearly the whole generation of Amateur Lady performers since Queen Bess's day) have in general musical ears of the worst class. [...] I except from my musical sentence of condemnation, all and every Lady "pianist" who can tune her own instrument, or her friends harp [...] or my guitar, in half an hour. I will even go a step further Sir and admit that Lady to be an exception to my rule, who will execute a decent extempore second, to any easy melody, an achievement by the way, of which (in spite of pains and penalties I must say), I scarcely ever knew a Lady Amateur capable — though I profess myself unable to give a solution to the phenomenon[7].

---

[3]. *MORNING HERALD* 1827.

[4]. GOOLEY 2018, pp. 106-108.

[5]. One review of a guitar method mentions that either the method or the «ladies instrument» is «remarkably convenient for getting up an extempore "tinkling" at garden parties and boating expeditions». *THE ATLAS* 1828.

[6]. *QUARTERLY MUSICAL MAGAZINE* 1827, p. 248.

[7]. *BOMBAY GAZETTE* 1820.

Improvisation Pedagogy in Nineteenth-Century Guitar Education

Whether this problem was real or imagined, 'the solution' was taken up earnestly by authors of all three of the instruments mentioned but the practice of teaching amateurs to improvise had been a concern in guitar and harp tutors at least as far back as 1760. It appeared often as an implicitly understood aspect of the performance culture of professional musicians and as these rules were disseminated to amateurs, certain conventions and devices were maintained well into the late nineteenth century. Often times, these teaching techniques grew out of the figured bass traditions used by professionals in the seventeenth and eighteenth centuries, and in the guitar tutors specifically, many sophisticated pedagogical devices were transformed and consolidated to fit dilettantes. Authors of guitar methods were very often musically trained in Southern Italy and Spain, and emigrated to France, the British Isles and the German confederation and their success coincided with a demand for Italian music. This Italian demand is mirrored in the publications of other educational tools, specifically a demand for those written by musicians trained in Naples[8]. Italian-inspired guitar playing reached Spain first in the seventeenth century via Gaspar Sanz and later Santiago de Murcia. Sanz travelled extensively in Italy and studied under composers such as Cristoforo Caresana (1640-1709) and Lelio Colista (1629-1680)[9] and states that he specifically learned his accompanying rules through his studies with the great masters in Rome and Naples[10]. In the late eighteenth century the demand for Italian, and specifically Neapolitan instruction first reached France and England through publications by Giacomo and Joseph [Giuseppe Bernardo] Merchi, and later, through Ferdinando Carulli and Nicolas-Raphaël Carli[11]. These guitarists travelled widely across Europe, transmitting their unique methods for teaching accompaniment and bringing improvised playing to a wider audience.

Preluding, Accompaniment and Variation Forms

The first commonly improvised activity a student would have engaged in were improvised preludes, but the pedagogical devices developed for preluding were also applicable to song accompaniment, and the ability to prelude and accompany the voice were often seen as mutually beneficial. The strong demand for simple songs with accompaniments on guitar, harp and piano

---

[8]. For more information on French publications of Neapolitan educational tools, see Cafiero 2007, pp. 137-159.

[9]. Strizich – Pinnell 2014.

[10]. Sanz 1697, p. 3.

[11]. Pierre-Jean Porro published many works and treatises from famous Italian composers in Paris. Nevertheless, it was the Neapolitan publisher Raphaël Carli (1764-1827) who arrived in Paris in 1807, and was vital for bringing Neapolitan and Roman educational materials to Paris. Macnutt 2001.

between 1780 and 1830 is attested to by the large number of popular song publications[12], and the standard trope of prelude and air necessitated certain skills be required to fulfil performance expectations[13]. Song accompaniments would have been the most popular music heard on the guitar and so accompanying the voice was, for most, likely the only skill a student would have endeavoured to learn when following a method of this time. The method books reflect this demand through the explicit teaching of how to vary accompaniments, and other grammatically important chord progressions. The primary chords of a key and basic right-hand arpeggios were the first skills learned, and many method books show how right-hand arpeggio patterns can be applied to existing song arrangements. This is a type of improvisation that involves changing preliminary right-hand movements over a static left-hand shape. As the student applies various right-hand patterns, different melodic and rhythmic variations are produced incidentally and a student discovers these gestures while reinforcing the basic motor-skill.

The earliest teaching of this type appears in both standard notation and tablature in *Méthode Pour Apprendre à Jouer de la Guitarre* published in Paris, c.1760. The anonymous author Don *** uses the term *batterie* to refer to specific right-hand patterns that guitarists now classify as right-hand arpeggios. The author also specifies which left-hand chord is being used to realise each note, which the author explicitly teaches on the pages before. This is one of the earliest uses of notation and it is evident that the *alfabeto* system, which built a technique centred around left-hand chords, did not disappear, but became assimilated into the newer standard notation. Right-hand variations are practised and worked out further by gradually changing chordal material in the form of the prelude. This provides first harmonic material for the left hand, then variation material driven by the right hand, in the form of arpeggios, and the two motor skills are then combined towards preluding[14]. By introducing techniques in this order, it leaves a student with a clear progression from chords to preludes, and eventually to vocal accompaniment. The anonymous author Don *** is explicit regarding preludes and the broken style: «these preludes should be played in the broken style; the letter or note detached from the agreement is added to the preceding agreement» but the notation the author employs is purely didactic (Ex. 1)[15].

---

12. STENSTADVOLD 2001, p. 11.

13. «There are [...] three kinds of preludes: one chiefly confined to the [...] diatonic scale of the key in which a piece is to be performed; one which passes through various modulations, ending [...] in the key of the composition; and also one that, from the key of the last movement or piece [...] serves to pass to that of the next». BOCHSA 1840, p. 49.

14. ANONYMOUS 1760, pp. 78-83.

15. «Ces prélude devrait se jouer dans un genre de batterie; la lettre ou la note détachée de l'accord, s'ajoute à l'accord qui la précède». *Ibidem*, pp. 82-83.

Ex. 1: Anon., Preludes in Perfect Chords, c.1760.

Blocked chord notation, sometimes even with tablature, was common in guitar methods around 1760 and is found as late as 1860. This notation leaves performers free to choose whatever arpeggio they wish, and inevitably entailed an easy and spontaneous (co)-composition — a preliminary form of structured improvisation. This type of notation is helpful for teaching improvisation as it leaves virtually all musical elements aside from harmony in the hands of the performer, a practice that might be described as semi-aural. Nevertheless, in order to learn what is often described as 'good taste' one must hear a professional either in concert or from instruction. For amateurs though, hearing professional musicians was not something that featured regularly in day-to-day life, a fact not lost on some authors sympathetic with the pursuit of music as a leisurely activity:

> [...] borne out in the belief I entertain, that such amateurs must employ far more
> of both [diligence and time], since professors enjoy advantages in the association
> with professional ability, by which they are hour by hour whetted, encouraged,
> and improved, and which facilitate acquisition incalculably. They practice with
> the most skilful musicians; they hear the finest music of every species; they join in
> the conversations, and mix largely in the remarks of scientific men; and above all,
> they are stimulated by every motive that the love of fame or the necessity as well
> as the desire of gain can inspire. In the meanwhile, the ambitious amateur drudges

patiently on in private perseverance, with the occasional brief lesson of the master, or the still less frequent benefit that is derived from the casual chance of hearing a good public concert, a chance rare indeed beyond the circle of the metropolis[16].

Le Guide des Ecoliers sheds much-needed light on the common thread shared between these method books; the *avertissement* gives instruction on the pedagogical purposes of including preludes «I made preludes in which we go through the 12 major modes and the 12 minor modes. [...] These well-thought-out preludes will give a lot of ease for accompaniment. Regarding the guitarist's favourite tune for playing arpeggios, the Spanish follies, 36 variations will give a sufficient idea. There are, however, also examples for preludes»[17].

These preludes are not there for the reproduction of written works as each prelude is written in blocked chords. Instead, they are pedagogical devices where improvisation is a central component. A student is free to perform any *batteries* over the chords and this practice not only helps refine the *batteries* but also explicitly develops skill in preluding and accompaniment. By transitioning this practice to Merchi's thirty-six variations on *les folies d'Espagne*, a student consciously learned how to use arpeggios to vary songs and airs. Merchi employs a type of statistical learning that has the student learn variation figures by practising composed models. New techniques are transmitted by discovering them in the works of established musicians, making them available for use in preludes or vocal accompaniments. Variation (spontaneous composition upon a pre-determined framework) is treated as an instrumental technique of its own importance.

Raccolta d'Ariette Francesi ed Italiane, Op. 4[18] provides insight into the sorts of decisions the Merchis and publishers had to make in the absence of a hegemonic form of standard notation and these decisions confirm that at least moderate skill in spontaneous accompaniment was required. The *Raccolta* features fifteen arias for guitar and voice as well as parts for two violins and small sections written in bass clef with figures simply labelled «basso». The guitar part alternates between tablature and switches to bass clef for the parts labelled *basso* indicating that a guitarist probably would have read and performed from this bass line in addition to any basso section that may or may not be present. The stringing of the guitar in Merchi's own method would not be able to realise the abundance of lower notes in the two arias with 'basso' parts. However, there is ample evidence to suggest a guitarist at this time would have overcome this by

---

16. *Quarterly Musical Magazine* 1818, p. 422.

17. «J'ai fait des préludes dans lesquels on parcourt les 12 modes majeurs et les 12 modes mineurs. Dans ces préludes, tous les accords se réduisent aux accords parfaits et de 7 mes de la note de basse fondamentale. [...] C'est préludes bien sucs donneront beaucoup de facilité pour l'accompagnement. À L'égard des arpègements air favori de la guitare, je veux dire les folies d'Espagne avec 36 variations en donneront une idée suffisante. On en trouvera cependant des exemples pour les préludes». Merchi 1761, p. 109.

18. Merchi 1760.

transposing any inaccessible bass notes up an octave. Merchi explicitly informs that variations are required when accompanying on the guitar: «The accompaniment of the guitar is the performance of a complete and regular Harmony, based on a basso continuo, in which each note performed on one of the strings, La, Re, Sol is also soon followed by the notes of its chord on the higher strings, in the form of arpeggios or batteries»[19]. Merchi also provides explicit instruction for varying accompaniments, which are too simple and provides a table of «exemples de variations» technique in the form of a diagram containing variations in two, three, and four notes (Ex. 2)[20]. These lists of variations were expanded in the methods of Federico Moretti, who offered over two hundred arpeggio figures, and they culminated in Mauro Giuliani's Op. 1[21], which became the *de-facto* leading text for right-hand technique. Both Carpentier and Merchi utilise *folies d'Espagne* as a tool for practising *batterie* variation, strengthening its use as a vehicle for improvisation.

Ex. 2: Merchi, list of variations for vocal accompaniments, 1777.

Volume 1 of Carpentier's method is the first to feature the term *canevas de prelude*[22] — a series of chords featuring modulatory embellishments in which the performer 'paints' over with right-hand variation. Carpentier's *canevas* are short chord progressions written without

---

19. «L'accompagnement de la guitare est l'exécution d'une Harmonie complète et régulière, fondée sur une basse continue, dont chaque note exécutée sur une des cordes, La, Re, Sol est aussitôt suivie des notes de son accord sur les cordes plus hautes, en forme d'arpèges ou de batteries». MERCHI 1777, p. 48.

20. «Lorsqu'on trouve que l'accompagnement d'un air est trop simple, on peut le varie dans le gout des exemples suivants; cela fait un bon effet [...]». *Ibidem*, p. 48.

21. GIULIANI 1813.

22. CARPENTIER 1771, p. 184.

rhythm on each tone organised in different keys, which invite students to employ their newly learned *batteries*. In the section on preludes, Carpentier shares what seems a commonly held belief in the late eighteenth century:

> It is too easy to practise preluding; nothing can advance students as much as this practice which results, among other things, from three advantages. The first is to develop your hand, the second to train your ear in harmony, and the third to learn a lot of positions, and to be sure of your hand on the instrument. Whenever we want to play a piece or accompany any song, we will have to prelude the key in which it is played, and similarly to practise playing it on the upper part of the neck where the chords are repeated; this is the way to learn to know it well[23].

His comments regarding the ease of use about preluding is in contrast with the attitude that amateurs were not expected or unable to improvise. These instruction manuals do not just provide deeper insight into the improvised performance practice of the period, but reveal the ways in which skills acquisition occurred. Carpentier suggests transposition for learning to prelude and contemporary improvisation pedagogy suggests actively, and routinely, transposing[24] fragments of music is one of the most important tools an improviser may use to further their craft. For Carpentier and most authors, learning to prelude was a holistic educational tool developing physical technique, aural skills and musical taste.

There were certain regional attitudes towards improvising and a notable difference between Spanish, French, English and German sources can be found. Moretti describes a few activities that bear similarities to the French authors, but curiously, the analogous term prelude is not used in the 1799 edition, or in the 1792 manuscript[25]. That a term as ubiquitous in the French methods as *prélude* would not appear in either editions by Moretti or any of the Spanish authors would seem strange. However, in a section on the various types of cadences, Moretti reveals an important distinction that bears significance for hundreds of methods published in the nineteenth century. After descriptions of the perfect and imperfect cadence, Moretti describes three species, *cadencia excusada*, *cadencia interrumpida*, and *cadencia falsa o quebrada* and cites Jean-Jacques Rousseau (1712-1778) and Nicolas-Étienne Framery (1745-1810) to

---

[23]. «On ne saurait trop s'exercer à préluder rien ne peut avancer les élèves autant que cette pratique dont il résulte entre autres trois avantages. Le premier c'est de se faire la main, le second de se former l'oreille à l'harmonie, et le troisième d'apprendre beaucoup de positions, et de s'assurer par la, la main sur l'instrument. Toutes les fois que l'on voudra jouer une pièce ou s'accompagner un chant quelconque il faudra faire le prélude du ton dans lequel on sera, et de même s'exercer à le dire sur la partie haute du manche ou les accords se répètent c'est la, la vraie manière de bien apprendre à le connaître». *Ibidem*, p. 185.

[24]. BERKOWITZ 2010, pp. 39-73.

[25]. MORETTI 1792.

draw comparison between the theoretical and practical definition of the word cadence[26]. Moretti does not use the term *cadencia* in the purely theoretical sense and instead makes clear that he uses this term in the more practical sense. *Cadencia*, according to Moretti, is the term for «the four chords which are generally played before performing a piece of music and serve to express the tone and mode in which the piece belongs»[27]. When reading through Moretti's method the implication is clear, there was an understood practice so widespread in Italy and Spain that Moretti describes the phenomenon in their colloquial terms, *dar el tono*, or *hacer la cadencia*. The comments in his *Explicación* reveal that the various cadences found in the 1792 edition are models for the student to learn, memorise and use to «give the tone»[28] — in all but name Moretti is instructing students how to prelude. Moretti, in remarkable clarity, describes the fore-meaning that would have informed the interpretation of terms like cadence, *modulación*, and variation. Moretti's use of *cadencia* for providing lightly improvised introduction agrees with J. F. Daube's comments on how useful transposing the «three basic chords»[29] can lead to improvising preludes and eventually the pinnacle of improvised art: the free fantasia.

Taken as a whole, early methods provide more cultural insight into the use of these terms and reveals the more improvisatory music making of amateurs in the late eighteenth and early nineteenth centuries. The practice-oriented approach of Moretti is echoed in Fernando Ferandiere's method, and a consensus is formed: being able to 'give the key' both in practice and in performance is an essential task. Yet, students must inevitably break away from the basic patterns offered by the methods and Moretti, in the explanation of the last table titled *arpegios generales*, recommends that each student takes the time to practise the arpeggios on all tones and modes in any position and any time signature (*compases*) that the student wants[30]. Moretti encourages learning through a practice that in the twentieth and twenty-first centuries would be called improvisatory play. Moretti is directing the student to practise by transposing (in different time and key signatures), recombining, and varying basic musical building blocks.

---

[26]. Moretti 1799, pp. 32-33.

[27]. «Uso de la palabra cadencia en mis principios de guitarra para expresar los cuatro acordes, que generalmente se hacen antes de ejecutar una pieza de música, y sirven para manifestar el tono y modo á que pertenece. Esta modulación se llama en español dar el tono, y en italiano hacer la cadencia». *Ibidem*, p. 33.

[28]. *Ibidem*, p. 61.

[29]. «I would advise that one try the three primary chords in all twenty-four keys; this is very easy because there is such a small number of chords. I know for sure that this practice would be of great use. [...] Through this small amount of practice [...] One also attains a great ease and skill in preluding [...] This would make preluding easier, and it would open the way to improvising [Fantasiren]». Wallace 1983, pp. 269-270.

[30]. «Esta tabla contiene 168 arpegios sencillos, que pueden executarse en todos los tonos y modos, y en qualquiera de las tres manos por estar combinados de manera, que el principiante de por sí los aplicará á las cadencias y compases que quiera». Moretti 1799, p. 63.

Cadenze Prolongate, Accompanied Scales, and Bass Motions

More advanced grammatical material appeared in the methods between 1800 and 1830, but accompanied major and minor scales, has a long history dating back to at least 1710[31]. Despite being written for both the five and six-course guitar, Charles Doisy's method established tropes and teaching techniques that featured throughout nineteenth century methods. Doisy's *Principes généraux* contains the first appearance of the accompanied scale in staff notation on the treble clef and is a precursor to the classical guitar style regarding texture and technique[32]. Prior to Doisy's method, the accompanied scales for the guitar were either written in bass clef with figures, tablature one, a unique hybrid utilising both found in Manuel da Paixão Ribeiro's method for the five-course guitar *Nova Arte de Viola*[33]. Ribeiro's studies with *Mestre de capela* José Maurício (1752-1815)[34] had a strong influence over his instruction on the guitar and, when considered alongside the work of Juan Antonio Vargas y Guzman, they demonstrate a strong cross pollination between organists and guitarists in the Iberian Peninsula.

The use of harmonised scales as found in nineteenth-century guitar methods, as with Doisy, often do not feature detailed explanation as to why they are included[35]. Instead, harmonised scales appear scattered amidst other sections containing cadences, prelude canvas' modulation patterns and singing exercises. François de Fossa, included harmonised scales as well as several harmonised bass motions in the appendix to Dionisio Aguado's *Escuela de guitarra* and provided the clearest example as to why these grammatically important harmonic patterns are included in his appendix: «If the exploited disciple wants to exercise his fantasy in prelude with modulations, in addition to the dexterity of his hands and the knowledge of the guitar fingerboard, he also needs to know the brief elements of harmony that I am going to indicate»[36]. De Fossa's bass motions are only the second examples of such a teaching device being used for the six-string guitar outside of Vargas y Guzman's method[37].

---

[31]. Campion 1716, fol. 14-15.

[32]. Doisy 1801.

[33]. Vargas y Guzman 1773, pp. 88-124. Ribeiro 1789, p. vii.

[34]. Stevenson 2001.

[35]. Doisy simply remarks that they produce harmony and strengthen your knowledge of the neck. «On appelle Gammes-Harmoniques celles qui produisent de l'Harmonie. Elles sont d'autant plus essentielles a travailler, qu'elles fortifient dans la musique et dans la connaissance du Manche, dont elles renaissent toutes les difficultés des Positions». Doisy 1801, p. 44.

[36]. «Si el discípulo aprovechado quiere ejercitar su fantasía en preludiar con modulaciones, además de la destreza de sus manos y del conocimiento del Diapasón de la guitarra, necesita saber también los sucintos elementos de armonía que voy a indicar». Aguado – De Fossa 1825, p. 103.

[37]. Vargas y Guzman 1773.

De Fossa provides six bass motions and demonstrates how the fundamental bass motion can be transposed liberally up and down to create new technical combinations resulting in eighteen distinct examples.

This instruction seems in keeping with many of the reasons why authors before and after included such small sections on harmony and for the copious amounts of chord sequences found in these methods. Doisy offers chord sequences similar to Carpentier's and provides clear instructions as to how they should be used: «Preluding is the best opportunity for the guitar to play beautifully. Here follow, as examples, a few chords that can be arpeggiated at will, and from which it is possible to make little preludes in the most common tones. They are all the easier to execute because they never go beyond the third position»[38].

The practice of including grammatically important chord progressions for improvising preludes did not fall out of fashion until well into the twentieth century, and eventually the terms used to describe them evolved. Francesco Bathioli used the terms *cadenze semplici*, and *cadenze prolongate*, with the former following Moretti's *cadencia*, and the latter resembling the *canevas de prelude*[39]. Bathioli's *cadenze semplici* are presented in each key with each example shown varied with a new set of right-hand arpeggios. *Cadenze prolongate* are extended chord sequences that indicate the key, and their presentation implies they are to be practised similarly. Bathioli's use of the word *cadenze* is clearly more similar to Moretti's use of the word than any purely theoretical definition. Salvador Gil, fourteen years after Moretti's *Principi*, provides another clear indication that the I, IV, and V chords are to be used to prelude (*formar el modo*) on every tone[40]. In this shared usage, Bathioli's *cadenze prolongate* can only be interpreted as material to be used for preluding — they feature chromatic passages, which serve to establish a key centre with modulatory embellishments (Ex. 3)[41]. The sustained importance of harmony as a practical skill can be seen developed further with the first method completely dedicated to harmony on the six-string guitar published by Ferdinando Carulli in 1825[42].

---

[38]. «Im Präludieren ist für die Gitarre vorzüglich die beste Gelegenheit schönem Gang zu machen. Hier folgen, als Beispiele, einige Accorde, die man nach Willkür arpeggieren kann, und woraus es möglich ist, kleine Präludia in den gebräuchlichsten Tönen zu machen. Sie sind umso leichter auszuführen, weil sie nie über den dritten Platz Gehen». Doisy 1802, p. 60.

[39]. Bathioli 1827, pp. 20, 25.

[40]. «Se acostumbra antes de tocar qualquiera pieza en la Guitarra, formar el modo en que está escrita con tres posturas consonantes: que son la de la primera del modo, la de la cuarta y la de la quinta, y aun á esta se suele añadir la séptima menor». «It is customary before playing a piece on the guitar to give the key in which the piece is written and this is done with three consonant chords: the first of the key, the fourth of the key, and the fifth of the key which can have added the minor seventh». Gil 1814, p. 18.

[41]. Bathioli 1827, p. 25.

[42]. Carulli 1825.

Ex. 3: Bathioli, *Cadenze Prolongate*, 1827.

Improvising, as a concert phenomenon, began to fall out of fashion around 1840 and the differences between Aguado's first method in 1825 and his last in 1849 hints towards the diminishment of improvisation as an explicitly taught skill in the nineteenth century[43]. Aguado changed his approach significantly between his first and last method and seemed to succumb to the pressure to accommodate more impatient amateur audiences. While Aguado's 1825 *Escuela de guitarra* ends with a lengthy appendix written by Fossa entirely devoted to cultivating preluding and modulating, Aguado's 1843/1849 edition includes a comparatively small section on preluding. Instead of consolidating the rules of harmony into several different bass motions, Aguado provides several written-out preludes and suggests transposing them into different keys[44]. The detailed instructions for composing one's own preludes found in de Fossa's appendix is absent, but Aguado still leaves the bulk of the work in the hands of the student as they must aurally transpose the preludes themselves. Despite transposition being used, this style of instruction largely reinforces the execution aspect of instrumental instruction, which became more central to instrumental technique and is a marked shift from the 1825 method. Nonetheless, the opinion was still held by Aguado that «the guitar is well suited for improvisation, or as they say, to play on a whim»[45]. Aguado's transition in teaching techniques

---

[43]. AGUADO – DE FOSSA 1825; AGUADO 1834; AGUADO 1843; AGUADO 1849.

[44]. AGUADO 1849.

[45]. «Llena de medios para representar las ideas músicas, la guitarra es a propósito para la improvisación, o como suele decirse, para tocar de capricho». *Ibidem*, p. 1.

epitomises the challenges authors encountered when faced with an increased demand from amateur learners. This transition moved from expecting the student to assimilate bass motions and compositional techniques into their preluding to simply indicating which preludes can be transposed into different keys.

MODULATION PATTERNS AND THE *LABERINTOS DE ARMONÍA*

The explicit instruction to develop more complex techniques like modulating and preluding is evident well into the 1840s and a variety of devices were used. The strongest and most direct device was to compose a model for how to modulate, which a student would memorise and use to create their own. In the tradition of varying harmonic progressions like the *folies d'Espagne*, guitarists created their own unique techniques to teach modulation by composing pieces consisting of long uninterrupted sequences of arpeggiated chords that modulated through many different keys. These pieces went by various names — *arpège modules*, *el laberinto* or *círculo armónico* and the earliest example is from 1760 described as a *suite de harmonie*[46]. Some are published separately, but most are unlabelled pieces found at the end of a method. *Arpeggio ovvero Giro d'armonia* is a four-page fantasia of modulations written by Antonio Nava[47] and features common right-hand arpeggios with clearly marked arrival points for each key. This type of modulatory etude appeared in methods by František Max Kníže[48], Johann Traugott Lehmann[49], Bartolomeo Bortolazzi[50] and several others and is often found at the end of a method. For Bortolazzi, it is the only written-out piece of music, and Carulli describes the six pages of modulatory arpeggios from his *Méthode complete*, Op. 27 as a *grand prélude*[51]. Some authors, like Leonard Schultz[52], Kníže, and Kirkman[53] provide suggestions for alternate right-hand variations (Ex. 4). That the *laberinto* appeared so frequently at the end of methods points to the cumulative effect of studying each method. The implication is that, if the method had been completed, a student should have developed a skill set capable of producing modulations.

---

[46]. ANONYMOUS 1760, p. 88.

[47]. NAVA 1830, pp. 2-5.

[48]. KNÍŽE 1820, pp. 34-38.

[49]. LEHMANN 1830, pp. 15-22, 26-30.

[50]. BORTOLAZZI 1805.

[51]. CARULLI 1810, p. 99.

[52]. SCHULTZ n.d.

[53]. KIRKMAN 1840, pp. 12-15.

Ex. 4: Kirkman, Modulations with Chord Canvas, 1840.

Fernando Ferandiere also wrote a *laberinto*[54] and describes its use for learning arpeggios and general modulation principles. *Laberinto* as an educational term used by guitarists can be traced back to Gaspar Sanz[55], and although his use is more as a table demonstrating harmonic possibilities, the persisting popularity of his term in Spain attests to a common intention with these devices. All of the three terms, *giro*, *circulo*, *suite* and *laberinto* imply not only a catalogue, but also a map of possibilities in which the exploration and movement within and outside of those possibilities is made through improvised play. By studying the *laberintos* of an instructor, students train their fingers and ears towards the principles of modulation. None of these principles should be learned by formal rules; instead, students carefully study these improvisatory compositions to learn modulatory technique. Antonio Cano provides a similar device and is explicit in its use; he illustrates the nuances of modulation technique and seems to end a pedagogical link of improvisation instruction, which lasted almost two hundred years (Ex. 5). The evidence provided by Cano is clear, *laberintos* were not meant to be performed as works, but to be learned from, to be used so that students would learn to modulate by principles and not routine.

> Once the Guitarist has penetrated all that is stated in this treatise, he will
> know how to modulate by principles and not by routine as is generally done, and
> will be able to analyse the works written for the Guitar and harmonise in a living way
> those he writes, since without having the presumption that this method is a perfect

---

54.   FERANDIERE 1799, pp. 13-14.

55.   An exploration of the term *laberinto* can be found in ROSAGER 2016, pp. 25-30.

work, I believe, however, to have filled a void that could contribute to the guitar occupying its rightful place in the Philharmonic world, and finally, if it deserves the approval of the lovers of our poetry instrument[56].

Ex. 5: Cano, Modulating Exercise, c.1869.

Using the *laberinto* as a canvas for learning what shapes to use when performing modulations was a useful endeavour, although more explicit techniques were used to improvise one's own. Similar to how bass motions, accompanied scales, resolutions or *cadenze prolongate* were used to prelude the key, small modulation patterns were memorised so an improviser could get *out* of the key. There is a historical precedent for this kind of instruction and in the

---

[56]. CANO 1869, p. 42.

mid-eighteenth century, the lack of practical instruction in the art of modulation was the catalyst for Francesco Geminiani's treatise *Guida Armonica*. By opposing more abstract and less practical rules[57], Geminiani offers a compendium of over 2,000 bass motions with figures and offers a method for combining and chaining patterns together. Certainly, a conceptual link to the *laberinto* is found in Geminiani's approach, but the more concrete connection is in the model-imitation format of instruction which exchanges learning from abstract rules for learning by the imitation and variation of prescribed grammatical figures. Daube too offered modulation prototypes[58] as opposed to abstracted rules and this practice was also employed by Georg Joseph Vogler[59] and later André Ernest Modeste Grétry[60] — both demonstrate the attempt to make modulation instruction more practical. Although Daube demonstrates the nuances of each modulation via a specific bass motion with figures, he also organises them by their fundamental root motion, an organisational tool found in several guitar methods found throughout Europe in the nineteenth century. Daube's position as a pedagogue concerned with teaching amateurs is confirmed by his seminal text *Der Musikalische Dilettante*, who's audience, the insular *Dilettantenkreis*[61] of late eighteenth-century Vienna would have likely passed his teachings on from one family to another.

The precedent of offering exemplars for modulations, whether influenced specifically by Geminiani, Daube, Vogler, or Grétry, became a hallmark of a guitar education as it is rarely found in any of the popular keyboard treatises aimed at preluding of this time[62] outside of Carl Czerny's Op. 300[63]. Guitarists, and harpists[64] used modulations for a variety of learning outcomes — Phillipe Verini states they (Ex. 6) are for «perfecting the pupil» and to give «the pupil a general knowledge of the instrument as well as to strengthen the left hand to undertake the difficult positions»[65]. Marziano Bruni is more practical expressing that once a student has mastered the cadences, modulations and resolutions found in his method one can accompany any air[66]. De Fossa continues the tradition of offering modulation patterns, but marks out one pattern as his sixth and last bass movement: the bass, which descends by third and moves to

[57]. GEMINIANI 1752.
[58]. WALLACE 1983, p. 198.
[59]. VOGLER 1776; VOGLER 1780-1781.
[60]. GRÉTRY 1801-1802, p. 50.
[61]. SNOOK-LUTHER 1992, p. 7.
[62]. Similar lists of modulations are not found in any of the following methods: CORRI 1810; KOLLMANN n.d.; VIERLING 1794.
[63]. CZERNY 1840.
[64]. RAGUE n.d.
[65]. VERINI 1825.
[66]. BRUNI 1834, p. 26.

remote keys[67]. Modulations following similar principles are included by Verini, Bruni, Antonio Cano, Kirkman and Ferdinando Pelzer[68] (Ex. 7).

Ex. 6: Verini, Modulations organised by root motion, c.1825.

Ex: 7: De Fossa, Bass Motion six and examples from various authors, 1825-1840.

67.   «Movimiento 6. Bajando por terceras mayores o menores, el bajo conduce a los tonos más remotos. / En el ejemplo siguiente, desde el tono de Do se hacen resoluciones en todos los semitonos dé su escala». AGUADO – DE FOSSA 1825, p. 149.
68.   PELZER 1836, p. 14.

The very concept of instrumental proficiency in the nineteenth century was not just the ability to execute musical works, rather the ability to freely recombine small musical ideas (scales, chord resolutions and modulations) in preludes, accompaniments and modulations. The overt effort to teach modulation found in the guitar methods is the logical conclusion of a culture where improvisation for pleasure is routinely cultivated. That a significant amount of this improvisation pedagogy was directed at amateurs, who wished simply to enjoy themselves on the instrument seemed to be a fluctuating pedagogical thought in the nineteenth century. Andre Grétry comments[69] that nineteenth-century education was too focused on mechanical exercises, which would «chain down the pupil» at the expense of «exercising his talents upon that which is essential. I call it the essential because it is thence that all our pleasure results». By linking music education with leisure, Grétry speaks to the over-emphasis in teachers' instruction on interpretation and the performance of works[70]. Grétry's followers, specifically de Fossa and Aguado, are contextualised by these comments into a debate over what should be emphasised in music education. Extempore playing was considered a skill that could elevate amateurs beyond the status of connoisseur. It was an ideal that was often explicitly taught in method books and must have been in demand throughout the early-nineteenth century given the number of methods published which include such devices. For nineteenth-century guitarists, the knowledge of harmony was not just an abstract theoretical knowledge demonstrable through discourse, but was a sense knowledge, which achieves its full understanding through spontaneous performance. Composition and instrumental technique were not separate concepts, but fell upon a type of spectrum where one influenced the other, and in an environment where composition is so closely tied to instrumental technique, free play and exploration were vital elements of a student's skill development.

BIBLIOGRAPHY

AGUADO 1834
AGUADO, Dionisio. *Nouvelle Méthode de Guitare Op. 6*, Paris, s.n., 1834.

AGUADO 1843
ID. *Nuevo método para guitarra*, Madrid, Benito Campo, 1843.

AGUADO 1849
ID. *Apéndice. Nuevo método para guitarra*, Madrid, Benito Campo, 1849.

---

[69]. GRÉTRY 1826, pp. 93-96.

[70]. A clearer contextualisation of his comments and the discussion surrounding it can be found here in LAOR 2016.

AGUADO – DE FOSSA 1825
ID. – DE FOSSA, François. *Escuela de guitarra*, Madrid, Autor, 1825.

ANONYMOUS 1760
ANONYMOUS. *Méthode pour apprendre a jouer de la guitare*, Paris, c.1760 [Facsimile reprint in: *Méthodes & Traités Guitare. 1: France 1600-1800*, Courlay, Editions J. M. Fuzeau, 2003].

BATHIOLI 1827
BATHIOLI, Francesco. *Kleine Gemeinnützige Guitareschule*, Vienna, Diabelli, 1827.

BERKOWITZ 2010
BERKOWITZ, Aaron L. *The Improvising Mind: Cognition and Creativity in the Musical Moment*, Oxford, Oxford University Press, 2010.

BOCHSA 1840
BOCHSA, Nicholas Charles. *The Harp Preludist*, London, Goulding & D'Almaine, c.1840.

BOMBAY GAZETTE 1820
The Bombay Gazette, Wednesday 5 April 1820.

BORTOLAZZI 1805
BORTOLAZZI, Bartolomeo. *Nuova ed esatta Scuola per la Chitarra*, Vienna, Tobias Haslinger, c.1805.

BRUNI 1834
BRUNI, Marziano. *Treatise on the Guitar Embracing the Rules of Harmony with Examples for the Guitar, Piano and Harp*, London, O. J., c.1834.

CAFIERO 2007
CAFIERO, Rosa. 'The Early Reception of Neapolitan Partimento Theory in France: A Survey' in: *Journal of Music Theory*, LI/1 (2007), pp. 137-159.

CAMPION 1716
CAMPION, François. *Traité d'accompagnement et de composition*, Paris, G. Adam, 1716.

CANO 1869
CANO, Antonio. *Método completo: con un tratado de armonía aplicada a este instrumento*, Madrid, Antonio Romero, c.1869.

CARPENTIER 1771
CARPENTIER, Joseph. *Méthode distribuée par leçons pour apprendre en peu de temps à jouer de l'instrument appelé Cytre ou Guitare*, Paris, l'Autheur-Melling, 1771 [Facsimile reprint in: *Méthodes & Traités Guitare. 1: France 1600-1800*, Courlay, Editions J. M. Fuzeau, 2003].

CARULLI 1810
CARULLI, Ferdinando. *Méthode complete op. 27*, Paris, Carli, 1810.

CARULLI 1825
ID. *L'Harmonie appliquée à la Guitare*, Paris, Ph. Petit, 1825.

CORRI 1810
CORRI, Philip Antony. *Original System of Preluding*, London, Chappell & Co., c.1810.

CZERNY 1840
CZERNY, Carl. *The Art of Preluding, Op. 300*, London, R. Cocks & Co, c.1840s.

DAUBE 1773
DAUBE, Johann Friedrich. *Der musikalische Dilettant*, Vienna, Johann Thomas von Trattner, 1773.

DAUBE 1797-1798
ID. *Anleitung zur Erfindung der Melodie und ihrer Fortsetzung*, 2 vols., Vienna, Täubel, 1797-1798.

DOISY 1801
DOISY, Charles. *Principes généraux de la Guitare à cinq et à six cordes, et de la lyre*, Paris, s.n., c.1801.

DOISY 1802
ID. *Vollständige Anweisung für die Guitarre*, Leipzig, Breitkopf & Härtel, c.1802.

FERANDIERE 1799
FERANDIERE, Fernando. *Arte de tocar la guitarra Española por música*, Madrid, Pantaleon Aznar, 1799.

GEMINIANI 1752
GEMINIANI, Francesco. *Guida Armonica*, London, John Johnson, 1752.

GIL 1814
GIL, Salvador. *Principios de Música Aplicados á la Guitarra*, Madrid, Imprenta de Sancha, 1814.

GIULIANI 1813
GIULIANI, Mauro. *Studio per la Chitarra Op. 1*, Vienna, Artaria & Comp., c.1813.

GOOLEY 2018
GOOLEY, Dana. *Fantasies of Improvisation: Free Playing in Nineteenth-Century Music*, Oxford-New York, Oxford University Press, 2018.

GRÉTRY 1801-1802
GRÉTRY, André Ernest Modeste. *Méthode simple pour apprendre à préluder*, Paris, l'imprimerie de la République, 1801-1802.

GRÉTRY 1826
ID. 'On Musical Education', in: *The Harmonicon*, VI (1826), pp. 93-96.

KIRKMAN 1840
KIRKMAN, Louisa. *Improved Method for the Guitar*, London, Mrs Joseph Kirkman, c.1840.

KNÍŽE 1820
KNÍŽE, František Max. *Vollständige Guitarre-Schule*, Prague, s.n., 1820.

KOLLMANN n.d.
KOLLMANN, Augustus Frederic Christopher. *An Introduction to the Art of Preluding and Extemporizing Op. 3*, London, R. Wornum, n.d.

LAOR 2016
LAOR, Lia. '«In Music Nothing Is Worse than Playing Wrong Notes»: Nineteenth-Century Mechanistic Paradigm of Piano Pedagogy', in: *Journal of Historical Research in Music Education*, XXXVIII/1 (2016), pp. 5-24.

LEHMANN 1830
LEHMANN, Johann Traugott. *Neue Guitarre-Schule*, Leipzig, Hofmeister, c.1830.

MACNUTT 2001
MACNUTT, Richard. 'Carli', in: *Grove Music Online*, 2001, <https://www.oxfordmusiconline.com/grovemusic>, accessed October 2023.

MERCHI 1760
MERCHI, Giacomo. *Raccolta d'ariette francesi ed italiane*, Paris, n.p., 1760 [Facsimile reprint Florence, Studio Per Edizioni Scelte, 1981].

MERCHI 1761
ID. *Le Guide des Écoliers de Guitare*, Paris, c.1761 [Facsimile reprint in: *Méthodes & Traités Guitare. 1: France 1600-1800*, Courlay, France, Editions J. M. Fuzeau, 2003].

MERCHI 1777
ID. *Traité des Agréments de la Musique*, Paris, l'Auteur, 1777.

MORETTI 1792
MORETTI, Federico. *Principj per la chitarra*, Naples, 1792 [Facsimile reprint, Florence, Studio Per Edizioni Scelte, 1983].

MORETTI 1799
ID. *Principios para tocar la guitarra de seis órdenes*, Madrid, Imprenta de Sancha, 1799.

MORNING HERALD 1827
MORNING HERALD, (London), Monday 4 June 1827.

NAVA 1830
NAVA, Antonio. *Arpeggio ovvero Giro d'armonia Op. 15*, Milan, F. Mantegazza e Fazini, c.1830.

PELZER 1836
PELZER, Ferdinand. *One Hundred and Fifty Exercises for Acquiring a Facility of Performance upon the Spanish Guitar*, not published, c.1836.

QUARTERLY MUSICAL MAGAZINE 1818
The Quarterly Musical Magazine and Review, vol. I, London, Baldwin, Cradock and Joy, 1818.

QUARTERLY MUSICAL MAGAZINE 1827
The Quarterly Musical Magazine and Review, vol. IX, London, Baldwin, Cradock and Joy, 1827.

RAGUE n.d.
RAGUE, Louis Charles. *L'Art de préluder sur la harpe*, Paris, Le Duc, n.d.

RIBEIRO 1789
RIBEIRO, Manuel da Paixão. *Nova Arte de Viola*, Coimbra, Na Real Officina da Universidade, 1789.

ROSAGER 2016
ROSAGER, Lars Christian. *A Humanistic Reading of Gaspar San's Instruccion de musica sobre la guitarra Espanola*, MA Thesis, San Francisco, San Francisco State University, 2016.

SANZ 1697
SANZ, Gaspar. *Instruccion de musica sobre la guitarra española*, Zaragoza, por los herederos de Diego Dormer, 1697 [Facsimile reprint, Geneva, Minkoff, 1976].

SCHULTZ n.d.
SCHULTZ, Leonard. *Modulations in Chords for the Guitar Op. 15*, London, Johanning & Co., n.d.

SNOOK-LUTHER 1992
SNOOK-LUTHER, Susan P. *The Musical Dilettante: A Treatise on Composition by J. F. Daube*, Cambridge, Cambridge University Press, 1992 (Cambridge Studies in Music Theory and Analysis).

STENSTADVOLD 2001
STENSTADVOLD, Erik. 'A Bibliographical Study of Antoine Meissonnier's Periodicals for Voice and Guitar, 1811-27', in: *Notes*, Second Series, LVIII/1 (2001), pp. 11-13.

STENSTADVOLD 2010
ID. *An Annotated Bibliography of Guitar Methods, 1760-1860*, Hillsdale-New York, Pendragon Press, 2010.

STEVENSON 2001
STEVENSON, Robert. 'Maurício, José (i)', in: *Grove Music Online*, 2001, <https://www.oxfordmusiconline.com/grovemusic>, accessed October 2023.

Strizich – Pinnell 2014
Strizich, Robert – Pinnell, Richard. 'Sanz, Gaspar', in: *Grove Music Online*, 2014, <https://www.oxfordmusiconline.com/grovemusic>, accessed October 2023.

The *Atlas* 1828
The Atlas, Sunday 12 October 1828.

Vargas y Guzmán 1773
Vargas y Guzmán, Juan Antonio. *Explicación de la Guitarra: (Cadiz, 1773)*, edited with an introductory study by Ángel Medina Álvarez, Granada, Centro de Documentación Musical de Andalucía, 1994.

Verini 1825
Verini, Phillipe Raphael Jean Baptiste. *Rudiments for the Spanish Guitar. Book 2*, London, J. B. Cramer, c.1825.

Vierling 1794
Vierling, Johann Gottfried. *Versuch einer Anleitung zum Präludiren*, Leipzig, Breitkopf & Härtel, c.1794.

Vogler 1776
Vogler, Georg Joseph. *Tonwissenschaft und Tonsetzkunst*, Mannheim, der kuhrfürstlichen Hofbuchdruckerei, 1776.

Vogler 1780-1781
Id. *Gegenstände der Betrachtungen, 3. Jahrgang*, Speyer, Bossler, 1780-1781.

Wallace 1983
Wallace, Barbara Kees. *J. F. Daube's «General-Bass in drey Accorden» (1756): A Translation and Commentary*, Ph.D. Diss., Denton (TX), North Texas State University, 1983.

Repurpose and Transformation of an Educational Material: Figured Bass as a School Practice in the Early Years of the Paris Conservatory

Justin Ratel
(Conservatoire National Supérieur de Musique et de Danse de Paris)

The Paris Conservatory, founded in 1795, exerted a considerable influence on music teaching both in France and elsewhere. It provided tuition in numerous disciplines including harmony, in which students were required to complete exercises in figured bass realisation both on paper and at the piano, even though, by the beginning of the nineteenth century, it was already an outdated practice. The Conservatory, as well as contemporary authors of music treatises, transformed the technique from one that had once had practical applications into a didactic method. Thus the figured bass evolved from being an end in itself to a means of providing the musical skills required by a nineteenth-century musician.

In order to understand how the figured bass was used in this context, we have also to understand the nature of the teaching of harmony at the Conservatory at this time. From its inception, a number of disciplines were grouped together under the title *composition*. These included practical accompaniment (*accompagnement pratique*), harmony, fugue, counterpoint and style[1]. At various times the written and practical elements were either considered together[2] or as distinct studies[3]; they were finally separated as individual disciplines in 1839[4].

---

[1]. «Loi portant établissement d'un conservatoire de musique à paris pour l'enseignement de cet art: 16 thermidor an III - 3 août 1795». PIERRE 1900, p. 125.

[2]. «En 1823, à la demande de Cherubini, directeur de l'École, on fondit ces deux branches d'études en une seule, afin "de former des élèves à la fois bons harmonistes et bons accompagnateurs". C'était limiter l'étude de l'harmonie aux seuls élèves qui cultivaient le piano». *BASSES ET CHANTS*, p. v.

[3]. «Des classes d'harmonie furent instituées dès la fondation du Conservatoire et, [...] Des classes distinctes, dites "d'harmonie et accompagnement pratique", existaient concurremment, dont le titre indique suffisamment le but et l'objet spécial». *Ibidem*, p. vi.

[4]. «En 1823, à la demande de Cherubini, directeur de l'École, on fondit ces deux branches d'études en une seule, afin "de former des élèves à la fois bons harmonistes et bons accompagnateurs". C'était limiter l'étude de l'harmonie aux seuls élèves qui cultivaient le piano». *Ibidem*, p. v.

This question of the separation of the disciplines was crucial as it conditioned both the approach to teaching and the pedagogical literature related to it. For authors of the literature, written realisation was held to be of great importance, and at the Conservatory, even after the disciplines had been separated, written harmony exercises were still compulsory as part of the practical harmony course, whereas the converse was not the case[5]. It was not until 1878, when the practical harmony classes were abandoned in favour of piano accompaniment classes, that the written exercises were finally abandoned[6].

Harmony was often considered as a preparation for the more serious study of composition[7]. François-Joseph Fétis claimed that harmony was the science of «chords taken in isolation»[8], thereby encapsulating an important theoretical concept that was central to the treatises on accompaniment from the early nineteenth century. For this reason, the authors of such books often included a 'chord catalogue' or a 'table of all chords', and this feature became a particular focus of the discipline. This idea of presenting chords as isolated entities first appeared at the end of the eighteenth century, and Fétis's definition indicates that it had already become an established component of the methodology[9].

While many writers considered that harmony was a subject that could be mastered through theory alone, practical harmony and accompaniment was a discipline that linked theory to practice. In order to understand how figured bass was employed, we need to understand the relationship between theory and practice in the teaching of accompaniment at the beginning of the nineteenth century. Some writers defended the need for a defined theory and clear rules that students could then apply, whereas others supported the idea that music should be learned, at least in the early stages, like a mother tongue without the application of theory. This was more than just an esoteric debate as it resulted in radically different methods of approaching the tuition of harmony at the keyboard.

---

[5]. «Dès le principe, le programme des classes d'harmonie et accompagnement pratique comporta l'étude de l'harmonie écrite comme pour les classes d'harmonie seule, et malgré le rétablissement de ces dernières, en 1839, on n'abandonna pas lesdites épreuves écrites». *Ibidem*, p. vi.

[6]. «Ce n'est qu'avec la suppression des classes d'harmonie et d'accompagnement en 1878, et la création d'une classe d'accompagnement au piano, uniquement consacrée aux épreuves instrumentales, que cessa cet usage de la réalisation écrite». *Ibidem*.

[7]. «Mais, comme le dit l'auteur, là s'arrête le cours d'harmonie et commence l'étude de la composition». Panseron 1855, p. 1.

[8]. «[...] des accords pris isolément». Fétis 1824, p. 2.

[9]. «Quant à l'harmonie proprement dite, je la considère sous deux rapports: 1° comme moyen d'exciter en nous le sentiment harmonieux, par l'usage de l'accompagnement au clavier. 2° Comme tableau synoptique des connaissances acquises par l'étude du contrepoint». *Ibidem*.

Henry Lemoine subscribed to the idea of an analogy between language and music[10]. He did not totally reject the need for theory, and instead agreed that such principles were necessary to grasp the beauty of music. The question was more the nature and order of presenting the stages of learning to the student. He suggested that students would better understand the importance of theory if they developed a curiosity in their approach to accompaniment: in tackling practical musical situations they would grow to feel the need for a knowledge of theory. In proposing a methodology akin to that of a learning language through practice, such writers encouraged an approach to accompaniment that involved the memorisation of passages of harmony.

Luigi Cherubini was one who supported the rote learning of harmony passages[11]. He acknowledged that it seemed contrary to the desire, shared by many at the beginning of the nineteenth century, to base learning on principles rather than reproduction, but the use of repetition was fully in line with way it was also employed at the time for tackling difficult passages in performance. He also used the term 'mechanics', which was reflected in the titles of several instrumental methods such as *Studies of Mechanism*. Thus it was that the concept of repetition was adopted into the methodology of instrumental teaching of the Paris Conservatory, of which, we may remember, Cherubini was director from 1822 to 1842. Cherubini also encouraged «intelligent use» and «scientific interest» in the use of repetition, however, meaning that understanding and the use of memory was also an important element. Other writers, by contrast, defended rules as a means of learning, one such being Pierre-François Moncouteau, who claimed that «Guided by these rules, the student will realise exactly what he must do, without stepping on the chance, as do those who transpose, so to speak, only instinctively»[12].

The teaching of practical accompaniment during this period focused on harmony and its direct application at the keyboard. It would therefore be useful to examine how the piano

---

[10]. «Dans cet état de curiosité et d'enthousiasme, les raisonnemens [*sic*] seront mieux accueillis et mieux saisis qu'ils ne l'ussent [*sic*] été primitivement, et c'est alors que mon traité les présente en petit nombre à la réflexion. [...] c'est ici le cas de rappeler le rapprochement que l'on a fait de la musique avec une langue ou il est besoin des principes pour en saisir toutes les beautés». Lemoine 1835, n.p.

[11]. «Quoique, à la première inspection, il puisse paraître assez étrange que des espèces de phrases toutes faites soient apprises, en quelque sorte par cœur; nous ferons observer que ces procédés, pour ainsi dire mécaniques, sont journellement d'un utile secours, non seulement dans les compositions spéculatives, mais encore dans la musique sacrée et dramatique, où, grâce à l'emploi intelligent d'une marche d'harmonie, d'une progression qu'un compositeur, homme de goût, sait rajeunir en la dissimulant par une facture élégante, les attaches qui lient la reproduction d'un motif principal, ou le retour obligé d'une phrase importante, acquièrent un intérêt scientifique qui n'est pas sans charme». Cherubini 1847, p. 1.

[12]. «Guidé par ces règles, l'élève se rendra un compte exact de ce qu'il doit faire, sans marcher au hasard, comme le font ceux qui ne transposent pour ainsi dire qu'instinctivement». Moncouteau 1845a, p. v.

was perceived in this context. One of the main advantages of the piano, as highlighted by many writers, was its ability to enable students to play the harmony: students were thus able to hear and correct any faults that escaped their inner ear. For this reason, its use was not reserved just for specialists[13] but for all musicians[14]. The employment of the piano by non-specialists prompted writers to find simple ways of practising harmony at the keyboard:

> C'est donc aussi, et nous en prévenons, par une conséquence nécessaire de cette base première que tous nos exemples pratiques y sont écrits, autant qu'on a pu le faire dans les deux seuls tons diatoniques, d'Ut majeur et de La mineur; lesquels exemples, par la raison qu'ils sont plus simples, c'est-à-dire moins chargés de signes, peuvent être analisés [sic], compris, et joués par l'élève qui commence s'il n'est pas que peu pianiste[15].

In this passage, Henri-Philippe Gérard used three verbs that summarised the way many writers envisioned learning harmony on the keyboard: analysing, understanding and playing. For these skills to be accessible to non-pianists, the author had to simplify the passages by choosing only simple keys. One advantage of studying harmony that appealed to many writers was that it enabled students to prelude, compose, accompany and adapt the music[16]. At the beginning of the century few keyboardists could improvise, even though the use of the prelude persisted[17]. Practising chordal sequences made it possible at the very least to improvise a short prelude in the key of the piece. Nevertheless, Zimmerman considered harmony to be a step on the way towards composition. He also emphasised another important ability it engendered, namely that of accompanying a vocal line. It also led to knowledge of ornamentation and how to correct faults. Knowing and practising harmonic sequences made it possible to engage in a more complex way with the most important elements of music.

Many writers aligned themselves with the educational philosophy and methodology of the Paris Conservatory[18]. There was a desire to construct a rationally organised pedagogy in

---

13. On the other discipline taught at the Conservatoire and especially piano see LA GRANDVILLE 2014.

14. «Le piano étant l'interprète par excellence de la composition, il est indispensable à tout musicien soit exécutant, soit compositeur, de le connaître assez pour manier facilement tous les accords de l'harmonie». BÉRIOT 1855, n.p.

15. GÉRARD 1834, n.p.

16. «La science de l'harmonie par laquelle je commencerai est d'un usage de tous les instans [sic] pour un pianiste, soit qu'il veuille préluder, composer, mettre une basse sous un chant, orner un passage, corriger une faute, faire une coupure, toucher l'orgue, accompagner la partition». ZIMMERMANN 1840, p. 1.

17. «Il est de bon goût pour un pianiste, surtout quand il va exécuter seul un morceau dans un salon, de ne pas commencer subitement par le morceau même, mais de s'essayer d'abord par un prélude, qui lui sert à préparer l'auditeur, et en même tems [sic] à s'assurer des qualités de l'instrument, qui la plupart du temps lui est étranger». CZERNY 1829, p. 5.

18. See HONDRÉ 1995; AUDÉON 1999.

whfich each discipline was taught through specific exercises. This thinking influenced many writers and was reflected in the separation of the disciplines: defending this rationalist ideal prompted authors to question the process of learning, leading to the suggestion that one should tackle one new element at a time and practise it until it was mastered before moving on to the next.

Figured Bass in the 19th Century

Figured bass played an important role in this teaching process. It was often seen as a step towards learning composition. As Johann Georg Albrechtsberger put it: «The study of the figured bass is the first stage of multi-part composition»[19]. One of the goals of this stage of learning was to «[...] practise assiduously to accompany a harmony indicated using the numbers [...] to be later able to realise without any indication»[20]. In other words, one learned how to create accompaniments or unfigured written compositions, as was required by the competitions run by the Paris Conservatory[21]. Study of the figured bass had to be accommodated within the structure of the separate disciplines as noted above, and writers sought to justify its inclusion within that framework:

> Ainsi donc, j'ai pris successivement et dans leur ordre progressif chaque accord et ses renversemens [sic], et après avoir énoncé leurs règles, leurs exceptions et leur emploi avec divers exemples, j'ai composé sur chacun d'eux plusieurs partimenti spéciaux ou exercices d'accompagnement avec la basse chiffrée seule, dans lesquels cet accord ou ce renversement se trouve fréquemment répété dans presque tous les tons [...] Quoique j'aie fait mon possible pour donner, en général, à ces PARTIMENTI une forme agréable, on appréciera, sans doute, l'extrême difficulté qui entravait mon désir à cet égard ; puisqu'au lieu d'avoir, de suite, à ma disposition, toute espèce d'accords (comme dans les PARTIMENTI de Fenaroli, Sala, etc.) le plan de mon ouvrage m'astreignait à composer la plupart des miens seulement avec un, deux ou plusieurs accords[22].

This passage by Alexis de Garaudé demonstrates a desire to apply progressive pedagogy to the figured bass. Each of the chords had been isolated so that the student could learn them, thus

---

[19]. «L'étude de la basse chiffrée est le premier degré de celle de la composition à plusieurs parties». Albrechtsberger 1830, p. 1.

[20]. «[...] s'exercer assidûment à réaliser une harmonie indiquée au moyen des chiffres [...] pour être plus tard en état [sic] de se passer de toute indication». Kastner 1841, p. 51.

[21]. Students had to be able to realise figured and unfigured bass and accompany a melody; Basses et chants 1900.

[22]. Garaudé 1835, p. 3.

applying the concept of chords seen as independent objects. This was part of a practical, and not just theoretical, harmonic approach by Garaudé in which chords were viewed individually and not in sequences. He specified that the exercises were designed to use all the chords frequently and in all keys, building an understanding that covered all possibilities and left no problem unresolved. It is notable that Garaudé named his exercises *Partimenti*[23], using the Italian term that he equated to the French *basse chiffrée*. In this we see the influence of the Italian conservatories, as we do also in the academics he mentioned in the passage: Fenaroli (1730-1818) and Sala (1713-1801) were transalpine composers active mainly in Naples[24]. Garaudé nevertheless contrasted his approach with Italian methodology: his exercises dealt with only one harmonic concept at a time, which gave them an element of pedagogic abstraction, whereas the Italian *partimenti* were more akin to the harmonic practices employed in actual works[25].

Numerical notation led inevitably to the consideration of intervals. The figuration proposed by the authors was linked to the intervals represented in the chord in question. As Colet put it, « The whole harmony is, therefore, about the study of intervals »[26]. He suggested beginning with exercises to learn the intervals in simple steps, first verbally, then on paper, then on the piano, and then finally on the piano without sight of the book[27]. As intervals were at the heart of harmony and figured basses, most treatises began with a 'Principles of music' detailing them, similar to those found in contemporary *Solfèges*. The inclusion of these in so many treatises indicates that they were intended for a readership not previously versed in music theory and without access to other books containing the principles of music.

The championship of the figured bass, together with a desire for simplification in the reading of scores, led some writers to propose its return in published works. Antoine Elwart, for example, suggested that if scores were to be published with a figured bass, this would allow

---

[23]. « [...] the term was in use during the seventeenth century as a synonym for the bass of a composition. About the end of the century, a semantic shift occurred: while officially retaining its identification with the bass, the term was being used to indicate a kind of notational shorthand for keyboard instruments. In the new meaning, a partimento was not only a bass; every clef could appear, as well as polyphonic textures, passagework, and imitations. In other words, every possible complication that might occur in a keyboard piece could be notated (or hinted at) in a partimento. Partimento became an alternative notational system, as opposed to today's more familiar two-stave, fully notated score; this latter system was called in Italy *intavolatura* (as the antonym of partimento; the term intavolatura has nothing to do with tablature). Obviously, partimento notation leaves ample space for improvisation ». SANGUINETTI 2012, p. 5.

[24]. See 'A genealogy of masters', in: *ibidem*, pp. 57-92.

[25]. « [...] the practice of partimento allowed a global composition training — thoroughbass, harmony, counterpoint, form, texture, motivic coherence — through improvisation. As a reward for a long and difficult practice, the student attained the highest degree of musical knowledge: a quasi-automatic, instinctive compositional skill, a way of composing "through the fingers" ». SANGUINETTI 2010, p. 71.

[26]. « Toute l'harmonie est donc dans l'étude des intervalles ». COLET 1847, p. 1.

[27]. *Ibidem*, p. 8.

singers to accompany themselves more easily[28]. Elwart was obviously aware that such a practice belonged to the past, but unlike some of his contemporaries, who criticised the complexity of the system, he viewed it as way to simplify musical language. He knew that he could not demand the same from singers as from pianists at the keyboard, but he suggested that if the student had practised the exercises and mastered the main chord sequences, he could play the harmony of the music from the figuration. This demonstrates that Elwart saw the figured bass as a synthesis of musical elements, allowing one to identify harmonic sequences as the fundamentals of the composition. It also shows that he did not discriminate between synthesising harmony through analysis of the figured bass or through the score.

Despite this wide acceptance of the figured bass as a teaching tool, there were still critics. Cohen explained his reasons for not adopting it:

> Je ne parle point de la basse chiffrée pour cinq raisons: 1° L'harmonie peut s'apprendre sans elle; 2° on n'écrit plus d'airs avec la basse chiffrée; 3° faute d'habitude, les plus habiles harmonistes ont de la peine à la remplir couramment; 4° il y a des différences notables entre les manières de chiffrer en France, en Italie et en Allemagne; 5° enfin, la basse chiffrée a toujours été un épouvantail pour les amateurs qui auraient désiré savoir l'harmonie, et peut-être une des plus puissantes causes qui ont contribué à en rendre la connaissance si peu répandue[29].

Cohen argued that harmony could be learned via other didactic means. He justified the abandonment of the figured bass by linking it with repertoire rather than with teaching. As he correctly stated at the time of writing in 1842, there was no longer any music published in that format and he therefore saw no point in it if the technique was not used in practice. He also noted that because no harmonists of his time knew how to use such an outdated process, it should be discarded (although this was the very reason why other writers, such as Elwart, thought it should be revived). There was also the fact that the variety of figuring conventions found in French treatises indicated that there was no one agreed approach to the notation. Cohen's point 5 is interesting in this regard: he described figuring as a «scarecrow» for amateurs, something that would put them off or frighten them away, and that it was responsible for the current state of knowledge of harmony. In this way, he refuted the notion of the simplicity that

---

28. «Il suffira seulement que, contrairement à l'usage actuel, la basse d'orchestre soit chiffrée, par un compositeur capable, ou par l'auteur lui-même, pour que le chanteur, privé d'un accompagnateur spécial, puisse étudier ses rôles avec promptitude et succès. Autrefois, les maîtres chiffraient les basses de leurs partitions scéniques et autres; témoins les œuvres gravées de Lully, Rameau, en France; Durante, Jomelly, en Italie; Sébastien Bach, Hændel, en Allemagne et en Angleterre. Cette excellente coutume s'est malheureusement perdue depuis longtemps; mais, il dépend de nos principaux éditeurs de la faire revivre ; et l'éducation musicale des chanteurs y gagnera efficacement». Elwart 1844, pp. 3-4.

29. Cohen 1842, n.p.

Elwart supported. Figured basses would not allow progress in harmony through a simplified method and a more global understanding of harmony. In his treatise, Cohen employed melody more extensively as a pedagogical means. Indeed, this was a general trend that we can observe among many treatises published during the century: the accompaniment of song became the main goal of teaching in the discipline in favour of the realisation of a bass, which was relegated to the practices of the past.

As we have previously observed, writers at this period sought to define chords as independent entities, and the use of chord tables was a teaching tool found in many treatises that corresponded to a rational ideal of presenting all the elements of music. The chords were presented on staves, with their name and (often) figuring supplied by the author. Some writers only presented chords in root position, while others supplied inversions as separate chords. The range of chords could vary widely in the tables published in treatises between 1820 and 1860:

- Only root position:
    - 12 chords: Bizot[30] and Lemoine[31];
    - 13 chords: Elwart, Damour and Burnett[32];
    - 15 chords: Elwart[33];
    - 16 chords: Kastner[34];
    - 17 chords: Concone[35];
    - 18 chords: Colet[36]: 6 «primitive chords» and 12 «derived chords».
- With inversions:
    - 38 chords: Plane[37];
    - 43 chords: Dauvilliers[38].
- Simultaneous presentation:
    - 21 chords Blein[39] who gives 54 versions with inversions.

We see that most writers only presented root position chords, which suggests that inversions were seen only as a different way of presenting the same chord. The variety in the

---

30. Bizot 1851, pp. 40-41.
31. Lemoine 1835, p. 102.
32. Elwart – Damour – Burnett 1838, p. 513.
33. Elwart 1839, p. 3.
34. Kastner 1842.
35. Concone 1845, p. 74.
36. Colet 1846, pp. 123-124.
37. Plane 1855, p. 9.
38. Dauvilliers 1834, p. 28.
39. Blein 1832, n.p.

numbers of chords included demonstrates the wide differences in the definition of a chord depending on the view of the writer, particularly in relation to the inclusion of notes from outside the triad. This example is taken from the treatise of Lemoine:

ILL. 1: LEMOINE 1835, p. 102.

From such a table, the student could identify the chords he might encounter with their name, figuring, and the notes to play on the keyboard. Lemoine encouraged the student to practise all the possible chords from the table. The inclusion of these tables, as well as figured bass exercises, in treatises radically changed the way students approached such exercises by developing their knowledge of chords as independent entities.

The theoretical nature of figuring was linked to the requirements of what it was intended to convey. Too much information prevented easy reading and realisation, whereas too little made realisation more difficult and required a considerable knowledge of harmony and greater input from the keyboard player[40]. Kalkbrenner required «[...] that the number indicates, not only the chord, but its position and the slightest alteration of the intervals which compose it»[41]. The type of figuring he specified was not meant to be a simplification, but rather an infallible guide to realisation. The figures in this case indicate not just the type of chord, but also its position or inversion. Conversely, other authors such as Plane criticised the fact that the «multiplicity [of figures which] is such, that instead of helping the reading of an accompaniment, they often only make it more difficult, and one who has acquired enough habit to read numbers well, is already skilled enough not to need them any more»[42]. The challenge here was to know if the pianists were capable of managing without figures, competence in which discipline, as we have seen above, was part of the necessary know-how in the competitions run by the Paris Conservatory. Some writers even suggested a completely new way of figuring, such as Moulet, who proposed alternative notation:

ILL. 2: MOULET 1821, p. 4.

---

[40]. On the figuring in the late 18th century see: «La querelle des chiffrages» in VERWAERDE 2015, pp. 145-195.

[41]. «[...] que le chiffre indiquât, non seulement l'accord, mais sa position et la moindre altération des intervalles qui le composent». KALKBRENNER 1849, p. 6.

[42]. «[...] multiplicité [des chiffres qui] est telle, qu'au lieu d'aider à la lecture d'un accompagnement, ils ne font souvent que la rendre plus difficile, et celui qui a acquis assez d'habitude pour bien lire les chiffres, est déjà assez habile pour n'en avoir plus besoin». PLANE 1855, p. 1.

Repurpose and Transformation of an Educational Material

New Ways of Practising Figured Bass

Several authors produced analytical exercises based on chord sequences. Moncouteau, for example, called the unfigured basses an «analysis lesson» and required students to analyse them to find the figures:

Voici les préludes précédents sans les chiffres. Il faut analyser tous les accords qu'ils renferment, ainsi l'on dira « Cet accord est un accord parfait majeur ou le premier renversement de la 7.ᵐᵉ de dominante de tel ton etc ».
Pour se rendre le travail plus facile on doit toujours chercher la basse fondamentale.

ILL. 3: MONCOUTEAU 1845B, p. 55.

In this example, Moncouteau provided «preludes» that the student was expected to analyse, as specified in the instructions provided. The chord was to be named (again, each was to be considered an object in itself) and the inversion and key given. We may see from this that Moncouteau required the identification of the fundamental bass which allowed the precise application of theory and an understanding of the inversions. This type of exercise was, therefore, the exact opposite of the realisation of a figured bass, and the student had to apply the opposite process: finding the figures from the chord. This demonstrated a desire to develop new exercises that would allow easier mastery of harmony at the keyboard.

In realising basses, some authors recommended a numerical analysis of the degrees of the scale. Concone, for example, suggested one should «add the indication of the degrees of the tones»[43]. Dauprat recommended one should «justify the chords indicated by the degrees of the scale, degrees which one indicates by the ordinal numbers, (at least at the beginning) by considering only the fundamental sound of each chord»[44].

Indeed, being able to identify the degree of the scale implies having perfectly understood the concept of fundamental bass and the concept that an inversion and a root position belong to the same chord. This theory seemed particularly to appeal to the authors of accompaniment treatises from the first part of the nineteenth century: it allowed them to conform to the rationalist

---

[43]. «[...] ajouter l'indication des degrés des tons». CONCONE 1845, p. 41.

[44]. «[...] justifier les accords indiqués par les degrés de la gamme, degrés que l'on signale par les nombres ordinaux, (du moins en commençant) en ne considérant que le son fondamental de chaque accord». DAUPRAT 1856, p. 132.

ideal already noted above. The fundamental bass was used, for example, by Zimmermann who indicated a line of «generating sounds» below the given bass line:

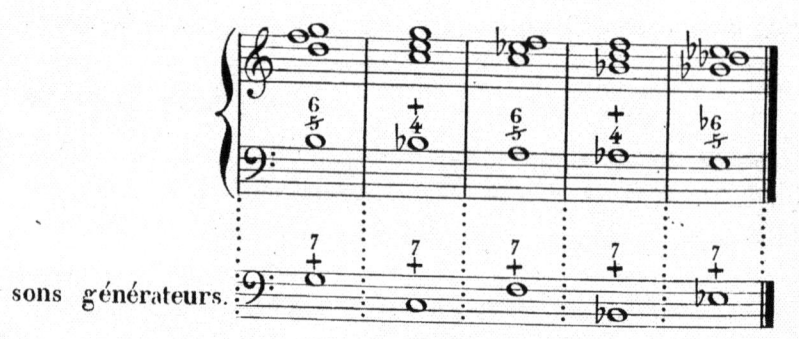

Ill. 4. Zimmermann 1840, p. 16.

It is clear that the fundamental bass was considered to be a theoretical tool, which made it possible to determine the degree of the chord within a given scale. Here is the way Dauprat recommended analysing the bass:

Ill. 5: Dauprat 1856, p. 132.

The analysis prescribed by the author was, therefore, a pedagogical tool for understanding each element of a whole that would then have to be synthesised to build the correct accompaniment. This skill was adapted to a step-by-step pedagogy as recommended in the methods of the nascent Paris Conservatory, with each element described and theorised so that the student could understand the realisation of a bass line.

At the beginning of the nineteenth century, France saw a significant increase in amateur involvement in the field of music. This involvement was encouraged by the new social and political contexts and by the development of musical printing, which produced many treatises and methods. From then on, the promise of simplification became an important sales pitch for authors, who sometimes even mentioned this aspect in the title. When teaching chords, reducing the number presented in a treatise allowed the promise that this would reduce the amount of study required, and this feature became a commercial attraction.

Several authors highlighted the fact that their works only employed three chords while still promising that this would allow the accompaniment of all music.

336

Poisson, among other theorists, called the three chords in question tonic, dominant and subdominant. These designations had already been introduced in Rameau's works[45] and the authors saw it as a simple way of presenting harmony in order to reach a wider audience. These chords were thought of by the authors not in terms of tonal function, as was the case in later theories, but in relation to the bass note on which the chords were built. Thus, the various possibilities for the sub-dominant, for example, included the addition of notes such as the sixth, so long as the chord was always built on the fourth degree. The authors presented the different harmonic possibilities on the four main degrees:

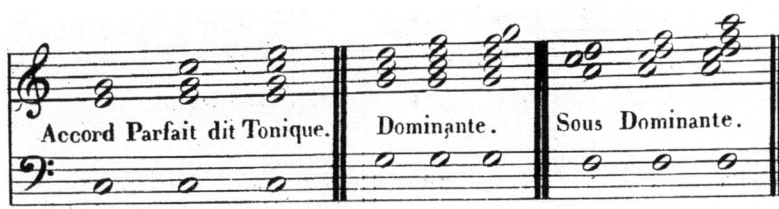

Ill. 6: Poisson 1838, p. 10.

To prove that these chords would suffice, Poisson used the octave rule, and by using this canonical formula, the author sought to show that the three chords he suggested were sufficient to accompany any type of music:

Ill. 7: Poisson 1838, p. 16.

---

45. «Selon Rameau, la grande majorité des enchainements harmoniques est basée sur l'alternance des fonctions d'accord-tonique et d'accord-dominante. Le théoricien introduit cependant une troisième fonction dans l'harmonie, à savoir la sous-dominante. Le terme même de sous-dominante n'apparaît pas dans le *Traité* [1722]. C'est dans son *Nouveau système* [1726] que Rameau le cite pour la première fois». Ceulemans 1990, p. 111.

From its origins as a method of notating music, the figured bass evolved into a school exercise championed by the Paris Conservatory from its foundation in 1795. The school, in its early days, created exercises and methods that disseminated the use of the figured bass as a pedagogical tool. As we have seen, the political and musical context was somewhat different from that of the previous century, requiring the figured bass to be thought of differently by writers and teachers. The development of amateur music making required writers to find new ways of teaching keyboard harmony. The figured bass was sometimes seen as a simplification, sometimes as an outdated and over-complex manifestation of musical notation. Theoretical considerations also influenced the use of the figured bass. The taste for rationalisation in music provided by the Conservatory's methods made authors adopt analytical exercises to help students practise figuring and learn the concept of fundamental bass as well as chord tables to describe all the possible chords. This use of figured bass as a pedagogical tool was, of course, not just a historic phenomenon, as more than 200 years later, harmony and keyboard harmony students still have to complete the realisation of figured basses in music schools today, as well as in the Paris Conservatory.

BIBLIOGRAPHY

ALBRECHTSBERGER 1830
ALBRECHTSBERGER, Johann Georg. *Méthodes d'harmonie et de composition...*, Paris, chez Bachelier, 1830.

AUDÉON 1999
AUDÉON, Hervé. 'Le Conservatoire et l'édition Musicale: L'activité du Magasin de Musique (1794-1814)', in: *Le Conservatoire de Paris, 1795-1995: deux cents ans de pédagogie*, edited by Anne Bongrain and Yves Gérard, Paris, Buchet-Chastel, 1999, pp. 205-225.

BASSES ET CHANTS 1900
Basses et chants donnés aux examens et concours des classes d'harmonie et d'accompagnement (années 1827-1900), recueillis par Constant Pierre, Paris, Heugel, 1900.

BÉRIOT 1855
BÉRIOT, Charles-Auguste de. *La Clé du piano ou méthode pour apprendre aux chanteurs à s'accompagner, Op. 95*, Paris, The Author, 1855.

BIZOT 1851
BIZOT, Charles. *Harmonie pratique, abrégé du Traité théorique et pratique de Henri Lemoine*, Paris, Lemoine, 1851.

BLEIN 1832
BLEIN, François-Ange-Alexandre. *Principes de mélodie et d'harmonie déduits de la théorie des vibrations*, Paris, Richault, 1832.

Ceulemans 1990
Ceulemans, Anne-Emmanuelle. 'La conception fonctionnelle de l'harmonie de J.-Ph. Rameau', in: *Revue des archéologues et historiens d'art de Louvain*, XXIII (1990), pp. 107-115.

Cherubini 1847
Cherubini, Luigi. *Marches d'harmonie pratiquées dans la composition produisant des suites régulières de consonnances et de dissonnances*, Paris, Heugel, 1847.

Cohen 1842
Cohen, Henry. *Traité d'harmonie pratique ou méthode facile et abrégée pour apprendre la composition, d'après un nouveau système fondé sur la mélodie*, Paris, Lemoine, 1842.

Colet 1846
Colet, Hippolyte. *Partimenti ou traité spécial de l'accompagnement pratique au piano*, Paris, Chabal, 1846.

Colet 1847
Id. *Conseils à mes élèves ou traité élémentaire d'harmonie servant d'introduction à la Panharmonie musicale*, Paris, Legouix, 1847.

Concone 1845
Concone, Paolo Giuseppe Gioachino. *Méthode d'harmonie et de composition préparatoire renferment la théorie et l'art de moduler, complétée par 40 exercices pratiques et 58 exemples analysés*, Paris, Richaut, 1845.

Czerny 1829
Czerny, Carl. *L'Art d'improviser mis à la portée des pianistes, œuvre 200*, Paris, Schlesinger, [1829].

Dauprat 1856
Dauprat, Louis François. *Nouveau traité théorique et pratique des accords ou préceptes et exemples d'harmonie et d'accompagnement de la basse chiffrée*, Paris, Quinzard, 1856.

Dauvilliers 1834
Dauvilliers, Jacques-Martin. *Traité de composition élémentaire des accords*, Paris, Janet-Cotelle, 1834.

Elwart 1839
Elwart, Antoine. *Petit manuel d'harmonie, d'accompagnement de la basse chiffrée, de réduction de la partition au piano et de transposition musicale, contenant en outre des règles pour parvenir à écrire la basse ou un accompagnement de piano sous toute espèce de mélodie...*, Paris, Colombier, 1839.

Elwart 1844
Id. *Le Chanteur-accompagnateur ou traité du clavier de la basse chiffrée, de l'harmonie simple et composée*, Paris, chez l'auteur, 1844.

Elwart – Damour – Burnett 1838
Id. – Damour – Burnett. *Études élémentaires de la musique depuis ses premières notions jusqu'à celles de la composition, divisées en trois parties: connaissances préliminaires, méthode de chant, méthode d'harmonie*, Paris, Au Bureau des études élémentaire de la Musique, 1838.

Fétis 1824
Fétis, François-Joseph. *Méthode élémentaire et abrégée d'harmonie et d'accompagnement: suivie d'exercices gradués et dans tous les tons, par l'étude desquels les amateurs pourront arriver promptement à accompagner la basse chiffrée et la partition*, Paris, À la Nouveauté, au Magasin de musique et d'instrumens de Ph. Petit, succr. de P. Gaveaux, 1824.

Garaudé 1835
Garaudé, Alexis de. *L'Harmonie rendue facile ou Théorie pratique de cette science et d'accompagnement de la basse chiffrée et de la partition, Op. 44*, Paris, chez l'auteur, 1835.

Gérard 1834
Gérard, Henri Philippe. *Traité Méthodique d'harmonie, où l'instruction pratique est simplifiée et mise à la portée des commencants par Gérard*, Paris, Launer, 1834.

Hondré 1995
Hondré, Emmanuel. 'Les Méthodes Officielles du Conservatoire', in: *Le Conservatoire de musique de Paris: regards sur une institution et son histoire*, edited by Emmanuel Hondré, Paris, Association du Bureau des étudiants du Conservatoire national supérieur de musique de Paris, 1995, pp. 73-107.

Kalkbrenner 1849
Kalkbrenner, Friedrich. *Traité d'harmonie du pianiste: principes relationnels de la modulation pour apprendre à préluder et à improviser, exemples d'études, de fugues et de préludes pour le piano*, Paris, l'auteur, 1849.

Kastner 1841
Kastner, Jean-Georges. *Méthode élémentaire d'harmonie appliquée au piano suivie d'un aperçu de l'accompagnement et de la transposition à l'usage des pianistes*, Paris, J. Meissonnier, 1841.

Kastner 1842
Id. *Tableau analytique de l'harmonie*, Paris A. Meissonnier et Heugel, 1842.

La Grandville 2014
La Grandville, Frédéric de. *Une Histoire du Piano au Conservatoire de Musique de Paris: 1795-1850*, Paris, l'Harmattan, 2014.

Lemoine
Lemoine, Henry. *Traité d'harmonie pratique et théorique*, Paris, L'auteur, 1835.

Moncouteau 1845a
Moncouteau, Pierre-François. *Manuel de transposition musicale*, Paris, Canaux, 1845.

MONCOUTEAU 1845B
ID. *Traité d'harmonie, contenant les règles et les exercices nécessaires pour apprendre à bien accompagner un chant*, Paris, chez Alexandre Grus et chez l'auteur, 1845.

MOULET 1821
MOULET, Joseph-Agricole. *Leçons d'harmonie et d'accompagnement au moyen du Cycle harmonique, tableau qui contient tous les accords dans tous les tons...*, Paris, Jouve, 1821.

PANSERON 1855
PANSERON, Auguste. *Traité de l'harmonie pratique et des modulations en 3 parties*, Paris, Brandus, 1855.

PIERRE 1900
PIERRE, Constant. *Le Conservatoire national de musique et de déclamation: documents historiques et administratifs / recueillis ou reconstitués par Constant Pierre...*, Paris, Impr. Nationale, 1900.

PLANE 1855
PLANE, Jean-Marie. *Cours d'harmonie divisé en 12 leçons claires et faciles, Nouvelle édition*, Paris, Richault, 1855.

POISSON 1838
POISSON, Toussaint René. *L'Harmonie dans ses plus grands développements présentée sous un jour entièrement nouveau ou Théorie de composition musicale*, Paris, The Author, [1838].

SANGUINETTI 2010
SANGUINETTI, Giorgio. 'Partimento-Fugue: The Neapolitan Angle', in: *Partimento and Continuo Playing in Theory and in Practice*, edited by Dirk Moelants, Leuven, Leuven University Press, 2010, pp. 71-111.

SANGUINETTI 2012
ID. *The Art of Partimento: History, Theory, and Practice*, Oxford-New York, Oxford University Press, 2012.

VERWAERDE 2015
VERWAERDE, Clotilde. *La pratique de l'accompagnement en France (1750-1800): de la basse continue improvisée à l'écriture pour clavier dans la sonate avec violon*, Ph.D. Diss., Paris, Paris-Sorbonne, 2015, <https://theses.hal.science/tel-04267902>, accessed December 2023.

ZIMMERMANN 1840
ZIMMERMANN, Pierre-Joseph-Guillaume. *Encyclopédie du pianiste compositeur en 3 parties par J. Zimmerman, 3ᵉ partie - Supplément Traité d'harmonie*, Paris, l'auteur, 1840.

Thorough Bass Made Easy:
The Pedagogical Value of Figured Bass
in Musical Education Today

Thomas Allery
(Royal College of Music, London)

I nterest in historically informed performance continues to grow, with performers, students and audiences alike; new graduates training in this specialist field enter the industry year after year from institutions across the world. Even amongst non-specialists, many of the core principles of historically informed performance are now commonplace in modern music pedagogy. The scene flourishes across the globe with the use of period instruments and original facsimile scores, with frequent performances of newly discovered music from archives continuing to be popular with audiences. Within this context, performance of basso continuo from figured bass notation has undergone a welcome revival over past decades, both in terms of research and its implementation in performance. However, as a pedagogical tool, it is taught primarily at specialist level and is rarely used in mainstream musical education. In the United Kingdom, where introducing the skill of creating realisations from figured bass notation usually takes place at tertiary level, it is often too late for students to benefit from the wider musical skills that performing from this notation can bring.

My work as a teacher involves bridging the gap between historical treatises and the teaching principles therein, and incorporating these into modern teaching practice from an early age, seeking to draw on the freedom of figured notation and its means of teaching voice-leading principles, texture, intervallic relationships, and other musical matters. The integrated approach of figured notation encourages the development of a broad musical skill set. Drawing inspiration from original sources, this research views such treatises from a new angle: their original purpose as teaching material. By sharing observations from practice-led research, I seek to illustrate some of my teaching principles and aims. In the context of the limited engagement with figured bass notation within music education in the UK, this paper endevours to investigate the gap between elementary learning and the flourishing historical performance scene, then to demonstrate some of the ways in which figured bass notation can be used as a teaching tool for junior and non-specialist students. The inherent space for creativity in figured bass notation is an opportunity to link theory with practice in a far wider field, away from the world of historical performance. Much of this research involves reflection and inquiry with the objective of stimulating meaningful discussion with teachers and educational institutions about research questions as such: What should be the role of the keyboard in music education in the future? How does the nature of the notation we use affect us as teachers, and shape the musical encounters of our students?

Teaching practice across the world was forced to dramatically change in 2020 as a result of restrictions during the coronavirus pandemic. A complete shift in focus was required: in my case, I chose to move away from the study of organ and harpsichord repertoire (as instruments in public spaces were unavailable), towards an emphasis on developing keyboard skills and an understanding which would make effective use of this period of time. My approach was to encourage students, ranging from beginners to conservatoire levels, to be able to use the keyboard (the main place of musical creativity during isolation periods) to understand and practice musical processes and to equip them to engage with a range of musical endeavours in the future. Soon into the process, it became evident that my keyboard teaching across the age range was unified by one main thread: the unique ability of figured bass notation to show harmonic processes and voice leading with clarity and ease, in a creative, flexible, and transferable manner. In my own teaching practice, both privately and in institutions, I regularly encounter advanced students who, even when they possess an advanced harmonic vocabulary in theory, lack the ability to implement it in a practical manner. This points to a serious and fundamental disjunction within musical training of young students between practice and theory, and has been the motivation behind this research and future work.

Situating this research within the existing body of scholarship requires care because there is little published literature on the specific principle of assessing the benefits of integrating figured bass notation and continuo accompaniment into music education at an elementary stage. This research sits within the realms of music pedagogy and improvisation studies. In terms of historical pedagogy, there is, of course, a wealth of translations and commentaries of primary sources from the seventeenth and eighteenth centuries, which provide valuable material for advanced students to gain a stylistic understanding of historical continuo practice from the hands of composers themselves. The use of these documents requires care and expertise, whether in formal teaching or self-study, with readers requiring a genuine understanding of the original function and aims of the document, ranging from tutors designed for amateur players covering rudimental principles, such as those by Pasquali (1757), Prelleur (1731), and Gasparini (1708) to the expansive compendium volumes of Heinichen (1728) or C. Ph. E.

Bach (1735), which act as tutors in composition and style as well as on figured bass. Even within the advanced study of continuo practice today, exactly how we use the information from these historical documents will naturally need to be adapted according to the nature of the source, and according to the needs of the individual student. The application of stylistic material from treatises to continuo performance is frequently the main goal for many players, but there are already many obstacles to overcome in this endeavour. There is, in addition, often a significant language barrier to overcome in many cases, which can prevent access to the material, and many treatises still lack a modern edition or translations. These issues mean that many continuo practitioners and teachers neglect one of the main features in figured bass practice: the fact that performing figured bass requires an advanced musical toolkit, which can be applied in any number of other musical situations.

Much research has been undertaken in the USA on the value of improvisation in higher education courses. Anna Song observes that «the use of improvisation in higher education outside the jazz curriculum remains minimal»[1]. She notes the difference between jazz and traditional courses in her survey, noting that «improvisation remains predominantly absent from many collegiate music courses. Excluding jazz related courses, a majority (82%) of the 209 courses do not incorporate any improvisation»[2]. She concludes by stressing «the need for continued discussion regarding the integration of varying forms and degrees of improvisation throughout collegiate music curricula»[3]. This research indicates the extent to which the development of improvisation skills is entirely absent from the majority music courses in her study, and is more associated with jazz and other styles. Improvisation in pedagogical environments is commonly considered a specialist or related skill, rather than key part of any musical training programme, which can unite different areas of study. As a form of structured improvisation, continuo practice could be implemented as a tool within such discussions on curricula, providing a useful pathway into developing musical material, which is not entirely notated.

It is crucial to consider the place of creativity and harmonic understanding as part of a music syllabus. Michael Palmer remarks that, when building connections between performance studies and musical analysis as part of his 'integral basic musicianship' course at Michigan University, he finds that tertiary level students are «motivated by their desire for an integrative, holistic approach to learning music theory»[4]. It is this sense of integration between composition, notation, harmony and creativity, which has stimulated my introduction of figured notation to young students in the very early stages of their musical education. In many cases, junior students

---

[1]. Song 2013.

[2]. *Ibidem.*

[3]. *Ibidem.*

[4]. Palmer 2014.

from the age of 11 were learning to recognise patterns and explore the placement of harmony in three or more voices above a given bass line. As will be explored below, learning harmony from figured bass requires integration between all of the major skills in music education, whether that be analysis, composition, harmonic theory, performance, chamber music, direction, or historical study. Steve Larson, in his paper 'Integrated Music Learning and Improvisation, Menus, Maps and Models', helpfully explores musical relationships and ways of mapping harmonic progressions while considering the content of theory courses. Improvisation and the seeking of creative ways to map and notate music in multiple ways is a key part of his teaching approach, with improvisation itself seen as a means of expression. He emphasises that «knowing facts about music is only useful if those facts can be brought to bear as quickly as the musical situation requires» and that «improvisation not only requires that those skills be accessible, but also makes them available»[5]. Improvisatory activities undertaken through the framework such as that provided by figured bass is a proven way of creating and consolidating theoretical relationships, integrating theory with practical skill. Ultimately, «music learning is best when it is integrated, when it combines different ways of understanding musical relationships»[6], but this sense of integration has been eroded in an era of increased specialisation.

AN ERA OF SPECIALISATION:
THE USE OF FIGURED BASS IN BRITISH MUSIC CURRICULA

In most Western music educational contexts, written notation is regularly valued above other disciplines, including improvised forms, as is evident through a survey of current exam specifications. Exam requirements and curricula often struggle to categorise and test non-written forms of music: we struggle to classify unnotated practice, and find implementing it into syllabi problematic for teaching and examining alike. Set against the background of a booming sector of historical performance, this may seem at odds with the fact that the very essential parts of this repertoire are unnotated, improvised or left to the discretion of the performer — whether that is continuo practice itself (including choice of instrumentation), ornamentation, dynamics, or even order of movements or use of repeats. Parallels might, once again, be made here with other musical traditions, such as jazz, to contextualise the sorts of issues at play in terms of placing this skill within curricula, syllabi and examination regulations. The Jazz examinations of both the Associated Board of the Royal Schools of Music and Trinity College London (the two major examination boards in the UK) both contain small amounts of improvisation in their jazz and performance graded examination requirements, yet even these are supporting tests or a 'quick

---

[5].   LARSON 1995.
[6].   *Ibidem.*

study'. Currently, figured bass notation is almost entirely absent from in within any music syllabi, with only brief encounters even within the highest level qualifications: ABRSM's grade 8 theory and in A level syllabi.

The Grade 8 examination in music theory contains this exercise: «Complete the upper two parts in the following extracts from a trio sonata following the figuring shown under the basso continuo»[7] (see Ex. 1 below).

Ex. 1.

Purcell

This question requires students to comprehend the harmony indicated by the figures, and the ability to create two independent lines, which conform to standard voice leading principles, with an understanding of the role of imitation between the violin parts. In order to answer successfully, students will need to be able to prepare and resolve dissonance correctly in two voices. This exercise requires an assured understanding of harmony and the language of figured bass to employ the correct notes in a three voiced texture, but it does not necessarily teach students taking the examination to understand the linear progression of harmony and of voices against the moving bass part, the function of chords, or any form of expression, which is conveyed by the composer in the use of dissonance in the figures. Although some students

---

[7]. CROSSLAND – GREAVES 2000, p. 20.

may use the keyboard to work out a practice solution, the examination takes place without a keyboard, so the exercise is entirely in written form.

The 2019 A level syllabus for AQA (Assessment and Qualifications Alliance, the UK's largest examination board) has only one reference to basso continuo, listing it as an example of a «sonority (timbre)»[8] which students might identify aurally. Here, it is thus not even taught as a performance tradition or form of notation. The examination board Edexcel gives a description of figured bass mentioning it to indicate that «[students] will not be required to add, or work to, a figured bass in the A level counterpoint exercise»[9]. Similarly, AQA mentions the concept of continuo in its baroque set works paper, pointing out that «the absence of any figured bass to provide the inner harmony would suggest that [the player] intended to play the keyboard himself»[10]. The common point in all of the cases above is that students are only encouraged to interact with this form of notation as either a written skill, or in the context of placing works in a historical context. Figured notation is purely considered a written skill, with no practical application encouraging students to play, experiment or experience the harmony physically at the keyboard or other instrument.

So, there is a fundamental gap here between musical skills understood in written form, and those required at practical level, forming a barrier to the linking of existing repertoire and practical musicianship, with students made aware of the existence of figured bass notation in a historical context, but without any real understanding of how it works. My own practice-led research seeks to build some of these links again, with students learning harmony first as a practical skill, subsequently supported by visual notation. Viewed primarily as a written discipline, the study of harmony may, in many cases, find no practical application in the lives and careers of students.

A more detailed survey of the syllabus requirements for A Level music[11] reveals that students studying Baroque works are required to understand fundamental harmonic concepts such as modulation, cadence formation, the use of chromaticism for expressive effect, changes in harmonic rhythm, pedal points, voice leading and forbidden parallel motion. However, the language used to describe harmony in this situation is generally written as Roman chord numerals, a system relying on the precise location of chords within a key at all times. Within this system, the identification of a chord and its position must be worked out in relation to the key of a passage — a process that can become complicated for students as music modulates across several keys. In contrast, using figures enables students to immediately associate a chord label as a position or arrangement of voices, which draws attention to the lowest voice, and

---

8. AQA 2016, (7272)
9. PEARSON EDEXCEL 2021.
10. AQA 2021, p. 21.
11. AQA 2016.

with dissonance observed in a linear manner. The lack of connection between theory and practice when using Roman chord notation prevents the development of cognitive resources that encourage a musical imagination of the musical discourse. I will go on to argue that figured notation encourages the musical mind to perceive the journey of music with reference to both horizontal and vertical awareness, allowing the means to realise it physically at the keyboard or other instrument. Crucially, figured bass notation is primarily designed to be a shorthand form of writing for the use of performers, and its key feature is its flexibility, which allows it to be realised differently in diverse musical situations. A review of examination requirements reveals that areas of music training are increasingly divided into smaller areas of specialisation with composition, improvisation, performance, analysis, figured bass all considered specialisms. The study of figured bass, however, encourages development of all of these areas together, with players developing their understanding of compositional principles through improvisation from this shorthand notation.

THE BENEFITS OF LEARNING KEYBOARD SKILLS FROM A FIGURED BASS

What can the characteristics of figured bass offers to students and teachers? In the call for papers, the Centro Studi Opera Omnia Luigi Boccherini, the Research Group Palma Choralis and the Dipartimento di Musica Antica 'Città di Brescia', in their 2021 conference *The Figured Bass Accompaniment in Europe*, asserted that figured bass accompaniment acts as «a halfway between composition and performance», putting those who use it in a unique and privileged position, required to add their own musical material to the composition through a realisation. Whilst learning how to play harmonic progressions as an accompaniment, students are simultaneously discovering the compositional process, encouraged to draw on the material and motifs from other parts of a composition and from stylistic features encountered during repertoire study. One extremely useful approach used by many teachers of continuo practice today is to learn, play and recognise common eighteenth-century bass patterns such as those laid out by the great Neapolitan maestri, including Fedele Fenaroli, Leonardo Leo, and Nicola Sala through their rules of partimento. The mind-set of students thence is at once that of an improviser (of counterpoint and melody), composer, and accompanist.

The nature of figured notation, with its 'incomplete' means of communicating harmony enables students, in essence, to relearn harmony, which they have previously heard and encountered in written form. In turn, this bridges the gap between theoretical understanding and practical experience — two levels of learning music, which are frequently considered separate skills. Larson emphasises that «to learn something, you must already know it»[12], and

---

[12].   LARSON 1995.

I would argue that figured notation makes use of this very principle in an entirely practical way. In the case of more advanced students learning to play continuo from figured bass, they have often encountered advanced harmonic processes through their study of repertoire, as well as in written exercises, yet this way of learning demands that students process such harmonic progressions physically and in a new way. They learn to build chords, understand principles of voice leading, how to treat dissonance, and gain an instinct for the texture of chords, often relearning known musical material through a physical process and a new encounter. In this way, the keyboard acts as a place of musical experimentation, as a physical musical map, which enables students of any discipline to discover harmony and voice leading practically, providing, through figured bass, a holistic link between notation (which is incomplete), composition, and physicality.

The physicality of playing and experiencing harmony is often overlooked in a world where written exercises are prioritised. Jerry Lowder's work draws on the development of fingering patterns, helping students accustomed to single line instruments to develop skills in playing harmony through considering the brain's ability to process shapes. He concludes that «precise and habitual fingerings for certain chord shapes and scale patterns should be introduced during [the] initial period of instruction»[13]. He assesses whether teaching the principles of figured bass would help with sight-reading skills, with positive results. There is a priority in this study of working towards an end goal of improving sight-reading quickly from notation, rather than just achieving a practical level of harmonic understanding, but the shift towards understanding the logic of harmony through hand shapes is a useful parallel, even though Lowder's study has a different aim to this.

Examining Larson's conclusion that «integrated music learning combines aural, vocal, visual, intellectual, digital, kinaesthetic, and emotional understanding of musical relationships»[14], it may be observed that the 'incomplete' notation can achieve all of these. Figured bass relies inherently on aural skills, with players listening to sounds, which are ever-changing and moving. Listening requires reacting to different numbers of voices in realisation, remaining aware of the voice-leading of several voices at once, noticing the quality of the melodic line created in the top voice, and discerning conjunct and disjunct motion. Equally, figured bass playing embodies a significant visual element, with the pedagogical logic we see in treatises such as Jean-François Dandrieu's *Principes de l'Acompagnement du Clavecin* (1718)[15] relying on training the eye to recognise patterns from a bass shape, and the associated chords. Dandrieu offers three versions of each exercise: fully figured, an outline, and finally, without figures. Similarly, the visual recognition of bass shapes a fundamental element of partimento training,

---

13.   LOWDER 1974.
14.   LARSON 1995.
15.   DANDRIEU 1718.

with students required to spot the *moti del basso* in order to provide appropriate harmony and decoration, then expanding the incomplete music away from the score and recognising them in future pieces. Larson's mention of the «intellectual» is also relevant here, with students using their fundamental and thorough understanding of chordal formation, including their positions, the rules on correct treatment of dissonance, and of forbidden motion. Students must understand these concepts in whichever form they find easiest and most appropriate to them, but it is in the practice and performance of figured bass that they are able to practice them and experience them physically. The concepts can then be processed and recalled digitally, allowing musical relationships to be consolidated. Fingering patterns of chords, likewise, physically reinforce musical relationships: with each repeated encounter of a chord position, the shapes are committed to memory and reinforced. Figured bass learning is fundamentally a kinaesthetic activity because the learning of theory is enhanced and supported by an awareness of the position of movement of the fingers and hand. Depending on the individual, students at some point learn through touch, movement and motion, and there is a crucial point at which the feel of this motion can be understood before a full 'written' understanding of the harmonies. The development of muscle memory can help students to play harmonies that they have encountered or heard before, because this takes priority over an intellectual understanding in a practical exercise. The huge amount of flexibility, which is an essential element of figured bass notation enables students to think actively about expression, especially with regard to texture and the qualities of intervals, both in the given bass line and melodic and imitative lines they create above.

Observations and Reflections from Practice

The materials I have designed guide students through a series of linked resources, all based on material from a range of historical sources and repertoire. Through the application of pedagogical logic from eighteenth-century treatises, exercises seek to teach and connect multiple core musical skills. In each case, the exercises are designed to lead from one to another, with each new principle introduced following a revision of previous material, in order to develop an understanding of the harmonic progressions as well as the role of the shorthand notation. Whilst the focus is on figured bass, exercises are supported by other skills such as reading open scores, transposition, free harmonisation, learning bass progressions, and playing chorales. Each exercise is designed to work with musical material across different notational layouts, with figured bass used alongside open choral scores and short scores. The objective is to use a combination of materials to produce multiple connections between musical material, which are often presented in fragments or shortened versions so as to allow time for repetition and reflection. In this material, the notation of figured bass can be used as a language to note harmonic progressions, whether they be presented in open score, improvised form or in a short score. The combination of written material and improvised exercises encourages students to draw upon their experience of voicing and texture in composed works. Having explored its use with my students, many of my organ students from age 11 upwards can now confidently play harmonies above a simple bass part, often adding of dissonance and decoration unprompted.

Ex. 2 shows the first exercise in the collection. The sequence of extracts is a progression from a simple four note bass part to a longer exercise requiring reading from a fully figured progression of root position chords. Having introduced the concept of chords in four parts, the sequence is displayed again in a 'choral' layout, encouraging students to think about the how the four voices are equivalent to four choral parts. From this introduction, students become aware of the sense of polyphonic lines coming together to produce harmony. The principle of the final exercise at the end is drawn from Dandrieu's *Principes de l'Acompagnement du Clavecin* (1718) with full figuring representing an exact voice leading. This exercise is followed by a review of these principles, still with 5/3 chords, but in a different key, a principle used by Handel in his figured bass exercises (c.1724).

Ex. 2.

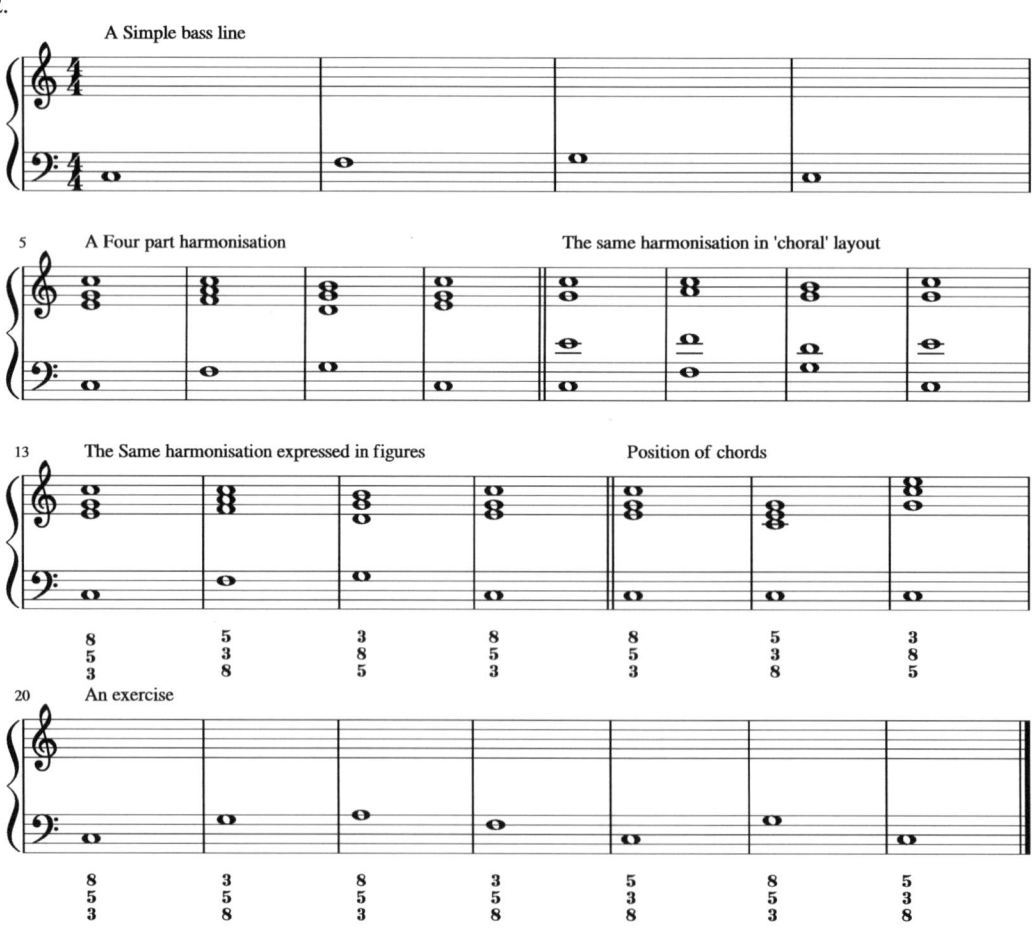

Ex. 3 shows a later exercise in the sequence, which teaches a common partimento bass line: the 'three down, one up' pattern. With the 6-3 chord having already been taught (including the different possible ways of doubling notes of the chord), this pattern is first introduced as a two part texture, with the right hand part having a clear melodic quality. The second stage shows a simple decoration in second species counterpoint, with the possibility of then encouraging students to improvise their own decorations with different rhythmic patterns, but with the figured notation then added as a guide. Next, the chordal version is introduced in an incomplete form so that students can confidently start the pattern using the notation before continuing unprompted. This has two objectives: firstly developing confidence away from fully notated music, and second, encouraging the moving hand position to be the motivating force, which takes the student through the exercise. Finally, the lesson ends with transposing the pattern and introducing one further decorative right hand part to begin, this time in third species.

Ex. 3.

Ex. 4 takes teaching principles of Pasquali's *Thorough bass made easy* (1757), whence this paper takes its name. The rising scale and cadential pattern are notated with subtle changes in the figuring, encouraging players to identify similarities and differences, and to understand the later, more complex, figures (such as the seventh chords, suspension) as a harmonic embellishment of earlier versions. This exercise revises the rule of the octave in the different positions, encourages the use of decorative passing notes and, once again, incorporates written in cues alongside blank staves where students continue without notation.

Ex. 4.

Young students, from age 11, have taken very quickly to figured bass using these materials, often seeing notation as a type of code to the unwritten or hidden material. Young students particularly enjoy recognising patterns they have seen before working out the solutions based on musical material they have previously encountered. The understanding of harmonic processes means that students also learn other important skills such as score reading and transposition. Ex. 5 shows a simple accompanying exercise in two-part score reading designed to build confidence in reading from score, consider two independent lines, whilst also introducing the cadential 4-3 as something they have previously heard or sung. This example is taken from the opening of William Byrd's 'Ave Verum Corpus', thus forming a direct link to known repertoire. Students find the activities more relevant and engaging when they can see that the material under study in exercises such as this creates links with other parts of their music learning.

Ex. 5.

Students using this material were learning harmonic process physically, not only in a written record. This was especially evident when recalling a common cadential 4-3 dissonance where the shape of hand was significantly different depending on whether the suspended voice was at the top, middle or bottom of the chord (see Ex. 4 above to see how this harmonic feature was encountered in a different context). After an initial period of study, many students built up the confidence to take skills they had learned in keyboard harmony lessons to other areas of their musical lives, partly because they were able to recall concepts more easily between lessons. Another significant observation was that advanced students started to keenly identify standard harmonic processes (such as 4-3 progressions, chains of 6-3 chords, cycles of 5ths, 6-4 to 5-3 progression) in their repertoire and in accompaniments such as hymns and chorales. Recognising them elsewhere, they are not slowed down by the need to work out the key area within the piece, as they might need to with Roman numerals, but can identify and recognise progressions and begin to engage with them as a musical gesture. Some students were able to start to experiment with concepts of stylistic awareness such as texture and voicing, and decoration, as a result of their being able to listen in a new way, relating their playing to expressive features they had seen in repertoire.

The benefits to students training in this material are manifold, particularly in terms of their ability to work with different elements of the music under study. Unlike in many textbooks on written harmony, where early exercises work on the harmonisation of a melody part, here the attention is on the bass part. Furthermore, making chords in the right hand and listening to the effects of different voicings draws attention to the contrapuntal lines present in harmony — a concept, which is more challenging to explain in written form. Finding a new way into teaching awareness of counterpoint, and how to craft melodic lines, has been a significant discovery. As highlighted above, learning figured bass means that students are learning not only harmony but also, through improvisatory exercises, the compositional process itself. Within this, students gain an awareness of musical expression through changing the number of voices, and are then able to identify such textural changes in repertoire. Today's musical world often views melody as the primary form of expression, with lower parts forming an accompaniment, whereas continuo playing gives students a real understanding of how melody is derived from harmony.

Ultimately, the main feedback from students and colleagues working with figured bass exercises with young students has been the fact that creativity is prioritised above notation, in a positive and approachable manner, which encourages confidence and independent musicianship. The approach is flexible: students are not encouraged to search for a single fixed 'solution', but taught to adapt material between iterations, learning to keep some elements between versions, and change others, rather than aiming for a final performance of a notated work.

The physical understanding of harmonic progressions is based on hand shapes and the positions of chords, not simply on visual representation, and the confidence gained by the freedom of notation encourages transferability to other styles of music. In particular, several students have immediately made a link to jazz and well known pop songs, simply observing the recurrence of harmonic progressions in a different context. Overall, learning figured bass notation encourages students to identify progressions and patterns, not simply chord by chord, or note by note. In this way, we can teach the relationships between chords, introducing them to key *moti del basso*, and encouraging the development of expressive playing in larger phrases and structures.

CONCLUSION: A WAY FORWARD?

The initial implementation of figured bass materials in my teaching have yielded encouraging and positive results. Using the same set of materials, students ranging in age from 11 to 18, at a variety of levels of previous experience, have taken to different aspects of improvising accompaniments. In each case, students have found that the physical discovery of harmony allows them to comprehend concepts more quickly than learning them only through written exercises. This may seem obvious to performers of basso continuo, yet the reality is that teaching using a bespoke combination of practical exercises and supporting written material (often tailored to the individual student) requires specialist knowledge and the correct circumstances and resources. The continual questioning by teachers and basso continuo players must continue if performances of much cherished repertoire are to continue in generations to come. What sort of role could figured-bass notation, or elements of it, play within modern music education, with the right resources? Through continued research and practice in this field, I hope to find new responses and reactions to the question of the role of the keyboard as a pedagogical tool in modern places of learning.

There are, however, many obstacles to consider. Today, the keyboard frequently suffers from being viewed as an elite instrument, often associated with the privileged environments of churches, private chapels, and elite conservatoires. Whilst we must cherish the tradition of basso continuo practice within the realm of historical performance, it is time to expand the benefits of this way of learning to a wider sphere. Practitioners of Early Music are uniquely placed today to make a significant contribution to the broader development of improvisatory activities within music education across the age range. The integrated approach to learning seen above can doubtlessly open musical opportunities to a range of students if introduced as a musical language early on. Much of the repertoire enjoyed by our performers and audiences is based on improvisatory practices, and so many crucial elements of our repertoire are improvised, yet there is still a sense in which to be able to create an accompaniment from a half way notation is exclusively a skill for specialists. Further studies in this area will naturally lead to questions on how we collectively define a sense of musical literacy in the modern world. At present, this often involves placing notation at the top of the agenda, with sight-reading, accuracy and the ability to perform with limited rehearsal time frequently remaining the main ambition of many teachers and directors. Figured bass, as an 'incomplete' notational system, can encourage an entirely different and more creative vision in its definition of literacy, moving beyond the idea of simply replicating information from the page, but requiring interpretation and understanding from the very start of the musical and creative process. With an open-minded approach from teachers and institutions, figured bass notation offers creative freedom, which will be rewarding and long lasting for many because it is supported by physical learning principles. This will require careful consideration of the priorities within teaching music and, in particular, in how to test, examine and grade students as they progress.

In the years to come, I hope to expand this area of research and create new methods and tutors for learning figured bass from a young age, taking examples and pedagogical logic from historical sources. This work will make advantage of part of the musical language, which students already know (aurally, in written form, or through previously learned repertoire) and encourage them to experience, process, and engage with harmony in a new way. Figured notation must remain a living teaching resource outside historical performance. Such research has a cyclical logic: work on primary sources often focusses on *what* musicians in former generations learned, not necessarily exploring *how* they learned. In order to teach fundamental principles to the next generation of young musicians, it is vital that we reflect upon learning methods employed in the past, to inform our practice today.

BIBLIOGRAPHY

AQA 2016
AQA A level Music. *Specification for teaching from September 2016 onwards, for exams in 2018 onwards, Version 1.1*, <https://www.aqa.org.uk/subjects/music/a-level/music-7272>, accessed October 2023.

AQA 2021
AQA A level Music. *Teaching guide: Area of study 1 (Baroque solo concerto)*, (2021), <https://filestore.aqa.org.uk/resources/music/AQA-7272-TG-AOS1-BSC.PDF>, accessed October 2023.

CROSSLAND – GREAVES 2000
CROSSLAND, Anthony – GREAVES, Terence. *Theory Workbook, Grade 8*, London, The Associated Board of the Royal Schools of Music, 2000.

DANDRIEU 1718
DANDRIEU, Jean-François. *Principes de l'Acompagnement du Clavecin*, Paris, chez l'Auteur, 1718.

LARSON 1995
LARSON, Steve. '«Integrated Music Learning» and Improvisation: Teaching Musicianship and Theory through «Menus, Maps, and Models»', in: *College Music Symposium*, XXXV (1995), pp. 76-90.

LOWDER 1974
LOWDER, Jerry. 'An Experimental Study of a Keyboard Sight-Reading Test Administered to Freshman Secondary Piano Students at the Ohio State University', in: *Contributions to Music Education*, no. 3 (1974), pp. 97-105.

PALMER 2014
PALMER, C. Michael. 'Learning Basic Music Theory through Improvisation: Implications for Including Improvisation in the University Curriculum', in: *College Music Symposium*, LIV (2014), n.p.

PEARSON EDEXCEL 2021
Pearson Edexcel Music. *Specification Pearson Edexcel Level 3 Advanced GCE in Music (9MU0). First teaching from September 2016 First certification from 2018, Issue 7,* 2021 <https://qualifications.pearson.com/content/dam/pdf/A%20Level/Music/2016/Specification%20and%20sample%20assessments/Pearson_Edexcel_Level_3_Advanced_GCE_in_Music_9MU0_specification_issue7.pdf>, accessed October 2023.

SONG 2013
SONG, Anna. 'Music Improvisation in Higher Education', in: *College Music Symposium*, LIII (2013), n.p.

Basso Continuo as a 'Concertato' Practice: Vocal-Instrumental Improvisation, Ornamentation and Counterpoint

Livio Ticli
(Conservatorio 'A. Vivaldi', Alessandria)

RECENT RESEARCH has established that instrumental accompaniment practices of the late sixteenth and seventeenth centuries were much more complex than scholarship had hypothesised even just thirty to forty years ago[1]. Alongside playing the intabulation for all the contrapuntal parts involved, we must also consider a set of improvisational practices that utilise various sources as starting points, including scores, short scores, *intavolature*, and the more customary forms of *basso seguente* or figured bass[2]. Therefore, it is challenging even to define what 'basso continuo' was, under which label we tend to group such diverse practices today.

Unfortunately, all too often, the focus has been solely on harmonic aspects and the simple performance of the four parts on the keyboard, neglecting the role of all instruments other than the keyboard that participated in ensemble music-making[3]. It is essential to remember, first and foremost, that the basso continuo phenomenon is primarily the result of an aural expression (both in practice and in its learning phases) and is not rigidly confined to its written form, which would serve as a stenography of a rebus to be reconstructed. For this reason, even apparently dry descriptions of concerts from the period, or treatises, which today we assume to have exclusively theoretical and retrospective relevance, should be reconsidered, as they often provide a vivid sonorous description of contrapuntal performance over the bass operated

---

[1]. Schubert 2012, Canguilhem 2015, Guido 2019, Campagne – Rotem 2022.

[2]. See Campagne – Rotem 2022.

[3]. Recent contributions that challenge this keyboard-centric conception can be found in Bahn – Barbati 2023, and in the article by Hilary Metzger in this volume.

by various instruments. The sources that constitute the core of this chapter will thus be re-evaluated with the aim of identifying those elements that give the practice of basso continuo a less rigid appearance, more akin to collective improvisation. At the same time, it becomes necessary to reconsider them diachronically, as testimonies of a living and ever-evolving practice that led from more 'spontaneous' forms of improvisation over a *cantus firmus* or *prius factus* (which over time increasingly took place in the lower part) to the codification, even in writing, of these habits, crystallising in the form of compositional rules and, over time, resulting in the modern concept of composition itself.

Without succumbing to the temptation to think of basso continuo as a simple 'mechanism' of feedback between visualisation-codification and the realisation of a pre-established harmonic scheme, the goal of this study is, on the contrary, to restore basso continuo to its aural foundation for the first time[4], rediscovering a collection of practices that break, transform, and readapt the rigid schematism and prescriptivism that we now attribute to musical notation, forgetting, on one hand, its symbolic function, and on the other, its nature as a selective note.

BASSO CONTINUO FACETS:
CONCERTI, *CONCERTATO* AND INTEGRATED PERFORMANCE

This study does not limit its discussion to thorough-bass treatises or works referencing a *Bassus pro organo* part-book. Instead, despite its undeniable peculiarity and innovation, I will examine the basso continuo in the context of ensemble music-making, focussing on earlier practices from the late sixteenth century and the first decades of the seventeenth century. As noted by scholars including Augusta Campagne and Gregory Johnston, amongst others[5], the historical evidence indeed shows a continuity of practice[6] regardless of the changes that also occurred in the editorial market and in the notation used for the instrumental parts to be included in the performance.

---

[4]. «[...] the majority, if not all, of studies on basso continuo technique concentrate solely on the visual element of the performance. However, this obviously represents just one aspect of many: it is of course necessary (and needs coordination with other performers), but undoubtedly it is not the most crucial factor for the success of the type of collaborative improvisation we are exploring». TICLI 2023A, p. 302.

[5]. JOHNSTON 1998, CAMPAGNE 2018, CAMPAGNE – ROTEM 2022.

[6]. This musical practice is intricately linked with the developing compositional style of the *concerto* or *concertato*. It is important to note that throughout this research, the terms *concerto*, *concertato*, *concento*, *conserto*, etc. are essentially interchangeable, although their usage varies depending on the historical period and on distinct stylistic and formal characteristics. For a discussion on its etymology and usage, see BOYDEN 1957, HALL 1958, KROSS 1970, KEYS 1971, REIMER 1980.

Such a wide range of practices can lead to different results depending entirely on the competence of the performers and the particular contexts, although the music notation does not capture this information with any precision (see Table 1)[7]. For instance, it is possible to notate relatively simple performances for non-professionals, often using printed intabulations for *chitarrina* or lute in the case of *canzonette* and *arie*[8]. When professionals performed (in ensemble but also in solos), historical accounts often describe complex, multi-skilled performances with at least one performer simultaneously singing and playing their instrument: I coined the term 'integrated performance' a few years ago to describe such practices[9]. When many expert performers gathered, they would concert pieces together or engage in a *dialogo*[10].

Table 1: Possibilities for Performances in Relation to Skills and Notational Supports

Beginners ('Non Professionals')	1. Performing in a 'simpler' way e.g. from Intabulations or *Alfabeto* Notation (for lute, *chitarrina*...)
Advanced ('Professionals')	
Solo: Integrated Performance	2. Singing-Playing with improvised ornaments and other kinds of improvisation e.g. from a Bass or Intabulations
Ensemble: Integrated Performance	3. Concerting/Performing *Concerto, Concertato, Dialogo* e.g. from a Bass or Intabulations

---

[7]. For instance, in his *Secondo libro delli Mottetti*, Bartolomeo Barbarino stated that the ornamented version («passaggiata») of the pieces he published (Barbarino 1614, 'Alli Sig. Lettori') was intended for those who, despite having acquired adequate vocal technique, were unable to improvise their own ornaments. The simple version («semplice») was suitable for novices as well as professionals who were skilled in counterpoint and improvisation, employing the written notation as a basic starting point for embellishment and rhetorical amplification. See Ticli 2022, p. 197.

[8]. The designations 'professionals' and 'amateurs' pose a challenge when applied without qualification to the Renaissance era. While they serve as convenient labels for historiographical purposes, it would be more consistent and correct to refer to the level of skills acquired by the performers, since such practices were widespread in many contexts across all social classes. For some considerations about Italian contexts, see Ticli 2021, p. 161, Mazzetti – Ticli 2023b, ch. 'Musica profana e corte'.

[9]. See Ticli 2021, pp. 177-178: «[...] categories such as monody, pseudo-monody, proto-monody, and self-accompanied singing, implying a hierarchisation and supremacy of the voice over accompaniment, are not at all effective in describing, at least throughout the course of the sixteenth century, the integrated performance between acting and setting to music a poetic text». As to the practice of self-accompanied singing, see Bier 2013, p. 9: «[...] the act of performing vocal music while simultaneously playing one's own accompaniment upon a separate instrument».

[10]. Prior to and in conjunction with the early stages of figured bass's development, notational devices like *spartitura* or *intavolatura* were more favoured due to their association with high-profile skills, as evidenced by the critiques of Adriano Banchieri and Girolamo Diruta, or the suggestions of Agostino Agazzari. See also below.

Indeed, the Renaissance, particularly in the Italian peninsula, saw the emergence of a diverse range of figures that would now be considered eclectic. Multiple accounts detail a plethora of polymath performances, including simultaneous singing-playing and acting. The repertoire showcased an expansive selection of expressive and performance possibilities, dependent upon factors such as the occasion, available musical forces, and their skills. Thanks to a multitude of scholars who have investigated the time period under consideration from various perspectives, including Anthony Newcomb, Martha Feldman, Nina Treadwell, Richard Wistreich, Laurie Stras[11], we have acquired valuable information in order to examine some key aspects of the phenomenon. Without claiming to be exhaustive[12], the following paragraphs present some preliminary cases that are relevant to this study and allow us to frame the issue, including sources that cover, and in some cases go beyond, the period under consideration.

The *Asolani*, published in 1505 but written between 1497 and 1502[13], often depicts multi-skilled courtiers singing to their instruments, and makes reference to *concenti*[14]. The context described by Pietro Bembo, though fictitious, seems to be one plausible, and perhaps even common, for such performances.

> [...] two gentle maidens holding hands, with joyful countenance at the head of the tables, where the Queen sat, came and greeted her reverently; and when they had greeted her, both of them rising, the eldest, took a beautiful lute which she held in one hand on her breast, and very skilfully playing it, after a while, with the pleasant

---

11. See NEWCOMB 1978, FELDMAN 1995, TREADWELL 2000, GORDON – FELDMAN 2006, WISTREICH 2007, STRAS 2018, and DURANTE – MARTELLOTTI 1989, WILSON 2019.

12. It should be acknowledged that the act of simultaneously singing and playing an instrument has been present since classical antiquity and persisted until the nineteenth century. Additionally, it remains prevalent in certain non-European musical genres and traditions, as highlighted by the enduring popularity of pop songs. To read two examples placed chronologically at the antipodes of this investigation, see at least KEENER 2014, BIER 2013.

13. PEROCCO 2014, MAZZETTI – TICLI 2023A.

14. See also: «Or with how much sweetness do our spirits search for a gentle song of our women, and especially one that is accompanied by the sound of some sweet instrument, played by their delightful and musical hands? With how much then, besides this, if they sing any of our songs, or by chance their own?» («O pure con quanta soavità ci soglia li spiriti ricercare un vago canto delle nostre donne, et quello massimamente che è col suono d'alcun soave strumento accompagnato, tocco dalle loro dilicate et musice mani? Con quanta poi, oltre a questa, se aviene che elle cantino alcuna delle nostre canzoni o per aventura delle loro?»); «O Love, and what lutes or lyres respond more concordantly than two souls that love each other? Which, not only when they're close together and one moves by some accident, both produce the same **concert**, but even when they're far apart and no more moved than the other, they make the sweetest and most conformable harmony» («O Amore, et qua' liuti o qua' lire più concordemente si rispondono, che due anime che s'amino delle tue? Le quali, non pur quando vicine sono et alcuno accidente l'una muove, amendue rendono un medesimo **concento**, ma anchor lontane et non più mosse l'una che l'altra, fanno dolcissima et conformissima harmonia», my emphasis). BEMBO 2003, bk. 2, secs. 25, p. 33.

sound of it, tuning her sweet voice and singing sweetly, she sang *Io pargoletta in festa e 'n gioco* [...]. After the young singer sang this song, the younger sister, after a brief course of sound from her companion, who was already returning to the first notes, on the tenor of those notes, as she sweetly unravelled her tongue, answered her in this way: *Io vissi pargoletta in doglia e 'n pianto* [...]. After she took one of her viols with a marvellous sound, but not without blushing, seeing herself having to sing in such an open place, which she was not used to doing, she sang this song with such pleasantness and with such a new manner of melody, that compared to the sweet flame that her notes left in the hearts of the listeners, those of the two girls were extinguished and cold coals[15].

We read that the older sister played the lute masterfully, and later sang very gently to it («piacevole suono»), with her sweet voice accordingly, three quatrains beginning with *Io vissi pargoletta in festa e 'n gioco*. After her sister interluded for a short while («un brieve corso di suono») and while the *canzone* was starting again, the younger one responded over the incipit of the tenor, singing sweetly («la lingua dolcemente isnodando») *Io vissi pargoletta in doglia e 'n pianto*. The younger *cantatrice* began to sing three different quatrains on the same tenor of her sister (very probably a polyphonic texture). Afterwards, another lady was asked to sing a *canzonetta* to her marvellous viol («una sua viuola di maraviglioso suono»): she sang and played eleven verses on the incipit *Amor la tua virtute*, one of her *canzoni* («n'aggiugnesse [una] delle sue»).

Some years later (1507-1512), Martin Luther, recounting his youth in Erfurt, recalled a sacristan singing-playing the Ordinary of the Mass to his lute and prompting Luther to respond with the presidential intonation of the Greater Doxology.

> "When I was a young monk in Erfurt", said Doctor Martin Luther, "and had to make appointments go to the villages for cheese, I came to one and said mass there. When I had dressed and was standing at the altar in my clothes and ornaments, the sacristan began to play the Kyrie and Patrem on the lute; I could

---

15. «[...] due vaghe fanciulle per mano tenendosi, con lieto sembiante al capo delle tavole, là dove la Reina sedea, venute, riverentemente la salutarono; et poi che l'hebbero salutata, amendue levatesi, la maggiore, un bellissimo liuto che nell'una mano teneva al petto recandosi et assai maestrevolmente toccandolo, dopo alquanto spatio col piacevole suono di quello la soave voce di lei accordando et dolcissimamente cantando, così disse. *Io vissi pargoletta in festa e 'n gioco* [...]. Detta dalla giovane cantatrice questa canzone, la minore, dopo un brieve corso di suono della sua compagna che nelle prime note già ritornava, al tenor di quelle altresì come ella la lingua dolcemente isnodando, in questa guisa le rispose: *Io vissi pargoletta in doglia e 'n pianto* [...]. Per che ella, presa una sua viuola di maraviglioso suono, tuttavia non senza rossore veggendosi in così palese luogo dover cantare, il che fare non era usata, questa canzonetta cantò con tanta piacevolezza et con maniere così nuove di melodia, che alla dolce fiamma, che le sue note ne' cuori degli ascoltanti lasciarono, quelle delle due fanciulle furono spenti et freddi carboni». *Ibidem*, bk. 1, chap. 3.

hardly refrain from laughing, for I was not used to such organ playing; I had to base my *Gloria in excelsis* on his Kyrie!"[16].

In 1542, Alessandro Piccolomini discusses in his philosophical and pedagogical work the role of vocal-instrumental *concenti* in educating Tuscan nobility's children[17]:

> [...] several kinds of musical **concerts** are being performed, some of which are for pity, others for gentleness, others for strength. And others lead to other acts [...]. And for this reason we can conclude that it is well done that children should be instructed in music **concerts** not only for the pleasure and recreation of the mind that should be their trade, but also for the adornment of good morals and the addiction to virtuous actions[18].

> We have thus far spoken of the musical division, with respect principally to that which derives from the **concert** of voices. We must now speak of the musical discipline, which proceeds from various instruments [...]. Other instruments are found, some with metal strings, and some with gut strings, of which I do not praise all, so as to avoid confusion in all things, and especially so as not to allow man to be perfect in all things, and also because some are too simple, and where different and various concords cannot be conveniently made. Therefore, leaving behind Harps, *Tricordi*, Lyres, *Cetere*, *Ribichinis*, and the like, I would only be content if Violas, Lutes, and Harpsichords, and the like, delighted you[19].

---

16. «"Da ich mich", sprach Doctor Martinus Luther, "zu Erfurt ein junger Mönch war und terminiren und nach Käsen gehen mußte auf die Dörfer, kam ich auf eins und hielt da Messe. Da ich mich nu angezogen hatte und für den Altar trat in meiner Kleidung und Schmuck, da fing der Kirchner an das Kyrieleison und Patrem auf der Lauten zu schlagen; da konnte ich mich schwerlich des Lachens enthalten, denn ich war solches Orgelns nicht gewohnet; musste mein *Gloria in excelsis* nach seinem Kyrie richten!"». Luther 1854, 8:399, no. 1923, p. 7. Note Luther's sarcastic and mocking tone at the end of the description, who evidently did not appreciate such a performance.

17. See Refe 2016, p. 96.

18. «[...] di più sorti **concenti** musicali si ritruovano, de' quali alcuni a pietà, altri a mansuetudine, altri a fortezza. Et altri ad altre operationi inducano [...]. E per questo si può concludere, che è ben fatto che i fanciulli siano instituiti ne i **concenti** della musica non solo per il diletto, et ricreatione di mente che debba lor fare di mestieri, ma ancora per ornamento de' buoni costumi, et assuefattion delle operationi virtuose» (my emphasis). Piccolomini 1552, bk. 3, chap. 10, fols. 56v, 57r.

19. «Habbiamo fin qui, della musical disciplina parlato, rispetto principalmente a quella, che dal **concento** delle voci deriva. Dovendo al presente di quella parlare, che da diversi instrumenti procede [...]. Altri instrumenti si truovano parte con corde di metallo, et parte di nervo, de' quali parimente, tutti non lodo, si per fuggire la confusione in tutte le cose, e massimamente per non concedersi all'huomo, d'esser perfetto in ogni cosa, et si ancora, per essene alcuni troppo simplici, et dove diversi, et varii concenti commodamente non possino fare. Lasciando dunque in dietro Arpe, Tricordi, Lire, Cetere, Ribichini, et simili, solo mi contentarei, che di Viole, di Leuti, et di Gravicembani, et simili vi dilettasse» (my emphasis). Piccolomini 1552, bk. 3, chap. 11, fols. 57r, 58r.

BASSO CONTINUO AS A 'CONCERTATO' PRACTICE

In 1543-1544[20], elite circles of exiled Florentines in Venice, overseen by Neri Capponi, engaged in practices where the South Netherlandish musician Adrian Willaert, Polissena Pecorina, and other performers played and sang simultaneously in a concert of voices and instruments. Antofrancesco Doni's *Dialogo* contains several passages that describe such performances.

> The Music, which is performed in Your Lordship's house, of lutes, instruments, *pifferi*, *flauti*, voices and in the house of the honoured Mr. Alessandro Colombo is most dignified, and the music of Mr. Guido dalla Porta's *violoni* is admirable: but if Your Lordhips could hear the divinity, which I have tasted with the ear of intelligence here in Venice, you would be astonished. There is a gentlewoman, POLISENA Pecorina (consort of a *cittadino* from my native town), so talented and refined that I cannot find words high enough to praise her. One evening I heard a **concert** of *violoni* and voices in which she **played and sang** together with other excellent spirits. The perfect master of that music was Adrian Willaert, whose studious style, never before practised by musicians, is so tightly knit, so sweet, so right, so miraculously suited to the words that I confess to never having known what harmony was in all my days, save that evening[21].

Seville's 1554 edition of Miguel de Fuenllana's *Orphenica Lyra* was designed to allow simultaneous singing and playing of collected polyphonic works, by providing lute intabulations with red-inked voices, mensural notation and text underlay[22]. The opening of the fifth section describes itself as: «fifth book, which contains *estrambotes* for five and four voices, sonnets and madrigals in Castilian, *villancicos* for three and four voices, *villanescas* and old *romances*»[23]: it

---

[20]. EINSTEIN – PIDCOCK – BONAVIA 1934, HAAR 1966, FELDMAN 1995, chap. 2.

[21]. «La Musica, che si fà in casa V.S. di liuti, di stromenti, di pifferi, di flauti, di voci, et in casa dell'onorato M. Alessandro Colombo, è dignissima, e quella dei violoni del S. Guido dalla Porta mirabile: mà se la S. V. udisse la divinità, ch'io ho gustato con l'orecchia dell'intelligenza qui in Vinegia, stupirebbe. Ecci una gentil donna: POLISENA Pecorina (consorte d'un cittadino della mia patria) tanto virtuosa, et gentile, che non trovo lode sì alte, che la commendino. Io ho udito una sera un **concento** di violoni, et di voci, dove ella **sonava, et cantava** in compagnia di altri spiriti eccellenti: il maestro perfetto della qual musica era Adriano Villaert di quella sua sua diligente invenzione non più usata dai musici, sì unita, sì dolce, sì giusta, sì mirabilmente acconcie le parole, ch'io confessai non avere saputo che cosa sia stata armonia ne' miei giorni, salvo in quella sera» (my emphasis). DONI 1544, 'Al S. Annibale Marchese Malvicino' (Tenor part-book, c. 1v). The last three sentences of the translation are from FELDMAN 1995, p. 32.

[22]. As pointed out in WISTREICH 2007, p. 175, at least seven Spanish mid sixteenth-century printed books of music for the vihuela contain texted intabulations of vocal music, all of which can be linked to courtly practice, ranging from Luis Milán, *Libro de música de vihuela da mano intitulado el maestro* (Valencia, 1536) to Esteban Daza, *El parnasso* (Valladolid, 1576).

[23]. «LIBRO QUINTO en qual se contienen estrambotes a cinco y a quatro. Sonetos y Madrigales, en lengua Castellana: villancicos a tres y a quatro. Villanescas: y Romances viejos». DE FUENLLANA 1554, fol. cxiv.

365

is noteworthy that when speaking of such a book in his prologue Fuenllana states «in the fifth section, you will find very graceful music also to develop the hands[24]: the **concierto** of which will be found in the table of the work, and below it is set out in more detail»[25].

Among the numerous sources from the mid and late sixteenth century, one notable instance is the Este court and the *Concerto segreto* of Alfonso II. The *Concerto* was composed of the famous ladies of Ferrara, who were a model for the practice of concerting the madrigal repertoire. Amongst their numerous talents, the ladies became renowned for their multi-skilled performances and the practice of singing to their musical instruments. We find in the correspondence between Alessandro Striggio, Francesco de' Medici and Belisario Vinta (July-December 1584)[26] that the performance (and subsequently composition) practices of the Ferrara circles had aroused the admiration and emulation of the Florentine court. The Grand Duke of Tuscany, intrigued by the Ferrarese *Concerto*, requested from Striggio «madrigals for three sopranos, with diminutions»[27]. Thus, fulfilling his patron's desire, Striggio composed a four-voice madrigal for three sopranos, with diminutions and then a «*Dialogo* for two fugati sopranos with diminutions»[28]. He had also prepared the lute intabulation but omitted to send it, though he expressed confidence that Giulio Caccini could «play flawlessly over the bass — either on the lute or the harpsichord»[29]. Striggio dispatched then additional pieces with performance instructions so that those madrigals could be perfectly performed and «consertati by Mr Giulio Caccini»[30]. Interestingly, the Grand Duke again requested madrigals for sopranos, but with a particular focus on challenging high and low runs[31], which Striggio was thus tasked with composing. Although no examples of these specific compositions have survived to the

---

[24].   See translation «para desenvolver las manos (to develop the hands)» in GRIFFITHS 1989, p. 23.

[25].   «En la quinta se hallara musica muy galana tambien para desembolver las manos: cuyo **concierto** se hallara en la tabla de la obra, y adelante le pone mas por extenso» (my emphasis). DE FUENLLANA 1554, 'Prologo al lector'.

[26].   Documents A102-119 gathered in DURANTE – MARTELLOTTI 1989. For a discussion on this material, see *ibidem*, pp. 75-76.

[27].   Document A102 in *ibidem*.

[28].   Document A106, A107 in *ibidem*.

[29].   Document A106 in *ibidem*. This was definitely improvised by the performer on the instrument as at the time no pieces with a specific part-book for the instrumental bass are known, while the majority of the madrigal repertoire is issued in a polyphonic setting through seemingly only vocal part-books. See MAZZETTI – TICLI 2023B.

[30].   Document A109 in DURANTE – MARTELLOTTI 1989.

[31].   «[...] the first of the four Madrigals [...] which is made in conformity with the notation in the margin [i.e. according the suggestions] of Mr. Giulio [Caccini], that is, with the runs which are very difficult and sought after on the top and bottom, and the end is repeated in various ways twelve times between both sopranos; however, if the music appears excessively lengthy to Your Serene Highness, Mr. Giulio [Caccini] may eliminate any parts desired, including the conclusion» («[...] il primo de quatro Madrigali [...] il quale è fatto conforme a la notatione in margine di ms. Giulio cioè con le tirate molto difficile e ricercano in alto e imbasso, et la fine replica in variati

present day, they bear a remarkable resemblance in terms of features to Luzzasco Luzzaschi's *Madrigali per cantare e sonare* of 1601[32].

John Florio — active as a linguist and cultural mediator in Elizabethan England in the early 1570s — printed his dictionaries in 1598 and 1611 respectively[33], providing us with further insight into the terms and practices relevant to this investigation.

TABLE 2: COMPARISON BETWEEN JOHN FLORIO'S DICTIONARIES

Florio 1598	**Florio 1611**
Concénto, a consort, or concordance in musick.	*Concento*, a consort, or concordance, a harmony, a tunable accord.
Concertare, to agree, or tune together, or proportion or accord together, to sing or play in consort.	*Concertare*, to proportion, or accord together, to agree or tune together, to sing or play in consort.
–	*Concertaménto*, as *Concerto*.
Concérto, as *Concento*.	*Concerto*, an agreement, an accord, a consort, or concordance.
Consertare, reduce to order, forme, tune or proportion.	*Consertáre*, as *Concertáre*.
Conserto, a consort or unison in musicke.	*Conserto*, joined, enterlaced, entermedled, set with, conserted. Also as *Concérto*.

At the turn of the century, as the *concertato* style and the *concerto* together with the emerging basso continuo practice began to establish themselves also as a distinctly Italian genre of composition, information is no longer so fragmentary and direct references to such practices are easier to find in treatises and written music, both in Italy and throughout Europe.

In 1619, the opening «Concerning Compositions with Sacred and Solemn Secular Texts, such as Concertos, Motets, and Falsobordoni» («Von denen Gesängen/ Welche Geistliche und gravitetische weltliche Texte haben: Als / Concerti, Motetae, und Falso Bordoni») of Michael Praetorius' *Syntagma Musicum* presents a range of definitions and references pertinent to this investigation. This is apparent from the description of the interplay between voices and instruments and the close relationship with the term *concerto*.

> *Cantio, Concentus,* or *Symphonia* is a composition of different numbers of
> voices. The Italians call it *concetto*[34] or *concerto*, which to the Latins is *Concertatio*,
> inasmuch as various voices or musical instruments are engaged in making a concert.

---

modi da dodice volte fra tutti dua i soprani; però se parerà troppo longo a V.A.S., ne potrà levare quante ne vorà ms. Giulio, non lassando la fine»). Document A115 in *ibidem*.

[32]. LUZZASCHI 1601.

[33]. See also FLORIO 2013, ROSSI 2018. Regarding dictionaries from the sixteenth and seventeenth centuries, see STARNES 1937B, STARNES 1937A, STARNES 1940.

[34]. This would seem indeed a misspelling according to Florio's dictionares: «*Concetto*, a conceit or apprehension of the mind. Also conceived» and «*Concetto*, conceived with child. Also a conceit or apprehension of the mind» in FLORIO 1598, p. 80a; FLORIO 1611, p. 114b. Praetorius probably read Giovanni Maria Artusi

The sweetness consists not so much in artifice as in variety itself. In German, it is called *ein Concert*. However, this designation *"concerto"* is applied: 1. In general, where there is any song of several parts [...]. In particular, [the designation is applied] from *concertando* it is when one selects from an entire company of musicians the best and most notable among them, including vocalists and all manner of instrumentalists such as [long list of instruments], and has them play in alternating choirs, vying with one another to see which one can outperform the other[35].

Praetorius goes further, exploring the concert, the utilisation of voices and instruments, and then even the practice of figured bass in his renowned homonymous chapter.

I call them concerted or, preferably, concerting voices, which respond to each other, so to speak, struggling among themselves to see who can outdo the other. Consequently, for such parts one must select the best singers, who are not only perfect and secure, but who possess a good disposition for singing in the current new manner, and who pronounce the words correctly and clearly as if reciting an oration[36].

The *Bassus generalis* or *continuo* is so called because it continues from the beginning of the piece to the end and, as principal part, contains within itself the entire motet or concerto. It is quite common in Italy, especially in the works of the outstanding composer Lodovico Viadana, the superb creator of this new art, who devised and published the method of having one, two, three, or four voices sing to the sole accompaniment of an organ, regal, or other fundamental instrument[37].

---

stating that S. Vito in Ferrara is «the most excellent, united, and well proportioned *Concetto* that Italy has» («il più eccellente, unito, e ben proportionato **Concetto** che habbi l'Italia», my emphasis)». ARTUSI 1600, fol. 3v.

[35]. «1. *Cantio, Concentus, seu Symphonia, est diversarum vocum modulatio. Italis vocatur Concetto vel Concerto, quod Latinis est Concertatio, qua Variae Voces aut Instrumenta Musica ad concertum faciendum committuntur: Suavitas enim non tàm in artificio, quàm in ipsa variatione consistit: Germanicé ein Concert. Usurpatur autem hoc Vocabulum Concert 1. in genere, quoquavis Cantione Harmonicae* [...] 2. *In specie à Concertando,* Wenn man unter einer gantzen Gesellschafft der *Musicorum* etzliche / und bevorab die besten und fürnembsten Gesellen heraus sucht / daß sie *voce humana*, und mit allerley Instrumenten als [...], einer nach dem andern Chorweise umbwechseln / und gleich gegen einander streitten / also / daß es immer einer dem andern zuvor thun / und sich besser hören lassen wil». PRAETORIUS 1619, pp. 4-5. Translation from PRAETORIUS 2004, pp. 18-19.

[36]. «Ich nenne es *Voces Concertatas, vel potius Concertantes*; die gleichsam einander *Respondiren*, und untereinander *Concertiren* und streitten / wer es unter ihnen zum besten machen könne. Darumb man denn zu solchen Stimmen die besten *Cantores* und Sänger außlesen / bestellen und ordnen mus / die nicht allein *perfect* und gewiß seyn / sondern auch auff itzige newe Manier und Weise ein gute *disposition* zu singen haben / also das die Wörter recht und deutlich *pronunciret*, und gleich als eine *Oration* vernehmlich daher *recitiret* werden [...]». PRAETORIUS 1619, p. 126 [*recte* 106] . Translation from PRAETORIUS 2004, p. 116.

[37]. «Der *Bassus generalis seu Continuus* wird daher also genennet / weil er sich vom anfang biß zum ende continuiret, unnd als eine *General*Stimme / die gantze *Motet* oder *Concert* in sich begreiffet; Wie dann solches in

Basso Continuo as a 'Concertato' Practice

In 1628, Vincenzo Giustiniani[38] gives us an account of these practices being used by Italian, Spanish (by the king himself, no less), and German performers. We can observe that they began to increasingly overlap in semantic terms with the corresponding compositional genre although the terms *concerto* and *concertato* were still associated with voices, instruments, and integrated performance.

> And we are used to singing to one or at most three voices **concerted to their own instruments** of Tiorba or Chitarra Cimbalo or with Organ, according to the circumstances and further, singing in the Spanish or Italian style has been introduced, being similar but with greater artifice and ornament, as much in Rome as in Naples and Genoa, with new inventions of the airs and ornaments; in which the composers are pressing, as in Rome the German of the Tiorba named Gio. Geronimo [Kapsberger]. In Naples Gutierrez began, followed by Pietro his son and Gallo and others; and in Genoa a certain Cicco who excellently composes and sings, giving great delight to those ladies in conversations and vigils, which there more than elsewhere are customary[39].

> King Philip IV of Spain and both his brothers are delighted with it, and they often **sing** by the book, and **play concerted** viols together, with a few other musicians to compensate for the competent number, amongst them Filippo Piccinino Bolognese, an excellent lute and Pandora player. Indeed, the King himself and his brothers write compositions, not only for their own enjoyment but also so that they may be sung in the Royal Chapel and in other churches during the Office [...][40].

Italia gar gemein / unnd sonderlich jetzo von dem trefflichen *Musico Ludovico Viadana, novae inventionis primario,* als er die Art mit einer / zween / dreyen oder vier Stimmen allein in eine Orgel / Regal/ oder ander dergleichen *FundamentInstrument* zu singen erfunden / an Tag bracht / und in druck außgangen ist». PRAETORIUS 1619, p. 144 [*recte* 124]. Translation from PRAETORIUS 2004, p. 133.

38. Regarding his *Discorso*, see MACCLINTOCK 1961.

39. «E si canta ad una o al più 3 voci **concertate con istrumenti proprii** di Tiorba o Chitarra Cimbalo o con Organo, secondo le congiunture e di più in questo stile si è introdotto a cantare o alla spagnola o all'italiana, a quella simile ma con maggior artificio e ornamento, tanto in Roma, come in Napoli e Genova, con invenzioni nuove dell'arie e de gli ornamenti; nel che premono i compositori, come in Roma il Tedesco della Tiorba nominato Gio. Geronimo. In Napoli cominciò il Gutierrez, e poi hanno seguitato Pietro suo figlio e Gallo et altri; et in Genova un tal Cicco per eccellenza compone e canta, porgendo gran diletto a quelle signore nelle conversazioni e nelle veglie, ch'ivi più che altrove si costumano» (my emphasis). SOLERTI 1903, p. 121.

40. «Re Filippo IV di Spagna et ambidue li suoi fratelli se ne dilettano, e sogliono spesso **cantare** al libro, e **sonar** di Viole **concertate** insieme, con alcuni pochi altri musici per supplire al numero competente, tra' quali con Filippo Piccinino Bolognese, sonatore di Liuto e di Pandòra eccellentissimo. Anzi di più lo stesso Re e i fratelli fanno le composizioni, non solo per loro diletto ma anche perchè si cantino nella Cappella Regia e nell'altre chiese mentre si celebrano li divini offizii [...]» (my emphasis). *Ibidem*, pp. 111-112.

[The one who carries all the glory] for the Tiorba, is Gio. Gironimo Tedesco [Kapsberger], who is also a composer and serves in palaces for private music and **concerts**[41].

[...] Mr. Cardinal Mont'Alto, who **played and sang** with much grace and *affetto*, despite his martial appearance [...][42].

In 1724, the anonymous *A Short Explication of Such Foreign Words*[43] allows us a glimpse of a now mature genre with distinctive features and related compositional and performative evolutions that from the mid-seventeenth century onwards began to characterise the *concertato*, and later the *concerto grosso* and the solo *concerto*.

CONCERTANTE, are those Parts of a Piece of Musick which play thoroughout [*sic*] the whole, to distinguish them from those which play only in some Parts.
CONCERTO, a Consort, or a Piece of Musick of several Parts for a Consort.
CONCERTO GROSSO, is the great or grand Chorus of the Consort, or those Places of the Concerto or Consort where all the several Parts perform or play together[44].

It is also worth noting the precise connotation of *basso continuo* provided in this context[45].

BASSO CONTINUO, is the Thorough Bass, or Continual Bass, and is commonly distinguished from the other Basses by Figures over the Notes; which Figures are proper only for the Organ, Harpsichord, Spinet, and Theorbo Lute.
N.B. A Thorough Bass is not always figured, tho' it ought so to be[46].

In 1735, at the beginning of his *Kleine General-Bass-Schule*, Johann Mattheson explains the relationship of the basso continuo to the *concerto*, basically following the definitions of Florio and the anonymous English print of 1724:

---

[41]. «Di Tiorba [porta fra tutti il vanto] il suddetto Gio. Gironimo tedesco, il quale anche è compositore e serve in Palazzo nelle private musiche e **concerti**» (my emphasis). *Ibidem*, p. 124.

[42]. «[...] il signor Cardinal Mont'Alto, che **sonava e cantava** con molta gratia ed affetto, se bene aveva un aspetto più tosto martiale [...]» (my emphasis). *Ibidem*, p. 115.

[43]. See also YOUNG 1982.

[44]. ANONYMOUS 1724, p. 23.

[45]. See also other definitions close to the same semantic field «BASSO CONCERTANTE, the Bass of the little Chorus, or the Bass that plays throughout the whole Piece; BASSO RECITANTE, the same as Basso Concertante; BASSO RIPIENO, is the Bass of the Grand Chorus, or the Bass that plays now and then in some particular Places; BASSETTO, is a Bass Viol, or Bass Violin of the smallest Size, and is so called to distinguish them from those Bass Viols or Violins of a larger Size». *Ibidem*, pp. 15-16.

[46]. *Ibidem*, p. 15.

Well then, my dearest, do you know quite thoroughly what the *General-Baß* is? Nothing else than numbered *Grund-Noten*, which indicate a full-voiced accord according to which full *Griffe* are made on the keyboard (or another instrument) so that they serve the rest of the **concert** in exact unity / for support and accompaniment[47].

In 1752, Johann Joachim Quantz made reference to the terms *concerto*[48], *parte concertante*[49], and their derivatives in multiple segments in his *Versuch einer Anweisung die Flöte traversiere zu spielen*. He openly acknowledged their Italian origins and provided extensive details about the nature of *concertare* by classifying and hierarchising what were then established as practices into distinct habits and crystallised into certain rules.

The concerto owes its origin to the Italians. [Giuseppe] Torelli is supposed to have made the first. The *concerto grosso* consists of an intermixture of various *concertante* instruments in which two or more instruments, the number sometimes extending as high as eight and above, play together in turn. In the chamber concerto, on the other hand, only a single concertante instrument is present[50].

What a Flautist Must Observe if he Plays in **Public Concerts**. [...] If a flautist has to **play in concert with a vocal part**, he must seek to match it as much as possible in tone quality and manner of execution. He must vary nothing except where imitations give the opportunity to do so. The graces must be of a kind that the voice can imitate; hence extensive leaps must be avoided. But if the voice has a plain melody, and the flute has its own distinct progressions above it, the flautist can add as much as he deems suitable. If the voice rests, he can play with still more

---

47. «Nun wolan! meine Wehrteste, wisset ihr denn auch recht gründlich / was der General=Baß sey? Nichts anders / als beziefferte Grund=Noten, die einen vollstimmigen Zusammenklang andeuten / nach deren Vorschrifft volle Griffe auf dem Clavier (oder einem andern Instrument) gemacht warden / damit dieselbe dem übrigen Concert / in genauer Einigkeit / zur Unterstützung und Begleitung dienen». Mattheson 1735, pp. 40-41, par. 6 ('Erste Anzeige').

48. The concert had come to be predominantly regarded as an instrumental form: «The principal types of instrumental music in which voices are not employed are the concerto, the overture, the sinfonia, the quartet, the trio, and the solo. Of these, the concerto, the trio, and the solo are each of two sorts. We have concerti grossi and concerti da camera». Quantz 2001, chap. 18, par. 29.

49. At this time the term was «regularly used to designate an undoubled part, that is, a solo part in a composition, or the performer of such a part. Thus undoubled parts in chamber works such as sonatas, trios, and quartets, or the performers of these parts. The antitheses of concertante part and concertante performer are ripieno part and ripienist». Further, as for the term 'Solo': «Quantz normally uses this word only as a noun, referring in nearly all cases to a solo sonata. It is rarely used to indicate a solo part, a solo section, or a solo performer». *Ibidem*, 'Preface to the Translation'.

50. *Ibidem*, chap. 18, par. 30.

freedom. If the voice is weak, and the performance is in a chamber, the flautist must play more softly. At the theatre, on the other hand, he can play a little more loudly, since there soft playing on the flute has little effect. In any case, however, he must not overwhelm the singer with too many variations, lest the latter, having to sing from memory, be thrown into confusion[51].

Of the Qualities of a Leader of an Orchestra. [...] The leader must take special pains to see that the instruments are correctly and uniformly tuned. The more prevalent the lack of correct common tuning, the greater is the damage done. Whether the pitch of the orchestra is high or low, the effect of a composition will always be considerably impaired if the instruments are not in tune with one another. Hence if the leader wishes to maintain correct intonation in the performance of a musical composition, he must first tune his own instrument truly with the keyboard, and then have each individual instrumentalist tune to him. That the instruments may not be put out of tune again if the performance does not begin immediately, he must not allow anyone to play preludes or other fancies as he pleases; they are very unpleasant to listen to, and often cause the players to alter the tuning of their instruments, and finally deviate from the common tuning[52].

Of the Duties That All Accompanying Instrumentalists in General Must Observe. [...] If there is a *concertante* part to accompany, each of the accompanists must regulate himself in all cases by the execution of the soloist, and always do his share[53].

Ritornellos in particular must be played entirely without extempore additions. These additions are permitted only to the performer of the concertante part. Some musicians have the bad habit of introducing at times all sorts of fopperies even in the ritornellos, and meanwhile forget to read the notes correctly[54].

Each accompanist need merely pay attention to whether he himself hears the concertante part. If he cannot, he can easily perceive that the accompaniment is too loud, and therefore requires moderation[55].

If a *concertante* part is accompanied by more than one other part, the fundamental part must be heard more strongly than the others. This rule must also be observed in a tutti, unless the middle parts imitate the principal part or the

---

51. *Ibidem*, chap. 16, par. 30 (my emphasis).
52. *Ibidem*, chap. 16, sec. 1, par. 8. See similar recommendations given by Agostino Agazzari or witnessed by Giovanni Maria Artusi as discussed in TICLI 2023A, pp. 297-298, 304.
53. QUANTZ 2001, chap. 7, par. 10.
54. *Ibidem*, chap. 7, par. 15.
55. *Ibidem*, chap. 7, par. 21.

bass, or have a melody in thirds or sixths with them. For parts that serve only to strengthen the harmony must never be more prominent than the principal parts. An elaborate or fugal piece that is imitative in all the parts must be played with the same volume in all the parts[56].

To become quite secure in both of these matters, you must begin by playing more middle parts than principal ones; you should play accompaniments more often than solos (since it is more difficult but also more useful to do the former); you should play more concertante and elaborate pieces than melodic ones; you should listen not only to yourself but also to the other parts, particularly the bass [...][57].

If the *tutti* following the completion of a principal cadence begins on the downbeat, discreet accompanists will do well, particularly in the accompaniment of a voice or a wind instrument, not to wait until the extreme end of the shake, but to interrupt it, entering rather too early than too late. Both singers and wind players may easily run short of breath towards the end, and if this were to happen, the verve of the performance would be disrupted. If, however, the tutti begins on the upbeat and during the shake, it is no longer a matter of discretion to interrupt the shake, but an obligation. In this regard you must be governed by the performer of the concertante part, and by the power of his lungs. Some singers and instrumentalists who have good lungs try to show a special bravura with long shakes after the cadence [cadenza]; thus one must not obstruct them[58].

As can be noted, at this stage the *concertante* parts have been definitively composed, put into writing and subsequently transformed into obbligato parts. We find precise roles between accompanists and soloists or between instruments and voices, as well as in the type of extemporaneous ornamentation to be utilised and the place in which it can be performed. At the same time, some earlier recommendations, such as attending to ensemble (orchestral) intonation and the aural aspects of the practice (mutual listening and balance of sonorities), are also echoed. We also receive specific instructions for commonplace interactions between ensemble members, informed by practical situations unique to the given repertoire — such as the final cadenza performed by the singer or the *concertante* part. Remarkably, despite some obvious differences in producing ensemble music-making, there are certain constants that are worth considering for this study.

---

56. *Ibidem*, chap. 7, par. 23.
57. *Ibidem*, chap. 7, par. 32.
58. *Ibidem*, chap. 7, par. 44.

Livio Ticli

Vocal-Instrumental Improvisation
in Solo/Ensemble Music-Making

Returning to the origins of the phenomenon and the aforementioned practices of singing-playing that form the basis of our discussion on the music at the turn of the century, it becomes clear that they were undeniably linked to the emerging *concertato* style, characterised by a solo voice and an independent instrumental part that showcase a close musical interaction. As Anthony Newcomb stated, «whenever a singer sang, accompanying himself on the lute, his performance was in this sense *concertato nel liuto*»[59]. However, as demonstrated through the aforementioned cases, multi-skilled performances can occur within an ensemble too, with *concerto* defined as a performative approach, an organisational attitude, rather than a compositional genre or form[60]. Such performances underscored the dynamic nature of a concert. Rather than being a severe execution of a normative and prescriptive series of rules (condensed into music notation), a *concerto* then allowed still for a flexible framework where performers could engage in a lively exchange. This involved the alternating presentation of musical elements, echoing themes or motifs between different parts, and fostering a dialogic interaction amongst ensemble members. In essence, a concert was a living, evolving entity that thrived on the interplay of elements as well as the unique connection between musicians and their listeners, making each performance a distinctive and expressive event. This approach was based on peculiar traits (e.g. alternation, echoes, and dialogic patterns) that were essential to the contrapuntal interplay both in a part within itself[61] (or between voice and instrument of the same performer) and among all ensemble members.

As the present survey will not address the *Concerto* or *Concertato* as a compositional style presented in writing, but rather as an (aural) practice specific to the performance even before the seventeenth century, the following paragraphs will examine features that resemble a plausible representation (in writing) of such improvisational practices.

---

[59]. Newcomb 1978, pp. 58-59, Ticli 2021, pp. 165, 179.

[60]. «[...] concerto non è un genere o una forma, bensì un atteggiamento organizzativo ed esecutivo caratterizzato fondamentalmente dalla contrapposizione e dalla collaborazione fra due elementi indipendenti ed eterogenei: voci e strumenti». Piperno 1991, p. 170.

[61]. E.g. an instrumental part — especially in the case of perfect (polyphonic) instruments such as keyboards, lutes or harps — has the ability to create a musical dialogue within itself, independent of other instruments. See below and Ticli 2023a. These dialogical features soon became a stylistic component of the instrumental repertoire and were included also in solo repertoire for viola da gamba, recorder, etc. (see e.g. Ortiz 1961 and Bassano 1585).

Basso Continuo as a 'Concertato' Practice

Ornamentation, Counterpoint and Vocal-Instrumental Interactions

In his *Regola da concertare cantando ogni sorte di compositione* from *L'antica musica ridotta alla moderna prattica* (1555), Nicola Vicentino emphasises the importance of utilising diminutions and 'effects' («*maniere*») to give a proper interpretation of a text and enhance the *affetto* of poetry in the first place.

> The singer [...] must [...] use different ways of singing, as there are different styles of composition, and when s/he uses these styles, s/he will be judged by the hearers to be a person of judgement, and to have many ways of singing, and s/he will show him/herself to be abundant, and rich in many ways of singing, with the disposition of the line, or of diminishing accompanied by the compositions, according to the passages, in his/her purpose: but there are some singers who demonstrate to the hearers their poor judgement, and little consideration, when they sing, and when they find a passage mournful, they sing it cheerfully; and then on the contrary when the passage is cheerful they sing it mournfully.

> [...] instruments [...] which will sound the right composition without diminution, and as will be noted, because with diminution one will not be able to lose the harmony that the instrument will hold the consonances in its terms.
> [...] when the player will diminish the composition; the one singing will together diminish the composition, which will be played, and which will be sung if both of them diminish at the same time not making the same passage together, in agreement, they will not make good agreement, but when they are well concerted, they will make a good sound.

> [...] in the compositions that will be sung without instruments, the diminutions will be good, in the compositions with more than four voices, because where a consonance is missing, the other part will put it back either with an octave, or with a unison, and there will be no poverty of harmony left[62].

---

62. «[...] il cantante dè [...] usare diversi modi di cantare, come sono diverse le maniere delle compositioni, & quando usera tali modi, sarà giudicato da gli oditori huomo di giuditio, & di havere molte maniere di cantare, & dimostrarà esser abondante, & ricco di molti modi di cantare con la dispositione, della gorga, ò di diminuire accompagnata con le compositioni, secondo li passaggi, in suo proposito: ma sono alcuni cantanti che à gli oditori dimostrano il suo poco giuditio, & poca consideratione, quando cantano, & che ritrovano un passaggio mesto, lo cantano allegro; & poi per il contrario quando il passaggio è allegro lo cantano mesto»; [...] «stromenti [...] i quali sonaranno la compositione giusta senza diminuire, & come sarà notata, perche con la diminutione non si potrà perder l'armonia che lo stromento terrà le consonanze ne i suoi termini»; [...] «quando il sonatore diminuirà la compositione; & colui che canterà vorrà insieme diminuire la compositione, che si sonerà, & che si canterà se ambo due diminuiranno in un tempo non facendo un passaggio medesimo insieme, d'accordo, non faranno buono

375

On the other hand, Vicentino affirms that a support for the harmony is required and usually entrusted to instruments, while the florid diminutions are performed by voices. We witness the presence of parts 'holding' the harmony (often instruments or the organ) and others ornamenting (usually and preferably voices). If voices and instruments want to give diminutions simultaneously, they have to 'concert' the piece and make arrangements, i.e. they all shall come to an agreement («facendo un passaggio medesimo insieme, d'accordo»). The concurrent presence of the same line in both a plain version and an ornamented one is something worth highlighting and we will comment on it below.

About fifty years later, Giovanni Maria Artusi describes the well-known *Concerto di S. Vito* in Ferrara, bringing back the necessary presence of instruments together with the extensive and appropriate use of diminutions within the famous ensemble[63]:

> What balance should the Singers have between them. [...] it is necessary in every way, that the Singers, and Players should listen to each other; for not a little deformity would be if the one sang with a powerful, gallant, and sonorous voice; and the other with a sweet, suave, and more quickly debile voice than otherwise.
> VARIO. Whenever they did not have this foresight to listen to one another, it might be said, that Music made thus was more soon disproportionate, than proportionate [...][64].

> Those who sing the part that brings them comfort perform beautifully, accompanied by many vague yet beautiful passages that leave the listener in admiration. However, this effect would be reversed if they were to sing a part that does not suit their nature of comfort[65].

The issues remain consistent with the previously mentioned sources: the challenges in performative processes and aural perception during the interactions occurring in ensemble

---

accordo, ma quando saranno ben concertati, faranno buono udire»; [...] «nelle compositioni che si canteranno senza stromenti, le diminutioni saranno buone, nelle compositioni à più di quattro uoci, perche ove mancherà una consonanza, l'altra parte la rimetterà ò con l'ottava, ò con l'unisono, & non li rimarrà povertà d'armonia». VICENTINO 1555, chap. 42.

63. See TICLI 2023A, p. 297.

64. «Qual proportione habbino d'havere li Cantori fra di loro. [...] bisogna à tutti i modi, che li Cantori, & Sonatori s'ascoltino l'uno e l'altro; perche non poca deformità sarebbe se l'un Cantasse con una voce potente, gagliarda, & sonora; e l'altro con voce dolce, soave, e più tosto debile che altrimenti. | VARIO. Ogni volta che non havessero questo antivedere d'ascoltarsi l'un l'altro, si potrebbe dire, che cosi fatte Musiche fossero più tosto sproportionate, che proportionate [...]». ARTUSI 1600, fol. 2v.

65. «Quelle altresì che Cantano quella parte che alla dispositione loro è di comodità; cantano con bella maniera, accompagnata da molti belli Passaggi tanto vaghi, che l'uditore ne resta tutto ammirativo; il che farebbe contrario effetto, se in vece di Cantare quella parte, che alla natura sua è commoda [...]». *Ibidem*, fol. 3v.

music-making (related to listening, sound levels and pitch accuracy) as well as the extensive implementation of embellishments.

One issue that comes immediately to the fore is the absence of compositions formally published as *concerto/concertato* for voices and instruments during the period of Vicentino. Neither did Artusi himself, in 1600, see the publication of Lodovico Viadana's *Concerti ecclesiastici*, which eventually paved the way to the development of the seventeenth-century *concerto* for voices, instruments and basso continuo — a compositional genre more familiar to modern scholars. The issue of whether the type of repertoire performed in those times can be defined more thoroughly is not easily resolved. The practice of «cantare et sonare d'ogni sorte di stromenti»[66] partially elucidates the phenomenon, but falls short in explaining certain aspects including the intricate interplay between voices and instruments, improvisation techniques, and ornamentation practices. Although there should be many issues to be addressed in terms of required musical skills and also of organological aspects related to the instruments employed and the possibility of adapting (or retaining) a polyphonic texture on the instruments, here we will keep our focus on the interactions between the different parts involved in the performance.

In 1607, Agostino Agazzari[67] provides a very clear definition of *concerto* in his treatise *Del sonare sopra'l basso* (On playing over a bass), in which he gives a linguistic cast to the well-established periphrasis of improvising (singing/playing/counterpointing) over a pre-existent voice (often a plainchant in the tenor)[68], associated with the flourishing tradition of sixteenth-century *contrapunto alla mente*[69]: «I say therefore that whoever wants to play well, it is necessary for them to possess three things: first to know counterpoint, or at least to sing confidently, and to understand the proportions, and tempi, and to read for all the keys, to know how to resolve dissonances with the consonances, to know thirds and sixths major, and minor, and other similar things»[70]. We read that the first skill one must have to play *nel Conserto* is counterpoint, and that means one needs to know how to resolve dissonances and, of course, rules for singing from mensural notation. We find both features within the professional requirements needed

---

66. See Mazzetti – Ticli 2014, p. 207: such an indication (or in Latin «tum viva voce tum instrumentis cuiusvis generis») — employed by Adrian Willaert (1559) and then borrowed by many others such as Orlande de Lassus (1562) and Andrea Gabrieli (1565) — suggests those pieces were meant «for singing and playing with every kind of instrument [at disposition]». See also Mannoia 2016, p. 27.

67. For a discussion on Agazzari's treatise and the related musical practices, please refer overall to Ticli 2023a.

68. For the training performers had to undertake in *contrapunto alla mente*, see Mazzetti – Ticli 2017, Ticli 2023b.

69. See Ticli 2023a, esp. pp. 299ff. and Canguilhem 2015.

70. «[...] dico dunque che chi vuole suonar bene, gli convien posseder tre cose: prima saper contraponto, ò per lo meno cantar sicuro, ed intender le proporzioni, e tempi, e legger per tutte le chiavi, saper risolver le cattive con le buone, conoscer 3. e 6. maggiori, e minori, et altre simiglanti [*sic*] cose». Agazzari 1607, p. 4.

to pass the examination at the Papal Chapel[71], where 'counterpoint' stands for *contrappunto alla mente* and was intended as an advanced skill acquired by the *cantor* for improvising[72]. In order to consider the aural aspects of the performance (i.e. from the performer's perspective), it is necessary to link Agazzari's statement to earlier widespread practices related to impromptu counterpoint.

In Diego Ortiz's 1553 treatise, «contraponti di consierto» there are specific techniques for the violone and harpsichord to use when playing a certain kind of «sonare di fantasia», including the extemporaneous incorporation («ciascuno buon sonatore [...] di sua testa») of graceful runs and figures («leggiadri passaggi» and «tirate»). It also stressed the importance of beautiful fugues and the need for both performers to respect each other's playing in order to avoid overlapping diminutions[73].

> This second Book discusses the various manners that should be played with the Violone, and the Harpsichord together. There are three manners of sounding. The First is called Fantasia. The Second over the plainchant. The Third over a composition for many voices. The Fantasia cannot be shown, as any good player plays it of his/her own will, and of his/her own study and habit, but I will well say what is required to play it. Let the Fantasia which the Harpsichord shall play be of well-ordered consonances whereupon the Violone shall enter sonorously with some graceful runs, and when the Violone lingers in some figures with flat bowing, then the Harpsichord shall answer it accordingly. And together they make some beautiful fugues having regard and respect for each other, as is usual in the **Contraponti di consierto**: and thus the one will know the other, and with the common exertion they will discover the many excelling and worthy secrets that are contained in this manner of playing Fantasia but of the two other manners it will be discussed at the proper time and in their own places[74].

---

71. Singing «sufficienter contrapunctum» was one of the requirements mentioned in the *Constitutiones Capellae Pontificiae* («si cantor examinandus»): see MAZZETTI – TICLI 2017, pp. 233ff.

72. On the Renaissance use of the term counterpoint, see TICLI 2023A, p. 299.

73. This closely reminds Agostino Agazzari's recommendations: see *ibidem*, p. 313.

74. «In questo secondo Libro si trattano le varie maniere che si debbano sonare col Violone, e col Cimbalo insieme, Tre sonno li maniere di sonare. La Prima si dice Fantasia. La Seconda sopra canto Piano. La terza sopra compositione di molte voci. La Fantasia non si può mostrare, che ciascuno buon sonatore la suona di sua testa e di suo studio & uso, ma ben dirò quel che si richieda per sonarla. La fantasia che sonerà il Cimbalo sia di consonanze ben ordinate ove poi entri sonando il Violone con alcuni leggiadri passaggi, e quando el Violone si trattiene in alcune tirate overo archate piane, allhora il Cimbalo gli risponda a proposto. & insieme faccino alcune fughe belle havendo risguardo e rispetto l'un all'altro, come suol haversi nelli **Contraponti di consierto**: e cosi l'uno conoscera l'altro, e con l'essercitatione commune si scopritanno li molti escellenti e degni secreti che si contengono in questa maniera di sonare di Fantasia ma delle due altre maniere si fara mentione nelli lor convenevoli e proprii lochi» (my emphasis). ORTIZ 1553, fol. 26r.

In Exs. 1 and 2 it is possible to find some contrapuntal patterns for improvising over a bass (so that imitation and fugues can be heard throughout the performance) as well as dialogue and echo effects produced by the solo instrument in a *recercada* for *violone*.

Ex. 1: Diego Ortiz, *Recercada primera*, incipit: solmisation syllables highlighting imitative patterns[75].

Ex. 2: Diego Ortiz, *Recercata terza*, incipit: solmisation syllables highlighting imitative patterns[76].

Other treatises from the context of southern Italy and the Iberian peninsula[77] elucidated the instructions for performing *contrappunto concertado* or *in concerto*, as is discernible in the

---

75. *Ibidem*, fol. 30v.
76. *Ibidem*, fol. 28v.
77. See CANNIZZARO 2011.

works of Vicente Lusitano, Pietro Cerone, or Scipione Cerreto[78]. This enabled performers to learn how to make impromptu consonances over a part and to create extemporaneous canons or imitative entries on one or more parts over a *cantus firmus*.

Ex. 3: Vicente Lusitano, Canon at fourth below over a bass[79].

Ex. 4: Scipione Cerreto, Canon at the unison over a bass[80].

Exs. 3 and 4 are canonical patterns utilised by Lusitano and Cerreto — i.e. mnemonic structures (interval successions) over specific bass motions: the entrances of the two voices *in concerto* over the bass show canons at the fifth and canons at the unison respectively.

Agazzari, besides talking about improvising counterpoint and playing from intabulations[81], also required the performer to have a very good ear («to hear the movement that the parts make between them, which I will not discuss, as I cannot make it better by my

78.   See Canguilhem 2011.

79.   Lusitano n.d.

80.   Cerreto 1601, bk. 4, p. 276.

81.   This second required skill is also connected to Banchieri's and Diruta's writings (1609 and 1622) on the topic (Ticli 2023a, pp. 301ff): there are players «really practised at doing concerts, but so boastful that they do not care anymore to work hard on *fantasia & spartiture*» (Banchieri 1609, p. 24). «They are easily satisfied with doing clumsily four pieces without any foundation, and with playing on a *Basso generale*» (Diruta 1609, bk. 4, p. 16): indeed, these *bassisti* «will be content with playing just the bass, as to the rest, then *tamquam asinus ad lyram*» Banchieri 1609, p. 25 and Bellotti 2023. On the practice of playing intabulations of sacred polyphony, see Mazzetti – Ticli 2014.

Ex. 5: *Regole di Canto figurato, contrapunto, e d'accompagnare* [c.1670], chap. XVI 'Che sia diminutione'.

speech if it is naturally flawed»)[82], which refers directly to the aural skills required by the kind of collective improvisation that was described in the treatise. It is essential the improviser understands what the other parts are playing and singing while they are performing. The author also pointed out that it is preferable to improvise each time something related to the *affetto* of the words, witnessing the freedom and versatility (in terms of a broad spectrum of instrumental possibilities, e.g. from tasto solo to big chords, or various instrumental gestures) that *basso continuo* could grant the performer for purposes of rhetorical and musical expression. As to the well-known division in instruments of *fondamento* and *ornamento*, Agazzari follows what we read in Vicentino's statement. The *fondamento* instruments support the consort and keep the harmony still, playing the bass as it is without needing to know much about counterpoint. The purpose of *ornamento* instruments is to embellish, beautify and flavour the *Concerto* through a great variety of good counterpoint depending on the instrument, which could be a polyphonic one such as a keyboard or a melodic one such as a violin. These players should be highly skilled in counterpoint as they have to improvise new parts on the same bass, *contrappunti*, and new and varied *passaggi*. Agazzari evidently is referring to improvisation, a sort of extemporaneous (re-)composition. Along with Vicentino, the contemporary presence of the same lines in two

---

[82]. «[...] buon orecchio, per sentir lo movimento, che fanno le parti infra di loro; del che non ne ragiono, per non poter'io col mio discorso farglielo buono, havendolo cattivo dalla natura». AGAZZARI 1607, p. 4; see also TICLI 2023A, p. 302.

versions (both plain and ornamented) is here openly stated again. The only difference is that Vicentino was almost certainly thinking of an instrumental intabulation of the parts or an instrumental doubling of the voices, which were giving ornaments, whereas Agazzari is talking about a recreated counterpoint over a bass played on the spot by a polyphonic instrument[83].

We can also observe further evidence of these practices later, as in the *Regole di canto figurato, contrappunto, d'accompagnare* (c.1670), which describe the florid diminutions for the bass line, explaining that the organ player should not play the ornamented version unless they are playing the simple bass on the pedal (Ex. 5)[84].

The necessary combination between *contrappunto alla mente* and ornamentation — documented in numerous manuscript sources such as Nanino's *Regola per imparare à fare Contrapunto à mente*[85] — is demonstrated also by Antonfrancesco Doni, who spoke of a *concerto* with voices and instruments, clarifying that it was essential to know how to produce fugues and not just chords and that playing without diminutions impoverished the harmony:

> [...] If all those who know how to make chords knew how to do it well, I would be in the number of masters. In a month one knows how to make a *zibaldone*, but invention and fugue must be united with harmony [...].

> And he, putting up with his insolence, began to play without diminishing: for the clumsy man, hearing that harmony was lacking, being ashamed to tell him that he should have diminished, or more likely not knowing anything about sounds, said presumptuously "You all play a little dance!"[86].

---

83. It is the same process as described by Luigi Zenobi: «But above all else, [they must use] some judgement in knowing how to harmonise with someone who plays a single-part instrument, or also sings with them». TICLI 2023A, p. 305. See also the survey of instrumental repertoire, regarding the formulas utilised by *ornamento* instruments in *ibidem*, pp. 312ff.

84. «The diminutions on the Organ are not laudable because they ruin the foundation of the music by moving the bass when it is the ground of all harmony, however by playing with the pedal they can be done. In the harpsichord, which seeks more motion as it cannot maintain the harmony, they will be allowed. One will even be able to make small diminutions as much in the soprano as in the bass» («Le diminutioni nell'Organo non sono laudabili perché si guasta il fondamento della musicha movendosi il basso come base di tutta l'armonia mà tenendovi il pedale si potranno fare. Nel cembalo che ricerca più moto per non havere il mantenimento dell'armonia si potranno concedere. Si potranno fare alfino piccoli diminutioni tanto nel soprano, quanto nel basso»). *REGOLE DI CANTO FIGURATO* 1670, chap. XVI 'Che sia diminutione'. This source considers the Harpsichord as a mere *ornamento* instrument.

85. The treatise lays emphasis on formulaic patterns clearly useful to such *concertato* practices: see MAZZETTI – TICLI 2017, pp. 246, 281ff.

86. «[...] se tutti quegli che san fare gli accordi sapessin far bene, io sarei nel numero dei maestri. In un mese si sa fare un zibaldone, ma l'invenzione e la fuga bisogna unire con l'armonia»; «Et egli, sopportando la insolenza sua, cominciò a sonare senza diminuire: perché il goffo, sentendo mancar l'armonia vergognandosi a dirgli che

Basso Continuo as a 'Concertato' Practice

Seeking Traces of Aural Practices and Performance Devices

For a full understanding of such improvisational practices, it will be useful to take into consideration also 'composed' pieces, which bequeath in writing some traces of the aural dialogue we are examining and reconstructing as a form of collective improvisation. Our focus will be on the patterns and formulas at the crossroads of contrapuntal and ornamental improvisation techniques mentioned above.

In Arcangelo Crotti's *concerto ecclesiastico* for Soprano and instruments *Pater peccavi* (1608)[87], the motif of four descending quavers in the vocal line is instrumentally imitated in contrary motion (see Ex. 6, highlighting the imitative patterns).

Ex. 6: Arcangelo Crotti, Excerpt from 'Pater peccavi' for soprano, instruments and basso continuo[88].

In Monteverdi's *Concertato* for solo voice and nine instruments *Con che soavità* (1609)[89] — which albeit with some variations reminds us of previous Florentine experiences such as the *Intermedii et Concerti* for *La Pellegrina*[90] — we notice that the same melody appears in the *viola da brazzo* over a very static bass line (see Ex. 7, highlighting the imitative patterns).

menasse pur le dita o più tosto non sapendo che si fusse suono, disse presuntuosamente: "Sonate un poco tutti da ballare"». Doni 1544, Canto IX and II.

87. Crotti 1608.

88. *Ibidem.*

89. Monteverdi 1619.

90. See 'Io che l'onde raffreno' sung by Vittoria Archilei at the beginning of the *Quinto intermedio* or 'Io che dal ciel cader' sung by Lucia Caccini at the beginning of the *Quarto Intermedio*. Rossi 1589, p. 49. See also Warburg 1932 and Walker 1963.

Ex. 7: Claudio Monteverdi, Final cadence of 'Con che soavità' for soprano, nine instruments and basso continuo[91].

In Luzzasco Luzzaschi's madrigal for three sopranos 'O dolcezze amarissime' (1601)[92], we find ornamentation formulas used on specific intervals echoed throughout the vocal texture of the three voices: in Ex. 8 the reconstructed contrapuntal lines of the polyphonic madrigal from the keyboard intabulation are highlighted.

In the case of integrated performers like the well-known Ferrarese ladies — that is, in performances including more than one skill at the same time — the continuo player is not separated from the solo singing. This can be a resource as the sought-after dialogue is unmediated, but it may be also a potential disadvantage as the player is not completely free and has to deal with vocal performance as well. In some collections, we see *concertato* pieces emphasise diminutions and ornamentations in the vocal line such as in *Madrigali et canzonette concertate* by Giovanni Bassano (1602) and the *Compositioni musicali intavolate* by Heteroclito Giancarli (1602). In both works for lute and voice, this choice is easily explained: performers needed a simpler instrumental part when they were already busy with singing diminutions to their lute (see Exs. 9 and 10).

---

[91].   MONTEVERDI 1619.

[92].   LUZZASCHI 1601.

Ex. 8: Luzzasco Luzzaschi, Excerpt from 'O dolcezze amarissime' for three sopranos[93].

Ex. 9: Heteroclito Giancarli, Excerpt from 'Lasso che desiando' for lute and voice.

Ex. 10: Giovanni Bassano, Excerpt from 'Placida herbetta' for lute and voice.

This fluidity between genres and practices, repertoire with basso continuo and the more traditional intabulated polyphony, poses no issues. For instance, we have already observed *dialoghi* and *madrigali* (such as the ones sung by the Ferrarese *Concerto*) could serve as pieces for few voices with a lute intabulation but could also be performed as basso continuo works *ante litteram*[94]. What the sources highlight instead is the persistent occurrence of multi-skilled

---

[93]. *Ibidem.*

[94]. See p. 366, especially fns. 29 and 31.

performances (involving singing, playing and acting, most usually), extensive embellishment and every kind of performative device that enhanced the ensemble music-making and made it distinctively outstanding, as is well articulated in Vicenzo Giustiniani's account:

> Giachet [Giaches de] Wert in Mantua, Luzzasco [Luzzaschi] in Ferrara. These were in charge of all the music of those Dukes, [...] to the utmost in making many ladies and principal ladies **play and sing** excellently; to such an extent that they sometimes spent the whole day in some *camerini* [...], and there was great skill among the ladies of Mantua and Ferrara, who competed, not only in the *metallo* [sound quality] and the *disposizione* [talent] of their voices; but in the ornamentation of exquisite runs [*passaggi*] drawn at opportune times and not overdone, (in which respect Gio. Luca [Conforti] falsettist of Rome, who also served in Ferrara, was wont to sin), and moreover in modulating the voice forte or piano, by thinning or swelling it approaching extreme sounds on the ledger lines, [they could achieve it] now by dragging their voice, now by dividing it with the use of a gentle interrupted short rest [*sospiro*], now by giving long runs [*passaggi*], well-performed, and distinct, now *gruppi*, [trill-like ornaments], now jumps, now long trills, now short, and now sweet runs sung piano from which, at times, echoes were suddenly heard in response, and most importantly **with facial expressions, and with glances and gestures** that appropriately accompanied the music and the concepts [of the poetry], and above all without any awkward movements of the body [*persona*][95], mouth, or hands, that were not directed to the purpose for which they were used while singing, and with making the words stand out so well that even the last syllable of each word could be heard, which was not interrupted or obnubilated by the runs and other ornaments, and with utilising many other particular devices and features that will be said by people more knowledgeable than myself»[96].

---

[95]. See GUALANDRI 2001, p. 22, discussing Giovanni Bonifacio's *L'Arte de' Cenni* (1616) and coeval treatises on acting.

[96]. «Giachet Wert in Mantova, il Luzzasco in Ferrara. Quali erano sopraintendenti di tutte le musiche di quei Duchi, [...] massime in fare che molte dame et signore principali apparassero di **sonare e cantare** per eccellenza; a segno tale che dimoravano talvolta i giorni intieri in alcuni camerini [...], et era gran competenza fra quelle dame di Mantova et di Ferrara, che facevano a gara, non solo quanto al metallo et alla disposizione delle voci; ma nell'ornamento di esquisiti passaggi tirati in opportuna congiuntura e non soverchi, (nel che soleva peccare Gio. Luca [Conforti] falsetto di Roma, che servì anche in Ferrara), e di più col moderare e crescere la voce forte o piano, assottigliandola ingrossandola, che secondo che veniva a' tagli, ora con strascinarla, ora smezzarla, con l'accompagnamento d'un soave interrotto sospiro, ora tirando passaggi lunghi, seguiti bene, spiccati, ora gruppi, ora a salti, ora con trilli lunghi, ora con brevi, et or con passaggi soavi e cantati piano, dalli quali tal volta all'improvviso si sentiva echi rispondere, e principalmente **con azione del viso, e dei sguardi e de' gesti** che accompagnavano appropriatamente la musica e li concetti, e sopra tutto senza moto della persona e della bocca e delle mani sconcioso, che non fusse indirizzato al fine per il quale si cantava, e con far spiccar bene le parole in guisa tale che si sentisse anche l'ultima sillaba di ciascuna parola, la quale dalli passaggi et altri ornamenti non fusse interrotta soppressa, e

In such a context, each performer concerted the piece not just within the ensemble but within their own part — i.e. their own voice and instrumental part in the first place. Such a dialogue could take place not only between different performers but also between different parts of the performance such as singing, playing and even acting, as seen at the end of Giustiniani's description. The performance habits remained quite consistent between the late Cinquecento and early Seicento. The only difference was the way of writing music (see *Giulio Caccini's Nuove Musiche et nuova maniera di scriverle*, 1614). A certain degree of freedom was allowed both in intabulations and basso continuo settings, although in the latter, the performer is freer to concert (see Agazzari's treatise) the different parts of the performance by also acting, playing etc. Every feature had to be at the service of the rhetoric of the *affetti*[97]: words and music serve the oratory art because they are an amplification of the meaning (as tools of the orator). Similarly, gestures and facial expressions to be featured during the performance played a central role in multi-skilled performances and in the imaginary dialogue of the *concerto*, too. We can imagine the density of the performance could change and be channelled amongst the parts — and performers — of the *concerto*: the four components we observed in terms of the required skills are Counterpoint/Ornamentation, Singing, Playing and Acting. Obviously, what can be performed on the instrument in such a context is vastly different from what a continuo player, who is playing just their own instrumental part, can achieve.

Manifest and Elusive Aspects of Concertato Practices

The present discussion is unable to cover all aspects of such extensive topics as *concertato* or integrated performance[98]. Therefore, before drawing conclusions, it is important to make a few remarks that highlight some of the cross-cutting themes that emerge from the source analysis presented above.

Firstly, it is essential at least to chart a chronological trajectory through the various sources and time periods surveyed during our investigation, in order to discern patterns of continuity amidst the ever-shifting tastes and styles of the respective eras. Compared to the earliest sources, which furnished only fragmentary reports and written accounts, we can note that the situation developed as we moved into the seventeenth century, providing us with more details, pedagogical precepts of improvisation techniques and concrete musical examples that, although not entirely faithful to the aural original, have allowed us to gain a more accurate idea

---

con molti altri particolari artificj et osservazioni che saranno a notizia di persone più esperimentate di me» (my emphasis). Solerti 1903, pp. 107-108. See also the discussion on Giustiniani's work at pp. 369-370.

[97]. Ticli 2021, pp. 174-175.

[98]. See fn. 9.

of the practices in question. Yet, even the so-called monody with basso continuo does raise questions concerning practices for accompanying the solo part, suggesting that seventeenth-century playing too could be more versatile than modern scholars might think: it is noteworthy that in cases such as the Carlo G. manuscript[99] the combination of voice and instrument was similar to the *concertato* practice we outlined above. As seen previously, the *concertato* was indeed based on particular traits such as improvised counterpoint over a bass (alternation, echoes, fugues and dialogic patterns); extensive ornamentation i.e. florid counterpoint in the shape of (often-short) motifs; instrumental gestures typical of each instrument; and stylistic features typical of the repertoire in fashion at the time. Thanks to a progressively systematic (and partly descriptive) use of notation, from the seventeenth century onwards, elements were incorporated in Italy and elsewhere, which gradually moved away from only the performative and improvisational realm towards either purely compositional approaches or improvisation with highly codified features. By examining well-studied practices such as Italian *partimenti*, which circulated widely throughout eighteenth-century Europe, it becomes clear that when ensemble performers possessed sufficient skills, their various roles in a performance (e.g., chamber music) could be more balanced or even equal: this is easy to observe thanks to the surviving written compositions, which shared an equally virtuosic style in all the parts involved. In this light, it is crucial to readdress in terms of skill requirements the relationship between instruments (accompaniment) and singing (solo), as demonstrated in *obbligato* pieces and later repertoire. This complexity is ultimately reflected in both notation and detailed indications (as seen in the works of J. J. Quantz), showing a much more multifaceted relationship amongst the performers (see Exs. 11 and 12, highlighting the imitative patterns).

Ex. 11: Aurelio Berettari, Excerpt from 'Exultent angeli'[100].

The second aspect that needs to be addressed relates to the degree of skills required for the performance. Depending on the performer's background and the various contexts, there are significant differences in performance outcomes, with notational aid being only of secondary

---

[99]. E.g., see recent studies on the Carlo G. manuscript and other sources in ROTEM 2019, CAMPAGNE – ROTEM 2022.

[100]. BERETTARI 1654.

Ex. 12: George Frideric Handel, Excerpt from 'Meine Seele hört im Sehen' (HWV 207).

importance. In view of all the above-mentioned considerations, TABLE 1 shows that the performance skills decrease from three to one and the texture shifts from a more contrapuntal one[101] to chords and simpler instrumental parts: from having *contrapunctum* as in the case of chapel singers, it moves towards simple accompaniments for those who needed *Regole* for accompanying[102] — which undoubtedly included enthusiasts and Banchieri's *bassisti*. These clues show, albeit very concisely, many potential intersections with different genres ranging from madrigals, motets to *canzonette, laudi sacre*, etc.[103] Indeed, the phenomenon under investigation is evidently multi-faceted, and it would be unwise to rely exclusively on the written sources at our disposal. Even skilled musicians and nobility could perform the same madrigals with strikingly different interpretations. For example, Countess Barbara Maggia from Brescia, or her son Francesco Gambara (whose studies, instruments, books, and commissioned music

---

101. Counterpoint (*alla mente*) is a customary expert skill of an accomplished musician, as substantiated by various sources including the Papal *Constitutiones*: see p. 378.

102. In the (late) sixteenth century, there was a proliferation of musical treatises, much like in other areas of knowledge. Those lacking knowledge of counterpoint required (simplified) *regole* for both 'accompanying', and beginners and non-professionals needed *regole* for learning how to sing or play counterpoint: see LORENZETTI 2003, pp. 1-2ff., MAZZETTI – TICLI 2023B, TICLI 2023A, p. 300. This is why treatises (even on basso continuo) are commonly directed towards those who are amateurs or at least beginner-level.

103. As can be seen in Simone Verovio's intabulations: see CAMPAGNE 2018.

have recently been reconstructed and reassessed in MAZZETTI – TICLI 2021), would have performed a madrigal differently to a professional like Giulio Caccini, who was active during the same period.

A comparison of editorial habits and notational practices in relation to ornamentation can effectively address the third point of this discussion, regarding the more fleeting aspects of aurality, specifically the relationship between improvisational practices and the written evidence they leave behind. As has already been discussed, Bartolomeo Barbarino gave two versions of each motet in his 1614 collection, a «Parte Passeggiata» for those who have *dispositione* but no counterpoint[104] along with a «Parte Semplice» for both those without *dispositione* (beginners) and those who have *dispositione* and counterpoint as they themselves could «create their own *passaggi* and everything else required by the good manner of singing» (see ILL. 1).

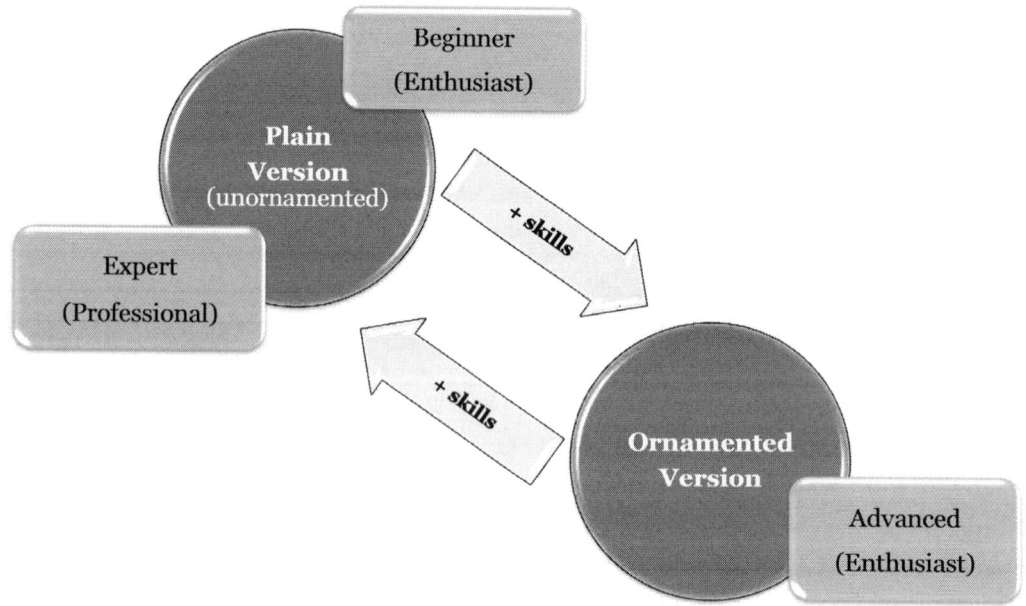

ILL. 1: Relationship between notational aids and skills: Ornamentation.

This information is pivotal for thinking about composers who were well aware of the needs of the music market and adapted their written works to their intended audience, while manuscripts often reveal a different status. Turning our attention to the instrumental practices under consideration (see ILL. 2), we can observe that basso continuo parts have similar characteristics to Barbarino's 'Parte semplice', in that the performer could easily improvise chords from a very simple and intuitive notation[105].

---

104. Again, it was intended as an advanced skill gained by the *cantor* for improvising.
105. See also the practice of «suonare schietto» in TICLI 2023A, pp. 305-306.

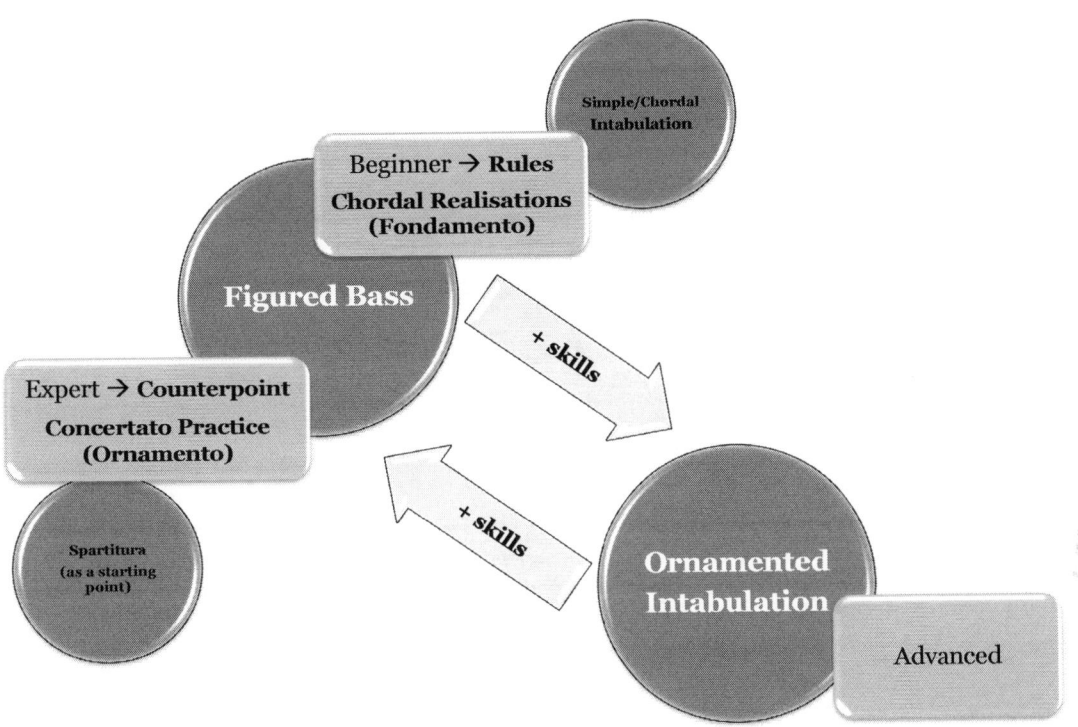

Ill. 2: Relationship between notational aids and skills: Concertato practices (basso continuo).

Our analogy can progress further by exploring the accompaniments provided by instrumental tablatures. For those with more advanced skills, an intabulated and ornamented arrangement of a piece could be created to produce a *concertato*, similar to Giovanni Antonio Terzi's madrigals («in concerto»)[106] or to the pieces from the above-mentioned Carlo G. manuscript. The expert musician, however, may use the basic basso continuo notation to present a highly complex and expressive performance. This highlights the innovation and fundamental characteristic of the basso continuo, which granted unparalleled freedom for creative expression.

Ill. 3 displays the connection between notated parameters and skill level. It can be concluded that the more musical features there are written in notation, such as ornamentation, the greater the skill level required for musicians to perform the music. Conversely, proficient players tend to prefer a simpler notation that allows them to showcase their mastery. This preference reflects a particular relationship with written music, as can be seen in Girolamo Frescobaldi's words. When talking about his *Capricci*, he confirms that «they are more challenging than other collections, but only if one knows them from reading»: one will understand their *affetto*

---

[106]. *Ibidem*, pp. 313-314.

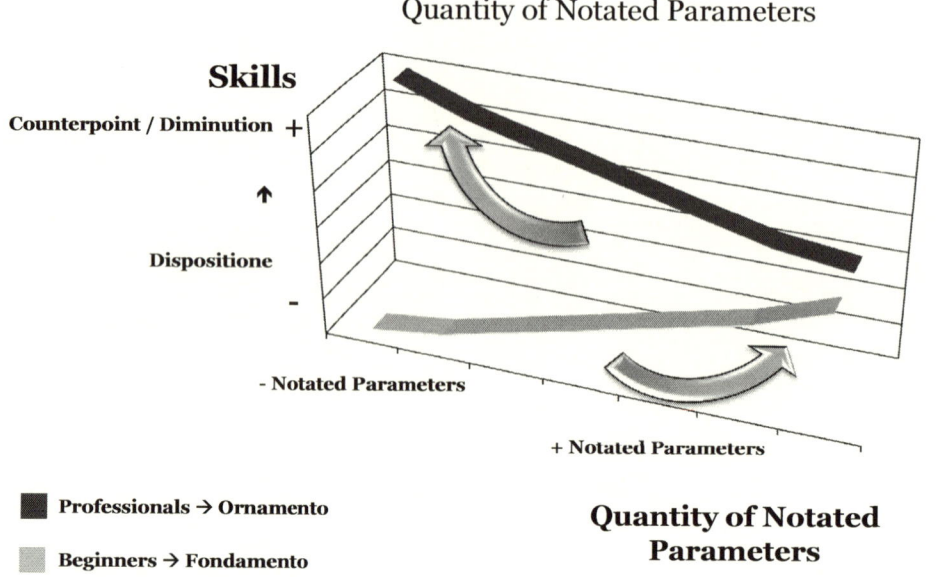

ILL. 3: Relationship between notated parameters and skills in concertato practices (basso continuo).

only «by putting them into practice on the instrument»[107]. Performers were capable of playing such a repertoire, but reading from written notation could obscure the music's sense and make it seem more challenging. As it was simpler for a professional to improvise a complicated piece of music than to read it from a 'complete score' or an intabulation, basso continuo is the perfect example of musical stenography or shorthand. Such a notation allowed the retrieval of an elementary contrapuntal texture on the spot, and at the same time the rendition of all the complex contrapuntal/embellishing practices, which flowed together into the terms *concerto* and *concertato*. This practice could thus easily be adapted to all skill levels. It suited several different kinds of instruments and potentially speaks to all of them, as instrumental idiomaticity was something players provided during the performance by themselves. In addition, it was so flexible that it could be employed with all styles, regardless of the genre and context.

***

Through detailed descriptions and written traces of practices, and the interpretation of selected labels, lists of ornaments and features of several instruments, we have observed a certain continuity of practices across the centuries and shed some light on the hierarchy of the different parts that are involved in sixteenth- and seventeenth-century collective improvisation, exactly

---

107. «In questi componimenti intitolati Capricci, non ho tenuto stile così facile come ne' miei Ricercari. Ma non si deve però giudicare la difficoltà loro prima di mettergli bene in pratica nell'instrumento dove si conoscerà con lo studio l'affetto che deve tenere». FRESCOBALDI 1624, 'A gli Studiosi dell'Opera'.

as suggested by treatises such as Agostino Agazzari's *Del sonare sopra 'l basso*. Nevertheless, it was easy to realise that versatility went along with expressiveness, as the same written notation permitted putting into practice radically different solutions, depending, as shown, on the *affetto* and the rhetoric of music and text[108]. Yet, the fluidity between performance and writing practices, recognised by musicians, composers and audiences alike, serves as a crucial gauge for assessing the significance of performers when enjoying music and poetry at the time. Indeed, the performance delivery necessitated a great deal of creativity in the interpretation of both the literary text and musical composition. The sole loyalty required of performers was aimed towards the empowerment of the rhetorical discourse they wanted to address through their artistic endeavours — not towards the composer, nor the musical composition itself. A collaborative improvisational approach, such as playing over a bass, namely the basso continuo practice, was able to fulfil all the performance requirements of the time. Its multipurpose notation could grant every conceivable kind of music expression at the service of *affetti*'s rhetoric, allowing the freedom for which, over the centuries, basso continuo was so highly praised.

BIBLIOGRAPHY

AGAZZARI 1607
AGAZZARI, Agostino. *Del sonare sopra 'l basso con tutti li stromenti e dell'uso loro nel conserto*, Siena, Domenico Falconi, 1607.

ANONYMOUS 1724
ANONYMOUS. *A Short Explication of Such Foreign Words, as Are Made Use of in Musick Books*, London, Joseph Brotherton, 1724.

ARTUSI 1600
ARTUSI, Giovanni Maria. *L'Artusi overo delle imperfettioni della moderna musica ragionamenti dui. Ne' quali si ragiona di molte cose utili, et necessarie alli moderni compositori*, Venice, Giacomo Vincenti, 1600.

BAHN – BARBATI 2023
BAHN, Catherine – BARBATI, Giovanna. 'The Partimenti of Rocco Greco: Reconstructing the Pedagogical Tradition of the Early Violoncello', in: *Basso Continuo in Italy: Sources, Pedagogy and Performance*, edited by Marcello Mazzetti, Turnhout, Brepols, 2023 (Musica Incarnata: Pedagogy, Performance and Market, 1), pp. 187-210.

BANCHIERI 1609
BANCHIERI, Adriano. *Conclusioni nel suono dell'organo*, Bologna, Heredi di Gio. Rossi, 1609.

---

108. «[...] consonances and all harmony are subjective and subordinate to words and not the other way round» («le consonanze, e tutta l'armonia, sono soggette, e sottoposte alle parole, e non per il contrario»). AGAZZARI 1607, p. 5. See also TICLI 2023A, p. 293.

BARBARINO 1614
BARBARINO, Bartolomeo. *Il Secondo libro delli Mottetti di Bartolomeo Barbarino da Fabriano detto il Pesarino, da cantarsi a una voce sola, o in sopra, o in tenore, come più il cantante si compiacera*, Venice, Bartolomeo Magni, 1614.

BASSANO 1585
BASSANO, Giovanni. *Ricercate Passaggi et Cadentie, per potersi essercitar nel diminuir terminatamento con ogni sorte d'istrumento: et anco diversi passaggi per la semplice voce*, Venice, Giacomo Vincenzi-Riccardo Amadino, 1585.

BELLOTTI 2023
BELLOTTI, Edoardo. 'Basso continuo e contrappunto nelle fonti seicentesche: un moderno approccio alla didattica musicale', in: *Basso Continuo in Italy:Sources, Pedagogy and Performance, op. cit.*, pp. 265-284.

BEMBO 2003
BEMBO, Pietro. *Asolani*, Rome, Biblioteca Italiana, <http://www.bibliotecaitaliana.it/scheda/bibit000035>, accessed November 2023.

BERETTARI 1654
BERETTARI, Aurelio. *Motetti a voce sola*, Venice, Alessandro Vincenti, 1654.

BIER 2013
BIER, Robin. 'The Ideal Orpheus: An Analysis of Virtuosic Self-Accompanied Singing as a Historical Vocal Performance Practice', Ph.D. Diss., York, University of York, 2013.

BOYDEN 1957
BOYDEN, David D. 'When Is a Concerto Not a Concerto?', in: *The Musical Quarterly*, XLIII/2 (1957), pp. 220-232.

CAMPAGNE 2018
CAMPAGNE, Augusta. *Simone Verovio: Music Printing, Intabulations and Basso Continuo in Rome around 1600*, Vienna, Böhlau, 2018 (Wiener Veröffentlichungen Zur Musikgeschichte, 13).

CAMPAGNE – ROTEM 2022
EAD. – ROTEM, Elam. *Keyboard Accompaniment in Italy around 1600: Intabulations, Scores and Basso Continuo*, Basel, Forschungsportal Schola Cantorum Basiliensis, 2022, <https://forschung.schola-cantorum-basiliensis.ch/en/forschung/keyboard-accompaniment-1600.html>, accessed October 2023.

CANGUILHEM 2011
CANGUILHEM, Philippe. 'Singing upon the Book According to Vicente Lusitano', in: *Early Music History*, XXX (2011), pp. 55-103.

CANGUILHEM 2015
ID. *L'improvisation polyphonique à la Renaissance*, Paris, Classiques Garnier, 2015.

CANNIZZARO 2011
CANNIZZARO, Diego. 'Legami tra Spagna e Italia Meridionale', in: *Revista de Musicología*, XXXIV/2 (2011), pp. 185-201.

CERRETO 1601
CERRETO, Scipione. *Della prattica musica vocale, et strumentale*, Naples, Giacomo Carlino, 1601.

CROTTI 1608
CROTTI, Arcangelo. *Il Primo Libro de' Concerti Ecclesiastici à 1. à 2. à 3 à 4. & à 5. Parte con Voci Sole, & Parte con Voci, & Instrumenti di Fr. Archangelo Crotti da Ferrara Agostiniano Eremita Osseruante. Nuouamente Composti & Dati in Luce*, Venice, Giacomo Vincenti, 1608.

DE FUENLLANA 1554
FUENLLANA, Miguel de. *Orphenica Lyra*, Sevilla, Martin de Montesdoca, 1554.

DIRUTA 1609
DIRUTA, Girolamo. *Seconda parte del Transilvano, dialogo diviso in quattro libri [...] Nel quale si contiene il vero Modo, & la vera Regola d'intauolare ciascun Canto, semplice, et diminuito con ogni sorte de diminutioni: et nel fin dell'vltimo libro v'è la Regola, la qual scopre con breuità e facilità il modo d'imparar presto à cantare*, Venice, Alessandro Vincenti, 1609.

DONI 1544
DONI, Antonfrancesco. *Dialogo della musica*, Venice, Girolamo Scotto, 1544.

DURANTE – MARTELLOTTI 1989
DURANTE, Elio – MARTELLOTTI, Anna. *Cronistoria del concerto delle dame principalissime di Margherita Gonzaga d'Este*, Florence, SPES, 1989.

EINSTEIN – PIDCOCK – BONAVIA 1934
EINSTEIN, Alfred – PIDCOCK, G. D. H. – BONAVIA, F. 'The «Dialogo della Musica» of Messer Antonio Francesco Doni', in: *Music & Letters*, XV/3 (1934), pp. 244-253.

FELDMAN 1995
FELDMAN, Martha. *City Culture and the Madrigal at Venice*, Berkeley-Los Angeles, University of California Press, 1995.

FLORIO 1598
FLORIO, John. *A Worlde of Wordes, or Most Copious, and Exact Dictionarie in Italian and English*, London, Arnold Hatfield for Edw. Blount, 1598.

FLORIO 1611
ID. *Queen Anna's New World of Words or Dictionarie of the Italian and English Tongue, Collected, and Newly Much Augmented by Iohn Florio*, London, Melch. Bradwood for Edw. Blount and William Barret, 1611.

FLORIO 2013

ID. *John Florio: A Worlde of Wordes*, edited by Luigi Ballerini and Massimo Ciavolello, Toronto, University of Toronto Press, 2013.

FRESCOBALDI 1624

FRESCOBALDI, Girolamo. *Il primo libro di capricci fatti sopra diversi soggetti, et arie in partitura*, Rome, Luca Antonio Soldi, 1624.

GORDON – FELDMAN 2006

GORDON, Bonnie – FELDMAN, Martha. 'The Courtesan's Voice in Early Modern Italy', in: *The Courtesan's Arts: Cross-Cultural Perspectives*, edited by Martha Feldman, Oxford, Oxford University Press, 2006, pp. 104-123.

GRIFFITHS 1989

GRIFFITHS, John. 'At Court and at Home with the Vihuela de Mano: Current Perspectives on the Instrument, Its Music, and Its World', in: *Journal of the Lute Society of America*, XXII (January 1989), pp. 1-27.

GUALANDRI 2001

GUALANDRI, Francesca. *Affetti, passioni, vizi e virtù: La retorica del gesto nel teatro del '600*, Milan, Peri, 2001.

GUIDO 2019

Studies in Historical Improvisation: From Cantare super librum to Partimenti, edited by Massimiliano Guido, Abingdon-New York, Routledge, 2019.

HAAR 1966

HAAR, James. 'Notes on the «Dialogo della Musica» of Antonfrancesco Doni', in: *Music & Letters*, XLVII/3 (1966), pp. 198-224.

HALL 1958

HALL, Robert A. 'Italian «Concerto» («Conserto») and «Concertare»', in: *Italica*, XXXV/3 (1958), pp. 188-191.

JOHNSTON 1998

JOHNSTON, Gregory S. 'Polyphonic Keyboard Accompaniment in the Early Baroque: An Alternative to Basso Continuo', in: *Early Music*, XXVI/1 (1998), pp. 51-64.

KEENER 2014

KEENER, Shawn M. 'The Giustiniana Phenomenon and Venetian Cultural Memory 1400-1600', Ph.D. Diss., Chicago (IL), University of Chicago, 2014.

KEYS 1971

KEYS, A. C. 'The Etymology of Concerto', in: *Italica*, XLVIII/4 (1971), pp. 446-462.

KROSS 1970

KROSS, Siegfried. 'Concerto - concertare und conserere', in: *Bericht über den Internationalen Musikwissenschaftlichen Kongress Leipzig 1966*, edited by Carl Dalhaus, Reiner Kluge, Ernst H. Meyer, and Walter Wiora, Kassel, Bärenreiter, 1970, pp. 216-220.

LORENZETTI 2003

LORENZETTI, Stefano. *Musica e identità nobiliare nell'Italia del Rinascimento. Educazione, mentalità, immaginario*, Florence, Olschki, 2003.

LUSITANO n.d.

LUSITANO, Vicente. 'Trattato grande di musica pratica', Paris, BnF, Esp. 219, n.d.

LUTHER 1854

LUTHER, Martin. *Dr. Martin Luther's Sämtliche Werke. Sechzigster Band Nach den ältesten Ausgaben kritisch und historisch bearbeitet von Dr. Johann Konrad Irmischer [...]. II. Tischreden. Vierter Band*, edited by Johann Konrad Irmischer, Vierte Abtheilung, Frankfurt am Main - Erlangen, Heyder & Zimmer, 1854.

LUZZASCHI 1601

LUZZASCHI, Luzzasco. *Madrigali per cantare et sonare a uno e doi e tre soprani fatti per la musica del già serenissimo duca Alfonso d'Este*, Rome, Simone Verovio, 1601.

MACCLINTOCK 1961

MACCLINTOCK, Carol. 'Giustiniani's «Discorso sopra la Musica»', in: *Musica Disciplina*, XV (1961), pp. 209-225.

MANNOIA 2016

MANNOIA, Valeria. 'Aspects of Performance Practice in Bologna in the Sixteenth and Seventeenth Centuries. A Study of Archival Sources', in: *Ensayos. Historia y teoría del arte*, no. 30 (2016), pp. 18-53.

MATTHESON 1735

MATTHESON, Johann. *Kleine General-Bass-Schule*, Hamburg, Johann Cristoph Kißner, 1735.

MAZZETTI – TICLI 2014

MAZZETTI, Marcello – TICLI, Livio. 'Reconsidering Floriano Canale's Works and the Role of Canons Regular in the late Renaissance', in: *The International Church Music Review*, XXXV/1-2 (2014), pp. 199-224.

MAZZETTI – TICLI 2017

ID. – ID. '«Quando de quintis terzisque calabat in unam octavam». Per una storia della prassi esecutiva della musica sacra a Brescia nel tardo Cinquecento', in: *Annalisi di storia bresciana*, issue *Cultura musicale bresciana. Reperti e testimonianze di una civiltà*, edited by Maria Teresa Rosa Barezzani and Mariella Sala, Brescia, Morcelliana, 2017, pp. 223-293.

Mazzetti – Ticli 2021

Id. – Id. '«I raggi della chiarissima Casa Gambaresca»: The Gambaras' Music Patronage and the Performance Practice in 15th-17th-Century Brescia', in: *Music Patronage in Italy*, edited by Galliano Ciliberti, Turnhout, Brepols, 2021 (Studies on Italian Music History, 15), pp. 267-314.

Mazzetti – Ticli 2023a

Id. – Id. '«Perché voglio cose vostre da cantar, non mi fate corociare»: Tracce sonore nel (e intorno al) carteggio Bembo-Savorgnan (1500-1501)', in: *Women Language Literature in Italy / Donne lingua letteratura in Italia*, edited by Elisa Curti and Franco Tomasi, v (2023), pp. 33-54.

Mazzetti – Ticli 2023b

Id. – Id. 'Società e culture: Musicisti', in: *Il Rinascimento in Italia. 1: Storia, società, culture*, edited by Giancarlo Alfano and Franco Tomasi, Rome, Carocci editore, 2023 (Storia, società, culture), forthcoming.

Monteverdi 1619

Monteverdi, Claudio. *Concerto: Settimo Libro de Madrigali*, Venice, Bartolomeo Magni, 1619.

Newcomb 1978

Newcomb, Anthony. *The Madrigal at Ferrara, 1579-1597*, 2 vols., Princeton, Princeton University Press, 1978.

Ortiz 1553

Ortiz, Diego. *El primo libro nel quale si tratta delle glose sopra le cadenze et altre sorte de punti*, Rome, Valerio Dorico, 1553.

Ortiz 1961

Id. *Tratado de glosas sobre clausulas y otros generos de puntos en la musica de violones: Roma 1553*, translated by Max Schneider, Kassel-New York, Bärenreiter, 3 1961.

Perocco 2014

Perocco, Daria. 'Caterina Cornaro: una corte, una regina e la creazione di un mito', in: *Modern Language Notes*, cxxix/3S (April 2014), pp. 35-44.

Piccolomini 1552

Piccolomini, Alessandro. *Della institutione di tutta la vita dell'huomo nato nobile, et in città libera. Libri diece in lingua toscana, dove et peripateticamente, & Platonicamente, intorno alle cose dell'Etica, & Iconomica, & parte della Politica, è raccolta la somma di quanto principalmente può concorrere alla perfetta, & felice vita di quello* [...], Venice, Bonelli, 1552.

Piperno 1991

Piperno, Franco. '«Concerto» e «concertato» nella musica strumentale italiana del secolo decimo settimo', in: *Recercare*, iii (1991), pp. 169-202.

Praetorius 1619

Praetorius, Michael. *Syntagmatis Musici* [...] *Tomus Tertius* [...], Wolfenbüttel, Elias Holwein, 1619.

PRAETORIUS 2004
ID. *Syntagma Musicum III*, translated by Jeffery T. Kite-Powell, Oxford, Oxford University Press, 2004.

QUANTZ 2001
QUANTZ, Johann Joachim. *On Playing the Flute*, edited by Edward R. Reilly, Faber & Faber, [2]2001.

REFE 2016
REFE, Laura. 'Istruzioni per l'uso e dichiarazioni di metodo nei volgarizzamenti aristotelici del Rinascimento (I)', in: *Philosophical Readings. Online Journal of Philosophy*, VIII/2 (2016), pp. 95-106.

REGOLE DI CANTO FIGURATO 1670
Regole di canto figurato, contrapunto, e d'accompagnare, [c.1670], ms., Bologna, Museo internazionale e Biblioteca della musica, E. 25.

REIMER 1980
REIMER, Erich. 'Concerto - Schlüsselbegriff einer musikgeschichtlichen Epoche?', in: *Bericht über den Internationalen Musikwissenschaftlichen Kongress Berlin 1974*, edited by Hellmut Kühn and Peter Nitsche, Kassel, Bärenreiter, 1980, pp. 503-506.

ROSSI 1589
ROSSI, Bastiano de'. *Descrizione dell'apparato e degl'intermedi fatti per la commedia rappresentata in Firenze nelle notte de' serenissimi don Ferdinando Medici e madama Cristina di Lorena, gran duchi di Toscana*, Florence, Anton Padovani, 1589.

ROSSI 2018
ROSSI, Carla. *Italus ore, anglus pectore: Studi su John Florio. 1*, London, Thecla Academic Press, 2018.

ROTEM 2019
ROTEM, Elam. 'The «Carlo G Manuscript»: New Light on Early Seventeenth Century Accompaniment and Diminution Practices', in: *Groß Geigen um 1500: Orazio Michi und die Harfe um 1600*, edited by Martina Papiro, Basel, Schwabe Verlag, 2019.

SCHUBERT 2012
SCHUBERT, Peter. 'From Voice to Keyboard. Improvised Techniques in the Renaissance', in: *Philomusica on-line*, issue «Con la mente e con le mani»: *Teaching and Learning the Art of Counterpoint on the Keyboard (1585-1671). Atti del Convegno (Smarano - Trento, 18-20 Novembre 2010)*, edited by Massimiliano Guido, XI/2 (2012), pp. 12-22. <http://dx.doi.org/10.6092/1826-9001.11.1449>, accessed November 2023.

SOLERTI 1903
SOLERTI, Angelo. *Le origini del melodramma: testimonianze dei contemporanei*, Turin, Fratelli Bocca, 1903.

STARNES 1937A
STARNES, DeWitt T. 'Bilingual Dictionaries of Shakespeare's Day', in: *PMLA*, LII/4 (1937), pp. 1005-1018.

Starnes 1937b
Id. 'English Dictionaries of the Seventeenth Century', in: *Studies in English*, no. 17 (1937), pp. 15-51.

Starnes 1940
Id. 'Literary Features of Renaissance Dictionaries', in: *Studies in Philology*, xxxvii/1 (1940), pp. 26-50.

Stras 2018
Stras, Laurie. *Women and Music in Sixteenth-Century Ferrara*, Cambridge, Cambridge University Press, 2018.

Ticli 2021
Ticli, Livio. 'Cantanti, strumentisti e improvvisatori. La poesia in musica e l'«esecuzione integrata» fra Cinque e Seicento', in: *Italique. Poésie italienne de la Renaissance*, issue *Il libro di rime tra secondo Cinquecento e primo Seicento*, edited by Valeria Di Iasio and Franco Tomasi, xxiv (2021), pp. 157-190.

Ticli 2022
Id. 'Ornamentazione vocale-strumentale e improvvisazione (secc. xvi e xxi): la sfida di una pedagogia storicamente informata', in: *ARTEDU 2021. L'Arte di Educare. Educare all'Arte*, edited by Alessandro Luigini, Chiara Panciroli, and Paolo Somigli, Milan, FrancoAngeli, 2022, pp. 192-207.

Ticli 2023a
Id. '«Contrapunto alla mente» or Basso Continuo? Agostino Agazzari and His «Sonare sopra 'l Basso»', in: *Basso Continuo in Italy: Sources, Pedagogy and Performance, op. cit.*, pp. 285-328.

Ticli 2023b
Id. 'L'*Organo de' cantori* e il lessico, vocale e strumentale di G. B. Rossi', in: Rossi, Giovanni Battista. *Organo dei cantori*, edited by Giovanni Caprioli, Ivrea, LeMus Edizioni, 2023 (Antichi Maestri), pp. 197-205.

Treadwell 2000
Treadwell, Nina. 'Restaging the Siren. Musical Women in the Performance of Sixteenth-Century Italian Theater', Ph.D. Diss., Los Angeles (CA), University of Southern California, 2000.

Vicentino 1555
Vicentino, Nicola. *L'antica musica ridotta alla moderna prattica, con la dichiaratione, et con gli essempi de i tre generi, con le loro spetie. Et con l'inventione di uno nuovo stromento, nel quale si contiene tutta la perfetta musica, con molti segreti musicali*, Rome, Antonio Barre, 1555.

Walker 1963
Les Fêtes du mariage de Ferdinand de Médicis et Christine de Lorraine. 1: Musique des intermèdes de La Pellegrina: Florence 1589, critical edition by Daniel P. Walker, Paris, CRNS, 1963.

Warburg 1932
Warburg, Aby. 'I costumi teatrali per gli Intermezzi del 1589 [Atti dell'Accademia del R. Istituto Musicale, 1895]', in: *Aby Warburg. Gesammelte Schriften. 1*, edited by Gertrud Bing, Leipzig-Berlin, Benediktus Gotthelf Teubner, 1932.

WILSON 2019
WILSON, Blake. *Singing to the Lyre in Renaissance Italy: Memory, Performance, and Oral Poetry*, Cambridge, Cambridge University Press, 2019.

WISTREICH 2007
WISTREICH, Richard. *Warrior, Courtier, Singer. Giulio Cesare Brancaccio and the Performance of Identity in the Late Renaissance*, Aldershot-Burlington, Ashgate, 2007.

YOUNG 1982
YOUNG, James Bradford. 'An Account of Printed Musick ca. 1724', in: *Fontes Artis Musicae*, XXIX/3 (1982), pp. 129-136.

Abstracts and Biographies

DAVID CHUNG, *The Significance of the Preludes with Figured Bass in F-Pn Vm⁸ 1139 for Keyboard Pedagogy in Early Eighteenth-Century France*

Modern research on French continuo practices has heavily relied on published sources, such as Jean Henry d'Anglebert's *Principes de l'accompagnement* (Paris, 1689), Denis Delair's *Traité d'accompagnement pour le théorbe et la clavessin...* (Paris, 1690), and Michel de Saint Lambert's *Nouveau traité de l'accompagnement du clavecin* (Paris, 1707). The continuo treatise in the manuscript Bibliothèque nationale de France, Vm8 1139, associated with the name of St. Georges, has escaped modern scrutiny until recently (Churchill, 2006). The manuscript was first known in modern scholarship in connection with original harpsichord pieces by seventeenth- and eighteenth-century composers, including Hardel, Louis Couperin, François Couperin and Jean-François Dandrieu, as well as arrangements of Lully's stage music. However, the source also contains a comprehensive figured bass method at the beginning (ff. 1r-31r), including 14 preludes for figured bass that conclude this method. Although Mr. St. Georges remains unidentified, the manuscript is closely linked to Dandrieu's *Principes de l'accompagnement du clavecin* (Paris, 1719), and was most probably copied during the first two decades of the eighteenth century. Following Churchill's first detailed study of this obscure treatise, this paper transcribes for the first time in modern history 14 preludes for figured bass, and provides a possible realisation based on the preceding method, the *Regles pour l'Acompagem[ent]*. Interestingly, the 14 preludes cover all tonalities in practical use, from C major to B minor, and a range of genres, including the overture, the menuet and the gavotte. By transcribing these preludes into modern notation, and providing a plausible realisation based on the method, this study assesses and evaluates what these preludes add to our understanding of French keyboard pedagogy in early eighteenth century. The detailed chord spellings reveal details of voice-leadings, and the harmonic contexts of dissonances and other aspects of French harmonic practice of the time.

DAVID CHUNG has contributed articles and reviews to *Early Music, Early Keyboard Journal, Journal of Eighteenth-Century Music, Journal of Seventeenth-Century Music, Music and Letters, Music & Practice, Notes, Revue belge de musicologie* and *Revue de musicologie*. His edition of unpublished keyboard arrangements of Jean-Baptiste Lully's music is available from the *Web Library of Seventeenth-Century Music* (<www.sscm-wlscm.org>) and his Online Thematic Catalogue of Lully Keyboard Arrangements (OTCL) available from <digital.lib.hkbu.edu.hk/OTCL/>. As solo harpsichordist and continuo player, Chung has appeared in the Festival d'Ile-de-France, Geelvinck Fortepiano Festival, Cambridge Early Keyboard Festival, Vesper Concert Series in Lubbock, Hong Kong International Chamber Music Festival, Le French May Arts Festival and Hong Kong New Vision Arts Festival, and performed in recital series of the Benton Fletcher Collection, the Cobbe Collection and the Handel House. Chung is currently Professor of Music at Hong Kong Baptist University.

***

ABSTRACTS AND BIOGRAPHIES

Clotilde Verwaerde, *The Three-voice Texture in Eighteenth-Century French Continuo*

Continuo realisation in eighteenth-century French music is traditionally associated with full harmonies in which at least four voices are heard consistently, or nearly so. The very notion of texture in the accompaniment, however, is found among the arguments opposing the supporters of Italian music and the defenders of French music. While Rousseau described the light chords of the Italians as precise and brilliant, Rameau saw in such an accompaniment a mutilated harmony. The studies carried out so far have shown that no rule or constant can be formulated concerning this parameter in French basso continuo, but it remains necessary to clarify the presence and the modalities of use of a lighter, three-voice texture, particularly in the second half of the century, following the Quarrel of the Bouffons and the writings of Rousseau. This study is based first on theoretical sources, from Saint-Lambert's *Nouveau traité d'accompagnement du clavecin* (1707) to Catel's *Traité d'harmonie* (1802). The use of a three-voice chordal texture is then considered in the context of the aesthetic debate and from the perspective of the choices and approaches of Italian(ate) composers. Finally, the written accompaniments are called upon as evidence of the accompaniment practice of this period in order to evaluate the implementation of this texture and its potential value for an amateur public whose harmonic skills may prove fragile in this acknowledged phase of decline of the thoroughbass practice in France.

Clotilde Verwaerde is a Lecturer at the University Vincennes - Saint-Denis (Paris 8) and a member of the Musidanse laboratory. She is the author of a Ph.D. thesis on the practice of accompaniment in France between 1750 and 1800. Her work focuses on harmonic theories and the analysis and performance of chamber music repertoires between 1750 and 1850, particularly the French genres of accompanied keyboard sonatas and romances. Trained as a harpsichordist and fortepianist, her research remains closely connected to historically informed practice.

***

Marie Demeilliez, *The «Encyclopédie ou Dictionnaire raisonné des sciences, des arts et des métiers» (1751-1772): A Source for Basso Continuo Accompaniment in Eighteenth-Century France*

In the 28 volumes of the *Encyclopédie ou Dictionnaire raisonné des sciences, des arts et des métiers* published from 1751 to 1772 under the direction of Diderot, D'Alembert and Jaucourt, several articles deal with accompaniment on the basso continuo. Like numerous articles on musical subjects, most of them were written by Jean-Jacques Rousseau, as a first draft of his *Dictionnaire de musique*. These texts address different aspects of accompaniment by keyboard instruments. The article *Accompagnement* (vol. I) defines the principles of its teaching and practice; *Règle de l'octave* (vol. XIV) teaches which chords are to be played on an unfigured bass; *Chiffrer* (vol. III) deals with the chord notation system; *Doigter* (vol. V) and *Face* (vol. VI) deal with the position of the hand and fingers, and their movement in the chord sequence; *Accompagnateur* (vol. I) lists the qualities one is expected to have in order to play the accompaniment; *Arpeggio* (vol. I) and *Harpègement* (vol. VIII) describe the ways of arpeggiating the chords, on the harpsichord and on the cello. This last article also examines the particular case of the accompaniment of recitatives. These texts testify to Rousseau's role in the dissemination of Rameau's theories, despite the quarrels that opposed them for several decades. Rousseau's predilection for Italian music also reveals that the aesthetic opposition between French and Italian music also affected accompaniment: the *Encyclopédie* can therefore be considered a rich source of information on how to accompany Italian or Italian-inspired repertoire performed in France in the mid-eighteenth century.

Marie Demeilliez is Associate Professor in Musicology at the Université Grenoble Alpes and a member of the Institut Universitaire de France. She graduated from the Conservatoire national supérieur de musique de

404

Paris (harpsichord, basso continuo and musicology) and defended a Ph.D. thesis at the Université Paris-Sorbonne. Her research bears on musical and theatrical practices at French colleges during the 17th and 18th centuries (*Musiques et danses sur la scène des collèges parisiens. 1640-1762*, Paris-Sorbonne, 2010; *Le Théâtre au collège*, Paris, Classiques Garnier, 2018), keyboard music, and French music theory. She contributes to the ENCCRE project — a collaborative and critical digital edition of the *Encyclopédie or Dictionnaire raisonné des sciences, des arts et des métiers* (1751-1772).

***

ISAAC ALONSO DE MOLINA, «*Acompañamientos con las llamadas del Baxo y lo que se puede tocar sobre cada uno de ellos*»: *Partimenti Diminuiti in Manuscript M/1188 of the Biblioteca Nacional de España (Madrid)*

The manuscript M/1188 of the Biblioteca Nacional de España in Madrid is a late 18th-century compilation of diverse didactic materials on thorough bass, for instruction in accompaniment on keyboard instruments. Two of its sections are ascribed to Félix Máximo López (1742-1821) and José Lidón (1748-1827), both of them musicians with careers linked to the Spanish Royal Chapel: López was organist there from 1775, while Lidón was also organist from 1768, assistant to the chapel master since 1788 and chapel master from 1805. Lidón also received his musical education as a choirboy in the Royal College, closely connected to the Royal Chapel. The college included, from 1738, specific training in the Italian style: Lidón himself occupied the position of «maestro de estilo italiano» of the college from 1771. A third section of the manuscript lacks any indication of authorship. Its title reads «Acompañamientos, con las Llamadas del Baxo, y lo que se puede tocar sobre cada uno de ellos», and it contains unevenly figured bass lines with hints for realisation in an idiomatic keyboard texture. These «acompañamientos», apparently *unica*, and possibly originating within the pedagogic practices connected to the Royal College, are nonetheless clearly analogous with the *partimenti diminuiti* of the Neapolitan tradition, especially with those of Francesco Durante. A comparative analysis shows the similarities, pointing to the presence of Neapolitan methodologies in the Spanish Royal Chapel during the 18th century.

ISAAC ALONSO DE MOLINA teaches Musica Practica (solmisation, improvised counterpoint, early notation) at the Royal Conservatoire of The Hague. He is founder and director of the ensemble *La Academia de los Nocturnos* (focused on Spanish music). He graduated from the Conservatory of Valencia in 2001/2002 in four majors (piano, cello, chamber music and music theory), afterwards obtaining a Bachelor in Music (harpsichord) and a Master in Music (maestro al cembalo) at the Conservatory of The Hague. Since 2019 he has chaired the Early Music task force of the European Association of Conservatories (AEC).

***

MICHAEL FUERST, *Hieronymus Praetorius, Multiple-Bass Notation in Organ Parts and Continuo Performance Practices of Polychoral Music in the Hanseatic Cities of Northern Europe*

Multiple-bass notation, used in the very first printed organ part in 1594, is simply a reduced portrayal of a polychoral work that presents a *basso seguente* for each individual choir in a score of as many lines as there are choirs. In 1618, the Hamburg organist Hieronymus Praetorius used this notation in his first printed *bassus continuus* for the *Cantiones variae*, the fourth volume of his *Opus musicum*. Four years later in 1622, the composer published organ parts for the three previous volumes using a single-line organ bass with a short preface. In the years before his own publications with a *bassus continuus*, Praetorius's own pieces appeared in anthologies that included organ parts of various kinds, perhaps influencing the composer's decisions in making his own parts. Also in 1622, he gifted a copy of all four volumes in a collector's edition to St. Peter's church in Lübeck, which, although incomplete, is still preserved in the city library there (D-LÜh). At some later time, a hybrid edition of the *bassus continuus* book of the *Cantiones variae* was made to augment the number of copies of the partbook. This and the Lübeck copy, which contains several handwritten additions including text underlay, are interpreted and put into context using forewords to organ books, treatises, other marked sources, and historical evidence regarding relevant musical performances to broaden the understanding of continuo performance practices of polychoral music in the churches of Northern Europe, particularly in Hanseatic cities.

MICHAEL FUERST, organist and harpsichordist, teaches at the Hochschule für Künste in Bremen and the Musikhochschule in Lübeck and performs internationally. He studied at the Eastman School of Music and was a Fulbright grant recipient for study with Robert Hill in Freiburg. He was a member of a Deutsche Forschungsgemeinschaft project to research German instrumental ensemble music. A resident of Hamburg since 2001, Fuerst regularly gives talks on Hamburg music history while demonstrating the historical keyboard instruments in the Museum for Hamburg History.

***

JOHN LUTTERMAN, *Partimento, German Thoroughbass Practice, and Improvised Solo Performance on the Cello*

As the burgeoning scholarship focused on Italian partimento pegagogy attests, continuo realisation served as a foundation of both written composition and improvised solo performance well into the nineteenth century. Until recently, little attention has been given to the striking similarities between early examples of unaccompanied cello music and Neapolitan partimento exercises. The fact that many of the partimento exercises were created by or attributed to celebrated cellists suggests a close relationship between the skills required for partimento realisation and solo improvisation. Partimento pedagogy may also have influenced (or reflected) similar German practices, which are given detailed and explicit verbal treatment in the thoroughbass treatises of Niedt, Kellner, Heinichen, Mattheson, C. P. E. Bach, Adlung and Wiedeburg. While these sources are aimed primarily at keyboard players, there is reason to believe that well-trained musicians would have employed similar techniques when improvising on the viol or cello. One of the most striking characteristics of the earliest cello treatises is that so many of them give instruction in chordal thoroughbass realisation, and traces of these practices may be discerned in several examples of seventeenth- and eighteenth-century music for solo viol and cello, traces which offer valuable clues to the idiomatic nature of improvised solo practices on these instruments.

Musicologist and cellist JOHN LUTTERMAN is currently Professor of Music at the University of Alaska, Anchorage, where he directs America's Northernmost period-instrument orchestra and viol consort. He previously served on the faculty of Whitman College, the University of California, Davis, the University of the Pacific, Lawrence University and the San Francisco Conservatory. He holds the Ph.D. in historical musicology from the University of California, Davis, as well as the DMA in cello performance from Stony Brook University. His post-doctoral work includes studies with Nicolaus Harnonourt at the Mozarteum, Christophe Coin at the Schola Cantorum, and Jaap ter Linden at the Royal Conservatory, the Hague. He has given solo performances throughout Europe and America, including the complete cello works of Bach, Brahms and Chopin, and has performed with the Wiener Akademie, Salzburger Hofmusik, Philharmonia Baroque, the American Bach Soloists and El Mundo. His research focuses on relationships between notation, compositional theory, and historical improvisatory practices.

Abstracts and Biographies

Hilary Metzger, *National Styles in Lower String Accompaniment of Secco Recitative in the Late Eighteenth and Early Nineteenth Centuries*

Several studies over the past 25 years have brought to light the role of harmonic realisation by cellists in bassline accompaniment generally, showing how pervasive this practice was in earlier times. After David Watkin's ground-breaking article on cello accompaniment for Corelli (1996) and Valerie Walden's seminal work on cello playing in general from 1740 to 1840 (1998), came many works on this subject, particularly, though not exclusively, in conjunction with secco recitative accompaniment: Claudio Bacciagaluppi (2006), Robert Smith (2009), John Lutterman (2011), Nathan Whittaker (2012), Christopher Suckling (2015), Giovanna Barbati (2019) Marc Vanscheeuwijck, (2020) just to cite a few. Thanks in part to these efforts, it is now less unusual to hear harmonic realisation by cellists in concerts today. Nevertheless, the work in the field thus far has not delved into a comparison of different national styles of harmonic playing by cellists and it has tended to concentrate on repertoire written before 1760. Furthermore, as a general rule, cellists have neglected the double bass, which also often accompanied secco recitatives, particularly in this later repertoire, and which has an important impact on the cellist's style of harmonic realisation. This article discusses national distinctions concerning styles of recitative accompaniment by lower string players in later secco recitative repertoire. First, it highlights national differences concerning the role and the image of the double bass in various 19th-century European opera orchestras. Then it discusses different national tendencies of arpeggiation, text synchronicity and voice leading by cellists in their harmonic realisations. The chapter includes a link to a short excerpt of a recitative from *La gazza ladra*, by Rossini, with the author proposing her own recitative accompaniment with only cello and double bass.

Hilary Metzger is a cellist who plays on period instruments throughout Europe and in America, specialising in late 18th- and 19th-century repertoire. As principal cellist with Teatro Nuovo (Will Crutchfield, Jakob Lehmann) and Opera Fuoco (David Stern), she has investigated various forms of harmonic realisation in later secco recitative repertoire. Ms Metzger is on the faculty of the École Nationale de Musique de Villeurbanne and the Pôle Supérieur de Musique et Danse in Poitiers. In 2020, she received a research residency grant from the Orpheus Institute in Ghent Belgium to study recitative accompaniment practice by continuo cellists throughout the world today.

***

Valeria Mannoia, *Per ogni tradizione il suo basso. I bassi seguenti italiani in alcune antologie tedesche del Seicento*

The formalisation of the figured bass in the printed German vocal repertoire spread at the beginning of the seventeenth century more slowly compared to the contemporary Italian production. Here, the Organ part-book appeared with relative regularity from 1594. The composers who worked in the transalpine regions considered the Italian sacred music as an essential point of reference for observation and study. Italian collections of *sacrae cantiones* for many voices, with and without figured bass, circulated during the German Bookfairs and in music bookshops. The *sacra cantio* or motet for many voices continued to arouse considerable interest until the 1620s while the Italian composers preferred to concentrate their attention upon the new repertoire for few voices. Several chapel masters and organists dedicated themselves to compiling and editing impressive anthologies of motet to intensify the study of counterpoint and Latin music in schools and in Catholic and Protestant religious congregations. Many texts were subjected to an inevitable reinterpretation, according to the author's taste and theoretical knowledge. This was an obligatory step for a positive transmission of the Italian musical phenomena in a different and new cultural context. Some anthologies printed between 1611 and 1621, the *Promptuaria musices* by Abraham Schade and Caspar Vincentius and the *Florilegium Portense* by Erhard Bodenschatz, hand down a significant portion of Italian motets for a large ensemble in which the figured bass was added, if absent, or updated according to more functional parameters to musical habits. The intervention proposed by Vincentius and Bodenschatz could have an exclusive impact on the written text, as in the setting of the parts, on the conceptual level, imposing a reworking of the melodic and/or rhythmic shapes or on a more technical level, introducing some figures belonging to a different organ practice. A general analysis of the attitude adopted in individual cases highlights the lack of a systematic approach and the need for the compilers to respond to specific needs and to a specific organ practice.

VALERIA M. R. MANNOIA graduated in Italian Literature (University of Catania), Musicology (University of Pavia, Cremona) and Baroque violin (Conservatorio 'E. F. Dall'Abaco', Verona). She received her Ph.D. in Sciences of the literary and musical text from the University of Pavia, Cremona, where she is attending a Post-Doc on the reception of Italian sacred music in seventeenth-century Flemish prints. In the same university, she is also an adjunct professor of History of Music for the single cycle master's degree course in conservation and restoration of cultural heritage. She is a member of the *Ex CATheDRA* research group and a member of the editorial staff of the *Bollettino di Studi Belliniani* (Centro Studi Belliniani e Fondazione Bellini, Catania).

***

FRANCESCA MIGNOGNA, *Il basso continuo nelle composizioni per i defunti di Pierre-Louis Pollio (1724-1796). Uso, notazione e problematiche relative all'edizione moderna della partitura*

Pierre-Louis Pollio (1724-1796) served as *maître de chapelle* in several *maîtrises* in the French region of the Northern provinces and present-day Belgian Hainault, dealing with the composition of music for religious services. Pollio's approximately one thousand two hundred works, preserved in sources of *descriptive* type (scores intended for preservation) and *prescriptive* type (separate parts intended for performance), and in which contrapuntal writing and Ramist harmony coexist, constitute a representative *cas d'étude* in relation to the use, notation, and practice of basso continuo. Pierre-Louis Pollio's comparison of the different sources of music highlights the ontological difference that exists between them: the scores, written for the purpose of preservation, turn out to be descriptive of the compositional idea; the separate parts, on the contrary, contain the information necessary for the musician to perform the work and have, for this reason, a prescriptive character. Particularly illustrative in this respect are the different versions of continuo lines available: in the scores, these appear melodically unelaborate; in the separate parts, on the contrary, the continuo line is a melodic elaboration of the structure provided in the score; moreover, when the separate part is available in several copies, these provide divergent versions of each other. Based on these observations, it is possible to say that the version of the continuo provided in the separate parts constitutes only one of the possible realisations of the virtual model provided in the score. Particularly representative in this respect are Pollio's compositions for the dead (about seventy compositions, including eight masses). Available in sources of three different types (manuscript scores intended for preservation, separate parts, and a *livre de choeur*) and composed for two different patrons (Saint-Pierre Cathedral in Beauvais, France, and Collegiale Saint-Vincent in Soignies, Belgium), these compositions allow us to explore not only the question of the implicit in the notation of the basso continuo, but also the relation of the latter to the *cantus planus*. In this study, we will investigate the relationship between notation and continuo practice in Pollio's funeral works and propose some possible strategies to distinguish the elements that characterise the work itself from those that belong to the specific manifestations of the latter, in order to obtain the tools for the realisation of a modern edition that reflects the 'virtuality' of Baroque notation.

FRANCESCA MIGNOGNA is an Italian musician and musicologist, currently a doctoral student at Sorbonne University. Her research focuses on Renaissance and Baroque music theory, as well as on 18th-century church music. She is undertaking a Ph.D. in Music and Musicology focusing on the funeral music of Pierre-Louis Pollio (1724-1796), under the supervision of Achille Davy-Rigaux. As a saxophonist, she graduated from the Conservatory of Music of Campobasso (Italy), where she also studied composition. She holds a Master's degree in Music and Musicology from Sorbonne University and has taught at the University of Lorraine.

***

ANTHONY ABOUHAMAD, *The Principles of Partitura Playing: An Introduction to Basso Continuo Instruction and Practice in Eighteenth-Century Salzburg*

Scholars have long known that basso continuo accompaniment at the organ was a standard feature of eighteenth-century Austrian church music practice. Despite this, few studies have examined this performance practice in detail. The aim of this essay is to contribute to our understanding of its performance by examining how court organists in eighteenth-century Salzburg realised a basso continuo when accompanying church music. Six manuals, written by five Salzburg court organists from the time of Georg Muffat to Michael Haydn, contain the foundations of this information. The purpose of this study is to ascertain the instructional method that these organists used to realise an accompaniment from a figured bass, which Austrian musicians called 'partitura'. As invaluable as the Salzburg manuals are, they contain very little textural commentary. In fact, they mostly consist of illustrations of standardised musical patterns, termed schemata in the academic literature. From an analysis of these schemata, I reconstruct Salzburg organists' method for improvising a partitura. I explain this method using two principles, which I label 'disposition' and 'exchange'. The two principles detail a Salzburg method for playing a partitura, which was practised by court organists working in a small, yet significant, city on the periphery of the Habsburg Empire. Besides being the home of Wolfgang Mozart, once a Salzburg court organist himself, the city boasted organists of the calibre of Georg Muffat and Michael Haydn. In addition to shining light on their methods of partitura playing, this study shows that Salzburg court organists understood basso continuo in contrapuntal terms. This challenges some of our fundamental conceptions of 'common practice tonality' and asks us to reassess how we analyse and perform basso continuo, a practice that was integral to eighteenth-century performance and compositional practice.

ANTHONY ABOUHAMAD is a recent Ph.D. graduate from the Sydney Conservatorium of Music (SCM). He has earned a bachelor's degree in harpsichord performance from both the SCM as well as the Royal Conservatory of The Hague. As a harpsichordist, Anthony performs regularly, including with his ensemble *The Muffat Collective*. Currently, he teaches in the historical performance and musicology divisions at the SCM.

***

MARTIN ENNIS, «*Quod licet Bacho non licet Francisco*»: *A New Perspective on the Continuo Realisations of Johannes Brahms and Robert Franz*

Much of the scholarship relating to nineteenth-century basso continuo playing, like accounts of the historical revival movement more generally, is built around binaries. On the one hand, we find purists who saw it as their mission to recreate as accurately as possible the practices of earlier ages. The other camp took its lead from Hegel's concept of «necessary anachronism», with adherents espousing the cause of renewal; from this standpoint, different instruments, different social environments — different sensibilities, even — demanded new approaches. The dichotomy is summarised in the titles of two recent studies: 'Progress and Historicism' (Glenn Stanley) and 'Evolution versus Authenticity' (Elaine Kelly). In the second half of the nineteenth century, the divide in Germany came to centre on two figures: Robert Franz and Johannes Brahms. Brahms is typically identified with historically faithful realisations, Franz with inventive, modern accompaniments. Their supposedly divergent approaches gave rise to bitter polemics, frequently involving proxies. Thus, Franz's friend Julius Schäffer accused Friedrich Chrysander, with whom Brahms collaborated on an edition of Handel's vocal duets and trios, of artistic impotence, while Brahms claimed that Franz's accompaniments were presumptuous, arguing that the freedoms Bach allowed himself were not appropriate for lesser mortals such as Franz («Quod licet Bacho non licet Francisco»). However, a binary divide is inadequate, as it can all too easily mask shared artistic practices. In this study, two realisations of basses from Bach cantata movements, one by Brahms and one by Franz, are used to demonstrate that Brahms's creative instincts could, on occasion, lure him far from what was seen as musicological orthodoxy to an aesthetic position very similar to that of Franz. In the process, I aim to refute the claim that, for Brahms, basso continuo was a puzzle to be solved as 'authentically' as possible.

MARTIN ENNIS is Associate Professor in Cambridge University's Faculty of Music (for which he served as Chairman for nearly a decade) and Fellow and Director of Music at Girton College. He studied in Cambridge and Cologne, writing a doctorate on the music of Brahms, a topic that remains his central research interest. He is principal keyboard player of the London Mozart Players, and has worked as continuo player and soloist with numerous ensembles, including the Monteverdi Choir and the Orchestra of the Age of Enlightenment. His compositions have been performed in Westminster Abbey and the Royal Albert Hall (in a Prom).

***

THOMAS CHRISTENSEN, *Figured Bass: Then and Now*

In his Handbook of music history published in 1912, Hugo Riemann eschewed the label of 'Baroque' (recently made famous by the art historian, Heinrich Wölfflin) to encompass music of the 17th and early 18th centuries in favour of a more prosaic term to describe its most characteristic ensemble component: «Das Generalbass-Zeitalter» — the Age of the Thorough Bass. Riemann did not mean it as a compliment. For Riemann, the introduction and spread of the figured bass as a common practice across Europe beginning in the 17th century was marked by its patently anti-intellectualist approach in treating harmony, one that inaugurated a catastrophic turn away from the brilliant insights of Zarlino. It thus may seem remarkable — and perhaps even perplexing — how this apparently mechanical shorthand of chordal notation for a continuo performer has enjoyed such a remarkable revitalisation in our own day, some two centuries after it ceased to be a part of any meaningful performance skill expected of a keyboardist. Whether we view the exalted place thorough-bass enjoys in the music theories of Heinrich Schenker and his acolytes, or the more recent and unexpected resuscitation of Neapolitan partimento practices, it seems that the thorough bass has become an indispensable key for understanding the creation, teaching, and analysis of tonal music. In my contribution, I will suggest some reasons why a practice that Mattheson once called pedestrian «Hand-Sachen» has gained such prominence in our own day, while also not failing to point out some of the many differences and contradictions between these competing historical notions of the *Generalbass* — then and now.

THOMAS CHRISTENSEN holds the Avalon Foundation Chair of Music and the Humanities at the University of Chicago, where he has taught for the past 25 years. The author of over 60 articles and a half dozen books, his scholarly research centres on the history of music theory. Among the most significant of these works can be mentioned his prize-winning monograph, *Rameau and Musical Thought in the Enlightenment* (Cambridge University Press, 1993), and his editorship of the *Cambridge History of Western Music Theory* (Cambridge University Press, 2002). His most recent book is *Stories of Tonality in the Age of Francois-Joseph Fétis* published by the University of Chicago Press in 2019. Professor Christensen's research has also received recognition from a variety of academic associations and funding agencies. He was a fellow at the Wissenschaftskolleg (Berlin) in 2011-2012 and the American Academy in 2002. Most recently, he received fellowships from the Guggenheim Foundation (2019) and the ACLS (2015) to support his current research projects. He received a Ph.D. in music theory and history from Yale University in 1985, studying with Claude Palisca and David Lewin. Before Chicago, he held teachings positions at the University of Pennsylvania and the University of Iowa. An active citizen in the broader intellectual community of music scholars, he has served as president of the Society for Music Theory (1999-2001) and worked for several decades to further international collaborative ties with colleagues around the globe.

***

STEPHAN LEWANDOWSKI, «*With regard to the Now Prevailing Taste in Music*»: *The Music Theoretical Work of Johann Gottfried Vierling (1750-1813)*

Johann Gottfried Vierling (1750-1813) was a Thuringian organist, composer and music theorist. His place of education, life and work was the small town of Schmalkalden, southwest of the musical centres of Weimar and Erfurt. In the course of his life, Vierling published several works on music theory, in which he focused primarily on the teaching of figured bass as well as on the art of preluding, which was gradually losing importance in its time. The theory of preluding in the transition from the 18th to the 19th century is an area that has received little attention to date, and in terms of its revival in contemporary discourse, Vierling certainly represents a more substantial chapter than one might possibly give him credit for at first glance. This text would like to help Vierling to regain a central place as a music theorist in the current scholarship. There will be a focus in particular on his *Attempt at an Instruction to Preluding for the Untrained* (orig.: *Versuch einer Anleitung zum Präludieren für Ungeübtere*) from 1794, with which the author makes a brief but substantial contribution to the preservation of the preluding practice in the late 18th century. Furthermore, this study aims to build a bridge to the compositional work of the author by taking its contents as the basis for the compositional and harmonic-contrapuntal analysis of selected works from the undated *xxx Easy Three-Part Organ Pieces* (orig.: *xxx leichte dreystimmige Orgelstücke*). These pedagogically motivated compositions are all three part settings, as are most of the examples of preludes found in the treatise und preluding. Such an approach – analysing Vierling with Vierling – has the potential to provide authentic insights into the mindsets during the processes of creating preludes (notated or improvised) in the late 18th and early 19th centuries.

STEPHAN LEWANDOWSKI studied composition and music theory at the Hochschule für Musik Carl Maria von Weber Dresden. From 2006 to 2012, he worked as a freelance lecturer in music theory at the Musikhochschule in Dresden, and from 2012 also at the Musikhochschule Franz Liszt Weimar. In 2012, he finished his dissertation on the combination of Schenkerian theory and pitch-class set theory as an analytical approach. In 2012, he received a permanent post at the Musikhochschule in Weimar, in 2012/2013 and 2016/2017 leading the center for music theory. From 2013 to 2015, he also held a substitute professorship in Dresden. Since 2019, he has been working at the Brandenburg Technical University Cottbus-Senftenberg. His research currently focuses on music theory of the late 18th and early 19th centuries.

***

Abstracts and Biographies

Matthew Paul Mazanek, *Improvisation Pedagogy in Nineteenth-Century Guitar Education*

In the nineteenth century, the guitar was in a fervent state of metamorphosis and experienced an unprecedented rise in popularity among lower- and middle-class amateur learners. As a result, music education was forced to transition, and guitarists increasingly turned to publishing methods which catered to a mass market of 'leisure' learners. This new educational movement was not immediately concerned with performing and reproducing musical works, instead, a wide variety of musical skill sets were cultivated of which improvisation was vital. Twentieth-century research in early music has revitalised the study of improvisation with a focus on the seventeenth and eighteenth centuries. Recent research has neglected the specific teaching techniques employed in the nineteenth century and this paper directs its analysis towards how, and why, lower- and middle-class amateur guitarists learned to improvise in the nineteenth century. Guitarists shared a unique concern with learning how to improvise as preluding, modulating between songs and spontaneously varying accompaniments were vital parts of the performance practice. By using a variety of techniques resembling those found in the *partimento* tradition such as bass motions, modulations, and the *canevas de prelude*, guitarists instructed fretboard harmony for its application in improvisation and accompaniment. Nineteenth-century guitarists developed unique ways of teaching students to improvise, and by exploring them they provided insight into the links that were cultivated between compositional and instrumental technique, revealing a curriculum centred around spontaneous composition. This research addresses the role pedagogy plays in the flourishing of improvisational skill and why, in the early twentieth-century, improvisation swiftly declined.

Matthew Paul Mazanek is a classical guitarist who received his Doctorate in Musical Arts at the Royal Irish Academy of Music in 2021. He has spoken at conferences across Europe and the United States and performed widely across USA, Ireland and the UK. His research interests include the cultural interpretations of instrumental technique in the nineteenth and twentieth centuries with methodologies that intersect historically informed pedagogy, hermeneutics and musical sociolinguistic. His doctoral thesis reassesses instrumental technique and its capacity to act as a medium for understanding.

***

Justin Ratel, *Repurpose and Transformation of an Educational Material: Figured Bass as a School Practice in the Early Years of the Paris Conservatory*

After having been an essential musical practice until the middle of the 18th century, basso continuo declined in the second part of the century and disappeared completely among keyboard accompanists at the beginning of the 19th century. In France, the figured bass was maintained only in certain *Solfèges* and in instrumental methods published at the beginning of the 19th century. One can observe that the study of this technique occupied a predominant place at the Paris Conservatory. During those years, French pedagogues transformed an educational material both from the Italian tradition of partimenti and from the 18th-century French practice of the basso continuo into a school subject integrated into harmony studies. We will rely on an examination of the 70 keyboard accompaniment treatises published in France between 1820 and 1860 to understand the pedagogical uses of this technique and its use in the school context. This analysis will allow us to understand how an exercise, which no longer corresponded harmonically to contemporary practices, continued to be useful in theoretical works and textbooks. The study of the teaching methods used by professors and treatise writers will also help us better understand the place of the Italian tradition in the organisation of harmony studies in the early history of the Paris Conservatory.

Singer, pedagogue and researcher, JUSTIN RATEL seeks to combine musicological research and pedagogy. He has studied at the Paris Conservatory (CNSMDP) in music history with Rémy Campos and music analysis and theory with Claude Abromont. His historical research focuses on the musical pedagogy of the 19th century, in particular on music theory, keyboard accompaniment and vocalisation.

***

THOMAS ALLERY, *Thorough Bass Made Easy: The Pedagogical Value of Figured Bass in Musical Education Today*

The flourishing interest in historical performance has led to a considerable body of research and interest in performing improvised continuo accompaniment from figured bass notation. However, less attention has been given to the role of basso continuo treatises in their related role as pedagogical resources. In the United Kingdom, figured bass notation and its associated performance practice is employed by specialists alone. It is almost entirely absent from British music syllabus requirements, and often taught first at tertiary level. This paper examines the role of figured bass notation as a teaching device outside of the realm of historical performance, through the exploration of a body of new teaching resources. Introduced to music students in the earliest stages in their musical education, this form of notation can provide a means of developing links with other parts of repertoire and, through encouraging confidence in improvisation, can develop a broader and more transferable musical skill set. Figured bass as a musical language enables students to comprehend harmonic progressions anew, and allows them to experience harmony kinaesthetically through practical application. The reliance on fully notated music is removed, encouraging a creative and flexible approach. Conclusions arising from this practice-led research may inform discussions between teachers, schools, and examination boards regarding the use of improvisation within music education. Figured notation is viewed here as a rich pedagogical resource, which develops transferable musical skills within the context of teaching traditions which are frequently too reliant on notation.

THOMAS ALLERY is a harpsichordist, organist and director based in London, active as a soloist and continuo player. Having initially studied music at Oxford University, and then at the Royal College of Music, Thomas was later awarded a scholarship to complete his studies as a harpsichordist on the Artist Diploma programme at the Guildhall School of Music and Drama, studying with James Johnstone and Carole Cerasi. Thomas is a founding member of the award-winning period ensemble, *Ensemble Hesperi*, a group known for their pioneering approach to performing eighteenth century Scottish repertoire. Thomas is organist of the Church of St Mary-le-Bow, Cheapside, in the heart of the City of London.

***

LIVIO TICLI, *Basso Continuo as a 'Concertato' Practice: Vocal-Instrumental Improvisation, Ornamentation and Counterpoint*

Recent research into the use of intabulations, scores, and *basso seguente* has demonstrated the multifaceted nature of instrumental accompaniment practices during the sixteenth and seventeenth centuries. The versatility of basso continuo accounts for its success, which is why unambiguous description also proves challenging. These practices could be utilised by both novices and experts in diverse settings, leading to varying outcomes based on musical skills and circumstances. This is illustrated in 'integrated performances', events featuring large musical ensembles, *concertati* works, and few-voice *concerti*, among other examples. By moving away from concentrating solely on harmonic aspects, the functions of all the performers and instruments other than the keyboard in ensemble music can be reassessed, as demonstrated by Nicola Vicentino's *Regola da concertare* (1555) and Agostino Agazzari's *Del sonare sopra'l basso* [...] *nel conserto* (1607). In this context, this contribution examines evidence from various geographic regions until the mid-eighteenth century to reveal a *fil rouge* of practices, despite inevitable variations in style and taste over the centuries. Although the *Concerto* or *Concertato* is not addressed as a compositional style, historical records, *contrappunto alla mente* treatises, compositions, and obbligato pieces provide insight and a plausible representation (in writing) of improvisational practices. Basso continuo in ensemble-making is considered within the framework of collective improvisation: by surpassing mere visualisation and realisation of a harmonic structure, this study aims at restoring the instrumental practices under investigation to their aural foundation for the first time, rediscovering complex techniques, which showcase elements of improvisation, ornamentation and counterpoint simultaneously.

LIVIO TICLI's interests range from historical musicology, researching the figure of the Renaissance virtuoso at the University of Huddersfield, to early music, performing with *Palma Choralis* and other international ensembles in prestigious venues in Italy, Europe and overseas, and organising international music festivals (*Tasso Music Festival, BIEMSSF*). He has dealt with early music performance practice and pedagogy, researching and giving lectures at universities in Italy, Europe, UK and USA. Since 2015, he has been co-chairing the Early Music Department of Brescia, now under the Istituto Italiano di Musica Antica. He was a visiting scholar at the University of Massachusetts and Mount Holyoke College, and Artist-in-Residence at the Folger Theatre (Washington D.C.). He is a member of the editorial board of the *Tasso in Music Project*, promoted by the University of Massachusetts and Stanford University and is the general co-editor of the series 'Musica Incarnata: Pedagogy, Performance and Market' (Brepols). He teaches music history, improvisation and ornamentation at the Conservatories of Alessandria and Vicenza.

INDEX OF NAMES

INDEX OF NAMES

INDEX OF NAMES

Index of Names